P9-DVQ-501

Voices for the Earth

VOICES FOR THE EARTH

A TREASURY OF THE SIERRA CLUB BULLETIN

Edited by Ann Gilliam

INTRODUCTION BY HAROLD GILLIAM

Sierra Club Books

SAN FRANCISCO

The Sierra Club, founded in 1892 by John Muir, has devoted itself to the study and protection of the earth's scenic and ecological resources — mountains, wetlands, woodlands, wild shores and rivers, deserts and plains. The publishing program of the Sierra Club offers books to the public as a nonprofit educational service in the hope that they may enlarge the public's understanding of the Club's basic concerns. The point of view expressed in each book, however, does not necessarily represent that of the Club. The Sierra Club has some 50 chapters coast to coast, in Canada, Hawaii, and Alaska. For information about how you may participate in its programs to preserve wilderness and the quality of life, please address inquiries to Sierra Club, 530 Bush Street, San Francisco, California 94108.

Copyright © 1979 by Sierra Club Books

Grateful acknowledgment is made to the following for permission to reprint material:

David Brower, Phoebe Anne Sumner, Lewis F. Clark, August Fruge, Ansel Adams, Allen Steck, A. Starker Leopold, Herbert Mason, Lewis P. Mansfield, Fred Gunsky, William Dunmire, Harold Gilliam, Vincent Butler, Eliot Porter, John G. Mitchell, Mrs. Avis deVoto, Edward Abbey, Nancy Wood, John P. Holdren, Volta Torrey, Garrett Hardin, Art Hoppe, Steven Johnson, Paul B. Sears, Leonard Woodcock, Philip Hyde, Bruce Barnbaum, Dave Bohn, John Trimble, James Powers, Michael Bry, James A. Mattison, Jr., Verna R. Johnston, Tom Frost, Roy Johnson, Bob and Ira Spring, Martin Litton, Paul S. Conklin, Harvey Richards, Bradford Washburn, Tim Thompson, George Rose, Paul Conrad, Jack Gainey, John Thomas Howell, Edgar and Peggy Wayburn, Tom Darcy, Wallace Stegner, and Jacques Cousteau.

"Wilderness and the Geography of Hope" from THE SOUND OF MOUNTAIN WATER by Wallace Stegner. Copyright © 1969 by Wallace Stegner. Reprinted by permission of Doubleday and Company, Inc.

Library of Congress Cataloging in Publication Data

Voices for the Earth.

Bibliography: p.
Includes index.
1. Sierra Nevada Mountains — Addresses, essays, lectures. 2. Sierra Club — Addresses, essays, lectures. 3. Mountaineering — United States — Addresses, essays, lectures. 4. Natural history — United States — Addresses, essays, lectures. 5. Conservation of natural resources — United States — Addresses, essays, lectures.
I. Gilliam, Ann. II. Sierra Club. III. Sierra Club. Bulletin.
F868.S5V63   917.94'4   79-530

ISBN 0-87156-254-5
ISBN 0-87156-211-1 pbk.

Jacket and book design by Anita Walker Scott

10 9 8 7 6 5 4 3 2

Printed in the United States of America

The Sierra Club has played an essential and effective role in preserving "the hills from whence cometh . . . (our) help." In gratitude, the editor dedicates her part of the book to the members of the Sierra Club, past, present, and future.

Contents

Foreword

THE SIERRA CLUB has made a transition from a hardy band of John Muir's followers in California to a national society of environmental activists. The link that holds the entire membership together is the Sierra Club *Bulletin*.

Unlike other organizations, people don't join primarily to get the magazine. They join to pool their efforts to protect the natural environment. But the *Bulletin* is the indispensable means of melding them into a club. It expresses the personality of the club; it reveals how we think about solving problems; it inculcates the basic values that characterize the Sierra Club, and is its instrument in setting forth well-articulated reasons for club positions.

Over the past two decades, the *Bulletin* has changed a great deal. By 1960, the club had become involved in a wide range of issues; the *Bulletin* called members to action on struggles to block dams, reform the Forest Service, and to protect more wilderness.

In the 1970s the club grew to such a size that its interests embraced hundreds of wilderness areas and objectionable dams. Moreover, we were now fighting the SST and worrying about national energy policy. There were broader stories to tell, and a national audience to reach with extremely varied interests. A vast and changing new membership wanted to know more about the club as an institution, too.

As a result, *Bulletin* articles of the 1970s ranged across the whole spectrum of environmental activism, using particular struggles to illustrate themes of pervasive interest. They provided the background on emerging issues so that calls to action would reach an audience that was already prepared. The articles were written in a highly readable manner, but also in a context which assumed some sophistication in understanding the political milieu in which public issues are decided. The *Bulletin* was not always the first to deal with a story, but its pieces were among the most solid accounts. Its scope was broadened in other ways too, with profiles of personalities, reminiscences about club history, pieces on outdoor experiences and natural history, letters to the editor, book reviews, and a column on club news. Advertisements were accepted for goods that seemed in keeping with the club's purposes.

Each editor left his or her mark in moving the *Bulletin* through these phases: David R. Brower introduced color to the covers of the magazine beginning in 1959; Bruce Kilgore and Hugh Nash focused the magazine on current events in the 1960s; James Ramsey added color to the inside pages as the 1970s began; William Bronson and his associate Roger Olmsted began the change toward a more outward-looking and broadly conceived magazine; and Frances Gendlin carried this change forward to fix the *Bulletin's* character more decidedly and give it more distinction.

While people don't join the Sierra Club to get the *Bulletin*, they come to be real members of the Sierra Club as a result of reading it. The *Bulletin* mirrors the mind and mood of the club.

MICHAEL McCLOSKEY

Preface

THE SIERRA CLUB BULLETIN was first issued in January, 1893—six months after the club was founded. Published at regular intervals ever since, the *Bulletin* has been the major voice of the organization for 86 years. The content of the journal has reflected the members' changing interests and commitments, but in thumbing through the volumes, one becomes aware of a persistent theme illuminating each page: the love for nature and the concern for a green integral world. That is the club's underlying spirit.

The *Bulletin* has been fortunate in its long line of distinguished editors, who have acted under the general guidance of the club's publications committee. Editors before 1960 volunteered their services. Many names could and should be mentioned, but among those who edited the *Bulletin* over a number of years and contributed much to its character are William F. Badè, a leading theologian and biographer of John Muir, who served as editor from 1911 to 1922; Sierra historian and club president Francis Farquhar, editor from 1926 to 1946; and David R. Brower, who edited the *Bulletin* from 1946 to 1952, when he became executive director of the club. Brower expanded the *Bulletin's* coverage from the Sierra Nevada to national issues in 1951 and continued to edit the handsome annual edition through 1968. We must also mention David Starr Jordan, president of Stanford University, who served as editor for only a few years (1900-1903), but continued to play a leading role as a member of the publications committee.

In the *Bulletin's* first decade of publication, traditions were established that have continued to this day.

Format and production have always received careful attention. Fine photography has been emphasized—not a difficult matter when a journal is fortunate enough to have such photographers as J. N. LeConte, Ansel Adams, Philip Hyde, and Cedric Wright contributing to its pages. The *Bulletin* has traditionally covered a wide range of subjects: conservation, always, but also geology, plant and animal life, philosophy, history, skiing, climbing—and the plain fun of outings. As environmental problems proliferated after World War II, conservation became the magazine's dominant theme, and so it is today in the larger context of concern for the life systems of the planet.

There is one tradition we have not mentioned—the effort to experiment with new ideas in format, presentation, and content. This tradition of innovation has been continued by the present editor, Frances Gendlin, who has introduced many new features and greatly broadened the concept of the *Bulletin,* which, in consequence, has received a new name, *Sierra.*

Now, a note about the *Bulletin* anthology itself, *Voices for the Earth.* To choose the most significant, interesting and well-written articles from the *Bulletin*'s nearly nine decades of publication was a difficult task. In fact, it was impossible, because many articles that meet these criteria have been published over the years—many more than I could include in a single volume. The choice in many cases was simply arbitrary.

Once the article was selected, there remained the tasks of fitting it into the anthology and providing the necessary background information. Most articles had also to be condensed. In the interests of format, deletions are not indicated; ellipses are used only when required by meaning.

A book is almost always the result of the ideas and insights of many people. Certainly *Voices for the Earth* is. But among those people who contributed the most to the book are the following: Jon Beckmann, Director, and James Cohee, Assistant Editor, Sierra Club Books; Michael McCloskey, Executive Director, Sierra Club; Christie Hakim, Librarian, Sierra Club; and Frances Gendlin, Editor, *Sierra.* Marjory Farquhar, Helen LeConte, Allen Steck, Henry and Ruth Colby, and the staff of the Bancroft Library were very helpful in locating pictures. For special assistance I would like to thank Harriet Parsons, David R. Brower, and Richard M. Leonard.

The following books were invaluable in putting the articles into context: *John Muir and the Sierra Club: The Battle for Yosemite* by Holway R. Jones; *History of the Sierra Nevada* by Francis P. Farquhar; *Wilderness and the American Mind* by Roderick Nash; and *Climbing in North America* by Chris Jones. Locating the articles was greatly aided by the *Fifty-Seven Year Index for the Sierra Club Bulletin, 1893–1949,* compiled by Dorothy H. Bradley and George Shochat, and *Sierra Club Bulletin Index (Annuals, 1950–1963)* compiled by George Stanley.

Last, I would like to acknowledge with love the constant help and encouragement given me by Harold, David, and Gregory Gilliam.

ANN GILLIAM

Introduction

THE CARTOON SHOWS Tarzan in the jungle, speaking into a phone. "Quick!" he says, "Get me the Sierra Club!"

To most informed Americans no further explanation would be necessary. Whatever may threaten the jungle, it would seem quite normal for the Sierra Club, as the defender of nature, to be called to the rescue. Yet the familiar picture of that organization as the advocate for the trees tends to obscure a role of far greater significance—the club as an expression of one of the major currents of American history.

The American dream of equal opportunity has meant, among other things, opportunity to share in the natural wealth provided by this continent. In this sense the American dream has been based on the conquest of nature. The perennial American effort for 350 years has been to build cities in the wilderness, to devise new technologies for harnessing natural forces, and to provide for each individual a chance to share in the resulting material abundance.

Yet there has been another American dream, far less publicized but almost as old, almost as persistent. It was the dream of a new Eden where one could walk in nature's garden with reverence and wonder, a place where one could find sources of renewal for the human spirit.

The two dreams have often been in conflict, and the result has been the Great American Ambivalence. The urge to conquer nature has been at war with the impulse to love and cherish nature for its own sake. Throughout our history the former drive has been dominant. Forests were logged; fields gave way to cities; mountains were mined. If there was a conflict between "progress" and nature, there was no doubt how it would be solved. The road went through; the dam was built; the meadows were paved; the bays and marshes were filled. The result of this imbalance was twofold: an unprecedented production of wealth and an equally unprecedented destruction of natural resources—the levelling of forests, the erosion of the soil, the annihilation of wildlife. But so abundant were the resources that for generations the destruction went almost unnoticed.

Meantime, the love of nature, even though subordinate to the dominant drive for conquest, persisted as a main theme of American culture and evolved progressively through several stages. Even among the Puritans, who faced the wilderness with complex and ambivalent feelings at best, there were the beginnings of reverence for some aspects of nature as manifestations of God. In the 18th century, pastor Jonathan Edwards wrote: "The green trees and fields, and singing of birds, are the emanations of His infinite joy and benignity. . . . The crystal rivers and murmuring streams are the footsteps of His favor."

The flower of this idea in the 19th century was transcendentalism, a meld of the American experience, as described by Emerson and Thoreau, and the ideas of the Romantic Movement in Europe. In art the painters of the Hudson River School celebrated the American landscape not only along the banks of that river but along the Mississippi and Missouri, in the Rockies, in the canyonlands of the Southwest, in the Sierra Nevada and on the California coast. Even pioneers in the wagon trains, beset by hunger, danger, and exhaustion, found time to record in their journals their awe at the scenic wonders along the trail.

Toward the end of the century the American nature concept again evolved into a new form. Under the influence of John Muir and the Sierra Club, among others, it expanded into the conservation movement, concerned not only with the enjoyment of nature but with its preservation. Americans were persuaded that at least in a few places of superlative natural beauty the drive to conquer the wilderness should be suspended and the love of nature should have full expression. One result was that distinctively American innovation, the national park system. The other American dream was at last beginning to have an effect on the political life of the nation and to be written into the laws of the land.

Two-thirds of the way through the 20th century, the idea broadened, again with the Sierra Club in a leading role, to become the environmental movement, concerned not only with isolated natural areas but with the entire biosphere, that thin film of air, water, soil, and organisms that surrounds the earth and makes human life possible. As a result of alarming evidence that rampant industrialism was not only devouring irreplaceable natural resources at an ever-increasing rate, but also poisoning the air and waters and threatening the earth's ecosystems, environmentalism has become a potent force in American culture and politics. It has not yet achieved full parity with the dominant drive to conquer nature — to build, to develop, to produce — but the gap is certainly closing.

In these pages you will find some highlights from nearly nine decades of Sierra Club writings. All of these accounts, in their own way, attest to the growing strength of that other American dream. You will find here not only reports of the well-known environmental battles but stories of people having fun and high adventure in the wilderness, experiencing wonder, coping with adversity, testing themselves on mountain peaks as well as in the political arena and thereby gaining invaluable insights into themselves and the world around them.

The articles are widely varied, from the expression of pleasure at the color of a mountain butterfly to the sounding of alarms at the global population explosion, but the essential continuity that runs through these pages is quite clearly the continuity of the other American dream as it has expanded through the past nine decades. In its present form it involves respect for the natural world as the context for human life, a desire to learn from the natural processes that sustain all life on earth, and a determination that those processes shall not be irretrievably damaged by reckless human intervention.

There are cynics who claim that the Sierra Club cares more for trees and animals than for people. They miss the point; trees and animals and their habitats are essential to people, not only for enjoyment but for survival. All of us — humans, plants, animals — are fellow passengers on this planet in its lonely voyage through space, and our destinies are inseparable.

The formative years of the Sierra Club were linked closely with the life and writings of John Muir. Before the club was organized he spent fourteen years in the Sierra Nevada, exploring the range, contemplating the splendor of the glacier-carved canyons and peaks, investigating their origins, scribbling in his notebooks impressions that were to become some of the most eloquent writings ever published about the American earth.

But he also found cause for alarm. The entire range was being ravaged by grazing sheep, and the giant sequoias were threatened with extinction by loggers. By temperament Muir was a loner who preferred mountains to cities and trees to crowds of people. But he put his inhibitions aside and went into the public arena to preach the gospel of wilderness like a latter-day John the Baptist. His brilliant articles in national magazines aroused the conscience of the nation and led to the creation of Yosemite and Sequoia National Parks in 1890.

Around the crusading mountaineer there gathered men and women who realized, as he did, that the establishment of the two parks was not the end of the battle but the beginning of a much longer effort to preserve the American wilderness from commercial interests.

One Saturday evening in 1892, Muir returned from a meeting in San Francisco to his home, near the Bay Area town of Martinez, and at the supper table triumphantly announced to his family that the Sierra Club had been founded. A guest at that table was Samuel Merrill, who years later gave his impressions of Muir in a campfire talk: "I had never seen Mr. Muir so animated and happy before. Up to that time, Muir had been waging a continuous war against selfish commercial interests which would exploit and destroy the forests and beautiful regions of our state and nation, fighting in his early years in the state, almost alone, with his back to the wall. Is it any wonder then, that Muir saw in the Sierra Club the crystallization of the dreams and labor of a lifetime, an organization which would carry on the good work for generations yet to come?"

The mountaineer's exuberance was well justified. The goal of legal protection for nature was an idea whose time had come; John Muir was its prophet, and the Sierra Club was his instrument.

On that Saturday, May 28, 1892, Muir and several others, including faculty members from the University of California and Stanford, had met for a planning session in the San Francisco office of Attorney Warren Olney; the following Saturday, June 4, the Sierra Club was created as a corporation, with Muir as president, "to explore, enjoy, and render accessible the mountain regions of the Pacific Coast." A list of the charter members of the club is almost a *Who's Who* of the San Francisco region in 1892; Charles F. Crocker, builder of the Southern Pacific Railroad; old William T. Coleman, who had been a leader of the Vigilance Committee of 1856; Professor George Davidson, pioneer scientist; William Hammond Hall, the founder of Golden Gate Park and California's first state engineer; landscape artist William Keith; President David Starr Jordan of Stanford; and San Francisco's mayor, Adolph Sutro. Shortly after the founding, William E. Colby joined the organization, became Muir's chief lieutenant, and served as the club's executive secretary for 44 years.

The fledgling organization successfully repulsed attacks on the parks by commercial interests, but in 1913 it lost the climactic, ten-year, nationwide struggle against a dam that would flood Hetch Hetchy Valley in Yosemite National Park. The defeat doubtless contributed to Muir's death from pneumonia the following year.

Nevertheless the Sierra Club had established itself as a force for conservation on the American scene. Later it played a principal part in the creation of other national parks, including Grand Canyon, Glacier, Kings Canyon, North Cascades, and Redwood. It has established fifty-three chapters that are carrying on local conservation battles in fifty states. It has introduced tens of thousands of people to the wilderness in its annual outings. It has published, on behalf of its cause, a widely acclaimed series of books and regularly, for 86 years, the Sierra Club *Bulletin* (now *Sierra*), the remarkable journal from which most of these selections were taken.

One of John Muir's most frequently quoted passages is his statement that whenever he tried to look at anything separately, he found it "hitched to everything else in the Universe." Step by step, as you will find in these pages, the concerns of the organization have extended quite logically from the Sierra Nevada to the whole earth.

No one would maintain that the Sierra Club has been infallible. There have been mistakes and there have been disagreements within its ranks. Yet its overall direction is clear. In an age of frenetic commercialism, the club's message is that nature's supreme sanctuaries for the human spirit must be kept inviolate. In a time of rampant technology, the club maintains that human survival requires there be limits on the power of the machine to damage or destroy man's natural habitat.

Each member, looking through these pages, can feel a sense of identification with a fraternity of people, living and dead, who have been united by shared experiences, by their love for the natural world, by their determination to defend it from the bulldozers, the polluters, and the destroyers. And each member can feel fraternal ties not only with those who have gone before but with those who will follow. For the most important function of the Sierra Club, in an era when immediate pressures seem overwhelming, is to affirm that the human race has a long future and that we are responsible to our descendants for maintaining a habitable earth. In a time when most of the world's leaders are preoccupied with this year's crisis and next year's election, the Sierra Club speaks for the needs of our great grandchildren and all the generations to come.

Partly as a consequence of that role, the two American dreams have begun, finally, to come together and interact in productive ways. In some respects the two will always be in conflict, but conflict can become creative tension, a source of insight and innovation. It may be that the most historic discovery of our time is the realization that the love of nature is not sentimental and irrelevant but an essential guiding intuition in all efforts to achieve a civilization that can sustain itself on this planet.

HAROLD GILLIAM

PART I   The Sense of
          Discovery:
          "Rushing
          Streams, Cold
          Sweet Air..."

FROM THE EARLIEST YEARS of the Sierra Club, its members have come from diverse backgrounds and occupations, but they have had one quality in common —a love for natural America, an affinity for the continent's mountains and scenic splendors. Almost invariably this common bond has been based on immediate experience —the sense of personal discovery that comes from the encounter with nature, particularly wilderness. On this bedrock the club was founded and grew. The ongoing struggle to preserve what is left of natural America continues to be based on the conviction that arises from deeply felt personal experience. We begin, therefore, with some varied accounts of that shared experience, the essential moment of joy and wonder and discovery.

The discoveries described here are of many kinds, some that can be put on a map, more that cannot. We sit with John Muir on the rim of the great Tuolumne Canyon and gaze at mountains "glowing with the Holy Spirit of Light"; we experience with Grant Smith the "peace that hangs over the Sierra in autumn"; we look with Theodore Solomons on the "sublime and awful sight" of the central crest of the range; we climb with George Gibbs down Tenaya Canyon, where he discovered inner resources that he had not known he possessed. The individual moments described here are the essence and heart of what the Sierra Club is all about.

Yosemite Falls.

1

Explorations in the Great Tuolumne Cañon

JOHN MUIR

1873

While living in Yosemite Valley in the early 1870s, John Muir gave "long and loving" study to the rocks of the Sierra. He contemplated domes, cliffs, boulders, and pebbles, and developed the theory that glaciers, long since melted, were primarily responsible for the carving of the mountains' crystalline topography. Muir's theory was in direct opposition to the theory of "catastrophism" held by Josiah Whitney, state geologist of California, and was only gradually accepted by professional geologists.

In his study of Sierra geology, Muir used imagination and intuition, as well as intellect, and integrated his findings with the whole of what he experienced as he collected evidence on his "rambles."

Following are excerpts from an article that was written for the 1873 Overland Monthly, *although not printed in the* Sierra Club Bulletin *until 1926, and then in excerpted form. The "lake-bowl" Muir describes was Ten Lakes Basin, north of the Tioga Road in what is now Yosemite National Park. The "stupendous precipice" was probably Grand Mountain.*

THE RIVERS OF THE Sierra Nevada are very young. They are only children, leaping and chafing down channels in which as yet they scarcely feel at home. . . .

In September, 1871, I began a careful exploration of all the mountain basins whose waters pass through the Yosemite Valley, where I had remained winter and summer for two years. I did not go to them for a Saturday, or a Sunday, or a stingy week, but with unmeasured time, and independent of companions or scientific associations. As I climbed out of Yosemite to begin my glorious toil, I gloated over the numberless streams I would have to follow to their hidden sources in wild, untrodden cañons, over the unnumbered and nameless mountains I would have to climb and account for — over the glacial rivers whose history I would have to trace, in hieroglyphics of sculptured rocks, forests, lakes, and meadows.

This was my "method of study": I drifted about from rock to rock, from stream to stream, from grove to grove. Where night found me, there I camped. When I discovered a new plant, I sat down beside it for a minute or a day, to make its acquaintance and hear what it had to tell. When I came to moraines, or ice-scratches upon the rocks, I traced them back, learning what I could of the glacier that made them. I asked the bowlders I met, whence they came and whither they are going. I followed to their fountains the traces of the various soils upon which forests and meadows are planted; and when I discovered a mountain or rock of marked form and structure, I climbed about it, comparing it with its neighbors, marking its relations to living or dead glaciers, streams of water, avalanches of snow, etc., in seeking to account for its existence and character. It is astonishing how high and far we can climb in mountains that we love. Weary at times, with only the birds and squirrels to compare notes with, I rested beneath the spicy pines among the needles and burs, or upon the plushy sod of a glacier meadow, touching my cheek to its enameling gentians and daisies, in order to absorb their magnetism or mountainism. No evil consequence from "waste of time," concerning which good people who accomplish nothing make such a sermonizing, has, thus far, befallen me.

. . . I began to guess that I was near the rim of the Great Tuolumne Cañon. I looked back at the wild headlands, and down at the ten lakes, and northward among the gaps, veering for some minutes like a confused compass-needle. When I settled to a steady course, it was to follow a ridge-top that extends from near the edge of the lake-bowl in a direction a little east of north, and to find it terminating suddenly in a sheer front over 4000 feet in depth.

This stupendous precipice forms a portion of the south wall of the Great Tuolumne Cañon, about half-way between the head and foot. Until I had reached this brink, I could obtain only narrow strips and wedges of landscape through gaps in the trees; but now the view was bounded only by the sky. Never had I beheld a nobler atlas of mountains. A thousand pictures composed that one mountain countenance, glowing with the Holy Spirit of Light! I crept along on the rugged edge of the wall until I found a place where I could sit down to absorb the glorious landscape in safety. The Tuolumne River shimmered and spangled below, showing two or three miles of its length, curving past sheer precipices and meandering through groves and small oval meadows. Its voice I distinctly heard, giving no tidings of heavy falls; but cascade tones, and those of foaming rapids, were in it, fused into harmony as smooth as the wind-music of the pines. . . .

The forces that shaped the mountains — grinding out cañons and lake basins, sharpening peaks and crests, digging out domes from the inclosing rocks — carving their plain flanks into their present glorious forms, may be seen at their work at many points in the high Sierra. From where I was seated, sphinx-like, on the brink of the mighty wall, I had extensive views of the channels of five immense tributary glaciers that came in from the summits toward the northeast. Everyone of these five ice rivers had been sufficiently powerful to thrust their heads down into the very bottom of the main Tuolumne glacier. I could also trace portions of the courses of smaller tributaries, whose cañons terminated a thousand feet above the bottom of

5

the trunk cañon. So fully are the lives of these vanished glaciers recorded upon the clean, unblurred pages of the mountains, that it is difficult to assure ourselves that we do not actually see them, and feel their icy breath. As I gazed, notwithstanding the kindly sunshine, the waving of grass, and the humming of flies, the stupendous cañon at my feet filled again with creeping ice, winding in sublime curves around massive mountain brows; its white surface sprinkled with many a gray bowlder, and traversed with many a yawning *crevasse*. The wide basins of summits were heaped with fountain snow, glowing white in the thin sunshine, or blue in the shadows cast from black, spiry peaks.

The last days of this glacial winter are not yet past, so young is our world. I used to envy the father of our race, dwelling as he did in contact with the new-made fields and plants of Eden; but I do so no more, because I have discovered that I also live in creation's dawn; the morning stars still sing together, and the world, not yet half-made, becomes more beautiful every day.

By the time the glaciers were melted from my mind, the sun was nearing the horizon. Looking once more at the Tuolumne glistening far beneath, I was seized with an invincible determination to descend the cañon wall to the bottom. Unable to discover any way that I cared to try, from where I stood, I ran back along the ridge by which I approached the valley, then westward about a mile, and clambered out upon another point that stood boldly forward into the cañon. From here I had a commanding view of a small side-cañon on my left, running down at a steep angle; which I judged, from the character of the opposite wall, might possibly be practicable all the way. Then I hastened back among the latest sun-shadows to my camp in the spruce trees, resolved to make an attempt to penetrate the heart of the Great Cañon next day. I awoke early, breakfasted, and waited for the dawn. The thin air was frosty, but, knowing that I would be warm in climbing, I tightened my belt, and set out in my shirt-sleeves, limb-loose as a pugilist.

Below, the cañon becomes narrow and smooth, the smoothness being due to the action of snow avalanches that sweep down from the mountains above and pour through this steep and narrow portion like torrents of water. I had now accomplished a descent of nearly 2,500 feet from the top, and there remained about 2,000 feet to be accomplished before I reached the river. As I descended this smooth portion, I found that its bottom became more and more steeply inclined, and I halted to scan it closely, hoping to discover some way of avoiding it altogether, by passing around on either of the sides. But this I quickly decided to be impossible, the sides being apparently as bare and seamless as the bottom. I then began to creep down the smooth incline, depending mostly upon my hands, wetting them with my tongue and striking them flatly upon the rock to make them stick by atmospheric pressure. In this way I very nearly reached a point where a seam comes down to the bottom in an easy slope, which would enable me to escape to a portion of the main wall that I knew must be climbable from the number of live-oak bushes growing upon it. But after cautiously measuring the steepness —

6

scrutinizing it again and again, and trying my wet hands upon it — both mind and limbs declared it unsafe, for the least slip would insure a tumble of hundreds of feet. I was, therefore, compelled to retrace my devious slides and leaps up the cañon, making a vertical rise of about 500 feet, in order that I might reach a point where I could climb out to the main cañon-wall, my only hope of reaching the bottom that day being by picking my way down its face. I knew from my observations of the previous day that this portion of the cañon was crossed by well-developed planes of cleavage, that prevented the formation of smooth vertical precipices of more than a few hundred feet in height, and the same in width. These may usually be passed without much difficulty.

After two or three hours more of hard scrambling, I at length stood among cool shadows on the river-bank, in the heart of the great unexplored cañon, having made a descent of about 4,500 feet, the bottom of this portion of the cañon above the level of the sea being quite 4,600 feet. The cañon is here fully 200 yards wide (about twice the size of the Merced at Yosemite), and timbered richly with libocedrus and pine. A beautiful reach stretches away from where I sat resting, its border-trees leaning toward each other, making a long arched lane, down which the joyous waters sung in foaming rapids. Stepping out of the river grove to a small sandy flat, I obtained a general view of the cañon-walls, rising to a height of from 4,000 to 5,000 feet, composed of rocks of every form of which Yosemites are made. About a mile up the cañon, on the south side, there is a most imposing rock, nearly related in form to the Yosemite Half Dome. About a mile farther down the cañon, I came to the mouth of a tributary that enters the trunk cañon on the north. Its glacier must have been of immense size, for it eroded its channel down to a level with the bottom of the main cañon. The rocks of both this tributary and of the main cañon present traces of all kinds of ice-action — moraines, polished and striated surfaces, and rocks of special forms. Among these mighty cliffs and domes there is no word of chaos, or of desolation; every rock is as elaborately and thoughtfully carved and finished as a crystal or shell.

The life of a mountaineer is favorable to the development of soul-life as well as limb-life, each receiving abundance of exercise and abundance of food. We little suspect the great capacity that our flesh has for knowledge. Oftentimes in climbing cañon-walls I have come to polished slopes near the heads of precipices that seemed to be too steep to be ventured upon. After scrutinizing them and carefully noting every dint and scratch that might give hope for a foothold, I have decided that they were unsafe. Yet my limbs, possessing a separate sense, would be of a different opinion, after they also had examined the descent, and confidently have set out to cross the con-demned slopes against the remonstrances of my other will. My legs some-times transport me to camp, in the darkness, over cliffs and through bogs and forests that are inaccessible to city legs during the day, even when piloted by the mind which owns them. In like manner the soul sets forth at times upon rambles of its own. Brooding over some vast mountain landscape, or among the spiritual countenances of mountain flowers, our bodies disappear, our mortal coils come off without any shuffling, and we blend into the rest of Nature, utterly blind to the boundaries that measure human quantities into separate individuals.

The next morning after my raid in the Tuolumne country, I passed back over the border to Merced, glad that I had seen so much, and glad that so much was so little of the whole. The grand rocks, I said, of this Tuolumne Yosemite are books never yet opened; and, after studying the mountains of the Merced Basin, I shall go to them as to a library, where all kinds of rock-structure and rock-formation will be explained, and where I shall yet discover a thousand waterfalls.

2

A Journal of Ramblings Through the High Sierra of California by the University Excursion Party

JOSEPH LeCONTE

1870

The Sierra Club owes a great debt to Professor Joseph LeConte, the University of California's first professor of geology. Affectionately known as "Professor Joe," the witty, speculative LeConte was the most sought-after teacher of his time at the university. Several Sierra features bear his name.

"Professor Joe" joined the club as a charter member, and served as vice-president and director until his death in 1901, when his son, J. N. LeConte, took over his seat on the board.

The following selections are from LeConte's account of a trip in the Sierra that he and some students made in 1870, not long after he arrived in Berkeley. The Journal *was reprinted in the* Bulletin *in 1900.*

One last note must be that in Yosemite, LeConte, still close to his aristocratic Southern background, met thirty-two-year-old John Muir and was amazed to find "a gentleman of so much intelligence tending a sawmill! . . . This is California!" The two became good friends. LeConte was deeply impressed with Muir and became one of the first geologists of international reputation to support Muir's theory that Yosemite had been formed by glacial action.

S UNDAY, August 7. 8:00 P.M. [Yosemite Valley] After supper, went again alone into the meadow to enjoy the moonlight view. The moon is long risen, and "near her highest noon," but not yet visible in this deep valley, although I am sitting on the extreme northern side, Cathedral Rock and the snowy veil of the Bride, and the whole right side of the cañon, are in deep shade, and its serried margin strongly relieved against the bright moonlit sky. On the other side are the cliffs of El Capitan, snow-white in the moonlight.

Above all arched the deep black sky, studded with stars gazing quietly downward. Here, under the black arching sky and before the grand cliffs of Yosemite, I lifted my heart in humble worship to the great God of *Nature.*

August 13. (Mono Lake). The general view of the range from this, the Mono, side is far finer than from the other side. The Sierra rises gradually on the western side for fifty or sixty miles. On the Mono, or eastern side it is precipitous, the very summit of the range running close to the valley. From this side, therefore, the mountains present a sheer elevation of six or seven thousand feet above the plain. The sunset view of the Sierra, from an eminence near our camp, this evening, was, it seems to me, by far the finest mountain view I have ever in my life seen. The immense height of the chain above the plain, the abruptness of the declivity, the infinitely diversified forms, and the wonderful sharpness and ruggedness of the peaks, such as I have seen nowhere but in the Sierra, and all this strongly relieved against the brilliant sunset sky, formed a picture of indescribable grandeur. As I turn around in the opposite direction, the regular forms of the volcanoes, the placid surface of Lake Mono, with its picturesque islands, and far away in the distance the scarcely visible outlines of the White Mountains, pass in succession before my eye. I enjoyed this magnificent panoramic view until it faded away in the darkness.

After supper I again went out to enjoy the scene by night. As I gazed upon the abrupt slope of the Sierra, rising like a wall before me, I tried to picture to myself the condition of things in the glacial epoch. The long western slope of the Sierra is now occupied by long, complicated valleys, broad and full of meadows, while the eastern slope is deeply graven with short, narrow, steep ravines. During glacial times, therefore, it is evident that the western slope was occupied by long, complicated glaciers, with comparatively sluggish current; while on the east, short, simple parallel ice-streams ran down the steep slope and far out on the level plain. On each side of these protruded icy tongues: the debris brought down from the rocky ravines was dropped as parallel moraines. Down the track of one of these glaciers, and between the outstretched moraine arms, our path lay this morning.

3

The Upper Sacramento in October

J. K. McLEAN

1893

The writer of this piece had an eye for color, and his references to Paradise were not only general in praise, but had a more specific meaning as well. Dr. John Knox McLean was president of the Pacific Theology Seminary (now the Pacific School of Religion) in Berkeley. In regard to the club, he has two distinctions: he was a charter member, and in 1903, he took Professor William Badè, a young colleague at the Seminary, along on the annual High Trip. Badè joined the club and later became one of its most effective leaders.

ON THE 11TH OF JUNE I had said, "This is the supreme day for Mount Shasta and the upper Sacramento. It never was so beautiful before and never will be again." On the 25th of the following October I was fully convinced of my mistake. And am now ready to aver that he who has seen the upper Sacramento only in June—magnificent as that sight is—knows little of its true glory. That compares to this only as green baize to cloth of gold.

As usual with all best glory, this was born in pain. October 14th to 16th was frosty, snappish, chill and gloomy. Grim Shasta refused to disclose himself at all. Apparently, the donning of his new suit he did not judge a transaction for the public eye.

But on Monday morning! Sky clear, low mountains steaming, higher ones

10

gleaming, and the great monarch resplendent in a suit of fleckless ermine, which covered his very feet. And such a golden hue to the air; such a clean-washed sky; such shining oak leaves and such glittering pine needles. And such faint hints and touches here and there of autumnal color. And withal, what fishing. Such fishing so environed! Paradise? Well, Paradise will have to start in early in the morning, and work late at night, to beat it.

And the growing wonder of it all is that each succeeding day was like its predecessor, only more abundant. The golden cast in the air deepened day by day, the halcyon tones grew subtler and more spiritual, and the colors upon the mountain sides and along the river much more vivid. A marvelous garment of green and gold, green and terra cotta, green and crimson, woven in the loom of ten luscious days was flung over the labyrinthined mountains in a perfect prodigality of splendor. I wish I could place all California — unequipped however with rod and tackle — along certain bends of the Sacramento which I was privileged to haunt from sun to sun all through those wondrous days. There are points where the mountain rises sheer out of the emerald stream to the height of hundreds of feet, and at an angle of forty-five degrees. These rises are somewhat thinly clad with loose growths of pine and cedar, leaving abundant openings, which dogwood, maple, oak and laburnum occupy. The steeps face northwestward. The sun seems to only just roll along their summit, but scarcely peeps over. Some days its shine did not find me till high noon.

Now just look. First of all the green, clear, rattling river. Growing out of its brink are the great umbrella-shaped, umbrella-sized saxifrage leaves, which, green in summer, are now gorgeous in all the colors of the rainbow. Next beyond these azalea bushes, that last June illumined the place with their pinkish, yellowish-white blossoms, and now irradiate it with their crimson leaves. Above them stands the dogwood of a deep, rich terra cotta. And higher yet — the crown and glory of it all — the large-leaved, soft maple, rising in broad blotches all the way to the mountain top. These show as great masses of pure gold, the goldenest sort of gold. And the dusky twilight of the overhanging, various-shaded green makes splendid contrast and background for it all.

This is beautiful all the day through, even before the sun has slanted his first beams up toward the ice-cap of Shasta. But as the morning goes on and the air grows warmer, and the light behind this grand decoration stronger — although the trout meanwhile are rising vigorously — why, one has fairly, now and then, to even stop his fishing and give himself up absolutely to admiration. Fishermen will understand how much is said in saying this, especially when I add that the trout landed in such surroundings by the hand which pencils this weighed, many of them, three-quarters of a pound apiece, a dozen at least a full pound each, one two pounds, and another a full two pounds and a half. To knock off fishing in favor of scenery at such a time stands for much.

But, increasingly beautiful is the scene as the day goes on, for the climacteric of the grand display is not reached until when at length, near noon, the

11

sun finally does glance over the apex of the ridge, and floods the entire amphitheater of the hillside. There's an illumination indescribable, unsurpassable! Each one of those brilliant masses of foliage is transfused with splendor. The fine gold of an hour ago is burnished now. The crimsons, terra cottas, and all the reds take on strengthened tints. It is a grand illumination without the jostle, a colossal pyrotechnic without smell or smoke. It is the coronation of the year.

4

A Tramp to Mt. Lyell

HELEN M. GOMPERTZ

1894

Only six women are listed among the 182 charter members of the club. Helen Gompertz, a teacher in Oakland, was one; Muir's daughter Wanda was another. According to Miss Gompertz, Galen Clark, Guardian of the Valley, "assured us that we"—she and her friend, Isabel Miller—"were the first ladies to make this ascent." At the end of the article is a glowing tribute to J. N. LeConte. In June, 1901, seven years later, Helen and J. N. "Little Joe" LeConte were married.

We take up the account on June 7, 1892, when "Miss Isabel Miller, Mr. G. M. Stratton, Mr. J. N. LeConte, myself" and Jingle, the burro, have arrived at Tuolumne Meadows and are standing on the banks of the Tuolumne River, northeast of Yosemite Valley. They had started from the Valley and are now on their way to Soda Springs, across the river.

THIS WAS OUR Rubicon, and how to cross it was the question. Heretofore we had always found a convenient tree spanning the swift mountain stream, but this broad current seemed to defy us.

We knew that Mr. Lambert, who stays at the Springs in summer, was already there, for he had passed us on his way thither the night before. He now appeared on the opposite bank, and called to us that he would cross. In a few minutes we saw him mounted on a small, gray, woolly mule, which looked much like a drowned rat when it emerged from the river. Its rider told us that it had been abandoned by a Government survey party on account of its vicious temper. The animal seemed determined to kick any one to death who attempted to mount it. Mr. Lambert had made the discovery that

12

if it were mounted on the right side, instead of the left, it made no resistance, and that in reality the mule was not vicious, but only capricious.

He kindly placed it at our disposal, and when the first lady was safely upon its back, said to the other: "Now, you get on behind, and keep your feet up when you get to the middle of the stream."

In vain were our protests that the poor little mule could not carry us both. The rest agreed that the mule was tough, and, encouraged by peals of laughter, the animal plunged into the broad but shallow stream.

"Oh, for a kodak!" was shouted after us as we proceeded. Then fainter came the warning: "Don't forget to get off on the right side!" In mid-stream we balanced ourselves as best we could on this mite of a quadruped, and finally made a safe landing, dismounting, as we had been warned to do, on the right side. We had to push it back into the river by main force, in order that our companions might cross. Then it was our turn to long for a camera.

Arrived at the Spring, we prepared for a feast. So did the mosquitoes. Legions of them, bred in the wilderness and thirsting for human gore, feasted upon us so that we fled, completely routed, and rested not till we had put miles between us and our foes. We camped on the river-bank that night, just where the Big Meadows begin.

July 8th. Although Mt. Lyell is the highest peak for many miles around, it cannot be seen until one reaches the very foot of the ascent. A sudden turn brought into full view the grand old mountain. What a perfect picture it made! And what a contrast to look, from the violet-strewn meadow under foot, upon its rugged flank, then upwards to the snow-mass, out of whose dazzling brightness rose a number of sharp, bleak peaks, towering against the bright blue sky! The highest of these marked the summit of our ambition.

There was now no possibility of a trail, and our faithful Jingle picked his way daintily over great boulders and fallen trees. But even he deserted us as we approached the snow-line. Leaving him staked out on a rich granite pasture, we pushed on, laden with our blankets and food enough for next day.

It was no easy task, at an altitude of 11,000 feet, to collect a sufficient supply of gnarled old pine stumps for a rousing camp-fire. But this being done, we each chose a slab of rock near the fire and "turned in" immediately. Before I slept, I looked out upon the amphitheater of bare peaks which, catching the last faint glow of sunset, took on a softer outline, and seemed to look down protectingly upon us daring mortals. As I looked, the full moon appeared above the summit; the rose-color changed to violet, then faded to gray, and made way for the silvery splendor which lit up the heavens and was reflected upon the glistening snow beneath.

But even the enchantment of this scene soon yielded to exceeding weariness, and 5 o'clock in the morning came all too soon. It was bitter cold, and we had to steep our coffee in melted snow. We had been told to shield our eyes and faces from the burning glare of the sun upon the snow, so we donned dark glasses and used the following mixture on our faces: Apply one thick coat of vaseline, then take the well-blackened coffee-pot and rub it gently over the smeared surface. The result is *not* a thing of beauty, but it saves the skin.

Now for a long, strong pull to the summit, 2200 feet above us. We scrambled for three hours, alternately up rocky inclines and across snow-fields. The absence of life and vegetation, coupled with a sense of absolute silence, oppressed us. The huge, jagged rocks seemed to have been hurled down one upon another, in dire confusion, by many an angry tempest. We crawled and leaped by turns from one to another, till we felt glad to reach the smooth and comparatively hard crust of the snow-fields.

At last we climbed upon the glacial moraine, where masses of bowlders move at our slightest touch, and where each must make the crossing singly, for fear of accident.

We were now on the lower side of the glacier, and looking across its white expanse and up the slender tongue of snow that reached almost to the sum-mit, we felt that the end was not yet. It was well that we crossed the glacier early in the season, when the snow was hard enough to bear us and when the smaller crevasses were hidden from view. We made straight for the almost perpendicular white streak; and as the sun rose high and melted the crust, we sank deeper and deeper, until it was a great effort to take each step in ad-vance.

The last few hundred feet were so steep that we had to dig steps for a foothold. At length our leader guided us safely to the left of the great cre-vasse, and lent us a helping hand as we struggled out of the river of snow on to dry land once more. We gazed at the little peak just above our heads, and little dreamed that it would take an hour longer to climb the last 200 feet. The masses of rock we had seen below were but fragments of this gigantic pile. We missed the best way up, and clambered from ledge to ledge, at times with the aid of a rope thrown down to us from above by our nimbler comrades.

At noon, on the glorious summer day, July 9th, 1892, we flung ourselves exhausted, but triumphant, upon the top-most rock of the slender peak which we had so longed to reach. We basked in the sunshine, not daring to mar by speech the sublimity of the moment. We were in the very heart of the Sierras, upon a mountain at whose base are the sources of four mighty rivers. Turn which way we would, long lines of bristling peaks stood out as if in battle array. Look down the face of the awful precipice and see the stern icy bosom in which the Merced River is cradled. How cold the blue of the frozen lakes, still half concealed by the snow drifts! Far beyond, to the westward, we saw the sunny plain where this same river meanders gently to its end, with not a hint of its pristine grandeur.

We now began to be conscious that we felt cold, wet and weary, yet happy. For had we not carried up an ample luncheon, a bag of pine-chips and our beloved coffee-pot? And should we not immortalize ourselves and Mt. Lyell by having a royal feast on its hoary summit?

Hours passed like moments, and, after a lingering farewell to this sacred spot, we prepared for our grand slide. We found our way to the point of the snow-tongue, and, letting ourselves down upon it, very gently shot down the dizzy descent amid the sheet of flying snow. How exhilerating it was to go down like a rush of wind, where we had toiled up step by step! After this first headlong rush, we all skimmed along delightfully as far as the snow extended. Then we slid over stock and stone, till we came to where we had left the blankets. These we shouldered, and we hurried on to find our pack. The piles of bowlders and clumps of trees looked confusingly alike in the waning light. Who knew but that a steady diet of rocks might not have brought Jingle to an untimely end, and then, alas, for us!

At last, to our great joy, we found him alive, but almost strangled in the coils of his long tether. Jingle and the pack represented "home" to us, and we expressed our joy over his preservation by feeding him with old kid gloves and newspapers —dainty morsels, in his estimation.

As for ourselves, "regardless of color and previous condition," we ate first, and removed our sable complexions afterward. There were not wanting those who declared that our cure for sunburn was worse than the disease. As night came on we looked in vain for a level resting-place —but too tired to care, because there was none, we chose perches on different elevations and at various angles of declivity, and soon sank into such a sleep as only those who have experienced it can appreciate. . . .

Those days made for me a pastoral symphony of which the theme lives always in my memory, and the cadences rise and swell, ever new and majestic to the inward ear. I can but recall it now, with added pleasure and grateful remembrance to Mr. LeConte, who made the trip possible and was largely responsible for its success.

A Search for a High Mountain Route from the Yosemite to the Kings River Cañon

THEODORE S. SOLOMONS

1895

No, Solomons did not discover "a high mountain route," but the explorations he did make were completed by J. N. LeConte, Walter Starr, and others, and eventually resulted in the construction of the John Muir Trail that runs from Mt. Whitney to Yosemite Valley.

A rotund, energetic man, Solomons made three trips into the Sierra in his twenties, attempting to locate and map a route near the crestline that could accommodate both hikers and pack animals. He was well read in science and literature, and in the course of his explorations named a number of Sierra landforms so well that the names have remained to this day: Vermilion Valley (now under Lake Edison) and the Seven Gables on his second trip; Disappearing Creek and Enchanted Gorge, Scylla and Charybdis, the Evolution group —including Mts. Darwin, Spencer, and Huxley — and Evolution Valley itself on his third trip.

It is his second trip in 1894 that he describes here. His first trip had taken him as far as the junction of the Middle and South Forks of the San Joaquin River. Now he proposed to explore south from that point to Kings Canyon, keeping as close to the crest of the range as possible. We take up Solomon's account at Bear Creek, the nearest he and his companion, Leigh Bierce, son of author Ambrose Bierce, came to the present John Muir Trail, the high mountain route of which he had dreamed.

A T A DISTANCE of perhaps ten miles from where we first struck the creek the valley ended and the stream forked, its larger branch coming through our pass—a term which we hasten to corrupt to "impass" — the smaller draining a remarkable group of chains of lakelets which lay upon a number of terraces, or plateaus, to the south and west. The south wall of the gap we found to be the side of a peak, the eccentric shape of which is suggested in the name Seven Gables, which we hastened to fasten upon it — the second and last of our gratuitous christenings. We climbed the Seven Gables on the afternoon of our arrival at the head of the valley — September 20th. There was a dash of snow on its chimney-like pinnacle, which must be upwards of 13,600 feet above the sea.

When we gained the edge of the slanting, roof-like crest of the peak and looked out east, we both experienced a sensation that is hardly to be described, though it will be understood by those who have traveled in the Sierra or the Alps.

I was too awed to shout. The ideas represented by such words as lovely, beautiful, wild or terrible, cold or desolate, fail to compass it. Words are puny things, and the language of description quite as impotent as the painter's brush. Roughly speaking, one might say that the sight was sublime and awful. I can scarcely conceive of another scene combining the peculiar qualities of that view in a higher degree, and I believe I was then looking upon the finest portion of the crest of the Sierra Nevada Mountains — their scenic culmination, their final triumph.

We were standing on the very edge of a thousand-foot precipice that ran on south for some distance. Below were some frozen lakes in a bare, glacier-swept basin between our peak and those immediately beyond. Stretching north-east, perhaps five miles, and north-west and south-east as far as the eye could reach, there lay a territory of solid granite and darker-hued metamorphic rock, the surface of which was rent, upheaved, and disheveled into a bewildering confusion of peaks, walls, detritus-piles, pinnacles, and cliffs, massed and fairly crowding upon the view; and among them, like jewels, were patches of snow and cold lakes, like black-blue eyes, and here and there a little, gnarled tree, which was almost painful in the landscape, because of its suggestion of a nether world of things that live. Yet, in spite of that remainder, you may imagine your world dead, cold, turned to a moon, and nothing from pole to pole but those hard, frigid monuments watching the eternal sky, oblivious of all other existence. It seemed the very end of terrestrial sublimity.

But the animal route! Well, our animals not being mythological beasts with wings, a glance sufficed to convince us that the Bear Creek divide was quite impassable. Yet, being within thirty miles, as the crow flies, of our destination, we determined to stick to our undertaking, and to dodge this ugly place by going a little farther from the crest and passing, if necessary, a little to the west of Mt. Goddard, which is the sentinel that guards the watershed between the two rivers.

I shall not have space to describe our movements during the next few days. Suffice it to say, that on the 28th day of September, after weathering several little flurries of snow, which were to be expected at that season of the year, and which therefore we did not seriously regard, we again found ourselves camped very near the Seven Gables. Not having been able to pass down the gorge of the lower Bear Creek, lack of provisions had forbidden any greater retrogression to a new starting-point, and we therefore determined to give our animals to a belated herder who was "feeding" up the creek, and to conclude the journey on foot, carrying our luggage on our backs. Experience in the Tuolumne Cañon had demonstrated that, hardened as we now were, we could carry fifty pounds and make good time; and allowing liberally for delays, we thought we could make the journey on the food we could carry, after subtracting from our combined capacity of 100 pounds the weight of camera outfit, blankets, and other absolutely necessary articles.

It snowed next day quite heavily as we neared the head of the valley, which was the place where we were to leave the jacks and strike out alone. Our fire-logs had to be pulled out of the snow, and, though we had no difficulty in maintaining a fire, the heat melted the steadily falling flakes and soaked our sleeping bags, so that we got almost no rest, and had to wait patiently for morning. The cheerless dawn came at last, and its gray light revealed to us a most alarming situation. From the edge of the melting circle of our fire out over the cañon, the surrounding crests, and as far as the vision extended—from horizon to horizon—Mother Earth was buried under nearly four feet of snow. Fully nine-tenths of it had fallen in the single night, and it was still falling. It enclosed us and our fire and the remnants of our outfit. We were on top of the Sierra, some seventy-five miles of nearly waist-deep snow between us and the nearest settlements. It was late in the year; the ground was cold; and, even assuming that no more snow would fall, fully two weeks must elapse before the mass already on the ground could melt. And then there would still be ahead of us the toilsome march across cañons and rivers to the lower mountains. On the whole, it was patent that our provisions were insufficient to warrant an attempt to weather the storm. How we hated to give in! But the silent, insidious enemy sifted deeper and deeper as we deliberated, and we surrendered to a cold and ominous necessity, and prepared to retreat. The "Kid" had strayed; "Lyell" we shot, to keep him from freezing or starving to death. Then we made up our packs, discarding everything we thought dispensable. When we struck out into the snow my camera-case and my companion's knapsack each weighed about eighteen pounds; and our sleeping-bags, wrung out as dry as we could get them, about twenty pounds each, or quadruple their weight when dry. After struggling through the drift about fifteen feet from camp, we stopped, obeying a common impulse, and looked at each other; and then, without a word, floundered back again to the smoldering logs. We were now fully alive to the gravity of the situation. It was a matter of life or death. Away went bedding; away went camera and the precious negatives secured at the pains of so many hours of patient climbing; away—flung out upon the snow—went everything except half of a threadbare saddle-blanket apiece, absolutely necessary cooking utensils, and some twenty-five pounds of food. Thus lightened, we took our last leave of the remains of a once proud camping outfit—I remember how yellow the flour looked against the absolute white of the snow—and struck out through the soft drifts.

Simply to walk was a complicated operation; for at every step the foot had to be raised clear of the snow before being reinserted, the body meanwhile precariously balanced on the other leg. We constantly ran foul of hidden snags, slipped from treacherous rock-surfaces concealed by the snow, and were tripped by logs too small to be indicated by long snow-mounds, as the larger ones were. Crystals showered down our necks as we jarred the laden trees; and often we could not see a hundred feet in front of us, and had to navigate by compass a creek-bottom, savagely rough and difficult to traverse when free of snow. The brawling stream had frozen over in the night; for the cold had been intense. It was yet snowing; our hands, though swathed in socks for mittens, were blue and stiff, and we had often to rest from the unwonted exertion of lifting at every step the weight of our legs, extra-weighted by the tenacious snow. We were sleepy; the hours went swiftly by, and our progress was alarmingly slow. Though we never lost hope—if we had, we should have been incapable of the exertions we were making—yet when discussing our chances, we were forced to admit that they were no better than about even.

At noon we succeeded in clearing a space, lighting a fire, cooking some oatmeal and chocolate, and drying ourselves. This consumed two hours and a half. In the afternoon it ceased snowing. We climbed the north wall of Bear Creek; and, as the dismal night closed threateningly around us, exhausted, cold, and dispirited, we stood in the snow prison that had clogged our limbs since early morning, and looked for the shelter and bed, by comparison with which all the things the great round world could then have offered us would have been contemptible. A big tree had fallen over two small bowlders, between which was a space only partly filled with snow. Bierce descried it; and we worked there till long past dark, scraping bare the ground of the cubby-hole, and roofing it with branches. Shelter we must have. As an effective preparation for slumber, we had previously found burrowing in the snow to be a delusion and a snare. The darkness deepened. Our shelter, when finished, was not snow-tight. Of the big pile of branches we had collected, little remained for firewood. My companion was taken with a severe chill, and I stood up, hour after hour, alternately warming the two rags of blankets, and making hot coffee. The night was freezing cold; the sky still ominous. Would it snow, or would it not? It was the critical hour of the whole adventure. At twelve o'clock, when nearly asleep, though still holding the blanket before the feeble blaze, I looked at the sky for the thousandth time, and thought I saw a star! I rubbed my grime-filled eyes. Yes, it was a star—three stars! As long as I live I shall never forget the shape of the triangle they formed. I shouted. Bierce and I watched that hole in the shroud of the sky. The three stars returned our steady gaze for a moment, then twinkled—twinkled alarmingly—and, finally, the shifting blackness blotted them cruelly out. But just then Bierce shouted, and pointed to the opposite portion of the sky. It was jeweled with stars! In ten minutes the whole firmament was lit with them. The storm was over.

Bierce's chill left him; we tore down the roof of branches, and converted it into fuel; we slept a little, and rested until late in the morning; ate breakfast,

19

and struck out for the South Fork in a glare of sunlight that was dazzlingly reflected from the snow. The great Sierra world was robed in virgin white. Never have I seen a sight so purely and transcendently beautiful. To feel one's self a mere animal, seeking warmth, food, and self-preservation; and suddenly, as upon that morning, to be confronted with a sight that touches to the quick the aesthetic nature, and thrills the immaterial soul within as it had never thrilled before—what a lesson in the duality of man!

The first day we had made perhaps five miles; the second, eight or ten; the third, we waded the icy current of the South Fork, and, climbing wearily up the other side, accomplished much less. By way of exercise, after our work of the day, each night we were compelled to devote two or three hours to collecting and arranging wood enough to keep us sufficiently warm to sleep. We had not a sufficiency of nitrogenous food to enable us to withstand these unusual inroads upon our strength, and on the fourth day we experienced the unique sensation of weakness without either sickness or particular fatigue. On the fifth we ran across a storm-bound sheep-herder; and mutton, in more than allopathic doses, restored us to full vigor. I venture to say that that sheep-herder had never got hold of more ostentatiously credulous listeners to his outrageous yarns. Generous with his edibles, superabundantly supplied with blankets, our pastoral Munchausen found us willingly—nay, anxiously—gullible; and in return for the contempt with which he doubtless contemplates our memory we continue to retain only the most innocent admiration, alike for his imagination and his mutton.

The next thirty miles was simply a run down the forests to the Pine Ridge settlements, on reaching which we learned that we had been overtaken by the most severe early storm that had ever occurred within the memory of the oldest inhabitant. Our satisfaction over the incontestable fact that we were still living, was such as to prevent any vain regrets over failure and loss of outfit; and we jolted indolently down the Pine Ridge road on a lumber team, reaching Fresno on the 8th of October.

As soon as circumstances will permit, the writer intends to resume the search for a high mountain route from the Yosemite to the King's River Cañon.

Solomons did reach the Kings Canyon on his third trip, a knapsacking venture made in 1895 on which he explored the Evolution country. After that he left for the Alaskan gold rush of 1898, and did not see the Sierra again for forty years.

6

A Woman's Trip Through the Tuolumne Cañon

JENNIE ELLSWORTH PRICE

1898

Jennie and her husband, "Mr. Price" as she called him, had been married a year when they made their trip through the Tuolumne Cañon. Robert M. Price had been through the canyon twice before, explorations which he described in the Bulletin *in 1894 and 1895. He was still in law school when he signed the Articles of Incorporation of the Sierra Club in 1892. Later he served in a number of club offices, including a term as president. He and Jennie lived in San Francisco and Nome, Alaska, before moving in 1904 to Reno, Nevada, where they spent the rest of their lives.*

The Prices had already had "four weeks of delightful experience" in the Sierra that had given them "strength and courage," when they began the trip related below. Theodore Solomons accompanied them on the first part of it.

TOWARD THE CLOSE of the afternoon we passed McGee Lake, reached the White Cascades, and, climbing to an elevation on the left of the river, gazed into the Tuolumne Cañon with greatest interest and expectancy. The scene was enchanting! The Tuolumne River, after dashing itself into foaming rapids, rushed on down the cañon in silvery masses until it spread itself out like shining ribbon amid the green foliage of the forest pines. The walls of the cañon rose ruggedly grand on either side, becoming higher and higher, closing nearer and nearer, and blending in the dim western horizon. Inspiring as was the picture, we could not linger long. So with considerable difficulty, we made our way, with our animal, down the slope along the White Cascades, and in a short time, were enjoying for a last time, until Hetch-Hetchy was reached, the warmth and comfort of our sleeping bags and blankets.

Break of day found us up making final preparations. Mr. Solomons had decided to accompany us on a photographing tour as far as Return Creek. So, after carefully staking our mule in the midst of a grassy marsh, we slung our knapsacks and began our journey. We were all well laden, for a camera and outfit burdened one back, Mr. Price carried twenty-five pounds, five days' provisions for our party of two, his sweater, and a revolver, and I followed with a knapsack containing the cooking utensils, my jersey, and a few other articles. Its nine pounds I found as much as I could manage. In fact, at first it seemed more than I was equal to, for it took some time to get the proper bend to the back and learn to descend a rock without going head foremost, or rather, pack foremost. But experience is quickly gained in the Tuolumne Cañon, and it was not long before our loads seemed a part of ourselves.

Having camped on the southern bank of the river, we decided to descend for some distance on that side instead of taking the northern bank, along which previous trampers had made their way. But before we had traveled far, we regretted we had not crossed the river at the start, for the rocky slopes, over which we were obliged to walk, grew both steep and smooth, and we could hardly find a safe foothold, while the brush became almost impenetrable, and we made discouragingly slow progress. But we were fully compensated for the delay, for walls had now appeared on either side of the river, whose masses of granite claimed our full attention. With the "Three Brothers" on our left, "Tuolumne El Capitan" and an adjoining bluff on our right, we felt the grandeur of the cañon had not been exaggerated.

On we went, over the glaciated surfaces of the rocks, often climbing up for several hundred feet in narrow cracks, or sliding down a distance as great, to advance only a few yards; then, scrambling over high talus and around bowlders huge as houses, and forcing a way through sharp, dense thickets—such was our course for several hours, along the mountain river, growing more beautiful in its series of small falls and cascades. Finally, about noon, we approached a point in the river where the water, as if having accumulated energy for a glorious climactic surprise, suddenly dashed over immense granite stairways in a wonderful succession of foaming cascades. The tremendous force of the water, the fearful roar, the tearing, dashing, whirling mass, beaten into snowy foam as it rushed down the granite inclines, were far more grand and inspiring in reality than any photograph could picture to the imagination. We lunched below the Le Conte Cascade, in full view of its foaming, whirling torrents, and were loath to leave the scene. A short walk brought us to the Upper California Cascade, the most beautiful and majestic of the whole series. We had great difficulty in finding a way down the glaciated surfaces of the rocks to a position near enough to see the full extent of the water. Seated finally on a buttress near the foot of the cascade, with the mist falling over us, we gazed with wonder and delight on the exulting, on-rushing mass of snowy torrent, spreading itself over waves of granite, while leaping high in the air with glorious whirls, or shifting from side to side, tossing, tumbling, roaring, with all the exuberance and sprightliness of young mountain energy. Most graceful, most picturesque, this cascade was for me the crowning glory of the Tuolumne Cañon.

Leaving our place on the edge of the buttress, against which the whole force of the water dashes, and then, unable to advance, turns abruptly to the right, we began to descend the gentle granite slope to the left of the river. We

22

advanced rapidly, for the face of the rock was rough, and there was no danger of slipping. Suddenly, when about half way down, we found ourselves on a glaciated surface, unable to advance or retreat one step without losing foothold and sliding upon the sharp rocks below. After many efforts, Mr. Price finally succeeded in swinging himself into a position where he had one good foothold, but I, too short of limb to follow his example, with no notch in which to place finger or edge of shoe, simply waited, with the palms of my hands tightly pressed against the rock, wondering how long I could keep myself from the fatal plunge. Just at that moment, Mr. Solomons, returning from a distance, and seeing our predicament, hastened to my rescue with a long pole, and just as I was beginning to slide, placed it beneath my slipping foot, and gave me hold firm enough to risk one step in the direction of Mr. Price, and grasp his outstretched hand.

At the confluence of Return Creek and the Tuolumne, the three crossed to the north side of the river, and Solomons left to follow Return Creek.

After an hour or more of rough scrambling through brush and over talus, we willingly confessed we had had enough experience for one day, and were ready to stop at the first comfortable camping place. Here a mild discussion arose between the two members of our party as to what constituted a good sleeping spot, when we must rest for the night with neither blankets nor down sleeping bags for a covering. Mr. Price declared himself in favor of a bed of leaves, with a great fire on either side, and I advocated the advantages of a sand bank, where the flame could not reach us unknowingly. But nature did not seem to heed my decision, for we traveled on and on, and found no sleeping place such as I desired. Finally an inviting spot under the trees near the river was selected, and tossing off our knapsacks with great satisfaction, we were soon enjoying a supper of corn-meal mush, dried apricots, and beef bouillon. After finishing our meal, I left Mr. Price to gather wood while I repaired to the river to wash our few cooking utensils. It was not long before I saw my husband in great distress, gesticulating wildly, and rushing toward the stream in strangest fashion, motioning me to leave the spot where I stood spellbound. For a moment I could not think at all; then a confusion of emotions passed through my mind, and finally I thought of snakes. The stories of rattlers and their abundance in the cañon had not been a pleasant prospect from the beginning; and now, on our first night, we had been attacked, and Mr. Price probably bitten. In great anxiety I awaited his approach, and, finally, above the roar of the water, I made out that the cause of all my fears, and Mr. Price's gesticulations, was nothing more dangerous than wasps. Sleep, we knew, in the vicinity of a disturbed wasps' nest, with a fire to keep the insects stirring, was next to impossible; so, quickly gathering our belongings, in the darkness we made our way along the stream in quest of a new sleeping ground. It was no pleasure at that late hour to drag our weary limbs over jagged rocks that often tripped our careless feet, or to slip every now and then, in spite of ourselves, into little pools of cold water;

but fortunately, we had not far to travel, and this time it was a sand bank we found. An ideal spot it was, sheltered on three sides by huge bowlders that acted as reflectors for the heat of the fire, and having ready, within reach, wood of all shapes and sizes, tossed there by spring torrents. Sleeping without blankets was a novel experience, but not as uncomfortable as would be expected. With leggings for a pillow, we managed to sleep the greater part of the night, rousing ourselves at long intervals to replenish our fire.

Morning found us somewhat stiff and sleepy, but, withal, refreshed, and ready for another day's experience. During the early hours, our tramp was a pleasant variety of open flats, rough climbing over talus, and hard scrambling through small clumps of trees.

We were now in that portion of the cañon where the walls began to rise higher and grow more perpendicular, until, in the distance, the double-peaked Tuolumne Castle seemed to pierce the very skies. We found ourselves gazing about us with ever-increasing wonder and awe, while a feeling of our own helplessness and insignificance took possession of us. Just before noon, from the terrific rush and roar of the water, we knew we were approaching the Muir Gorge, where the angry river, after rising and falling for miles, transforms itself into a hissing, seething mass of churning water. Fascinated, we stood on a great bowlder and watched the frothing water hurl madly past into a veritable prison of granite. Out of this chasm rose, side by side, two bare gray walls to the height of a thousand feet, where the northern wall suddenly turned and swept back to the side of the cañon, forming a great rocky spur. Over this rough point we began our scramble about two in the afternoon. On reaching the summit, we found the Sierra Club register can buried under a substantial monument, and to the records added our names, the first since '94. We camped soon after reaching the river again, and slept the sleep that only the tired mountaineer can enjoy.

The third day was our hardest, for the forest fires, which were raging in the adjoining sections of country, made the air close and sultry. Our ambition seemed to vanish, and we advanced only because it was a necessity, and with the perspiration fairly dripping from our faces. Fortunately, however, we had reached Pate Valley, and had delightful walking all morning over small garden-like openings and level flats, through groves of trees and bushes heavily ladened with ripe thimble berries.

In the afternoon, after leaving Pate Valley, we met with rough work once more, and had several hours of difficult scrambling over talus that seemed almost impossible to climb around or over, through brush that pierced our clothing, and over rounded, polished stones by the waterside. The heat was most oppressive, and by five o'clock we were worn out and ready to camp. Just then a sight met our eyes that will long remain in memory. We were on the talus, piled several hundred feet high, and silently struggling along, when, suddenly to our right, and only a few feet away, there fairly shot into the air from out the shelter of huge blocks of granite, two large snakes. They seemed to stand on their very rattles, while, with heads erect, all unmindful of our observations, they twisted their long bodies around about each other, and sported in the most playful manner. The sight was uncanny, yet we stood fascinated for some moments. A second later a shower of missiles made known our presence, and in an instant, rattling loudly as they went, the two reptiles disappeared in the rocks below. A short walk brought us to the river once more, and to a comfortable camping place; but no sooner had our knapsacks reached the ground, than from our very feet came the penetrating, unmistakable rattle again, and two more reptiles were before us. It did not take long to despatch the snakes and secure their rattles, but the place had lost its charm for camping purposes, so we slung our knapsacks and started on. More weary than ever, now, we were glad to drop into the first inviting place we came across, and before many minutes had passed, supper was over and we were fast asleep. About twelve o'clock we aroused ourselves to set fire to the great pile of wood which had been collected during the evening, for up to that time the atmosphere, warmed by the burning forests, had made other heat unnecessary. As the first dry twig cheerily crackled in the silence of midnight, from the rocks beyond the fire, and only a few yards away, came once again the same warning note of the rattler. Another snake had been disturbed. But, feeling that all efforts, at that time of night, to escape our unpleasant neighbors were useless, we calmed ourselves as best we could, and in a short time had forgotten our fears in quiet sleep.

We were off on the morning of the fourth day at half-past five, and by seven were delightedly gazing on one of the most beautiful and varied water scenes in the whole cañon. The river, after dashing in small, picturesque whirls for a hundred feet or more, suddenly fell over a perpendicular wall, then dashed on over a silvery apron, smooth and regularly inclined, and then threw itself, with tremendous force, down a great stone stairway in foaming, whirling, tumbling cascades. An hour later, we could see dimly, but unmistakably outlined, far into Hetch-Hetchy, the massive Sugar Loaf; but, before reaching the valley itself, we had to cross one of the roughest spurs that we had met during the whole journey. It was a veritable hauling ourselves up for long distances, then crawling with greatest precision around slippery ledges, only to let ourselves down the rocky cliffs as best we might, jumping, sliding, or slowly edging away; but by ten o'clock we had camped for the day at the entrance to Hetch-Hetchy.

Our journey was over; regret and gladness mingled — gladness, that an end had come to constant labor; regret, that so much of grandeur and magnificence was far behind us in the cañon. A feeling, almost of indignation, rose within us, when we thought of the glorious cascades, the sheer granite walls, the great Muir Gorge, all pent up within a narrow mountain cleft, inaccessible to the great majority. But anyone who is anything of a mountaineer can see this region, and should journey through the entire length of the cañon, for it is a scenic wonderland, with never a dull step in the whole distance.

[*Editor Sierra Bulletin:* The Sierra Club is developing some capital mountaineers, and Mrs. Price must be one of the best. The Tuolumne Cañon is perhaps the roughest of all the Sierra streets, and her quiet walk through it was a fine, notable performance. As far as I know, she is the only woman who has traced it through its entire length. The Club should make some sort of a trail through this magnificent cañon. Simply cutting lanes through the densest of the chaparral tangles would go far to render it accessible. Very truly yours, JOHN MUIR.]

7

The Descent of Tenaya Cañon

GEORGE GIBBS

1901

It was not always easy to follow in the footsteps of John Muir, as George Gibbs found out. Who was George Gibbs? A college student who camped with three friends at Tenaya Lake on July 23, 1894. As with many writers in the Bulletin's *pages, we cannot say more than he tells us himself; we know him for a vivid moment, and then no more.*

The discovery George Gibbs made was about himself: what he could do if he really had to. Like many of us, he found that the frontiers of the self cannot be found until sought. That discovery is one made over and over again, in wild areas the world over; it is part of what Nancy Newhall meant by, "Wilderness holds answers to questions man has not yet learned how to ask," an axiom the club has lived by.

WE HAD BEEN on the road some fifty-six days, and had tramped over 500 miles. Our trip had taken us into some of the grandest and wildest parts of the Sierra. Corbett, one of our party, and I wished, as a climax to the tour, to attempt a dangerous and exciting bit of mountaineering, and so decided upon the descent of Tenaya Cañon into Yosemite Valley. Neither of us knew anything about the cañon, though we had heard that Mr. Muir had successfully passed through it. Had we, before starting, known the extent of the difficulties to be met, we might have hesitated some time before undertaking the trip.

Lake Tenaya is a beautiful sheet of water situated at the head of the stream which supplies Mirror Lake below. To reach the Yosemite from here by the usual trail, one travels twenty-odd miles; by way of Tenaya Cañon the distance is eight. While Corbett and I made the attempt through the cañon, the other two of our party were to take our mules into the valley by the usual route, and all were to meet below at Mirror Lake.

At six in the morning we started, carrying with us a bite of lunch and about fifty feet of stout rope. We expected to reach the Yosemite by noon — the others intended to arrive in the valley at four in the afternoon — so little did we realize what was before us! It took us fourteen hours of the hardest and most trying work to cover the eight miles of cañon.

Leaving Lake Tenaya, we followed along the right bank of the stream. For a mile or two we made our way through thick underbrush and over trunks of trees which lay all about the ground. We were congratulating ourselves on the easy work we were having, when we found that the way was growing gradually steeper and the cañon narrower. The traveling soon became very difficult. The glacier which had passed through the cañon had left the walls and floor in places as smooth as glass. Suddenly the way grew precipitous. There were no signs of brush, and the highly polished rocks were very slippery. Ahead of us we heard the sound of falling waters, and knew that we were approaching a precipice. A precipice it proved to be, and a frightfully steep one. We were puzzled, for if Mr. Muir had gone down the cañon, he had certainly not descended the waterfall before us.

Sliding down on my back thirty or forty feet along the smoothly polished rock surface, I barely succeeded in reaching a small projecting ledge. To this I clung, and looking over saw that a single step would have taken me over the edge of a perpendicular cliff hundreds of feet in height. The sight appalled me. I started back to join Corbett. Then I realized that, while there had been little difficulty in sliding down, to return was another matter. Unaided, I could not do it. I shouted to Corbett. Fortunately he had the rope, and after two or three attempts threw me an end, and with this help I was drawn up to the higher level where he stood. We were at a loss as to the method of reaching the floor of this chasm before us. Mr. Muir could never have gone down on the side of the stream which I tried, neither could he have descended the bank directly across the stream, for that, we found, was similar to the left side. The only thing to do was to leave the stream and to attempt the descent from a point about two hundred feet to the right. The wall was broken by two or three broad ledges and several narrower ones. Our only hope seemed to be in dropping from ledge to ledge, by means of the rope, down the steep wall on to the level below. This we finally accomplished, though it took us three hours of climbing, sliding, lowering, dropping, and falling. We would double the rope around some thick shrub or around a sharp-pointed rock which protruded sufficiently, and then, gliding down on the rope, would seek a footing at some point below. Thus, considerably exhausted, we came to the bottom. Here a plunge into a deep, cool pool refreshed us.

For a mile or more we now walked through underbrush or waded through the creek. Wet, tired, hungry, and a great deal less exuberant than in the morning, we trudged along, knowing that to go back now was impossible. With only four biscuits and a couple of cold rice-fritters in our pockets, the outlook was not cheerful.

It was now noon. Calculations showed that we had made about four miles. We must reach the Yosemite by night. The descent again grew steeper and steeper, and the walls of the cañon gradually narrowed, so that we were compelled to walk in the middle of the stream. The most exciting and dangerous incident of our descent now followed. The walls were not more than a hundred feet apart, and rose a thousand feet or more above us. The stream suddenly plunged into an extremely narrow gorge. We seemed to have reached the final jumping-off place. It was as impossible to climb out of the cañon as to go back, and to go straight ahead seemed out of the question. After a survey of the surrounding wall, we found only one solution to our difficulty. That was to make our way along a very narrow ledge on the right. This ledge, about two feet in its broadest places, sloped downwards toward its outer edge, constantly giving us the sensation, while moving along it, of slipping into the gorge below. Corbett thought that with the aid of the rope he might reach a ledge below, and while I secured and held the end, he lowered himself some distance down the side of the gorge. He was completely hidden from sight, and kept me in constant dread lest he should slip and be dashed against the granite rocks below. All at once the top of his head, followed by an extremely pale face, reappeared above the ledge. He had gotten down fairly well, but had found no good footing below, and had just been able to return by means of the rope. So to descend at this point was impossible, and it seemed as though nothing were left but to crawl farther along the ledge we were on — a very disagreeable alternative, as the ledge grew narrower at every step. We made a few yards on our hands and knees, and then came to a nearly perpendicular slope along which for a distance of thirty or forty feet ran a small ledge. It was about half the width of a man's shoe. Corbett started across, leaning against the wall and placing one foot directly before the other. Slowly, step by step, making each move with the greatest deliberation, he crossed, and finally with a shout of joy reached a level spot beyond. It was now my turn, and, trying to forget the danger, I advanced, keeping my eyes always before me, directed on the spot where my companion stood. In a few moments — a period which seemed a hundred times longer — I joined him, with a feeling of relief and pleasure that is hard to describe.

For a half-hour or more our descent continued to be a hard one. We let each other down and pulled each other up over ledges and difficult places, the rope seemingly indispensable. At last, about three o'clock, we reached the bed of the stream once more. We then sat down to a lunch and well-earned rest. We knew we were nearing Mirror Lake, because the Half Dome, a guiding-point throughout the day, seemed now not very far distant. The most dangerous portion of the trip was over; the remainder was merely vexatious and tedious. It was a continuous climbing over bowlder after bowlder. The brush and trees became so thick on the sloping sides of the cañon as to drive us again and again into the stream, compelling us to wade.

It was now about 6 P.M., and we were faint and tired. There seemed no end to the bowlders, brush, and undergrowth, and our arms and legs ached from the repeated strains. We were on the left-hand side of the stream and were walking along a grateful level stretch when it abruptly ended in a fall of sixty or seventy feet. We did not want to turn back and search for a means of getting around the fall, and so we looked for a place near by. Standing on a projecting bowlder some yards to the right, we saw close at hand a branch of a huge pine whose base was not far from the foot of the fall. Corbett again took the lead, and after some hesitancy swung himself upon the branch, which bent almost double under his weight. He clung to it, dangling in mid air fifty feet above the ground. Hand over hand he reached the main trunk, then slid quickly to the ground. I followed him, and in a few moments our last difficulty had been overcome.

It was growing late, and we knew the boys in the valley would be anxious about our safety. We now came into a dense forest in which we had to struggle through ferns and underbrush and where we were constantly stumbling over dead trunks of trees and creeping vines. It was not until it was evening and completely dark that we finally emerged and found ourselves before Mirror Lake. A few moments more and we joined the other two, who welcomed us as if we were the dead come to life. For once they were glad to see us, and to say that they were thankful—and we also, for that matter—would be putting it mildly.

We learned from Mr. Clark, the Guardian of the valley, that Mr. Muir, and one other party, consisting of two men, had made the descent of the cañon. Our trip was the first for over twelve years.

If one loves excitement and peril, he may rest assured that he can find it in the trip we took. As an example of dangerous mountain-climbing, it will serve as one of the best; but neither Corbett nor I would wish any friend the doubtful pleasure of some of our experiences.

8

The Great Spruce Forest and the Hermit Thrush

VERNON KELLOGG

1902

The wilderness experience is not only macroscopic—evoked by the grand panoramas of ranges and valleys—but well-nigh microscopic, like John Muir's surprise at seeing the blossom of a single gentian in a remote Canadian forest or the climber's delight at spotting, amid the granite pinnacles at the summit of a range, the sudden appearance of that alpine phenomenon, the polemonium. And the wilderness experience is not only visual but auditory. There are certain sounds that are heard so rarely as to evoke a sensation of mystery that cannot be remotely conveyed to one who has not heard them. One of these sounds, audible to the keen-eared listener in most American forests, is described here by Stanford Professor Vernon Kellogg in a prose that for all its Victorianisms will awake deep recognition in anyone who has had the good fortune to experience a similar moment of austere beauty.

THE GREAT SPRUCE FOREST is characterized chiefly by its very many trees and its dreadful stillness. As we reluctantly poked our heads from beneath the covering blankets and peered about through the heavy gray of a June dawning, the ghostly trees and the absolute silence struck first into mind.

It is cold on the mountain-side. High up on the eastern flank of a mighty mountain range, a small group, perhaps half a dozen, of spruces had succumbed to some great wind and their fallen shafts were slowly returning to the soil the rich stores they had formerly taken from it. A tiny pool of clear, cold water with a half-invisible rivulet seeping away through the dense green mat, quickened the plant life for some little space around. Bright yellow splashes of buttercups and trembling wind–flowers reared their dainty white faces from among the cool green leaves; near a half-imbedded stone dashed with soft shades of color by the abundance of some microscopic plant form, a handful of odd-faced columbines, half-white, half-purpling, bent languidly toward us.

With all the charm of the camp surroundings, the almost intolerable silence tended to create a feeling akin to depression, and our weak attempts at jest over the night's unrest were so foreign to the spirit of the morning that they died on our lips. There was needed the voice of the Great Forest, the utterings of the wood-spirits. And as we lay with straining ears and tense nerves, of a sudden the voice came. High over head and down the trail half a dozen rods burst forth a single lyric measure, the notes rolling, trilling, gurgling, and clear and strong as befits the voice of a great forest's spirit. The short carol was repeated, and again. The last liquid *tur-kwill-ah-illah-ée* was barely dying away when from far away in the direction of the silent green lake which one may seek for a day and never find, came faintly the answering voice, trilling back the same joyous strain, and more faintly still, floating up the mountain from far below, where the tumbling rill makes soft music all the day, came, half unheard, the song's sweet repetition. 'Twas the matins of the hermit thrush, rare minstrel of the mountain forests. Garbed in soft brown friar's frock, a monk well content to worship lone at Nature's shrine! Naturalists have told and poets sung of the hermit's wonderful song. It is in truth a marvelous measure, containing all those characteristics of liquidity and bell-tone which make the thrush-song the highest expression of bird-music. But it is largely the always-enhancing circumstances which give it special credit above other thrush carols, although it has its own peculiar and indescribable special characteristics. Haunting the dense woods of the whole North American continent the hermit thrush is yet rarely heard, and worse, if heard, more rarely recognized.

9

Late Autumn in the Sierras

GRANT H. SMITH

1924

Grant Smith's litany of late autumn evokes that time of year when we know that nature has its endings—as well as its beginnings in the season still to come.

THE DAYS ARE GOLDEN; the rain-washed air is clear and sparkling, the warm rays of the south-sloping sun fall like a benediction. Not a leaf stirring save those that drift down from the whitening branches. No sound of insect or of bird except the occasional harsh note of the jay.

The opening lines of a famous sonnet come to mind:

> "That time of year thou mayst in me behold,
> When the yellow leaves, or none, or few, do hang
> Upon those boughs which shake against the cold;
> Bare ruin'd choirs, where late the sweet birds sang."

The only music is the unceasing murmur of the streams.

The short days pass all too soon, with reading, dreaming, and untiring contemplation of Nature's majestic handiwork.

Often a ride up the steep trails, with their infinite variety; along flashing streams and deep gorges, through primeval forests, up to the high ridges, commanding wide views of dark cañons and range on range of forested mountains.

At the close of day, a stroll along the brook fringed with poplars, where yellow leaves lie deep, rustling underfoot and giving forth a fragrant, pungent odor; returning through the tree-encircled meadow, to enjoy again the play of light and shadow on the ragged peaks of the great mountain that seems to block the wide cañon opening to the west.

Long, solitary, restful evenings in the cabin, with pipe and book, where a glowing fire warms like the presence of a cherished friend.

Before bed, a walk in the starlit night, to marvel afresh at the wonders of the heavens, whose shining lights hang so low that vision seems to penetrate far beyond.

Late rising in the frosty mornings, a wash in the ice-cold waters of the brook, and then to breakfast with appetite that makes simple fare a feast.

All nature is preparing for the snows and the long winter sleep.

The birds have all flown southward except those undaunted by harsh weather. The grouse have taken to the high ridges.

Tree-squirrels and chipmunks noisily gather their winter stores; severing pine-cones with their sharp teeth, which fall with resounding crash in the silent woods.

The ground-squirrels are already half-dormant in their warm, dry nests.

Everywhere the fresh-turned earth tells of the industry of the gophers, gathering grass and roots for storage in deep cellars.

Scarcely an insect passes through the air save a few belated butterflies, unmindful of their early demise.

Such of the grasshoppers as have postponed death crawl slowly in the sunshine.

The ants and wasps and bees have ceased their labors.

The trout, no longer sprightly, lie in the deep pools, scarcely feeding.

Dark and cold run the swift streams which in summer seemed so gladsome. Now they are brightened only by the yellow leaves that come floating along, resting lightly on the water.

On the mountains above the bears are making ready for their long sleep, while the deer await the first fall of snow before departing for the foot-hills, whence the quail have already gone.

The few mountain-lions that remain all winter are having their last fill of venison until the return of the deer in the spring; meantime they will grow thin and hungry on a slight fare of snow-shoe rabbits, porcupines, and other small animals.

With the first heavy snow, the fat, stupid, shambling porcupines will betake themselves to the tops of tall pines and firs, there to cling through the blasts of winter, barely subsisting on the tender bark, whose removal kills the tree-tops.

Only the eagles, hawks, grouse, woodpeckers, kingfishers, water-ouzels, jays, owls, chickadees and snowbirds, and the lions, bob-cats, coyotes, martins, mink, porcupines, foxes, rabbits, flying squirrels and tree-squirrels will brave the winter weather for a precarious living.

On the earth brownness everywhere; the flowers and grasses have long since died; the tender plants and shrubs, blasted by frost, hang in tatters.

Nature — ever seeking to make amends — for lack of beauty elsewhere has glorified the landscape with the flaming banners of autumn.

Along the streams the maples, cottonwoods, and willows are all green and gold, intensified by an occasional crimson splash of dogwood.

The mountains, towering on every hand, adorned with stately pines and firs and cedars, interspersed with aspens, oaks, maples, and dogwood, present a gorgeous spectacle of intermingled and contrasting colors.

A great peace hangs over earth and sky, inviting and satisfying the soul.

10

Trail Song: Giant Forest and Vicinity

CEDRIC WRIGHT

1928

The earth spoke to Cedric Wright with clarity and grace, and he gives these words to us intact as he heard them summer after summer in the Sierra. Wright was a violinist, a poet, and one of the finest nature photographers of his time. He began to experiment with the camera in the 1930s, and sought to bring out of film not only images, but the spirit that lay behind them. Words of the Earth, *a collection of his poetry and photographs, published after his death in 1959, shows how he succeeded.*

33

R USHING STREAMS, cold sweet air, tingling sun and freezing shade, pine needles, big busy black ants, content! Not merely to enjoy this world for ourselves, but to do our bit to leaven the human world with some draught from these forests, through thought, through example, through music, and in a thousand ways; to aid no matter how little the great process of change toward reality.

Melting snows, firm moist granite sand, fragrance of trees in the crystal air—something of these things sinks into us because their individuality is true beauty. Lace patterns on the snow of pine needles, fragrance of fallen boughs, old wood! These are the "words of the earth," so filled with quality that their mere existence is enough. There is a direct meaning in them—"No argument, screaming, persuasion."

Every foot of earth so beautifully draped, laved in such exquisite light and sound, full of serene beauty. "Consider the lilies of the field." We come here to gain the richness, quietness, and content of the earth, through paths of leaf-mould and bark-mould, in half-swampy stretches through the shady wood. There is always the living richness of contrast. Each elevation has its own growths and personality. But continually, all around, are symbols of grim stateliness and character, because the free processes of unhampered nature flow here, producing this unimpeded loveliness. These dead branches and pine needles on the snow, their patterns dictated by the action of subtle natural laws—the care-free instinct of the forest—the wind, gravitation, and deep momentums, past understanding. How remote we humans keep ourselves from these influences in our towns and colleges!

These quantities of freshly fallen trees tell the stern story of last winter. Trees in all stages of decay intensifying the richness of the forest. Tragically broken trees, yet each dead stump fulfilling beauty. No sorrow there, only beauty. Here again, as everywhere, exhibited clear, the great river, life, the passing show, forever flowing, fading "out of the embraces of its names." So the liquid river, kindred to the life river, through some faint analogy suggests its weird charm.

No one's writing, no one's pictures, ever tell the intimate spirit of a camping trip in the Sierra. They are too much in love with the *big mountain* and the *big tree,* and with what *they did.* But when we see the exquisite charm of little intimate rivulets, their moss gardens and little separate worlds, is it any wonder to feel the need of being closer in spirit to this sort of thing, to collect into ourselves all the intimate touches of a mountain trip—the pictures that have never been taken—and to try to translate the phrasings of mountains into the phrasings of music and human life? To love this beauty so that one becomes it! To see in each rock, each weather-beaten dead tamarack and juniper, each bit of needle-strewn earth, a beauty inviting a lingering look. A mountain trip distills this love of rustic free beauty, sculptured and formed by majestic momentums and laws divine.

So along these mountain paths a continual harmony of care-free influences surrounds us. A siren call to adopt more and more the fundamental laws which are God and the spirit of Democracy. When this clearer understanding of true existence and law comes, sympathies will be more common, love more universal, democracy more established. Though diversity of opinion may always exist, yet an underlying sympathy, or at least tolerance, will be more prevalent and human love will crave the setting of the woods and hills, because a great love is so in tune with them.

Here we learn the primitive and authentic joys of closeness to natural vital running water, fire, wind. We lie on the ground resting or enjoying ourselves tremendously, oblivious to sun or rain. After many days of mountain communion, it dawns that you have sensed things which appeal to the mind and heart as being—God—the composite spirit of everything that is, working together toward a deeper beauty.

Suddenly along these trails I find myself thinking some music— Beethoven violin concerto, Andante from Tschaikowsky string quartet, or what not. And it comes with a richness of interpretation I have hardly known, with a tone-quality which glows. Beauty advances on such a broad front, "the growing mind of God." To outline that front and advance it is the eternal world problem after we are free from necessity. This is certainly necessary to the essence of great music. Without the feeling of the wilderness there is no interpretation. This can hardly be gained in a city. But here in the mountains we are directly in the midst of the elemental rhythm and pulse which is the high tide of this drift eternal.

When the mountains evoke a melody, a song, a thought, sing it with you—it is that spirit back of mountain and song which is the precious new world we need to find. It is in wave-lines of checkered sunlight and shimmer of wind flicking across some high green snow-lake. Or, appearing suddenly, while watching mountains, a cold effervescence in the heart, a touch of . . . what else than a glimpse of cosmic reality. That tingling spirit haunts all the high country like a majestic hymn, for those who see and feel beneath the surface of things. It is in the cold sunny air—the brilliant mountain air. It is in the streaming billowy clouds, filtering changing floods of light and shadow, in patterns ever clothing the mountain anew. It is accompanied ever by things which to sight and sound include this thrilling quality, swelling the chorus, giving it universal breadth.

And the sound in the air, the deep hum of river and of wind in forest! It has a flow and roll, an elastic depth, a kindliness infinitely soothing, yet majestically great. Oh, to emulate the personality of this mountain music! It is Beethoven, Bach, and Brahms—or, rather, they are like it.

In these mountains, all that we see there, think there, is through the filter of these influences. Everything good is magnified and glorified through this mountain democracy and blend. The shimmer of wind over mountain lakes, the sadness of distant ranges, the brilliance of quiet clear water—all these I see in the faces of mountain-lovers; a certain wistfulness and determination seem there. For there is a mighty contagion in the qualities of things.

Stop and listen to the birds on one of these high ridges. What I said of the contagion of the quality in things seems true here between their song and the sunlight. The depth of beauty in the sunlight filtering through the forest

35

seems mirrored again in the song of the birds, like streams of elastic gold weaving through the trees. On warm quiet days, a bell song in minor shadés, weird rhythms and intervals, all music, through the forest, through the magic of great spaces, through the stateliness of the growth of the soil.

But one must be greatly alone.

These mountains and cloud halos by day, at night their dim silhouettes against huge stars, set in a depth of silence no lowland ever exhibited. Tuned to the beloved mountains, fairly humming their key and clef, we return to the mild and petty expressions of civilization. Distant thunder reverberant over violet ridges bids us good-by.

Indelible in our memories, the fusion song of all nature solemnly and serenely flows over the waves of forest ridges and gleaming granite heights. It is a continual Chopin C Minor Prelude. These mountains seem the scaffolding of creation, tuned to things a million times their breadth and grandeur, linked to other planes than ours.

11   Last Citadel

PHOEBE ANNE

SUMNER

1950

All of us have dreamed of finding a "last citadel," as Phoebe Anne Sumner does, a place where we can perceive what nature was like before human intrusion. Whether such a place exists or not, we need to think it does, and if we find it, leave it as Phoebe Sumner does, unnamed, unchanged.

WHEN WE FIRST SAW the basin on our map of the southern High Sierra, its striking topography fired our imagination and raised a challenge. Remote from any trail, apparently inaccessible from any direction, it was bounded on three sides by a semicircular wall of giant peaks, and on the fourth by a drop-off equally forbidding and sheer. We had long hoped to enter this primeval area, and when last summer's High Trip brought us near it, we seized the chance to knapsack in.

Eight of us spent the greater part of the first day in working up over the vast, steep fields of rock which provide natural protection for the basin. As we traversed the seemingly endless jumble, we became aware of a sensation new to most of us: at a time and in a part of the world where the opportunity to do so was rapidly vanishing, we knew that this was the way it felt to be pioneers, bound for a land so little visited that it was as if no man had come this way before.

By mid-afternoon the view behind, of wooded slopes, tall peaks, and shadowed canyons, had receded and was forgotten. If the map was right, we were close to our single point of entry to the basin; we had climbed to 13,000 feet and were approaching its rim. To our left now were the summits of its towering, serrated, upper wall, the westernmost of which would soon obscure the sun. A cloud stole briefly over a low point on the crest, and dissolved.

Soon afterward we stood triumphant on the basin's rim; far below us lay its rugged wilderness — barren in its upper reaches, with twisted trees and green meadow patches farther down, its gray rocky surface broken by small, shining lakes. But what made it all unique in our experience was that great wall, which revealed to us no other breach. The invulnerability of the wall was in its height and its loose and treacherous rock — rock which mountaineers shun gladly.

An eagle circled high in the slanting light as we started down; and by the time we had made our way, over rocks which slid with every step, to relatively level ground, it was almost dark. As we looked around this mountain fastness in the twilight, hunting for a place to camp, our sense of isolation and remoteness grew. There were no old campsites here, no marks of axe or fire. There was only the murmuring of the stream, the faint night wind, the light of the stars.

When we awoke next morning, it seemed to us as if each separate beauty of the High Sierra had been gathered here, to be preserved and guarded for all time. This hidden stronghold formed a self-sustaining world; the white snow patches where the streams were born, the pines and willows and soft meadow grasses watered by these streams, the little animals and birds protected and fed by the plants and trees — all these things in perfect equilibrium, requiring nothing from outside their granite home except the sun which brought them warmth and light, the clouds which brought them rain.

First reactions to this untouched loveliness retold another story. "If only we could live here!" someone cried. "If only the others could see this too!" The fisherman mentally stocked the stream with trout; the skiers stocked the slopes with down-mountain courses. But to such thoughts the basin and its living things had answers. We sensed these answers as our feet pushed through the waving meadow grass, untrampled since time began, and we thought of other meadows we had known; as we walked through clumps of giant foxtail pines, unblazed or thinned by man, blackened only where lightning had struck; as we picked our way along the stream bank and shining lakes, past waters as clear and pure as they had been a thousand years ago; as we watched a cony busy in the piled-up rocks; as we listened to a rock wren's song — and thought of forests, waters, and creatures known no more.

Slowly we understood the implications of the knowledge, now made real, that here was something which once a continent had possessed, something which had thrilled men's hearts as they looked over the unbroken western prairie; the great marshy valley of the San Joaquin teeming with wildfowl and big game; the untrodden Yosemite — something which had retreated and retreated until now it must hide between a sheer precipice and a giant wall, deep in the lonely reaches of the mountains.

We found ourselves doubling our usual care to leave no sign that we had passed. We spoke less frequently of coming back some day; stopped planning to tell others by what route we had come. Better perhaps if we could tell them why.

Late on this second day, while we stood beside a quiet lake and looked back toward the far end of the basin, an uneasiness which had grown steadily upon us took shape in words. It was as if the spirit of the place were speaking, within its voice the echo of other voices which were silent now, because men had not heard.

"Here is a different wealth from that which most men understand. It may not be gained by blasting these rocks, felling these trees, damming this stream; it could be lost forever in an hour. To try to take this treasure is to lose it. Leave it unchanged; the gain will not be yours alone, but every man's.

"You who have walked otherwise through all the earth, walk gently here."

38

PART II   Heritage: Men
and Women to
Match Our
Mountains

THE EARLY YEARS

IN ITS NINE DECADES of history, the Sierra Club has been action and symbol, fact and legend, catalyst and gadfly. From a group dedicated in 1892 to exploring and enjoying the mountains of the Pacific Coast, as well as to preserving "the natural features of the Sierra Nevada," it has become a national organization concerned with both a livable and beautiful Planet Earth.

How did this transformation come about? Part of the answer lies in the beginnings of the club—in the caliber of the men and women who founded it, and their far-reaching concept of what it should be. In this section we look at the founders and their successors, men and women "to match our mountains"—and to enjoy, revere, and preserve them.

The Sierra Club

J. N. LeCONTE

1917

The Founding of the Sierra Club

ETHEL OLNEY

EASTON

1969

In his history of the first twenty-five years of the club, J. N. LeConte tells of the events that led to its founding. LeConte, who was just completing a term as president, begins with Yosemite Valley and the Sierra Nevada that stretched north and south. To the generation that founded the club, the peaks and canyons, the forests and meadows that were the Sierra formed a superb symbol of natural beauty around which they could rally.

LeConte's account of the club's founding has been merged with an account by Ethel Olney Easton, Warren Olney's daughter. She was born in San Francisco, raised in Oakland, and graduated from the University of California in 1897. She was well into her nineties when she wrote these reminiscences.

We begin the story with LeConte. Although, as LeConte notes, Yosemite first became "open to the world" in 1851, it is likely that scout Joseph Walker and his men camped near the northern brink of the valley and saw it in 1833.

THE TRUE GRANDEUR of our Sierra Nevada was first opened to the world by the discovery of the Yosemite Valley in 1851. In spite of the difficulties of travel, a great many people found their way into this famous valley during the early fifties, at a time when access was possible only on horseback and over the roughest of trails. It is not surprising then that these hardy pioneers soon discovered that the Yosemite was only the gateway to a vast alpine region whose equal was not to be found within the boundaries of the United States.

In 1868 John Muir came to California and immediately made his way into the Yosemite Valley, which by this time was renowned throughout the world. He at once began his travels and studies in the high Sierra, and his first contribution to the literature of this subject was published in 1871. From then on to the time of his death, his writings, more than any one thing, have directed the attention of the public to the wonders of the Sierra.

Beginning about 1870, expeditions were formed by enthusiastic mountain-lovers simply for the purpose of exploring and enjoying the high Sierra. But these also were but pioneers, and each party was obliged to work its own way through independently, making use of the trails of the sheepmen who at a very early date began using the rich pasturage of the alpine meadows. Practically no detailed information was to be obtained then in any published accounts. All descriptions so far were of a general nature and lacked that accuracy of detail of route and trail so necessary to the traveler.

It finally became evident that some organization was needed whereby the experiences and practical results of travel might be brought together and preserved for the use of others to follow. . . . The first definite move in this direction seems to have been made by Professor J. H. Senger, of the University of California, in 1886. . . . Professor Senger's first idea was to establish a library of mountaineering literature in the Yosemite Valley, bringing together not only all books relating to the California mountains, but collecting all published maps, as well as sketch-maps and notes and itineraries made by travelers. His idea was evidently that Yosemite would be the natural starting-point from which all trips would be made. Later the idea expanded, and by 1890 the proposition of forming a club or association was widely discussed, particularly among the students and faculty of the University of California, and the name "Sierra Club" seems to have been thought of at that time. Professor Senger discussed the matter with many of his friends, notably with Professor William D. Armes, of the state university, with Mr. Warren Olney, of San Francisco, and with John Muir. I myself realized the importance of such a club during a trip through the Kings River Sierra in 1890. At that time nothing was popularly known of the trails in that section, and our party knew nothing from day to day of what lay before us.

The one thing which finally brought matters to a head was the creation of the Yosemite, Sequoia, and General Grant national parks in October, 1890. The idea here was first conceived by Mr. Robert Underwood Johnson, editor of the *Century Magazine*. He visited Yosemite during the summer of 1889, and was persuaded by Mr. Muir to accompany him to the high Sierra region about the headwaters of the Tuolumne and Merced rivers. He noticed the sad destruction caused by sheep in the meadows and wild-flower gardens, descriptions of which he had read in Mr. Muir's articles, and on his return he urged the formation of a great national park which should include this upper region, offering to Mr. Muir the use of the *Century Magazine* to put before the public a proper description of this and other scenic wonders of the Sierra. Right gladly Mr. Muir took up the work, and, energetically backed by those who afterward were founders of the Sierra Club, the necessary bills were passed through Congress and signed by President Cleveland.

The formation of the Sierra Club was now no longer a matter of doubt. It was decided to abandon the idea of headquarters in Yosemite Valley, as that was obviously inappropriate to the broader idea, and to make the place of business San Francisco.

Thus the Sierra Club was founded not around a campfire in Yosemite, but in a law office at 101 Sansome Street in San Francisco, blocks from where its headquarters are today.
We will hear about the next stage from Mrs. Easton.

In 1889 or '90 my father, Warren Olney, began meeting John Muir at William Keith's studio which was located above the California Market in downtown San Francisco.

Keith was a well-known landscape and portrait painter and an active lover of the outdoors. He was an intimate friend of Muir and had accompanied him on outings in the Sierra and elsewhere. My father had come to California from Iowa in 1868 because of the climate and the mountains, as well as to practice law. He had tramped and camped over hundreds of miles in the California back country and had known Keith for many years but had never met Muir, who was not then by any means as widely known to the general public as he later became.

Coming to San Francisco from Martinez (not far north of Oakland, where he had a fruit ranch) Muir would often visit Keith's studio. On receiving word from Keith, my father would walk over from his office in the nearby First National Bank Building, 101 Sansome Street, and the three would talk about the outdoors.

The creation of Yosemite National Park in 1890 and of the Federal Forest Reserve System in the following year must have given impetus to these conversations. There was increasing concern over the future of "the Sierras," as we usually called them, and over encroachment of "civilization" and of private interests on wild places.

After their talks the three would often go downstairs for lunch in the California Market restaurant, the market then extending from Pine to California streets at the site of the new fifty-three story Bank of America Building.

Others soon joined the conversations and lunches. I remember my father saying that the meetings were growing too large for Keith's rather small and cluttered studio and were being held in my father's law office. Among those included in the group were probably Professors Joseph LeConte, J. H. Senger, William Dallam Armes, Cornelius Beach Bradley, and John C. Branner of the University of California and Stanford faculties, and David Starr Jordan, President of Stanford, all then or later friends of my father. At about this time I recall both Muir and Jordan coming to our house on 29th Street in Oakland.

Muir certainly played a leading role in the meetings. I remember my father's speaking of this.

Keith evidently provided a sympathetic context and atmosphere. He was a genial man of great personal charm and wide acquaintance. He had painted his favorite view (perhaps it was Muir's too) of Mt. Tamalpais from the west: It was a watercolor which my father had purchased and which is now in my home. Keith had painted as a gift the portrait of my father that is now at Mills College.

My father's particular contribution to the conservation meetings was his practical, legal, business and political knowledge. He had been a Bay Area resident for nearly twenty-five years. He would soon consent to run for mayor of Oakland but only on condition he receive both Democratic and Republican nominations, which he did. In addition to law, business, and politics, he was in touch with administration and faculties at California, Stanford, and Mills [College] and could thus help create a broad and practical base for an effective organization.

All those working for what became the Sierra Club shared a common love and concern for California's natural beauty. My father and Muir had a small additional bond in that they had arrived in California the same year.

The articles of incorporation of the Sierra Club were drawn up by my father and signed in his office on June 4, 1892. Muir was named president and my father first vice-president. Keith was a charter member, as was my brother Warren Olney, Jr.

We return to J. N. LeConte. Muir had replied with the following, to Professor Senger's invitation to attend a meeting at which founding a "Sierra Club" was to be discussed.

MARTINEZ, May 22

PROF. SENGER,

Dear Sir: I will gladly attend the meeting on Saturday next at Mr. Olney's office. I suppose it will not be best to have a large number present at the first meeting. Hoping that we will be able to do something for wildness and make the mountains glad, I remain

Cordially yours,
JOHN MUIR

LeConte then gives the famous article III from the articles of incorporation in which the purposes of the club are stated. As drawn up by Warren Olney, the statement of purposes served the club well in its beginnings, and, in an expanded form, serves the club equally well now.

That the purposes for which this Corporation is formed are as follows, to-wit: To explore, enjoy and render accessible the mountain regions of the Pacific Coast; to publish authentic information concerning them; to enlist the support and co-operation of the people and government in preserving the forests and other natural features of the Sierra Nevada Mountains.

He remarks:

It will be noticed in reading the above purposes of the club that they show two distinct points of view, which seem to reflect the characters of the two most active organizers. A club to "explore, enjoy and render accessible the mountain regions of the Pacific Coast; to publish authentic information concerning them" was evidently the first idea conceived of by Professor Senger, while the purpose of "enlisting the support and co-operation of the people and the government in preserving the forests and other natural features of the Sierra Nevada Mountains" shows the legal mind of Mr. Olney.

The club began its work in a modest way with a charter membership of 182, but from the first it began developing along all the lines laid down by its founders. The first publication, issued in the summer of 1892, has already been referred to as containing the articles of incorporation and by-laws. The first *Bulletin* appeared January, 1893, and the second in June of the same year.

In 1893 also there were published two outline maps, one of the Yosemite and the other of the Kings River High Sierra, which were the only maps of the high mountains at that time showing trails and routes. From the first also the club took an active part in the protection of the national parks. As early as October, 1892, the club considered, took action against, and by its influence defeated the so-called Caminetti Bill which proposed to cut down the boundaries of the Yosemite National Park, and it also protested against certain illegal timber-cutting in national parks. Money was also appropriated for the improvement of trails and marking of routes in the Tuolumne Sierra.

The question of a seal came up at an early date. When first organized a simple seal was adopted, showing a pine tree within a circular margin, with the words "Altiora peto" below. In the spring of 1894 Mr. Willis Polk designed the present seal, with the *Sequoia gigantea* in the foreground, Half Dome and a typical alpine group, Mount Ritter and Banner Peak, in the distance.

The most important piece of work in which the club has ever engaged was the passage of a bill through the legislature receding the Yosemite State Park to the Government, and the subsequent acceptance of it by Congress as a part of the national park.

The club is now in a flourishing condition. It has over 1800 members, and its income from dues and advertising is some $5000 per annum. Its publications fill nine volumes, and these contain practically all the results of exploration in the high Sierra during the past twenty-five years, as well as work in other mountain regions. Let every one then put his shoulder to the wheel, so that, as Mr. Muir says in his letter, "We will be able to do something for wildness and make the mountains glad."

All the men mentioned by LeConte and Mrs. Easton are remarkable, but two stand out.

William Keith, a fine landscape painter and fellow Scotsman, had met Muir in 1872 in Yosemite. They became the best of friends. At his request, Muir took him to Tuolumne Meadows, pronouncing to him: "The crown of the Sierras is a picture hung on the sky, and mind you, it needs none of your selection or 'composition.'"

Willis Polk, designer of the club's present seal, does not enter the story again, but

he must have electrified the early members with his dramatic and tempestuous person-
ality. As an architect, Polk was a brilliant innovator who designed the first glass-
walled building in the United States; as a personality he took delight in astonishing if
not affronting as many wealthy members of society as he could. One does not think of
Polk as fond of the out-of-doors, and yet, in Golden Gate Park, there is a tree
dedicated to him by the Garden Club: "To Willis Polk, lover of trees."

13 Hetch Hetchy

ETHEL OLNEY

EASTON

1969

Most of J. N. LeConte's history of the first twenty-five years has been reprinted
here. It is a little amazing that something has been left out: LeConte does not once
mention the all-out, decade-long battle the club waged to prevent the damming of
Hetch Hetchy Valley in Yosemite National Park. The majority of members sup-
ported Muir, Colby, and other club members, including LeConte, in their fight to
preserve the Yosemite-like valley and to establish the inviolability of national parks.
However, there was a bitter dissident faction in the San Francisco Bay Chapter that
felt the city of San Francisco needed Hetch Hetchy water and promoted damming the
valley for a reservoir and for generating power. Warren Olney himself held strongly
to this opinion. The club lost the battle in 1913 and the dam was built. However,
feelings had run so high on both sides of the issue that J. N. LeConte, writing in
1917, still did not feel free to mention Hetch Hetchy.

In this excerpt from The Founding of the Sierra Club, *Mrs. Easton tells how*
her father felt about the issue.

I SHOULD LIKE TO ADD that in the unfortunate Hetch Hetchy controversy
my father played a leading, and I believe a mistaken, role in dividing the
Sierra Club, a division that led to his resignation and to temporary
estrangement from some members of the club he had worked with, including Muir and Will Colby.

My father honestly believed that the Hetch Hetchy project—aimed at
damming the Tuolumne River in a magnificent valley adjacent to Yosemite—was necessary to the Bay Area's water supply. As a longtime Bay Area
resident he had experienced the years of water rationing which many old-

timers still remember. Wells and windmills in back yards were common. As mayor of Oakland he had had to face "the water problem" and be responsible for its solution. He had battled the private interests then controlling the Bay Area's meager water supply. He had become convinced that a public source, and in particular the Hetch Hetchy source, was the best available solution to a problem which he had had long personal and painful experience with. He felt that since Yosemite Valley was assured, a compromise on Hetch Hetchy "in the public interest" was advisable.

He did not foresee the day when the Sierras would be so crowded, and unspoiled natural grandeur in such short supply, that Hetch Hetchy Valley would loom in retrospect as a bit of paradise lost. Besides—he had once fallen while fishing in Hetch Hetchy and cracked three ribs. Perhaps the painful experience marred his appreciation of the Valley's grandeur and beauty.

His resignation from the Club after nearly twenty years of pioneering service and close friendship became such a painful subject to him that the Hetch Hetchy project was never afterward a permissible topic of conversation in our household.

Hetch Hetchy around 1900. *Hetch Hetchy after the dam was built.*

14

Sierra Club
Then and Now

FRANCIS FARQUHAR

1972

One of the most thoughtful, authoritative — and personal — accounts of the club's history was given by Francis Farquhar in an interview with Dave Bohn in 1972. Farquhar was eighty-four at the time and could look back over more than sixty years of close association with the club. For twenty of these years he was editor of the Bulletin; *he served as president of the club in the mid-thirties and late forties; in 1969 he was made honorary president. He received the club's highest honor, the John Muir Conservation Award, in 1965, the same year that his definitive* History of the Sierra Nevada *was published.*

The people to whom Farquhar refers are identified elsewhere in this book, except for Walter Huber, Francis Tappan, Ernest Dawson, Phil Bernays, and Alexander Hildebrand, all past presidents of the club.

CERTAINLY there is a distinct difference between the Sierra Club as it was in the 1890's and the first part of this century, and what it is now. It's just a different Club, but the seeds of its present activities were there in the beginning and it was from those seeds that the Club sprouted and grew, and it was adherence to the high ideals that made this possible.

My view of it depends very largely on personalities and I was fortunate in knowing the leaders of the Club, or most of them, from the beginning. I met John Muir once in Will Colby's office and had a little talk with him but can't say that I really got acquainted with him. I never was in the field with him. I joined the Club in 1911, and Muir had been on the outing in 1909 and was still active in the Club for the next few years, but the people I knew, were Joe LeConte (Little Joe, as we called him), Will Colby, William Badè and Walter Huber, Duncan McDuffie, Bob Price, and a few others of that caliber. It is about their influence on the Sierra Club that I'd like to speak.

The Sierra Club was founded in the early nineties by a remarkable group of men, mostly from the University of California and Stanford. The intellectual quality of the members was high, and they in turn attracted others so that we had, at that time, a strong national membership. It was these mem-

Francis Farquhar—portrait taken by Dave Bohn directly after the interview.

bers who established the ultimate ideals of the Club. John Muir was, of course, the recognized leader and was ably supported by such people as J. N. LeConte, Vernon Kellogg of Stanford, and David Starr Jordan of Stanford, among others. In 1910, I came out from the East, my first trip out of New England, and fell in love at once with California's High Sierra on the 1911 outing. Not only the character of the country itself, but the people associated with it, convinced me that this was the place I wanted to live for the rest of my life, which I have done. My recollections of the leading members of the Club in those days are still very vivid.

Will Colby was one of the strong influences in my life, and I shall ever be grateful to him for his kindness. He was a professor of Mining Law at the University of California. Colby was a devoted follower of John Muir, and never failed to bring up Muir's name in any talk that he gave to members of the Club. His wife was Rachael Vrooman, who was also a lawyer in her own right, and once in a while when Colby was unable to give his lectures at his law classes in Berkeley, she substituted for him. A remarkable team.

In the 1890's, the Sierra Club's first decade, the exploring of the great river systems was the main feature.

Quite early it became obvious that the Club should have a publication, and it began under the editorship of Professor J. Henry Senger of the Uni-

49

versity of California, one of the real founders of the Club. Also, the Club fortunately invited Charles A. Murdock, one of the pioneers of fine printing in California, to do the printing of the initial *Sierra Club Bulletin*. Murdock had the highest ideals of typography, and this was centered around simplicity, a quality that characterized the *Bulletin* for the next 25 years.

When I came into the editorship of the *Bulletin,* I was already interested in typography, largely through the leadership of my younger brother Sam, who established the University of California Press in its modern character. I had become acquainted with Taylor and Taylor, who were the successors of Charles Murdock in fine printing in California, and I brought the *Bulletin* into their offices and it continued there for some time.

My own personal connection with the *Bulletin* came after the summer of 1911. William Badè was then the editor, and throughout his long period of editorship he brought the *Bulletin* to be one of the finest mountaineering publications in the country. Badè was an extraordinary man. He was educated in Pennsylvania in the Moravian pastorate, and was active in the Pacific School of Religion in Berkeley. He later produced one of the great contributions of Sierra Club literature, *The Life and Letters of John Muir* in two volumes. In contrast with this was his work on the Old Testament and the life of today. Later on he conducted archaeological work in Palestine. In the early numbers of the *Bulletin,* Badè was ably assisted by Miss Marion Randall, later Mrs. Parsons, who added much to the quality of the publication.

In the early years of the Club as reflected in the *Bulletin* articles, three figures stand out above the rest; Will Colby, Joe LeConte and William Badè. Their influence continued for many years and really established the character of the Club. . . .

The early articles dealt primarily with exploration of the river systems and with the opening up of the unexplored regions of the High Sierra.

Mountaineering was another feature of the early-day articles, particularly the exploits of J. N. LeConte and Jim Hutchinson. In 1903 they climbed the North Palisade, which was a notable achievement then, and I would like to add the name of another member of that party, James K. Moffitt, who was a California banker. Another outstanding event in the history of mountaineering in the Sierra Nevada was the first ascent of the east face of Mt. Whitney in 1931. I was with the party that approached the face, but was overtaken with a temporary illness and had to wait while the others made the ascent. It was accomplished by a group of remarkable mountaineers. The older ones were Norman Clyde and Robert Underhill of the Appalachian Mountain Club, but they were ably supported by some younger Sierra Club members, notably Jules Eichorn and Glen Dawson. They climbed with precision and always with the belays necessary for safety. I recovered enough to go up what we call the mountaineers route, which was rather to the right of their route, and got up there just before they did. There were some Boy Scouts on top, who had come up by the ordinary route, and I asked if they had seen anybody come up over the east face. They answered that nobody could do that because it was a precipice. Just then Jules Eichorn popped his head over the top and refuted the boys' statement.

But the men I have been mentioning were not only interested in the physical activities of the Club. They were also much concerned in the objects of the Club, one of which was the development of the conservation movement. The concept was not nearly as widely recognized as it is today. The natural resources then seemed to be unlimited, and only beauty spots were the ones that needed to be preserved. But as these beauty spots became occupied by hotels and campsites, it became apparent that a much wider range of preservation was necessary and I think that the Club took the leadership in that area. It was not any change in the thought, but rather a development and expansion, and I think that the influence of the early leaders and so many others who were associated with them at the time. Thus, the Club was active in the protection and expansion of Sequoia and the establishment of Kings Canyon National Park. There is a clear line of continuity from the very beginning in this direction, but in all those years the Club was primarily a California organization, divided, I should say, about two-thirds from the northern part of the state and about one-third from the Los Angeles and San Diego areas.

Later on, attention was turned outward and in 1905, for instance, the Club made an expedition to Mt. Rainier, and it is notable that a large number of Club members reached the summit. Among the Rainier climbers was a very remarkable man who was just an ordinary Club member at the time, Stephen T. Mather, graduate of the University of California, but then from Chicago, I believe. Mather was one of the founders of Smith's Twenty-Mule-Team Borax Company but his great claim to fame was that he was the first director of the National Park Service, and the character and quality of the service is greatly indebted to his influence. He was a native Californian and grew up in the traditions of the Sierra Club, and these traditions unconsciously persisted throughout his career. It is a remarkable coincidence that the National Park Service should be founded and developed by three Californians, all of them graduates from Berkeley: Mather, Horace Albright, and Newton Drury, all members of the Sierra Club who were motivated by the ideas developed by the Club. I do not mean to say that these were the only ones who were responsible for the development of the park service, but they were evidently the leaders.

I was fortunate in being very close to Stephen Mather and accompanied him on many of his visits to the national parks, particularly a memorable excursion to the North Rim of the Grand Canyon in 1923. Mather invited me to join him at Salt Lake City and motor down through the Southwest.

One thing that developed from that trip was the concept of what was then called the President's Forest, the protection of the great primeval forest that spreads back from the North Rim. Mather was able to enlist the enthusiastic support of George Horace Lorimer, editor of the *Saturday Evening Post,* and the idea was given wide publicity. The Kaibab Forest eventually became a forest preserve and only part of it went into the Grand Canyon National Park. But the concept served its purpose in preserving the trees.

With the passing of Colby and LeConte and Badè, the leadership fell into new hands, and some of them very capable. I have not dwelt on the influence

51

of Walter Huber and Bob Price, as well as southern members Clair Tappaan and his son Francis, Ernest Dawson and his son Glen, Phil Bernays, and later on, Professor Joel Hildebrand and his son Alex. Although I have mentioned the men whom I consider to have been the great leaders of the Club in its early years, I have omitted a great many who were less prominent, but these others were very active and effective in their work.

I kept up my editorship of the *Bulletin* for 20 years, but finally, by 1946, I found other responsibilities taking precedence and I needed assistance more than ever. I was fortunate in having David R. Brower, a very good writer and staunch conservationist, take over the editorship. From that time on his ideas dominated and I had very little to do with the *Bulletin*. Outstanding among Brower's new ideas was the use of colored illustrations. These tended, in my opinion, to obscure the textual part of the *Bulletin*. Also, the printing today conforms to present-day ways of doing things, but it would not be appropriate to carry on the original plans. The same is true of the contents of the textual matter. There are entirely new problems today and they cannot be treated in the same tone and the same rate of expression as pertained in the early days. The needs of today require different treatment, and the point that I want to emphasize is that the same type of high ideals and leadership pertains today that did in the past, although quite different in outcome.

Today we have a kind of book that did not appear in the early days. Well, there are two different kinds that the Club has produced. One is the great, illustrated format book that is largely due to the activities of Dave Brower, with beautiful photographs by members of the Club, particularly Ansel Adams, Phil Hyde, Eliot Porter and others. The other type of book is the paperback produced for large consumption at moderate prices. These are reflections of the times, and again I emphasize that the Club has kept its leadership in these things as well as it did in the early days. The illustrated format books are a great achievement and they will remain for a long time as records of the Club. They are beautiful books that stimulated the world at large to join the work of preserving our primitive country and to prevent despoliation by modern industry.

And speaking of photography, I would like to talk about Ansel Adams. Ansel was a very important person in the Sierra Club for many years, and still is. He was a musician at first, trained to be a concert pianist. But afterwards, as time went on, he became interested in photography and he developed the techniques much along the line of his musical education. The concepts of beauty and order that prevail in music carry into Ansel's photography with remarkable results, not only in the pictures themselves, but also in the techniques that produced them. There is a clarity and precision in Ansel's work that is comparable to the performance of a Beethoven piano sonata. Of course, the reproduction of so many of Ansel Adams' photographs in the *Bulletin,* and in other publications of the Club, had a wide effect in stimulating public interest in the natural scene. Ansel can dramatize the beauty of the scene and carry it through to the public. He was closely identified with Yosemite Valley, for there is where he began his photographic work, and then he married Virginia Best, daughter of the artist Harry Best, who had a studio in Yosemite. Together, Ansel and Virginia had a great influence on visitors to the valley.

But Ansel was a good deal more than a photographer. He had a philosophic mind that gave him insight into what he was photographing, and I think he always had in mind with every photograph a concept aside from and above the actual physical subject. He also had a great influence on other photographers, particularly Cedric Wright, who accompanied him on many Club outings. Ansel's keen intellect was also a valuable asset on the board of directors, of which he was a member for many years.

Mention of the board brings up another point. Throughout the early history of the Club, members of the board were intimate friends and were able to reach others personally at any time. But in the latter part of my editorship of the *Bulletin,* namely in the 1940's, more and more attention was given to parts of the country other than the Sierra Nevada. The Club up to that time had been almost entirely Californian, although we had members from other parts of the country, particularly some very strong members from New England who helped broaden the views of the Club. But at last, some of the members from the Northwest wanted to establish a chapter of their own. Hitherto the only other chapter outside of the Bay Area was located in Los Angeles, and then one in San Diego. Now we had a chapter in the northwest and later on there was expansion all over the country. The Atlantic Chapter was established, which took in New York and New England.

For many years most of the members knew each other well, largely through the outings, but now there were hundreds of new members who never knew the pioneers of the Club and were having no personal contact with present-day leaders. In other words, my personal feeling is one of regret that the Club expanded. I wish that it had devoted its efforts to expanding some other organization, such as the Wilderness Society, and that the Club had been kept small and compact. However, there is no use in speculating on that now. The deed has been done, and it is up to us to make the best of it. I am certainly not one of those who wants to live in the past. I believe I have demonstrated that I live in the present and have an eye to the future, and that I wish to continue and not regret the loss of things that are irretrievable.

Today there are perhaps 50 different Sierra Clubs with some ideas in common but different ways of expressing them. Whether this is a good thing or not I am not prepared to say. It certainly has brought into the conservation movement thousands of people who would not otherwise participate, and I think we should not think too much about the fine history of the past but rather rejoice that the original Sierra Club has produced such a vast group of conservationists throughout this country.

In the following section we present some of the remarkable men who founded the club, and those who carried on after them. The Sierra Club's pantheon is a large one, and we can only offer a few of the innumerable men and women who have symbolized the club's high purposes. We have not attempted to include any living leaders and offer our apologies to them and to the memories of scores of others who are entitled to recognition here.

From the first, the Sierra Club's most important asset was its members. While the club leadership came mainly from the faculties of the new universities, the 183 members who signed the charter lists included engineers, lawyers, politicians, inventors, artists, and ranchers. Among the names found are Andrew Hallidie, inventor of San Francisco's famous cable cars; George Perkins, later to become governor of California and U.S. senator; geologist Andrew Lawson, discoverer of the San Andreas fault; and the venerable Galen Clark, Guardian of Yosemite, who must have mailed his signature from his cabin in the valley.

Diverse as they were, these first members held much in common. They shared a love for the Range of Light, and a commitment to keep these and other mountains in the West as wilderness. Transcendentalists all—or so it seems from reading the early Bulletins—the founding members were firmly grounded in the basic philosophical and cultural outlook of their day. Yet, they could see beyond to days and years when the outlook might be different, but human needs for wilderness and a green world would be the same.

15   Personal Recollections of John Muir

SAMUEL MERRILL

1928

Who founded the Sierra Club? John Muir would have denied that the honor belonged solely to him, but more than any other person he created the commitments in his generation that led to the founding of the club, and he served as its spokesman until his death in 1914.

Therefore, the club's pantheon, its role of honor, begins with Muir.

For a view of Muir's life, we listen first to his friend, Samuel Merrill, talking in the flickering light of a campfire on the High Trip of 1927. Merrill, a member of the Indianapolis family that befriended Muir in 1866, when he was temporarily blinded by an accident, stayed at the Muir ranch the summer of 1892 before entering Stanford University as a freshman. The ranch, at Martinez, near San Francisco, is now open to the public under the National Park Service.

AS MANY OF YOU KNOW, John Muir came to this country from Scotland when he was a lad of eleven years. His father settled on a piece of wild land in central Wisconsin. Muir received the usual education afforded by the country schools of those days, which was very limited. He educated himself, however, by reading all the books in his father's home and in the homes of neighbors for miles around. With very little financial assistance from his father, he succeeded by his own efforts in putting himself through the University of Wisconsin, at Madison. While in college he became greatly interested in the science of botany, and on leaving the university he made many extensive trips to nearby states and to Canada to study the flora of these regions. In order to carry on these explorations, he secured work from time to time, and in this way he came to Indianapolis in 1866, when he was twenty-eight years old. He found employment in a wagon factory. There he received a serious injury to one of his eyes. While adjusting a belt, a sharp tool slipped in his hand and pierced his eye, causing temporary blindness in both eyes.

It was at this time that John Muir became known to our family. Professor Butler, of Madison, Wisconsin, one of Muir's teachers at the university, hearing of the accident, wrote to my aunt, Miss Catherine Merrill, asking her to do what she could for the young man. Miss Merrill took charge of the case, employing the best oculist in Indianapolis. It was necessary for Muir to remain in a dark room for many weeks. During this enforced imprisonment, Miss Merrill and her sisters, Mrs. Moores and Mrs. Graydon, gave much of their time in reading to him and in keeping his room supplied with flowers; while my cousin, Katherine Merrill Graydon, to whom I am much indebted for material in this sketch, recalls to this day the wonderful stories he used to tell her. This story-telling ability, in later life, culminated in that classic dog story, "Stickeen."

Muir stored the herbarium and notes of his first botanical trips in the attic of my aunt, Mrs. Moores, where they remained for more than a half-century until brought to light and examined by Muir's biographer, Dr. Badè. Saying good-by to his Indianapolis friends, Muir set out on that famous thousand-mile hike through the South to Florida. It was his intention to continue the journey to South America, but a fever, contracted in the South, caused him to change his mind and his destination to California.

Arriving in San Francisco by water in the spring of 1868, he lost no time in getting out of the city, headed for Yosemite Valley on foot; not that he had any aversion to San Francisco, but, as he puts it, "I cared not to spend time in a city when I could be in the open and see God making a world." Muir

55

describes his tramp to Yosemite in these words: "It was one of those perfectly pure, rich, ripe days of California sun gold, where distant views seem as close as near ones, and I have always thanked the Lord that I came here before the dust and smoke of civilization had dimmed the sky and before the wild bloom had vanished from the plain. Descending the Pacheco Pass, I waded out into the marvelous bloom of the San Joaquin, when it was in its prime. It was all one sea of golden and purple bloom, so deep and dense that in walking through it you would press more than a hundred blooms at every step. In this flower-bed five hundred miles long, I used to camp by just lying down wherever night overtook me, as if I had sunk beneath the waters of a lake, the radiant heads of compositae touching each other, ray to ray, shone above me like the thickest star clusters of the sky, and in the morning I sometimes found plants that were new, looking me in the face, so that my botanical studies would begin before I was up."

For the next ten years Muir buried himself in the Yosemite Valley and the High Sierra, living much of the time absolutely alone, in close communion with nature, studying the flowers, trees, and rocks of this region, not that he loved man the less but Nature more, as Byron expresses it. During these years Muir gathered the material that later appeared in book and periodical form bringing him fame as an author and making him the foremost defender of the beautiful regions of the state which later became national parks.

Muir's life in the Sierra was interrupted by an eastern trip to his old home and to Indianapolis. Muir consented to give a talk on the mountains and big trees of California at my father's home before a number of invited guests. Although I was only a boy, Muir's visit and talk at our home made a deep impression upon me. I am sure that we all, both grown-up people and children, realized that John Muir was a great man—unlike any man we had ever known before. His language was simple and easily understood by a child, and yet had a charm for the most highly educated.

Years passed before I saw John Muir again. During the years which had elapsed, he had carried on extensive explorations on the Pacific Coast and in Alaska. On my return to California from India, in 1892, I made a pilgrimage to John Muir's ranch near Martinez. Muir had only recently returned from an expedition to Alaska, and, though but fifty-four years of age at this time, he showed by the lines in his face and his general appearance that he had endured and suffered great hardships and privations. He was glad, however, to make the sacrifice that these trips entailed and did not complain, and referred to it once in this way, saying, "I have made a tramp of myself; I have gone hungry and cold; I have left bloody trails on sharp ice peaks to see the wonders of earth."

In spite of the deep lines in his face, Mr. Muir's personal appearance was most attractive. He was above the average in height, slender, lithe, and active as an Indian. His eyes were as clear and blue as California skies; his head was well shaped and covered with curly brown hair. He was modest in telling of his adventures—adventures which must have tried the soul of the bravest man. No woman could have been more tender than he, particularly to

56

animals. He even went so far as to express regret for having killed a rattle-snake, saying that he hoped the Lord would forgive him for taking the life of a creature loved only by its Maker.

The family at this time consisted of Mr. and Mrs. Muir and their two young daughters, Wanda and Helen. Occasionally at the table were his brother David and wife, who lived on the upper part of the ranch, or friends from San Francisco, Oakland, or Berkeley.

Muir's study, or den, was on the second floor, in the front of the house. He was allowed to have his own way in this particular room and no one dared to put it in order. It was so full of his books, manuscripts, and sketches that it was difficult to find a chair unoccupied. Muir appreciated the best in art, as was evidenced by the pictures on the walls. I particularly recall a fine painting by William Keith on the wall to the right as one entered the study. Mr. Muir showed me many sketches of his recent Alaskan trip, and I realized that he was no mean artist himself. In fact, Muir was very versatile, a man learned in more than one branch of science, particularly in botany and geology, pre-eminent in his specialty of glaciers, a naturalist, a poet who wrote no verse, a great prose writer, a wonderful conversationalist, a natural-born story-teller, a successful farmer and fruit-grower, and an inventor of considerable ability.

Like Dr. Samuel Johnson, John Muir never appeared to better advantage than in conversation, but unfortunately he did not have a Boswell to preserve his sayings for posterity. It was a rare privilege to be included in a group in which Muir was a member.

I am sure that you will pardon me for being proud of the fact that I was a member of Mr. Muir's household when the Sierra Club was born. I recall the day in the summer of 1892 when Mr. Muir returned from San Francisco and announced to us all at the supper-table that the Sierra Club had been organized and that he had been chosen its first president. I had never seen Mr. Muir so animated and happy before. . . . It was not Muir's success as an author, or the honors that were conferred upon him in this country and abroad, that gave him the keenest pleasure, but the happiest day in his life, I venture to say, was the day in San Francisco in the summer of 1892, when he found himself the center of a devoted and loyal group of citizens who organized themselves into the Sierra Club and made him president.

Up to that time, Muir had been waging a continuous war against selfish commercial interests which would exploit and destroy the forests and beautiful regions of our state and nation, fighting in his early years in the state, almost alone, with his back to the wall—yes, with his back against the granite walls of the Sierra which he loved so well. Is it any wonder, then, that Muir saw in the Sierra Club, the crystallization of the dreams and labor of a lifetime, an organization which would carry on the good work for generations yet to come? But an organization is only what its members make it. Our great leader, after a long life of public service and self-sacrifice, has fallen, like some giant *Sequoia sempervirens* which has gone down before the storm. But, as there springs up around the base of the redwood a circle of vigorous young trees to take its place, so, my friends and fellow members, it devolves upon us to close in and fill up the breach in our ranks caused by the loss of our gallant leader. As we are gathered here about the camp-fire under the stars and beneath the shadow of these lofty lodgepole pines, let us here and now resolve to be more worthy disciples of this inspiring man.

16 — John Muir and Ralph Waldo Emerson in Yosemite

SAMUEL T. FARQUHAR

1934

Muir was not always the relaxed speaker who held forth at Sierra Club meetings, or the easy companion who conversed so readily with the teen-aged Samuel Merrill. In this selection, compiled by Samuel Farquhar from the writings of Emerson's friend, James Bradley Thayer, and of Muir himself, we see him as the shy and awkward, yet eager and engaging young man he was when he met Emerson in Yosemite in the spring of 1871. Emerson, honored, old, and tired, was on a tour of California.
Samuel T. Farquhar, Francis Farquhar's brother, was an editor at the University of California Press. The selection by Thayer is from A Western Journey with Mr. Emerson *(Little, Boston, 1884); Muir's speech at Harvard is quoted from* The Life and Letters of John Muir *(William Frederic Badè, Houghton Mifflin, Boston and New York, 1923–4); the last quotation is from Muir's notes.*

THE BEGINNING of Emerson's acquaintance with John Muir is told by Thayer, one of Emerson's companions, as follows:
On the evening of Monday the eighth there came an admiring, enthusiastic letter for Mr. Emerson from M., a young man living in the valley, and tending a sawmill there. He was a Scotchman by birth, who had come to this country at the age of eleven, and was a graduate at Madison University, in Wisconsin. Some friends near San Francisco had written him that Mr. Emer-

son was coming, and they had also told Mr. Emerson about him. He had read Mr. Emerson's books, but had never seen him, and wrote now with enthusiasm, wishing for an opportunity to come to him. The next morning Mr. Emerson asked my company on horseback for a visit to M. So he mounted his pied mustang, and we rode over, and found M. at the sawmill alone. He was an interesting young fellow, of real intelligence and character, a botanist mainly, who, after studying a year or two at Madison, had "zig-zagged his way," he said, "to the Gulf of Mexico, and at last had found this valley, and had got entangled here — in love with the mountains and flowers; and he didn't know when he should get away." He had built the sawmill for Hutchings, and was now working it. He had heretofore tended sheep at times — even flocks of twenty-five hundred. Occasionally he rambled among the mountains, and camped out for months; and he urged Mr. Emerson, with an amusing zeal, to stay and go off with him on such a trip. He lodged in the sawmill, and we climbed a ladder to his room. Here he brought out a great many dried specimens of plants which he had collected, and hundreds of his own graceful pencil-sketches of the mountain-peaks and forest trees, and gave us the botanical names, and talked of them with enthusiastic interest. All these treasures he poured out before Mr. Emerson, and begged him to accept them. But Mr. Emerson declined; wishing leave, however, to bring his friends to see them. Other calls were interchanged that day and the next; and when we left, two days later, to see the great trees of the Mariposa Grove, M. joined our horseback party. . . .

On the next morning, May 11, we left the great valley before seven o'clock. . . . It was pleasant, as we rode along, to hear him sound M. on his literary points. M. was not strong there; he preferred, for instance, Alice Cary to Bryon. . . .

Clark's was a plain country tavern on a fork of the Merced River, at about the same level as the Yosemite Valley. It was full, but we were somehow crowded in. In the morning we were off at eight o'clock for the Mariposa Grove. Galen Clark, our landlord, a solid, sensible man from New Hampshire, was the State guardian of the great trees, and now accompanied us, *honoris causa.* It was a sunny and pleasant ride. M. talked of the trees; and we grew learned, and were able to tell a sugar pine from a yellow pine, and to name the silver fir, and the "libocedrus," which is almost our arbor-vitae and second cousin to the great sequoia. By and by M. called out that he saw the sequoias. The general level was now about fifty-five hundred feet above the sea; the trees stood a little lower, in a hollow of the mountain. They were "big trees," to be sure; and yet at first they seemed not so very big. We grew curious, and looked about among them for a while; and soon began to discover what company we were in. . . .

We sat down to lunch near a hut, and had a chance to rest and to look about us more quietly. M. protested against our going away so soon: "It is," said he, "as if a photographer should remove his plate before the impression was fully made"; he begged us to stay there and camp with him for the night. After lunch, Mr. Emerson, at Clark's request, chose and named a tree.

59

Drawing of John Muir about 1872.

This had been done by one distinguished person, and another, and a sign put up to commemorate it. Mr. Emerson named it [his tree] Samoset, after our Plymouth sachem. He had greatly enjoyed the day. "The greatest wonder," said he, "is that we can see these trees and not wonder more."

We were off at about three o'clock, and left M. standing in the forest alone; he was to pass the night there in solitude, and to find his way back to the valley on foot. We had all become greatly interested in him, and hated to leave him. His name has since grown to be well known in the East, through his valuable articles in the magazines.

John Muir has described his meeting with Emerson in a warmer, more personal manner than that of the matter-of-fact Thayer. Badè quotes a memorandum of after-dinner remarks made by Muir twenty-five years later when Harvard University conferred upon him an hononary M.A. degree.

I was fortunate [he said] in meeting some of the choicest of your Harvard men, and at once recognized them as the best of God's nobles. Emerson, Agassiz, Gray—these men influenced me more than any others. Yes, the most of my years were spent on the wild side of the continent, invisible, in the forests and mountains. These men were the first to find me and hail me as a brother. First of all, and greatest of all, came Emerson. I was then living in Yosemite Valley as a convenient and grand vestibule of the Sierra from which I could make excursions into the adjacent mountains. I had not much money and was then running a mill that I had built to saw fallen timber for cottages.

When he came into the valley I heard the hotel people say with solemn emphasis, "Emerson is here." I was excited as I had never been excited before, and my heart throbbed as if an angel direct from heaven had alighted on the Sierran rocks. But so great was my awe and reverence, I did not dare to go to him or speak to him. I hovered on the outside of the crowd of people that were pressing forward to be introduced to him and shaking hands with him. Then I heard that in three or four days he was going away, and in the course of sheer desperation I wrote him a note and carried it to his hotel telling him that El Capitan and Tissiack demanded him to stay longer.

The next day he inquired for the writer and was directed to the little sawmill. He came to the mill on horseback attended by Mr. Thayer and inquired for me. I stepped out and said, "I am Mr. Muir." "Then Mr. Muir must have brought his own letter," said Mr. Thayer, and Emerson said, "Why did you not make yourself known last evening? I should have been very glad to have seen you." Then he dismounted and came into the mill. I had a study attached to the gable of the mill, overhanging the stream, into which I invited him, but it was not easy of access, being reached only by a series of sloping planks roughened by slats like a hen ladder; but he bravely climbed up and I showed him my collection of plants and sketches drawn from the surrounding mountains, which seemed to interest him greatly, and he asked many questions, pumping unconsciously.

He came again and again, and I saw him every day while he remained in the valley, and on leaving I was invited to accompany him as far as the Mariposa Grove of Big Trees. I said, "I'll go, Mr. Emerson, if you will promise to camp with me in the grove. I'll build a glorious camp-fire, and the great brown boles of the giant Sequoias will be most impressively lighted up, and the night will be glorious." At this he became enthusiastic like a boy, his sweet perennial smile became still deeper and sweeter, and he said, "Yes, yes, we will camp out, camp out"; and so next day we left Yosemite and rode twenty-five miles through the Sierra forests, the noblest on the face of the earth, and he kept me talking all the time, but said little himself. The colossal silver firs, Douglas spruce, Libocedrus and sugar pine, the kings and priests of the conifers of the earth, filled him with awe and delight. When we stopped to eat luncheon he called on different members of the party to tell

61

stories or recite poems, etc., and spoke, as he reclined on the carpet of pine needles, of his student days at Harvard. But when in the afternoon we came to the Wawona Tavern. . . .

The memorandum ends abruptly, but fortunately the story is continued elsewhere in Muir's writings:

Early in the afternoon, when we reached Clark's Station, I was surprised to see the party dismount. And when I asked if we were not going up into the grove to camp they said: "No; it would never do to lie out in the night air. Mr. Emerson might take cold; and you know, Mr. Muir, that would be a dreadful thing." In vain I urged, that only in homes and hotels were colds caught, that nobody ever was known to take cold camping in these woods, that there was not a single cough or sneeze in all the Sierra. Then I pictured the big climate-changing, inspiring fire I would make, praised the beauty and fragrance of sequoia flame, told how the great trees would stand about us transfigured in purple light, while the stars looked down between the great domes; ending by urging them to come on and make an immortal Emerson night of it. But the house habit was not to be overcome, nor the strange dread of pure night air, though it is only cooled day air with a little dew in it. So the carpet dust and unknowable reeks were preferred. And to think of this being a Boston choice. Sad commentary on culture and the glorious transcendentalism.

The poor bit of measured time was soon spent, and while the saddles were being adjusted, I again urged Emerson to stay. "You are yourself a sequoia," I said. "Stop and get acquainted with your big brethren." But he was past his prime, and was now as a child in the hands of his affectionate but sadly civilized friends. It was the afternoon of the day and the afternoon of his life, and his course was now westward down all the mountains into the sunset. The party mounted and rode away in wondrous contentment, apparently, tracing the trail through ceanothus and dogwood bushes, around the bases of the big trees, up the slope of the sequoia basin, and over the divide. I followed to the edge of the grove. Emerson lingered in the rear of the train, and when he reached the top of the ridge, after all the rest of the party were over and out of sight, he turned his horse, took off his hat and waved me a last good-by. I felt lonely, so sure had I been that Emerson of all men would be the quickest to see the mountains and sing them. Gazing a while on the spot where he vanished, I sauntered back into the heart of the grove, made a bed of sequoia plumes and ferns by the side of the stream, gathered a store of firewood, and then walked about until sundown. The birds, robins, thrushes, warblers, etc., that had kept out of sight, came about me, now that all was quiet, and made cheer. After sundown I built a great fire, and as usual had it all to myself. And though lonesome for the first time in these forests, I quickly took heart again — the trees had not gone to Boston, nor the birds; and as I sat by the fire, Emerson was still with me in spirit, though I never again saw him in the flesh.

17

John Muir and the Alaska Book

MARION RANDALL

PARSONS

1916

Marion Randall Parsons writes of her experiences as editor, secretary, and friend to John Muir during the writing of his last book, Travels in Alaska. *She was an extraordinary person herself, as we shall see.*

I N NOVEMBER, 1912, not long after his return from his last long journey across South America and Africa, Mr. Muir came to Berkeley to begin work on his Alaska notes. For a month he worked at my home with a stenographer, getting an exact transcription of the journals. The travel-worn, weather-stained little books carried on those memorable exploring trips of nearly forty years before were crammed with sketches and voluminous notes, jotted down perhaps in the canoe, or around the camp-fire, but oftenest in the solitudes of the great glaciers in whose study he cheerfully underwent so much cold and hunger and hardship.

It was most amusing to watch Mr. Muir at work. His intense interest in his subject led him to make many a long digression as his notes brought this or that incident to mind. Time meant nothing to him. Household machinery might stop, food grow cold on the table, and the business members of the family miss their morning trains while Mr. Muir pursued the tranquil course of his subject to the end. And so for an hour or more he might discourse while the stenographer sat with her hands folded. Her stolidity and indifference exasperated him beyond measure. To have no curiosity about the "terrestrial manifestations of God," above all to have no interest in glaciers, was to him both incomprehensible and sinful.

Once started on a task Mr. Muir was a tireless worker. The book in hand might have lain fallow for thirty years, but when it began to take form and substance he was all afire with eagerness to see it finished. Long evenings he spent poring over the notebooks or drawing from them the texts of the monologues he delighted in. His mind, indeed, dwelt with such complete absorption on his work that his conversation nearly always indicated its trend. His speech had all the beauty of phrase, the force and vigor of style of his written word, but with an added spell of fire and enthusiasm and glowing vitality that made it an inspiration and never-ending delight. Many a page of this Alaska book is for me a living record of our fireside hours of companionship.

Not until many months later, however, did I have any close acquaintance with *Travels in Alaska*. After working on it only a short time, Mr. Muir laid the book aside to take an active part in the fight for Hetch Hetchy. A few weeks after the final defeat a severe illness, from whose effects he never fully recovered, again interrupted the book. In his weakened condition the mere sifting out of the enormous mass of material was a task almost beyond his strength. Finding him one day utterly discouraged over it, I offered to go to him a day or two each week to help him until he could find the secretary to his mind. The arrangement proved unexpectedly happy and congenial to us both, and lasted until within a week of his death.

No one unacquainted with Mr. Muir's habits of work and living could appreciate the difficulty, nor, indeed, the humorous nature of the task. He was living alone in the dismantled old home, unused save for his study and sleeping porch. He went to his daughter's home for his meals, but neither she nor anyone else was allowed to touch the study, overflowing as it was with books and papers. Confusion was no word for the state of the manuscripts. He had been collecting material for over thirty years. In the interval that had elapsed since he began real work on it the two typewritten copies of the journals had become mixed, and in some cases both had been revised. Material from certain parts of the journals, moreover, had been used in newspaper letters and again in magazine articles, so as many as five different versions of some passages were in existence. Even had they been collected together and in order, to read and compare and reject would have been sufficiently hard, but fresh versions were constantly coming to light, or in my absence Mr. Muir would unearth a copy of some version already disposed of. He was in the habit of making notes on anything that came to hand — an opened envelope, a paper bag, the margin of a newspaper. No scrap of manuscript could ever be destroyed, and I could devise no system of putting the rejected material aside that served to keep him from "discovering" it at some later date. Finally I took to hiding copies and rejected sheets alike inside a great roll of papers conspicuously tied with red ribbons and labeled in huge capitals "Copied!" and little by little the orange-box full of manuscript and the piles of scattered notes littering desk and table were reduced to a single working copy.

By seven o'clock each morning Mr. Muir had breakfasted and was ready for the day's work, usually lasting, with but the interruption of an hour at lunch and dinner and another at mail time, until ten at night. Composition was always slow and laborious for him. "This business of writing books," he would often say, "is a long, tiresome, endless job." To read his easy, flowing, forceful sentences, as rich in imagery and simple in diction as Bible English, no one would dream what infinite pains had been taken in their creation. Each sentence, each phrase, each word, underwent his critical scrutiny, not once but twenty times before he was satisfied to let it stand. His rare critical faculty was unimpaired to the end. So too was the freshness and vigor of his whole outlook on life. No trace of pessimism or despondency, even in the defeat of his most deeply cherished hopes, ever darkened his beautiful philosophy, and only in the intense physical fatigue brought on by his long working hours was there any hint of failing powers.

Mr. Muir himself, however, seemed to know that the end was near. Very touching were his attempts to rehabilitate the old house, whose forlorn emptiness and desolation were never allowed to weigh upon his own serene spirit, to put it in readiness for whomsoever should next live there. During the latter months of his life he often expressed the conviction that he would never live to write another book. His plan had long been to have his books tell the story of his life and travels, and in the early days of our work together he would often speak of the volumes of this wanderer's autobiography that he hoped yet to complete. But he was curiously untroubled about leaving his work unfinished. To a most unusual degree he seemed to feel that his had been a glorious life, wholly worth while. "Oh, I have had a *bully* life!" he said once. "I have done what I set out to do." And again: "To get these glorious works of God into yourself—that's the great thing; not to write about them." That nature's beauty had a deep and lasting influence on character was one of his most earnest beliefs. No impassable gulf between things material and spiritual ever existed for him, and scientific study only served to deepen his natural reverence and faith. Throughout this book, as through all the others, rings his triumphant belief in the harmony and unity of our universe, its imperishable beauty, its divine conception, "reflecting the plans of God."

18

Joseph N. LeConte: Some Recollections

J. S. HUTCHINSON

1950

"He has since become the best camper and mountaineer I ever knew," wrote Professor Joseph LeConte about his son, Joseph Nisbet, while on a trip in the Sierra in 1889. The nineteen year old had tramped "four or five hundred miles in the Sierras every summer and probably knowing them better than any other living man, unless possibly Mr. John Muir."

J. N. "Little Joe" LeConte, who was to serve the club for fifty years, possessed two qualities that were to be important to the club in its first decades: a profound love for the mountains and a profound love for his fellow man —the latter inspiring, said his fellow club member Ansel Adams, "a quality of friendship for which he is beloved by all."

It is surprising how much of the Sierra was still unmapped at the time of the club's founding, even though the Whitney survey party of 1864, in which Clarence King participated, had explored, described, and mapped large areas. With determined zeal, young LeConte set himself at filling in the blank spaces that remained on the maps of the time. In 1908 with James S. Hutchinson and Duncan McDuffie he completed the first high mountain route from Yosemite to Kings Canyon, a venture Theodore Solomons had begun in 1893. The route later became the basis for much of the John Muir Trail, completed in 1938. LeConte published many accounts of his explorations in the Bulletin, *each written with careful attention to detail and accompanied by accurate maps.*

LeConte's feelings for the mountains were reflected both in the poetic descriptions found often in his writings, and in his photography, which he began in 1889 with a Kodak that made round images two-and-a-half inches in diameter. On most of his trips he carried a camera at a time when cameras were not lightweight equipment. He produced the finest photographs of the Sierra made in the early decades of the century. Many of his pictures were published in the Bulletin, *thus starting a tradition of publishing outstanding nature photography that has included works by Ansel Adams, Cedric Wright, Philip Hyde, and other masters of the camera.*

A professor of engineering at the University of California, LeConte served as a director of the club from 1898 to 1940. In 1931 he was made honorary president, a post he held until his death in 1950.

Here J. S. Hutchinson writes on "Little Joe," his old hiking buddy. Hutchinson was a director of the club and served as editor of the Bulletin *in 1903 – 04 and again in 1925.*

I F YOU WANT his autobiography, particularly that relating to the high mountains, read the *Sierra Club Bulletin* commencing with Volume 1 — he was a Charter Member — down to the most recent — he was made the club's Honorary President in 1931 and he made a valuable contribution to the *Bulletin* as recently as 1941. Besides he kept a diary of every single trip he made into the mountains; there are forty-four of them. Some day, someone should publish these.

I have taken many trips with Joe. On many of these trips I have often felt as though I was his man Friday; I was always learning so much from him and doing the best I could to help him. When he was measuring the movement of the Nisqually Glacier on Mount Rainier he set up his transit and directed me where to drill a long line of auger holes in the ice. I helped him carry his transit and his plane table to the summits of many high peaks in the Sierra when he was making observations and rechecking locations for his valuable maps of the Sierra. When he made the survey of the Sierra Club property at

Joseph N. LeConte, 1945.

Tuolumne Meadows I was with him to help him by holding the rod and by locating the old corners and blazes. We had lots of fun.

I believe the two very high spots in Joe's mountaineering in the Sierra are the ascent of the North Palisade and his working out of the High Mountain Route.

He had often said to me that the region of the Palisades was the wildest and most rugged part of the whole Sierra. He had climbed Split Mountain (South Palisade) with his wife Helen in 1902. The North Palisade was still a very definite challenge to him. Finally—1903—we were camped at Lake Marion: Joe, Helen, Jim Moffitt, Bob and John Pike, and I. We were now within striking distance of the North Palisade. Leaving Helen and Bob in camp, the rest of us started on a knapsack trip across country to the North Palisade. We camped on Palisade Creek and next day started to climb the peak. We went up to the main crest with the idea of working north along the knife edge, but on arrival considered this to be unsound. So we all climbed Mount Sill. The next day, Joe, Jim Moffitt, and I reached the summit of the North Palisade by another route and let out a mighty shout of joy. Joe gives further details in his memorable article in the 1904 *Bulletin*.

The High Mountain Route was something Joe had had in mind for a long time—a pack-animal trip from Yosemite to Kings River Canyon, along a route as near the Main Crest as possible. Theodore S. Solomons had covered part of this route. Finally, in 1908, Joe asked Duncan McDuffie and me to go with him. Joe wrote about this in the *Sierra Club Bulletin* for 1909. This was a marvelous trip and he loved to talk about it. The real tough parts were from Mammoth Pass to Fish Creek, from what is now known as Muir Pass down to Little Pete Meadow, and from Palisade Creek to Cartridge Creek.

In his "Diary, 1908" he describes this trip down from Muir Pass. Nobody had been over before, not even the sheepmen: "On July 18th we were up at ten to four and off at 5:30. We first passed the lake and crossed the creek at its head. Then continued on up the creek on its west side to the outlet of Crystal (Wanda) Lake, and then crossed again. There was no serious trouble to the summit of the pass over the Goddard Divide (this pass is now Muir Pass). Puss (one of our mules) floundered in the snow at one point but got out without unpacking. From the summit down to Kings River side the going was very rough. We took the mules across talus slopes and down the bed of the creek. Ate lunch at 11:30 when we thought the worst was over, but after that had to go down 1,000 feet of talus. In the river canyon again the going was rough. We had to cross the river four times to avoid cliffs and huge talus. Finally made a large meadow by 3:30 and camped for the night. It was a beautiful camp and we had a fine dinner." This meadow is Little Pete Meadow and the Canyon now appears on the Geological Survey maps as LeConte Canyon. Joe wrote, "This was one of the most glorious trips that I ever took in my life."

When Joe and I would get together we would frequently trade a lot of "Remember when's" but I will only give you just one of the anecdotes which relates to the Sierra.

In 1913 Joe, Charles Noble, my nephew "Din" Hutchinson and I were camped at Bullfrog Lake. One afternoon I said "I've often looked down to Independence from the pass, but I've never been down over that trail and I'd like to go." Din said at once, "I'll go with you." Charles was noncommittal but showed favorable signs. Joe said, "I've been over that trail many times, I'll keep camp if you fellows want to go." I knew that Joe liked beer, so around the campfire I said, "Joe, if you'll go down, I'll buy beer for all." Joe dreamed of beer that night and next morning early he said he'd decided to go down with us.

Helen Gompertz, LeConte's first wife, died in 1924. Five years later, LeConte married Adelaide Graham, Helen's best friend, who had nursed her in her final illness.

"By the Summer of 1930," Joe said, "I saw Adelaide could stand a Sierra Pack trip so we made one last grand trip to the Kings River Canyon, Simpson Meadow, Grouse Valley, and Kearsarge Pass, where Adelaide climbed Mount Gould, 13,001 feet."

"On this trip," writes Joe in his diary, "as on those of the last two preceding years I was troubled again with aching and numbness in my feet when walking. In the fall I began to have heart pains when exercising violently or walking rapidly. I saw that it was all off, and my doctor and my common sense told me that there were no more High Sierra packing trips for me. There could be nothing more strenuous than an automobile trip to the Ski Club. So that 1930 trip was my last, but nothing can ever efface the memory of those forty-four glorious Sierra trips."

I last saw Joe on February 1st. My daughter and I went down from Berkeley to see him. As we entered his room his eyes were closed. I went to his bedside and said: "Joe, here are Jim and Marjorie." He opened his eyes and held out his hands toward us. Adelaide lifted the curtain of his oxygen tent and put on his glasses. He grasped our hands firmly. I began to talk to him, and Adelaide said: "Talk to him about the mountains. He loves that."

I asked, "Joe, remember our climb of the North Palisade with Jim Moffitt?" He looked up at me through his intensely keen and intelligent eyes and smiled. He tried so hard to talk to us. His tongue moved but he could not articulate.

"Do you remember our Mount Brewer climb? Remember your High Mountain Route? You and Duncan and I?" I talked of our camps on the Merced, at Porcupine Flat, at Tuolumne Meadows. All this time he was looking intently at me smiling, his bright eyes full of intelligence and delight. It was a great joy to him to hear about his beloved mountains.

That afternoon Marjorie and I drove back to our Berkeley home. An hour after we arrived the phone rang. It was Adelaide, to say that Joe was gone. This was the earthly end of a great and good man; a man who was fond of his fellow men, who loved his friends dearly, and who was beloved by all who knew him; a man whose influence for good will last long. I loved that man dearly and I know that he loved me.

19　　　　　　# Marion Randall Parsons

B. H. LEHMANN

1953

Novelist, musician, painter, mountaineer, Marion Randall Parsons infused her Sierra Club activities with a remarkable range of interests and accomplishments. She was the first woman elected to the board of directors and served for twenty-two years. A member of the editorial committee, she wrote often for the Bulletin, *recording the high trips she loved so well with wit and perception. Her portrait of John Muir at work on his "Alaska book"—his last—is a classic.*

MARION PARSONS was a remarkable woman. She had the talent for life, and she had the temperament of the artist which transmutes life into forms that deepen the insight and enlarge the horizons of others. As musician, as writer, as painter she succeeded notably; as companion and friend, her interest and quality rose to that true distinction which derives from great imagination, swift sympathy, and a genuine intuition of the nature of reality. Those who knew her will not forget her delighted laughter or her quiet and often saddened comprehension. On a mountain trail, in a garden or by a fireplace, she unfailingly responded to life, its predicaments and aspirations. And in the extended solitudes which suited her she made the stories, the pictures, and in earlier years the music which were outward aspects of her inner life. . . .

In 1902, upon reversed fortunes, the family left the great estate in Piedmont, moved to Berkeley, and there through Wanda Muir, oldest daughter of John Muir, began for Marion that interest in The Sierra Club which was to last to the end of her life. Her first Outing was in 1903. After John Muir's death, she edited his *Travels in Alaska*.

In 1907 Marion married Edward Taylor Parsons, director and moving spirit of The Sierra Club. He died in 1914. She succeeded him as director, and was continuously active until she resigned the responsibility in 1936. Through all this period she worked steadily in the cause of conservation, and had her historical part in establishing the National Park Service. It was, however, on the Outings that she had those experiences which were later to be so fruitful in her painting. Immediately, they were reported in a series of articles in the *Bulletin*. The first of these, in 1905, characteristically dwells upon the human side: "the lost trail, the bridgeless river, the firm-willed beast of burden, the camp-fire that will not burn . . . the crowd . . . comradeship and chivalry, simplicity and joyousness, and the care-free life of the open." But through the years, the mountains—rock, light, forest, stream, glacier—are there: the great names: Grand Canyon of the Tuolumne, the Merced, Mount Ritter, Kings River, Kern Canyon; and the lesser: Huntington Lake, McClure Meadow, Gnat Meadows and Jackass Meadows, Tehipite Valley, Marie Lake, often with touches from the painter's imagination. From beyond the Sierra came her reports too. Of her more than fifty ascents of major peaks, a fair half were in the Cascades, the Olympics, the Selkirks, and the Canadian Rockies.

There is in all these works [her novels], published and unpublished alike, something private, almost secret, suggested but not fully communicated—the delight of life in whatever form. One seems to overhear, rather than to hear, the word. It is as it was with her music. She could not free herself to play for an audience; but if one sat in another room, unrealized, the Beethoven Sonatas came from the piano with absolute dominion—the beauty enclosing and transcending the tensions which made them.

About 1930 Marion Parsons began to be interested in sketching. After her illness, in 1936, she set to work seriously, and was mostly self-taught as a painter. Discerning critics took her work seriously. It is proper to have a painter's judgment of it.

Ariel Parkinson writes: "These paintings convey those secrets of high mountains, storms, trees, water, that have to do with volume, mass, masked

Marion Randall Parsons and her husband, E. T. Parsons, left, on an early High Trip. The High Tripper on the right is unidentified.

71

and moving light, organic form bleached down to death again. They reveal a sense of fundamentals, creation, destruction, force."

Marion Parsons moved, remembering and researching, in the past that she might reach into the future. Her growing time had been in an era of limitation upon the young. Though modest and even shy, she avoided limitation for herself, in her thinking about life and in her living of it. She was one of the not very conspicuous people who quietly operate to make civilization.

20 Cedric Wright

DAVID R. BROWER

1959

Cedric Wright photographed all aspects of nature in the Sierra, but he seemed to have a particular feeling for water. One of his pictures, included in Words of the Earth *(and chosen by Edward Steichen in 1955 for the back cover of* The Family of Man*), shows water brilliant with light, as it leaps, foams, moves in innumerable patterns through a rapids. The text, written by Wright, reads: "Human life must know ecstasy."*

WE HAVE A NEIGHBOR who had not known Cedric Wright personally at all, yet tears welled up when she heard that he had died. "He left so much beauty for so many people," she said. He did.

He sought out this beauty in the course of some thirty-five High Trips that he took with the club back into the High Sierra wilderness country that is the climax of what John Muir liked to call the Range of Light. Wright fell in love with this high world even as Muir had, and each summer brought him closer to its forms, its moods, its tones, its light—and to the thousand textures that unfolded as the trail turned or as a trailless slope opened up on a broad sweep or an intimate glen that no man had seen before.

Oh, others may have stood there, yes. But none could see what he saw, not until with black cloth and box he had worked his magic, had captured and carried away the essence of beauty without harming a hair of it, had printed and fixed its image, had let others see it at last, far from where it was, and had led them, in that way, to look for it and find it next time.

On many of these High Trips Wright served as official photographer, meaning that the check he sent in for a reservation on the trip was returned to him in gratitude for what he had already contributed, worth many times a trip's cost, in exquisite display prints of the previous year's trip. These became the mainstay of the club's permanent photographic collection; they were augmented by Wright's gift to the club of all his Sierra negatives.

From these prints and negatives came the illustrations for Cedric Wright's book, "Words of the Earth"—the High Sierra earth. The text comes from the same piece of terrain. People who knew Wright in his mountains—and there are hundreds who did—know that the text came to him by osmosis as he lay up on some choice piece of Sierra, in between his exposures of film, and was himself exposed to inaudible words and music.

One of the nicest of all memorials to Cedric Wright, however, is the picture so many friends carry in their mind's eye of Cedric before the first of a series of strokes grounded him and impaired his eyesight. For in that picture he is the Good Samaritan of the trailside, bringing music to a campfire, pouring a warming cup of tea from his billycan for the weary traveler, brightening the tired end of a day with his good humor and his good heart. Above all, we his friends are grateful that because he saw clearly, we can begin to see clearly, or at least be less unseeing.

Cedric Wright.

21

Norman Clyde: Old Man of the Mountains

HAROLD GILLIAM

1961

This account of one of the club's greatest mountaineers was reprinted in the Bulletin *from the San Francisco* Chronicle, *where it first appeared in Harold Gilliam's regular Sunday column,* This Land.

WHEREVER MEN GATHER around blazing campfires in the cold nights of the high country and talk of the history of mountaineering, there are certain names that inevitably come into the conversation—Mallory, Irvine, Mummery, and among Americans John Muir, Clarence King, Norman Clyde.

In terms of pioneering climbs on American peaks, there is never any doubt that the all-time champion was Norman Clyde. There are a good many old-timers in the Sierra Club whose eyes shine with recollections of the great bear of a man who always carried a mountainous pack—often weighing 100 pounds or more—never removing it except to sleep. One wag dubbed him: "The pack that walks like a man."

The tales of Clyde's endurance are Bunyanesque. He held the speed record for racing up 14,000-foot Mount Shasta, climbed Mount Whitney some fifty times over a period of years, often without pausing for breath, and once in Glacier National Park scrambled up the thirty highest peaks in as many days.

Many a mountaineer has struggled up some remote Sierra crag for what he believed was a first ascent, only to find on the summit, beneath a cairn of rocks, an empty camera film box with the signature "Norman Clyde" and the date scrawled on the cover. Kilroy himself never turned up in more unexpected places.

Understandably there was genuine excitement at the 1961 Sierra Club Base Camp above Lake Sabrina when into the camp walked a big grizzled man with a giant pack and a thick swatch of white hair showing from beneath the back of his battered campaign hat. This was indeed Norman Clyde, the legend, still living, climbing and telling his tales of adventure in the high country.

His appearance caused a flurry for another reason as well. Camper Barbara

Norman Clyde as a young climber.

Vye was brushing her teeth one night when the bushes parted and she was suddenly confronted with a shadowy figure she thought was a bear. It was the embarrassed Paul Bunyan of the Sierra, who apologized and asked for directions. "I know my way around the mountains pretty well," he said, "but when I get into camp I'm completely lost."

Clyde had consented to lead Sierra Club hikers into the high country to share with them his lore and techniques. Although he could have had his equipment carried to the base camp by pack animals, as did the rest of the campers, the elderly climber preferred to lug his huge pack on his back to the camp on Baboon creek at 10,600 feet elevation, seven miles and some 1500 feet above the roadhead at Sabrina.

But the pack was a light one, he said—a mere 55 pounds. Most guesses placed his age near 80, although he reckoned with a grin that he was 350.

Clyde was always at home in the mountains in winter and in summer.

Overtaken by a storm, he burrowed into a thicket until the weather cleared, then bulldozed his way out.

One time he headed up the precipitous east side of the range and over one of the passes in late October, intending to go out over another pass. But he was caught—without his skis—by the first big storm of the season. The storm lasted several days, and by the time it was over, all the passes were buried under six feet of soft snow, making the return trip impossible.

There was only one thing to do. He slogged down the western slope of the range some 70 miles into Fresno. The most difficult part of the trip, he said later, was trying to get checks cashed in Fresno to buy food.

Whenever someone was lost in the Sierra or whenever a plane crashed on a seemingly inaccessible mountainside, almost inevitably there was a call for the man who knew the range as no one had known it since John Muir.

In 1933 when Clyde's young friend Walter A. Starr Jr. failed to return from a solo climbing expedition in the Minarets, south of Yosemite, parties of the Sierra's best mountaineers combed the area without success. After the other searchers had given up, Norman Clyde persisted.

Searching the steepled Minarets with his field glasses, foot by foot, he finally detected a spot high on a 12,000-foot pinnacle from which a slab of rock had recently peeled off and fallen.

Clyde's surmise turned out to be correct. In a notch hundreds of feet below he found the body of his young friend.

To many of the Sierra Club campers who listened to Clyde's tales at Baboon Creek, the biggest surprise was his splendid command of the language, his felicitous turn of phrase. The secret was in his famous pack. It developed that in that mysterious mountain of gear he customarily carried volumes of classical literature in half a dozen languages. That summer of 1961 he was re-reading Goethe's Faust in German.

Under questioning he confessed that he had worked for his Masters Degree in the classics at the University of California more than half a century ago. Then, because of his disinclination to write a thesis, he deserted the groves of academe for the forests of the Sierra, sometimes returning to civilization long enough to earn a grubstake by teaching.

For a time he was a school principal in the Owens Valley town of Independence but lost the job when he fired a gun over the heads of some students perpetrating a destructive Halloween prank.

Under the lodgepole pines of glacial-carved granite basins and along the high trails where for years he had led hikers on club outings, he talked not only of Palisade Glacier and Kearsarge Pass, of aretes and cols and couloirs, but of Virgil, Homer, Emerson, Boccaccio, Dante—all of whom he read in the original. His eyes were on the summit peaks—both of landscape and literature.

The campers recognized an extraordinary phenomenon—an American prototype, a man of the wilderness in the mold of Daniel Boone, Jim Bridger, Kit Carson and Jedediah Smith, yet a man as much at home in the world of literature as many a university professor.

Perhaps Norman Clyde's real prototype is not the wilderness scout but Henry David Thoreau, the learned Yankee individualist who would have no truck with social conformity but stubbornly went his own way in his cabin at Walden Pond. Clyde's Walden was the entire Sierra, and his cabin was carried on his back.

Although Clyde often climbed with parties of mountaineers — always as the iron man of the group — most fellow climbers agree that he was hardly an organization man. He was happiest when climbing alone, setting his own pace, looking for new heights to conquer.

In the years after World War II, a new generation of climbers came to the fore. By the use of co-ordinated teamwork and specialized equipment — ropes, pitons, expansion bolts — and mathematical calculations, they were able to scale perpendicular cliffs, such as those of Half Dome and El Capitan, where even Clyde, using only his native endowment, could not go.

Yet there is little doubt that long after the expansion-bolt climbers have ascended the last "inaccessible" pinnacle, the legend of Norman Clyde will continue to be related with awe around mountain campfires for generations to come.

22

Walter A. Starr, Jr.

VINCENT BUTLER

1934

The LeContes are not the only father-son team in the club's pantheon. Around the turn of the century, Walter Starr, Sr. and his hiking companion, Allan Chickering, made some of the pioneer explorations along what is now the John Muir Trail. Three decades later Starr's son, a brilliant young attorney and superb mountaineer, began work on his Guide to the John Muir Trail, *which has probably been carried in more knapsacks than any other publication. He died at thirty before the work was completed, and his father, a club president and later honorary president, prepared the material for publication.*

Here is part of an account of "Pete" Starr's life by his good friend and law associate. It first appeared in early editions of "Starr's Guide."

HE SPENT ALL OF HIS vacations and many of his holiday week-ends in the High Sierra. Although he was rich in social grace and charm, and thoroughly enjoyed people, he shared with John Muir the love of

77

solitude in the high mountains. In 1929 he conceived the idea of a comprehensive Guide to the High Sierra, and he set about compiling data for it in a studious and well-ordered way, doing the job himself. There was no thought of glory or personal prestige in his concept or in his work. He knew the need and he wanted others to share his enjoyment of the great range that was his second home. His plan was to give the Guide to the Sierra Club, of which he was a life member.

In his short span, he climbed forty-two main peaks between Yosemite Park and Sequoia Park, and covered at least two thousand miles of trails and knapsack routes, some of them several times. His endurance and enthusiasm were almost without parallel. A remarkable example is given in his diary of a holiday week-end knapsack trip in the Yosemite region in 1930. He left the valley at noon, Saturday, September 6, 1930, and returned the following Wednesday morning at six. In the interval he had traveled alone, with his pack on his back, taking notes, distances, altitudes, and observations, over one hundred and forty-three miles of mountain trails and passes. His route led via Merced Lake over Isberg Pass to the Middle Fork of the San Joaquin, and thence to the Devils Postpile under Mammoth Pass. He came back via Thousand Island Lake, Island Pass, Donohue Pass, Tuolumne Meadows, and Lake Tenaya to Yosemite. Some of the travel was at night under a full moon. The return from the Devils Postpile to below Tenaya, forty-eight miles, was made between 1:30 A.M. and 8:00 P.M. of the same day. The finish of ten miles to Yosemite was made by 6:00 A.M. the following morning.

When the word went out in August, 1933, that Peter was missing in The Minarets, many heroic companions, whose names are first in California mountaineering, responded to lead the search. Among them were Norman Clyde, Jules Eichorn, Glen Dawson, Oliver Kehrlein, and Dick Jones. The President of the Sierra Club, Francis Farquhar, made the search from the air. . . .

There was something of true genius in "Peter" Starr. This book gives evidence of it, and there were other signs. Peter was a poet in his heart and in his music as well as in his mountains. He found solace in solitude and he often attained the heights—where he now rests.

Mountaineers recognize that Peter was a really great one among them, whose physical capacity was matched only by his spiritual sense. It is deep tragedy that this volume should appear as his posthumous work. It is none the less a part of the permanent record of California that this is the enduring gift of a young man who gave his life at the age of thirty in completing the first Guide to the High Sierra.

There is special meaning in the name of Peter Starr. He chose "Peter" himself for reasons of his own. His patronym suggests his scintillating radiance and his home in high places. His adoptive name is from the classic word for rock.

If Peter were to have chosen his resting-place, he would have asked for his present one. He is untimely there, but he is eternally embraced by his youthful love, and the two have become one.

23

Francis P. Farquhar

DAVID R. BROWER

1974

Among the Sierra Club's latter-day leaders, few had as great an impact on the organization as Francis P. Farquhar, an accountant by profession but by avocation a mountaineer, editor, director, and president of the club and historian of the range from which it takes it name. He was honorary president at the time of his death at eighty-six in 1974. He is seen here in a role that was vitally important to the club in his middle and later years—encouraging younger people to devote their talents to the cause.

David R. Brower, former executive director of the club and founder of Friends of the Earth in 1969, was elected a Sierra Club honorary vice president in 1972. This selection originally appeared in Not Man Apart, *published by Friends of the Earth. The Middle Palisade, referred to here, is one of the Sierra's major peaks and is near the eastern boundary of Kings Canyon National Park, which Farquhar helped create.*

FRANCIS P. FARQUHAR joined the Sierra Club in 1911, two years out of Harvard, served on its Board of Directors from 1924 to 1951, was its president twice (1933–35, 1948–49), and edited the *Sierra Club Bulletin* from 1926 to 1946. He loved the Sierra Nevada, became the authority on its history, and was particularly fond of the Middle Palisade, of which he and the late Ansel F. Hall made the first ascent in 1921. He had a major hand in introducing the techniques of modern rock climbing in the Sierra. More than anyone, he dissuaded people from improperly calling the Sierra the Sierras. In Spanish, he explained, *sierra* means "range of mountains"; "The Sierra Nevada is distinctly a unit, both geographically and topographically, and is well described as '*una sierra nevada*' " in early accounts. To say "Sierra Nevada Mountains," he added, would be as bad as saying "Saint San Francisco."

He invited me to his house in San Francisco in 1933 three months after I had joined the Sierra Club. The previous summer I had been on a seven-week backpack and climbing trip, and he wanted to ask me a few things about Sierra routes that might help with a forthcoming Sierra Club book, *Guide to the John Muir Trail and High Sierra Region*, written by Walter A. Starr, Jr., who had, before quite completing the work, fallen to his death in

The Minarets that same summer. Francis also asked me to write a note about my trip for the *Bulletin*. It was pleasing to be in print and to be introduced into Sierra Club ruling circles. I soon learned that Francis made a point of doing this for young people, and it brought important continuity to the club program and to mountaineering. Marjory Bridge, a mountaineer he was soon to marry, followed suit (and put me on my first club committee).

Then Francis got me in deeper. In the summer of 1934, I made a ten-week backpack and climbing trip with Hervey Voge and submitted "Far From the Madding Mules" to the *Bulletin*. Francis did some masterful editing, ran it in the 1935 Annual, and for all the editing he had to do, nevertheless appointed me to the club's Editorial Board that year. He guided me in digging up, editing, and writing material for the battle to establish Kings Canyon National Park. I found out how to steer things through the printer, forever trying to keep Error from fixing its sly imprimatur on the final work — as Error did to Francis one time with extra slyness when he was carefully distinguishing between two spellings of a proper name — Thompson and Thomson — and the printer stopped the presses to insert the missing *p* and blow the whole point.

There was also much to be learned from the man who had undertaken the first out-and-out conservation lobbying task for the club in its effort to extend Sequoia National Park (an effort not quite completed yet, in spite of

*Francis Farquhar
on the summit of
Mount Whitney, 1930.*

80

the designation of Kings Canyon National Park). And Francis was the man who knew where and why the Sierra got its names (*Place Names of the High Sierra,* 1926), who revived Clarence King's classic *Mountaineering in the Sierra Nevada,* who teamed with Ansel Adams to bring fine photography to the *Bulletin* and earn it the accolade "that model of all mountaineering journals" (given it in England), and whose writings about the Sierra's discoverers and protectors culminated in his *History of the Sierra Nevada.*

Francis had an extraordinary love for fine books and built the most remarkable mountaineering library in the West. It was a place for pilgrimages. Indeed, whenever a mountaineer of note, whether the degree was earned on a Sierra wall or in a distant range, dropped by the San Francisco Bay Area, Francis and Marj invited him or her to their Berkeley home—along with 40 or 50 of the Bay region's active climbers. What memorable reunions they were!

In the course of all this, the Farquhars and their growing family helped me through various prewar nadirs, giving me the run not only of the library but also of the beautifully equipped Farquhar darkroom. With Francis' concurrence and help, I worked part-time for the club, ostensibly trying to prepare a member's handbook, but getting deeper and deeper into helping him with the *Bulletin.* In May 1941, he sensed that I knew enough to go professional and suggested that I ask the University of California Press about an editing job. The manager of the press, Francis' brother Sam, gave me a chance for a full-time paid job. Whereupon Francis filled my volunteer time by delegating the 1942 Annual to me and saying he was ready to pass the editorship on. The Army, however, had precedence and whisked me off to the US Mountain Troops.

When the war was over, it was quite clear that Francis had bent the twig. I was back at the Press, back on the Board and *Bulletin,* and full of ideas about Sierra Club books. The club was now ready to break new ground by publishing the superb exhibit that Ansel Adams and the late Nancy Newhall had put together to tell the world a conservation story it needed to know and to tell it beautifully. This required transforming the exhibit into the first Exhibit Format book (a term invented for the occasion), *This Is the American Earth.*

The message of *This is the American Earth,* and the Exhibit Format books that followed, was one that Francis had himself been developing for decades, presented in a way that, in its appearance and attempts at clarity, was informed more by Francis than by anyone else. Conservation-through-publishing was thereafter promoted and pushed by many. I, as one of the promoters, would never have given the idea a second thought had it not been for Francis' particular concern: new people must be sought out, their interest engaged, and their roots in wilderness watered with understanding, tolerance, and kindness. In a long and fruitful life, the Sierra Club's late Honorary President, Francis Peloubet Farquhar, was a grand coach. He brought honor to the club, to mountaineering, to conservation, to accounting, and to the graphic arts. That honor will last a long, long time.

24

A Fractured History of the Sierra Club

WILLIAM E. SIRI

1966

As a last note on the club's history, we present a look from a lighter viewpoint, excerpted from a "misaddress" presented by William E. Siri at the Sierra Club Annual Banquet in 1966. Siri has served as a director and president of the club, and is a dedicated climber.

IN 1892, just 400 years after Columbus discovered America, the Sierra Club was founded by John Muir and some friends. His friends in the venture were members of the faculties of Stanford University and the University of California. That was the first and almost certainly the last collaboration between these schools.

In this brief essay there is space to touch on only a few highlights of the Sierra Club's history. In doing so it is illuminating to examine battles lost as well as won, and thus learn from the mistakes that were made. Hetch Hetchy in Yosemite was the first great battle lost. In that campaign, the Club, led by John Muir, fought valiantly but in vain. The good intentions of the dam builders were misunderstood, as was the importance of the dam to the preservation of wilderness. The misunderstanding, of course, was the Club's failure to comprehend that when the dam was built, a magnificent canyon would be preserved in perpetuity, under water, for future generations. It would no longer be threatened by freeways, mining, timber cutting, and overgrazing. But the Club learned slowly. Years later it fought again unsuccessfully against the damming of Glen Canyon. Today the Bureau of Reclamation can smile with pride as thousands of young people enjoy a wilderness experience at Glen Canyon on their water skis.

At the turn of the century it became evident that a population explosion in California was in the making. With characteristic resourcefulness, Will Colby set about to remedy this menacing problem. He conducted groups, at first small and then progressively larger, into the wilderness with the object of displacing or misplacing them and thus reduce the population pressure on San Francisco and Los Angeles. The scheme never worked; they all returned. Worse still, they told friends in Iowa and New York about it, with the inevitable consequence that even more people came to California. Ironically, Will Colby, one of the Club's greatest and most devoted leaders, unwittingly abetted the population explosion in California.

However, the practice of hiking with packs in the mountains, or outings as they came to be called, naturally spread with alarming speed as does any slightly masochistic activity, for as everyone knows, "suffering builds character." Outings continued to grow in number and size until they reached the point where reliable witnesses reported that during the summer months hundreds of thousands of Sierra Clubers bearing backpacks marched shoulder to shoulder in great hordes up and down the Sierra Nevada, each tugging two or three burros laden with canned foods and equipment. Their numbers were so great according to my informant, a company forester, that some, even in the middle thirties, had to take to the vertical walls of Yosemite, led there by Francis Farquhar and Dick Leonard. This practice quickly became known as rock climbing and, as fortune would have it, rock climbing was even more masochistic than backpacking. For this reason most of the directors of the Sierra Club were, until recent years, rock climbers. It was assumed that anyone who would endure the self-inflicted suffering of rock climbing would also qualify as a director. Now, of course, there are additional means of qualifying, like neglect of family and profession for committee meetings and hearings.

The Club considers population growth the major long-term conservation challenge and is exploring every possible approach to a solution.

My own studies on population have confirmed projections that are now widely known; for example, that the population will double in 37 years, and that by 2764 there will be standing room only on the earth's surface, but they also revealed new facts of considerable significance. Among them, it is of some interest to know, for example, that because of the Club's growth rate, the membership will exceed the population of the United States in the year 2093. Moreover, in the year 2562 the Club's membership will be three times the population of the world.

It is becoming clear that the Americans with red skins may have been right all along. They had lived here for 50,000 years without getting themselves into the desperate plight that confronts Americans with just red blood. What is more baffling, however, is the mystery of how the Indians managed to preserve 3,000,000 square miles of wilderness extending from coast to coast without the Sierra Club.

83

PART III   "To Explore,
Enjoy, and
Preserve . . ."

NINETEEN HUNDRED AND ONE *was the Year One not only of the twentieth century but of the Sierra Club outings. The first trip to "Camp Muir" in Tuolumne Meadows was the ancestor of the hundreds of trips the club now sponsors each year around the world, from the Sierra to the Galapagos to the Himalaya.*

Although, as we have seen, the club has its impelling inner force in the experience of wonder in the wilderness, its unity of purpose and the human relationships that could transfer that purpose into effective action were formed or deeply strengthened on the club's annual outings during the early decades. To share that experience of wonder provides an added dimension.

Wonder, of course, is not the only sensation felt on the outings. Inevitably there are others—exaltation and fatigue, excitement and weariness, affection and anxiety, friendship and friction, adventure and drudgery. Walk a trail through dust, heat, rain, mud, and snow; climb interminable switchbacks and scramble up steep slopes in the thin air of the high altitudes; swat mosquitoes; dodge lightning; sleep shivering; ford streams; gaze at sunsets; cluster around campfires; all amid the intense beauty of forests and meadows, lakes and streams and snowy summits—share these experiences with old friends or with strangers, and in a few days you develop personal bonds unknown under the circumstances of routine life in the lowlands.

A large proportion of the participants on the early month-long outings, which came to be known as "High Trips," returned year after year and developed the camaraderie that carried the club through its later struggles to preserve pristine wilderness sanctuaries as an inviolable American heritage. John Muir and William E. Colby originally saw this "cementing of the bonds" as one of the purposes of the trips. They also assumed that the more people who experienced the wilderness, the greater the constituency that would work for its preservation.

25

How It All Began—or Almost Didn't

WILLIAM E. COLBY

1931

It is amusing to learn that when Colby first proposed the idea of annual outings, the club's leaders had serious doubts, as this account indicates. One of the greatest of club leaders, Colby fought hard in the campaigns to enlarge Sequoia National Park and create Kings Canyon National Park. Yet, what hundreds of men, women, and children have always remembered best are the High Trips, which he organized in 1901 and led for twenty-nine years. The traditional High Trips were the start of what has become an outing program operating around the globe. Particularly at the beginning, without the guidance offered by the High Trips, many people would never have experienced the mountains and become fighters for the wilderness they knew and loved.

Colby became secretary of the board of directors in 1900, and held this position for forty-seven out of the forty-nine years he served on the board; the other two years he was club president. In 1950 he was elected honorary president.

WHEN I first became secretary of the Sierra Club, some thirty years ago, the Mazamas, with headquarters in Portland, Oregon, had just been conducting some very successful summer outings into the mountain regions of the Northwest. Reading of these expeditions made me realize that this strengthening feature was entirely lacking in the life of the Sierra Club. I presented the possibility of such outings to the directors. Some were favorably inclined, but others expressed great pessimism, stating that individual members preferred to organize their own parties, and that there would be no great response to an outing which involved a crowd where members would be forced to "rub shoulders" in a strange group. Rather dubious about the outcome, they finally granted the authorization to conduct such an outing, but with the distinct understanding that the club treasury was not to be in any way responsible for any obligations incurred.

It was from John Muir, however, the president of the club, that I received the warmest encouragement. He was highly enthusiastic, and told me that he had long been trying to get the club to undertake just such outings.

William E. Colby.

The first outing announcement was a remarkable product. In the advice regarding outing costumes suitable for women to wear in the mountains, it was suggested that skirts should reach "halfway to the knees," and this at once provoked the natural question as to whether the measurement was to be made from the ground or from above. It illustrates the fact that in the year 1901 it was difficult for women to get a comfortable and serviceable costume without having it specially made. A few emancipated females wore bloomers on mountain climbs. These garments gave the desired freedom, but transgressed all laws of esthetic standards. For many years skirts persisted, but they grew scantier in length with each succeeding year, and finally the yoke was entirely thrown off, though not without much amusing opposition on the part of those who thought that somehow or other fundamental modesty rather than mere custom was involved. The present-day knickerbockers, or hiking trousers, have now been accepted as altogether the most comfortable and fitting garb for high-mountain travel, and women are now clad as appropriately as men.

Pioneering on untrodden ground, the Outing Committee had much to learn, and it took several outings, in which extensive pack trips were involved, and many sad experiences, before the basic problems were solved. Had I realized all the grief that was to follow, as well as the nervous strain of the tremendous responsibility, I probably would have reconsidered and canceled the plans. But, blissfully ignorant of the perplexing problems, youthful enthusiasm carried the day. Many abnormal conditions arose to make the task all the more difficult. A heavy snowfall in the winter of 1900–1901 had broken most of the important bridges on the Tioga Road. Fortunately the owners of the road put a crew of men to work and saved the day by repairing these bridges in the nick of time, and our freight-teams were delayed only two or three days in consequence. We even had to blast out heavy drifts of snow to get the teams through.

The trip as a whole, however, proved such a success that, instead of deterring me from further efforts, I immediately began planning for a much more ambitious outing the following year [to the Kings River Canon]. . .

On the 1901 outing, we had used a famous "Buzzacott Army Range," made particularly for Philippine service, which weighed almost 250 pounds. We have since evolved what is known as the "Sierra Camp Stove," a light sheet-iron stove with a detached aluminum sheet top and telescoping stovepipe which fits in the oven. The total weight is only 125 pounds, and with careful packing it can be readily transported on muleback.

Most of the cooking utensils are aluminum, and so far as possible are made to nest one within another. They have given excellent service and wear. The cups are made to order, of pressed tin, with a wire in the rim and forming the handle, which is made so the cups will nest or can be hung on the belt. Each has the name of the club stamped on the bottom. They are patterned after similar cups made for the famous Appalachian Mountain Club of Boston. At the outset of the trip each member of the party is provided with a cup and a spoon, which are carried at all times. Besides their regular use at meals, they have on several occasions proved particularly useful in emergencies.

It is of prime importance that food for such a trip be of good quality and of sufficient variety, yet without undue weight. In the earlier years I made a careful study of this vital problem, reading books on dietetics and consulting lists of army rations, as well as investigating suggestions by authorities on outdoor life and camping. The character of the meals and the balance of the rations served on Sierra Club trips have received the highest praise from expert dietitians and physicians who have been on these outings. . . .

Of course, even the best of food can be ruined by poor cooking, and a good cook has always been one of our most important considerations. In the early days of the outings — for thirteen years, in fact — we were fortunate enough to have the services of dear old "Charlie Tuck." He grew to be very fond of the mountains, as well as of the members of the outing parties collectively, and while he lived nothing could have induced him to miss a trip as chef of the Sierra Club. Of all the Chinese I have known, he had the jolliest, the most jovial disposition, and he was usually joshing or joking with some member of the party, even while he carried on his work. He called the girls by their first names, and surprised many of the staid members who had been on previous outings by telling them a lot of their family history, which he had learned the winter before, in Chinatown, from Chinese employees of their families. I shall never forget the night he rode into the light of our blazing camp-fire above Lake Merced, in 1907, when it was still a real wilderness. He had missed the trail, and had ridden in the saddle thirty-two miles over rough mountain country, the last hour or two of it in pitch dark, and it was between eight and nine o'clock at night when he arrived. His sense of responsibility and loyalty had kept him going under circumstances in which others would have given up and turned back. Nor shall I soon forget the morning in 1913, in Tehipite Valley, when he appeared in camp garbed in long yellow slicker and broad sombrero, both of which he had acquired through the "Lost and Found," and with a very sheepish look on his face. He had missed a crossing log on the Middle Fork of Kings River and had spent the night out in a drizzling rain. Unfortunately, gin was at the bottom of this mishap, for though at one time Charlie Tuck reformed, it was only for two or three years following the earthquake fire, during a period of conversion by a Baptist mission. This fall from grace did not happen often, however, and the result was usually more ludicrous than otherwise. When Charlie Tuck passed away, in the winter of 1914, he left many devoted admirers in the Sierra Club.

Considering the character of the outings which the club takes into the High Sierra, involving traveling for long distances on mountain trails, the pack-train is probably the most vital institution of the whole trip. Upon the satisfactory transportation of food and personal equipment, including the all-important sleeping-bag, the success or failure of the outing depends. On the outings with maximum attendance of 220 regular members and 50 packers and members of the commissary staff, it has been necessary to transport more than ten tons of provisions and over five tons of dunnage bags and commissary equipment. On the earlier outings, missing dunnage bags and delayed pack-trains were a common occurrence. In spite of precautions based on sad experience, many were the occasions for all-night vigils around the camp-fire.

Many have commented on the low cost of these outings per person — about $80 for four weeks. This is due to the fact that the institution is a co-operative affair, each person contributing a share of the expenses, and also to the fact that a great deal of the labor in planning the trip and its active conduct is volunteered. Many can testify that it is impossible to obtain a more delightful and beneficial vacation for less cost.

What is it that appeals to people and draws them year after year like an irresistible magnet into the High Sierra? Those who have joined repeatedly in the outings have doubtless done so in part, at least, because of fine comradeship under delightful surroundings. But important as this is, friendship is not all. We may not consciously realize it, but it is quite certain that one powerful reason which induces us to go back to the high mountains year after year is their cleansing effect on body, mind, and soul. They take us far from the jarring, jangling noises and jazz of modern life — where we are forced to be constantly on the alert to avoid the real dangers which confront us at every crossing. Telephone-bells constantly ringing, automobiles honking, newspaper headlines screaming deeds of crime — these are not conducive to the best life. It is little wonder that our nerves get on edge.

Crystal clear air, crystal pure water, pine-needles for a bed after a day of healthful hiking along trails that unfold inspiring views to delight the eye, all combine to give us fundamental relief and cure for our many ills. The early rising which becomes the custom during that all too short month enables us each morning to see the increasing light fill the eastern sky until it spills over the crest of the mighty range in a perfect flood as the sun itself finally appears from behind the shoulder of some sublime peak. We live and sleep alongside of the companionable streams. And during the nights from our high-mountain camps we can look up at the heavens crowded with myriads of stars that no mere lowlander can ever hope to see.

Somehow or other we find ourselves for the time being dwelling nearer to God, and it is little wonder that when we return we unconsciously bring back with us some of that rare peace and contentment which pervade the high places the world over.

William E. Colby with club outing leaders at the start of the 1939 High Trip at Hutchinson Meadow in the Sierra. Left to right: Oliver Kehrlein, Colby, Richard Leonard, and David Brower.

91

26

Camp Muir in the Tuolumne Meadows

ELLA M. SEXTON

1902

The first Sierra Club outing in 1901 was historic for several reasons, including the distinguished roster, on which we find John Muir; his daughters, Wanda, 20, and Helen, 15; painter William Keith, whose Sierra landscapes are still prized; C. Hart Merriam, director of the U.S. Biological Survey; historian Theodore Hittell; and a number of prominent faculty members from both Stanford and Berkeley.

The latter was to have included the elder statesman of the club, Professor Joseph LeConte, who thirty-one years earlier had made an exploratory trip to the same region. In June of 1901 "Professor Joe" had attended the wedding of his son and Helen Gompertz and then gone to Yosemite Valley in preparation for joining the club trip. He was jubilant at his return to the scenes he had first seen three decades earlier. E. T. Parsons, one of the organizers of the trip, wrote: "Those who were with him will never forget their visit to the foot of the lower Yosemite Fall, where, standing on a rock in the spray from the falling waters, he raised his arms aloft and shouted in the exuberance of his joy and delight at the magnificent spectacle before him."

The seventy-eight-year-old professor was stricken and died the next day. "After his passing," Parsons wrote, "the outing continued as planned, for there could be no doubt what his wishes would have been. To those who loved him and revered his memory it was as if his kindly presence had been with them on the trip, and the voice of Nature seemed to speak a more forceful message of the wonders and magnificence of creation which had been the study of his life."

Parsons wrote a vivid description of the trip in the Bulletin: "It was a sight to see dignified college professors, wily limbs of the law, deft doctors, and reverend clergymen join gleefully in rolling rocks, lifting logs, and shovelling snow to make way for the commissary."

Parsons' greatest surprise, like that of most men in the camp, was how women sweetened the trip. "Nearly all of the women in his party were Berkeley or Stanford girls, and their vigor and endurance was a revelation to all of us. . . . At no time during the outing did the college women give out or find fault, nor did they delay or prove a drag on the progress of the excursion. One confirmed mountaineer said that it was the first time he had ever been camping with women, and that he had started in with serious misgivings, but after this experience he would never go to the mountains again without the added pleasure of the companionship of women. . . ."

For a woman's view of the trip we offer here the account of Ella M. Sexton, one of the ninety-six adventurers who began the steep trail up Yosemite Falls in 1901. Miss Sexton's prose is Victorian and characteristic of the writing of the period, but we can feel across the years the verve and freshness and sense of high adventure that animated the outing.

"South Dome," which she refers to here, is better known as Half Dome. The "soda spring" is Soda Spring in Tuolumne Meadows.

COME, ALL YOU HIGH SI-EERYS! was the slogan that called us to the camp-fire—a slogan first heard in Yosemite Valley from mighty lungs that sent this cheerful cry echoing from South Dome to Glacier Point, three thousand feet above us.

"Come, all you High Si-eerys!"—and a circle of eager, expectant faces gathered under the tall pines and round a splendid cone of leaping flames. Myriads of sparks shot up to the dark sky and brilliant stars, while grave professors, giddy co-eds, the poet, the historian, and sundry medical, clerical, and legal lights blushed alike in the camp-fire's rosy glow. For here was the Sierra Club of mountain-lovers, equipped and more than ready for this its initial expedition to those high meadows where the Tuolumne River, new-born of Mt. Lyell's glacier, lingers among the wild flowers before taking its long series of playful slides and swift rushes to the Grand Cañon miles below.

None of these "High Si-eerys" knew when the party was to start, for alarming rumors of great snow-drifts, of broken bridges and washed-out roads delaying the freight-teams had reached the camp. The real exodus, however, came three days later, and then what a girding on of knapsacks and tin cups, what a marshaling of alpenstocks there was, since the way lay upward along the steep Yosemite Falls trail to the rim of the valley.

Under great oaks and by dewy, fragrant hay-fields, with the valley dust rising as the sun dried up the dew, we "hiked along," in mountain parlance, with the cool spray of the lower fall greeting us, and soon the zigzag, rocky path led upward. An hour's climb brought the procession to the cañon between the two great falls, and with the thunder of Upper Yosemite throbbing in the warm golden air, we rode through this grassy vale sweet with laurel and wet with misty spray.

Up again, while the roar of the torrent in its sixteen-hundred-foot plunge drowned our feeble shouts. Scarcely daring to look down over the slippery rocks or up to the sublime wall of overhanging granite, we clung in desperation to the saddle and hoped to behold the top. The distressed mules panted and heaved, but never failed to set each little hoof securely; the last turn came, and there was a long sigh of relief. We looked silently down three thousand feet and more to the floor of Yosemite's wonderful chasm, and then pressed forward over bare heights where the glacial markings were plain, crossing the foaming Yosemite Creek hurrying to its drop at the falls, and over endless great rolling hills.

We reached the advance-guard of walkers at Porcupine Flat, and there, under magnificent firs and cedars, was our first camping-spot. The supper-call was the melodious whanging of a tin pan, and in line, like soldiers, we held out the individual and ubiquitous tin cup for the first course of soup and hardtack. A log or handy stone was the dining-chair, and no true mountaineer ever rinsed his cup for the following black coffee or nut-brown tea. A tin plate heaped with beans, potatoes, and a remarkable corned-beef stew was the next course, and this progressive dining permitted conversation with a second partner and a different seat for this part of the feast. Our mountain appetites disposed of everything, and ladies used to nibbling bonbons, chicken-wings, and sweetbreads ate what was in sight, polished up their tin plates, and called for more.

So the chilly dusk fell upon us, and the first truly Sierra Club "pow-wow" was held round its own glorious camp-fire. Almost too tired to enthuse much, we scorched our faces while the snow-drifts sent cold blasts against our backs, had a little singing, an announcement that Sunday was to be spent at Porcupine Flat, and then each leg-weary or mule-jolted pilgrim hunted repose under the stars.

Most amusing were the elaborate preparations for the slumber all sought and few found. One lady near me donned two sleeping-robes, one pink and one black, a pair of yellow slippers, tied a blue bandanna over her head, and then crawled into a sleeping-bag with much pinning of giant safety-pins and tying of countless strings. In five minutes she suddenly sat up in her chrysalis of blankets (with great damage to pins, strings, and feelings) to say "Shoo!" to a wandering horse that fancied a tender bunch of grass near my lady's head.

The bell-mare roamed up and down with maddening persistence, too, and stones, sticks, and pine-cones made themselves prominent in the fir beds. On the whole the frosty morning was welcomed, though dressing and a dip into the melted snow of the brook resulted in much shivering.

Some six miles' tramping through fir-woods and tamaracks was the next day's trip. While plodding along over granite hillsides and ridges strewn with bowlders literally as large as a house, we caught a glimpse of blue Lake Tenaya in the distance, and on descending to the meadows skirting that body of water a race of savage and hungry mosquitoes presented their ready bills. Having been forewarned of these pests, our "High Si-eerys" went into the temporary retirement of head-nets. These were a sort of maddening bird-cage of white bobinet and wire rings, very hot and blinding, but mosquito-proof at least.

Lake Tenaya was a pretty sheet of clear, shallow water, lying under the shadow of a great mass of snow-flecked granite, and in the forest beside it was our halting-place for the night. Not till cold twilight did the belated baggage get in, and then there was a great scurrying to unpack blankets and make hasty sleeping-quarters in any old place. Camp-fires blazed near every group of sleepers, and no wandering horses, nor even the alleged cry of a mountain lion, could rouse the tired ones.

The following day tried our souls indeed, and incidentally blistered not a few tender feet; but finally we struck the first of the Tuolumne Meadows and could hope for a goal at last. Between us and the invisible river lay stretches of grass, marsh, and mosquitoes, the most distracting variety of this interesting family we had yet encountered. A magnificent panorama of Sierra mountains walled in the horizon — grand Cathedral Peak with its long roof-shaped summit, crowned at one extremity with cathedral spires; Unicorn, whose sharp horn to the right of the snowy bulk had earned its fantastic name; Echo Peak and others to the south, and the Dana group we were drawing nearer to in the eastern end of the valley. The way was musical with brooks and swirling, foaming streams, each having a perilous crossing of slippery logs or widely separated stepping-stones where most invitingly the cold waters rippled over weary feet. So the last of the ten-mile tramp was traversed and permanent camp was reached in tired thankfulness.

Next day the creamy-white tents were pitched picturesquely on rocky knolls or under the pines and tamaracks on the southern bank of the Tuolumne, here a rushing river some fifty feet wide. Army cots were unfolded for the sybarites who found Mother Earth's bosom rather a hard one, the two excellent Chinese cooks set to work at a range warranted to bake for a mess of a hundred, and the "High Si-eerys" were in regular possession of their dreamed-of mountain-camp.

Then came delightful lazy days, when brilliant sunshine, an enchanting view of eternal snows on Mt. Dana or Mt. Gibbs, and the music of the cascades near by made lounging round camp perfection enough. Or there were trifling three-mile tramps to an ice-cold soda spring bubbling up in its iron-reddened basin across the river and effervescing with lemon-juice and sugar into a draught fit for the fabled gods.

There were solemn hours, too, when the mountaineers looked disdainfully at us feeble "tenderfeet" as we set off with trusty alpenstocks, a light lunch, and much courage to conquer the jagged peaks, loose talus, and snow-fields of Mt. Dana. That proved an exciting day for even the "stay-in-camps," since the party had to be ferried over the Tuolumne on a primitive log-raft which dipped to the swift current and elicited shrieks and wet feet from the feminine passengers and laughter from the party on shore. Then the climbers were so delayed by ten long miles to the foot of the mountain, the hard ascent and a weary ten miles back to camp, that relief-parties had to go out to kindle fires at stream-crossings, and it was nine o'clock before the last straggler was ferried over on the shaky raft.

For several days thunder-storms gathered in the afternoons, and showers capriciously drenched the camp and avoided other localities a mile or so away, while the sunsets on piled-up clouds and snowy peaks were the admiration and despair of our artists and poets.

Down the meadows and rock-ribbed banks of this newborn, tourist Tuolumne, as John Muir calls the river, to the great fall at the opening of the

95

Grand Cañon proved a day to be remembered. Muir, the prince of mountain-lovers, was guide and apostle, and his gentle, kindly face, genial blue eyes, and quaint, quiet observations on present and past Sierra conditions impressed us unforgettably with the "sermons in stones, books in the running brooks" he knows so well.

All too swiftly flew the days, each ended by a gathering round a glorious blazing camp-fire, while Professor Dudley, of Stanford, talked on the Sierra forests, C. Hart Merriam, the eminent biologist, explained his system of classifying the animals of these high altitudes, John Muir, as president of the "High Si-eerys," modestly introduced others, and many lesser lights told incidents of the day's happenings, or songs and stories.

So the inevitable day came when we looked our last on snowy mountains and rushing river, and with precious cameras loaded with snap-shots or time-exposures, and more precious memories Time himself cannot obliterate, went out cityward assured of the Sierra Club's successful expedition.

27

Why Camp with a Crowd?

MARION RANDALL

1905

Marion Randall was a close friend of John Muir's daughter, Wanda. The third Sierra Club outing (1904) was her baptism into the wilderness. One result was her marriage three years later to fellow hiker E. T. Parsons, a member of the club's board of directors. Another, spread over the years, was a series of Bulletin *articles in which she captured, as well as anyone ever has, the spirit of the annual High Trip, as well as other club outings.*

Here, after her 1904 trip, she addresses a question that still is raised by outsiders and newcomers to the club: How is it possible to enjoy the wilderness in a crowd? Nowadays the "crowds" are smaller (twenty-five is often the limit when necessary to minimize the impact on the land), but the spirit of the trips is unchanged. Marion Randall here distills an experience that has been shared by succeeding generations for three-quarters of a century. The "aristocrat of cleanliness" she refers to is William Badè; the "aristocrat of good fellowship" is her future husband, E. T. Parsons.

OUNTAIN TRIPS the world over bear a certain intrinsic resemblance to one another; the lost trail, the bridgeless river, the firm-willed beast of burden, the camp-fire that will not burn—all these are tribulations to test the qualities of the mountaineer as well in the Cevennes as in the Sierra. But there is one feature of a Sierra Club outing which tends to make it unique, a feature much derided by the doubting Thomas whom you wish to convert, much defended by you if you are a loyal Sierran—namely, the "crowd."

It sounds rather alarming at first—to camp for a month with a party of one hundred and fifty persons, strangers for the greater part, gathered from all quarters of California and from distant points throughout the world, representatives of every profession, every science, every art, who have only one common bond, the love of nature. They are very queer-looking people too, some of them. They bear a few hallmarks of civilization, it is true; they take off their hats when they speak to you, and smoke pipes and cigarettes; they possess tooth-brushes and mirrors and back-combs—but you never heard of anything like them in song or story nor saw them upon the stage.

You rashly decide that you don't care very much about making indiscriminate acquaintances. You have a few tried friends in the party, and, though they strongly resemble the other desperadoes, you have a comfortable remembrance that but a few days ago they were orderly and respected citizens, that they still possess bank accounts and have reputations to maintain. But soon you begin to realize that some of these old friends are not quite the companions you would have chosen for the woods. Your friendship is perhaps more superficial than you thought it, or is based upon some common interest which is absent here, and while it costs you something to admit it, they jar upon you. And then you discover that the unshaven gentleman in spotted khaki with a scratch on his nose has seen the same beauty and thought the same thought that you have, and you know he is a kindred soul, though you don't like to acknowledge the kinship.

As day after day passes, and you learn to waive ceremony and accept the easy comradeship of the trail, you find that the bearded ruffian is a learned scientist, the untidy girl in the strange bonnet is an artist of promise, and the neat man in khaki who quotes Shakespeare is one of the packers, and you begin to distrust your powers of discrimination. At last you make the discovery that you yourself look as queer as your neighbor. You are a Sierran by that time, body and soul, ready to find your place in the socialist's Utopia which you inhabit for a few short weeks.

But, strange to say, even in this democratic society the aristocrats are sooner or later bound to appear. There is the aristocrat of cleanliness. On the dustiest trail, over the smokiest camp-fire, he is seen always fresh and immaculate. He must have been born clean, for he spends no more time in the washing of face and raiment than the rest of us do, and yet the result is so different!

Then there is the aristocrat of good-fellowship. He can hike too, if he wants to, but he knows that one hour of the trail is worth two in camp and that "to travel hopefully is better than to arrive." He may come late into camp, but you may be sure he will come with a smile and be ready on the instant to help cook dinner or to carry half the dunnage-bags to their abiding-places for the night. He will cobble your boots for you, he will mend your clothes, and lend you his blankets when yours are lost; and though he will talk very little about it, his name will be found on the highest peaks and the trout will have reason to remember his rod.

Life in the main camp is a degree more formal than when on the trail. The main camp is a place where Charley Tuck has stoves on which to cook, where you have a tent in which to dress, and where you get fresh bread instead of galetta. Your days are less strenuous there. Breakfast is obtainable from six until nine, and you do not have to walk abroad unless you wish.

Dinner is quite a function. It is there, perhaps, that you catch most fully the charm, the picturesqueness, and the jollity of the outing. Behind the long table stand eight girls dressed in the brightest and best their dunnage-bags can offer — shirt-waists fresh from the river, skirts a shade longer and cleaner than the well-worn regimentals, and caps, aprons, and kerchiefs of gaudy bandanas.

Each girl has charge of a kettle and a spoon, and for an hour or more hungry people file past the table for a second, third, even a fourth, helping — soup, fresh meat, potatoes, bread and butter, rice, tomatoes, pudding, gingerbread, tea and coffee à la tin cow, surely a meal fit for the gods. They think so anyway, these sunburned people in their gay sweaters and bandanas, as, laughing and joking the while, they move along the line, turn from the table with filled plate to join a chosen group of diners on the ground near by, busily wield fork and spoon, and then patiently join the line again for a further supply.

A lazy hour follows until the camp-fire is built and you gather round its circle of red light. The entertainment offered you may be grave or gay, quiet or noisy, but it is never twice alike. Songs, instrumental music, impromptu rhymes, original ballads, and talks on many topics relating to the mountains and the purposes of the club are among the things you hear nightly, and once at least in the course of the trip a grand vaudeville performance calls forth all the talent in camp. These camp-fire gatherings hold a place among your dearest recollections of the summer. The faces that you have seen illumined by the leaping flames can never be indifferent to you, and wheresoever you may meet them, in crowded streets or dingy offices, or in the heat and babble of an afternoon tea, they will bring to you a little thrill of joy as if you caught again a breath from the pines.

By common consent the day after you arrive in camp is devoted to a general washing. Shortly after breakfast the girls return to their camp, and procuring a pile of clothing, go down in groups of three or four to the river. As the morning's programme includes a bath, the favorite costume for laundry work is a bathing suit. It is a pretty though often a humorous sight to see the lassies lined up along the river-bank diligently scrubbing and sousing until the garments have assumed that appearance of uniform griminess which passes in camp for cleanliness.

Fourth of July dinner on the 1903 High Trip to the Kern River.

There seems to be a prevailing impression that the entire club travels day in and day out in one indissoluble "gang." Nothing can be further from the fact, for save when climbing a mountain you travel to suit yourself. You start at whatever hour you wish, walk alone or in company, and spend the whole day or a few hours in covering the distance. It is possible to travel all day without meeting a sign of a fellow Sierran save his footprints in the trail.

And what a spell the forest weaves for you when you are alone! Each turn of the trail has its message. The little woodland creatures, the birds and squirrels and chipmunks, so suspicious of the sound of laughter and voices, look at you with their quick, bright glances and hardly seem to think it worth their while to hide. After all, these are the moments which live. The grandeur of the summit peaks thrills you into awed stillness while your eyes behold it, yet, like remembered music, when the image returns to the mind, something of the stir and the exaltation is irrevocably lost. But the glint of the sun on the river, the meadow knee-deep in flowers of the shooting-star, the creeping shadows and the lingering light in the forest at nightfall—all these little half-noticed charms of the wayside sink deep into the memory to flash forth again, fresh and undimmed, with a certain haloed brightness.

The Sierra Club has great and noble purposes, for which we honor it, but besides these its name has come to mean an ideal to us. It means comradeship and chivalry, simplicity and joyousness, and the care-free life of the open.

For a little while you have dwelt close to the heart of things. You have lain down to sleep in a wide chamber walled about by mountains rising darkly

99

against the lesser darkness of the sky, where stars looked down on you between the pines, stars more brilliant than on the frostiest night in the lowland; you have awakened to the laughter of streams and the songs of birds. You have lived day-long amid the majesty of snowy ranges, and in the whispering silences of the forest you have thought to hear the voice of Him who "flies upon the wings of the wind." And these things live with you long after the outing has passed and you are back in the working world, linger even until the growing year once more brings around the vacation days, and you are ready to turn to the hills again, whence comes, not only your help, but your strength, your inspiration, and some of the brightest hours you have ever lived.

28

The High Trip of 1925

BERTHA CLARK POPE

1926

Any Sierra Club trip — any wilderness trip — is but the tip of an iceberg. The time spent on the trail is the result of long days and nights of planning, finding equipment, packing and repacking, and getting to the roadhead. (Up through the 1920s most hikers still traveled to the Sierra by rail and stage.) Even during the outing itself, the experience of wonder in the wilderness occupies a relatively small proportion of time, compared with the problems of "survival" in an unfamiliar environment without the common conveniences.

There are times when merely keeping track of the necessities of life may be maddening, and fear of what may come next — rain or mosquitoes or exhaustion — may crowd out of the mind all esthetic considerations. John Muir, to judge by his writings, seemed to live in the mountains effortlessly, but most of his followers have been plagued by the normal mortal fears and weaknesses and disabilities.

Bertha Pope's account gives some notion of the problems of mountain housekeeping and the trials and trepidations of freshman hikers. Yet there emerges from this and all trip accounts the feeling that the hours of stresses and strains, which at the time may seem well-nigh intolerable, are worth enduring for the moments of sublimity.

Clair Tappaan was a judge from southern California, and Colby's right-hand man on the High Trips. Judge Walter Fry was superintendent and then U.S. commissioner for Sequoia National Park, and one of the great figures in the park's history.

WE ALL GOT OUR Sierra Club paraphernalia from the box in the garage or the bag in the wall-bed closet or whatever makeshift it is that now supplants the good old-fashioned attic. Yet, we got it out, and we regarded it more or less dubiously. But as we regarded, as we were inspired with notions of cunning weight reductions, especially as we haunted camping-goods, hardware, and five-and-ten-cent stores, we became first assured and then exalted. We were somewhat deflated, certainly, when we finally weighed the mass on the friendly drug-store scales, but we deflated the mass and felt proportionately better.

And oh! that day when we finally put on what was intended to be put on — that was about half the aggregation — and rolled up our shelter; bed; extra shoes; extra wardrobe for four weeks, business and society; soap, laundry and toilet; kits, writing, sewing, and medical; library, technical and *belles-lettres;* gastronomic delicacies and so on — that was the other half — and said good-by to our families! . . .

And then as in a dream we were in a long line, the cynosure of neighboring eyes, in a railroad station somewhere, and then in a Pullman car, still as in a dream till a four-o'clock call at Exeter, doubtless benevolently intended to get us inured to hardship, no other reason appearing. Then, after a goodly motor-trip, presently we were plodding along a dusty road through Giant Forest to our first camp at Wolverton Creek.

Possibly we all kept our city gait and some of our city thoughts in the next two days. This seemed but the gathering of the clans and the prelude. All the good camp-fires that were to be were presaged in those first evenings. Cedric Wright and Dorothy Dunyon played violins — are violins ever so poignant as under fire-lighted great trees? — there was community singing, interesting talk by Mr. Colby, "comic relief" by Mr. Tappaan, a fine talk by Judge Fry on the life history of the *Sequoia gigantea,* and one by Colonel White, Superintendent of the Sequoia National Park, on his work. "The Sierra Club," he said, "is the truest democracy left in America. It is America as it was."

But in the gray dawn of the 13th, when that strange cry rang out, when we weighed our dunnage for the first time on the official scales and found how dismayingly severer was their standard than that of the aforementioned friendly drug-store, when we all — one hundred pack-animals, one hundred and eighty Sierrans — set our faces toward the hinterland, where there are higher mountains and purer skies, then everything was different. The route lay across Marble Fork, Willow Meadow, Silliman Creek [in Sequoia National Park]. This day saw the first of those alpine meadows that were to make the days to come so beautiful. In these the cyclamen *(Dodecatheon)* was particularly large and tall, and with the abundant white alpine smartweed gave the effect of an old-fashioned garden full of flowery spires. For the sake of tenderfoots (or -feet? — neither ever sounds correct, yet in our case both seem applicable) that first trek was planned mercifully short, so short that the impetus of certain ardent souls swept them onward a considerable distance. All, strenuous and unstrenuous alike, slept at Clover Creek that night — or, at any rate, they went to bed.

That was the last night on the entire trip, however, that the entire party was together. Next morning the first knapsackers set out with Francis Farquhar and Bob Lipman up over J. O. Pass, down Sugarloaf Creek to Roaring River, and down the wall of Kings River Cañon, rejoining the club the second day after. The majority went up over J. O. Pass to the next main camp at Horse Corral Meadow.

At the camp-fire that evening—July 14th—we sang the Marseillaise, listened to a most informing talk by François E. Matthes, of the United States Geological Survey, on the geology of the region to which we were going, and then, trustfully, with our wardrobes and earthly possessions spread out under the starry twinkling eye of kindly heaven, we all went to bed and to sound slumber. Up came one of the most complete and magnificent electric storms imaginable. The lightning was none of that mild yellow glimmering we sometimes know in the lowlands; it was deadly white, like liquid iron poured in the foundry; the thunder was no agreeable bass growling in the distant horizon; it was a crashing, cracking, terrific tearing of the heavens as if they were silk, and simultaneously of the shuddering branches of your particular tree—obviously the tallest in the region. Also the rain was of an unusual wetness.

The morning was gray and threatening, and one stood, damply, at breakfast, but everyone seemed happy in the opportunity of voicing his impressions of the storm. And as the day advanced it was clear and beautiful. The trail was long, but it was downward, and wonderful views were to be had by a little side scramble up Lookout Peak and all along the old trail down the side of the cañon. There was one heavenly little stream with a pool and waterfall, all set in ferns and trees and sparkling moss, where sooner or later most pilgrims came to kneel. And, of course, there was the rushing river for a judicious swim, but somehow these cool delights were forgotten in that last dusty, interminable seven miles along the valley.

Camp was made at Kanawyers in the Kings River Cañon. Here for four days by that swift green river were all the delights of a fixed Sierra Club camp, which, it may not be generally known, are climbs, swimming, and song. Also there are laundering parties: for a picture of fundamental democracy, regard, say, the colonel, the co-ed, the millionaire, the professor, chummily washing their garments in borrowed pails with one bit of soap in common. And the rapture of mere solo bathing in soft cold mountain water has never been sufficiently sung. Those emerald, those aquamarine floods are soft and soothing as chilled velvet, exhilarating as sparkling light. As a small child I used to play with a boy named "Bill," who had an ill-concealed contempt for the weaker sex as he knew it. At the age of eleven, he wrote a poem setting forth the disadvantages of girls. I remember two withering lines:

> They cannot climb up trees for fruit,
> Nor bathe without a bathing-suit.

Across the years we salute you, Bill, and tell you times have changed.

On the morning of the 20th the majority of the club remaining at Kanawyers arose after shower-baths served in bed, took breakfast standing, for the sake of drainage facilities, and set their faces toward Granite Basin. To do this they must have turned them straight up, for the ascent for the day was 5490 feet, although the miles were but five.

The Granite Basin camp, at an altitude of 10,400 feet, was a strange beautiful place, with gray rock scenery that looked like that of the moon. There was a moon, too, shedding a weird loveliness down upon our camp-fire gathering. And that night a heavy frost. In the morning a few long-haired women had to shatter the ice from their rigid locks while the bobbed-hair sisterhood was jauntily off for hot coffee.

Simpson Meadows for the next four days were Elysian fields in which the Blest wandered. It is impossible to ascribe cause for the pure and peculiar happiness one feels in the High Sierra. Of course, freedom from care and distractions, a natural life in the open, constant draughts of intoxicating air, are potent. Then, too, for once in one's life one may be non-competitive, non-acquisitive; a blackened tin tomato can, a few prunes mixed with dried beef crumbs in a bandana, a divine scene, the laughter of a friend—these seem to be the elements of a perfect happiness, refined of circumstance; happiness having the quality of the sparkle of a mountain stream, the crystal atmospheric overlay on glittering foliage, the peace the Redeemed know their first day in Paradise.

But when does a Sierra Club trip end? With the last great peak? or the last long trail? or the final camp and farewells? Surely it does not end with any one of these; surely in the years to come it does not end. From time to time we shall live again "hours when from the circling faces, veils pass, and laughing fellowship grows warm"; we shall hear again that mountain bell-note ringing to the touch of the last ray of the sun; see meadows stroked with silver, peaks terrible and eccentric thrown against the sky.

29

Knapsacking Across the Kings-Kern Divide

WILLIAM E. COLBY

1912

There is another answer to the question of how it is possible to enjoy the mountains in a large group: The knapsacker can use the main camp as a base for cross-country forays far beyond the well-traveled trails. Here is an account of one such trip by the club's executive secretary and one of its preeminent mountaineers.

The chief difference between this trip and today's knapsack excursions is that much of Colby's hike was a journey of exploration through almost unknown territory. Although today's knapsacker may be closer to well-mapped trails, for the venturesome there remain numerous wilderness areas that still offer solitude and the sense of exploration.

The east-west ridge known as the Kings-Kern Divide separates the headwaters of those two rivers, the Kings flowing north and the Kern flowing south. There is a classic account of crossing the divide by Clarence King (who evidently chose the hardest possible route) in his Mountaineering in the Sierra Nevada, *where he described adventures there in 1872. (The Kings River had been named in 1805, for the three kings of the Nativity, by Spanish explorers, who saw only its lower reaches in the San Joaquin Valley.)*

Kearsarge Pass, crossing the Sierra crest in the climactic southern part of the range near Mount Whitney, is east of the Owens Valley town of Independence. The point at which Colby first crossed the Kings-Kern Divide is now known as Foresters Pass and is part of the John Muir Trail. His return trip, from the Kern-Kaweah Basin over the divide to Roaring River, was approximately the route later named Colby Pass, as a consequence of this trip and explorations he made two years later.

THE CLUB was encamped on one of its main side trips at the upper end of the Vidette Meadows, near Kearsarge Pass. The exquisitely sculptured granite pyramid of the East Vidette towered into the sky on the one hand and the jagged crest line of the Kearsarge Pinnacles enclosed us on the other, while the lace-like tracery of Vidette Falls dimly seen through the sturdy Alpine forest and the flower starred meadows close by, added a delicate touch to the otherwise stern and forbidding grandeur. Out-fitting ourselves from the convenient Club commissary with those light weight but nourishing foods which are the knapsacker's delight, a small party of us started up the main stream toward Center Basin and taking the westerly branch where it forks at the base of Center Peak, kept on up the left-hand side of the stream skirting the slope of the Peak.

We took two pack animals and four five-gallon fish cans with us intending to try to cross the main Kings-Kern Divide through the second gap to the west of Junction Peak and bring back some of the famous Golden trout to plant in the main stream which was fishless above Vidette Meadows.

The fish cans and the animals themselves had to be abandoned near a point where Colby and the group found themselves "standing at an altitude of about 13,000 feet on a sharp edge of the main Kings-Kern Divide amid a bewildering array of splintered and jagged 14,000-foot peaks, while to the southwest is stretched out the grand panorama of the Kern river basin. . . . The Kern side of the divide drops away with an appalling steepness."

They scrambled down the precipices, camped in the canyon, and the next morning continued to Crabtree Meadow. "As we descended into the meadow, Mount Whitney and its neighboring summits were aglow with the early flood of morning light and out of the brilliance, sailing majestically toward us, as if a messenger from the mountain itself, came a Golden Eagle, which soon disappeared in the immense void of the Kern canyon to the west."

They found some golden trout, the result of a Sierra Club planting in 1908, ascended Mount Whitney, continued down the Kern canyon to the mouth of the Kern-Kaweah river, a tributary flowing into the Kern canyon, not to be confused with the Kaweah river farther west.

We climbed into the lower end of the magnificent Kern-Kaweah Cañon. Except for the absence of any extensive level floor, it is strikingly Yosemite-like with its towering cliffs and sculptured walls. Stains on the faces of these sheer cliffs give evidence of wonderfully picturesque waterfalls which, ear-lier in the season, to one below must seem to pour from the sky. We fol-lowed up the bed of this wild and trackless gorge past several beautiful glacial lakes and finally darkness forced us to camp. We selected a fine grove of two-leafed pines beside the roaring stream whose banks were thickly carpeted with Bryanthus heather.

Early the next morning we were on our way and soon reached the lower end of the main amphitheater where the stream heads. Here it makes a sweeping curve back on itself and almost parallels its original course. We were planning to cross the Kings-Kern Divide and drop into the headwaters of Roaring River. We found the wall of this upper basin to consist of sheer savage-looking cliffs all along its southerly side. We had expected to clamber up a narrow cleft indicated on the map but found it blocked by a foaming series of falls. A little further along the wall, we started up a steep talus slope and by carefully picking our way managed to climb out onto the ridge above. We found this ridge separated the main basin from a small amphitheater in which headed the stream forming the series of falls which had just blocked our progress. We easily crossed this amphitheater and reached a pass on the main Kings-Kern (Great Western) Divide just north of Triple Divide Peak. The distance of but a few inches determines whether raindrops falling on this peak will flow into the Kern, Kings or Kaweah watersheds. As may be imagined, the view from this culminating portion of the divide is superb. A wilderness of peaks, snow fields, lakes and cañons greets the eye. Unless I am greatly mistaken, we saw some of the "Big Trees" of the Giant Forest.

While sitting in the notch of the pass (12,500 ft.) a hummingbird, probably attracted by a gaudy trout fly which I had fastened in my hat-band, poised itself in the air within a few inches of my ear and remained there several seconds, when, discovering the deception, it darted off to sip honey from the throats of the brilliant Alpine flowers which grow in sheltered sun-exposed nooks of even that wild and forbidding region.

Descending a steep chimney of loose rock, we plunged rapidly across a huge snow field and down a talus slope where we found, to our surprise, a well built trail. We followed this down to the head of the main Deadman

William E. Colby and his sons, Gilbert, left, and Henry, at Colby Pass in 1927. Colby discovered the pass on the 1912 knapsacking trip which he describes here.

106

Cañon, the more easterly of the two nearly parallel branches of Roaring River. Here we found the ruins of a mining camp. It would be difficult to describe all the beautiful features of our trip that day as we hurried down the cañon, between sculptured walls, following the foaming river. The succession of flower gardens, groves and meadows that we passed through was bewildering in its beauty and variety. I shall always recall the spot where we rested at noon. Up the cañon, Whaleback formed a perfect pyramid in the center distance, with snow-capped peaks in the background. We had thrown ourselves on the long velvety grass of a wonderful meadow and the stream here had widened out almost to a tranquil lake. Half a dozen partly grown wild ducklings, probably Golden Eye *(Clangula clangula Americana),* came working their way up stream close to the grassy bank within a few feet of us, and their cheery notes as they talked to one another indicated that they were utterly unconscious of our presence.

Climbing to the saddle between Avalanche Peak and Sphinx Crest we dropped down the steep cañon of Avalanche Creek, and began to cut across diagonally just above the steep cliffs of the Kings River Cañon, intending to reach the head of the rocky chute which leads down to the cañon floor just to the East of the Grand Sentinel. But darkness overtook us and fearing that we might mistake the right gully and be led to the brink of the dangerous precipices which intercept all the other numerous gullies which lead down from above, we camped where we were. Never have I spent a night anywhere just like that one! We were on an unusually steep mountain side and the only ground we could discover approaching a level character was an area of a few square feet behind a large boulder. By building up a rude wall of stones and logs to keep from rolling down the mountain side, we managed to pass the night in comparative comfort. At daybreak we were up and ate the few crumbs of food left in our knapsacks. As we hastened down the rocky chute leading to the floor of Kings River Cañon, we witnessed the wonderful effects of early morning as the light poured over the jagged crest of the Sierra and filled cañon after cañon with its brilliant flood. We reached camp in time for an early breakfast and were glad indeed to throw down our knapsacks which had burdened us during these strenuous days.

Some day there may be well traveled trails crossing the passes just described. Considerable work will have to be done first, but only a short distance remains to be made passable. I think it is an entirely feasible and probably the best route for the future from Kings River Cañon to Mt. Whitney.

30

The Lore
of the Cup

BLANCHE STALLINGS

1940

If there is a badge and symbol of this organization it is that most useful of all mountain tools, the Sierra Club cup, first used on early High Trips and patterned after a similar design used by the Appalachian Mountain Club. It has a wire handle that stays cool when the cup is full of hot soup and that enables it to be looped under the belt in such a way that the bottom faces out and can be emblazoned with the wearer's first name.

The sign of a genuine old-timer in the club is a cup that reads, as Blanche Stallings notes below, "Sierra Club of California." Cups made shortly after World War II bore only the words "Sierra Club" with a line underneath. In later models the line was omitted, and the owner is likely to be a relative newcomer — along with most of the club members.

IF I HAD TO BE a cup, and wanted a delightful, varied, interesting, and useful career, I think I'd say, "Make me neat and smooth, out of tin, stamp these words on me, 'Sierra Club of California,' and hang me on the belt of a good mountaineer."

Bright, Sierra Club cups! Over the mountains they go, dipping water for thirsty high-trippers. They dip from streams — streams over trails, streams over granite, streams in forests, streams in meadows, white streams cascading down from the blue sky, clear streams bubbling up from the ground. They dip from lakes — blue, wind-ruffled lakes, quiet, reflecting lakes, green-blue, half-frozen lakes, dark, silent, star-filled lakes. From streams and lakes, changing and changeless in sunshine and shadow, cups of cold water.

But what do the cups do when the high-trippers aren't thirsty? They are by no means idle, as the following observations disclose.

Gathered about campfires, in various choice spots, small groups of friends rest and talk. The fires burn brightly, and the billy cans get blacker. Around the circles go the tea bags, the sugar lumps, the precious lemons. The tea parties are on, and the cups have become teacups.

But have they? Listen.

"This is the top!"

"What a climb!"

"What a view!"

"That's Mt. So-and-So, and there's Lake Such-and-Such."

"Here's a snowbank! Got any jam? I have a lemon. Let's have sherbet."

The high-trippers are on peaks and passes, and the cups are sherbet glasses.

Water dippers, teacups, sherbet glasses—delightful. The cups are also seen, frequently, in less cuplike aspects.

For example, two high-trippers are crossing a stream on a small, wet, slippery log. As soon as they are safely across, one of them, to make the way easier for other log-walkers, scoops a cupful of sand and scatters it over the log. Thus a thoughtful mountaineer discovers that the cups qualify for heavy duties, such as sand-shoveling.

Again, high-trippers are going over the snow. The way grows steep, and the leader suggests using the cups to scoop out better steps. The cautious climbers find that the cups make excellent snow shovels.

What's that flashing on the top of the highest peak over there? Looks like mirror signal-flashes. Just another Sierra Club custom; a party of climbers has reached a summit, and is announcing its achievement by means of flash-signals, not from mirrors, but from Sierra Club cups!

Now high-trippers are making camp. They need hip-holes and shoulder-holes for beds, and reach for the cups. The resourceful campers want to be comfortable, and the cups dig hip-holes.

Oh, look! Where the party is crossing the snow! A woman just slipped at the top, and is sliding face-down, head-first, down the steep grade! But something is holding her back. What can it be? Why, it's the cup! Hanging on the front of her belt, it has become, in this moment of extremity—a brake!

Useful, adaptable, versatile, indispensable, shiny, cups! What are they up to now? At campsites, beside various streams and lakes, there are great numbers of them, for the most part sitting on the edges of aluminum plates. Some are full of soup, some of salad, some of stew, jello, bread, pudding, stewed fruit, vegetables. No question about what's going on. The high-trippers are hungry, and the cups are full of food!

In a large assembly of mountaineers and cups, such as this, there must be some good close-ups. Yes, here's one.

It's day-in-camp breakfast time. The sun shines warmly on trees, rocks, stream, meadow, and high-trippers.

"Is this the hotcake line?"

"Yes, this is the hotcake line."

Everyone has a plate. But no; there's the club chief, and he has no plate. Only a cup and spoon. What's he doing in the hotcake line with only a cup and spoon? How can he get hotcakes into a cup without ruining them? Will he fold them, crush them, or let them droop over the edge? The syrup will all run off if they ——. He's getting his cakes now. Well, look at that!

Into the cup go the hotcakes. They sort of fold in neatly. Wonderful cups! Adequate even for hotcakes, as the president proves. Or perhaps he just knows how, like the "diamond hitch," or his "way with a burro."

Here's another close-up.

It's dinner time, the sun is behind the mountains, and the air is crisp and cold. Down at the end of the line, coffee is being ladled out of a big kettle into Sierra Club cups. Along comes a member of the Outing Committee. He is busy talking to someone, and sticks out a cup. Oh, what a sight this will be! The cup has obviously served as salad plate. As the hot coffee fills the cup, the lettuce floats wiltingly. Still deep in conversation, the committeeman walks away, apparently unaware of anything unusual about his coffee.

Quite a cupful, but the Sierra Club cup can take it! On second thought, perhaps the honor should go to any man who can help plan outings, lead trips, rescue lost hikers, do rope tricks, play an accordion—and drink coffee which is flavored with salad dressing and garnished with limp lettuce.

What is the vital and eternal question connected with Sierra Club cups? There must be one, else why is the handle, the sturdy loop of wire which slips over the belt, curved in a perpetual question mark? Every cup-user would have his own answer to the question, "what is the question of the cup?"

Well, the only way to find out, for sure, about the cups is to go with them. That means pack up the dunnage bag, pull on the boots, shoulder the knapsack, and get out on the trails that climb to the high country. Enjoy the snow-streaked, rain-washed, sun-drenched mountains with the unofficial, shining Sierra Club insignia!

31

A Wartime High Trip

WELDON HEALD

1941

The 1940 High Trip was held under the cloud of World War II, which had broken out in Europe the previous fall and prompted these musings of narrator Weldon Heald, an architect and climatologist who was for many years the club's unofficial predictor of snow depths in the Sierra. We omit here his lively description of the trip, which began at Cedar Grove on the South Fork of the Kings, but the names he mentioned in that account constitute a familiar cast—photographer Cedric Wright and his violin on their twenty-eighth High Trip; Charlotte Mauk, a long-time member of the board of directors, in charge of the commissary; Norman Clyde and David Brower leading peak climbs; Ike Livermore playing his accordion at campfire; Fran-

cis Farquhar explaining Sierra history; Oliver Kehrlein organizing base camps, all members of the club's pantheon; plus what appears to be a record number of hikers.

TAKE 275 SIERRA CLUB MEMBERS.
Add eighty mules and sixteen packers.
Season with a resourceful management and an inspired commissary.
Stir constantly for twenty-eight days of perfect July weather.
Shake well up and down the peaks and valleys of Sequoia and Kings Canyon national parks.
Result: an unsurpassed High Trip — 1940.

There were so many superlatives during this memorable month on the headwaters of the Kings and Kern that it is difficult to choose one above another. But I think the outstanding theme this year was coöperation. There was generous coöperation between the personnel to produce a smooth-running organization; unselfish coöperation on campfire entertainment; full-hearted coöperation during the trying days at Milestone; and even natural coöperation by the elements which smiled upon us from blue skies throughout the trip.

In these days we cannot help feeling that the energies of men are turned towards hatred and destruction. But our faith in human nature is restored when we find that a group of people, isolated from the world and held together only by a common love for the mountains, is composed of kindly, helpful, good-natured beings, each willing to contribute his share in a true and voluntary democracy. Probably all humans are coöperative at heart, but sometime in the past we took the wrong turning and are now caught in a vicious circle of doubt and misunderstanding. Perhaps the prescription for rebuilding a saner world is for each of us occasionally to forget the clamors and divided counsels of warring humanity and to camp out under the stars. There is room for one more initialed government activity, the RTNA — the Return To Nature Administration. . . .

32   The Work Trip

ELIZABETH ROGERS

1969

By the 1960s the felicitous custom of writing up trips for the Bulletin *had come to an end. By then the Sierra Club was no longer primarily a California organization, and the trips began to number in the hundreds, extending to wilderness areas all over the U.S. and overseas. If trip write-ups appeared anywhere, they were in the publications of local chapters around the nation, although space seldom permitted the literary excursions indulged in by earlier* Bulletin *writers. But one new type of outing, which became highly popular among the younger set, seemed to warrant an exception to the rule against trip write-ups in the* Bulletin.

The Work Party trip was originated in 1958 by former club director Fred Eissler. In the following decade Clean-Up and Trail Maintenance Party trips became immensely popular with young backpackers, offering both economic and social advantages: the lowest cost and the opportunity to meet and work with other young people, from age 16 up.

WE DIDN'T LAUGH MUCH on the way up the trail. It was hot and our packs were heavy. Then, too, we didn't know each other well. Half the fun was watching a lone guitar change hands along the trail. By the time that instrument made camp late that night it had become the unifying element of the group. Music and wilderness do not always mix, but Bob Dylan couldn't have done a nicer job at the strummed-out nightcaps of a young, curly-haired singer. Molding each other, she and guitar became one. No one talked when she sang. We just keep adding wood to the fire.

"Why did I come? Well, I had some free time at the end of the summer and wanted to go to the mountains. My brother had been on a Trail Maintenance trip before and really loved it, so I thought I'd come on a clean-up trip. I wanted to meet people, too. When you're in the mountains for a week you get very close to people. My parents dropped me off and here I am."

We worked one day and played the next. The beauty of the trip was in the cleaning up. Everyone helped. We smashed cans, picked up litter, garbage and broken glass. We erased all traces of old campfires and overturned fire-blackened rocks. We cleaned for refuse under bushes, in open meadows, and on lake bottoms. The trash collecting gradually became a game. (The bits of junk people leave behind can be hilariously funny if the altitude is high enough and the collectors have a sense of humor.) There was satisfaction in the job, too. To see litter along a wilderness trail and to walk past without doing anything about it can be frustrating. But to backpack with thirty-four companions into beautiful country with one purpose in mind—to clean it up—can be amazingly gratifying. It's an immediate step towards puting right the things that are wrong; it's also a way of getting close to fellow cleaner-uppers.

There was only one person, a girl, left in camp the second day of work.

"It's funny. I thought I was going to have to work all day and I've been playing the guitar and reading the whole afternoon. The cook wanted the afternoon off and someone had to stay and guard the commissary. The marmots won't leave it alone for a minute." She hummed softly to herself. It was breezy and the tune flew into the wind.

A lot of people who saw us working wanted to know why we were cleaning up. Were we being paid, how often did groups do such a thing, were we going to be in this spot very long? When we told them the purpose of the trip, and of the organizing force responsible for our being there, most gave understanding nods. They offered thanks and some wanted membership information. They were quick to inform us that the trail was filled with rocks and needed clearing. As the trip went on, we even did trail maintenance work.

At night we talked. Sierra nights are cool and the best place to be was close to the fire.

"Yes, I have a twin sister," said a boy as he flipped his hair from his eyes and straightened his glasses that had broken that morning. "When we were born my parents got a free washer-dryer set from G.E. It was a publicity kick where G.E. offered 'twin' sets to every set of twins born on a certain day in September. Our doctor held us up till then. G.E. lost a lot of money 'cause doctors all over the country did the same thing."

Mt. Whitney stood only seven miles above camp and its challenge faced us all the time. Many licked it. We hiked to nearby lakes and lush meadows and some boulder-hopped through parts of Inyo National Forest. Glissading was fun, although declared off-limits. And every day was hot enough to test the lake water that only days before had been covered with a thin sheet of ice.

"Umm, yea. I got pretty scratched up. Geez, I'm so mad at myself. I got going fast and couldn't stop before the snowfield ended. I flipped over and bumped my head on a rock. I don't think it's very deep. I had Jennifer look at it. If it's still bleeding in the morning I'll ask Kevin what I should do."

The group was young and it was easy to see they felt at home in the high country. Everyone on the trip had backpacked before and for many wilderness was a household word. The air was clean and delicious to breathe. Every day brought a sky of deep, deep blue and nights were bright with a full moon reflecting off granite walls. Quiet places were easy to find and we often crept away to secret spots, nourishing the stillness of aged rock.

"It's so strange when I first walk into my house after a trip. Everything seems closed in. Out here there is space to move around. At home walls seem silly and the T.V. box makes me groan."

·Twice a day we gathered around the commissary for meals. In one sense we were guinea pigs. All of our food was freeze-dried, which is a rarity for work party trips. Rumor had it that the store where fresh food was ordinarily purchased was closed the day the commissary shopped for supplies, so they brought dried food instead. Our leader explained, however, that we were testing the feasibility of a proposal for 1970 trips. One type of clean-up trip would offer the traditional fresh food packed in by mules, and the other would entail extensive backpacking, with each person sharing part of the load. This type of trip would permit hikers to cover greater distances, and

113

because large quantities of trash are not always concentrated in small camp-grounds, work parties would be able to cover miles of trail not yet touched by clean-up crews.

"I'm not even worried about the future. I may be a doctor and work in the country someplace. There is a shortage of small town doctors and you can get exempted for it. There are all kinds of ways to get out of the draft. I only know I'm not going to go."

It was Whitney's second clean-up in only four years. In 1965 a group collected 60 sacks of trash. We collected nearly 50, but ran out of sacks and turned to trail maintenance work. Our trip ended Labor Day and, because Mt. Whitney registered more visitors then than on any other weekend of the year, a lot of our work was probably undone. Even clean-up trips — that exist for one reason — cannot clean everything. The Forest Service latrines that were falling apart roof, floor, and walls couldn't be helped much. No doubt heavy winter snows were the main causes of destruction. But with the camping area as badly overused as it was sanitation conditions were ap-palling.

"It's inevitable! They'll have to outlaw cars from city streets during rush hours within the next twenty years."
"Yea, I know. Why should some guy drive a big, fat car on the road when he takes up the same amount of space in which twenty people could fit on some kind of public transportation, like a bus or something? They could improve buses and then cars wouldn't have to stink up the air."

More than just hikers appreciate clean-up trips. The National Park Service and Forest Service budgets are limited for trail repair and clean-up work. In Idaho the Forest Service foots the entire cost of packing for Trail Mainte-nance parties, figuring they save many times that amount. They take charge of packing out all collected trash. A story goes, however, that a clean-up worker returned to a spot he had helped scour a year before only to find the same burlap sacks sitting in the spot where they had been left a year ago.

"My blisters don't hurt anymore. They popped and are okay." The hiker carefully removed her socks and examined her taped heels. "Dad said it would save money if I had one pair of boots for both hiking and skiing. I just didn't have time to break them in before I came."

The trip passed quickly. Bundled sacks lay at trailheads all over the Whit-ney area. After our final play day we headed back to San Francisco on Interstate 80. It was dark and we were tired after the day-long drive. One sunburned hiker caught the mood — we knew the trip was over.

"Have you heard about plans to build a boat harbor and marina on the ocean near the Audubon Wildlife Sanctuary?"
"Wow, you're kidding. That place is beautiful."
"Right. A lot of people are really up tight and the local Sierra Club people are fighting it. You know, there are lots of conservationists in that area. I hope they win. I think there is going to be some sort of public hearing pretty soon."

114

33 Burro Tripping

DANIEL H. CONDIT

1945

By the late 1930s, the High Trips had grown so large as to be unwieldy, so beginning in 1938, the club began to add new kinds of outings to the schedule year by year: saddle trips, knapsack trips, base camps, burro trips, and, later, river trips. Burro trips were especially planned for families.

A burro trip from Cedar Grove resulted in the following paragraphs by Daniel H. Condit. His three-year-old son, Philip, like some others of the younger generation, rode along happily atop a burro.

THE CAR, which had been stuffed beyond its reasonable capacity, pulled up at Cecil's pack station and disgorged its load of five excited humans. In a few minutes we had piled on the ground the amazing miscellany collectively referred to as "our equipment." Then the cool morning air encouraged us to seek out spots where the slanting rays of the early sun were an earnest of heat to come. There is something in the atmosphere of a pack station which contrives to quicken the heart beat and heighten anticipation. It is in a sense an outpost of civilization; the end of the road. The time of preparation is ended. Check lists, purchasing of food, weighing supplies; these are things of the past. The trail lies ahead and we are on our own.

The dappled shadows shortened and the air took on warmth as we went about our packing. There was a sense of leisure in the air. Birds twittered in a subdued fashion as they hopped about, scratching for seeds. The burros with philosophic calm kicked up gobbets of dust which drifted lazily away — over our food, of course. Against the sleepy hum of countless flies we gossiped with the packers. Time passed. Later, strung out along the trail, really in motion, all delays were forgotten. Cedar Grove was behind. Now for Bubbs Creek, East Lake, Bullfrog Lake, Center Basin, and Foresters Pass! Two care-free weeks, ours to spend without hindrance.

Late in the afternoon of the third day we arrived at East Lake. The trip thus far was an easy one but not without those troublesome incidents that lend spice, particularly to the telling of the tale at a later date. *Item:* Just as we reached our camp at Junction Meadow, Buck snagged his pack and, burro fashion, fought his way forward regardless. There came a sonorous rip, and Buck shot ahead, his pack dangling at an odd angle. When he was unpacked we found that the canvas of one kyack was torn almost completely across; so, most of the evening was spent punching holes in the canvas with a nail and lacing up the tear with a strip of rawhide. *Item:* We found Bubbs Creek

115

fifty feet wide and very swift at the East Creek trail junction. So, watches, cameras, and pants were shed, and Philip, as custodian, rode across dry shod while the grown-ups gingerly felt their way, step by step, with much waving of arms. *Item:* Philip got his dose! The ford across East Creek was deceptively narrow. Buck crossed over without incident, so we started Philip's burro Judy across. But Judy turned down-stream and promptly stepped in a deep hole. Philip flew off with a large splash and when extracted was one wet little boy.

There are pleasures and delights peculiar to a day in camp. Awakened at dawn, one can snuggle a little deeper in one's sleeping bag and doze in luxury while the exploring fingers of the sun gently reach into each shady corner. The burros, seeking to remove the chill of the frosty night from their bones, stand broadside to the sun, now and again tossing up showers of dust which drift away, giving a golden substance to the shafts of sunlight. It was Philip, the three-year old, who finally aroused us. He saw no point to such lazy ways. A leisurely breakfast was followed by an equally leisurely stroll around the lake. We took time to see, hear, touch and smell a few of the many, many things that unite to make up the Sierra scene. Then came washing and cooking. We baked two loaves of crusty, yeast-bread in the dutch oven and set them out to cool. By the time John and Harriette came in from their trip to Reflection Lake we were dressed in newly washed apparel, ready to serve dinner, complete with soup, trout, fresh-baked bread with lots of butter and jelly, and a dessert of jello.

Bullfrog Lake, Kearsarge Pass, University Peak — these are names that stir up a rustling host of memories in the minds of many Sierrans. Three of us had camped at Kearsarge Lake in 1939 and to have missed a return visit would have been inconceivable. Leaving the pack-burros to enjoy a lazy day in the meadows, we set off for a leisurely side trip. What a climb! We felt like flies on a wall as we trudged up the interminable zigzags. The Starr Guide, aided and abetted by the topographic map, calmly states the distance is 1.2 miles and the climb 1000 feet. If that climb is only 1000 feet we will never in this world get up the 5000 foot pull to Granite Basin on some future trip!

Back at Vidette Meadow, the burros were strangely unappreciative of their day of ease. Obviously they considered burden-bearing as something they could do without — every day. Despite their displeasure at leaving such pleasant feeding-grounds we were away early the next morning.

On any vacation trip there is always a superlative. It may be some scene or experience to be treasured above all others. Or it may be such a day as the one on which we climbed to Foresters Pass, a day perfect in every detail. Our hearts were light as we felt the first rays of the morning sun. Under foot, thin sheets of ice shattered beneath our swinging feet. Overhead, a flawless indigo sky seemed to rest lightly on the shoulders of the thrusting peaks. East, south, and west, granite spires soared majestically heavenward, and in the crystal morning light each pinnacle, cleft, and crest stood out in sharpest clarity. To the north the canyon fell away, its inhabitants still slumbering in shadowed quiet.

116

Burro beginners, Tuolumne Canyon, 1967.

Beyond the old trail-makers' camp, nestled under the *albicaulis* pines at timberline, the trail was visible only at infrequent intervals. Under the long shadow of the eastern cliffs the snow still lay deep and the silence was broken only by the crunch of our boots and the subterranean murmur of hidden streams. The sun found us again as we crossed the last of the glacial moraines and stood looking across the frozen lake which lies at the foot of Junction Peak. Here only a few boulders were visible, but on the ridge above the lake we found the trail nearly clear and the alpine polemonium in bud.

Our first glimpse through the pass into the upper Kern was thrilling. Sixteen hundred feet below lay several frozen lakes at the headwaters of Tyndall Creek. We could hardly believe that there was a trail down the sheer east face of the Kings–Kern Divide to those remote lakelets. Desiring a wider view, we pushed on up the granite slopes of a nearby peak, until, near the top, we found a sheltered nook where we could have our simple meal spiced with some of the most rugged scenery in the Sierra.

The next day, after a morning in camp, a trout lunch, and a siesta for all, we were ready for the trail once more. The burros were now eager to be away and jogged along at a lively pace. Pots and pans, flashlight and hand-axe, dutch oven and cutlery, rattled and clattered with a merry sound. At Vidette Meadow, we were delighted to find our previous camp site, including wood pile, unoccupied. Dinner over, dishes washed, beds made, and the campfire laid, we strolled to a point where we could look down Bubbs

Creek Canyon and at the same time see Kearsarge Pinnacles and East Vidette. The thunder of distant cascades was like the throb of kettledrums forming a background for the delicate tones of the evening symphony. Deep green trees, silhouetted against the darkening sky, were the strings of our orchestra. East Vidette delicately traced with snow, yet glowing as with an inner fire, held us entranced with its soaring melody.

Slowly the sunset fires burned to ashes, golden rays turned to silver, night crept up the sky. A new theme, accentuated by the muted roar of falling water, was introduced. The leaping flames of our fire soon sent the shadows dancing and we sat late, gazing at the embers and talking of things near to our hearts. When at last we arose the moon was flooding down through the forest aisles to fill the meadow with its silvery light.

Many months have passed, but now and again there comes a day when the wind is out of the north and the skies are especially blue. The air is clean and dry and it carries some secret message, for our hearts beat faster and our thoughts turn again to the high mountains. Patience! The day will soon come when all who will may again walk the High Sierra in full freedom of spirit, and "The mountains shall bring peace to the people."—*Psalm 72.3.*

34   Homecoming

CHARLOTTE MAUK

1947

John Muir called the Sierra the most hospitable of ranges, with its open, park-like forests and meadows and its sunny summer weather, usually free of the rains that deluge the more northerly ranges. But sometimes it does rain in the Sierra, as the following paragraphs by the late Charlotte Mauk indicate.

Mauk was a long-time director of the club and was in charge of High Trip commissary for many years. The article's title derives from the fact that this was the first High Trip after the hiatus during World War II. She starts with food.

WITH PLANNING, any comparison [between the housewife and the High Trip commissary] ends. In the ordering and the transportation and the preparation—the housewife has all the advantage. For one thing, she always knows, from day to day, just where her stove is going to be, and that her kettles and pans will retain their normal shape — an assurance which a pack-trip cook cannot enjoy. For another, the food she is going to use can be kept in good condition in the refrigerator. She probably has been able to purchase what she needs within a day or at most a week of use, thus taking advantage of a changing market and fluctuations in supply; and she has had a better chance to get scarce items because she needs only a small quantity. But for the High Trip — well, we took what we could get, and were thankful. We hope we were also sufficiently ingenious. For variety, the diners could look at the scenery, even though they could not always find it (the variety *or* the scenery) in the food. The sameness of the meals was not the fault of the planners, but of *(a)* supply houses which couldn't supply, *(b)* supposedly cold storage which wasn't cold enough, and *(c)* a gamble into which we were forced — and lost. Six-weekers still shudder at the thought of macaroni, and sympathize with the serviceman's views on spam. However, commissary did its collective best, and the campers were gratifyingly cheerful and good-natured. Maybe they, too, were thinking, "It will be different next year."

If food is near the top of the list of campers' recollections, then weather is scarcely less important. Spam and rain, rain and macaroni!

The storm that started just after we had all got safely over Foresters Pass was something we could take in our stride — for the first couple of days. But when it followed us to Charlotte Lake, old-timers began to talk about the solid week of rain at Milestone in 1936. "That," they reassured one another, and tried to tell newcomers, "was a *lot* worse." People who had not been at Milestone in 1936 were skeptical but on the whole polite; they permitted themselves only a few fishy glances from under dripping hats or hoods. By the time we had made our sodden way down from Glen Pass and had splashed past most of the Sixty Lakes, even the storms of 1936 seemed to be growing milder. By the seventh wet day we had begun to wonder if there were to be thirty-three more, but the next afternoon brought sunshine at last — glorious, golden sunshine to steam out the puddles and to dry wet clothing and lift our spirits as high as the domed clouds that floated, brilliant, in a blue sky. And maybe the 1936 storms weren't such pikers, after all.

Just so the last-two-weekers wouldn't have to carry their rain gear home unused (or, as in 1940, incorporate a rain-fashion show into Carnival Day so the girls could show off pretty raincoats), the management arranged to have the dust laid at Colby Meadow. Of course, no one would have thought that thunder and lightning and hail were necessary to lay the dust — but at least no innocent freshman will believe you now if you try to tell him that "it never rains at night in the Sierra."

35   Knapsaga

ROBERT R.

BRECKENFELD

1947

The first club knapsack trips were organized in conjunction with the High Trips. In 1946 both trips began on the same day at Onion Valley, the roadhead above Independence. (And both were pelted by the same rainstorms.) But the mountain "elitists" were soon separated from the more sedentary High Trippers, as the following excepts from Breckenfeld's account make clear.

C AN YOU carry twenty-five pounds in the mountains and still have fun? I was just home from the Navy and was casting about for a mountain vacation when I read this query. I read the Sierra Club trip announcement over more carefully, was reasonably convinced, and as a result, floated into Onion Valley in late July. Floated is the correct word; for ninety high-trippers and fifteen knapsackers were all sure that this particular July 20 was the wettest Sierra day on record. True, the showers that afternoon were just a warmer upper for the weather to follow, but we didn't know it yet. Several eyebrows were raised at the management, which assumes the responsibility in these matters.

The knapsackers were all but lost among the High-Trip crowds, the herds of mules and piles of foodstuffs; but worse, the four hundred pounds of food—all we had—was lost somewhere between Berkeley and Lone Pine. Happily, the all-important shipment arrived, but only after I had frantically returned to Lone Pine to assemble a complete new commissary. The rain abated and we set about sorting the supplies into the three caches to be packed in by Ike Livermore, finally finishing the job by Coleman light just before the rains came again.

With an early 10 A.M. start, we shouldered those twenty-five pounds we were supposed to have fun with—the heaviest twenty-five pounds ever—and went up the trail past Heart and Pothole lakes. At the expense of some perspiration, we climbed out of the east-side sage, traveled through the sparse pines, across the treeless nivated slopes below the pass, and finally reached the top of Kearsarge Pass about two o'clock. Pausing only long enough for a brief look at the clouds swirling around the peaks, we hurried down to our camp at Kearsarge Lake. Gone were the mules and crowds. What difference would a little rain make now that we were away from the cars, telephones, and other hindrances of modern civilization? Any difference the rain could make, it did; it was with us for the next six days.

At Kearsarge Lake we organized the commissary to the extent that the first one up in the morning must make the fire. Thereafter, even in the face of countless insults hurled by the insomniacs who invariably rose with the sun, I broke all records for sleeping.

A few hardy souls set out for University Peak, but the scree slopes near the summit discouraged all but the most hardy; later, a small party climbed Mount Rixford and traversed to Mount Gould. The ascent of Gould was notable chiefly in that it was the first of several summits we climbed in dense fog, identifying the top only by the presence of a register.

After some discussion it had been decided to make the next camp at East Lake. That was fine but it involved less cache and more carry than most of us would have considered ideal. We found the food cache in Vidette Meadow with no trouble at all, selected what we thought would be a good menu, loaded our packs, executed a modified right shoulder arms, and started down the trail. We paused above Junction "Meadow" to admire the cascades

Where to? What next?

in Bubbs Creek, the heavens meanwhile opening up again with a cascade of their own. The air was moist for the rest of the day.

At Junction Meadow we met Jules Eichorn, Norman Clyde and Joe Brower, who were leading a group of boys south along the Sierra crest. They had cheered the landscape noticeably with a large fire—ample reason not to hurry away. From Junction Meadow we and they took the branch trail leading up to East Lake, where we found a plot of ground that wasn't a puddle and immediately set about dispelling the cold and dampness with hot soup and an odd assortment of tents and ground sheets. The rain did let up enough for a relatively dry meal. I was sure that the Onion Valley night had been a complete freak—everyone knows that it never rains at night in the Sierra—nevertheless, the ensuing night reminded me all too much of the South Pacific. By morning, well daunted, we moved our sleeping bags under the protection of a large overhanging rock. Here we were safe against the most devilish storm. There was no more rain during the trip.

The fishermen did well in East Creek during our five-day stay, providing amply both for themselves and for those parasites who merely ate the fish. The culinary artists had their field day too. All manner of tasty bakery products were produced in the tiny reflector oven. The apple turnovers were the crowning achievement, superior to any commercial product.

On the first day with a ceiling higher than fifty feet Norman Clyde led a twenty-man ascent of Mount Brewer. The weather finally was as ordered—just the right amount of clouds for the photographers, comfortably cool, yet pleasantly warm. The summit made a very pleasant lunch spot, where with legs dangling over a rock, a soft boulder for a back rest, we enjoyed a jagnificant* view of the clouds scudding over the Kaweahs and the main crest north to the Palisades.

After talking it over we decided to make the jump to Sixty Lakes Basin in one day, instead of the originally planned two. It turned out to be a long long way with a lot of uphill. Our appreciation of the lovely trail up the south side of Glen Pass was somewhat dimmed by the great distance. We were sorry to be leaving the Kings-Kern Divide area, but the region ahead looked very inviting indeed. Descending from the pass, we found a duck line leading off in the direction of Sixty Lakes Basin, a short cut which we later learned was used—not without comment—by most of the High Trip party. It was rather late by the time we found the cache. Dinner was made and eaten by flashlight. The day after was meadoweer's day. A few of the very energetic did a little fishing. Most of us were content to sit in the sun and absorb vitamin D.

Our two weeks in the Sierra seemed to be dwindling rapidly. In the time remaining a party of six climbed Mount Clarence King, not finding the right route until the descent. Two parties of four went up Fin Dome. Then we went out to Onion Valley. This time the sun was shining.

---

*A typographical error—but we're letting it stand.

122

Breckenfeld must have enjoyed his trip with or in spite of his twenty-five-pound pack, because when he returned, he promptly signed up for a knapsack trip in the Grand Tetons. He ends:

We had collectively enjoyed an unprecedented Sierra Club backpacking summer — 784 man-days of it. As the outing announcement promised, we had been independent of trails — although certainly not contemptuous of them. We had eaten no grass and had therefore presented no recreational-grazing problem; we had been our own packstock and had fared well enough in this year of food shortages and experimental biscuits. We had even had fun. As for the twenty-five pounds — well, it would be better to blame the men's overweight on chivalry and not to mention at all those luxury items we were carrying because we might want them. I should have to leave firm ground before I could criticize anyone else for the "personals" in his pack. It could have been twenty-five.

36 Instant Vacation

ANON.

1960

An anonymous Bulletin *staff member, obviously experienced in the ways of wilderness outings, was stricken in 1960 by "a flash of inspiration which we think is sure to revolutionize wilderness attitudes and travel habits." It has not yet revolutionized them, but it still seems like a good idea.*

THE IDEA IS SIMPLY to provide a prefabricated do-it-yourself wilderness experience in one convenient package at nominal cost. One important advantage of the Instant Vacation is that the purchaser, by applying the various accoutrements of the vacation package during his spare time, can enjoy a complete two-week vacation without any time off the job. We are so elated with these possibilities that we had a subcommittee appointed immediately to decide upon what each instant vacation package should contain and report its findings to the Outing Committee.

The report on this brilliantly conceived project is now ready, and we hasten to publish excerpts from the list of items for the Instant Vacation.

ESSENTIAL

a) Pants ripper
b) Pants patch
c) Pants patch ripper
d) Finely ground charcoal for knuckles, knees and elbows
e) Abrasive crystalline quartz sand for scuffing shoes
f) Steel rasp for shredding backsides of trousers
g) Super ultraviolet sunburn lamp
h) Two snowblinder flash bulbs

OPTIONAL

i) Soiled band-aids for use with the world's dullest pocket knife
j) World's dullest pocket knife
k) Super soup heater for intolerably hot soup
l) Instant acting coffee cooler for intolerably cold coffee
m) Pre-exposed roll of 35 mm. color film, including several out-of-focus informal portraits and several double exposures.

The total list covered 14 single-spaced typewritten pages and cannot be reproduced here. It is understood that compelling fiscal considerations and problems of tax status give the project a limited feasibility, even though the Outing Committee is expected to approve of the project in principle.

37

Down the Narrows of the Virgin River

LEWIS F. CLARK

1951

In the post-war years, club outings expanded not only in variety but in locale, from the Sierra to other parts of the U.S. and ultimately to other continents. The canyons of the Southwest were among the first areas outside the Sierra to be explored by club parties. Many trips were not official outings but expeditions organized by club members on their own, such as this two-day hike in 1950 down the Virgin River in Utah—not alongside it but in it.

Henry David Thoreau a century earlier had made similar "fluvial walks," as he called them, in the Concord River. However these hikers walked in the water not by choice but by necessity: with canyon walls rising straight up from the stream, fluvial walking was the only way to make the trip. Also unlike Thoreau, they faced a serious danger —flash floods from which the only escape would be straight up.

At the time, Lewis F. Clark was president of the Sierra Club, a position held later by his brother Nate, organizer of this trip.

THE COLORADO RIVER country is famous for its scenic canyons. Its major tributary from Utah, the Virgin River, has carved chasms that are probably unrivaled for a combination of deepness and narrowness. There are deeper canyons and narrower gorges but where will one find any that combine these dramatic features in such colorful union? In 1872 G. K. Gilbert traversed the North Fork of the Virgin from a point near its head to its junction with the East Fork (Parunuweap). These spectacular miles of canyon, in places less than twenty feet wide between sheer walls 2,000 feet high, he named "the Narrows—the most wonderful defile it has been my fortune to behold."

Zion Canyon has been visited by white men in increasing numbers for almost a century yet relatively few persons have penetrated all the way through the Narrows, particularly their upper reaches. Reliable information about these mysterious depths is so scarce that we felt like explorers.

There were the inevitable questions about what to take, who would go, and when. Zion Park has two definite dry periods, early summer and late fall. We hoped that the first week in July would still be in the so-called dry period. That was important for two reasons: freedom from flash floods was an essential safety factor, and dry weather would simplify our camping gear.

In Zion National Park, as in a number of other national parks, all persons who wish to go climbing or exploring off the trails are required to register with the ranger headquarters. Notices to this effect are posted in campgrounds and other places in the park. This requirement is intended, of course, as a safeguard for visitors.

As soon as we had briefly outlined our proposal the ranger's first reaction was that we should not make the trip because of the hazard, and explained that from early July through August trips through the Narrows are inadvisable because of the threat of thunderstorm and flood. He pointed out that the thunderstorm season was imminent, that there had been no rain for weeks and it was overdue. This opinion, although quite reasonable under the circumstances, was unexpected, and to us an abrupt setback. Our leaders talked with the ranger and the park naturalist (who had been in the upper North Fork country) for a good hour and a half, going over the perils of the gorge, the experience of the party members, possible alternative trips. Finally it was agreed that our whole party would drive that evening to the chosen starting point on the uplands of the North Fork and the next day would consider the weather and the recommendations of the local residents.

Next morning the party was astir at dawn. No clouds — a good sign. Now the decision must be made. If we were to go down the river there was final packing and the car shuttle to be arranged, and we ought to get going. At the ranch we talked with Mr. Chamberlain, a genial man who with his family spends the summer with their cattle and pigs and orchard, and the winter in the town of Orderville east of the Park. We also talked with a prospector (rumored to be hunting uranium, although this remained unconfirmed). He claimed he had been down through the gorge and his assurances strengthened our determination to try it.

The valley was broad and open, the stream meandering through a series of meadows with pine-clad hills on either side. Soon, however, the valley became narrower and deeper. Instead of occasional little cliffs suddenly there was a huge vermilion precipice with tall dead trees leaning against it. The stream lapped its very base. Down logs jamed across the stream and we had to clamber around or over them. But mostly we zigzagged downstream through water which averaged a foot in depth. There were, of course, deeper pools. After half the party had passed one sloping bank, Jonnie, always alert for live things, saw a coiled rattlesnake and caught it with a forked stick. After that we were more careful to watch beside our steps as well as ahead. There were several low waterfalls which we got around easily at this stage of water. One narrow fall plunged into a pool of unknown depth. To get past this we scrambled up the left wall through trees and brush about forty feet and slipped through a two-foot cleft in a huge rock, then descended a sloping ledge to the shallow end of the pool below the falls.

The last mile and a half before the junction with Deep Creek was an extremely narrow gorge with vertical walls rising in weird undulations to the sky. In the narrowest parts two persons side by side with outstretched hands could touch the opposite walls. Alternating with these sections there were alcoves and bays with more sloping sides and gardens of ferns in the fractured rock terraces. We kept our eyes alert for escape ledges. There were many, we thought, although there were also many sections of several hundred yards where no one could climb out. We are still wondering how high the water could rise here. Opinions vary from a few yards to a hundred feet, all in a matter of minutes. Some say you can smell the musty downdraft before the flood. Others say there are walls of water coming down like a wave crest. I remember having once been caught in the canyon of Bright Angel Creek in the Grand Canyon Park during an hour-long thunderstorm with an accompanying deluge of rain; and the stream rose rapidly, but there was no wall of water. No doubt, however, in the Virgin River occasionally a log jam is broken and water and bouncing logs come tumbling down the gorge as though a dam had burst.

Suddenly the hugging walls parted as if we had passed through a doorway in an ancient temple. Sculptured walls, ranging in color from reds, orange, and amethyst to white, rose skyward for thousands of feet. On our right through another portal a clear stream, wider than the one we'd been wading, flowed across the sandy floor of our temple, the bed of the new stream filled

126

with round stones, some of them granitic in appearance. We were sure this was Deep Creek. Ahead on the far side of the amphitheater, through a narrow gorge, the confluent streams disappeared around a bend. We paused here to rest a moment and consider the situation. Soon there would be no more light in our deep canyon, although it was several hours before sunset on the open country above. We wanted to find a safe campsite, if that were possible. After scouting around and debating alternatives, we camped on a sandbar in Deep Creek a couple of hundred yards above the junction. Here was one 45° escape ledge on which we cached our cameras and extra food; then we prepared supper on a huge flat rock resting on the sandbar.

Jim thought each person should take turns sitting by the campfire so we could be warned if the water started rising. Deep Creek has its source in the highlands of Cedar Breaks, and a shower miles away could cause a flood where we were even with a clear sky overhead. Then we felt raindrops! Above, the sky was cloudy in spots. We finished our supper while Nate, the engineer, mentally calculated acreage, precipitation, and stream flow, and finally announced that it would take eleventy gillion cubic feet of water falling over the basin of Deep Creek to raise the water in our spot in the canyon ten feet—we figured we had that much leeway. Before the debate on this had run its course, half the party had hit the sack. From where I lay on the sand I could look straight up and see three pine trees far above silhouetted against the faint glow of the sky. On my left, to the north, the stars were blanked out by clouds. I wondered if it was raining up in Cedar Breaks. Then there was a roaring sound. Water? It grew louder, like a plane. It was a plane. There were the winking lights. Moonlight now bathed the upper walls of the chasm with a soft wondrous light, but beautiful though it was it couldn't hold my attention, and I slept.

Next thing I knew, the sky was getting light, someone had the fire burning, and the doubts of night were forgotten in preparations for the day ahead.

Even before the direct sun hit the stream, how much more cheerful the canyon was, with sunshine on the cliffs above and a bright blue sky overhead! Two water ouzels chirped and flitted from rock to rock, as though to draw us on—and perhaps away from their nest. Some of the party had never before seen this bird and especially enjoyed its odd dipping motion and its playfulness in the water. Where Kolob Creek enters from the north, and downstream from here, we found a number of good-looking campsites: benches twenty to forty feet above the stream with a width of canyon that would seem to afford more safety than our Deep Creek site. The best one was between the entrances of Kolob and Goose Creeks. Below this the main stream snakes around so that we seemed to head in every direction in turn. We had lunch and a swim beside an alluring pool, ten to twelve feet deep, with a cool spring seeping from the east wall. Warm rocks tempted us to a siesta, but only too soon we were packed up and sloshing down the stream again.

The real box canyon of the main river begins abruptly, about a fifth of a mile below the entrance on the right of a beautiful spring-fed creek which drains out of Corral Hollow. Part of the water poured out in a fan shower from beneath brilliant orange flowers. As we rounded a turn, the walls closed in and were vertical for many hundreds of feet, then, stepped slightly, continued to rise precipitously in a series of ledges. Far down the nearly straight canyon the water extended from wall to wall, except for a gravel bar now and then. The contorted walls were generally about twenty feet apart, and in many places curved in toward the center of the stream fifteen feet or so above low water. The variation in the amount of erosion may be due to different amounts of resistance in successive layers of sandstone, perhaps to fluctuations in the number of flash floods, and undoubtedly to the effect of water seepage through fractures in the walls. There was much seepage. Often there would be a horizontal line of delicate ferns growing apparently out of solid rock; only a close inspection would reveal the faint seepage crevice. Around a bend the gorge widened but the way was blocked by huge boulders fallen from the heights. The pool was too deep to wade, so we put cameras and wristwatches into waterproof plastic bags and walked — packs and all — until there was no bottom. The packs buoyed us up surprisingly well. On the shoal below the amphibians walked out and burst into laughter as one after another poured gallons of water out of his knapsack. Along here we had striking evidence of how the canyon had been widened yet the verticality of the walls preserved. We saw a jumbled pile of huge rock fragments several hundred feet along the left bank, and near by the wall of the gorge curved skyward to an overhanging rock cornice.

Again the walls closed in over us on either side. Over the rushing waters of the stream I heard a very deep gurgling sound; mysterious and ominous. I peered around and found its source — a spring above the level of my head, pouring a stream into a dark pool. We would like to have paused, but the afternoon was getting on. Besides, there were passages where for forty to fifty minutes of normal travel there was no possibility of climbing up off the bottom of the gorge. The sky was clouding and we felt a compelling urge to keep moving. From time to time we did stop a moment to take the sand out of our shoes. The riverbed was mostly roundish boulders, from the size of a man's head down to gravel, and with occasional rocks as big as a dinosaur. It seemed many times as if we were going through high vaulted tunnels. In some places one can, they say, look straight up and see the stars in mid-day. Not so for us; either we didn't look in the right place or the growing overcast hid the stars.

The narrowest portion of the defile was just above the junction with Orderville Creek. This tributary from the east entered on mainstream level through an even narrower gorge; a short way from the junction one person could almost touch its opposing walls with outstretched hands.

About a quarter of a mile below Orderville Creek the gorge became roughly twice as wide, but even here the water extended from wall to wall. This is the portion of the river that is marked on the map "The Narrows." Soon we heard voices which were not ours. On the east side was the end of

128

the trail that comes up from the loop road at the Temple of Sinawava. As we walked out of the river, a crowd of tourists watched the ranger point out The Narrows beyond and heard him tell of the hazards which lurked there.

Several weeks after our trip a big flash flood inundated the whole canyon at the Temple of Sinawava. Such a sight would be thrilling to see—from anywhere but the box canyon!

38

River Journal: Yampa and Green Rivers

AUGUST FRUGE

1954

The club's river trips, float style, began as a specific effort to save specific rivers. The U.S. Bureau of Reclamation had plans for dams on the Yampa and the Green, tributaries of the Colorado, within Dinosaur National Monument, and the club waged a national campaign against them. To build up a constituency of people who had seen the wonders of these canyons, the club sponsored three trips in 1953 and others in the following years. Following is an account of one of those trips by August Fruge, director of the University of California Press, a club director and long-time chairman of the club's Publications Committee.

The trip began in Vernal, Utah. The historic first boat exploration of the Green and the Colorado from Wyoming to the Grand Canyon had been made by Major John Wesley Powell in 1869. Frederick Dellenbaugh, also referred to here, was on Powell's second trip, in 1871.

JULY 5. We gather at the house of Bus Hatch, the river boatman, where we check in and the dunnage is weighed. Packed in an old school bus, we rush down Highway 40 like a runaway stage coach, cross the now placid Green River at Jensen, Utah, and pass the state line into Colorado. A side road takes us north seven miles to Lily Park on the Yampa River. Here, a few miles upstream from the eastern boundary of Dinosaur National Monument, the Yampa breaks out of the narrow Cross Mountain Canyon and runs slowly through an open valley with scattered grassy flats and groves of cottonwood. We walk under the hot sun to the lower end of the Park where the river disappears into the main Yampa Canyon. Here the boats are waiting to be launched.

Without thinking and with recollections of Powell and Dellenbaugh in the back of my head, I had somehow expected wooden boats. Nearly all river running nowadays is done in rubber landing craft or life rafts, essentially giant black inner tubes shaped into blunt-nosed boats and divided into compartments so that a puncture is inconvenient but not fatal. The floor or bottom (deck doesn't seem to be the right word) is a single piece of heavy rubberized canvas, adequate but not very stable. Stepping on it, you learn the sensation of walking on the water. The small boats hold four or five people and their luggage; the larger ones are about twenty feet long, have two sets of oars, and hold ten or twelve people.

Almost immediately we enter the mouth of the canyon and float along quickly between red sandstone walls several hundred feet high. Neal and I are in Bus Hatch's boat, a small one named the *Plesiosaur.* We sit easily on the stern, ten inches above the water, and watch the little fleet move down the river. The large boats flex with the waves. Instead of cutting through the water, they fit themselves to it, undulating, and from a distance they look like big caterpillars. The small boats act in the same way, only less so. There are also two small folbots, or kayaks, in the party.

Bus is of medium height, with round figure, red face, glasses. Probably he doesn't look at all like a riverman during the winter in town, where he has a construction business. But we soon see that he knows what he is doing. Experience and skill are evident as he directs the other boatmen, steers his own boat with a quick dip of the oars, no waste motion, detects a hidden rock by the lines in the water, watches the waves and the shoreline for tell-tale evidence of the river's behavior. And all the time joking, answering questions, offering to hold the boat still for pictures. He is an old hand at the game. Several years ago he was with the first party to get through the Middle Fork of the Salmon River in Idaho. Another time he and Jim Orr, also one of our boatmen, tried to run the still unconquered Cross Mountain rapid in the upper Yampa, had their wooden boat smashed, lost all their equipment, and spent two hungry days getting out of the canyon and across twenty miles of desert.

July 6. We are off early for our longest run, about 22 miles to Harding's Hole. The big rapids come early in the day. I say big because they are much rougher than anything we had yesterday, but when we act impressed the old hands smile and tell us to wait for Split Mountain. Nevertheless, the boatmen are taking no chances. They stand up and peer ahead at each rapid, they row like galley slaves for what seems the best passage, they go down correctly, stern first, and every now and then a sharp rock rushes by so close I can reach out and touch it. The water has a smooth, deceptive way of gliding over the upstream side of a rock and falling away sharply on the downstream side, revealing naked points and sudden drops. They tell a hair-raising story about one of the large boats on an earlier trip; the front end slid smoothly over a big rock and suddenly dropped several feet, out of sight of those in the rear. Then the stern snapped up, catapulting the rear passengers into the water. This may be only a story but it illustrates the trickiness of the waves and shows how hard it is to see the rocks from above. The incident pops into my mind again when Bus beaches his boat and stands on the shore ahead, shouting directions to the others.

Today we are riding with Dave Allen, the 16-year-old son of one of the regular boatmen. This is Dave's first trip down the river: he is a little nervous at first but his confidence grows measurably as we get through the difficult parts successfully. His father is easily the most imperturbable and confident of the boatmen and already has a loyal following in one of the large boats, unofficially named the *African Queen.*

The method of taking the rapids stern first seems so obvious and right that it is easy to think rivers have always been run thus. The boatman faces his adversary, he is continually watching the water before him and is in the best position to check speed or to pull away from dangerous spots. Nevertheless Ellsworth Kolb says, in his book, that this method was first introduced on the Green and Colorado rivers by Nathan Galloway, a trapper and a member of Julius Stone's expedition down the two rivers in 1909. Presumably Powell and the other early voyagers went head first with a steering oar behind.

Both Powell and Dellenbaugh point out that river waves are the opposite of sea waves. That is, the river wave or the foam of it remains in one place while the water rushes through it, but a sea wave moves along the surface of the ocean while the water stays in one place.

Tepee Rapid is long and pretty rough. Big Joe, which we take just after lunch, is short and mean, the closest thing to a waterfall we have seen, and here we almost lose one of the folbots. A large rock lies in the center of the stream and the water rushes through in two passages, one probably impossible to run and the other swirling and twisting close under a steep cliff. The only way is to stay in the middle of the left-hand stream and go with the main current.

July 7. Today we have an easy run of ten miles to Mantle's Ranch at Castle Park. All our stopping places on the Yampa and Green are named either *park* or *hole,* and one of them has two names, Echo Park or Pat's Hole; take your choice. The name *parque* or *park* was scattered across the map of the Rocky Mountain region by the French trappers of the 1820's and 1830's. It seems to mean any large open or grassy place among the mountains or along a river bottom. It doesn't appear with the same meaning in any of the Pacific Coast states nor, I think, is it used in the East. If Tuolumne Meadows were in Colorado, it would certainly be a *park.*

Hole must be American in origin and pretty unlettered American at that. I don't know whether there is any other distinction between the two terms although one might well expect a *hole* to be smaller. According to Dellenbaugh: "In the old trapper days when a man found a snug valley and dwelt there for a time it became known as his 'hole' in the nomenclature of the mountains."

Today the cliffs are higher, more imposing, and I begin to feel that we are getting close to the Green River. Indeed we are not far away as the crow flies, but the Yampa chooses to make its way slowly in great horseshoe bends, running three miles to gain one.

July 8. The day is hot and still and we keep cool by alternate dunking and evaporation, swimming alongside the boat in the quiet water and then riding again until dry.

This is the day for water fights. Yesterday first blood was drawn and vengeance has been sworn in more than one quarter. We are reasonably well prepared: a small boat that is easily maneuvered, a good man at the oars who can splash water as well as row, bailing cans for the passengers, and a spare oar which I learn to use with good effect at a distance of fifteen feet or more. The big boats have more guns, in theory, but they get in each other's way and the boats are awkward. We give some of these sitting ducks a good drenching and, while we get away, another small boat, which scorned an alliance with us, is boarded and almost swamped. Still another big boat, full of comfortable photographers, buys us off with soft words and candy. We sell out too cheaply but our hearts are big today.

The river is slow approaching its marriage with the larger Green, swinging in one wide curve after another, detouring left or right before each minor advance. Above us the red sandstone cliffs are more magnificent than ever, towering vertically for 1500 feet or more, carved by wind and water into outlandish forms, faces, and towers. Here and there great exfoliation shells have peeled off and fallen into the canyon; the exfoliation seems to be on more vertical lines than in the Sierra granite and hence does not leave the same rounded domes — at least we do not see them from the river. Some of the great cliffs overhang the water for many hundreds of feet — this on the outside curves where the river has swept against the rock for millions of years. And there are small, deep overhangs almost like caves; we run the boat under these and stand up to touch the rock over our heads. Life has never been so easy. We swim in the pools under the rock or lean back and try our voices on the echoing cliffs. We load our cameras in the semi-darkness of the caves and head out into the stream for more pictures. We slide close by the plastered bird nests on the stone walls. . . .

Straight ahead rises a long cliff of lighter red — Steamboat Rock, the great landmark of Echo Park and the sign that our day's run is nearly over. Here the small dark Yampa and the heavier, lighter Green slide together easily and move beside each other under the vertical cliff until in the distance they mingle in the same bed and sweep around the prow of the Rock, doubling back. On our side of the river, opposite the Rock, is a wide open park with grass and scattered trees — here we tie up the boats and make our camp.

Powell named the massive cliff Echo Rock for the echoes that bounce back from its smooth wall, and from that came Echo Park. I do not know how or when Echo Rock was changed to Steamboat Rock. A short walk along the grassy park shows the end of the rock rising out of the water like the prow of a stone ship, six hundred feet high.

Dellenbaugh, the chronicler of the second Powell expedition of 1871–72, tells that the party camped here several days. Major Powell, with four men and one boat, spent three days exploring the Yampa while the others stayed in camp. One evening they rowed up the Yampa in the moonlight, singing *Softly and Sweetly It Comes from Afar* and other songs and listening to their words echo from canyon wall to wall.

July 9. We must be rested for we are up early and willing to walk a couple of miles before breakfast to hunt petroglyphs and visit a cave. Our group doesn't see the petroglyphs (although others do) but we find the cave, which is different from any I have seen before. A huge exfoliation shell, several feet thick, has been warped out from the sandstone cliff, leaving a space between shell and rock body, with a small opening at ground level. Within, a cool wind blows from somewhere. We find that we can walk to either side for an indeterminate distance, with the passage narrowing gradually until we can just move sideways, the rock touching us fore and aft.

In the boats again, we swing around Steamboat Rock and enter Whirlpool Canyon. Here the walls are higher, perhaps 2,000 feet, and the rock formation has changed to a rougher kind of sandstone that is eroded into broken, jagged cliffs, set back tier after tier with towers and pinnacles on several levels. At the water level the cliffs come close together, leaving little or no room to walk in the event of a wreck, and as we go into the first rapid I am aware that this is no longer the little Yampa but a big, muscular river, quite capable of inspiring fear. The water runs deep, with whirlpools, and the waves are high. But we are in one of the large boats again and we go through swiftly, easily.

July 10. This morning we have Jones Creek trout for breakfast and start

*Lodore Canyon on
Green River, Utah.*

133

down the river in a light rain. In the fast water we soon pass out of the high canyon walls, tilted, terraced, and banded with colors, and float slowly into Island Park. Through this open valley the river winds for several miles, dividing itself into channels, making islands, spreading out over sand bars so that we are sometimes hard put to find the deep water. Once or twice we get out and pull the boat through the shallows, with the sand and the pebbles under our feet.

The river cuts through a low ridge to Rainbow Park, really a part of the same valley; here we have lunch and regroup the boats for the Split Mountain run. The rain is no longer falling but the skies are somber and the color of the open cliffs is duller than it would be in bright sunshine.

Split Mountain looms in front of us with its arching, rainbow-colored cliffs — a magnificent geological exhibit. The river, seeming to avoid an easier course, runs straight into the end of the mountain at ground level, splitting the ridge in two for a distance of six miles. An amateur geologist explains that the mountain is an *anticline,* a thick layer of hard rock that has buckled up in a great curve. Once the anticline was underground; the river ran over it on a nearly level course and began cutting into the hard rock. Later the soft surrounding sediments were worn away, leaving the mountain with the river running through it. The stream, still cutting away the rocks, now descends swiftly through the canyon, dropping in a long series of rapids that are the biggest and roughest that we shall see. Throughout the trip we have been hearing sidelong remarks about them, particularly about the one called the S.O.B. or the Dirty Sob.

Before we take off, the excess gear and the folbots are loaded into a truck for the long way around by road, and a few people choose that way too. The small boats are limited to three passengers but fortunately many people (particularly the photographers) prefer the large boats, and we have no trouble staying with young Dave Allen. Naturally he is nervous; we might be worried if he were not. For the first time we put on life jackets, and I get rid of some extra clothes that might be awkward in the water.

We are the fourth or fifth boat away. A few pulls of the oars bring us into the current and soon we pick up speed going into the first waves. Several hundred yards away, the head boat is bucking and twisting where the dark water breaks white, and the muffled sound of the rapid, echoing off the canyon walls, rings in our ears. Stern first we lurch down before a wave and up again with a few gallons of water in our laps; some still bigger waves break too soon or too late and we ride over them dry; we are poised high on the swelling water between two huge rocks and then rush down into a tall curling wave that wets us again and swings us around while the boatman lays on one oar to point the stern downstream again; we bob through the long choppy end of the rapid, and some of the little waves slap the boat and throw their tails in our faces. Up come the buckets at our feet and we bail like good landlubbers. All at once the fear is gone and we go into the next rapid with a whoop.

They come one after the other, no two the same, the best channel to the left, to the right, down the middle, or take your choice when they are all

134

bad. No time to sit still: ride with your whole body when it's rough and bail the water out when it's easy. In one place Bus stands on shore, pointing to the middle of the stream and shouting. Dave stands up to get the directions, sits again and rows like a demon for the single open channel. Suddenly he stops and we race down past a big rock with thin water spilling over a three-foot drop, then into the rough stuff below, bouncing but untouched. Pulling up near the shore, we watch the others. One of the big boats finds the channel but swings around and comes through sideways, down deep and thrown up again with heads jerking and water over everything. A wooden boat might have capsized but the rubber rides high. A few yards downstream, another boat runs head-on into a rock, bounces back a few feet, and goes around it unhurt.

We are as happy as children, shouting, intoxicated by the motion and by the rushing water so close to us, but young Dave carries the responsibility. Concentration holds his face as he works the oars and watches the rocks ahead. We have known that he approached today's run with a healthy mixture of fear and desire and with a lot of natural pride. And he has done splendidly. Now, in a quiet stretch of water we come close to Bus Hatch's boat and Dave calls over to ask when we reach the S.O.B. rapid. "Passed it two rapids back," says Bus, and there'll be no holding us from here on in. We head for the biggest waves, scorning all others, and the little boat has the roughest ride we can give her.

39

O Tempora! O Mores! Recollections of a High-Trip Tenderfoot

PEGGY WAYBURN

1975

Peggy Wayburn's initial confoundments and blisters will be recognized by many another tenderfoot who has taken a High Trip. The ending of her story will be, too. For reasons the author mentions—the impact of so large a group on the fragile

Sierra meadows—the traditional High Trips were discontinued in the '60s. The High Light Trips have taken their place. The number of trippers is kept to twenty-five or so, and they carry a part of their dunnage.

Peggy Wayburn is a club leader and conservation writer. She has written Edge of Life: The World of the Estuary, *co-authored* Alaska, The Great Land, *and edited* The Last Redwoods and the Parklands of Redwood Creek.

THE HIGH TRIP was a particular Sierra Club invention. It was never meant to be purely a pleasure trip that moved crowds of humans and mules through the mountains just for the fun of it. It always had another purpose. The High Trip was designed to take as many people as possible into John Muir's Range of Light, to acquaint them with its beauty, and to send them back as fervent, and hopefully articulate, disciples of his wilderness.

From its inception in 1901, the High Trip prospered. Not only did it make many converts, but it acquired a devoted coterie of repeaters who filled its rolls every summer. Since it was a large trip and covered a lot of ground, the High Trip always had an inevitable impact on the mountain terrain. As other people and groups moved into the Sierra Nevada, this impact became more critical. By the late 1940's, the Sierra Club was becoming sensitive to the problems the High Trip posed: already the trip was taking fewer mules, and the packers were carrying extra feed; and already the itinerary of the trip was being planned to avoid heavily used or fragile areas. Still the Club Fathers had to question whether the High Trip was really worth it. Had it outlived its purpose? Was it time to end its sunny days? David Brower presented the club's decisions on these matters in a graceful apologia for the High Trip, which appeared in the March, 1948 *Bulletin.* "Are Mules Necessary?" Brower asked. The answer was "yes." In 1948, the High Trip was still a valued Sierra Club institution.

I was unaware of any of this when I went on the High Trip that year. I had recently married a man who loved the mountains, and I embarked on that summer's outing with him only because I was trying to be a good wife. It was my first outdoor venture and secretly I thought the whole idea was crazy. I was also scared. I was a New York City girl who had grown up thinking that a mile's walk on the level was a good hike. I had never slept outside. Until I married, I had never seen a **sleeping bag,** let alone owned one. For many years, in fact, I had thought a sleeping bag was something like, well, a large laundry bag that you got into and tied around your neck.

As it happened, a sleeping bag was the first piece of High Trip equipment that I acquired. I was surprised and not entirely pleased one evening a few weeks before the trip when my husband came home with an Army surplus mummy bag, which he gave me for my own. It was an ugly shade of mud-brown, stuffed with feathers, and both limp and lumpy. My husband also brought me a long narrow plastic air mattress. (He had an old, beloved and obsolete Hodgeman, a big tan rubber waffle that was as heavy as lead but better than a Beautyrest.)

In those days, outdoor footgear was a problem. Virtually no shoe manufacturer made boots for women. I was advised to get Boy Scout shoes, but they didn't fit me. For weeks I persevered until I finally located a pair of Bass ladies' boots in Spiro's Sport Shop on Market Street. They were five inches high, a smooth and genteel leather, and they had cuffs. The salesgirl, also city-bred, was pleased for me. "At least your feet will be stylish up there," she said.

There were a lot of other things I had to get for that trip. My husband and I—and most of the people on the High Trip—took along pine-tree chiffoniers to tie around a tree near our camp. These contrivances, something like outdoor shoebags, held our combs, brushes, mirrors, toothpaste, and other miscellanea. We also took canvas basins and buckets and khaki-colored towels. We had light underwear, heavy underwear (wool that itched), pajamas, sheets for our bags, numerous changes of socks and shirts, sweaters, jackets, extra jeans, gloves, hats with brims, day packs, bandannas, and raincoats. I had to get them all. We also took lots of rope, a medicine kit, a mattress-repair kit, a sewing kit, and a large groundcloth and tarp. (We took no tent because it never rained at night in the Sierra Nevada, my husband told me.) After a good deal of packing and repacking we ended up with exactly 30 pounds of dunnage apiece, the amount allowed each person on the High Trip. For some reason, it was a point of honor for every High Tripper to weigh in at precisely the limit, no more and no less.

We left for the 1948 High Trip on a sunny July evening and stopped in Palo Alto to pick up a friend and have dinner with his family. Our hostess, a veteran mountaineer, looked at me and knew at once that I was a tenderfoot and a coward. "I hope you're prepared for the ants," she said pleasantly. "That's one thing about the Sierra. The ants are everywhere."

After dinner, we drove through the warm velvety valley night. Our windshield got plastered with flying insects. Some time around midnight, we found a schoolyard and rolled out our bags. The insects thrummed and fiddled around us. My bag was extraordinarily hot and I spent the night on top of it trying to balance on my air mattress. When I slept, I dreamed of ants.

The next day we made it to Zumwalt Meadows with only two stops for the engine to boil over. Although we left the car where the meadow was quiet and waist-deep in grass, the trailhead of that High Trip was bedlam. The air was full of sunshine, noise, and dust. People were milling about everywhere, except for a few weatherbeaten men in boots and Stetson hats who were lounging around looking like characters out of a Western movie. Strings of mules and several horses were tied to trees nearby. There were piles of rope, slings, pack boxes, crates of lettuce and eggs, more pack boxes, nests of enormous kettles, stoves, metal boxes of assorted sizes, guitar cases, fishing rods, rolls of canvas, and many other odds and ends, including two large shellacked wooden boxes, which were curiously shaped like truncated pyramids and had holes on top. Throughout, there was a sense of happy and total confusion.

That was deceptive. For although I did not know it, this was the staging

137

area of a highly organized and thoroughly equipped traveling camp that would have put many an army to shame. Indeed, the old High Trips provided quite a few of the simpler comforts of home. We took along two privies (the wooden boxes I had seen) with a commissary member to set them up. (These sanitary facilities were called "burlaps" after the burlap curtains that were strung from trees to provide them with privacy.) We carried a large and fully utensiled kitchen, whose capacious wood-burning stoves required a specially trained mule to haul them lengthwise on her back. We also had a cook, a cook's assistant, and other kitchen-crew members. We took along huge tarps for rainy weather. We had a cobbler's box to repair boots that might give out. We had enough food to dish out a quarter of a ton of it a day, and tin plates and silverware to eat it with. We had a first-aid tent with medical supplies, and we even had a doctor (on this trip, it was my husband). Fishing gear and musical instruments were carried for anybody who wanted to take them along. Added to all this, of course, were a few tons of dunnage for the guests as well as for the packers and commissary. It was a formidable array.

That was the 43rd High Trip, and that night 173 guests, a couple of dozen commissary members, and as many more packers gathered around the leaping flames of a big, bright campfire. Francis Farquhar, then the club's president, had driven down from Berkeley just to wish us God-speed. Eivind Scoyen, superintendent of Kings Canyon Park, had come over for the same reason. Dave Brower was our leader. By the light of the fire we all set our watches with his, and then we listened to him tell where we were supposed to go the next day. I was bemused. It was all too much. Everyone seemed to know my husband. And while they were all nice to me, I thought the other High Trippers looked oddly at my stylish boots, my stiff jeans, and my new shirt.

The next morning, while it was still dark, there was a terrible screaming and beating on pots and pans. I thought the camp had been invaded by bears and leapt from my sleeping bag to find a way to escape. But the noise stopped and nothing happened. It was cold. I stood there shivering in my pajamas and, in the ensuing moment of quiet, I thought I heard a large hissing sigh all around me. My husband said that it was everybody letting the air out of their air mattresses. The screaming and banging on pots was the get-up call.

We packed up our dunnage bags and weighed them in on a hanging scale slung between two trees under the watchful eyes of a weighmaster, one of the guests. Then we had a breakfast of stewed fruit, hot cereal, toast, fried Spam, and coffee strong enough to pave a road. I had envisioned that we would move out of camp all together, like an army advancing up the trail. But people left in twos and threes and my husband and I traveled by ourselves. It was just as well. The morning was one of pain and misery for me and I told him so—frequently. It started out well enough as we walked beside a stream through cool, gentle forests. But by the time we reached the switchbacks to Paradise Valley, the sun was up and it was getting hot. It

138

grew hotter as we made our endless way up that steep rocky slope. My feet hurt dreadfully, and as I put one cuffed boot in front of the other, I resigned myself to dying young.

But Paradise Valley proved to be incredibly lovely, with aspens twinkling their leaves, great cliffs soaring upward, and the pure bright waters of the Kings River racing beside us. I was for camping at the first grove of trees, but Dave Brower took us to the upper limit of the valley. (Dave always took us to the upper limit of places, I soon found out. Before long we got to measuring our travels in "Brower-miles," and the altitude we climbed in a day's hike in "Brower-feet.")

At Paradise Valley, I learned some of the niceties of the High Trip. There was a separate men's camp, a separate women's camp, and a married couples' camp, usually in between. You found your camp site, dropped your cup to mark it, and then waited for the mules to arrive with your dunnage bag, which you would now haul yourself. The "burlaps," one for each sex, were set up as far from camp as possible. This could mean a long walk or even a scramble in certain places. And during popular hours, there was an inevitable wait, and queues formed. Next to meals in camp, this was one of the best places to get acquainted with your fellow campers, albeit of the same sex.

In that first camp, we put down our groundcloth where we could see the high rocks outstretched above us like the wings of some great bird. Ed went off to help chop wood, and I lay down on my bag and started to cry. But I soon became aware that a tide of darkness was rising in the valley. Commissary called for dinner, and we had marvelously hot and salty soup. That night the skies swarmed with stars. I heard a rock avalanche roll down the slopes like thunder. More tired than I had ever been in my life, I closed my eyes and was immediately asleep. I had forgotten to worry about the ants.

That was only the beginning, of course. We stayed at Paradise Valley for a layover day while the mules went back for another load. I took my first teetering steps on talus, and inched my way across a wet log above a stream. I felt like a child learning to walk. We had steaks for dinner that second night, and we sang around the campfire until it burned down to embers and the shadows crowded around us. We sang a lot on that trip, songs that I'd grown up with—Oh, Susannah, I've Been Workin' on the Railroad, Swing Low Sweet Chariot, Danny Boy, Greensleeves. They had never sounded so sweet.

After leaving Paradise Valley we went over a high, windy pass to Twin Lakes. That day I saw my first high-mountain meadow with a stream-like pure liquid glass curling through it. I felt the springy turf beneath my feet and had my heart stopped by the wild beauty of the shooting stars that stood in the wet places. We slept cold at Twin Lakes, and I remember the scum of ice on the water in my cup the next morning.

Twenty-six years later, I remember many other things about that High Trip. Even for those days, it was a strenuous trip: I expect we hiked close to 100 miles and climbed a total of nearly 20,000 feet before the two weeks were over. One day we climbed 4,000 feet straight up out of Simpson

Meadows and then did another 2,000 feet of ups and downs before we finally made camp at Granite Pass. I remember that a private party camped next to us at Simpson Meadows had deck chairs and tables, and they had ice cream flown in and air-dropped for their children. Alongside them, we felt like virtuous Spartans.

We camped two nights at Bench Lake and I will forever remember the reflections of Arrow Peak catching the first soft glow of morning light. I don't recall in which camps the mules wandered around us all through the night—it happened more than once—but the sound of their bells is still with me. So is the clank my Sierra Club cup made on the rocks as I first learned to scramble. I remember the cold, utterly delicious taste of pennyroyal and bourbon crushed together in snow. More painfully, I remember the ascent and descent of Cartridge Pass, a wicked ordeal for people and mules. Going down that impossibly steep pass, two ladies twice my age sped past me, as fleet and sure-footed as deer. I hated them as I picked my careful way among the huge unstable boulders that formed the trail. Later I came to count them as dear friends. One was Ollo Baldauf, whose rich haunting voice heightened the beauty of the mountain stillness each time she sang for us.

I remember many other people on that trip. Cedric Wright was one of them, gentle genius, artist, and mountain spirit. He loved to travel ahead of the crowd and wait at the foot of a pass with hot tea, or the offer of a foot bath for a weary wayfarer. Cedric was a violinist as well as a photographer: he called the "burlap" a "Straddlevarius." Jim Harkins was the cook, and Charlotte Mauk his assistant, and between them brewed hundreds of gallons of coffee and they fried thousands of pieces of bacon and flipped twice as many pancakes. We never ate better.

The packers on that High Trip have a special place in my memory. Some were college boys working through their summer vacations, but others were old-timers like Bud Steele, who claimed he helped the Devil pack in the rocks for the Devil's Postpile. Bud nearly lost his life coming down Cartridge Pass and said he stayed alive to feed the mosquitos at Marion Lake.

There were a number of ladies of uncertain age on that trip, veteran High Trippers who traveled together. They might wear hats with enormous brims, rubber bathing shoes on the granite, or old-fashioned (unstylish) knickers, but they were true mountaineers. Before the trip was over, all of us had become acquainted, and some of us had made friendships that would last for lifetimes. We gathered together on the last afternoon for the traditional bandanna show, art exhibit, and what was called the social tea. We shared what was left of extra goodies people had brought along, and we began to share reminiscences, too, of the days behind us, which had ended far too soon.

The High Trip is no more, of course, and never will be, the world having become what it is. But it fulfilled its purpose for me. As I expect it did for many other people, it changed my life. When we made our way 6,000 feet down from Granite Pass to Zumwalt Meadows on the trip's last hot day in July, 1948, I had never felt more alive or free. I could skip over the talus and walk a log across a stream. I had drunk the waters of cool, clear mountain streams, skinny-dipped in an icy mountain lake and sun-dried beside it. I had drowsed in a mountain meadow breathing in the sweet smell of wild grasses. I had seen the Sierra's pale granite peaks stained apricot and gold and blue as the sun's afterglow swelled and faded. I had awakened to the song of mountain birds. The love of the wilderness had entered into me. I was, and forever would be, one of John Muir's disciples.

40 A Carol in Praise of the Hat Monticolous

PEGGY WAYBURN

1961

As we know, Peggy Wayburn's first club trip was in 1948. By 1961 she was a veteran, able to note with her customary eloquence some of the finer points of mountain travel and the spirit of sheer fun that prevails along the trails.

WHAT IS A HAT? N. Webster said:
"The hat's a cover for the head."
With due respect to Webster, that is
The merest part of what a hat is.

> The hat's an emblem of our mores,
> Evokes tradition, signals glories.
> On top of all, a hat reveals
> The secret way its wearer feels.
> And so it is that mountain lids
> Have much to tell of certain ids:
> Both lid and id may run the gamut
> With some quite staid, while others ham ut.
> And though they're often called ridiculous,
> I love the hat (and id) monticolous.
>
> So someone else can write a sonnet

In honor of milady's bonnet,
Or rave about new headgear urban.
I'll sing my song to alpine turban,
To happy hat that gets to shade
Those cheeks that have not felt the blade,
To hats that wear an eagle's plume,
The hair of goat, or primrose bloom,
That ride so well o'er slopes precipitous—
I tip my own to hats monticolous!

I say "hurrah" to neat beret,
To coolie hat, and skimmer gay,
To cowboy hat, fedora nifty
And tam-o-shanter neat and thrifty.
I offer "hi" to broad-brimmed flopper,
A yodel to Tyrolean topper,
A hearty "hey, and a hey-nonny-nonny!"
To knotted kerchief, sun-hat bonny
To helmet pith, to beach hat batty,
And to the bowler small and natty.

I take a bow to brim unraveled,
To dashing tilt of hat well-traveled.
A loving pat for hat grown crusty
From dirt kicked up on paths so dusty,
And for that hat that's warm in camp
(The one you sit on when sitting's damp)
The good old hat that won't talk back
When squashed and rolled and stuffed in pack.
Applause for hats with veils delightful
That save the day when bugs are biteful.
Though on a street you'd be conspicuous
On peaks you're peerless, hats monticolous!

I'd like to make a nice remark a-
Bout the fur-trimmed hood of parka;
And all those hats that match each other
On father, son, on sister, brother.
And while I'm at it, I would praise
The common hat of uncommon ways:
The swanky Stetson, the good tweed cap,
The visor neat—for each, a clap!

A particular cheer for the mountaineer
And the hat that goes with him year after year,
Taking its drenching and taking its drying,

142

Faithfully sticking in spots that are trying,
Until, like a feature, its curving brim
Becomes, as it were, a part of him.
(And when you see him sans his hat,
You stop and wonder: "*Who* is that?")
Truly togetherness reaches its zenith
With mountain hat and face that's benith.

Though alpine hats may be expressive
Of traits more often kept recessive,
They have a lilt and spirit of revel
That's seldom found in hats at sea-level.
So let who will choose hats all decorous,
I'll take the charming, mad, disarming, functional,
   versatile, absurd, glorious, crazy, uproarious,
   preposterous—hats monticolous.

Will Colby's Last High Trip

41

MARION RANDALL

PARSONS

1930

Here we depart from chronological order for a flashback to 1930 and some excerpts from Mrs. Parsons' account of the last High Trip led by Will Colby in 1929. Her story is redolent of passing time and the changes taking place in the Sierra Club; one generation was giving way to the next and old traditions were falling by the way as new ones began.

A few years after this account was written, a serious illness ended Mrs. Parson's own hiking days. The rising younger members she lists as the "second generation" have now themselves passed the conservation torch along to succeeding generations. Although today's trip participants have multiplied in number by many hundreds and although their "High Trips" may not be in the Sierra but the Himalayas or the Pyrenees or under water in the Virgin Islands, they carry with them a venerable heritage and an awesome responsibility for the generations that will follow them.

Mrs. Parsons' message is of the continuity that flows through decades and unites wilderness-lovers of all the club's eras.

The twenty-eighth High Trip began near Florence Lake on the South Fork of the San Joaquin River and followed the John Muir Trail to Tuolumne Meadows. As a finale, Colby led a memorable side trip in Northern Yosemite. Among the members of the party were such veterans as J. N. LeConte, Nathan and Lewis Clark, Cedric Wright, Virginia and Ansel Adams.

"Dunnageless St. Laurences" were hikers whose sleeping bags had not arrived by muleback, and the "aviation corps" were those who slept on the new-fangled air mattresses.

A CERTAIN SMALL BOY had been brought up on stories about the Sierra Club. He had heard of Army Pass and the trail through the snow that was scooped out by a battalion of tin cups; of Charley Tuck, riding by night over Vogelsang Pass to save a side-trip from the disaster of a cookless camp; of the flood year, earthquake year, and the bridges that were built and swept away and built again. And he had heard, of course, of our devoted leader and chief. So when at last he was presented to the chief in person, his elders sensed, they thought, the full importance of the event. Amused, they watched the widening of eyes, the solemnity, the awed silence, and when the guest had departed awaited comment. It came, devastatingly.

The child said, "Was *that* guy—Mr. *Colby?*"

Hero-worship has its perils, one observes from this incident. One overshoots the mark, dresses the wearer of khaki in football trappings, endows him with a panache. Nevertheless, how can the story of the twenty-eighth outing, which Mr. Colby claims is to be the last he will himself conduct, begin without due tribute to his foresight and patience, his command of detail, his imperturbability, and especially his faculty of directing all and controlling all without having one person, not the youngest, rawest, least amenable of freshmen, feel irked by rules or discipline? For it is this rare quality in leadership, more than any other one factor, perhaps, that has given our outings their special tone. At once the most detailed and the least arbitrary of governments, its essence is that every member, put squarely on his own mettle and initiative, is made individually responsible for the mountaineering fame and general good repute of the club.

Our critics complain that this policy tends to make us a little egocentric at times. The stranger within our gates, they say, or the weaker brother, finds himself treated rather more cavalierly than in other clubs. And it is true that with us fewer trips are "officially" planned, more is left to one's own enterprise, less overt attempt is made to fuse the crowd into a homogeneous whole. The spirit of the organization is somewhat Spartan, in fact—a miscellaneous horde of two hundred-odd left to lose the trail or keep it, cross the log or fall off, leap into camp or limp in, love the life or loathe it, all at their own sweet wills. One may question a little anxiously the success of such a

144

Will Colby, July, 1938.

policy under a leadership less magnetic, less able to fire the rank and file with a kindred idealism and zeal; dread to have it in the future become a source of disorganization rather than of strength. But that under Mr. Colby it has served to build up an unparalleled enthusiasm and loyalty and to create competent, hardy mountaineers, let this year's devoted throng of "old-timers" and the army of climbers that swarmed up black Ritter by every conceivable approach abundantly attest.

As one of the old-timers aforesaid, I find the story of the twenty-eighth outing coming to mind most readily in terms of comparison. Considering the fact that my first outing, the club's third, was so very far from perfect that perhaps only Mr. Colby's determination not to "quit on a failure" saved it from being the last, it is especially pleasant to record that this year mountaineering hazard, the crowd, the packers, the commissary boys and girls, the cook, and the weather all conspired to make the month a perfect one in every way. It is pleasant, too, to reflect that while in 1903 a score of dunnage-less Saint Laurences, grilling night-long beside a camp-fire, was no unusual sight, in 1929 not once did even a recreant member of the "aviation corps" miss the luxury of his six-cylinder bed. Pleasant further to recall a certain far in the past luncheon of dried applies and drier crackers for the purpose of contrasting it with the salad and chocolate cake with which Dan Tachet regaled us when we took a day off and lunched in camp.

And the clothes! Compare my first costume and its heavy denim skirt "not many inches from the knee" —below that member of course understood—

145

with the "shorties" and the "sun-backs" of that more progressive element amongst us belligerently christened by certain conservatives the "nudes"! Over the costume question, indeed, schism almost rent the camp. To wear 'em or to bare 'em became the subject of a hotter contention than Smith versus Hoover or Wet versus Dry. And even to the conciliatory observation overheard among the veterans when the ferment had begun to subside: "After all, when you remember what was said of *us* barely twenty years ago when we wore knickerbockers to knapsack down the Tuolumne . . ." was appended acrid foreboding regarding the costume of twenty years hence. Nor were sartorial changes limited to the women's ranks. The one-time protective coloration is no longer the only mode for men. Ensanguined shirts, plaid blazers, the gaudiest of neckerchiefs are "in." Brilliant color, it seems, is no longer the sole prerogative of the packers or the flappers, or even of the "scenery."

We in the lower camp, meanwhile, had been honored by a visit from the sheep-herder whose great flock we had seen—and deplored!—earlier in the day, in the upper reaches of Mills Creek. He was a Basque, he told us, and he had been in this country for some eleven years. A good part of this period, one may assume, had been spent after the manner of sheepmen in mountain solitudes. At least, he had never seen the like of us before—so his lively curiosity about our food and equipment betrayed. Not at all an offensive curiosity; on the contrary, his manner had the courtesy and gentle naïveté that the European peasant so quickly loses, ordinarily, when he comes to America. This young fellow, too, differed so far from most Sierra Nevada sheepmen that he was willing and even anxious to talk.

The encounter with this friendly herder moved me to somewhat regretful consideration of the human contacts, so frequent in Europe's mountain regions, which the Sierra, in these days, so signally lacks. For since Indian and trapper and miner, and even derelict old hermits like Lembert and his kind, have passed into history, there remains no group of men indigenous, so to speak, to the Sierra soil. Rangers and trailmen, engineers, construction gangs, agents of power companies—these, indeed, one meets with increasingly. But they mark the encroachments of civilization on the wilderness, while the men of old Lembert's type and day, on the contrary, were wilderness men, seeking refuge from cities among the last sanctuaries of the pioneers. Marking especially the sordid changes that the last eight years have brought about in the then virgin country around Shadow Lake, one may be forgiven, perhaps, a faint nostalgic reaction toward that earlier menace to the mountains, the always picturesque Sierra sheepman and his flocks.

This must not be construed as any indorsement of grazing in forest lands or national parks, nor of drowning our mountain meadows in reservoirs. Rather as a groping, perhaps too personal expression of an uneasiness that must assail every loyal Sierra Club member with each new visit to the mountain regions his efforts have helped to preserve—even to such admirably regulated and administered regions as the Giant Forest or Yosemite Valley or Glacier Park. One wonders sometimes whether the time has not

146

come for a certain restatement of our aims. "To explore, enjoy, and render accessible our mountain regions," our articles of incorporation run. And in the earlier years it was in the last degree important to make known to an indifferent and ignorant public the very existence of the fast-disappearing mountain beauty that our generation was only just in time to save. But time has turned the tables on us a little disconcertingly. Our problem is no longer how to make the mountains better traveled and better known. Rather, it would seem, how from the standpoint of the mountain-lover "to render accessible" may be made more truly compatible with "to enjoy."

The club's statement of purposes was changed to "explore, enjoy, and pre-serve. . . ."

We hurry on to the climax of our journey, Mr. Colby's "mystery" side-trip.

Out of his exploring days alone he had "saved" this region for us, to crown the last day that he will play the leader for us in quite the old way — so he has claimed, at least, though this none of us can quite believe. A high plateau region adjacent to Wildcat Point, bounded by the Tuolumne Cañon, Virginia Cañon, Return and Conness creeks — a region unpenetrated by trails, its forests and meadows virgin, its beauty wholly untouched.

We did not know our destination until the very moment of our start. Two hundred strong, largest perhaps of all the side-trip parties that ever have set forth under his leadership, we left our camp in Cold Cañon early on the morning of August 4th to follow him through hemlock aisles, across yellowing meadows, along languid streams, up rocky slopes aromatic with pennyroyal, along lake shores, up mountain crags — a peerless day of swimming in Virginia and Mattie lakes and basking on sun-warmed rocks and nooning in nests of heather . . . a peerless day, and yet for many of us rather a melancholy day, too.

For we cannot bear to think that the old days may be passing! Rebelliously we told each other so over and over again that day, we, the old-timers, who have followed Mr. Colby for a quarter of a century or more. Yet — what are we going to do about it? Time has not stood still with any of us, alas! We still tread the mountain trails, it is true, and flatter ourselves that we will continue to do so yet for many a year. We still climb the passes and lay siege to the lesser peaks; but the days of highest rapture, the real climbing days, the more arduous knapsacking days, become fewer and fewer, and soon necessarily must be past.

But does that mean that the Sierra Club is waning — that the days of its usefulness, too, are passing, or past? One might have thought so, listening to some of the trail talk that day. Talk of the value of old traditions; gloomy doubt concerning the new ideals — or lack of them! — in possible days to come. Yet to feel this, it seems to me, is not only to pay a very poor compliment to Mr. Colby's personal influence, but also to deny the lasting worth of all the struggle and effort that he, and we, may have put into the

147

club. And if we, the pioneers of yesterday, are not to be branded as the old fogies of today, how can we take our proud stand on the old victories and concede nothing to problems existent or to come? We banished the sheep from the national parks, it is true, and limited the herds that might browse in the forest reserves; yet the parking areas and vast spreading camp-grounds are treading down the mountain meadows no less surely, no less devastatingly than the trampling hooves. We "preserved" the forests from the lumberman's axe; yet a cigarette-stub flung from a passing motor may destroy a century's growth of timber just as irrecoverably. We conquered black Ritter in the course of a fifty-mile knapsack trip over mountain passes deep in snow and ice, and thought quite well of ourselves — deservedly so, we still think! Yet the uneasy suspicion will not down that today's nonchalant Ritter-scaler, bred to high-diving, tennis-playing, pole-vaulting, motor-racing, surfboard-riding, may have had none too easy a scramble of it either, yet honestly may have found it less of a feat because of his better-trained body and more nimble, quick-acting mind.

For those who fear that Sierra Club prestige in the future may wane, let us list a few names familiar to old-timers and freshmen alike: Francis Tappaan, Helen LeConte, Henry Colby and Gilbert Colby, Ann Wyckoff and Steve, Glen Dawson, Harry Miller, Elizabeth Currier, Augustine Allen, Llewelyn Bixby II, Leland Chase — second-generation Sierrans, all of them, their ways necessarily not our ways, their philosophy not ours, nor their climbing methods — nor their clothes! And yet who is to say that their work to maintain the parks and forests may not count in the end for as much as ours?

Days come and days go. Problems we once grappled with have gone into limbo with seven-gore hiking skirts. And I for one am all for yielding up our tradition graciously, confidently, not as something static and finished to be passed on to the younger generation intact, but as something living and vital that still may grow and gather honor.

PART IV

Rocks, Trees, and
the Experience of
Wonder

A PERSON ENTERS A LARGE, *crowded room where he knows no one; he is conscious only of a sea of faces. Gradually he may learn some names and backgrounds. To each new face he may attach an identity, an origin, an occupation, an association or a mutual interest. In time he is likely not only to cultivate acquaintances but may make friends who will enrich his life for years to come.*

The person who enters the wilderness for the first time is in much the same situation. At first he sees only anonymous trees and rocks, plants and flowers, birds and animals. Then he begins to distinguish, for example, between the conifers and the broad-leaved trees of the forest. Later he is able to tell a pine from a cedar and a maple from an aspen. Then he begins with some delight to identify a ponderosa pine, a sugar pine, a lodgepole. He learns that the lodgepole pine was named by Lewis and Clark when they observed the Plains Indians using the saplings as supports for their buffalo-hide lodges or tepees; that it is also called a tamarack; that it grows in diverse forms from saplings in a thicket at the edge of a meadow to gnarled timberline veterans.

Most of us never develop the sensitivities of John Muir, who could examine a pebble on a river beach and detect which high-mountain area it came from, or could close his eyes and distinguish the species of tree by listening to the sound of the wind in its leaves. But anyone can learn to name the flowers and rocks and birds, to know their backgrounds and habits and characteristics. To do so is to be at home in the wilderness, to cultivate associations and "friendships" that add immeasurably to the enjoyment of the wilderness experience, to participate more fully in the richness and diversity and beauty of the natural world.

No people were more at home in the wilderness than the native Americans. To them nature was a continual source of wonder, the focus of their culture and religion. We include here the poignant story of the last surviving member of the tribe that lived in Yosemite Valley.

In the previous section of this book, on Sierra Club outings, there was considerable discussion of the advantages and disadvantages of going to the wilderness in groups of various sizes. One advantage of a group is that it may well contain people who are versed in the natural sciences and can add to other travelers' knowledge and enjoyment. Through the outings, through informal walks and campfire discussions, through leadership training courses, and through the Bulletin *and books, the Sierra Club has sought to spread knowledge of the natural sciences, not only to enhance the wilderness experience of its members but to develop that constituency for the wilderness. The assumption is that the more Americans know about the workings of the natural world, the more likely they are to preserve it, and to build a society that will endure because it respects the nature of the planet on which we live.*

42

The Water-Ouzel
at Home

WILLIAM
FREDERIC BADÈ

1904

"Among all the mountain birds," John Muir wrote, "none has cheered me so much in my lonely wanderings —none so unfailingly." His essay on the dipper or water-ouzel (The Mountains of California), which has been called "the finest bird biography in existence," has tended to intimidate other writers who might try to describe this remarkable creature that makes its home in Sierra streams. But Professor William Frederic Badè, later Muir's biographer, was unable to resist recording in the Bulletin one of his own experiences with this bird at the time of the 1903 Sierra Club outing on the headwaters of the Kern at "Camp Olney." Coyote Creek enters the Kern southwest of Mount Whitney.

Badè was a professor at the Pacific School of Religion in Berkeley, and a theologian whose liberal views confounded many in his day. He served on the club's board of directors for nearly three decades, was president for three years, and editor of the Bulletin for twelve. It was his skilled editorship that transformed the Bulletin from a periodical of primarily local interest to a leading national publication on wilderness and conservation. The Muir daughters chose Badè to edit their father's unpublished papers.

ONE MORNING I was casting the fly on a few foam-flecked pools near Coyote Creek's junction with the Kern. Fed by the melting snows of the Great Divide, every morning found the creek at its fullest, for then it was carrying past Camp Olney the increment of the previous day's thaw. A keen ear could easily detect in the thunder of its falls a fuller crescendo, and the water leaped from the escarpments with greater abandon. True to her name the water-ouzel was there in her favorite environment of alder, pines, and flying spray.

My efforts to beguile the excessively wary trout made me an object of much suspicion to a pair of these birds, who seemed to claim exclusive hunting rights on that part of the creek. Evidently they had never seen a man do so insane a thing as to whip a stream with a make-believe fly at the end of a long string. Was he fishing for ouzels? Did he expect their nestlings to bite on that fly? Their behavior made it apparent that a brood of nestlings must be hidden away behind one of the many cascades. It required but little observation to locate the nest — a moss-built affair sunk in the floor of a niche behind a heavy sheet of falling water.

The site had been cleverly selected. No increase of volume in the stream could endanger the nest, for the pool had enough fall to spill all the water above a certain level. The diaphanous liquid curtain effectually screened it from observation and protected it from attack by bird enemies. Few carnivorous birds would venture to seek their prey behind a waterfall. The ready accessibility of this nesting-site for purposes of observation at once suggested to me the possibility of photographing the birds as they came and went in pursuance of their family duties. Their excessive shyness was the only obstacle. In order to overcome this I continued to fish for two days near their particular cascades, pretending not to see them; and yet it was only the occasional unwary trout that found his way into the creel. My interest for the time being was more ornithological than piscatorial. The ruse succeeded, for the ouzels decided that I was harmlessly interested in my own business, insane though it was, and began to go about theirs with confidence. This probation period afforded abundant opportunity for the study of their habits and manners. My recollection of Mr. Muir's classic study added zest to my observations.

What a winking, bowing, busy little creature the "dipper" is! In what far-off period of time did this "humming-bird of California waterfalls" acquire the bowing and scraping habit which one is accustomed to think the peculiar accomplishment of the snipe family and a few other water-birds? The possession of a nictitating membrane, which gives the bird an air of winking at the observer, is evidence of long and intimate acquaintance with the water. In his search after food he often lights in midstream on some rock over which the water dashes at intervals. Not infrequently I saw him swept off the rock into a churning pool. But his short wings enabled him to rise from the water with ease, or he swam complacently to the nearest bank and waded out.

Several pair of them had set up housekeeping in more inaccessible places under some of the higher falls. As with short and rapid wing-stroke they darted in and out among the flying spume and spray, often directly through the swaying sheet of water, they seemed the very embodiment of the spirit of the waterfall. The two sprites which I had under particular observation were quite generous in showing off their varied accomplishments. They swam, dived, waded, sang; they pirouetted from rock to rock, slipped into the current by intention or accident, flickered in the sunlight, and washed their slate-colored plumage in the crystal water of the falls. Four hungry mouths kept them extremely busy. Every few minutes they appeared with their bills full of insects that live in and beside the water. In fact, a young water-ouzel seems to be quite as bottomless as a baby robin. Both continue in the begging habit as a fine art long after they ought to be finding their own grub.

Not the least interesting and commendable feature of a water-ouzel's family life is the fact that husband and wife expect to assume equal shares of the

152

family burdens. How they apportion their duties during the period of incubation I was not able to observe. But both minister with equal assiduity to the needs of the fledglings. What is more important, they seem to hold each other to the performance of this duty under untoward circumstances.

The following incident occurred at the time when I was preparing to photograph the birds at close range. I had concealed my camera within six feet of a place where they were accustomed to perch before entering the niche behind the cascade. Such close approach again excited suspicion and alarm. For considerably more than an hour they refused to carry food to their nestlings. Then the female began to reconnoiter. Seeing that I was apparently only whipping her home pool as I had whipped many another pool in the neighborhood, she decided to risk a visit to her nest with a load of tidbits.

The distribution must have been made with unseemly haste, for she immediately appeared again through her doorway of spray. She was, however, in no haste to leave the neighborhood, but lit on a boulder a few feet away and warbled the equivalent of a "Coast clear" to her lubberly husband, who was still nursing his suspicions on a distant rock in the stream. He would not come. His bill was full of May-flies. A second and a third time she signaled, and now he very circumspectly approached the cascade that hid the nest, flitting hesitatingly from rock to rock until he was almost beside her. But suddenly his fears again overcame his courage and he darted precipitately back to the place from which he had started. He wasn't going to risk his neck, not he! This churlish behavior seemed to rouse the ire of his spouse. Instantly she lit beside him and running her bill several times vigorously into his fluffy plumage she took his catch of May-flies from him and carried them to the hungry nestlings. Her example no less than the little explosion of wifely indignation seemed to recall him to a sense of his duty. My presence was soon ignored, and he came and went as regularly as she.

His whole attitude — the uptilt of the stubby tail, the poise of the head and body — suggested something of the alertness that characterizes the water-ouzel at all times. The grace and swiftness of the mountain stream have passed into the bird's movements. The dash and music of its waters have sung themselves into his being. And there are moments, even in his busy life, when he likes to stand on a moss cushion and watch the stream glide by.

In the case observed it was the female whose stronger maternal instincts made the demands on the conduct of the male. But the obligations and the demands are no doubt reciprocal. Such evidences of domesticity give the water-ouzel no mean place among birds that have an admittedly high emotional development. Long may this charming singer continue to dwell in the cascaded mountain fastness of the Pacific Coast — his inalienable home!

43

Butterflies of the Mountain Summits

VERNON L. KELLOGG

1913

Like the forms of the rocks and the varieties of trees, the animals offer clues to the deeper meanings of the wilderness. To the novice, butterflies, for example, are bright patches of color fluttering across the landscape, but to the eye of such a biologist as Vernon Kellogg, they may also be evidence of the larger forces that move through the eons to mold the crust of the planet and shape the lives of plants, animals, and humans.

Besides butterflies, Dr. Kellogg refers here to the marmots and conies, rabbit-sized mammals of the alpine zone (conies are also known as pikas or rock rabbits) and leucostictes, the gray-crowned rosy finches that are the only birds nesting in the summit regions. The Erebia *and* Chionobas *species have no common names.*

Dr. Kellogg was professor of entomology at Stanford from 1894 to 1920 and author of several books on insects. Shortly after writing this article he was recruited by Stanford alumnus Herbert Hoover to be director of the American Relief Administration in Europe and later became permanent secretary of the National Research Council.

THE INSECTS OF THE high mountains have a particular interest both to special students of insects and to mountaineers. This interest comes not so much from any particular appearance or modification of body, or extremely unusual habits or modes of development, as from the simple fact of their being where they are. Finding delicate little butterflies clinging to the great rocks of a mountain peak, or fluttering in the brief sun over the rare fragrant beds of dwarf forget-me-nots and buttercups at the oozy edge of a glistening snow-bank above timber-line, has all the thrill of discovering such flutterers far out at sea. Someway the high mountain top seems a foreign place for such frail creatures. And you pity the poor things blown up the mountainside by some untoward wind, or drifted there by their own wayward wandering. But you waste your pity. They are neither compelled expatriates nor foolish inquisitives from softer, safer climes below. They belong here, they find their food and shelter here, they rear their young here, and as butterfly happiness may be imagined to go, are happy here. That is, they live and live as successfully among the rocks and snowbanks of the mountain summit, as their less strenuous fellow species live in the meadows of the lowlands. Like the marmots and the conies, representing the mammals, and the leucostictes, representing the birds, these Erebia and Chionobas species are the high-altitude representatives of the butterflies. They are alpine residents, and snow and icy wind and bleak brown rock are their habitual associates.

It was twenty years ago, when I used to spend my camping and climbing summers in the Front Range of the Colorado Rockies, that some of these summit butterflies first became familiar friends. So that when I had got above timber-line or even to the very top of the peak — and the high points in the Colorado Rockies run from 13,000 to 14,000 feet just as in the California Sierra Nevada — I did not give all my attention to distant scenery, but spent part of it making acquaintance with the lofty summit butterflies. I would unlimber a little butterfly net with jointed handle, and chase about over the rough surface in an atmosphere about one-half as dense as that of sea-level, until I would sink breathless and exhausted on the soft flower-studded turf by the side of a great snow-bank, and then content myself with watching my would-be victims take their dainty sips of nectar and hunt eagerly for the right little plant on which to lay their eggs.

The most successfully elusive flutterers, in this life and death game of hide and seek, were certain small velvety dark brown butterflies which belong to a species, *Erebia magdalena,* limited to Colorado's mountain tops. Whenever I flushed one it always made for the roughest patch of jagged rocks anywhere near, and there it slowly fluttered invitingly over them until after violent and painful scrambling I was ready to strike with my net, when it would dive swiftly down to safety into the dark openings among the uneven stones. I have seen specimens go down into one of the pit-like refuges and then come out ten or a dozen feet away from another opening connected with the first by a dark sinuous way among the rocks.

No Erebias have yet been found in the Sierra Nevada, but it is highly probable, nevertheless, that one or more species occur there. And some Sierra Club member should be first to find them. They cannot be mistaken; small, velvety, dark brown butterflies, expanding about one and a half inches. The species found may have a single small eye-spot with yellowish ring for a margin on either fore or hind wings or even on both. Two or three species occur in Alaska and one in the Yellowstone. They may occur anywhere above timber-line to the summits.

A group of alpine butterflies which is represented in California is the interesting genus *Chionobas* (or *Oeneis*) of which species occur on Mt. Katahdin in Maine, on the White Mountains of New Hampshire, on the Rockies and on our own Sierra Nevada. This curious and suggestive distribution of these alpine butterflies, appearing as they do on mountain summits from the Atlantic to the Pacific, but wholly absent in the great regions between these mountains, and the further extraordinary fact that the Katahdin, White Mountain and Rocky Mountain representatives of the

155

genus all belong to the same species (showing only certain slight variations which have given them separate sub-species ranking), present to us one of the most important and interesting special biological problems in butterfly life. Nor is it a problem limited to butterfly distribution, but it is one that arises in the consideration of the distribution of any other mountain-top insects or other animals.

The problem has had much attention, and its solution seems to be that most of these mountain peak species are the persisting representatives of almost unmodified descendants of Glacial Epoch forms, the offspring of stranded individuals left on the summits at the time of the retreat of the great ice-fields. The glacial species extended across the continent in glacial times. With the retreat northward of the ice-sheets some animal and plant kinds retreated with it, but others followed the withdrawing local glaciers up the mountain cañons. The ones that went north are to-day Arctic species ranging across the northern part of the continent. The ones that went up the mountains are to-day alpine species existing in little isolated groups on widely separated mountain summits in mid-continent latitudes. Some alpine forms extend north along the summit of a mountain range, as the Rockies or the Sierra Nevada, until they reach Arctic or sub-Arctic conditions and then range across the continent. Altitude equals latitude as regards biological environment, and our little butterflies of the mountain tops in sunny California are really living in and enjoying the Arctic conditions of their glacial time ancestors, and of their far northern cousins of to-day.

We find Chionobas represented on the peaks of the Sierra Nevada by at least one well-recognized species, *Chionobas ivallda,* with the probability that one or two other species, so far recorded only from the Rocky Mountains, or from the Coast Mountains of British America, will be found in California. Chionobas is larger than Erebia, and is of a wood-brown color, with one or two small blackish eye-spots in the apex of each fore wing. It is, even more strictly than Erebia, a thing of the bare rocks of the mountain's summit. It is rarely seen upon flowers or sipping water from a snow-bank's edge. It alights on the rough rocks, balancing itself in the harsh wind, with many a tipping and righting, but ever clinging fast with delicate legs and tiny claws. Or it settles with curious, hesitant, then suddenly certain manner on the little lee patch of bare soil made by the weathering of some great rock. The wings seem curiously large for the frail body, and there is something in all its appearance that makes it different from lowland butterflies, just as its strange life as hermit on the bleak peaks is so profoundly different from all that we conceive the life of the gregarious, dancing, painted flutterers of the flower-strewn valley meadows to be.

Chionobas, like Erebia, will drop down into a crevice between rocks to escape when closely pressed. The under sides of the wings are mottled and marbled in dull color tone, and *semidea* [found on Mt. Washington] has the habit of tumbling on one side with a sudden fall, as soon as it alights, thus especially exposing the under sides of the wings with their mottled markings next the gray rock mottled with brown and yellow lichens. It is an obvious

156

case of protective resemblance, with a special habit to aid the color pattern to become effective as a concealment.

Another strictly mountain summit California butterfly is *Papilio indra,* one of the swallow-tails. It is one without much tail, and with no very great size or brilliancy of appearance. The wings, which expand only about two and one-half inches, are dark velvet brown with two broken yellow bands across each one. These bands, one very near the margin and one farther in, are made of separate small yellow blotches, those in the marginal series being much smaller and more widely separated than those in the inner series, and the marginal band itself thus much more broken than the sub-marginal one. I have never seen this adventurous swallow-tail alive, although I have looked closely for it on many peaks and especially on the top of Mt. Tallac, reputed to be one of its favorite resorts.

The veteran butterfly collector Wright says that it is at home on sharp rocky peaks of 10,000 to 12,000 feet in height, never coming down the mountainsides lower than 9000 feet. "It is peculiar in its habits as well as in its habitat," he writes, "in that while most Papilios are good feeders, Indra spends its time on those high, bare rocks in sunning itself when the sun shines, and in occasionally starting up energetically to flirt with or to fight some other butterfly, but never wasting any time in feeding on flowers to prolong its life.

"It is the most difficult of all California butterflies to capture, as it frequents the most inaccessible places, and is moreover exceedingly wary. I have spent much valuable time (for on the top of a peak 10,000 feet high, time is always valuable), in watching it to learn if possible the secret of its food plant, but always unsuccessfully. Because it does not feed on flowers, and for other reasons, I believe that the life of the individual butterfly is very short, indeed, say from three to eight days, according to the weather, and that its life as a butterfly is wholly spent in play and in the reproduction of its species."

A single species of the familiar group of yellows *(Colias)* is occasionally found on, or at least near, the summits. Its scientific name is *Colias behri,* thus bearing with it the memory of one of California's early and most active butterfly hunters, Dr. Hermann Behr, curator of insects, for many years, in the Academy of Sciences. While most Coliads are bright yellow and of some size, Behri is a tiny little thing of little more than an inch in expanse, and of a curious dusky greenish-yellow, or dusky yellowish-green color, characteristics making it seem something well removed from its warmer-climate larger cousins. . . . As a rule, indeed, all high altitude butterflies are darker than their near relations of the lowlands.

When one extends one's attention from the very summit to those still bleak but a little less cruel parts of the mountain, its flanks above timber-line and just below it, meeting with more kinds of butterflies is likely. This becomes certain if one works still a little further down the mountain slopes and comes to the shores of the upper glacial lakes in the great cirques and cañon heads, and to the still lower, but still alpine, upper glacial meadows,

157

those smooth green playgrounds in which grasses have supplanted water, and fragrant flowers grow lush in the short season of summer sun.

Here you will find one or two other yellow and orange Coliads, a few adventurous checker spots, and two or three gossamer-winged, iridescent little "blues," species of *Lycaena*. These tiny dancing blues that flit along the wet edges of the lake, alighting daintily on the mud or rocks for a rest, or on the flowers for a sip of nectar, are among the most attractive of mountain butterflies. But neither they nor the yellows, nor yet the various abundant silver spots, meadow browns, checker spots and skippers that occur in the lower glacial meadows are particularly different in appearance or general habit from their related species of the lowlands. Indeed, some of them are only rather bold, errant individuals belonging to species which belong normally to the lower mountain flanks and foothill valleys.

There is, however, a single group of odd, aberrant butterflies all of whose species occur only in Arctic or mountain regions, and when in mountains usually at altitudes that range from five to nine or ten thousand feet. They never, or rarely, get up to the very summits, but also they never, or but rarely, get down to the real lowlands, at least in California or the Rocky Mountains. These butterflies, of which but few species are known, compose the family Parnassiidae and are commonly called Parnassians. The family is world-wide in its range, characteristic members of it occurring in the Alps, the Caucasus, the Himalayas and elsewhere in the great mountain groups of the globe.

All the Parnassians are rather large butterflies, expanding from two and a half to three and a half inches, but showing much variation in size, specimens from the higher altitudes being often much smaller. The wings have a curious, almost translucent, solid white ground color—in one Alaskan species the color is pale lemon-yellow—and the heavy body is clothed with gray and dark hairs. The hind wings bear on both upper and lower sides a few irregularly circular reddish spots, sometimes with a whitish center. One or two of these spots occur also on the fore wings of certain varieties. There are also, especially on the fore wings, a few blackish spots or small blotches, and the inner margin of the hind wings is broadly bordered with blackish. There is usually a faint dark band across the fore wings near the outer margin.

The flight is irregular and jerky, usually rather slow and near the ground. They are easily seen because of their large size and whitish color, and are not difficult to catch. They occur in the Rocky Mountains in considerable numbers at about 8,000 feet altitude, in the characteristic glacial parks of the Front Range. In California they range from much lower altitudes to much higher ones, records of captures at nearly sea-level and at 12,000 feet having been made.

The peculiar faintly smoky translucent appearance of the wings of the Parnassians is due to the fact that the "butterfly dust" or scales which cover the wings and on which all color and pattern of butterflies depends, are not, as in other butterflies, short, flat and broad, and closely and regularly arranged in a complete shingling covering over the wing surfaces, but are narrow, rather sparse, and irregularly arranged, and thus do not form a complete flat color layer on the wings. This curious and wholly unusual character and disposition of the scales in the Parnassians is associated with several other structural aberrances which are hardly of a nature to interest the general reader, but which add to the interest that these strange butterflies have for students of insects.

I should make an end of this paper, and yet I have said nothing about the life of the larvae, or caterpillars, of the mountain butterflies. There is indeed not much to be said about them, for not much is known. Of *Papilio indra,* for example, the eggs, caterpillars and chrysalids are still wholly unknown. And this is true of some of the others. But of others, still, some little is known of the immature life, and it all agrees in revealing a high tolerance of low temperatures on the part of the caterpillars. There is indeed little doubt that most of them can be frozen and then thawed out with perfect safety. The eggs are laid on dried grasses or on the proper food plant, and the whole immature life is gone through with very swiftly. Just as some mosquitoes of desert regions are able to condense their larval life into one or two days and their pupal life into a few hours, the whole keeping pace with the short existence of a swiftly drying pool formed by one of the rare desert rains, so the butterflies of the mountain-tops have had their life-history adapted to the short alpine summer season. With the oncoming of this season when the sun burns hot and melting, through the thin atmosphere, on the great snow-banks, small grasses and flowers spring up swiftly by the wet edges of the snow and along the tiny rivulets that run away from it. On these low green plants the caterpillars feed voraciously and grow rapidly. The chrysalids are formed, either on the ground or attached to plant stems, nearby, and the issuing butterflies quickly expand their wings, have a few sips of nectar, and a few dancing flights over the rocks and fragrant flower patches, then mate, lay their eggs and die. A week must be a fair old age for most of the summit butterflies; a fortnight is octogenarianism, and any longer is the miracle of Methuselah.

44

The Little "Lost Valley" on Shepherd's Crest

FRANÇOIS E. MATTHES

1933

It is an amazing quirk of Sierra geography that craggy peaks often have flat summit plateaus big enough for small cities. Matthes' story of such a valley atop Shepherd's Crest gives a view of a previous epoch and an earlier, lower Sierra. The valley is a clue to the origin of the tabular summits on other parts of the range and makes dramatically clear that the mountains are as changeable in the longer spans of time as the sea is in shorter terms. Our view of the mountains is like a single frame of a motion picture that has been running since the Earth's beginnings.

Shepherd's Crest is in the northeastern part of Yosemite National Park. The scoutmaster Matthes travelled with is the same Richard M. Leonard who later became a High Trip leader, a rock climber expert, and president of the club.

This article is abridged from the Bulletin *of 1933. It appears in full in* François Matthes and the Marks of Time: Yosemite and the High Sierra, *edited after Matthes' death by his colleague, Professor Fritiof Fryxell. In addition to many technical papers, Matthes' works include* The Incomparable Valley: A Geological Interpretation of the Yosemite *and* Sequoia National Park: A Geological Album.

L AST SUMMER, while roaming over the High Sierra with the Scout Naturalist Expedition, it was my good fortune to become acquainted with a piece of mountain sculpture of a very exceptional sort. Though presumably not without parallel in the Sierra Nevada, it is nevertheless of a type that from the very nature of things cannot be represented by more than a few rare examples. The feature in question is on the top of the mountain known as Shepherd's Crest, which stands forth prominently on the east side of Virginia Cañon, a mile or more above the McCabe Lakes. To many members of the Sierra Club, doubtless, this mountain is a familiar landmark; for all I know, it has been climbed and explored from end to end; but to me it was new and its summit sculpture a revelation, the more unexpected since the small-scale topographic map, which I had duly scanned in advance, gave scarcely a hint of its unusualness.

Viewed from any low point to the southwest, Shepherd's Crest appears surmounted by a row of blunt pinnacles, all curved in the same direction, and rising from a sheer wall that is cleft at almost regular intervals. Not having seen the mountain before, one might readily suppose these jagged teeth to constitute the main summit crest; but on viewing it from other directions and from higher vantage-points, one perceives that there is a second crest, higher and smoother, some distance to the north of the first. Between them lies a bit of rolling upland that seems wholly unrelated to the sheer glacier-trimmed sides of the mountain, and, what is most remarkable, this bit of upland consists of a V-shaped valley instead of a convexly moulded summit. From each of the two confining crests the surface slopes inward to an old stream-channel that drains out at the western point of the mountain. This channel is, however, much nearer to the low southern crest than to the high northern crest, which culminates in a summit almost 400 feet above the valley, and so the feature as a whole is strikingly asymmetric.

The little upland area is roughly triangular in outline, and measures three-quarters of a mile in length from northwest to southeast, and one-quarter of a mile in greatest breadth. Its lowest point, at the lip of the valley, is just above the 11,500-foot contour line; the highest point on the northern crest reaches an altitude of 11,860 feet. The floor of Virginia Cañon, near by, is somewhat below 9000 feet.

Its isolated position amidst the titanic environment of craggy peaks and profound cañons is almost dramatically revealed. It seems like a little secluded skyland realm, cut off from the fierce world around it by impregnable cliffs.

That this little "lost valley," as the boys called it, is a lone remnant, a surviving bit of an ancient landscape of moderate relief that once had wide extent, but that has been largely consumed by the incision and widening of the deep newer cañons, readily suggests itself to one who observes it critically. Certainly to a geologist trained in the interpretation of topographic forms the fact is at once manifest from the very contrast between the flowing contours of the little upland valley and the stark sculpture of the cañon walls below. Moreover, from Mount Conness one beholds the smooth westerly slope of North Peak, which is in the same general range of altitudes as the valley on Shepherd's Crest and represents another remnant of the same ancient landscape. On the west it connects with still other smoothly curving remnants on Sheep Peak. To the southeast of Mount Conness, again, one looks down upon a gently sloping tableland that exhibits the same subdued style of topography at the same general level. Farther to the southeast is the long flattish top of White Mountain, and beyond that the nearly level Dana Plateau, the largest tabular summit of this type. To the east and the northeast of Mount Conness, finally, are the smoothly rounded summits of the Tioga Crest, about three miles in aggregate length.

Though these different fragments of the ancient landscape (or erosion surface, as geomorphologists would term it) lie so far apart that the missing portions between them can hardly be reconstructed in imagination, it is possible, nevertheless, to make local restorations and to visualize to some extent the progressive destruction of the old topography by the development of the new. There can be no reasonable doubt, for instance, that the long attenuated arête which ties Shepherd's Crest to the main divide of the Sierra Nevada was once a massive ridge broad enough to bear a strip of the ancient topography throughout its entire length. By the glacial enlargement of the deep cañons on both sides to capacious cirques it has been gradually reduced in width until now there is left only a thin, sharp knife-ridge, a cleaver, as such a feature would be termed in the Mount Rainier country. By the divergence of the two cirque glaciers Shepherd's Crest and its little upland valley happily were saved from a similar fate, but the broadening of the cirques nevertheless has progressed far enough to destroy in large part the two spurs of the upland topography that originally flanked the little valley. The two crests that now enclose it are not the tops of those ancient spurs—they are merely the sharp edges in which the encroaching cirque walls without cut the gentle slopes of the valley within.

But has not the little valley itself been glaciated? you will ask. No, it exhibits none of the characteristic signs of glaciation—that is, of erosion by a moving ice mass shod with rocks. According to the report of Scoutmaster Richard M. Leonard, who with several of the boys climbed up to the little valley by way of the spur that leads to its lip, polished and striated, or even simply smoothed rock-surfaces and rounded ledges, such as are common features of glacier-beds, are wholly absent from it; neither are there any accumulations of rock débris resembling moraines. On the other hand, he found its slopes encumbered throughout with angular blocks, large and small, loosened and heaved by the freezing of water in joints and crevices; and most of these blocks, he observed, lie on or near their places of origin—no forces other than those of frost, snow-pressure, and gravity, apparently, have acted upon them. Such a mantle of frost-riven fragments is a characteristic feature of high mountain slopes that have borne no active glaciers, but only inert drifts or fields of snow. It is the product of that slow and unspectacular rock-shattering process due to oft-repeated alternations of frost and thaw, unaccompanied by any adequate transporting agency, for which some years ago I proposed the term *nivation,* in contradistinction to *glaciation.*

While alternating freezings and thawings occur almost everywhere at high altitudes, the special combination of conditions that results in nivation occurs typically only on high summits and slopes that annually bear snowdrifts for long periods. For both the recurring drifts and the porous rock mantle tend to prevent the melt-water from gathering into vigorous transporting and eroding streams, and instead to distribute it into many feeble rills. Nivated slopes, accordingly, not only are mantled with rock débris that remains *in situ* (except as it is affected by local creeping movements known as "soil flow"), but they are devoid of sharply cut stream-channels as well.

162

The little valley on Shepherd's Crest exhibits both of these effects of nivation. Its sides are rock-strewn throughout, and also unfurrowed by stream-worn ravines. Nevertheless, these facts alone cannot be accepted as absolute proof of its non-glaciation, for it is conceivable that the little valley was glaciated at a very early date in the Ice Age—so long ago that the nivation process has since had time to obliterate all traces of ice wear. At least three, and possibly four epochs of glaciation have been recognized in the Sierra Nevada, and the earliest of these occurred presumably not less than half a million years ago. Such a span of time might have been long enough to give the little valley a thoroughly nivated aspect. However, it is to be observed that the valley retains the V-shape characteristic of stream erosion as well as remnants of a stream-channel, now apparently no longer functional, at the bottom of the V. These facts constitute almost irrefutable proof of non-glaciation, for even moderate glacial action would have sufficed, considering the jointed structure of the granite of Shepherd's Crest, to remodel the valley into a fairly smooth U-shape and to wipe the central stream-channel out of existence; and no amount of nivation would have transformed a glacial U-shape back to a V-shape, or would have produced a new central channel. Its distinct V-shape, therefore, together with its nivated aspect, proves conclusively that the little valley on Shepherd's Crest has remained unglaciated.

Perhaps it will seem as though this conclusion had been reached with needless caution; but it is to be borne in mind that a hollow feature such as a valley is inherently well-adapted for the catchment of large quantities of snow and for the generation of a glacier—much better adapted than a tabular or convex summit. The non-glaciation of the little valley on Shepherd's Crest therefore seemed rather unexpected, and it called for particularly convincing proof.

Such proof having been found, there opens at once a new vista of thought on the subject of the non-glaciation of the high tabular summits of the Sierra Nevada in general. All the tabular summits I have been able to examine bear the earmarks of prolonged nivation, yet corroborative evidence of their non-glaciation is not in every instance afforded by their topography. However, if the valley on Shepherd's Crest has definitely escaped glaciation, then the presumption is all the stronger that these tabular summits—or at least a large proportion of them—have escaped glaciation also.

Now, these summits, mark you, are situated in the highest parts of the range, whence emanated the mighty ice-streams of the glacial epoch—ice-streams that attained lengths of thirty to sixty miles and depths of 2000 to 4000 feet. How then, it may be asked, does it happen that all these high-level tracts have escaped the heavy hand of the ice which wrought destruction all around them?

One reason readily suggests itself from the fact that they are all so oriented as to be exposed to the heat of the midday sun as well as to the southwesterly winds—which are the prevailing winds in the High Sierra, as is so eloquently attested by the asymmetric and even recumbent forms of the timber-line trees. Everyone of the tabular summits and slopes before mentioned is inclined to the southwest, the west, or the south. Even the little valley on Shepherd's Crest, although its axis trends northwestward, has in the main southwesterly exposure, for the row of pinnacles on its southern edge is too low to create a "wind shadow" of any consequence. Moreover, any westerly air-currents that enter the little valley at its lip must in part be deflected by the high northern crest so as to turn directly up the valley.

Now, it is a fact of observation that the southwesterly winds blow the bulk of the snow, while it is still in a powdery state, from the exposed slopes up over the mountain crests, and fling it in great banners, as Muir aptly called them, out to the northeast, to let it swirl down at last in the sheltered valleys below. Whatever snowdrifts remain untouched by the wind are later consumed by the rays of the sun, and so toward midsummer all southwesterly and southerly mountain sides are wholly bared, whereas the northeasterly and northerly sides are still generously flecked with snow, and in some places even retain perennial ice bodies.

During the Ice Age this markedly unequal distribution of snow, due to the combined action of wind and sun, must have tended to minimize glacial action on the southwesterly and southerly sides of the mountain crests and to intensify it on their northeasterly and northerly sides. As a consequence, many of these crests are now decidedly asymmetric in form, their southwesterly and southerly sides sloping at moderate angles, and their northeasterly and northerly sides being very abrupt, in part composed of unscalable cliffs.

Remains the question: How old is the little valley on Shepherd's Crest? Or, more generally, how old is the "ancient landscape" of which it and the numerous tabular summit-tracts in the High Sierra are the remnants? Is it possible to determine its age in any way? Yes, it is possible, though only roughly and by roundabout methods.

It will be remembered that the Sierra Nevada consists essentially of a vast block of the earth's crust that lies tilted to the southwest, so that its eastern edge forms the crest line and its western edge lies deeply buried beneath the sediments in the great valley of California. This great earth-block gained its tilted attitude not at one bound but by successive hoists separated by long intervals of relative stability — intervals to be reckoned in millions of years. With each uplift the streams coursing down its west slope were tremendously accelerated and intrenched themselves in narrow steep-sided cañons. During each interval of repose their downward cutting slackened, the cañons widened out to valleys by the weathering and erosion of their sides, the tributary streams cut ramifying valleys, and there was developed a landscape or "erosion surface" with a topography of its own. Naturally the cañons and valleys of each new cycle of stream activity were cut into the topographic forms left by the preceding cycle, and so each new landscape was developed at the expense of the previous one.

On the west slope of the Sierra Nevada there can be distinguished four sets of topographic forms recording the work of as many cycles of stream erosion. The newest forms are the narrow V-shaped cañons in which the main streams now flow. Less than a million years old, they are still being actively deepened by the streams and remain youthful in aspect.

To a close observer it is patent that these Pleistocene cañons were cut into the broad floors of mature valleys of an earlier cycle. The Big Meadow flat, which lies more than 2000 feet above the Merced River at El Portal, is a remnant of such an older valley and so is the entire Illilouette Valley, which has never been trenched. These older valleys, which attain great breadth on the lower slope of the range, are the products of a much longer cycle of erosion—a cycle that comprised probably all of the Pliocene epoch and lasted more than 7,000,000 years.

Big Meadow, Turtleback Dome, and the Illilouette Valley in their turn lie 2000 to 2500 feet below the general level of the little valleys on the uplands that flank the Yosemite. These billowy uplands are, indeed, portions of a still earlier landscape—a landscape that was produced during a very long cycle of erosion comprising most of the Miocene epoch and probably large parts of the preceding Oligocene epoch. Its age cannot be determined in the Yosemite region for want of telltale fossils, but it is indicated as probably late Miocene by fossils found near the old mining town of Columbia, north of the Tuolumne Table Mountain.

High above the Miocene landscape, which remains preserved on many of the extensive intercañon tracts, stand the peaks and ranges that give the High Sierra its alpine character; and it is on some of the loftiest of these peaks and ranges, 2000 to 3000 feet above the Miocene hills, that are found the gently sloping, tabular remnants of the ancient landscape to which the little valley on Shepherd's Crest belongs. The age of this landscape is indicated approximately by the fact that in the northern parts of the Sierra Nevada remnants of it lie 1000 to nearly 2000 feet above the "fossil stream-beds" that contain the earlier gold-bearing gravel. These stream-beds, which were preserved by masses of indurated volcanic ash (a rhyolitic tuff), have yielded fossil plant remains of middle Eocene age. It follows that the ancient landscape in question cannot be less than 50,000,000 years old.

That any parts of a landscape so ancient could remain preserved on exposed mountaintops may at first seem incredible. Yet in the Sierra Nevada the fact is hardly open to doubt. Three circumstances, it would appear, have operated to preserve those bits of the early Eocene landscape that form the tabular summits of the highest peaks—namely, the resistant nature of the granitic rocks of which those peaks are made; the position of those peaks at the extreme heads of the rivers, where the streams are smallest and have the least cutting power; and their complete exemption from glacial erosion. Of course, it is not contended that these residual summit tracts have suffered no degradation whatever since early Eocene time; but the fact is stressed that they have suffered but very little change as compared with the deep cañons that surround them—so little, that they retain the gentle slopes and rounded contours that were imparted to them when the Sierra region still was a land of moderate elevation.

Of all the ancient summit-tracts in the High Sierra, certainly the little valley on Shepherd's Crest seems most remarkable; for a valley, being the pathway of a stream, is inherently more likely to be cut away during the uplift of a mountain range than is a ridge or a summit. Only some special circumstance could have saved it. Perhaps the streamlet on Shepherd's Crest was unable to compete with its neighbors because its water was entrapped by vertical fissures that developed across its path—the same fissures that separate the pinnacles of the south crest from one another. Again, the little valley seems remarkable because it has escaped glaciation, although valleys inherently afford good sites for glaciers. And, finally, to a student of the High Sierra it seems particularly precious because its non-glaciation, so well attested by its form, confirms the non-glaciation of many of the lofty tabular summits of the Sierra Nevada.

45

Carbonated Landscape

JOHN THOMAS

HOWELL

1946

This forest fire took place in the hills and mountains immediately north of the Golden Gate in 1945, but Howell's insight into the role of fire in the natural order of things applies to most wilderness landscapes. Three decades after the Marin fire, a hiker in the same areas strolls through a lush growth of large trees and chaparral, with only the occasional blackened snag of a big Douglas fir rising above the new vegetation to testify to the holocaust that swept these lands a generation ago.

Howell is the retired Curator of Botany at the California Academy of Sciences in Golden Gate Park and the author of such definitive books as Flora of San Francisco, California, *and* Marin Flora: Manual of the Flowering Plants and Ferns of Marin County, California.

LATE IN SEPTEMBER, 1945, masses of dry cold air accumulated as an atmospheric "high" over the northern part of the Great Basin in Idaho and Utah while at the same time to the south a deficiency of air created a "low" that extended northward and westward from Arizona through California. The cold northern air, reacting to the unequal pressure, poured southward and westward across Nevada: wind whipped to foam the broad expanse of Mono Lake and across the summit ridges of the Sierra Nevada a gale roared beneath a blue cloudless sky. Down the slopes of the range and out to the west across California the air pushed, getting even denser, hotter, drier as the altitude decreased. This is the air that dried to tinder the forests and chaparral of Tamalpais, the air that spread the flames through the heart of the Marin County hills, the air that dusted with ashes the buildings and streets of San Francisco across the Golden Gate.

Within the week the fire was controlled, but not until after it had swept over more than 20,000 acres, a roughly rectangular area extending from upper San Anselmo Creek west to Bolinas Lagoon and from San Geronimo Ridge south to Laurel Dell and the Mountain Theater on the very crest of Mount Tamalpais. Change of wind did much to check the blaze: the reëstablishment of a dominant North Pacific High and resumption of the cool moisture-laden westerlies quickly counteracted the northeast wind from the Basin and, with the increased humidity, the hazard lessened.

On October 21, three weeks after the fire, I went into the heart of the burned area with a group of Club members from the San Francisco Bay Chapter.

The desolation was like that which one associates with the desert after prolonged drouth, when even burro bushes look dead and cacti shrivel. The blackened, ashy front of Pine Mountain above Lagunitas Canyon resembled nothing so much as some sun-baked canyon side above Death Valley. Lagunitas Canyon was, in its way, a canyon of Death. Along the trail were the charred carcasses of squirrels and deer which failed to escape the flames, and the untold numbers of animals, large and small, furred and feathered, that were entirely consumed cannot be estimated.

My companions who made this trip into the burned area did not share my optimism on the recovery of the vegetation; to them the beauty of the Douglas fir in Lagunitas Canyon and of the manzanitas on Carson Ridge was gone and they could not visualize the return of the plants. But for countless ages the hills and lower mountains of California have been ravaged by fire, and plant communities have evolved which are actually benefited by recurring burns. The brush or chaparral which is so characteristic of the hill country below the forest belt is such a plant association, and quickly following a fire the shrubs again cover the slopes, the new growth coming either from fast-growing seeds or from root and stump sprouts. Annual and perennial herbs also recover rapidly and put forth a special show of vigor and profusion which may result from thermal stimulation but which is more probably due to the fertilizing effect of ash in the soil. In fact some rare herbaceous species are not seen except after burns and it is only in the ashes of their parents that manzanitas and mountain lilacs germinate extensively. Strange but true, the chaparral as a plant community is rejuvenated by fire (a fact that is not appreciated by stockmen who would improve their range land by burning brush).

The destruction of the forest, on the other hand, is to be regretted because

167

its beauty is usually gone for a longer time. The redwood, one of the trees most tenacious of life, is injured by fire but usually not killed, even if entirely denuded of its widely branched and finely leafy crown. From living tissues protected beneath the thick fibrous bark, new growth buds arise and immediately begin to repair the damage. The promptness and speed of this reaction of the redwood was observed in Big Carson Canyon on November 11, just six weeks after the burn, when the charred trunks and limbs were already decked with dense bunches of vivid green shoots.

The great loss in the Marin fire was the fine forest of Douglas fir in Lagunitas Canyon, because, unlike the redwood, the fir is killed by the flashy blaze which destroys its crown but which leaves the trunk that for years will bear mute testimony to the holocaust. Not only is the death of the trees a loss but the passing of the fir forest is something that only time can repair. Like other highly developed plant communities, the Douglas fir forest is the last of several steps in the recovery of a denuded area; first will come the herbaceous vegetation in which the "fire weeds" of different kinds will be especially numerous; then will follow a shrub formation which, in Marin County, will consist chiefly of poison oak, mountain lilac, and sticky monkey flower; and finally in the shade and protection of these shrubs will germinate the seeds of the firs which, after several decades, will produce again a forest like the one that is gone, the climax plant formation of the region.

In the burned area, there are two other conifers, a pine and cypress, which, oddly enough, should be benefited by the fire. The former is the prickle-cone or bishop pine, one of that small group of pines in which the cones remain attached to the trunk or branches for years and only open to shed their seeds after being roasted. By this remarkable habit the tree is especially fitted to live where fires recur periodically and since many seeds may be shed by a single tree, the density of the forest where they grow may be increased by fire. In the next few years it will be interesting to watch the reëstablishment of the bishop pine on San Geronimo Ridge and to see if a larger number of individuals replaces the relatively few which have grown there heretofore.

The second conifer having a reaction to fire like that of the bishop pine is the Sargent cypress, a picturesque and characteristic feature of the serpentine barrens on Mount Tamalpais and Carson Ridge. In the cypress, as in the pine, the numerous cones generally remain closed and attached to the branches until the tree burns, and since reproduction following fire is usually abundant, the denuded serpentine areas should soon be re-covered by dense cypress thickets. The youthful cypresses seem to anticipate a recurrence of fire for they frequently bear cones when only three to six feet tall, another of the remarkable adaptations of this plant to a highly specialized condition.

In March, 1946, six months after the fire, I revisited that part of the Carson country where such desolation had been noted the preceding October. After heavy winter rainfall, the vegetation was flourishing, and although it would not be true to say that the scars of the burn were effaced, it was possible to prophesy a normal and rapid recovery for the region. Vigorous sprouts growing from the crowns of shrubs or around the stumps of trees were seen in the following species: California hazel, chinquapin, coast live oak, leather oak, chaparral oak, gold-cup oak, tanbark oak, California laurel, chamise, toyon, service berry, California false locust, chaparral broom, buckeye, California coffeeberry, silk-tassel bush, western azalea, huckleberry, Cushing manzanita, and madroño. Other shrubs were sending up suckers from roots or underground stems: wild rose, chaparral pea, poison oak, yerba santa, and snowberry; while abundant seedlings of chamise, mountain lilac, yerba santa, and manzanita were seen on slopes formerly covered by chaparral.

Among the herbaceous species, the early spring perennials were putting on a fine show, especially on slopes that were formerly wooded. Here were brilliant masses of Indian warrior, azure hound's tongue, yellow snake root, and pale milkmaids. The star lily, at times over four feet tall, was unusually abundant, not only where there had been woods but also brush. So numerous were the many-flowered stalks in places that the plant imparted broad splashes of creamy white to distant fire-swept slopes.

Although the perennial herbs were very fine, the annual herbs which carpeted the slopes and crowned the ridges were the most abundant and colorful. Rose-flowered calandrinias and lavender-flowered phacelias covered steep gravelly slopes between the charred stumps of chamise, while here and there were the brilliant rose-red corollas of a couple of diminutive monkey flowers *(Mimulus Douglasii* and *M. modestus)*. At even so early a date about twenty annual herbs were noted, but of all, the finest was a pink-flowered relative of miners lettuce, *Montia exigua*. The densely tufted plants, covered with numerous flowers, crowded over the gravelly slopes of serpentine outcrops and produced a most beautiful display. Especially effective was the contrast between the bright pink of the montia and the lush green of grassland where the serpentine dipped beneath the sod of meadowy uplands.

That anything good should come from a devastating fire in the California chaparral might seem paradoxical, but even the smoke clouds of the conflagration have a silver lining, be it ever so thin. Apparently certain plants have become specially adapted to grow on burns and although they may occur sporadically and rarely in disturbed soil amid the brush between fires, they frequently come up in vast numbers over broad areas that have been laid waste. Sometimes, as in the case of the montia described above, the flowers may be showy and the display may rival the desert's best; but not infrequently the fire weeds may have an inconspicuous flower, which, however, does not in the least decrease the scientific interest the plants may have for the botanist. On the Marin County burn, *Calandrinia Breweri,* a plant of rare occurrence in the central and southern Coast Ranges, carpeted hundreds of acres; *Silene multinervia,* a choice but weedy-looking catchfly, appeared in numbers after an absence of about thirty years; *Campanula angustiflora,* an inconspicuous and wholly inornate relative of the blue bells, competed for place on rocky knolls; *Phacelia suaveolens,* with foliage smelling like strong

169

honey, graced an ashy flat after an absence of four decades; and *Papaver californicum*, the real California poppy, the rarest of the rare fire flowers, in all the burned acres traversed was seen only in a restricted gully on the side of Pine Mountain above Little Carson Canyon. These are but a few of the botanical treasures which constitute for the botanist, expert or tyro, that silver lining on the smoke clouds of the brush fire.

Since only the kiss of the flame is needed to rouse dormant seeds from decades-long sleep, is it not strange that botanists do not turn arsonists on occasion that some floral phoenix might arise from the ashes? Since none is more avid for the new, the rare, or the unusual among Marin flowers than I, was it not for me the perfect alibi that, on September 27, 1945, the day the fire started, I was far away, struggling to a Sierran summit in the face of that bitter desert gale which a few hours later would fan the flames transforming Marin's cool green wilderness into a scorched and carbonated landscape?

46

Mono Mesa, Sierra Sky-Island

JOHN THOMAS

HOWELL

1947

The remnants of ancient flat or gently sloping landscapes among the crags of the Sierra intrigue the botanist no less than the geologist. Mono Mesa, described here by botanist Howell, is one of the same type of geologic anachronism that Francois Matthes found on Shepherd's Crest in the Yosemite region. It is in the middle latitudes of the Sierra above Mono Creek, which flows west into the South Fork of the San Joaquin River.

PERHAPS the gently sloping sand- and rock-covered plain is five million years old, or perhaps it is only half that old, but the fact remains that it is much older than the spectacular escarpments and canyons that bound it. Although it is a very small part of what was once an extensive landscape, even in its present fragmental condition it represents what is probably California's oldest land surface that is unaltered by erosion. This bit of ancient plain is not found in the deserts nor in the valleys nor on terraces along the ocean, but, remarkably enough, it is situated on the very crest of the Sierra Nevada at an elevation of more than two miles above sea level. Historically it is part of a region of low relief, an area of plains and undulating hills, which were once found at low elevation where today the Sierra raises its forest-covered flanks and snow-flecked summits. For it was by a series of fault movements along the eastern edge of this matured landscape that the present mountain mass was lifted to form one of the largest and noblest fault-block ranges in the world. Profound erosion, first by water and later by ice, carved the slopes of the new-born sierra, but here and there along the summit crestline small restricted areas remained relatively unaltered, in general continuing to look much as they did long ago when they were so much nearer sea level.

One such area is Mono Mesa, a high granitic tableland that dominates the region immediately north of Mono Pass about the headwaters of Mono Creek. The climber, emerging on Mono Pass from the narrow and precipitous gorge that leads upward from Rock Creek, is confronted by this conspicuous topographic feature as he looks northward beyond the shallow glacial basin immediately below the pass and across the head cirque of Mono Creek. In the midst of a scene of superbly glaciated slopes and canyons, the gently sloping and finely graded expanse of the mesa stands in arresting contrast. Here is an island in the sky whose surficial features bespeak an ancient landscape, whose smooth rock- and sand-strewn expanse is alien to the adjacent avalanche chute, raw talus, and roche moutonnée, and whose very extent is as limited by thousand-foot glacier-carved escarpments and declivities as is a true island by water. Pre-Sierra relic, alpine nunatak: what secrets does it hold that antedate the very mountains; what living things did it sustain when close begirt with gnawing ice?

Like similar areas in the Sierra, Mono Mesa is both thrilling and monotonous. Its sandy slopes, stone-paved flats, and shallow swalelike hollows are quite like those of Dana Plateau or the broad gently sloping southeastern shoulder of Mount Conness, while at no place on the mesa are there the steep rocky slopes similar to those encountered in the ascent of such unglaciated slopes as those on Mount Dana or Mount Kaweah. The broad open area, devoid of trees and shrubs, gives one the sense of unlimited space, and from the matchless blue of overarching sky and from the cleanness and propriety of everything below it comes a sense of primal purity and simplicity. Atop a peak, the struggle of ascent carries over in a yearning restlessness of spirit: on the mesa there are calm, relaxation, and repose.

During the 1946 Base Camps from July 14 to August 10, a number of parties visited the mesa to investigate its remarkable geological and topographical features and to enjoy its unique panoramas of the High Sierra. Bent on botany, I was fortunate to make two visits. On these two occasions I found seventy-three kinds of plants, this figure not including the ten I found growing on the precipitous glaciated side of the mesa above Gold Lake. Since an approximate estimate of the number of all species of ferns and seed plants occurring in the Sierra Nevada above timberline is about three hundred, it will be seen that nearly one-fourth of the alpine flora of the entire range grows on the limited area of this sky-island. This, of course, is presuming that I found all the vascular plants growing on the quarter-square-mile of mesa-top. I did collect intensively; for, when not walking from place to place and when not looking at the scene, I spent much of the time on my hands and knees searching for some elusive alpine that might otherwise escape unnoticed.

Most of the plants were not spectacular and some were downright minute. There were only four woody plants—two pines, an alpine currant, and a granite gilia. The pines, whitebark and lodgepole, were extremely dwarfed where they nestled among sheltering boulders along the southern margin of the mesa and obviously they were not reproducing themselves. Of the herbaceous plants, more than one-third belonged to the ubiquitous alpine grasses, sedges, and rushes, with frequently attractive forms but with inconspicuous greenish or brownish flower clusters. The beautiful and really showy Sierra alpines were represented by the columbine, polemonium, Davidson penstemon, and hulsea, although there were other attractive species among the eriogonums, drabas, phloxes, and various daisies.

But botanically speaking, the most exciting plant on the mesa was one of the pygmies, a tiny mosslike sandwort, less than a half inch tall, which had not been reported before in California. Isolated on this alpine Sierra tableland when most of its kind are found in Arctic latitudes and in the Rocky Mountains, what a venerable and far-flung history this plant proclaimed! The migration of an Arctic flora, the orogeny of a new sierra, the glaciation of its juvenile slopes, the preservation of a pre-Sierra surface, the survival of a floristic fragment. Such is the story of *Arenaria Rossii,* and so far as its California sojourn is concerned, a historic epitome of Mono Mesa and all Sierra sky-islands.

47   # Native Daughter

HAROLD E. PERRY

1952

Over most of the American wilderness there hovers an air of tragedy, the spirit of the first Americans. Of those who made the Sierra wilderness their home and their livelihood, there remain only some mounds marking the sites of their villages, and an occasional scattering of obsidian arrowheads, such as those that may be found near some of the Sierra passes.

Of the Indian place names that linger, some of the best-known are in Yosemite, which takes its name from a tribe that once lived there and from the grizzly bear they hunted. The Indians themselves called the valley "Ahwahnee," now the name of the luxury hotel there. Other Indian names are Hetch Hetchy, Illillouette, and Tenaya.

The latter was the name of the chief of the tribe at the time the valley was first entered by whites in 1851. The invaders chanced upon the valley while pursuing some of its inhabitants. The whites were members of the Mariposa battalion and were, like most of the pioneers, highly ambivalent toward the natives. They attached Indian names to natural features, an honor the residents doubtless would have declined in favor of being left alone.

Chief Tenaya, who served as a guide, was kept tied to a tree to prevent him from escaping. The following poignant story of Tenaya's granddaughter, who had witnessed these events, was written for the Bulletin *by a ranger-naturalist of the National Park Service.*

THE FIRST TIME I saw Maria Lebrado I was aware of a strange reaction within myself. I was looking at an old, old squaw, wrinkled, shrunken, defiant; a stolid soul burdened with memories which reached back to the antagonism and misunderstanding that existed for so long between her people and pioneer Americans in California. But I thought of a charming, carefree Indian girl, one who laughingly enjoyed the freedom allowed the granddaughter of Chief Tenaya in Ahwahnee, the village which flourished in Yosemite Valley a century and more ago.

It was on the occasion of Maria's return to Yosemite, after an absence of seventy-six years, that I first met her. The day was warm, one of the radiantly clear days so common in summer in the Sierra Nevada. The usual flow of visitors was coursing through the exhibit rooms in the Yosemite Museum where I was on duty. When I was informed that Maria Labrado was entering the museum, that third day of July became historically significant. The last full-blood Yosemite Indian who was alive when the Valley was discovered in 1851 had come back to her ancestral home.

Some ninety years before that day in 1929, Maria was born in Ahwahnee, the village governed by her grandfather, Tenaya. The mother must have been appreciative of the majestic setting, for she named her daughter To-tu-ya, meaning "Foaming Water." To-tu-ya's childhood joy was destined to have a short life. Before she had reached her teens, rumblings of trouble echoed through the foothills west of Yosemite. The discovery of gold marked the end of Indian sovereignty in central California, for immediately prospectors swarmed to the deposits along the fabulous Mother Lode and rudely brushed aside any natives who were unfortunate enough to stand in their way. Soon the dispossessed Indians grew resentful; their mutterings of discontent finally exploded into violence which thundered against the walls of To-tu-ya's valley. The miners, organizing to meet Indian resistance, implored the Government to remove these trouble makers, and themselves volunteered to perform the task. Friction at last flared into war, and history records the entry into Yosemite Valley by an expeditionary force of prospector-soldiers on March 25, 1851. Three times between 1851 and 1853 the Indians were driven from the Valley.

To-tu-ya's childhood fortunes ebbed and flowed on the tide of this unhappy conflict. Twice she and other members of her village were escorted to a reservation in the foothills. On two other occasions she fled from Yosemite, once to escape surrender to a military detachment and again to avoid capture and possible death during a brief period of intertribal warfare.

The most tragic experience of the girl in these early years occurred in 1851, soon after the Mariposa Battalion arrived in the Valley. Soldiers had captured three of her uncles, sons of Chief Tenaya, near the base of those rocks which have since been known as the Three Brothers. In an attempt to escape, one of these men — her favorite uncle — was killed. Bitterness and hatred filled the heart of the little girl. Small wonder that she fled at last with a determination never to return to the scene of such desecration. This vow she faithfully kept until that long-delayed visit in the summer of 1929.

While still in her teens, To-tu-ya married a full-blood Yosemite Indian and become the mother of four sons and a daughter. During the next few years all four sons as well as her husband met tragic deaths. In the sorrow of these experiences her resentment continued to rankle.

Later To-tu-ya married a half-breed Mexican miner named Yerdies Lebrado. She made her home a few miles east of Mariposa, close to what is now the All-Year Highway. Maria Lebrado — as she was known thereafter — gave birth to four daughters and her life was full once again.

Although she had been invited repeatedly to visit the valley, Maria steadfastly refused. You can imagine our surprise and delight, therefore, upon learning that she was finally coming home.

After her arrival in the valley, several days passed before Maria responded to an invitation to visit the museum and see what was being done to preserve the story of her people. At first she refused, but later she reconsidered.

Thus on that third of July Maria appeared at the Yosemite Museum. I shall never forget the half hour that followed. Visitors were quickly ushered from the Indian Room so that the sanctity of Maria's experience would not be violated by curious eyes or flippant remarks. Exhibit cases were swung open and everything within them was made accessible to her hungry fingers. She walked slowly from one display to the next. I studied her reactions, and tried to imagine the emotions which were flooding her consciousness. Haunted by a lifelong bitterness yet responsive to a newly awakened urge, Maria seemed to have a rebirth of interest as she viewed the contents of the Indian Room. She was reticent and uncommunicative at first, but the sight of so many familiar things swept her mind back to girlhood days. Enthusiastic now, she began to chatter in a mixture of Indian, Spanish, and English words. Her delight was unbounded; several times her laughter echoed through the Museum as some exhibit struck a chord of reminiscent pleasure. But in every moment of the short encounter I detected a deep, underlying note of pathos.

When Maria was ready to leave, she noticed the curious tourists who had congregated at the door, and reverted to her old unyielding attitude. She emerged from the Museum with all the dignity and reserve one might associate with the granddaughter of an Indian chief. In a few days Maria left the valley, never to return.

A year later, in August of 1930, I met Maria Lebrado for the second and last time. With my family and the Museum Librarian, I journeyed to her home on Bear Creek. We found the little cabin at the end of a winding dirt road, a mile or so from the highway. Old Mary came out to welcome us—the daughter of Maria's first marriage some seventy years before. Mary announced us to her mother and soon we were all seated at the front step. I could glimpse the interior of the cabin. It was almost bare, but very neat. Several sacks of acorns lined one wall, a backlog of primitive food against a rainy day. Because of language difficulties, our conversation was limited, but we sensed a warmth in Maria's countenance that needed no interpreter.

As we became aware of Maria's interest in our baby and realized her unexpressed longing, we laid him in her arms. She clasped him to her breast and swayed slowly back and forth. Time rolled back for Maria to the days of her own active motherhood and her face was radiant. Then a faraway look came into her eyes. Maria sadly remembered, "All gone, long, long 'go, my all gone." She was an old, old woman again and she complained that her eyes were poor and her teeth were "all gone." We jokingly pointed out that our baby had no teeth either and she laughingly prophesied, "He get some, by 'n' by."

Our visit soon ended and we thanked Maria for her hospitality. As we drove back—to her valley—we felt that in seeing her again we had been privileged and that our lives had been lastingly enriched.

Less than a year later, on April 20, 1931, Maria Lebrado slipped quietly away to "El-o-win," the Far West of the Yosemite Indians. She had requested an Indian funeral. When the time came, tom-toms beat for an hour or more while relatives and friends circled Maria's body as they joined in a funeral dance and song of Chief Tenaya's day. Late in the afternoon the body was placed in a casket. Following the last kiss and the final farewell, the casket was closed. Eight young Indians—grandsons and relatives—led a procession of more than one hundred persons as they bore the body of Maria Lebrado to its resting place in the family cemetery. With more ceremonial singing and swaying, the casket was lowered into a muslin-lined grave, the sides of which were softened with fern fronds. Articles dear to the dead woman were placed in the grave, and finally it was filled and wildflowers were placed on the mound.

I like to believe that Maria's attitude toward the white race had mellowed during her later years. Long before, with great bitterness in her heart, she had fled the valley with a firm resolution never to return, but finally she did. On her visit to Yosemite she had no intention of going to the Museum, but she did. Above all, she had never permitted anyone to take her picture. Even in that instance, the warmth and understanding of a white woman—the Museum Librarian—melted this resistance and several pictures were made, one of which hangs today in the Indian Room. Perhaps the most convincing proof of Maria's change of heart was manifested at the time of her funeral, for among the cherished possessions laid beside her in the grave was a woolen blanket, a gift to Maria from this same warm-hearted white woman.

Maria Lebrado's physical form will never be seen again, but I find it easy to believe that To-tu-ya's liberated spirit has returned again to the scenes of her childhood—to Yosemite, the home of "Foaming Water."

175

48

Too Many Deer

A. STARKER LEOPOLD

1953

> When Daniel Boone goes by, at night,
> The phantom deer arise
> And all lost, wild America
> Is burning in their eyes.
>
> Vachel Lindsay

For generations of city dwellers the deer have been the ultimate symbol of the American wilderness. Their lithe grace and beauty have been celebrated by poets and painters as well as naturalists, and hunters have developed their own special mystique about the animal. When overgrazing by sheep and cattle, and the reckless destruction of the forests and wildlands in the late nineteenth century, destroyed habitats and threatened to wipe out entire species, public opinion was aroused to protect wildlife; saving the deer as a symbol of "all lost, wild America" became a National Purpose. The method was to set aside wildlife preserves and, outside the reserves, to limit hunting to a certain season, and to outlaw the taking of does.

When A. Starker Leopold's article appeared in the Bulletin *in 1953, a good many conservationists were shocked by the title alone. The notion that there could be too many deer was for many people as unthinkable as the idea that there could be too many redwoods. But Leopold's article emphasized John Muir's discovery that everything in nature is "hitched" to everything else, as well as the later findings of the ecologists that interference in the balance of nature sets off chain reactions of unintended consequences. The solution is not always clear, as Leopold's article makes plain. Sometimes the best that can be done at any given moment is to learn more about how to minimize the damage wrought in the past.*

The author, a former vice-president of the Sierra Club, is professor of zoology and forestry at the University of California, Berkeley, and in the 1960s was chairman of a special Advisory Board on Wildlife Management appointed by the Secretary of the Interior. The resulting "Leopold Committee Report" has become a classic in the field. Professor Leopold is a son of Aldo Leopold, author of A Sand County Almanac, *and a brother of Luna Leopold, an outstanding hydrologist.*

SINCE 1925, the year of the great die-off of Kaibab deer, there has been blowing in conservation circles a minor gale of controversy over the hows and wherefores of managing our deer herds. Eddies of the storm have swirled through legislative halls in all the northern and western states, where deer are most numerous, and even into the southern provinces of Canada and, more recently, southeastern Alaska. Sometimes the winds of oratory have reached cyclonic proportions, as in Wisconsin in 1948 when Governor Rennebohm vetoed a bill to permit the shooting of female deer (and consequently was defeated for re-election), or in Pennsylvania when an irate public protested the kill of 171,000 does during the hunting season of 1938. More often the gusts are local and puffy, as fish and game commissions from coast to coast listen to arguments for and against liberalizing the deer kill.

The center of the tempest hinges on a seemingly simple point — should we legalize the killing of female deer as well as bucks?

Arguments in favor of doe hunting are all based on technical and biological grounds. The contrary view is not so simply defined — it springs from tradition, sentiment, and fear, and to understand it one must retrace the whole evolution of wildlife conservation in this country.

When Theodore Roosevelt and Gifford Pinchot came forth in 1904 with plans for the conservation and wise use of the nation's resources, there was quick and grateful acceptance on the part of the American public. Already there existed a growing awareness that the waste and slaughter of frontier days could not continue indefinitely. Although perhaps few people really understood the economic (much less the ecologic) significance of the butchering of the forests or the overgrazing of the grasslands, nearly everyone grasped the implications of the disappearance of bison and passenger pigeons. There crystallized rapidly a philosophy of conservation based on fear of resource exhaustion by overuse. In the specific province of wildlife conservation this concept was championed by such popular figures as William T. Hornaday, John M. Phillips, T. Gilbert Pearson, and others of lesser rank, and within a short time nearly all of the states had plunged enthusiastically into the crusade to protect remaining breeding stocks of game from threatened extinction. Indeed, nothing could have been more salutary at the time, for many species, especially of big game, were dangerously reduced in number.

The accepted techniques of restoration were (1) legal regulation of hunting, with necessary enforcement, (2) establishment of refuges or special preserves, and (3) control of predators. In the case of deer, this combination of devices was applied almost universally as *the* formula for deer management. The rapidity of its success was proof of its soundness and further was a source of gratification and encouragement to the conservationists of that day. From about 1910 on, deer increased steadily — sometimes spectacularly — over much of their former range, and one by one the states began cautiously to permit more hunting of the thriving herds.

One widely adopted phase of the protection program was to limit the legal kill to bucks only and to save all the does as breeding stock. Since deer are polygamous in mating habit, this procedure was biologically sound and served to sustain and perhaps even to stimulate the rate of increase among deer by enlarging the proportion of females in the herds. Much play was made of this differentiation of the sexes in presenting the problem of deer

177

conservation to the public. Hornaday for example, and many others, depicted the true sportsman as a clean-shaven gentleman of high principle who went afield to match wits with the noble stag and who looked solely with affection on the limpid-eyed doe and her spotted fawn. Only the ruthless game hog would slaughter a female. Wardens preached this gospel in country stores and administrators expounded it in the banquet halls. It became at length a part of our national creed.

And then came the Kaibab. The north rim of the Grand Canyon had been set aside as a National Game Preserve by Roosevelt in 1906 and particular attention was devoted to restoring the remnant of native mule deer. By eliminating hunting and closely regulating the numbers of large predators, the herd of about 4,000 deer was built up to an astonishing 100,000 by 1924. In the interim the area of the original game preserve had been reallocated to Grand Canyon National Park and to Kaibab National Forest. In 1918 the forest officers first noted severe damage by the deer to forage plants on the range, and by 1923 they were urgently requesting that the Arizona Game and Fish Commission open the area to hunting, not only of bucks but also of does, for the purpose of reducing the deer herd. This was the first demand for reduction of deer and it came as an unpleasant surprise to the conservation-minded public. There followed a series of investigations by special committees, and several court cases regarding jurisdiction over the deer, but before a new policy could be formulated the deer herd had largely perished. In the winters of 1924–25 and 1925–26, sixty per cent of the deer died of starvation on the depleted range. By 1930 the herd numbered only 20,000 and even then it dwindled slowly until in 1939 there were only 10,000 left. The Kaibab herd and the range had been sacrificed, but the point was borne home that there could be too many deer.

The spotlight shifted from Arizona to Pennsylvania where white-tailed deer were becoming locally overabundant. In 1905 the sportsmen of the state had fought against the adoption of a Buck Law, but in 1925 they opposed even more bitterly a plan to repeal that statute and to permit a limited kill of does to hold down the growing herd. It is to the everlasting credit of the Pennsylvania Game Commission that they followed the advice of their field men, despite sportsman opposition, and periodically from 1925 to the present day have legalized a sufficient kill of does to hold the deer at least partly in check. That is not to say that the people of Pennsylvania are in full accord with doe shooting. There is still much disagreement over the efficacy and morality of killing potential mothers.

In rapid succession parallel problems developed all over the United States—in Michigan and Wisconsin, Utah and Colorado, Washington and California. The technical literature on wildlife came to be almost dominated by reports of too many deer, damage to ranges or crops or forest reproduction, wholesale losses of deer to starvation or in warmer climates to disease, all leading to professional recognition of the need for herd control. But so deeply had the philosophy of protection and restoration penetrated public thinking that challenging the sacred position of the doe called forth a pitched battle in nearly every state, county, or local community where the issue was raised. And usually the sentimental view prevailed over the biological. Only Idaho and Minnesota were immune—the two deer states that were fortunate enough to have escaped the Buck Law. Parenthetically it might be added that these two states have plenty of deer today and only a few trouble spots— mostly in parks and refuges.

Fortunately, controversy in conservation affairs always stimulates field investigation and research, with the result that today we know a great deal about deer biology and range relationships. First let us examine the evidence pertaining to the causes of deer irruptions and secondly that regarding the biological after-effects, both on the deer and on the range.

In the mushrooming of deer herds in the first half of this century there was more involved than mere overprotection. North American deer generally thrive best in certain *secondary* stages of forest succession; that is to say, there is much more food for deer in cut-over or burned-over forest than in virgin forest, and as a consequence there are usually more deer. Virtually all deer studies have shown that the quantity and quality of forage, specifically of winter forage, ultimately limits deer numbers on any given range in the absence of other controls. The indiscriminate slashing and burning of forests that occurred during the past century inadvertently created almost ideal food conditions for deer, so that when protection from both hunters and predators was offered, the deer were able to increase at a rate little short of their biological potential. Shrubs such as species of *Ceanothus* (deer brush), *Purshia* (bitter brush), and *Cowania* (cliff rose) grew in seemingly unlimited amounts through the western mountains where once were lofty stands of conifers with little deer food beneath. In the East and Lake States were thickets of succulent young maple, white cedar, and hemlock growing among the stumps of Paul Bunyan's pines. The timing of the protection program could not have been better conceived to assure a response from the deer. Actually, in many areas deer have achieved much higher densities in the past two decades than were ever seen by the pioneers. To take one example, perusal of the journals of Jedediah Smith, Walker, Frémont, and John Work leaves little doubt that deer originally were scarce in the Sierra Nevada as compared with what we have today.

When the natural predators of deer were removed from the range by government hunters, bounty payments, and by the sheer weight of popular sentiment to the effect that "the only good varmint is a dead one," and when further no provision was made to substitute hunting for predation as a regulatory force over deer numbers, the stage was set for our present crop of difficulties.

Without outside control, deer tend to increase beyond what the range will carry in security and health. In excess numbers they punish the very elements of the forage which support them, just as too many cattle in a pasture will overgraze the palatable and nutritious grasses and create finally a field of weeds. No matter how good a deer range is to start with, it will deteriorate with overuse as the better food plants are killed out. Over a period of time, therefore, the density of the deer population is bound to decline. In some cases, like the Kaibab, the exhaustion of the range and consequent collapse of the herd is sudden and spectacular. This is especially true in arid regions. In more humid climates the critical forage plants tend to be more resistant and the course of an irruption is usually longer and the decline more gradual. The fruit of overprotection of deer is a long-term loss in population.

On a short-term basis, there is a loss in year-to-year harvest of deer which if not taken by hunters or predators will die anyway from malnutrition or some secondary effect of malnutrition. For example, a recent study of the Jawbone deer herd on the west slope of the Sierra Nevada, just north of Yosemite Park, showed that the annual production (net increase) in the herd of 32 per cent per annum was dissipated as follows: 23 per cent to starvation, 7 per cent to hunters, and 2 per cent to predators. The 32 per cent represented a biological excess that could not possibly have survived, because there was not enough nutritious food. Had these animals all been killed by hunters there probably would have been no loss to starvation. But California has a Buck Law and although the herd was heavily hunted, the harvest took only a small part of the surplus. Other studies have yielded more or less parallel results. Where only bucks are killed, the harvest is usually from 4 to 9 per cent of the population each year, whereas net production normally runs from 20 to 35 per cent, at least two-thirds of which is wasted.

In some areas like the northern Coast Ranges of California and the shinnery thickets of Texas, excess deer die from disease and parasites rather than starvation. But basically this appears to be but a modification of the same phenomenon, since epidemics occur only in overpopulated ranges where the animals are weakened by competition for food. The cure for disease in deer, just as for starvation, is in limiting numbers of deer to fit the food supply.

Research on the physiology of the individual animal has yielded additional pertinent information. The productivity of a given herd is by no means a constant. Studies in New York State and more recently in California have shown that well-situated deer on good range have a decidedly higher crop of fawns than overcrowded deer on poor range. The quality of food obtained by a given doe will influence the age at which she breeds (earlier on good ranges), the number of ova released from the ovary, the probability of successful implantation and pregnancy, and even the strength of the fawn after it is born. This means that on a given range with forage capacity for say 1,000 deer, the total production of fawns may be greater if the herd is held to 1,000 than if it is permitted to increase to 1,200 or 1,500. Since production of deer for hunters to shoot is one of the main objectives of managing deer, this point is important.

Furthermore, studies of starvation losses on overcrowded range indicate that it is mostly fawns and old deer that die under conditions of severe competition, and that the big majority of fawns lost are *males*. The reason for this is obscure—it is associated apparently with the higher metabolic rate of young bucks and the more rapid growth of skeleton and muscle with less storage of reserve fat than in young does. Be that as it may, an overcrowded

180

herd will tend to produce fewer bucks than a smaller balanced herd on the same range.

All of these are cogent arguments for regulating deer numbers, but they are reluctantly accepted by a public conditioned to think only of protecting and increasing numbers of wild animals. So we shall probably continue for some years to starve more deer than we shoot. The dyed-in-the-wool buck hunter, who professes indignation at the very thought of killing a doe, is losing as much as the summer vacationist who wants only to enjoy seeing the deer. There will be fewer deer for both a decade hence.

Alternate proposals have been offered to ease the situation. Attempts to trap and move deer from overcrowded ranges have proved exorbitantly expensive—$30 to $80 a head. All experiments in artificial feeding have ended in failure. When natural browse foods are exhausted the wild deer die even with bellies full of alfalfa or cottonseed cake, which is curious since deer are easily kept on such foods in captivity. Anyway extensive feeding of deer is economically out of the question. Perhaps the most practical idea is to permit some recovery of the large predators, but this proposal meets with even more vehement opposition than shooting does. If there is a workable formula for coping with excess deer, other than by hunting, no one has discovered it.

Certain it is, however, that as conservationists and sportsmen, Americans will have to take a realistic view toward regulating deer numbers. The success of deer restoration in the past will have carried with it the seeds of its own destruction if we do not heed the example of the Kaibab and of the countless other ranges that have deteriorated in the last two decades.

In the years since this article appeared, Professor Leopold's predictions have been confirmed: The "deer explosion" of the 1940s and early '50s overtaxed the food supply, and the herds were depleted by starvation. Deer populations have dwindled in all eleven western states to the point that Leopold no longer recommends doe shoots. The diminution of the herds has been caused not only by overgrazing by excess numbers of deer but the elimination of their habitat by clear-cut forestry that destroys the undergrowth as well as trees, by overgrazing cattle in National Forests, and by fire control, an issue almost as emotion-laden as the doe shoot.

Clearly, there are no quick and easy answers. Scientists and laymen alike still have much to learn about how man and nature can work out a peaceful coexistence.

181

49

Do We Want Sugar Pine?

HERBERT L. MASON

1955

Good intentions may be their own worst enemy. Well-intentioned overprotection by parents can spoil the child; well-intentioned overprotection of deer, as Dr. Leopold has indicated, can wreak havoc; well-intentioned overprotection of wilderness from fires can result in elimination of whole species, as Herbert Mason here points out. Certain species of trees are not only more fire-resistant than others; they actually require periodic fires to eliminate the aggressive competitors that would otherwise take over the forest. To protect them from all fires is to seal their doom, and the longer a forest is protected from fire the more destructive an eventual fire will be. In the forest, as elsewhere, human interventions in natural processes set off unpredictable chain reactions. To paraphrase Sir Walter Scott:
>   *Oh, what a tangled web we spin*
>   *When nature's process we butt in.*
Mason is Director Emeritus and Professor Emeritus of the Herbarium of the University of California.

IT HAS BEEN SUGGESTED that any attempt to preserve the sugar pine in the condition in which it is now found is futile; that through natural processes the sugar pine is rapidly being replaced by incense cedar and white fir; that the sugar pine is therefore not a part of the ultimate stable forest community, but must give way to the dominant incense cedar and white fir. This argument is based on correct observations and sound reasoning.

But let us look at another set of facts. When man came to California he found throughout the length of the Sierra Nevada a magnificent sugar-pine forest—the sugar pines mixed with ponderosa pine, white fir, and incense cedar. This forest had all the appearances of a stable forest community. The evidence of reproduction was only of a replacement type with all characteristic species reproducing in this manner. . . .

Now, however, such a forest, dominated by white fir and incense cedar, exists. This brings us to the anachronistic conclusion that both the forest as found by civilized man on the west slope of the Sierra Nevada and that which seems now to be replacing it satisfy the definition of a relatively stable forest community and the concept "climax forest" as employed by the ecologist. In these facts we have what on the surface seems to be a paradox — on the one hand, evidence that the sugar pine throughout much of its area is not a member of the stable climax community, on the other that the sugar pine was and, in some places as least, still is an integral part of the stable climax community. Can this seeming contradiction be resolved in terms of phenomena that we can understand?

First let us consider the climax theory. It is a part of the logic employed in the interpretation of what we find in nature. We owe the climax theory to the late Frederick E. Clements, who developed it to explain the end point in the natural sequence of plant succession. Clements conceived the progression toward the climax condition as being predominantly under control of environmental conditions classifiable as "climatic." He pointed out that the word "climax" as he employed it in ecology was not to be construed in the then current dictionary sense, but had the same etymological roots as the word "climate." He argued that all other conditions of the environment, whether edaphic or biotic, were themselves either the result of climate, or their influence was controlled by climate, or in the course of earth changes would at length disappear and the prevailing climate would then dominate the situation. He did not deny the influence of other factors, but to him none had the relative permanence of climate.

But it is now generally conceded that no single group of conditions is adequate to explain every community that displays the characteristics of a climax community. Some communities are dominated by one set of conditions, others by another, and the fortuitous nature of the course of the succession may influence what ultimately prevails.

What does all of this suggest for the sugar-pine paradox? It suggests that some environmental conditions have changed, because the practices of civilized man in his association with the sugar pine differ from the practice of aboriginal man. This difference tends to create conditions favoring incense cedar and white fir at the expense of sugar pine. One cannot, of course, exclude the possibility of variation in climate, but this variation hardly seems to have exceeded the range that was evident when civilized man first came; also its effect would be manifest as a gradient across the area of sugar pine, but the effects we note are evident throughout the sugar-pine range.

We may assume that the climatic potential for fire initiation through lightning in the forest has been relatively constant throughout prehistorical and historical time; also that both aboriginal man and civilized man have been responsible for fire in the forest. The most important difference in man's relation to the forest has been that civilized man has built up a rather effective method of protecting the forest from all but the most devastating fires. In spite of many disastrous forest fires, the persons charged with fire protection are doing a very effective job against increasingly serious odds. Furthermore they have been responsible for one of the most amazingly successful educational jobs on record — of making the average man conscious of the danger of fire. In this set of facts we may have the key to the sugar-pine problem.

Fire protection has, on the one hand, apparently increased the selective potential of the environment for incense cedar and white fir and militated against sugar pine; and, on the other, created a condition which in turn increases the probability of devastating fires.

In semi-arid climates such as ours with summer thunderstorms, fire is a natural and characteristic feature of the environment. In addition, fire was set by aboriginal man. The natural vegetation in such areas becomes the product of a natural environmental relationship with fire. There is evidence that fire, whatever its cause, has occurred frequently enough in forests to have resulted in a relatively stable "fire type" vegetation. This was pointed out long ago by Jepson. In other words, certain types of vegetation cover are able to maintain themselves in the face of recurrent fire so long as the fire is not of too great intensity at any one time. Most low- and middle-altitude vegetation of California has this "fire-type" character. The recurrence of minor fires prevents the building up of conditions conducive to disastrous high-intensity fires. Thus recurrent fire, regardless of cause, is and has been a part of the normal disharmonic fluctuation of environmental conditions.

Recurrent fire has played a role in the history of the sugar-pine forest, which is attested by readily observable facts. The trunks of many trees of different ages are scarred by fire around their bases and often to considerable height. The scars observed in any forest are of different ages, indicating several fires. The name "sugar pine" itself attests a fire history, because the most available source of sugar from which the tree derives its name is from the surface of burns where sugar sometimes exudes and crystallizes. These fires were ground fires of low intensity, which is attested by the basal position of the scars and the fact that the trees were not killed. That a "fire climax" was able to develop indicates that the fires recurred at irregular intervals depending first on a source of ignition and secondly upon the accumulated undergrowth. The fires must have occurred often enough so that no hazard sufficient to promote disastrous crown fires developed, yet been of low enough intensity locally so that some of the young trees were able to survive to an age at which the thickness of the bark would protect them.

By our efficiency in fire protection we have removed a natural environmental condition that appears to be significant to the regeneration of the sugar pine. In its place is a hazardous climax not under the developmental regime of fire. Something of the nature of these changes can be gained from an incident in my experience. In the summer of 1923 I stopped a little above the present entrance to Yosemite National Park on the Big Oak Flat road to admire a magnificent panorama of columns. Two years ago I took my wife and son to see this panorama and found that although the trees were still there, the panorama was gone. In its place, and obscuring it, was a thirty-years' growth of trees and brush. Some of the trees are no longer small. Here is a fire hazard to frighten anyone charged with the protection of this area every time a thunder storm passes over.

The situation presents a great dilemma. Nobody wants fire in our forests, however small its extent or however low its intensity. Yet everybody seems to want sugar pine. Well, what is the answer?

The answer is not entirely black, although it may leave some charcoal. Our desires, ideals, and prejudices are going to have to give way at some point in this problem, either on the precarious side of no fire or on the side of sugar pine. To have sugar pine means to have to accept some tampering with the sequence of the succession either by controlled fire or some means that will accomplish the same result. In the long run the cheapest method will be to maintain a forest in low-fire-hazard condition through controlled burning at intervals that will prevent the fire hazard from building up. This can be done in a manner that will protect sugar-pine regeneration; it certainly need not be done every year. If we choose to keep sugar pine, the situation has already reached such a state that we may have to do more than passive protection—we may have to remove and reduce fire hazard artificially if our enterprise is to have the only kind of fire insurance that will pay off in sugar pine.

Our efforts to manage our forests without fire have not been entirely successful. Nature before us successfully managed the forest with her own system of controlled burning. As fire seems inevitable in our arid climate, would not the wisest course be to see that fire occurs only at such times and in such places as we choose? Under such circumstances the fire would no longer present a threat to our forests.

A decade after Dr. Mason suggested the heretical notion of setting fires in the national parks as well as the national forests, the National Park Service began doing precisely that in Sequoia National Park. It had been discovered that sequoia seeds were not resulting in new trees; they were intercepted by the overly thick underbrush before they reached the ground. Controlled burns cleared the ground for seeding.

50

Wilderness Fungi—The Silent Scavengers

WILLIAM BRIDGE

COOK

1957

Perhaps the Save-the-Redwoods League, concerned with the tallest trees, should have a counterpart concerned with some of the smallest plants in the forest, a Save-the-Fungi League. Functionally, if not esthetically, they are even more important to the forest than trees, and they have their own beauty and fascination, as well. They may even save human lives, as a substance found in the fungus Penicillium *has done. Who knows what equally beneficial uses may be discovered in the future?*

The last word in ignorance is the man who says of an animal or plant: "What good is it?" If the land mechanism as a whole is good, then every part is good, whether we understand it or not. If the biota, in the course of aeons, has built something we like but do not understand, then who but a fool would discard seemingly useless parts? To keep every cog and wheel is the first precaution of intelligent tinkering.

Aldo Leopold, in Round River (Oxford, 1953)

I WOULD TAKE YOU for a walk in a wild forest, hardly disturbed but for a man-made trail. At this particular point there has been no disturbance to the trailside woodlands because there is no special incitement here for such tourist depredations. The trees are unscarred by the boyish knife blade or the messages of young lovers. The flowers have been left alone since they are just like those unthinkingly picked down the trail. The berries appear to be inedible so the bear and the deer may eat their fill. Only the occasional chirp of a hidden bird, or the song of a warbler from a small opening in the woods by the creek, or the chatter of a squirrel scared up by our passing, break the silence.

But these things are visible and audible as we wander along. Let us stop by this log beside the trail. We can see that it fell a very long time ago. The space this tree took in the forest canopy is being rapidly filled by saplings arising from the cavity it left in the forest floor and by the branches of its former neighbors.

Growing on the end of the log are little shelflike projections. These have concentric rings of varicolored hairs; the under side is pure white with many holes like a sieve. There is another shelflike structure but here the white growing margin is bordered by a red belt. Farther along the log is a cluster of delicate, bright orange mushrooms, and where the trickle of a spring keeps the wood moist a group of small scarlet cups with fringes of brown hairs adds color to the darkened day. A piece of transplanted coral shows yellow against the dark-brown decaying wood, and near the upper end of the log, where the mosses have moved onto the wood from the neighboring soil, a crust of grey-green scales with bright red-tipped fingers covers part of the old wood.

Over on the forest floor, apparently growing on the litter which has accumulated from the falling of leaves and needles, twigs, and bits of bark, we can see the shapes of numerous kinds of mushrooms. Maybe some of these are toadstools but we will not try them to find out. These are sometimes very colorful. Some are pure white, others have splashes of red, yellow, brown, purple, green, and blue. Near a few sticks are some black fingers protruding from the soil, some with a thin coat of white flour on their pointed tips.

If we were to look with a magnifying glass at the decaying wood, or litter, or bits of material in the soil, we would see still other growths actively working on these materials, producing variously colored or colorless, delicate or coarse fruiting structures which are very small in size and which may be distorted by the crowded conditions in which they live.

As we wander over to the creek along which willows, alders, and many herbs and grasses are growing, we discover that the willow leaves are supporting a rusty growth which does not appear to belong to the leaf. Most of the cones on the alder brushes appear normal, the scales of others have become distorted into numerous little purple tongue-like processes. One patch of pretty yellow monkey flowers appears to be stunted, and on its leaves are olive-colored spots half the size of a dime. A sedge growing along the creek has peculiar catkins of fruits, for every once in a while the single seed in the ovary is replaced by a large grey ball which, when broken, sheds its many black spores. In the flowers of some of the grasses along the miniature meadow are large purple hornlike structures which do not appear to be natural for the plant.

These organisms, the fungi, are most ubiquitous. Many species are world-wide in distribution and carry on the same life processes whether found in New Zealand or in Nova Scotia. Let us go back to the log. Bracket fungi are among the best known of the wood-decay fungi. They work relatively quickly on the cellulose and lignin in the wood and reduce them to their body tissue, or to substances they cannot use but which are readily used by other fungi, bacteria, and other organisms of the habitat. The fungi, themselves, of course, are prey to other organisms as are all living things at one time or another in the period of their existence. Thus we see moldy mushrooms, mushrooms and bracket fungi covered with incrusting yellow and orange fungus growths, and mushrooms with maggots, beetles, springtails, and other organisms eating them away. The tiny varicolored bracket-producing fungus is using the lignin in the immediate vicinity of its fruiting body, the bracket, while the larger red-belt conk is using the cellulose. The vegetative part of the red-belt conk probably inhabited the heartwood of the tree before it fell, and its fall may have been caused in part by the weakening of its structure as the fungus used up the cellulose in the heartwood, leaving only brown cubical chunks of lignin.

It is certain that the vegetative parts of the fungus producing the little orange mushrooms and the scarlet cups are using some of the materials left in the rotting log but it is not certain just which of these materials is their choice food. The same is true of the coral mushroom which was growing on the wood and of which other species grow on the forest floor.

The gray-green scales with the red-tipped clubs belong to a lichen which grows on soil and decaying wood. Other species of lichens are hanging like long gray, black, or green beards on the tree branches or clinging like bright yellow-green antler complexes to the bark of the tree trunk and to its branches. The bark of the trunk also supports other tiny hidden lichens, and still others are to be found on a rock outcropping up the trail. These lichens are made up of a fungus and an alga growing in close harmony, and in some

187

situations they may help to pave the way for the growth of other organisms.

The most obvious fungi of the forest floor are those whose fruit bodies are large, colorful, fleshy, and of diversified form. Many of these live directly upon the decaying litter on the ground. Others have a more complex design for living. They form a union with the roots of the trees of the forest which is called a mycorrhiza, or "fungus root." The tree benefits from this union as well as the fungus, because the fungus in decomposing materials obtains for its nourishment some substances which are also taken in by the tree. In many areas they are a critical source of nitrogen and other nutrients for the tree. On the practical level, forest nurseries in central Oregon need such fungi; Monterey pines planted in New Zealand had to be imported as started seedlings with the proper mycorrhizae attached; a forest plantation started in Brazil failed because after planting the seeds it was found that the proper mycorrhiza-producing fungi were not present.

Mushrooms are to the fungus organism much as apples are to the apple tree. The main body of the growing organism lies buried or otherwise concealed in the soil, the duff, or the litter where it is continually obtaining its nutrients, and only under the most favorable conditions does it produce the mushrooms which are the fruits in which are produced the structures on which the tiny spores are produced. Together with these mushrooms, which may have fruit bodies looking like the conventional mushrooms or toadstools, pieces of coral, cups, heads of cabbage, or other more peculiar shapes, are many other types of fungi whose fruits are less obvious. Some of these fruit underground, either singly or in "hills" like potatoes; these are the truffles and the false truffles. To attract the rodents who use them as food and in this way help to spread them through the forest, they produce different odors, some of which are vague and others as strong as garlic or rotten eggs.

Besides these two types of fungi, there are many whose size makes them invisible to the naked eye. These can be seen only after samples of the soil or litter are placed in special nutrients in which those fungi present can grow luxuriantly and then can be studied with a microscope. They are known best as the molds which get on bread, damp walls, damp paper, cloth, shoes, or any other place which can get moldy or mildewed at any time of the year under proper environmental conditions. Some of these fungi cause our greatest losses. They produce molds in seed bins and in bales of clothing dropped to a jungle battalion; when their spores are present in the air in large enough quantity, they are the cause of some of the different types of allergies people suffer. Yet at home in the soil or in the decaying log and litter on the forest floor they are extremely beneficial because they constantly remove various parts of the organic matter as their food supply.

In any natural community the ecology system is very delicately balanced. If one member of the community is removed (even with the best intention), the balance may be upset and the end result may be harmful. The practicing forest pathologist is interested in preventing the spread of wood-decay fungi in the forests from which the timber crop is being removed. It is difficult for him to understand that in an adjacent area, set aside for complete preservation of the forest type as a natural museum, the older, potentially infected, trees should not be removed. To him their removal would lessen the chance of infection occurring in the harvestable timber, although conks of infecting fungi occur throughout the nearby unprotected areas. An epidemic of spruce budworm is itself subject to an epidemic of a bacterial disease which eventually eliminates the budworm, sometimes in a dramatic manner. The removal of lodgepole pine in one area by a rust parasite or a mistletoe need not be controlled or sanitized since the natural removal of this tree can give living space to other trees in the climatic climax for the area. The indiscriminate removal of currant and gooseberry bushes from the region of a white-pine or a sugar-pine forest by the use of hand grubbing, bulldozing, or 2,4-D application may help to control the white-pine blister rust to which both plants are host, but at the same time it also eliminates potentially important members of the understory communities, and plants which are completely innocent of "wrong doing" may thereby be needlessly destroyed. Such plants may have been important forage plants for the larger mammals of the region, or they may have been host to insect members of food chains whose existence had been little suspected until the balance was upset.

The fungus microbe can thus be seen to play one of two important roles in the development, and continuance of the forest. It is either a parasite causing disease in plants, removing whole populations by destroying them, and thus eliminating its own food supply; or it is a saprobe, policing the forest as a scavenger, removing the dead organic matter, making way for the following year's layer of needles on the forest floor, or removing the results of yesterday's wind storm. In the wilderness there is room for both types of activity; in the wilderness both types of activity can be studied from beginning to end of each type of cycle; in the wilderness we can learn principles to apply in more satisfactory types of land management.

In the forest primeval the pines and the hemlocks bearded with moss and in garments of lichens stand like Druids — but the unknown diseases of age will remove the older trees, and as the younger trees come to maturity the trunks of the dead trees will be removed gradually to make room for more. With changes in climate, and the changes accompanying man's intensifying use of the land, the character of the forest may change, but that of the parasites and the scavengers which accompany it will probably continue indefinitely.

Fungi may not be the wheels that Aldo Leopold cautioned us about, but if not, then they are surely the cogs that help move the wheels. As we tinker, we can be thankful that in wilderness we can keep both.

51

Yosemite's Disappearing Meadows

EMIL F. ERNST

1961

Visitors to Yosemite Valley are likely to assume that it has always appeared as it does today. Even if they are aware of the changes that have occurred in geologic time, they may assume that in historic time, the natural features remain the same, and only roads and buildings have changed the scene from what the Indians looked upon. In reality, the valley landscape has changed markedly since its "discovery" in 1851 and continues to change, as photographs and written testimony indicate.

L. H. Bunnell, quoted here by Emil F. Ernst, was a member of the Mariposa Battalion, which entered Yosemite in 1851.

THE YOSEMITE VALLEY has been called for many, many years, "The Valley Incomparable." Just what is it that entitles it to this appellation? It is not the high waterfalls alone, nor the towering, shining cliffs, the magnificent forests, or the peaceful meadows; for each of these are exceeded in height or in volume, or extent, or beauty elsewhere in the world. The thing that makes the Yosemite Valley "incomparable" is the balancing of all these scenic features in one magnificent and sublime composition.

The question arises, "Has it always been thus, and shall it always be thus?" Nature, constantly changing, answers in the negative. The meadows are one of the two features of the valley which can be radically affected by the efforts of Man or of Nature in a relatively short time. The other feature, the forests, will expand or retreat as the meadows retreat or expand, and they can be considered as a corollary of the meadows.

Dr. Bunnell, in an article evidently prepared for the *Century Magazine,* and not published, but which was included in the Yosemite Valley Commissioners' Report for the year 1889–90, says that, "The valley at the time of discovery presented the appearance of a well kept park." He goes on further to say, "There was then a little undergrowth in the park-like valley, and half a day's work in lopping off branches along the course enabled us to speed our horses uninterrupted through the groves."

The next reference, in period of time, to the condition of the valley is given by Galen Clark in 1894. He says, in part, "My first visit to Yosemite was in the summer of 1855. At that time there was no undergrowth of young trees to obstruct clear open views in any part of the valley from one side of the Merced River across to the base of the opposite wall. The area of clear open meadow ground, with abundance of luxuriant native grasses and flowering plants, was at least four times as large as at the present time."

The next reliable information occurs eleven years later, and refers specifically to conditions at the time when, in 1866, Professor J. D. Whitney, State Geologist, made a careful survey of the bottom of the valley for the Commissioners. The data was plotted on a scale of ten chains (660 feet) to the inch, and it showed the number of acres in each tract of meadow, timber, and fern land. Galen Clark, in his letter of August 30, 1894 to the Commissioners [of Yosemite Valley], says that:

In 1866 when Professor J. D. Whitney, State Geologist, made a segregated tabulated map of the floor of the valley, there were seven hundred and fifty acres of meadow ground. Since then the forest growth has so far encroached upon the borders of the meadow land that there is not one-fourth of that amount, and what there is left is becoming so thickly covered with young willows and cottonwoods of four and five years' growth that there are really not fifty acres of clear ground except such as has been under recent cultivation.

In 1907, Clark wrote:

A great change has taken place in Yosemite Valley since it was taken from the control of the native Indians who formerly lived there. In the early years, when first visited by white people, three-fourths of the valley was open ground—meadows and grasses waist high and flowering plants. On the dryer parts were scattered forest trees—pines, cedars, and oaks—too widely separated to be called groves of underbrush, leaving clear, open, extensive vision up and down and across the valley from wall to wall on either side. The Indians kept the valley clear of thickets of young trees and brushwood shrubbery, so they could not be waylaid, ambushed, or surprised by enemies from outside, and to not afford hiding places for bears [it should be remembered here that grizzlies then inhabited the valley] or undesirable predatory animals, and also to have clear ground for gathering acorns, which constituted one of their main articles of food. At the present time there is not more than one-fourth of the floor of the valley clear, open ground, as there was fifty years ago. Nearly all the open ground between the large scattering trees is now covered with a dense growth of young trees, which also extend out over hundreds of acres of the dryest portion of meadow land. Every pine tree of the valley less than seventy-five feet high has grown from seed within the past fifty years.

The written story goes on and on. If the observations and writings of the men quoted can be accepted as shown, then there is no question but that the meadows of Yosemite Valley at the time of, and shortly after, the discovery by the white man, were much larger than they are today. The statements recorded are substantiated fully by photographs that have been taken from time to time beginning with Watkins' great photographs of 1866. After 1870, photographs are more numerous and show the meadows being continually encroached upon by the forest trees.

191

The question naturally arises that if the Yosemite Valley was an open, brush-free, and park-like valley at the time of the arrival of the white man, why is it today so heavily screened with forest trees? Any one or all of several things may have been responsible for the radical change that has occurred since its discovery by the white man in 1851.

The first thought would be that something has occurred in the character of the meadows themselves. Generally, meadow conditions are primarily dependent upon an abundance of ground water. Perhaps a drying-out is occurring in the Yosemite Valley meadows which permits the more xerophytic trees to gain a foothold which is secured by the further drying-up capabilities of trees exerted upon the lands upon which the foothold has been obtained. The original drying out may have been the result of the lowering of the water table sustaining the meadows of the valley.

[But] speaking of the Miwoks, of which the inhabitants of Yosemite Valley were a branch, Barrett and Gifford, in a bulletin of the Public Museum of Milwaukee, 1933, say:

The only other control of vegetation which they (the Miwoks) attempted was the burning off of dry brush about August. This was said to have been done to get a better growth the following year. Underbrush was less abundant anciently than now, so informants said, and perhaps was due to periodic burning.

A photograph of the upper end of Yosemite Valley taken from Columbia Point in 1899 by H. G. Peabody. The meadows were much larger in extent then than today.

192

According to Barrett and Gifford the Miwoks used fire for another purpose, and that was hunting. Hunts were staged by the inhabitants of a single community. Fires were set around the meadows which the deer frequented. New fires were built from time to time and the deer approached these fires out of curiosity and were noiselessly shot with arrows by the Indians from their places of ambush.

M. C. Briggs, Secretary of the Commission to Manage Yosemite Valley, in the Report of the Commission to the Governor of California, dated December 18, 1882, makes the following statement:

> While the Indians held possession, the annual fires kept the whole floor of the valley free from underbrush, leaving only the majestic oaks and pines to adorn the most beautiful of parks. In this one respect protection has worked destruction.

During 1881 State Engineer William H. Hall made an extended professional visit to the valley. He submitted a report to the Commissioners dated May 20, 1882, in which he says:

> . . . and the area of meadow is decreasing, while the young thickets of forest or shrub growth are springing up instead. Members of your Board have observed this change; it is very marked, and it may be regarded as in a degree alarming, sufficiently so, at least, to prompt measures calculated to check it.
>
> The cause is alleged to be the abolition of the old practice of burning of the thickets, which practice formerly made new clearings almost every year for grass growth.

The State of California assumed jurisdiction over the Yosemite Valley in 1864 following President Abraham Lincoln's magnificent gift to the State of the "gorge or cleft known as the Yosemite Valley." Although it was reported to the Committee of The Congress handling the bill authorizing this grant that there were no settlers in the valley, this was not in accord with the facts. Attempts at settlement began in 1858 with the construction of permanent living structures. James Lamon became the first all year around resident in the winter of 1862–63, to be followed by James Mason Hutchings and his family on the 20th of April, 1864. Since then the valley has been in continuous habitation by the white man.

In the early days of occupation by the white man several small areas were given over to farming activities. Hutchings' garden helped to supply fresh vegetables for his hotel, his orchard provided fruits, and an Aaron Harris had a farm in the vicinity of the present Ahwahnee Hotel for a number of years. In fact farming activities were so much in evidence that the November 26, 1888 edition of the San Francisco *Daily Examiner* likened the valley to a "hay ranch" and published a map showing how practically all of the upper portion of the valley was enclosed in barbed wire. Records exist showing that most of the meadows have been plowed at one time or another mainly to produce hay or for some truck farming.

The grazing, farming, and hay production activities undoubtedly helped to retard the advance of forest encroachment on the meadows, and in this respect the activities of the white man paralleled the crude meadow retaining endeavors of the former Indian inhabitants.

Previous to the assumption of control by the State of California in 1864 there is no evidence that the white man engaged in any extensive or periodic burning of the meadows or of the forest land in Yosemite Valley. Since that time and to the present day, fires have been quickly suppressed and fire prevention measures actively prosecuted. Up until about 1906 this policy of fire suppression was openly and actively condemned by the highest responsible officials who, however, disregarded their own opinions and carried out the fire suppression and fire prevention policies with which they heartily and honestly disagreed.

There are thousands upon thousands of wet and dry meadows in the Sierra Nevada. The number of acres lost to forest encroachment in the Yosemite Valley is so small as to make concern over their loss appear ridiculous. But the Yosemite Valley is no ordinary valley. It is outstanding among the very few similar valleys of the world and valleys of this type are called "yosemites." As stated at the outset, that which makes the Yosemite Valley "incomparable" is the blending of the waterfalls, the shining cliffs, the forests, and the meadows into a composition of supreme beauty in Nature. The small area of the meadows which is the leaven of this product of Nature is being progressively weakened as the years pass.

In conformity with the basic policy, the National Park Service has done little or nothing to halt or delay Nature in the encroachment of the forests upon the small meadow areas of the Yosemite. This policy was established by The Congress in the enabling act creating the National Park Service. The policy has made the American national park a living and incontrovertible symbol of the idealistic political philosophy of preserving for the people in their natural state areas of outstanding natural significance.

The day of the Indian and his burning is long past. In these days burning is not the tool to use, or to have natural wild fires run unhampered, in order to preserve the remaining meadow areas of the Yosemite Valley. Nor is it practical economically by any other means to attempt to recapture or to entirely stay further forest encroachment.

Fortunately it is now recognized that protection can work destruction. Outstanding scenic views can be preserved from obliteration from forest encroachment through judicious application of vista clearing methods. And in some instances vista clearing could recapture, with relatively small expenditure, now obliterated superb views.

The problem is not unique to Yosemite Valley. What is unique is the fact that we have a written and photographic record covering a period of more than 100 years of an area which shows profound ecological and esthetic changes.

52

What Colors the Mountain Snow?

ROBERT POLLOCK

1970

From whole biotic communities, we turn to some of the smallest living things, from macro-organisms to micro-organisms, from the complex to the simple, from the upper strata of evolution to some of the lowest and oldest. For the one, the environment may be an entire mountain range; for the other, it is a single snowbank. In this article on the colors of mountain snow, biologist Robert Pollock of the University of North Dakota reports on studies he and others have made at the University of Colorado's Institute of Arctic and Alpine Research. In doing so, he provides a clear explanation of that little-understood but all-important concept, the ecosystem, the basic living unit of the human environment. In the snowbank ecosystem we find one of the frontiers of evolution, between the primitive, chlorophyll-bearing plants known as algae and the single-celled creatures that reproduce by splitting themselves, protozoa, literally "first animals."

SUMMER VISITORS to alpine areas often notice that the surface of some of the snowbanks is colored. Orange and various shades of red are commonly observed; the extent of the colored snow varies from a small patch to an entire bank. The color has often been attributed to wind-blown dust, but in most instances it is due to the presence of large numbers of algae which are adapted to live in the austere environment of the snowbank. Besides the algae, which are visible to the naked eye because of the pigments they synthesize, the snowbank also contains cold-adapted bacteria, fungi and protozoa, all of which can be detected by microscopic examination of fresh snow or by various culture methods commonly used in microbiological research.

The ecosystem is the basic functional unit of ecology; it is defined as an area of nature composed of interacting living and non-living components. For example, a pond is a natural ecosystem while a test tube of synthetic culture medium inoculated with various microorganisms is a man-made ecosystem. A summer snowbank is also an ecosystem. The non-living components of the snowbank include water, dissolved atmospheric gases, various other inorganic and organic ions and molecules, and several types of radiation including visible light, ultraviolet light and ionizing radiations.

Water in the liquid phase must be present in the snowbank for several days

195

continuously before substantial growth and reproduction of snow microorganisms occur because metabolism ceases when the water freezes. Accordingly, a snow microorganism community does not begin to develop until May or June in the mountains of North America. The temperature of the liquid water in the snowbank is always 32°F since energy coming into the snowbank is used to melt snow rather than to raise the temperature of the water already present. The snow microorganisms are adapted to grow at a temperature of 32°F, but many microorganisms cannot grow at a temperature below 45°F. Microorganisms which can grow at 32°F are classified as psychrophiles or cryophiles (cold-loving). Mesophiles can grow at temperatures from 45-115°F while thermophiles, such as those found in hot springs, can grow at temperatures up to 175°F.

Dissolved oxygen from the air is required by all of the snow microorganisms that have been studied. The oxygen is utilized primarily in a metabolic process that releases energy from organic molecules such as carbohydrates in a form that is readily available to the organisms. Carbon dioxide dissolved in the liquid water of the snowbank is of importance to the algae in particular because carbon dioxide and water are the raw materials from which these organisms photosynthesize carbohydrates with the aid of energy from sunlight. The carbohydrates are then used by the algae for the synthesis of various chemical components of protoplasm and also as a source of energy for cellular processes. In this way energy from the sun is made available directly to the algal component of the snow microorganism community.

Snow water contains both inorganic and organic ions and molecules. Some were dissolved from soil or organic debris at the snow-soil interface or from debris which was blown onto the snow while others were components of the dust nuclei in the atmosphere around which snowflakes formed. Phosphates, nitrates, and several other of the inorganic ions are essential for all living organisms. The organic ions and molecules can be absorbed and used by various snow microorganisms to provide energy and the chemical components of protoplasm in much the same way as the carbohydrates photosynthesized by the algal cells.

The role of visible light in photosynthesis has been mentioned above. Ionizing and ultraviolet radiations generally have deleterious effects on snow microorganisms. A small proportion of the cell population in a snowbank will be either mutated or killed by these radiations in any given period of time. If, as seems likely, the snow microorganisms evolved from others which were not capable of growth at 32°F, then these same radiations were in part responsible sometime in the past for the production of the mutations which allowed cells to grow in the snowbank. Evolution is probably going on in snowbank communities at the present time but, now as before, the great majority of new mutations are deleterious. To understand why this is so, one must keep in mind the fact that, regardless of their small size, microorganisms are complex, intricately regulated structural and functional entities. A mutation randomly changes some aspect of structure or of func-

196

tion; most mutations, therefore, will upset the complex functioning of the cell rather than render it more harmonious.

Algae are the most conspicuous of the snow microorganisms because they synthesize pigments of various kinds which render them visible to the naked eye when the cells are present in a high concentration. Red-colored algae are commonly observed but orange- and green-colored algae are also found in summer snowbanks. The majority of the red- and green-colored algae are members of the genus *Chlamydomonas* and the orange-colored algae include members of both the genera *Scotiella* and *Chodatella*. A total of 15 to 20 species of snow algae have been described for North America and Europe.

Research done at the University of Colorado's Institute of Arctic and Alpine Research has resulted in a classification of summer snowbanks which correlates the algal species present with the amount of sunlight the snowbank receives during the day. Banks at timberline or below which are shaded throughout most of the day generally are populated by green algae, while banks in the alpine which are fully exposed to sunlight for at least one-half the day usually contain red algae. The orange algae are found in banks which receive an intermediate amount of sunlight. This is the main reason why mountaineers see red and orange algae more often than green algae: banks which contain the former persist sometimes for the entire summer while banks inhabited by the latter melt completely in the early summer. The reason for the correlation between exposure to sunlight and pigment color is not clear, but there is evidence that red pigments protect cells from the deleterious effects of intense visible light. Hence, the ability to synthesize the red pigments may have evolved as one of the adaptations which allowed algae to colonize alpine snowbanks.

The concentration of algal cells may be as high as 500,000 per milliliter of melted highly-colored red snow. The red footprints made by mountaineers are primarily due to an increase in concentration of the cells resulting from compression of the snow. Most of the red cells are resting stages or spores which are passively distributed by flowing meltwater in the banks and tend to be concentrated in low areas and in depressions. Intensely colored red snow smells and tastes like watermelon; the curious should remember, however, that for some individuals red snow is a laxative of considerable strength.

Algae are the only members of the snowbank community which photosynthesize. Hence they and they alone can obtain energy directly from the sun while the other microbes must get their energy second-hand by eating other organisms or by absorbing organic molecules present in the liquid water of the snowbank. For this reason algae, and green plants in general, are classified as the producers of the ecosystem. In the case of snowbanks, some of the energy available to the other microorganisms comes from windblown organic debris and from debris on the soil surface beneath the bank.

The protozoa are the consumers of the snowbank ecosystem. By definition, consumers are generally animals which obtain their energy by ingesting other organisms or particulate organic material. Very few studies have been done on the protozoa, the fungi, or the bacteria of snowbank communities. Work done at the Institute of Arctic and Alpine Research revealed that there are four or five species of protozoa in the snow of the Colorado Rockies. They are present in a very low concentration relative to the algae: there are an average of about 100 protozoa per milliliter of melted snow water. When observed through the microscope most of these protozoa are transparent. A few, however, appear opaque and, and, as the slide warms up, they burst and release up to twenty or more algal cells which they had previously eaten. The majority of these cells are green algae; the basis for choice by the protozoans may be that red and orange snow contain primarily spores encased in a tough coat while green snow contains cells which are growing and reproducing and which lack this coat. Accordingly, it was predicted that more protozoa would be present in snow which contained algae, and in particular green algae, than in snow which lacked algae. This was found to be true: green snow contained about ten times as many protozoa as red, orange, or white snow, in spite of the fact that the red and orange snow had approximately the same concentration of algal cells as the green snow. The presence of protozoa in snow other than green suggests that although they eat algae, they are not dependent upon them as a sole source of food. Since protozoa are known to eat bacteria and since bacteria are widely distributed in the snow, it seems likely that they as well as the algae are the major source of food for the protozoa.

The bacteria and fungi make up the decomposer class of the ecosystem. Decomposers break down the complex chemical compounds in the bodies of dead organisms into simpler compounds. Some of these compounds are then utilized by the decomposers for their metabolic processes and the remainder are released into the environment and are available to other organisms. Thus, there is a fundamental difference between the flow of energy in the ecosystem and the flow of matter. Energy comes ultimately from the sun in the form of visible light. It is converted to chemical bond energy as the result of photosynthesis by the producers. The consumers and decomposers obtain their energy from producers: algae photosynthesize, they are eaten by protozoa, and the protozoa are decomposed by bacteria and fungi—a simple food chain. However, at each nutritional level within the chain and in the transfer between levels, energy is continually being lost to the environment in the form of heat. If the sun did not perpetually supply energy to the chain, eventually all of it would be converted to heat and lost, and life would cease to exist. The flow of matter, on the other hand, is cyclical: atoms are taken into the food chain from the environment and eventually are returned to the environment to be utilized again. If a cyclical process did not exist, our environment would eventually be depleted of certain essential atoms and there would be a vast accumulation of dead organisms. Returning atoms to the environment is carried out primarily by decomposers.

The concentration of bacteria in the snowbank is approximately the same as the concentration of algae except in white snow where there are about ten times as many bacteria as algae. There are at least ten to twenty species of bacteria adapted to living in snowbanks. Along with the bacteria there are a small number of fungi. So far only one of the bacteria has been classified to the species level and it turned out to be a variety of the common soil and water organism *Pseudomonas aeruginosa.*

It may be asked why snow microorganisms should be studied. There are several answers to this question. The snowbank ecosystem could be of considerable importance in the study of ecosystems because of its relative simplicity and the rapidity of growth of its components. It is characteristic of science that a phenomenon is most easily studied when conditions are the simplest possible and that the results thus obtained may convert chaos to order when the same phenomenon is studied under more complex conditions. In view of the direct relation that ecology has to man's survival, the more that can be rapidly learned the better. Also, research aimed at understanding the physiological characteristics of psychrophiles which allow them to grow and reproduce at low temperatures has a direct application to the frozen food industry and to the low temperature storage of human cells for medical purposes. Finally, snow microorganisms are interesting to the biologist simply because of their ability to survive in an austere environment. And the beauty of the environment makes the study of this much neglected group of microorganisms even more rewarding.

53

The Seashore: Wilderness Between the Tides

TODD NEWBERRY

1967

In the early years, as we have noted, the Sierra Club was concerned almost exclusively with the Sierra itself. When its interests broadened, they extended first to other mountain areas—the Cascades, the Rockies, the Appalachians. It has only been in recent years that other types of wilderness—and areas other than wilderness—have come into the club's official purview.

It seems odd that, although most of the club's members live in coastal cities, there was so little early attention to preserving the coastline. But that oversight has been remedied in recent years by increasing numbers of shoreline outings and tidepool explorations. Whole new worlds have thus been revealed, as biologist Todd New-berry of the University of California at Santa Cruz made clear in this article. Since the article was written, new federal and state laws have been enacted for coastal protection. One of the most noteworthy, and one in which the club played a major role, has been California's Coastal Plan, which creates a "constitution" for shoreline planning and sets up strong means of enforcement. This Bill of Rights for the creatures Newberry describes provides a heartening postscript to his article; his "awakening of improbable proportions" is evidently taking place.

THE SIERRA CLUB admonishes us against "blind opposition to progress" and urges us to explore and judge reasoned arguments for and against the conservation of our natural heritage. America's seacoast is a part of this heritage, yet our protection of it is a challenge that often evokes more visceral sympathy than reasoned understanding. This understanding can grow out of the sympathy only as we become more knowledgeable about what it is we are trying to protect. In view of this, I would like to suggest some aspects of the seashore—and, by implication, of its conservation—that are especially cogent to my perspective as a marine zoologist. Hopefully, this will stimulate others, as well, to write from their acquaintance with our coasts. For a thoughtful conversation about the general prospects of seashore protection is long overdue, and many of us consequently have been hard-put to fathom the issues of this complicated matter beyond the pros and cons of specific and local controversies.

We can begin by making some rather obvious observations about the seashore—but then take them further or look at them differently than we usually do. We shall restrict our attention to the intertidal region of the seashore, to the zone that is covered at the highest high tides and uncovered at the lowest lows. This encompasses some eight vertical feet along cliffs in central California, while on beaches and mud-flats the zone may stretch horizontally over a belt many yards wide before this vertical difference of eight feet is included.

This intertidal region is at once the edge both of the sea and of the land. But when we go tidepooling, we feel far more that we are venturing onto the periodically exposed bottom of the sea than onto some periodically submerged surface of the land. This sensation seems to arise largely from the living things around us there. The familiar animals and plants of dry land stop rather abruptly at the uppermost reaches of the surf, sometimes a good many feet above the water on exposed coasts. From there down to where the sand and rocks are permanently covered by water, what we encounter are marine beings, not terrestrial ones, and marine animals often are bizarre to our eyes. Why should marine animals seem so strange to us? One sure reason lies in our unfamiliarity with many groups of marine animals that are rarely or never found on land. A little arithmetic quickly bears this out. When we categorize the world of animals into its major groups—for example, into arthropods, molluscs, annelids, vertebrates, flatworms, sponges, and so forth—we thereby devise about 27 such major groups, or phyla. Surveying the distribution of representatives of these phyla in the sea, in fresh water, and on land, we find a very unbalanced picture. All but one or two of the 27 phyla are found at least in part in the sea, 17 of the 27 nearly or quite completely so. And the dominantly or wholly marine assemblages include some large and conspicuous animals: the echinoderms, such as the seastars and sea urchins; most coelenterates, such as the anemones and jellyfish and colonial hydroids; the sea-squirts or tunicates; most sponges; most moss animals or bryozoans, just to mention a few. In contrast, only five phyla have representatives that we would expect to find with any frequency on dry land in these latitudes: arthropods, annelids, vertebrates, molluscs, and roundworms. Consequently, despite the overwhelming *superficial* diversity of animals on dry land, especially of insects, we encounter a very restricted range of *basic* varieties around us. We are, in a way, protected from zoological unfamiliarity by this conservative range of basic animal types. But at the seashore we suddenly confront a panorama of other phyla, often in great abundance. So it is no wonder that we feel in unfamiliar surroundings, for much of the seashore's living element is basically, not just superficially, beyond our usual acquaintance.

The unfamiliarity of what we encounter in the intertidal zone goes beyond the anatomy of its inhabitants to include, as well, the ways in which they make their living; that is, how they gain food and protection and reproductive success. Taking feeding as an example, we see right away that land animals are forced to go to their food—to catch it, crop it, search for it actively—in order to eat. Thus, the cat goes to the mouse, the horse to grass, the bird to the worm. We do not find many instances (aside from parasites) where food goes to the feeder. This need to move in order to feed is so commonplace that many people even characterize animals by this capacity of

Wilderness explorers.

movement itself: "Animals move, plants don't." Why should this be so? One reason is that, were food carried to the feeder, air would have to carry it, and air is simply not dense enough to carry much for long in suspension.

In the ocean and in its intertidal fringe a very different situation exists. There, the counterpart of our air is water; and moving water can carry very large amounts of substantial particulate matter for virtually indefinite lengths of time. As a result, the sea carries enormous quantities of food in suspension, both in the form of planktonic floating life and in the form of detritus, life's debris. Many bottom-dwelling animals in the sea simply rest in place and, by means of diverse and elaborate filters, strain the water around them for this food. A tremendous abundance of animals that we encounter intertidally—such as sponges, barnacles, bryozoans, many worms, and tunicates—spend the great bulk of their lives firmly attached to the substrate, as sessile as plants, admirably adapted to feeding this way. In fact, once we get over our initial fixation on familiarly free-moving animals (such as crabs) in the intertidal region, we notice that great numbers of the animals around us are either attached or planktonic—in other words, are living in ways that find no animal counterpart on dry land.

This leads us to the sobering realization that, insofar as we cut ourselves off from the seashore or overrun it with our essentially terrestrial influences, we impoverish our range of experience with the diversity of the living world in basic, not just superficial, ways. We cut ourselves off not only from encountering a large variety of living things, but also, perhaps most strikingly, from experiencing the extraordinary range of ways that lives are led in the natural world. We cut ourselves off a little more from finding astonishment in the world around us.

The seashore, then, is unparalleled in the diversity both of the animals that live there and of the ways they live. It is also unique in being a zone of dramatic transition and conflict between the ocean on one side and the land on the other. Again, an obvious fact—but perhaps so obvious that we do not usually recognize some of its significant implications. We have already seen that the living organisms of the intertidal seashore are more part of the sea than of the land. But they endure conditions of life that are neither wholly marine nor wholly terrestrial. For example, while we associate waves with the sea, waves are relatively unimportant to most animals out in the open sea. Waves take on enormous significance, though, where they become surf, a phenomenon restricted largely to the shore. In contrast to the usually gently rocking movements of waves at sea, surf generates ceaseless scouring, cannon-like blasts, shearing, sedimentation, and incessant stress. Along our Pacific coast the energy of the breaking waves has accumulated over a fetch of thousands of miles and is utterly expended in a matter of yards amidst extraordinary violence. The often exquisitely delicate animals that live in this maelstrom thus face conditions that are clearly not terrestrial in character yet substantially different, too, from the open sea.

Periodic exposure and submersion by the tides is another condition unique to the intertidal environment. This tidal rhythm, inconsequential on land or

202

at sea, dominates the ecology of the intertidal zone. Consider, for instance, the lot of an anemone attached to a mid-tidal rock. It is exposed beneath the water to the rigors of the surf, to the physiological demands of life immersed in the medium of sea water, and to a marine set of predators, amidst all of which it must carry on its activities of feeding and reproduction. With the ebb of the tide, it is exposed to air—to drying out; to overheating or chilling; to winds; to the fresh-water of rain; and now to a whole new set of predators, this time terrestrial (birds, insects, rodents, people). Then, perhaps with a severe shock, the flooding tide sweeps the sea over the animal again. As if this were not enough, the 25-hour tidal cycle combines in continual variation with the 24-hour day-night one, with the monthly lunar cycle of spring and neap tides, with solar cycles that add their own substantial influence to tidal fluctuations, and with the seasonal cycles. The resultant interplay of rhythms is such that intertidal organisms are exposed to their environment in almost every possible combination of conditions. Neither in the open sea nor on dry land is the rhythmic interaction of dominant environmental forces so remarkably complicated. In this respect, too, the intertidal seashore is actually a linear realm *between* sea and land.

Consequently, to the extent that we destroy this linear realm, we wipe out the possibility of our knowing not just the fringe of something but rather the whole of it. If this unique belt, often only a few yards across, is overwhelmed by construction or polluted or chopped to pieces or filled by dumping, we have not just encroached on the seashore, we have destroyed the whole thing. It simply has no room for give in the face of such misuse.

The intertidal region holds not only unique and unfamiliar treasures but also tremendous variety within its limited expanse. But surveying the intertidal zone from six feet up (in other words, walking about and looking down at it) is rather like looking at the earth from an airplane and reveals roughly the same relative detail. Only by coming down out of the skies—by crouching or crawling or sprawling to get our eyes and ears and noses into the intertidal zone, too, along with our feet—do we really join the seashore world. When we do this, we quickly learn that, like a great city, a seashore is made up of neighborhoods, each with its own distinctive traits and peculiarities, each with a recognizable life of its own as well as a place in the life of the whole. But by and large, these intertidal neighborhoods are cryptic, hidden ones. Their real spectacles are under boulders, inside grottoes, beneath ledges, tucked away from drying, from too much sun, from wind, from the full force of the surf, from the rain of sediments or of fresh-water— and from the view of people standing above them.

Such explorations reveal that conditions of life in one grotto are not quite like those in the next, nor is either pocket like an adjacent exposed surface or a nearby patch of sand. The actual activities of the shore, the ways in which the organisms confront and interact with their surroundings, are everywhere fragmented and diversified into neighborhoods, into microhabitats. This awareness deepens the fascination of the seashore as it draws us on to compare such microhabitats and to try to discern and comprehend the ways in which they differ. Superficially (but deceptively) this seems a rather simple enterprise, but it is the sure route to the frontiers of understanding and into the wilderness beyond.

But close acquaintance is bound to impress the visitor with the vulnerability of the seashore, too. Despite its endurance of the rigorous consequences of surf and tidal rhythms, the intertidal seashore is a delicate place, as sensitive as an alpine meadow to unnatural disruptions. One of the most common agents of disruption and destruction is the visitor who rolls rocks over, to see the marvels underneath, but does not roll these rocks back carefully into their original positions. By our analogy of the city, this disruption would be virtually tantamount to bombing neighborhoods. It results in shifting to upper surfaces those organisms that need the protection of undersurfaces to survive, and in casting underneath boulders those species that are adapted to conditions atop them. Whole microhabitats are turned topsy-turvy, and it is no wonder that they are destroyed as effectively as they are. Rocks that are rolled back carelessly may be almost as badly scarred by consequent instability in the face of surf, changed circulation of water, and suddenly altered patterns of biotic interactions. So a lot of damage is done to the intertidal region by people who do not realize that they are merely intruders into a region that has no real place for them and suffers, often drastically, from every human touch.

Seashore life is also jeopardized by being so often within reach of visitors. It is thereby exposed to the inexplicable greed of people who feel compelled to make a trophy of whatever interests them. In an earlier era, we could all collect our share of curiosities at the shore. But now virtual armies of adults and children are beginning to devastate regions in the name of education or intellectual stimulation or sport. The fate of their collections is almost always the garbage can, about as unfortunate and useless and absurd a fate as an intertidal animal can possibly have. The resulting destruction of the seashore makes some sort of restriction on this pillaging already well overdue. In fact, we already have some collecting laws on the books. But the impossibility of their enforcement, as well as the pressures of well-meaning people who have just not thought the matter through, eventually will seal the fate of some rich and biologically magnificent parts of our shoreline.

The seashore is vulnerable to more than the depredations of individual visitors. Its historic use for commerce imposes another whole order of disruptions. By this I do not mean the appalling ravages of commercial exploitation that abound above the high tide line. Rather, I refer to the effects of commerce that reach below high tide. Necessary though it usually is, commercial development has almost totally destroyed California's natural quiet-water seashores, usually converting them into marinas, harbors, factory and power-plant sites, and other such facilities. Intertidal mud-flats, for example, have been frequent victims of this "progress." True, mud-flats are not especially pretty and they often smell bad. Consequently, it is hard to find friends for them. The recent controversy over an oil refinery's proposed installation at Moss Landing, for example, focused on many issues, but not on the fate of the mud-flats there. Yet these mud-flats are the last of any extent in the entire stretch of coast from San Francisco to Morro Bay. For all their lowly appearance, they are as unique a natural habitat as a desert gorge, a cascade, or a coastal promontory. And when they are gone from Moss Landing, the loss will be as complete as would be the loss of all the alpine meadows or cattail marshes — or even redwood forests — over a major extent of the state. Again, by our own actions, we hem ourselves into a narrower world of natural experiences.

Finally, the seashore is vulnerable to the time-honored assumption that the sea is a safe and stable place for all the pollutants that are too noxious or, worse, too dangerous for disposal on land. It is certainly not a stable realm, for currents of enormous dimensions churn the sea throughout its depths. And it consequently is not a safe place to dump any materials that remain dangerous while they are borne far and wide, as they will be by these oceanic currents. Yet we witness the dumping at sea of sewage, explosives, atomic wastes, factory leavings, and now apparently quantities of pesticide-contaminated irrigation water as a presumably effective way to be rid of them. Particularly in the case of pesticide residues, presumptions of safety have no basis in fact. Sea life is as exposed as the land's to the disruptions of chemical pollution. Pesticides properly used and controlled are essential, but no less poisonous, agents in agricultural management. But pesticides in the sea are as wholly out of control as they are out of place. Organisms concentrate these substances many-fold, despite their dilution in the surrounding water, and doubtless suffer the same results in the sea that they demonstrably do on land. Knowing what we do about the dangers on land of uncontrolled dispersal of pesticides, the idea of spewing these agricultural toxins into our coastal waters, for subsequent general spread along the shore, at first seems too grotesque to be taken seriously. But the funds of ignorance and arrogance that would permit such misuse of our environment are as ample as they are powerful. Consequently, we are likely to sow a whirlwind in this domain — as we have with our fresh-water resources — before good sense intrudes.

As in so many instances of our society's destructiveness, the retort to worried scientists is that science will solve it. Science becomes what the biologist Marston Bates has dubbed "white magic." But it is the scientists who recognize most keenly their simple incapacity to salvage things beyond a limit. So it is often the marine biologist who is most concerned and most pessimistic about the needless and arrogant destruction of our seashore.

What is the outlook? While the characteristic resiliency of the natural world will reward every easing of man's pressures upon the seashore, these pressures themselves are growing. The seashore's prime defense of sheer isolation is now largely gone, and accessible regions find no alternative protection. Perhaps because the intertidal realm does hide its treasures, it most likely will never evoke widespread and sustained public concern about its destruction. Most people will simply never know what they have lost. This destruction would be an immense misfortune. If we are to avoid it, an awakening of improbable proportions will be called for, and soon.

54 # Sea Otters

JUDSON E.

VANDEVERE and

JAMES A.

MATTISON, JR.

1970

Along California's Big Sur coastline, the sea otters stage a delightful show. You can watch the mammals frolicking in the water, floating on their backs, diving for food, holding shellfish in their forepaws, and eating the meal like a human munching corn on the cob.

Vitus Bering, exploring Pacific coastal waters in 1742, was accompanied by naturalist Georg Wilhelm Steller, who was intrigued by the human-like qualities of the sea otters: "They prefer to live together in families. . . . The male caresses the female by stroking her, using the forefeet as hands; she, however, often pushes him away from her for fun and in simulated coyness, as it were, and plays with her offspring like the fondest mother. Their love for the young is so intense that when the young are taken away they cry bitterly, and grieve so much that after ten or fourteen days they grow as lean as skeletons and become sick and feeble and will not leave the shore."

Despite Steller's fondness for the animals, Bering's interest in them was primarily economic. Their fur was soft and thick, ideal for European markets. For decades after Bering's expedition, Russian, British, and American fur-trading ships arrived on the Pacific coast in such numbers that the animals were slaughtered by the thousands. One trading company took home 15,000 pelts in one year—a market value of a million dollars. By the end of the nineteenth century, there were no more to be seen on the California coast. They were believed extinct.

A few had managed to survive along the Big Sur shoreline, and by the late 1930s they had begun to reappear. By that time they were protected by treaty, and the California coast for 100 miles south of Monterey is now a Sea Otter Reserve. The otter population is large enough now that in recent years commercial fishermen have blamed otters for declining shellfish harvests.

Judson E. Vandevere is a marine biologist specializing in the sea otter and Dr. Mattison is an underwater naturalist and photographer. Both are on the Advisory Council of Friends of the Sea Otter, founded by Margaret Owings of Big Sur, who has been a leader in attempts to save the mountain lions, as well.

Since this article was written, the sea otter has been placed on the Federal govern-ment's threatened species list, owing primarily to the danger of lethal oil spills as increasing numbers of tankers from Alaska move down the California coast.

ONLY THIRTY-TWO YEARS after its exciting rediscovery, the rare south-ern sea otter, opening its polluted shellfish with pop bottle, rock, or beer can for tool, is faced with new threats to its survival. In the southern portion of their range otters are not infrequently shot and, in the north, with increasing small craft traffic, more are being fatally injured in boating accidents. Females continue to bear pups within sight of oil tankers whose frequency of passage and potential for spills increase yearly.

Since 1954, the Point Lobos State Reserve, south of Carmel, California, has offered interested observers from all nations some of the finest views of the behavior of sea otters.

Recent observations of mothers with newborn pups reveal a part of the appeal this mammal has for residents of California's Monterey and northern San Luis Obispo counties and for the tourists who flock to the area. The

Sea otter and kelp.

constancy of body contact during early maternal care has been demonstrated for a number of mammals. Sea otters should be the least neurotic of all mammals, for they apparently enjoy the most body contact and early maternal care of any mammal. One mother kept her pup constantly upon her chest and abdomen from sunrise to sunset for three weeks. Occasionally she held the pup by the side of the head and rotated her own body in the water or floated her sleeping baby off her chest and groomed alongside it without awakening it. Frequently during the otter's toilet she would float her baby back onto her chest and then gently re-float it, resuming her grooming without having disturbed the baby. Not once for these three weeks was the nursing mother seen to feed during daylight hours. Each evening, at dusk, she swam on her back, with her pup asleep on her chest, to an in-shore feeding area. On a few occasions, just before darkness, we saw the mother float her pup off her chest and commence her feeding.

Why would a nursing mother forego nourishment during the long day while floating in a 53°F environment? Could she "remember" predation by the bald eagle? Man has essentially spared her from that threat by greatly reducing the number of bald eagles in California. A well-developed pup will dive with its mother finding some of its own food, and occasionally a rock, which it will use as a tool in opening shellfish. Often, when its mother surfaces with a large, tasty object, it will discard its tool and shellfish and rush to its mother who generously hands out large sections of tissue which she has removed from the shell. Occasionally mothers and pups lose track of one another. The worried one begins issuing alarm calls which are soon answered by another.

In March, 1970, as many as 140 otters would rest simultaneously in a kelp bed off Pacific Grove. This "raft" of sea otters constituted the largest group yet observed in modern times in one kelp bed in California. More otters could be seen resting in mid-morning than at any other time of the day as the peak hours for feeding were early morning and late afternoon. In mid-afternoon many of the otters would begin active grooming, rubbing their heads and chests with their paws, rubbing their feet together, rolling in the water, and interacting with each other. They would then move off singly or loosely in two's or three's.

As they left their resting area to forage for food, approximately half of these otters would swim south, the other half swimming north. A similar, almost fifty-fifty division of north and south foraging otters from a resting area off Cambria Radar Station, California, in the southernmost extension of the sea otters' range was also observed. Not all of the otters moved out of the rafting area to feed. Some dove in the bed in which they were resting while others came to shore opposite the resting bed and began foraging close to shore for food items. Some would swim several miles before commencing their feeding bout. However, most otters fed within a half mile of their resting area.

Most food-searching dives require from forty-five seconds to a minute-and-a-half, and although otters generally obtain their food from the bottom,

Sea otter ready for action.

kelp crabs and turban snails are removed from the kelp canopy by otters who forage just beneath the water's surface. When collecting turban snails, as many as ten are pressed down and back against the fur and loose skin of the chest, forming a pouch which secures the snails until they are removed for eating. The temporary chest pouch thus formed is continuous with a pouch formed under the arm for the purpose of securing a rock-tool. While surfacing, the left paw often pushes the rock from the left auxiliary pouch to a position over its left, lower rib cage. The snails are removed one at a time, held between the paws, and with repeated fast arm swings, the shells are cracked; the otter's head being thrown back or turned to one side during the banging.

One otter was observed breaking a bottle open on its rock-anvil and the occupant, a shellfish, consumed. Rocks are also commonly used to open large mussels when they are obtainable. Occasionally an otter may be seen clinging to a mussel bed on a nearly vertical cliff face, having been carried to a high bed on an incoming swell. The otter is then left by the outgoing surge, clinging to a clump of mussels until the force of the next swell assists him in tearing free the gold, byssal hairs by which the mussels adhere to the rock.

During our months of close observation, we have identified 25 food species in the southern sea otter's diet. The red and black abalone are but two of these. However, the otters' consumption of these two species [has resulted in state legislative proposals] to permit the netting of unlimited numbers of otters south of Cambria and north of the Carmel River, California, for the purpose of tagging and removal to scientific institutions, such as Marineland of the Pacific, Sea World and Stanford Research Institute.

The excessive human take of both abalone and spiny lobster near the

209

Channel Islands and in Southern California, where sea otters do not occur, is causing the decline in these fisheries, but the otter is being blamed for it. Also, recent public health awareness of chorinated hydrocarbons (such as DDT) and heavy metals (such as mercury) appearing in many species of marine life has resulted in the suspension of landings in some affected fisheries. Some fisheries are close to collapse because of overfishing and this may well be the plight of the commercial and sport abalone fishery both in and outside of the southern sea otter's range.

Unfortunately, attempts of some commercial and sportmen's groups to encourage legislation that would "manage" the sea otter so as to avoid "resource conflicts" may be unnecessary. On September 24, 1970, three commercial abalone divers were each sentenced to three years probation and $1,000 fines for shooting sea otters. Far more subtle forces than these may threaten the otters' survival. Extremely high cadmium concentrations in their livers and kidneys have prompted us to begin a search for its source. The accumulation of toxic levels of pesticides and other environmental poisons may eventually cause such a reduction in the number of sea otters as to make man's efforts to reduce their numbers seem ludicrous. One of the sea otters killed by the three commercial abalone divers sentenced on September 24 contained thirty-six parts per million total DDT residues in his fat. A food item with seven parts per million total DDT residues is considered unfit for human consumption.

Although the fate of the California brown pelicans is well-known, most readers are unaware of the large numbers of aborted California sea lions that were discovered in May 1970. Karl Kenyon of the Fish and Wildlife Service told us that 1200 parts per million DDT were discovered in one sea lion fetus on San Miguel Island. Concentrations of this magnitude can cause reproductive damage.

In this kind of crisis situation it is extremely unlikely that sport and commercial abalone fishermen will recognize the country's profligate use of dangerous chemicals and their own over-fishing as the real culprits in the decline of their fishery.

If the sea otter can overcome the effects of environmental degradation and the threat of the abalone fishermen, this remarkable animal has something to offer man besides being one of the more photogenic members of the animal kingdom. This pitiful remnant of a once abundant population actually adds to our marine resources by reducing sea urchin populations, thereby enhancing kelp growth which in turn supports rock fish nurseries. Also, lush kelp beds permit harvest by the kelp industry which makes a far greater contribution to the world's economy than does the abalone industry. Significant users of kelp colloids include the beer, ice cream, dairy, textile, cosmetic, pharmaceutical, paper and paperboard industries.

But the sea otter's right to existence should not be dependent on his usefulness in relation to man's activities. As a life species on earth, he should be subject primarily to natural law, and not the whims of a consumer, or an abalone fisherman, or a fur hunter.

55

Puma

J. LLOYD CAHILL

1971

By whatever name it might be called, mountain lion, cougar, puma, this member of the cat family plays an essential role in the chain of life. Perhaps it was in recognition of this fact that most states removed bounties on the animals in the 1960s —but puma can still be legally hunted. And it is much easier to kill one now than it once was, as a University of California zoologist notes here.

THE MOUNTAIN LION is a large cat with the characteristic grace and beauty of his family. Tawny or ferruginous to gray in coloration, males range in weight from 145 to 225 pounds or more while females are considerably lighter at 80 to 135 pounds. The apotheosis of American carnivores, the cougar's strength and agility are legendary. Exceeded in size only by the jaguar among the 12 species of wild felids in the Western Hemisphere, he has proven more than the equal of even the grizzly bear in staged combat. Ernest Thompson Seton has said, "of all the beasts that roam America's woods the cougar is the big-game hunter without peer." Typically feline, the mountain lion has an extraordinarily fast muscle-reaction time which, coupled with his great strength, gives him the power to high-jump at least 14 feet and broad-jump more than 40 feet as reported by reputable observers. Cougars can kill and drag away animals weighing more than 750 pounds, yet they are of negligible danger to man. Even 75 years ago when mountain lions—or "pumas" as the ancient Peruvians called them—were apparently more numerous than they are now, attacks on humans were almost unheard of. Indeed, the cougar was revered rather than feared by the early inhabitants of Lower California. Whenever discovered, the animal's unconsumed prey had, for centuries, formed a part of the annual subsistence of the Indians of that region.

The puma had the largest range of any native mammal in the Americas, occurring from northern British Columbia through Middle and South America to Patagonia—a total of more than 100° of latitude. Records exist of the cougar's former presence in every state except Indiana and Alaska and from the east to west coasts of Canada, with the possible exception of the province of Manitoba. It is likely that it inhabited every part of the United States in which cover and a "year-round" food supply could be found, from sea level to the higher mountain slopes. In South America it occurs in dense tropical jungles and has been recorded above 15,500 feet in the Andes. Originally abundant on both continents, it was being bountied in South America in the last century and was classified an outlaw and shot, trapped, and sometimes poisoned in North America for more than 300 years. Currently restricted, in much reduced numbers, to 12 western states, British Columbia, Alberta, New Brunswick and Florida, with very infrequent sightings in the Midwest and South in the last decade, the cougar's position is still not secure.

The Bureau of Sport Fisheries and Wildlife Committee on Rare and Endangered Wildlife considers rare any species or subspecies that "although not presently threatened with extinction is in such small numbers throughout its range that it may be endangered if its environment worsens." As human population increases in the West, it seems likely that the cougar's environment will worsen, and that through habitat loss and overexploitation it may shortly, if not already, be endangered.

Numerous virtually inaccessible and seldom frequented mountainous regions as well as broad expanses of high desert and rimrock permitted the cougar to survive in the western United States despite callous and thoughtless persecution. Judging from the available literature, the frontiersman almost always attempted to kill the big cat wherever he found him. Later, the cattlemen and sheepmen attempted eradication but, finding the cost high, sought and obtained governmental assistance with public funding. In part because of our cultural denunciation of nearly all carnivores and partly because a cougar does occasionally kill a cow or sheep, the species has been, and in regions of some states still is, the object of a vindictive extermination campaign.

Cahill says that bounties were used in Western States in an effort to eradicate the lions. Between 1947 and 1969, 5,454 lions were reported killed in Arizona, and $350,685 in bounties paid out.

Imprecations were flung at the entire species because of the stock-killing of a few individuals. The first reasonable study of mountain lion food habits was in fact prompted by the observation that cougars often passed by easily procurable horses and cattle in order to capture more difficult deer. F. C. Hibben in 1937 reported checking 32 claims by ranchers of stock loss to cougars in New Mexico and finding 30 of them false. The ubiquitous deer is the mainstay of the puma's diet across the continent, with partial substitution of elk, porcupines, rabbits and miscellaneous other creatures in certain regions. The well-known Jawbone deer herd study on the west slope of the Sierra Nevada showed an annual net increase in the herd of 32% with 23% of that lost to starvation, 7% to hunters and 2% to predators. The annual increase could not be supported by the habitat and the 23% lost to starvation could have been removed by predation—to the benefit of the survivors. Although D. D. McLean of the California Department of Fish and Game stated in 1954 "it should not be a policy to eliminate mountain lions from any area entirely unless a sudden rise in deer population is desired," the bounty approach to lion management continued. He cites the rapid increase in the deer populations in Santa Clara County, California after the killing of

22 lions in a 550 square mile area of the Mt. Hamilton Range between March 1934 and March 1936. By 1940 deer were spreading into the agricultural area of the county "and feeding on vineyards, orchards and other crops. By 1941, disease became active in high deer population and by 1944, deer numbers reached a low of probably not over 40 per cent of the total of 1939 or 1940."

In many of the Western states, bounties were finally discontinued in the '70s. But the effort to eradicate lions was not finished.

Despite the esteemed position in which the mountain lion is held by many, political expediency caused those who did not favor lion hunting to seek game classification as a substitute for a complete lack of protection. Protected status was in most instances opposed by cattlemen, sheepmen and, more often than not, hunters in general. Although there have been no complaints of mountain lion depredations filed with the Division of Wildlife Services in California for more than two and one-half years, livestock associations and their representatives apparently still oppose protected classification for the puma. The Fish and Game Department is also opposed, even though only a tiny fraction of the hunting fraternity—let alone the general public—hunts lions. Some departments of fish and game have stated no desire to maintain abundant cougar populations and consider legalized hunting (at a fee) a form of control. One wonders if our resource managers realize that, in the words of A. Starker Leopold, "for every deer hunter there is a mountain hiker for whom the track of a lion would be the high spot of a summer's adventure."

Mountain lion, western U.S.A.

213

Although elevation of the cougar from "varmint" to "big game" status makes management possible, no department of fish and game has the necessary biological information to properly do so. Assuming that sport hunting of lions is a wise use of a very limited resource, those invested with the responsibility of husbandry should have, at the outset, objective data on numbers as well as age and sex compositions of populations within the management areas. In addition to periodic censusing, population trends indicated by natality and mortality should be continually monitored. Wildlife managers should only permit a certain kill based on a knowledge of lion abundance. Present procedure is usually to estimate lion abundance on the basis of the number killed. Since cougar kittens spend about 2 years with their mothers learning the skills of stalk-and-pounce predators, killing an adult female may mean death for from one to six young also. Local seasons, based on a knowledge of maximum littering times in various regions, would give females with recently born young some leisure. Since a few hunters with dogs can eliminate the territorial lion over hundreds of square miles in a single winter, the number of hunters in an area and the number of cougars they may take must be restricted. No lion hunting should be permitted at any time of year in appropriate zones around National or State Parks or Monuments which serve as winter range for the cougar's prey. Each state should have a lion study area. Current "management," not based on informaton derived from research, is unwise and argues strongly for completely closed seasons in many states until adequate data are available.

Seventy years ago, mountain lion hunting in the western United States was a vigorous enterprise demanding a rugged constitution and often requiring skillful horsemanship. Today, lion hunters normally drive sandy or snow-covered back country roads until cougar tracks are found. The hounds are then loosed and, baying vociferously, they trail the cougar until it climbs a tree. The hunters may then walk to the base of the cougar's refuge and shoot the large, usually immobile target. Some guides advertise guaranteed hunts — and may then release a captive lion to be shot by a client only recently out of his business suit. But the cougar's aesthetic value to society must surely rank him with the bald eagle and sea otter among our most treasured forms of wildlife.

56

Native Mollusks: Little Known and Little Loved

BARRY ROTH

1972

Issue a call to save the redwoods or save the condors or save the whooping cranes, and increasing numbers of Americans will flock to the cause and donate time and money. But raise the cry "save the snails" and you are likely to elicit guffaws from the public and trenchant barbs from satirists who are ready to ridicule all efforts to preserve unloved species as the demented activity of little old ladies in tennis shoes.

Nevertheless, even those lowliest of creatures cannot escape the attention of conservationists. Biologist Barry Roth's concern here is not with the common garden pests, or with escargots, *but with the snails that are part of natural ecosystems. And as conservation broadens from concern with particular species to concern with ecosystems —and with the global ecosystem known as the biosphere —we are likely to find that any animal or plant has its place in the chain of life and the "balance" of nature and is worthy of respect and consideration. In their rightful place, snails, too, can be beautiful.*

ROLL OVER AN OAK LOG in the limestone belt of the central Sierra Nevada, between Tuolumne and San Andreas. Or poke in the humus under a salmonberry thicket on the California north coast. If the season is right, temperature and moisture conditions correct, you may find, clinging to the decaying bark or nestled among the leaf litter, one of the country's silent, aboriginal residents; a native snail.

This discovery may or may not excite you. Most people think of snails as garden pests, unpleasant creatures to be squashed underfoot or killed with snail bait; and it is true that certain snails and their shell-less cousins, slugs, do thousands of dollars' damage annually to crops and gardens. Less commonly known is the fact that virtually all commercially important snail and slug pests are *introduced* species —kinds which naturally inhabit other parts of the globe but have hitchhiked here, generally unnoticed at first, with the comings and goings of man. This is a continuing process, and potentially troublesome species are still intercepted regularly by inspection and quarantine officers.

Far less familiar is the large and diverse fauna of mollusks native to North

America (*Mollusca* being the great phylum of animals which includes snails, slugs, clams and squid). Each climate-zone and floristic province is inhabited by a characteristic group of mollusks. In the rivers, lakes and streams, particularly those of the eastern half of the continent, live roughly half the known species of river snails and half the known species of naiads (freshwater clams) in the world. Popular opinion correctly associates snails and slugs with damp, shady places; but the deserts of the western United States support a unique and highly interesting snail fauna. Some of the desert species live in a state of suspended animation for most of the year, becoming active only during the brief seasonal periods of rainfall and subsequently raised humidity. They are of interest also as "relict" species—the scattered survivors of more favorable conditions in geologic ages past. Between the extremes of desert and boreal zones live most of the North American native mollusks, some species ranging over considerable distances, others narrowly restricted.

In contrast to the introduced mollusk pests, the native varieties do practically no damage to cultivated plants. Conversion of land to agricultural use, in fact, is likely to eliminate them from a district. Having evolved in natural, undisturbed habitats, they prefer, and generally require, the specific combination of environmental factors which only an undisturbed biotic community provides. The delicate and beautiful snail, *Helminthoglypta allynsmithi,* for instance, has been found only in a few mossy rockslides in the canyon of the Merced River below Yosemite National Park. It occurs there because the particular combination of shade and exposure, temperature, moisture, soil chemistry, and vegetation is to its liking. The choice rockslides are "islands" in the midst of territory which, at least under present climatic conditions, is uninhabitable to the species; and the snail does not have the ability to pack up and migrate to other places which might be suitable—even if these do exist, some miles away. Obviously, construction of a highway through the rockslides, or quarrying for their stone, would work great hardship on *Helminthoglypta allynsmithi,* and probably bring about its extinction.

It is fortunate for most native snails that they do go generally unnoticed. Pressure from amateur herpetologists has brought many similarly narrow-ranging reptiles and amphibians to the brink of extinction. A few species of snails which, because of their attractive coloring and form, have attracted the attention of hobbyists, have been nearly wiped out by intemperate collecting.

As the speed with which man changes the American landscape increases, simply noting the presence and location of certain rare or narrowly endemic species of mollusks will not be enough to save them from extinction. A case in point is that of the freshwater clams, or naiads, which at one time existed in great numbers and variety in the waters of the Mississippi and southeast coastal drainages. These were discovered by pioneer naturalists and thoroughly described and named, their ranges for the most part well charted. In these areas, man has worked such great changes on the habitats that from 40 to 50 percent of the naiad species living in those streams and rivers are considered in imminent danger of extinction. Dr. David H. Stansbery, a malacologist at the Ohio State University Museum of Zoology, has summarized the processes at work here in the following account:

> With the initial clearing of the forests and tilling of the soil great quantities of humus-rich topsoil were washed into our streams. This loss to early agriculture was also a loss to stream life through a reduction of dissolved oxygen and an increase in organic acids. The removal of topsoil decreased the ability of the land to hold water, hence producing greater floods in the wet seasons and dryer droughts in the dry part of the cycle. . . .
>
> The fine silts and clays which followed the topsoil into our streams may well have had a smothering effect on some species by the simple effect of clogging of gills. . . . In the early days the rivers were commonly the direct recipients of lumbermill sawdust, brewery slops, and slaughterhouse refuse. With the coming of community sewage systems, raw domestic sewage was added without benefit of treatment. The discovery of new energy resources in the form of coal and petroleum led directly to an upsurge of technology and a mushrooming of industry. Not only did the mining and drilling operations add new pollutants in increasing amounts to our waters but the industries they supported contributed a whole new spectrum of soluble and insoluble wastes to our already overloaded rivers.
>
> The advent of the chemical pesticide industry over the past 20 years has given additional cause for concern since the bulk of most of these toxins are washed into our streams.

A natural watercourse is a complex system, fostering varied habitats and supporting a diverse fauna. Stream channelization and damming simplify the pattern, reducing some habitats and eliminating others outright. Thus fewer species of animals can survive. Commerce has taken its toll of the naiads too; from the 1890's until after World War II they were harvested for the production of pearl buttons. More recently, pellets cut from their shells have been used as nuclei of cultured pearls. Placed in the tissues of a Japanese pearl oyster, the pellet accumulates a coating of pearl. Capture of naiads for this purpose has depleted one species after another.

No mollusk of North America has yet appeared on the Department of the Interior's official Endangered Species roster—in fact, no American invertebrate of any kind is listed. But many species, both terrestrial and freshwater, are as definitely endangered as the more publicized California Condor or Trumpeter Swan. A recent tabulation listed 11 naiad species known to be extinct, and 213 species of freshwater mollusks considered "rare and endangered." Of these latter species, 82 are snails and 131 are clams. A study sponsored by the Sierra Club Foundation turned up 127 species of terrestrial snails and slugs in California which also can claim the dubious distinction of being "rare and endangered."

Until recently, mollusks, and invertebrates in general, have been animals without advocates. They have, however, had their enemies, both in the field and in the lobbies—if not the actual halls—of government. The exclusion of the entire class Insecta from the Endangered Species Conservation Act of

1969 can probably be laid to pressure from the pesticide industry, which did not want the responsibility for vanishing species of butterfly laid on its carpet. Mollusks, however, are specifically included in the act, and the Office of Endangered Species and International Activities of the U.S. Fish and Wildlife Service, with the assistance of the American Malacological Union, is maintaining a tentative list of endangered native mollusks. With interest rising in the preservation of ecosystems — rather than just the management of conspicuous species of animals — this list is sure to be enlarged. . . .

A new concept of sanctuary, if it were to gain official acceptance, would help the picture. Land set aside as ecological reserves can sustain the native mollusks living there. Designation of molluscan habitats as ordinary game refuges or public recreational areas will not suffice. The management of marshland for the benefit of waterfowl, as in one instance uncovered by the Sierra Club Foundation study, may as a side effect exterminate terrestrial mollusks originally living in the area. Several species of rare snails, considered during the same study, inhabit national parks and monuments; but the needs of a snail, and of a natural biotic community, are different from those of a game animal alone, or of a vacationer, and a different sort of refuge is required.

The story of man's alteration of the landscape is largely a story of simplification and the loss of diversity. Mollusks have been on the earth for 600 million years. Major groups of North American land snails have been present on the continent at least since the Upper Cretaceous period, some 80 million years ago. During their stay they have diversified and proliferated to occupy the various habitats open to them — from hardwood groves in Florida to high-altitude forests in the mountain states and the arid mountain ranges of the Mojave and Colorado deserts. The combination of ecological factors which enables a given species to inhabit a given place usually represents a delicate balance. The ecologist Kenneth E. F. Watt has recently written, "An argument for preserving anything, particularly something rare, often turns out to be an argument in disguise for diversity." The argument for preservation of our mollusk fauna is a perfect example. And in the case of mollusks, preservation means not merely leaving them alone, but arresting the processes which cause deterioration of their habitat. In saving snails, slugs and clams, we shall be saving a good many other things, too, not the least of which may be the vital diversity of the natural world.

57

The Rings of Life

GALEN ROWELL

1974

Until twenty years ago, the bristlecone pine was a little known tree battling for survival on the arid summits of mountain ranges in the Great Basin. Now, study of the rings of the tree has revealed not only that it is the oldest living thing yet discovered, but has caused the history of Stonehenge and other megaliths in western Europe to be rewritten.

Galen Rowell is a free-lance writer and veteran mountaineer.

A GUST OF WIND brightened the campfire as two men warmed themselves high in a remote California mountain range. They were above 10,000 feet, where the air that rose hot from the desert floor blew cool and clear on a September evening. One man pulled a brand from the fire and examined it closely. "1277 to 1283 A.D.," he said with assurance. "This six-year ring pattern never repeats itself."

When Edmund Schulman finished studying the flame-blackened ring pattern, he tossed the wood back into the fire. It burned hot and even and long.

Schulman was in the process of proving that bristlecone pines were the oldest living things. He already believed it, but proving the age of trees is far harder than just counting rings. Intensive statistical correlation must establish the ring-producing tendencies of a certain species in a certain location before the number of rings can be interpreted into years of growth. Some trees commonly grow multiple rings in wet seasons; others miss rings in dry years. Schulman's book, *Dendroclimatic Changes in Semiarid America,* is a maze of graphs and statistics. Like nails to a carpenter, these were the tools of his trade.

While most foresters contemplated long lives dealing with third and fourth growths of a "renewable resource," Schulman dealt with trees already more than 1,000 years old when King Tut ruled Egypt. His poor health magnified this contrast. Although only in his forties, his bad heart made him realize that his own life might not be very long. The high mountain home of the bristlecone, with its steep terrain and thin air, was among the worst places for his health, yet year after year he persisted in his research.

Schulman was basically a practical, scientific man. Perhaps his fascination with the "Methuselahs," as he came to call the oldest trees, was the contrast between their longevity and his own tenuous claim on life. Perhaps, like all of us, his mind occasionally wandered in an unstructured, mystical, superstitious fashion. Whatever the emotional trigger, he gradually restated the goals of his bristlecone research, depending on his audience and the evolution of his thought. For the scientific journals he wrote that the primary goal of tree-ring research was the record of rainfall and temperature in times before man recorded such things. For a more popular magazine he said, "The capacity of these trees to live so fantastically long may . . . serve as a guidepost on the road to understanding longevity in general."

Weeks before these words appeared in the March, 1958, issue of *National Geographic*, Schulman died of a heart attack. One of his friends is convinced that behind the facade of a dedicated researcher was a doomed man hunting for an elixir. Like Ponce de Leon, he never found his fountain of youth.

Appearing in the same magazine and during the same decade as an article conferring the title "Oldest Living Things" on the giant sequoia, the bristlecone story brought world attention both to Schulman and the trees. In April of that year the U.S. Forest Service established 28,000 acres of the White Mountains as the Ancient Bristlecone Pine Forest Botanical Area, naming the area with the oldest trees, "Schulman Memorial Grove."

Like Schulman, I too have warmed my hands over the hot, even coals of bristlecone wood in more than one Great Basin mountain range. Since the days of prehistory, man has used trees for tools, weapons, shelters, and fires. Bristlecones have not escaped this use. Power poles on the road to Goldfield, Nevada, were originally made of bristlecone, as were poles on the powerline to the Barcroft Laboratory at 12,500 feet in the White Mountains. Forest Service signs, a cross in a Bishop, California, church, and the firewood in many local homes were all bristlecone. A basic dilemma exists when modern man comes in contact with bristlecone: the idea that wood is useful and ornamental versus the inescapable conclusion of any sensitive individual who walks through a grove of bristlecone that there is something very special about these twisted trees. On a mountain pack trip more than 20 years ago, my mother jotted down these words:

"Why is the ugly in Nature so beautiful? Why do we notice and reverence the jagged, rocky, forbidding peaks more than the smooth symmetrical ones? Why do we carry in our minds the picture of the knotted, twisted tree, or the dead tree hit by lightning and forget the sedate, proper trees that have grown according to pattern?"

Why indeed? Why should bristlecone become protected with the reverence of the Lincoln Memorial while coast redwoods are being clearcut to the very boundaries of Redwood National Park?

Bristlecones are a very rare combination. They combine scientific evidence of age and climate with a mystical appreciation for their form. The Governor of California may have gotten away in some circles with saying, "If you've seen one redwood, you've seen them all," but he could never say that about bristlecone pine. Each tree is unique, both in its scientific and spiritual importance. . . .

Should age, and age alone, give bristlecone protection over other timberline species? Logically not. We have only to view the way the human race treats the aged of its own kind to appreciate that the mere factor of age could not protect the bristlecone pine. Perhaps this is why legal protection has not worked perfectly. The exact location of the Oldest Living Thing By Default, the 4,600-year-old Methuselah Tree in the White Mountains, is kept a secret for fear that tourists will desecrate it or carry off souvenirs.

Charles W. Ferguson, a successor of Schulman, decries the loss of dead bristlecone wood. In an article in *Science* he wrote:

The beautiful sculpturing of the bristlecone wood makes it particularly desirable, and even in areas where collecting is restricted, wood is still disappearing. In our research in the White Mountains and other bristlecone areas, we have noted that the more accessible the area is, the less wood on the ground and the more saw cuts there are on trees. As a dendrochronologist, therefore, I must compete with the public for my basic research material: a small, often quite attractive piece of wood that may hold the solution to a dendrochronological problem may become someone's personal memento.

Even Schulman, who dreamed of elixirs and clues to longevity, would not have predicted the far-reaching effects of his bristlecone chronology. For many years, tree-ring dating was primarily an archeological tool for dating timbers from sites in the American Southwest. Then it became accepted as a scientific tool for understanding world climate before man kept records. It gained popular acclaim for pointing out the locations of the oldest living things. Eventually it ran headlong against the scientifically accepted carbon-14 dating system—and won. But as the story of bristlecone and radio-carbon unfolds, it returns to archeology, where the twisted trees in the Great Basin ranges have brought about a revolution in Old World prehistory. The previously accepted theory of cultural diffusion, which explained that culture in early Europe spread from prior civilizations in Egypt and Mesopotamia, has now had its complex chronology reassembled. Bristlecone-corrected carbon-14 datings now show that many aspects of European culture are actually older than their assumed Mediterranean progenitors.

It has been but a single century since the theory of evolution altered the framework of biological and social sciences—a change that is still incomplete. Modern archeological theories tracing European cultures to Egypt and Mesopotamia are, in part, vestigial conglomerates held together by a cement of Judeo-Christian beliefs. Because of their own culture, early scientists unconsciously stacked evidence behind the remnants of their biblical heritage, guessing at dates to order the spread of civilization in Europe. When carbon-14 dating came on the scene in 1949, it was little used by Egyptologists. They already had a highly functional ancient calendar derived from the written records of astronomical events. This record took them to 1900 B.C., beyond which they depended on the "king lists," which did not include astronomical events. Carbon 14 was used extensively for dating European artifacts of the Neolithic period. By coincidence, C-14 did little to upset the theory of cultural diffusion. Only a few discrepancies were found, and their sharp edges were rounded off to make them fit the overall pattern.

221

A skirmish developed between the C-14 physicists and the Egyptologists. Datings agreed reasonably closely until 1500 B.C., beyond which the physicists claimed that the Egyptian calendars read too old. By 3000 B.C. the discrepancy was on the order of five centuries. Tree-ring researchers in the United States had noticed similar discrepancies in C-14 datings of bristlecones, but there were very few 4,000-year-old living trees. Mainly through the research of Charles W. Ferguson and the University of Arizona Laboratory of Tree-Ring Research, an absolute chronology of more than 8,000 years was developed for bristlecone. This was accomplished by cross-dating the ring patterns of dead wood with those of established age in live wood, often using computers to match the complex patterns.

Science has now accepted the bristlecone-corrected radiocarbon clock. Bristlecone research indicates that the production of C-14 in the atmosphere has not been constant. The corrected C-14 dates now agree closely with Egyptian calendars. The new clock has, however, pushed back the dates of many artifacts in Europe to the point where they now predate their Mediterranean counterparts.

Bristlecone may hold the key to other secrets, locked from man by the doors of time. As Renfrew has called for a shift in man's attitude toward archeology, bristlecones themselves speak for a new perspective on trees. Sequoias are strong and healthy into old age. Scientists can find no reason for them to die from aging. They don't. Every one of them topples in muddy soil or otherwise suffers a catastrophe before approaching the age of the oldest bristlecones. Tall fir and pine rot and tumble earthward only a relatively short time after death.

Bristlecone rarely die in natural catastrophes. With the exception of an occasional lightning strike they grow too high and too far apart for fire to threaten them. A few have toppled after their roots became exposed from the gradual erosion of the mountain surface around them. A few large trunks with bark on them lie in the bottoms of the steepest canyons in the White Mountains, apparent avalanche victims from the colossal 1969 winter. Their only real threat is modern man.

In the 20-odd years since man "discovered" bristlecone, he has wreaked more change than the previous 2,000 years. The cool, clear wind that brightened Schulman's campfire now has measurable air pollution. Some of the oldest snags are gone—in the interest of science and kitchen cabinets. Others have found their way into campfires, wood stoves, and curio shops.

Depending on how man treats the bristlecone, age can be their downfall or their salvation. With growth rates often less than an inch in diameter per century, they cannot recover from the pace of human society like rabbits or eucalyptus. Their survival, and man's too, depends on slowing down the frantic scramble we call civilization. Only then will man be able to look beyond the blindfolds of time, realizing that compared to a bristlecone pine, he himself is a renewable resource.

Say What You Want About Me, But Spell My Name Right

1976

The following letter appeared in the April, 1976, Yodeler. *The* Yodeler *is published by the San Francisco Bay Chapter of the Sierra Club. The letter is self-explanatory.*

I MUST GENTLY PROTEST the misspelling of my name in the March issue. On page 12 you refer to the plural of octopuses as octopies. The plural of eskimo pie may be eskimo pies, but this rule does not apply to our species. The preferred plural is octopuses, which has a rather nice squishy sound to it. Octopodes is another choice, although some think it rather pretentious and formal. Octopi is fine, too, but it is plural as it stands. Do you refer to antennaes or deers or sheeps or (horrors) squids?

We here at Deep Six believe that you Sierra Clubbers are generally nicer and smarter than most homo sapiens. We realize you must be terribly handicapped at the typewriter, having only two arms, but next time please spell our name correctly. Thank you.

D. CEPHALOPOD

Voices of Spring

ELIOT PORTER

1967

To the city dweller the most readily apparent — and sometimes the only — signs of nature are the birds. To one who may never enter a wilderness area, a knowledge of bird life can be a window to the wonders of creation, to the cycles of the seasons, and to what John Muir called "the grand shows of nature." As Americans increasingly turn to nature for refreshment and relief from the onerous demands of the urban routine, the number of bird-watchers has increased faster than the population.

We conclude this section on natural science as we began it, with one person's experience of birds in a particular setting. The observer this time is a pioneer in color photography of nature. His early interest in birds led him to photography originally and to the creation of some of the most beautiful books ever published, beginning with "In Wildness Is the Preservation of the World." This article was drawn from his book Summer Island, *an account of his experiences on an island off the coast of Maine.*

WHEN THE MONTH of May is well advanced, a New Englander may look for the arrival of the first great wave of migrating birds. It is an event of considerable consequence and involves in its most spectacular aspect that colorful family of new-world birds, the wood warblers. As the leaves unfurl, the vanguard of the later-migrating hordes begins to arrive, a few early warblers and many sparrows of different species. The casual observer of the spring realizes that birds are singing again. He will say, "I heard a song sparrow today"; or "What was that new song I heard this morning for the first time?" But to those for whom birds are a hobby or a profession these events will long have been noted. These people are out early with their binoculars to identify every new arrival by sight and by song. They have also been waiting for a certain morning, that morning on which the trees are suddenly alive with birds, all busily foraging for insects that have appeared with the first leaves. Through the short moonlit night the new arrivals have flown. They are hungry after their exertions and must renew their bodies for the next lap of the journey north. Were it not for the food they find during their daytime pauses they would not continue their flight, and would perish from starvation. The next year their numbers would be less, and after that, if the shortage of food continued, there would be silence in the spring.

In incredible thousands, birds occupy every tree, fluttering from branch to branch in a feverish search for insects. Warblers by far outnumber all other birds. The first waves are the males, identifiable by their gay plumage and their songs. All day long on the Island, and day after day for several weeks, I have watched them, sought them out, and determined their kind. They come in all colors: orange, yellow, brown, greenish hues, blue, and occasionally red. Of the many combinations and patterns, blue and yellow predominate in myrtles, magnolias, Canadas, and parulas. With few exceptions though, they all are marked with some yellow, which varies from the total yellow of summer warbler to the crown, rump, and small yellow flank-spots of the myrtle. The songs, too, seem infinitely varied. Some, high-pitched and buzzy, are near the limits of hearing, like those of the blackpoll and bay-breasted; others are rich and melodious, like the yellow warbler's or

224

the throaty song of the Canada. And in between these extremes—a multitude of other songs.

At dawn the chorus begins. I awake early, and from my bed listen to the announcement of spring and count the number of songs I can hear. Some, right outside the window, are loud and insistent. A black-throated green warbler is trying to get me out of bed with his strident, simple notes, and farther away another is singing a different version of the same theme. Faintly, in the distance, I hear a magnolia, and can also make out the sibilant buzz of a parula and the weaker, warbly song of the myrtle. Then nearer again I hear several redstarts. But behind and through all these separate songs a constant chirping, peeping, and rustling forms a background of indistinguishable sounds that attest to the thousands of night arrivals. Since the waves of birds began—for several mornings now—I have been hearing new songs at the start of each day. I identify some old friends who have returned for the summer; and I recognize, too, the songs of Blackburnians and Cape Mays, birds who pause at the Island only for a rest and are gone with the night in a day or two. Warblers are not all I hear, however, for mixed with their songs are those of red-eyed vireos, whitethroats, purple finches, wood pewees, crossbills, and the cheerful, ebullient ruby-crowned kinglet. I am unable to lie in bed, for I must see as well as hear the throngs that have taken possession of the Island during the night. Once out, I find it hard to concentrate on any particular bird. Everywhere, in all the trees, especially among the tender new leaves of the birches, is a seething mass of active, brilliantly-feathered little bodies. My eye is caught by a flash of orange and black, and my subconscious automatically registers "redstart," but my mind cautions, "Are you sure it is not a Blackburnian?" As I hastily try to bring the creature into the field of my binoculars I catch a glimpse of a black necklace about the yellow throat of another bird. I switch to him to make sure I saw a magnolia and not a Canada, and now the orange one is gone. In desperation, I lower my glasses and stare at the tree, not knowing where to look next and not really caring because I know they are all there; I have heard their songs. Sooner or later it is certain each kind will pop into view, and unless I hear a strange song my eyes would only confirm what I already know. Nevertheless, for a long time I wander, hungry for breakfast, but unwilling to return to the house, unwilling to disengage myself from this wondrous phenomenon of life that recurs each year.

From the jungles of South America, over thousands of miles, these tiny birds wing their northward way, undaunted by the hazards of ocean wastes, or the wastes of civilization. Instinct impels them to reproduce their kind in their ancestral lands. To what is this annual two-way mass movement a response? Perhaps it is an adaptation to the advent of the ice age scores of thousands of years ago. But think of the casualties there must have been in those past eras; how few must have survived the year-long winters of snow. And from those that escaped have evolved the present families and species. Every year since the retreat of the ice these growing families have returned to their old homes, and by so doing have given to their kind the scope to multiply freely, away from the overcrowded tropics. Perhaps somewhere buried in the depth of their brains there has survived through these ages an ancient memory, an intense, vital spark, a pattern of cells that initiates and controls their return. Here they all were, returning by the billions, like waves beating against the retreating winter, now only a symbol of the ice that covered this land not so long ago. They occupied every available island, gathered in unusual concentrations along the coast, and spread over the whole breadth of New England. Every wood, hill, and farm was this day ringing with the songs of these uncountable numbers of birds. This is indeed the mystery and miracle of spring.

PART V

To the Utmost Crags

WHEN THE NON-CLIMBER contemplates those athletes who risk their lives struggling up "inaccessible" cliffs and crags, the inevitable question is "Why do they do it?" The venerable answer, "Because it's there," no longer satisfies, and the skeptic may be right when he claims that the Mot de Mallory is a cop-out. Perhaps the motivation for such activity can never be explained and the only answer is that any of true believer: "You just have to feel it."

Nevertheless, climbers have sometimes struggled to express their feelings about the sport with as much effort and anguish as they have expended ascending the Lost Arrow or Everest. Some of these expressions appear toward the end of this section. But the mystique of climbing has probably never been set forth more succinctly than in the words of Mr. and Mrs. J. W. Hood in 1947 in memory of their son:

JOHN HOOD (1926–1947)

Many of our friends have written to us about our son John, who recently met his death in a rock-climbing accident. No one should feel that words are futile at such a time. Words are the vehicle of the spirit and have the power to dispel the dark clouds and reveal the light which makes it possible to trace the deep pattern concealed in the tangled web of fate. We will always remember with deep gratitude.

John lived richly and well. He loved to hear fine music, to read great books, to spark class discussions in history, to solve tough problems in mathematics, to talk far into the night with friends. Above all he loved to climb mountains.

Earthbound men have often wondered why climbing appeals deeply to so many of the finest souls. We believe that it is for them the enactment on a physical plane of the eternal ascent of the human spirit in the quest for truth and beauty, justice and freedom. It demands the conquest of fear and triumph over the weakness of the flesh in a united assault on the ramparts of nature. The reward is an ecstatic experience of beauty and a supreme sense of exaltation.

It is the high destiny of every one of us actively to participate in that slow and magnificent evolution of which mountain climbing is a symbol.

MR. AND MRS. J. W. HOOD

THE EARLIEST CLIMBS

The first recorded ascent of a peak in North America was by Francisco Montano. A soldier of the Cortes expedition, he huffled up 18,000-foot Popocatepetl in 1522. His feelings on the summit of the volcano were not preserved for posterity, but he was doubtless triumphant on his return. He and his companions staggered back into camp with 300 pounds of sulphur from the crater, which was used to make gunpowder. Cortes was elated and gave him a hero's welcome. Presumably Montezuma was less enthusiastic.

Nearly 300 years passed before the first recorded ascent of a major peak in what is now the United States. In 1820 Edwin James, a twenty-three-year-old botanist on a topographical expedition, climbed 14,110-foot Pike's Peak in Colorado.

But these two climbs, arduous though they may have been, were walk-ups. Aside from any unrecorded ascents by Indians, genuine hand-over-hand climbing began in the U.S. in the 1860s, about the time British adventurers were making similar forays in the Alps. Whymper and Hudson made the first ascent of the Matterhorn in 1865, the year after flamboyant young Clarence King began to scramble up Sierra peaks in adventures described with florid embellishments in his classic Mountaineering in the Sierra Nevada.

60

An Ascent of Half Dome in 1884

A. PHIMISTER PROCTOR

1946

A decade after Clarence King's first climbs came one of the most notable first ascents in history. George G. Anderson, a Scotch carpenter, trail builder, and sailor, made an assault on Half Dome, which rises 4800 feet above the floor of Yosemite Valley. Josiah Dwight Whitney of the California Geological Survey had described the summit as "perfectly inaccessible, probably the only one of all the prominent points about the Yosemite which has never been, and never will be, trodden by human foot."

Anderson, a man not easily discouraged, set up a forge in the saddle north of the monolith, drilled holes in the granite, and hammered in eye-bolts. He stood on each eye-bolt to drill for the next one, attached a rope to the bolts, and over a period of weeks attained the summit. There is no record of how many people used Anderson's ropes to scale the dome (John Muir was one of the first), but nine years later, winter ice and snow, sliding down the dome, carried away most of the rope and a number of bolts.

The next chapter of the Half Dome story occurred in the summer of 1884. As told by Phimister Proctor, it appeared in the Bulletin *in 1946. Editor Francis Farquhar knew "Phim" Proctor, a successful sculptor, when he was living at the Bohemian Club in San Francisco and writing his memoirs. The book was never finished, but Farquhar persuaded Proctor to let him publish this chapter in the* Bulletin. *For the occasion "Phim" drew a picture of himself lassoing the pins, as he had done sixty-one years earlier, climbing barefooted.*

In his introduction to the article Farquhar wrote: "His eyes sparkle as he demonstrates with a wave of the arm the technique of throwing the lasso that made possible the successful outcome of the 'danger-defying exploit.' "

Proctor's companion in the adventure was appropriately named Alden Sampson.

I WAS SITTING on Overhanging Rock, with my feet hanging over the Yosemite Valley, 3,000 feet below. Turning I saw, standing near by, a man who turned out to be Galen Clark, one of the pioneers of the valley. He told us how, several years before, an intrepid sailor named Anderson had with great labor and danger put up a rope cable on Half Dome. A year or so before our advent, he said, Anderson had died, and during the past winter an avalanche had taken down most of his cable and had torn out many of its supporting pins. "Now," he said, "we are waiting for some Swiss Alpine climbers to come over and replace the rope."

At that last remark our ears went forward. The thought passed through both our minds at the same instant: "No foreigner will do that job till we have a try at it."

We camped half a mile from Glacier Point for some days, enjoying the wonderful valley views, then moved to Little Yosemite where we established a base for our attempt on Half Dome.

A day or so later we were standing at the bottom of the fifteen-hundred-foot, smooth, granite pitch. The only side it was possible to climb appeared to be as smooth as writing paper. At our feet lay the remains of the bale-rope cable which had been torn down by the snow slide.

As we studied the face of the mountain, we saw how the dare-devil sailor had accomplished his work. Wherever it was possible to climb, and he was a past master at that game, he went without pins, taking advantage of toe-holds. Then, when the rock was too smooth and steep, another pin was put in and the cable fastened as he went. This helped him to come and go. He had built a cabin at the nearest spring, a mile away, where he lived and kept his forge for making bolts.

We returned to camp that night after our tour of inspection to get ready to tackle the cliff in the morning. We had carried with us all of our pack and picket ropes that could be spared, and both of us were looking forward to the attempt with considerable anxiety.

Everything ready, we started on the ascent. The first two hundred feet were accomplished, all the rope hauled up and fastened, and then our troubles began in earnest. We tried every expedient we could think of, one after the other, to get up that smooth steep rock. We could see clearly enough now why all the others had failed, for no matter how hard we tried we kept slipping back. Yet, forty feet or so above our heads a rock jutted out. If we could only reach it! Beyond, the surface looked rough enough for finger-holds for some distance. But there was no joy in that, for we couldn't get there. We had failed! There was one satisfaction—no one would know of our failure, for we had told no one of our intentions. In silence we began to gather up our ropes.

Suddenly I had an inspiration. "I'll lasso it," I yelled. No one had thought of that—the only possible solution, except for Anderson's laborious method. Luckily I was a pretty fair hand with a lariat. Tying a loop on a lash rope, I made a throw. After several false pitches I finally got the range. The knot caught in a crack of the rock and stuck. It didn't look particularly good to me, but I started crawling up the steep slope supporting my weight on the rope. Just before I could grasp the projection, the knot slipped and down I slid for about twenty feet before it caught again. This gave me a bad scare, and while I was collecting my scattered nerves, Sampson climbed up. Soon we were both standing on the jutting rock and could survey the problem ahead.

We found that the slide had not only carried away all of the rope and some of the pins but had loosened some of the pins that were left. This was an unlooked for handicap. Wherever a pin had been pulled out, the only way to reach the next one was to lasso it and then pull oneself up to it with the help of the rope.

As we proceeded we found that some of the pins had been bent over by the snow and were difficult to rope. Often my loop would roll over a ring twenty times before I caught it, even though I had made a good throw. Several of the pins pulled out when my weight was put on the rope. Moreover, our ropes had been used in packing and picketing horses for the past six months and were rather thin and frayed. By this time I was barefoot, for I had discarded my shoes which had a poor set of hobnails.

When I reached a pin, my method was to climb up on it, always leaning against the wall of the mountain, and hook my big toe over the pin. That was my only support. I would straighten myself up slowly, still leaning against the face of the mountain, and throw for the next pin. And I repeat, I was standing on a two-inch pin, with my big toe the only support between me and the valley below. There was never a handhold. The only way that I could get my big toe over the ring was to double up like a jackknife, put my toe on the fingers by which I was holding to the pin, and when I was balanced all doubled up, pull my fingers out with all my weight still resting on them. This was not too easy, as I soon found out. Early in the day my right glove got away from me and went tobagganing down the mountain. This made changing my weight from fingers to toe much more painful.

We at length reached a place where there were no pins, but there were a few rough surfaces. It was now Sampson's turn to go ahead. I doled out the belt rope as he cautiously crawled aloft. If he had slid down past me there wasn't a chance in the world that I could stop him, and we would both have been swept to the bottom. Finally, he reached a ledge where he was compelled to slant off to the side, and this was impossible without something to hold to. As he hung on desperately to small cracks in the rock, he worked a piece of bale-rope from his pocket and tied it to a small bush just above him. I held my breath. Then, putting just enough pressure on the rope to keep himself from slipping, he moved cautiously along till the angle was too great and he had to let go of the rope. But he managed to drag himself to a little hump in the rock, where he cupped his hand over it and clung for several minutes to get his breath. Several yards farther he reached a safe spot, where he fastened the rope and I pulled up to him.

By noon we had reached the only ledge on the mountainside where we could rest and eat lunch. It was all of six inches wide and had been forced

232

away from the main rock so that we could push a leg down in it and rest without holding on. I tell you, that felt good.

By the end of the first day we had made about half of the distance. Just before sunset we slid down the cable, mounted our horses and rode to camp some three miles away. My feet were mighty sore from climbing about on the rocks. To tell the truth, I looked at that mountain with a heap of dread, though I didn't let on. Later I found out that Sampson was scared, too, but as I didn't show any signs of fear, neither would he.

Bright and early the next morning we were back at the starting place with all the rope we possessed. It wasn't hard to reach the upper end of the cable, but there our troubles began. It was tedious work pulling all the spare rope after us. I don't know the exact pitch of the mountain, but everything slipped off the moment we let go of it. Every minute we had to lean against the mountain, which always seemed trying to push us away.

From then on, the surface was the deadly smoothness that I dreaded — there were few pins, and I had to go ahead with the lasso. About a hundred and fifty feet above the spot where I took the lead, I was clinging by my big toe to a pin and lying on my side against the steep cliff, trying to rope the next pin. There was a wind blowing, and this made roping difficult. Finally the rope caught. I put my weight on it, and it held. Then just as I was about to let go on my toe-hold I gave another yank and out came the pin! It rolled down past me, still in my lasso loop. That gave me a chill, and no mistake.

Luckily the next pin was only five feet above the one I had just pulled out. But the tedious work had to be done all over again. After half an hour of trying, the loop finally caught on that pin. It was a great relief, for if the little pin I was then on had given way, or if my knee had caved in, it would have been all over, for there was nothing between me and the bottom of the canyon.

The next pin was the worst of all, for it was thirty-five feet above me on a ledge of rock which stuck out over me about two feet and a half. It seemed next to impossible to make the rope fly up those extra perpendicular feet and hold. We both yelled when the loop finally settled over it. Right there was the fiercest spot I had to conquer. I crawled up on hands and knees, holding like grim death to the rope, until I got to the ledge. There I had to pull myself up on the rope hand-over-hand until I got hold of the pin with my fingers. Then I had to worm myself up over the pin in the "jackknife" movement while I held my weight on the pin with three fingers of my right hand. With my right big toe over my fingers, I slid my body up against the face of the mountain, first painfully yanking my fingers out from under my toe with all my weight on said toe! I lost some skin, but that couldn't be helped. As I stood leaning against the sloping granite catching my breath, that hellish old mountain seemed more than ever determined to push me off.

Once my right toe was hooked over the little pin, there it had to stay. I couldn't change my position, for there was absolutely nothing above to cling to. But before I could catch the next pin, which was a long throw above, my leg trembled so that I simply had to go down — and that was even more difficult than going up! I had to push my index finger under my toe to get hold of the pin, meanwhile hanging over that empty mile of space. It seemed almost impossible to keep from pitching headlong into the blue. I had to climb up over that hellish corner three separate times before I succeeded in roping that next pin. Every time, under the intense strain, my leg would begin to quiver, and I knew that I would either have to go down or get a cramp and fall down. How I cursed the day that I undertook such a fool stunt.

At last, after an hour and twenty-five minutes of unbroken hades, my loop held. This pin still had a bunch of old rope caught around it, which made roping it difficult. Four times it caught, but when my weight was put on it the loop had slipped off. I was anything but happy as I put my weight on that worn rope and, on hands and knees, cautiously climbed up the polished surface of the rock. How anxiously I watched the rope for signs of giving way and the loop for signs of slipping off the pin. If either had happened, you wouldn't be reading this story. To the left, through the corner of my eye, I could see Little Yosemite 3,000 feet below, while at the right, bathed in purple mist, lay the grand Yosemite Valley. Below me, clinging to the cliff, Sampson looked little bigger than a chipmunk. Curiously, while lying there against the side of the mountain I thought to myself, "Now I can face the biggest grizzly in the wilds."

Finally I reached a safe pin, and to it fastened the rope. Sampson climbed up then, and we pulled the cable after us. From here up we had to use about two hundred feet of our own rope to piece out the sailor's cable. There just wasn't enough to finish the job. Sampson still had some ticklish work to do, but we made the top at last.

The view from the top of Half Dome is, I suppose, one of the most wonderful in all America. The valley was spread out below us in all its blue, hazy beauty. We sat for awhile enjoying the wonders of the valley under the glow of the setting sun, and then built a fire on the highest point in view of the whole valley, to let people know that Half Dome had been conquered! At last, reluctantly, we left, slid down the cable and reached safety just at dark.

There are times in a young man's life that a great experience changes it. Those two days on Half Dome were for me the divide between careless youth and serious manhood. My mind had been made up long ago to become an artist. There was nothing else for me in the way of a profession. Those hours of anxiety and danger, trying to accomplish something which in itself was of little value to the world, had crystallized in my mind the ideals that had vaguely been floating in it. After a month's visit in San Francisco with an artist friend, I returned to Denver and was soon launched upon the career that has claimed me ever since.

61

First Ascent of the Middle Palisade

FRANCIS P. FARQUHAR

1922

Anderson's pioneering ascent of Half Dome in 1875 and the follow-up climb by Proctor and Sampson in 1884 pioneered a method that was not used again extensively until the 1930s. For more than half a century after Anderson the major ascents were made without mechanical aids, although climbers were occasionally roped together, alpine-style, for safety, particularly on glaciers and snowfields. The first ascents of most of the higher Sierra peaks were made during this period, while the range was being explored. The only technical improvement was the use of rubber-soled or cleated boots in place of smooth leather, making possible steeper ascents through "friction climbing."

Francis P. Farquhar's account of the first ascent of the Middle Palisade in 1921 is typical of these unaided climbs. The Palisade peaks are the high points of a spectacular ridge located west of the Owens Valley town of Big Pine. They are reached from the west by way of the headwaters of the Kings River.

Placing the register in a cairn at the summit was a solemn ceremony observed with pride in all properly recorded first ascents. John Muir, to the despair of later climbers, never bothered to record his achievements in this way, so it is possible that he climbed numbers of peaks whose first ascent is credited to others. Norman Clyde, with more recorded first ascents than any other individual, habitually left in the cairns he built not a register but a yellow film box with his name scrawled on it.

The "ducks" Farquhar refers to here are not waterfowl but small piles of rocks left to mark a route for future climbers. Albicaulis is the whitebark pine which grows near timberline, affording welcome shelter for the mountaineer.

A FIRST ASCENT of a high mountain has a thrill all its own that can never be duplicated by any subsequent climb on that particular peak. There is an uncertainty about what is ahead and a consequent satisfaction when the doubts have been dissolved. It is a sort of game in which the climbers' resources are matched against the resistance of the mountain, and, as in any game, victory is cause for elation.

During the Sierra Club outing of 1920 in the Middle Fork of Kings River, the Middle Palisade was frequently in view, and there were many inquisitive glances cast at its fluted sides in search of a possible way up, for it was reputed to be still unclimbed. Closely resembling its neighbor, the North Palisade, it is one of the prominent landmarks of the Sierra Crest, attaining an altitude of 14,049 feet, ninth in order among the thirteen peaks in California over fourteen thousand feet. . . .

Farquhar says that he was "eager to attempt the climb," but was unable to do so until the following summer. In August, 1921, he and a friend, Ansel F. Hall, Yosemite Park Naturalist, were knapsacking through the Kings River region and decided to try their "luck at an ascent."

At seven o'clock on the morning of August 26, we left our little clump of *albicaulis* and started for the mountain. We traveled light, carrying only a little lunch and our cameras. The climb over the solid granite was quickly made, and we soon came to the pile of talus below the chute we had selected as the most promising route to the summit. Our examination of the mountain the previous evening had led us to the conclusion that one of the sharper peaks near the extreme right of the ridge was the highest point.

The climb up the chute proved easier than we expected. Our principal concern was to avoid injuring each other by dislodging loose rocks. We made good progress and were beginning to exult in what seemed the certainty of a successful climb when we received a blow to our expectations. A little pile of rocks on a ledge, and another above, and beyond still others, meant that someone had preceded us. We wondered who were our forerunners and envied them the experience of a first ascent.

By quarter-past nine we had reached the top of the ridge at a point only a few hundred feet below the summit. Here several slabs of granite leaning against one another formed a triangular window through which we thrust our heads and beheld a large glacier far below us. This view revived our enthusiasm and we eagerly resumed the climb. The signs of our predecessors continued to the very summit, and as we climbed nearer to that point we beheld the monument that indicated their victory.

Increasing our speed, we reached the top at half-past nine, and looked upon a sight that filled us with mixed emotions. The view was spectacular enough, but it contained a quite unexpected element; for not only were we not the first to reach this point, but there, standing clearly before us only a short distance away to the northeast, was another peak unmistakably higher than the one on which we stood.

At first we were chagrined at our mistake, but presently another thought occurred that somewhat lifted the gloom; for as we looked at the gulf that separated us from the true summit we were confident that no one had passed that way. Although we had not reached the highest peak, neither, perhaps, had our predecessors; and at least the question of a first ascent was still an open one. With calmer feelings, we examined the monument and found a little can containing an envelope addressed, "To the Next Man." Within we found the following record:

July 20, 1919—The undersigned made a first ascent of this peak this day and were disappointed not to find it the highest point of the Middle Palisade. We hereby christen this summit "Peak Disappointment." We made the ascent by the south face from the head of the chute just south of the peak. We entered the chute by crossing the knife-edge on its farther side.

J. Milton Davies, San Francisco;
A. L. Jordan, Berkeley; H. H. Bliss, Berkeley.

We added our testimony to the record and lingered for a few minutes to enjoy the view, which we could not help feeling would have been more impressive if it were not for that point fifty or a hundred feet higher, so near to us in distance, but so far away by the measurement of time and effort. We began to discuss the possibility of attempting to climb the higher peak that day. It was not a very serious intention, but we thought we might at least go down and take a look at the approaches. By eleven o'clock we were back at the talus, where we stopped for luncheon and considered our next step. With a large part of the day still ahead of us, and, refreshed by a rest and a little food, our ambition increased and we determined to try the climb.

The route that we chose for our second effort was by another chute parallel to the one we had ascended in the morning and occupying the same relative position to our goal. Almost immediately, however, we found that the climbing was much more difficult than before and we had to use the utmost care. Most of the lower ledges were covered with deposits of loose gravel so that we found it wise to climb side by side or take turns in standing by while gravel and rocks cascaded down.

It seemed a very long way to the top of this second peak, and the climb did not become any easier as we progressed. Several times we were discouraged and considered abandoning the climb, at least until another day. But the feeling of discouragement never seemed to attack us both at the same time, and on each occasion we turned again to the task and continued upward. About three-fourths of the way up we found, to our disgust, another small pile of rocks, and then we had little doubt that our predecessors on Peak Disappointment had also preceded us on the main summit.

Presently I found myself standing on a ledge to the right of Hall, who was in the main chimney. I had reached the point with difficulty and was now absolutely blocked from further progress upward. The way across the ledge toward Hall did not seem very inviting, and I studied the rocks carefully, with the thought of descending a few feet and rejoining him by a lower route. But the more I looked the more impossible seemed a descent, and presently I became unnerved and thoroughly scared. The longer I looked at the enormous depth below the worse I felt. Even the ledge to which I was clinging began to seem insecure, although, as a matter of fact, I had a perfectly safe hold. This feeling could not have lasted long, but I did a good deal of scared imagining during the time.

Hall, too, seemed to be in a situation from which further progress was doubtful. He was only about fifteen feet away, but that seemed a long distance to me just then. At length I pulled myself together, subdued my fears, and began to concentrate my attention on the firm granite close at hand, paying no heed to what was below. I promptly recognized how easy it was to work along the ledge, and in a moment I was across.

We then held a brief consultation and, after examining the rocks above, concluded that we had had about enough and definitely decided to go down. We looked around for a route for the descent, and then, instead of climbing down, we both began to climb up. It was one of those spontaneous impulses that sometimes occur at critical moments. We found tolerable handholds and footholds, and in a few moments were safely above our ledge; and from that moment, although the climbing was sometimes difficult, we did not stop until we reached the summit.

The route was somewhat complicated, and we frequently had to change from one chimney to another, traversing around the precipitous ridges. As we approached the summit we carefully searched for further evidences of a previous climb. We had not seen any ducks for some time and not a trace of any previous ascent was to be found near the crest. With a shout we greeted the summit as its first visitors. We subsequently learned that Bliss, Jordan, and Davies had been forced by a hail-storm to abandon their attempt on the day after their climb of "Peak Disappointment."

The summit of the mountain is an extremely narrow knife-edge. We had to use great care in moving about, as there were many large blocks just poised on the brink. Selecting a favorable spot, we gathered a few small rocks and constructed a monument. In this we deposited a Sierra Club register encased in two photographic film tubes placed end to end and bound with adhesive tape. We made the following entry in the record:

From camp at about 11,500 ft., climbed southerly peak this morning, only to find that it was lower than this one and had been ascended by a party in 1919. We descended 2000 ft. to the foot of the cliff, ascended another chimney to the peak just south of this one, thence along the crest to this point.
Ansel F. Hall: University of California 1917;
Park Naturalist, Yosemite National Park; Sierra Club.
Francis P. Farquhar: Harvard 1909; San Francisco;
American Alpine Club, Sierra Club, California Alpine Club.

We took several photographs and then at three o'clock began our descent.

In our effort to reach the summit, we had neglected to leave any signs to indicate our return route. During the early part of the climb it had not been necessary, as there were no alternative routes. But now we wished that we had left ducks at the points where we had traversed from one chimney to another, for the rocks which we had studied so carefully on our ascent seemed to be missing and to be replaced by total strangers. We proceeded with deliberation and caution and seldom went down many feet without being positive that we were on the right route. Our progress was steady, and at length we reached the main chimney, where our chief concern was to avoid slipping on the gravel and hitting each other on the head with bounding rocks. It was nearly five o'clock when we reached the top of the talus, and we then proceeded as rapidly as we could over the huge rough blocks of granite until we reached the firm benches, where we increased our speed and arrived at our camp-site at half-past five.

62

An Ascent of North Palisade from the Glacier

OLIVER KEHRLEIN

1929

The following account of a party on the North Palisade in 1929 does not record a first ascent; the peak had first been scaled from the west side in 1903 by Sierra Club stalwarts J. N. LeConte, James S. Hutchinson, and James K. Moffitt. The 1929 climb was nonetheless notable; the route, from the precipitous east side, took the climbers across the mile-long Palisade Glacier, largest in the Sierra and the most southerly glacier in the U.S. The party was led by Norman Clyde, who had pioneered the route the previous summer. Oliver Kehrlein was a Sierra Club director for many years and founder of the club's base-camp outings. Bestor Robinson has also been a director and president of the club and was one of its pioneer climbers. Ropes were used for safety on the North Palisade glacier crossing, as customary in the Alps, and later for a rapid descent.

THE GLACIER and eastern face of the North Palisade is easily approached from Glacier Lodge, situated eleven miles west of Big Pine. An unfinished trail leads almost to the edge of the ice-field, which in the late season is free from snow and presents many characteristic glacial formations so familiar in more northerly mountains.

Great grottoes, deep greenish-blue in color and filled with icicles, tempt one to tarry. Many yawning crevasses have opened in the body of the ice both transversely and in the direction of the flow. These crevasses are often thirty feet deep and over a hundred feet long. The surface of the glacier inclines so gradually that there are no icefalls, seracs, or even hummocks. Great boulders that have fallen from the rocky cliffs have been carried by the ice to a well-defined terminal moraine. Some of these rocks stand on pedestals of snow ten feet high, like mammoth toadstools. In one spot we found a group of them resembling a gigantic mushroom garden. Not fully aware of the arduous nature of the task ahead of us, we explored the glacier from one end to the other, for none of us had expected to find such a wonderful example in our own Sierra Nevada.

By the time we reached the bergschrund, the sun had crept around and into the couloir upon which we were focusing our attack. Rocks were already falling and we feared that the ice-cliff might start cracking. Crossing an ice-bridge, we presently came to a wall of ice some thirty feet high overlooking a gaping bergschrund. We were all equipped with crampons, ice-axes, and ropes; without them we could never have succeeded. Here I began to learn something of the technique the others had acquired with the Sierra Club on the glaciers of Bennington, Robson, Resplendent, and other peaks during the summer. Cutting notches up the face of the ice-wall was slow and tedious work, the brunt of which fell upon Clyde and Robinson.

Above the cliff we found the couloir exceedingly steep and the ice free from snow and hard and brittle. As cutting steps up its entire length was out of the question, we kept as much as possible to the rock-wall, where we felt more at home. Most of our climbing, therefore, was at or near the juncture of the ice with the rock-wall. There was a great deal of loose rock at this juncture, and the least touch would start these rocks bounding down the glare ice to the glacier far below. This couloir lies directly east of the first chimney one ascends in attacking the mountain from the western side and reaches the large notch in the crest southeast of the peak.

After a late lunch in the great notch at the head of the couloir, Clyde dropped down the western side a few hundred feet, then led us up by way of a hardly perceptible crack onto a shoulder that brought us back to the ridge. Thence to the summit was merely a matter of working along the knife-edge—a real pleasure after the tedious and insecure climbing up the ice.

Four of us signed the register at the top: Norman Clyde, Bestor Robinson, Oliver Kehrlein, and Oliver Kehrlein, Jr., September 9, 1928.

It was well after four o'clock when we started back. Realizing the short time before sunset, we hurried over the rocks using the rope as much as possible to let each other down. By the time we reached the ice-cliff we were working by flashlight. There we found our steps filled with detritus and frozen over. On the very brink, with only thirty feet to go, we went into a "huddle" and decided that the prospect was unfavorable. To try to locate in the dark, with our toes, a series of notches on a slippery ice-wall that might have changed through melting or cracking during the heat of the day, with a yawning bergschrund below, was more than we cared to undertake. The chances seemed a hundred to one against us. So we climbed back up the couloir to the rock-wall, where we found a shelf just big enough to accommodate one man. The flashlight revealed a nearby crack in the rocks into

240

which the thinnest of the party managed to squeeze after taking everything out of his pockets and doubling up like a jack-knife. One man sat on the ledge, another sat on him, both as a matter of economy of space as well as conservation of heat; the last man sat on the ice. Soon, however, the draught coming down the couloir and the frozen perch proved too much for the ice-sitter, so the man in the crack pulled himself together another few inches and made room for two.

As the bergschrund was directly below, ready to receive anyone who might become drowsy, we deemed it advisable to unwind the trusty rope and make it secure upon a rocky projection and lash ourselves together as tightly as possible. This was a wise precaution, for we soon found it impossible to keep awake. In fact, we spent the night alternating between cat-naps and convulsive shiverings. These shivers involved every muscle and were quite violent. A temporary warmth then pervaded the body, and we would doze off, only to be awakened by another fit of shivers and shakes. As our limited space prohibited any exercise, we aided the automatic endeavors of our reflex systems, by beating each other in turn until we were black and blue.

As we look back upon the experience, there were many amusing incidents, the humor of which did not appeal to us at the time. For instance, Robinson announced that he had an extra pair of socks in his rucksack. As cold feet seemed the least of our worries, they went begging until one man said he could make use of them. Next morning this individual, who had held himself in place on his perch by driving one heel into the frozen ground, found his heel badly frostbitten. What had he done with the extra pair of socks? One he had tied about his neck as a muffler, the other he had placed across his stomach to retain body-heat. The night was one of those clear, sparkling ones, when the stars appear large and brilliant, and Clyde did his best to keep us awake with a dissertation of the Pleiades, Orion, Ursa Major, and other interesting topics.

With the first break of dawn, we anchored our rope and Clyde went ahead to cut new steps. Our descent was easy and simple enough by daylight. We had a hot breakfast in camp and by noon were at Big Pine, with the temperature over one hundred degrees.

THE BEGINNINGS OF MODERN CLIMBING IN THE SIERRA

In the summer of 1930, Francis Farquhar, who had maintained his Harvard connections after coming to California in 1910, joined other members of the Harvard Mountaineering Club in the Selkirks of British Columbia and there met Harvard philosopher and mathematician Robert Underhill. Underhill had learned to climb in the Alps a year or two earlier, using rope techniques then unknown in the U.S., and he taught these methods to the Harvard climbers. In 1931 Farquhar tried some of the same methods in leading a party up Unicorn Peak, above Yosemite's Tuolumne Meadows, where he had made a first ascent twenty years earlier.

At his invitation Underhill arrived from the East later that summer and organized a climbing school for Sierrans, teaching them the alpine techniques on Mount Ritter and Banner Peak (immediately southeast of Yosemite National Park) and leading a party on a first ascent of the precipitous East Face of Mount Whitney, at 14,495 feet the highest point in the range. With Underhill on this historic trip were Norman Clyde and two young Californians who would later leave their names in the climbing annals of the club, Jules Eichorn and Glen Dawson.

And so began a new era in Sierra climbing. The rope techniques inevitably led to new assaults on the previously inaccessible walls and spires of Yosemite Valley. Essential to these ascents was not only the rope but the piton, a spike with a sharp point, which can be hammered into cracks in the rock. It has a ring or eye in the other end. Once secure in the crack, the piton can be used for direct handholds or footholds or for support of a rope connected to it with a safety-pin-like ring known as a carabiner. When a climber is attached to a rope secured by pitons, he is "belayed."

The first successful major ascent in Yosemite by use of these techniques was made in 1934 by three members of the Sierra Club's new Rock Climbing Section, Jules Eichorn and San Francisco attorneys Bestor Robinson and Richard Leonard, who had carefully trained themselves in the new techniques on Cragmont Rock and other outcrops in the Berkeley Hills. Their goal was the higher of the two Cathedral Spires, across the valley from El Capitan. Their gear consisted of several hundred feet of various kinds of ropes, fifty-five pitons, thirteen carabiners, and two piton hammers. They proceeded methodically up the nearly vertical walls of the spire, using a double-rope technique they had devised, known as tension climbing. While the leader pounded in his piton and snapped one rope into it, the second rope, which was looped through a previously driven piton and held tight by his teammate below, gave the leader support, freeing his hands. (Both ropes were tied to the leader's waist.)

If the leader should fall, the belayer, with the rope passed around the back of his hips and secured slackly at the other end, was to let the rope slide slightly through his hands to ease the sudden wrench when the line tightened at the end of the fall. This latter method, which had also been devised and practiced by Leonard and others on the Berkeley rocks, was known as the "dynamic belay." It was developed not only to ease the strain on the leader but more important to prevent the rope from snapping, as it would almost inevitably do under the strain of a serious fall.

This new technique was a substantial advance over the old Alpine "static belay"—tying the rope to a rock or piton below the leader. If he fell, the rope would probably snap and his fall would continue, but the rest of the party would be safe. The Alpine method could only be used successfully in conjunction with the Alpine rule: "The leader must not fall." A leader operating under that solemn injunction would obviously be less daring than one who could proceed knowing that if he did fall, he would have a reasonable chance of survival.

Fortunately, there was no need to test the dynamic belay in action on Higher Cathedral Spire. It had been amply tested on the rocks of Berkeley. But the confidence that it afforded the leader was undoubtedly a major reason for the success of the climb *and others that followed. A few months later the same team used the same techniques on Lower Cathedral Spire. One of the club's first women climbers was Marjory Bridge, later Mrs. Francis Farquhar, who was a member of a three-person party that ascended the Higher Spire later the same year.*

63

The First Ascent of Shiprock

BESTOR ROBINSON

1940

Shiprock is a volcanic plug rising 1800 feet above the New Mexico desert. In one of the major climbs of the 1930s, it was tackled by a Sierra Club team including Bestor Robinson, Raffi Bedayan, John Dyer, and David Brower, who later became the club's Executive Director. Robinson, the team's "rock engineer," had a new piece of equipment—a modification of Anderson's eye bolts on Half Dome. These were "expansion bolts," eye bolts used in the construction industry for drilling into concrete. Unlike pitons, which must be hammered into cracks, these could be drilled into any part of the rock. By using them, climbers could go straight up almost anywhere, as Anderson had done. But out of deference to the ethics of mountaineering, the Shiprock team relied principally on pitons and placed the bolts only where absolutely essential for safety.

The ascent itself was a superlative example of the teamwork necessary in the new age of technical climbing. Each man had his specialized role, but there was no permanent leader. All decisions were made democratically after careful discussion.

WE WERE ENCAMPED at the eastern base of Shiprock. Dinner was over. The embers of our sagebrush campfire sporadically came to life as gusts of desert wind fanned them into flame. We were all looking at the silhouette of Shiprock outlined against the evening sky. The wind–driven clouds gave the mountain the appearance of motion—it was no longer a mere rock in the desert but a full-rigged barkentine carrying triangular skysails atop its three masts. It must have been under conditions such as these that the early wanderers named the peak. Under the full glare of the desert sun it is not a ship, but just another fantastically shaped rock in a land filled with weird erosion forms.

I was jarred out of my nautical musings by Dave Brower's strictly military remark, "Seven o'clock tomorrow morning is our zero hour."

Looking backward it seemed that the military analogy was appropriate. Like an army staff we had developed our plans of attack deliberately and in detail. A mountain which had repulsed a dozen attempts could obviously not be conquered in any other way, if it could be conquered at all.

Dick Leonard had served as intelligence officer. He had corresponded with most of the earlier parties as to their routes, difficulties and suggestions. He had collected photographs from both climbers and non-climbers. These had been examined under the microscope for routes and under a protractor for angles. A folder jammed with photos, notes, letters and maps was the result. Unfortunately, the necessity of attending an important National Park conference prevented his joining the climb.

Since climbers, more literally than armies, move on their stomachs, it was necessary that a small, but efficient, quartermaster corps be organized. Raffi Bedayan pulled the most tasty and nourishing foods off the shelves of his grocery. Florence Robinson enlisted as commissary sergeant.

A list of equipment finally emerged from a plethora of arguments and experiments. It included over one thousand feet of rope, dozens of pitons of varying shapes, thicknesses and lengths, and carabiners of three sizes, including the screw-jawed type for excessive strain. Lastly, and with some concern over the mountaineering ethics of our decision, we included several expansion bolts and stellite-tipped rock drills. We agreed with mountaineering moralists that climbing by the use of expansion bolts was taboo. We did believe, however, that safety knew no restrictive rules and that even expansion bolts were justified in order to secure the firm anchorage that would prevent a serious fall from imperiling the lives of the entire party.

The climbing party had been organized on the theory that men who varied greatly in their special climbing abilities would make a stronger team than a group of good all-around climbers without such special abilities. Although three men would ordinarily have been considered ideal, the plans finally called for four men in order to be able to handle complicated anchorages and involved rope techniques. And so the party consisted of Dave Brower, John Dyer, Raffi Bedayan, and me.

Dave was the friction climber, the advocate of dynamic balance who seemed somehow to be able to move on slight discolorations of the rock. His long orangutan arms added to his normal height of six feet two made him valuable where holds were far apart.

Dyer was our lightweight lead man. Chipmunk-like, he could scramble up cracks; his lack of weight enabled him to make use of rotten rock and insecure pitons which could not be relied upon with safety by a heavier climber; and, if he should be unfortunate enough to fall, he would strain neither the rope nor the belayer holding it.

Bedayan, like Brower and Dyer, was an all-around climber. His particular ability, however, lay in the establishment of bombproof anchorages. With his two feet firmly planted, he was as immovable as a stubborn burro, and as reassuring for lead men.

Why I was included in the party still remains a mystery, unless it is explained by my love of ropes, pitons and other technical gear in their

244

manifold combinations, which had earned me the doubtful appellation of "Rock Engineer."

Finally perfecting our military preparations, we had decided that the attack would have to be along the lines of methodical siege tactics, instead of the now famous blitzkrieg. In one important particular the military analogy was totally abandoned. There was no general, no captain—not even a lance corporal. The party was deliberately leaderless. The assumption of responsibility for decisions by the entire team does of course take time, but it brings into play the conflict of opinions without the presence of a dominating voice. In the long run, with an experienced party the judgment of such a "composite mind" is more likely to be right than the quick decisions of even a brilliant leader.

"Yes," Dave repeated, looking at Shiprock's silhouette against the sky, "Seven o'clock tomorrow morning is our zero hour. I wonder if we'll get over the top?" Being a navy man, I could not, from pride, restrain the contentious rejoinder, "This is a ship we are boarding—it's not an army maneuver. The job is to get around the fire control tower and climb the mainmast."

Came sleep—then breakfast, followed by the lugging of much gear around the stern of the ship to the western side—to the basalt dike which yielded a satisfactory, but at times airy, route to the bottom of the north tower. Halting only long enough to admire the work of our predecessors, as well as their ambition in attempting a frontal assault on its perpendicular wall, we went over the ridge to the east side and looked down toward camp. Three hundred feet below lay a sloping ledge which could be reached only by roping down a steep chimney. There was, however, no possibility of climbing back on the smooth-polished, holdless rock.

An improvised block and tackle appeared the appropriate technique. A loop of rope was securely anchored to two pitons, a large carabiner tied into the rope and the loop adjusted so that the carabiner would hang just beyond the lip of our ledge. Dave roped down, grumbling a bit when the large carabiner passed over his shoulder. John and I followed, but Raffi remained behind using up valuable calories maintaining body warmth against the snow-chilled winds which blew from the San Joaquin mountains. We were not convinced that we could trust our hoist for the return journey and wanted a human donkey engine at the upper end of the rope.

We were now on a ledge as large as a city lot, sloping outward at an angle of thirty degrees to the brink of the eastern cliffs. This ledge continues, like the roof of a lean-to, almost the entire length of Shiprock. It forms the bottom of the great bowl and also the top of the south shoulder. The only difficulty is that this roof is cut into three sections without apparent provision for a connecting trail.

Reconnaissance indicated two possibilities, a high route which would land us in the bowl, and a low one which ended thirty feet under its lower lip. Although both contained extensive gaps of nothing, the lower route looked preferable except for its termination. Lack of piton cracks and adequate anchorage made it necessary to bring down Raffi, who by this time had made it clear that as a hoisting engine he was completely useless because of the cold. We did not feel concerned, however, so long as he could complain so loud and lustily.

Using all of our available rope, and even tying Raffi into the bottom of our hoist for better anchorage, we tackled the traverse. It was a friction problem, so Dave took the lead and demonstrated the effectiveness of his theory of dynamic balance by arriving at a secure ledge almost halfway around the tower. I came up and took over a fair sitting anchorage, aided by an insecure piton. Even such a piton is helpful when one is dangling his feet over a desert more than a thousand feet below. I knew I could not fall for I was tied to Raffi by a new rope, the breaking strain of which was over three thousand pounds; and Raffi was tied into the double hoisting rope. My mind told me that all was secure and that the worst that could happen would be a pendulum swing around the nose of the tower and onto the sloping ledge. This conclusion was irrefutable. I looked down on the desert, drove in a second, equally useless, piton and then, and not until then, felt secure.

Dave tried the high route but found it impossible. There was not even a prayerhold. (Next day he tried again but got no further.) Dropping onto the lower route he found it better than expected, leading by way of a small, but secure, shelf to an eight-foot wall, which was climbed by use of a single piton.

Dave reported that if he could get over a thirty-foot cliff he would be in the giant bowl, but that he was figuratively at the end of his rope. Looking at the single coil of the one hundred twenty foot climbing rope remaining in my hand, I called from my well-ventilated anchorage that he was literally at the end of his rope and almost at the end of the day.

Johnny would have to lead over such a wall, so Raffi and I shuttled him over to Dave to have a look. Half of our composite mind was now in operation at the actual battle front. However, gnawing feelings in our midriffs and the lengthening shadow of Shiprock warned that it was time to return to camp. An hour later we were stowing away the excellent grub Florence had prepared.

The second day of climbing found all four of us at the base of the thirty-foot wall well before noon. We were on a broad but sloping shelf. Not a single secure piton crack could be found. Holding a fall from above would not be easy—so in went an expansion bolt.

Dave unsuccessfully attempted to detour the wall by way of a large crow's-nest. There was only one alternative left; a job of pure rock-engineering with two-man stands, pitons, foot slings and tension ropes. I had such an enjoyable time pounding pitons into the overhanging, outward sloping crack, that I hated to turn the job of going over to Johnny. However, prudence dictated that a two hundred pound man should not fall on questionable pitons, so Johnny took over. A delicate traverse on rotten rock, a second expansion bolt for safety, and Johnny reached the base of the second crack on our resisting wall. Then, back to camp. We had climbed only twelve feet that day. Too much time was being spent going to and from camp. The lure of good food and air mattresses was wrecking our mountaineering technique; at least so we concluded.

Next day, the third on the mountain, witnessed our carrying, over our well worn route, a light tent, extra grub, and six pints of water. Johnny finished his overhang, well enmeshed in ropes, pitons and slings. A few minutes later the entire party was in the great bowl scrambling over easy slopes to the south side of the thin transverse fin. There, alongside the same lava dike which witnessed Ormes' fall a year before, nature had fashioned an excellent bivouac cave. Surely it was not more than forty feet from the back of this cave to the opposite side where we had arrived more than three days before. Forty feet in three days. Raffi thought that next time we had best tunnel through.

Caching our equipment in the cave we hurried to scale the mainmast itself—the scantiness of our water supply or a cold night might disable the party for difficult climbing on the morrow.

After preliminary surveying of routes, the composite mind came to a two to two impasse. Dave and Johnny voted for the north side, the rest of us for the south arête with its overhanging horn. Dave, belayed by Raffi, performed in topnotch style. The north face begrudgingly yielded a perpendicular route to within seventy feet of the summit and then flatly refused to permit further progress. An overhang without a piton crack or a place for a two-man stand ended a valiant attempt.

Darkness had fallen before we arrived at our bivouac cave. Starvation rations were prescribed for dinner because digestion would waste much-needed water. Crawling into our light tent to conserve body heat, we spent a reasonably comfortable night on the hard rock, turning over, however, only by unanimous consent. The night was chilly, but we did not especially miss our sleeping bags.

The next morning the remainder of our water was partitioned under watchful eyes intent on democratic equality. After much scientific argument a little food to allay stomach emptiness was distributed and we were ready to tackle the mainmast.

Again we climbed to the upper edge of the great bowl at the base of the south arête of the main tower. Here I put a long line of pitons into the overhanging crack that wormed its way upward toward the horn. Johnny took over, threw his auxiliary rope over the horn and, after making sure he was anchored both above and below, climbed out over eighteen hundred feet of sheer western cliff and up the holdless side of the horn.

On the broad ridge atop the nose safe anchorage could be secured only by another expansion bolt. Up came the rest of the party. Dave took over the lead on the friction slopes ahead and soon we were all sitting on the summit of Shiprock. A rock cairn was built; a Sierra Club register with room for a thousand names was safely tucked away in its center.

"We've gone over the top," said Dave.

"No," I insisted, "we've climbed the mainmast."

64

Climbing the Lost Arrow

ANTON NELSON

1947

The Shiprock ascent was a triumphant expansion of the new technique that had been pioneered on Higher Cathedral Spire. Nevertheless, there were those in the mountain climbing fraternity who looked on the elaborate technology with disapproval. They had the feeling that the use of so much equipment was not quite sporting. The controversy between the traditionalists and the "rock engineers" was to come to a head after World War II with the climactic assault on the most spectacular of the "impossible" Yosemite climbs—the Lost Arrow. Meantime, during the war, little climbing took place; the club's mountaineers served with distinction in the armed forces, many of them with the army's famed 10th Mountain Division.

When climbing resumed after the war, the Lost Arrow was one of the first objectives. It is a sharp spire immediately to the right of Yosemite Falls, rising 1300 feet above its base, about twice the height of the Washington Monument and almost as steep. Its needle-like summit is about 150 feet from the rim of the valley wall behind it, and it is joined to the wall at a point 200 feet below its summit. The notch between the Arrow and the wall is the point where a legendary Indian princess found the body of her lover, who had shot the arrow that gave the spire its name.

The notch is also the goal of all climbers looking to an ascent of the pinnacle. The story of the first ascent was told for the Bulletin *by one of the climbers, Anton "Ax" Nelson, a tall, rangy carpenter. It is significant that most of the "trail" had been pioneered a couple of weeks earlier by John Salathé, who became a legendary figure in Yosemite climbing. He was a small, wiry, Swiss-born wrought-iron worker and natural-living enthusiast, who devised the new equipment that made his climbs possible. He began climbing in his mid-forties, a living denial of the axiom that climbers are old at thirty. There have been stronger, more agile climbers on Yosemite's walls but none who was more of a technician and master of equipment, a rock engineer par excellence. Ironically, he was denied the first ascent of the Arrow, even though he showed the way to the top; Nelson explains some of the reasons.*

The "Prusik sling" referred to by Nelson is a stirrup attached to a rope by a knot that slides until it is loaded, then holds fast, giving the climber a secure foothold.

MANY A HARDY HIKER, having viewed with awe and fascination the leaping waters at the top of Yosemite Falls, walks on up the trail to near-by Yosemite Point to look at Yosemite Valley's majestic panorama. As he gazes about in reverent appreciation, his eye is attracted to an upsoaring block of granite out in the space where logic suggests nothing could possibly stand. Yet there below the rim a little, poised in impassive solitude, is the top of a mighty pinnacle. Carefully moving to a better vantage point, he sees the sleek shaft drop away toward the swirling mists of the falls. Twitches of respect and fear well from his stomach and, stepping back, he declares, "Now there is a spire no man can possibly climb!"

This is the Lost Arrow, lost indeed to a world of creatures who live in the horizontal dimensions. In recent years, however, rock-climbers of the Sierra Club, driven by high spirits and aided by piton, carabiner, and rope, eagerly sought the more vertical routes up the inviting cliffs and spires of Yosemite. They began to wonder even about the Lost Arrow, the most challenging spire of all and, according to some, the last difficult unclimbed summit in America. In the early 'thirties, David R. Brower and George Rockwood surveyed a possible route from the base. Brower returned in May, 1937, with Richard M. Leonard. They started up the polished trough at the west side, their aim to reach the narrow, vertical chimney, 800 feet high, that cut in behind the shaft. At the chimney's upper terminus was the notch separating the last 200 feet of the shaft from the cliff.

After twelve hours of delicate and strenuous work, Brower swung out onto the first noticeable ledge 350 feet from their starting point, the two men alternately having placed 40 pitons for protection or direct aid. It was still 200 feet to the entrance to the chimney. In "A Climber's Guide to Yosemite Valley," they described the prospect from the base in all simplicity, "The route from here is terrifyingly clear." The first ledge was dubbed First Error. Another was the Second Error. The notch became Third Error and the summit suggested that it would be the Last Error of any climber brash enough to attempt to reach it.

Four more attempts by the persistent trio of Jack Arnold, Robin Hansen, and Fritz Lippmann followed the same route. They even entered the great chimney. The polished granite holds became increasingly scarcer; the angle verged sharply toward 90 degrees; the sun's direct rays turned the walls into an oven, and lassitude sapped the will. The route above would require days of continuous climbing if, indeed, it was possible to go any higher at all. The Lost Arrow waited in noble serenity, an incomparable prize, the winning of which made any method honorable.

An alternative method of getting onto the spire had been suggested by an Indian legend. Bestor Robinson attempted to lasso the summit from the near-by rim, but it wasn't near enough by. Brower, with Rolf Pundt belaying, climbed down from the valley rim to a point level with the notch, but a blank wall some fifty feet wide separated him from it. Then in 1946 two new climbers, John Salathé and I, turned our minds to the problem.

One day in August, Salathé arrived on the scene ready to join two others in a new attempt from the rim. Through a misunderstanding the others did not arrive. Undaunted, Salathé decided to try out a system of solo climbing worked out by Italian alpinists. This he had practiced on local climbs in the

Bay area. He descended on one rope and, by making an intermediate traverse across the face of the cliff, was able to rig a second rope which dangled to the notch itself. Some two hundred twenty feet below the rim he minutely surveyed the beetling upper shaft of the spire. It was incredibly flawless and holdless. The only place left on which to move was a narrowing ledge running out to a corner of the east face and overhanging talus 1,000 feet or more below. It was like stepping out the window from the hundredth floor of the Empire State Building onto a window ledge. He edged out to the end of the ledge. There, in the corner, a slight crack ran upward a few feet. He must see what lay beyond its terminus. Placing pitons he had manufactured especially for the smallest cracks, Salathé ran his climbing rope through carabiners hooked in several pitons and passed it about his own body again. He could now belay himself in case one of his pitons jerked out. Patiently he tried to pound pitons into the almost inadequate crack. Most climbers would not even have attempted to do so. At last twenty feet was won.

Rising high above his last piton where the crack ended he could just reach one of those strange solution pockets which climbers sometimes thankfully find in the most necessary places. It looked to Salathé like an "eagle's nest," and was just big enough to wedge his body into. Holdless granite above necessitated drilling holes for two expansion bolts. Then he could reach a loose crack beyond, which offered enough help to bring him to a resting place.

In forgetful absorption, such as only a climber can know, oblivious to time and danger, he worked his way upward, inch by inch. He passed an overhanging spot where the rock was rotten, stepped onto a granite flake, thin as a board but attached to the main mass several feet below. Then, testing each piton, and using several together when one alone was not strong enough to hold his weight, he passed another overhang on rotten granite, his anchor pitons ten feet below. A second ledge appeared on the face above, and Salathé built a cairn upon it to prove that the apparently unbroken walls could be climbed. He was sitting hundreds of feet higher than anyone had ever before climbed on the Lost Arrow. It was only 100 feet farther to the top.

Now, however, as he rested after the furious concentration of his efforts, Salathé realized the peril of his solitary endeavor and wisely returned to the notch. Using Prusik slings he ascended once more to the safety of the rim. Deciding that further solo climbing was indiscreet, he enlisted John Thune as a partner and on the following week returned with him to the outer ledge. He worked slowly upward all day, with patient assistance from Thune. By swinging from one slight crack to the next, he was able to gain perhaps 90 feet to the end of the last crack. A ranger a mile away marveled at the sight revealed through his telescope.

This was the situation as evening fell: In the fading light, Thune, out of sight 90 feet below, called that Salathé must come down, for the end of the rope was at hand. Having drilled a hole for a bolt, Salathé answered that he would just look over the bulge of rock above.

And in the last light of day he looked—up onto the smoothly polished

250

angle of the monolithic tip of the Arrow, a surface which tapered to the summit 30 feet away. The remaining interval could not be covered without some drastic kind of artificial aid. It was high time to retreat. They did.

Now it must be admitted that competition is the essence of sport and the spur to thought. When Fritz Lippmann and Jack Arnold heard of these astonishing successes they decided something ought to be done to finish the task. Robin Hansen and "Ax" Nelson were hurriedly consulted. A new idea was born, and, on Labor Day week end, a route to the top of the Lost Arrow was devised and climbed. . . .

It is Saturday morning. Hansen and I have joined Lippmann and Arnold at base camp in the now dry and silent bed of Yosemite Creek above the falls. Finishing breakfast, we gaily march up the swells of granite to the rim. The Arrow's cold response to our welcome is sobering. As the first breezes of the day swirl up the cliffs we make ready to try out our new idea. It is this: From the brow of the cliff just west of Yosemite Point it is but 100 feet or so laterally to the top of the Arrow, which stands somewhat below the level of the valley rim. If a light line can be cast over the top and down the far side, and then reached by climbing around to it, heavier ropes that would support a man may possibly be pulled over and anchored. Then the last unclimbable pitch can be surmounted by climbing up the rope itself, and a unique and spectacular means of returning to the rim can be rigged—an aerial traverse.

All day Saturday we take turns at casting and throwing lines and ropes weighted with lead sinkers. First short of the target, again onto a two-foot level space on the summit, then to one side of it, fall the leaders. Then, swinging into the cliff beneath, they catch in fissures, and the line breaks when we pull. Hundreds of feet of line are thus lost. The ever-present updraft capriciously foils nearly successful casts. Some even land on top, but fail to drag the rope on over, or slide off sideways. Late in the day the skill and luck of Hansen increase until we know he has the range. Again and again Bob lets "just one more last try" sail out with a snaking of rope behind. Then suddenly one cast settles over the correct place and slithers over without sliding off. With gleeful shouts we run down the rim to where we can see the guide line hovering over the outer ledge. At camp we sit around the fire and eat a watermelon brought along for a treat. We sleep light-heartedly as if tomorrow would bring an ordinary day's work.

Sunday morning is frosty. We must split the team. Who will go down onto the Arrow itself and climb out to the valley side to reach the guide line? Who will take the responsibility of staying on the rim to supervise the engineering of our complex rope system? We all look at each other and sense the decision. Jack and I will climb. We heft our hammers and carefully select what we need from our copious and varied supply of hardware and ropes. An hour later Jack and I stand at Third Error, the notch, contemplating our formidable adversary.

The day's climb is much like Salathé's, except that it is filled with successive unexpected difficulties, each of which almost stops us. The route is obvious and inevitable.

A buzzard circles patiently in the sky viewed between our feet.

The first pitch turns out to be as difficult as any we have ever seen. Direct mechanical aid is 90 per cent of the task, and we devoutly wish our pitons were as good as Salathé's, which have wide, short blades and hair-thin points. Moreover, we would like it if the previous climbers had not largely ruined the barely usable crack when they hammered out their pitons. But we must use what we have. As we further diminish the crack's possibilities it becomes doubtful that many others will ever climb the Lost Arrow. After 15 feet of tediously trying to place sound pitons Jack drills a hole for an expansion bolt, but is still unable to reach the immediate objective, the "eagle's nest." He comes down to rest.

I take up the lead directly into the sun. The day is half over. I must make full use of my extra-long reach or lose precious time placing another bolt. By placing my left foot in a short loop from the bolt and pressing my arms and body close against the wall, I can rise in delicate balance on one foot. My right foot and finger tips search for any helpful rugosities in the rock. At full length I stretch up and place two fingers of my right hand over the lower lip of the eagle's nest. Pulling up on one hand and then placing the other on top of it for added strength calls up all my glandular resources. With a sudden pouring of sweat I squirm into the shallow and narrow hole and wedge my knees and one arm and elbow. Swiftly I search for the needed security of another hold.

A tiny hole which once received a piton to aid previous climbers proves now to be damaged and unusable. The angle is too steep to balance on, the rock too smooth for my finger tips or nails to dig into.

My judgment tells me I will need the rest of my strength to get back down safely. Then, ten inches from my face I see a small, round hole and jam a little finger tip into it. A "thank God hold," if ever there was one! It turns out to be a hole drilled by Salathé, for whose help I am grateful. Then more trouble. My bolt fits the hole only loosely. However, I can put just enough weight on this slight aid to free my hands for drilling another hole. The unnatural strains start leg muscles quivering uncontrollably. I screw in the bolt twenty minutes later. My temples pounding and clothing soaked with sweat, I am lowered from it as from a pulley by Jack. Our troubles are only beginning as Jack resumes the lead. It has taken us eight hours to cover the fifty feet to the first ledge.

The route to the second ledge is not a route at all. It looks like sheer folly, for the wall is overhanging, the granite rotten. We must hold a council of war. Communication with Fritz and Bob is another problem. The distance engenders confusing echoes from the opposing walls and the rush of the wind buffets our voices into gibberish. If it were earlier in the year and the falls were roaring, nothing would be audible between us. Nevertheless, we reach the understanding that our five nylon ropes will not suffice for the job we have planned for them even if Jack and I do reach the guide line. Fritz and Bob must go down for more. Leaving a fixed rope, we return to the notch and hollow out two level holes in the broken rock in which to sleep. Our sleeping bags and food, even a primus stove, are lowered to us.

As the sun sets, the peaks of the High Sierra are illumined with the day's last lovely smile. Hot soup and tea round out a royal meal for such an airy dining room. Time, which seemed to race through the day, now seems to stand motionless in this never-never world of the perpendicular whose creatures we have become. A magic silence we are reluctant to break fills the world between our dark cleft and the purple sky. The battlements of Yosemite loom about us in all the mystic presence of a hundred centuries. Our reverie is startlingly broken as a furry, mouselike creature scurries past and scampers straight up the cliff, his claws scratching the tiny flakes of granite as confidently as if he were on a level table top. Through our rock picture frame we see the campfires flickering in the valley below our feet. The Glacier Point firefall makes for us a display such as few men will ever see. There is nothing to do but regain strength for the completion of our task. We sleep.

For Bob and Fritz it is far different. With each hour the responsibility for success rests more heavily upon them. They run down through the twilight to the valley, covering the four miles in half an hour, and set out to hunt for nylon ropes. They spend all evening tracking them down, and it is late as they slowly mount the way again with leaden feet.

Labor day comes cloudily. Will the good weather continue? A thunderstorm can ruin our chances and imperil retreat. We ascend the fixed rope and go to work in deadly earnest. First Jack attempts to pass the rotten overhang. Then I try. It seems as though Salathé and Thune used the last poor piton cracks for the last time. Without piton aid we cannot hold onto the rock, which pushes us outward. The whole trip is at stake. However, two men, for whom we have the greatest of respect by now, have gone ahead; we must, also. Anything is fair now.

An idea! Yes, it is worth trying. We weight an end of rope. Twenty-five feet above our ledge is an outjutting horn of rock. After many awkward casts our rope settles over the horn and does just what we did not want it to do: it wedges tightly! To climb it now would be sheer folly, for if it pulled out a fatal fall might drag us both down. Then we look around the overhang and discover that we can just reach the other end of the rope from our highest piton. We tie onto that end and make it fast. We both hang on the ropes and jerk them to see if the horn is solid; it seems to be.

I look at Jack, who is furiously puffing a cigarette. The stern code of the climber decrees that the lightest man shall lead doubtful pitches. Our fans atop the cliff cannot see what we are doing and to them the maneuver appears incredible as Jack, apparently climbing on nothing, mounts the fixed rope on Prusik knots. To me, braced below for a fall, he appears to be climbing right into the sun. The rotten overhang passed, we easily move to the second ledge where, after swaying in the winds for 40 hours, our guide line miraculously awaits us.

At the rim end of the guide line Bob selects the best spots to anchor one of the nylon ropes and belay with the other. The nylon in 850 feet of half-inch rope would fashion thousands of stockings, but to us it is more precious than that. It provides reliable support under tensions which may approach 3000 pounds. In case of a heavy fall its elastic property offers additional cushioning.

Time is now our greatest opponent. In the stillness of the noon air we four discuss and determine the exact method of executing the coming maneuvers. To the upper end of our light guide line is attached a heavier rope, and to that two strands of nylon, each three rope-lengths long. Double bowline knots that will neither slip nor seriously reduce the rope's effective strength unite the individual ropes. At last comes the order to pull. Jack and I comply. Every time a knot reaches the summit it catches and must be see-sawed back and forth with anxious care lest it slip off sideways. Bob maneuvers from side to side to keep it running over the exact center of the Arrow tip.

The nylons arrive at our ledge. Bob anchors his end of one. Three hundred feet of nylon stretches exasperatingly, so Jack and I pull it down tight before looping it about a large block of rock. This stretches the rope some 20 feet. We now have a new route by which to overcome the final unclimbable summit rock.

To the left the slight cracks of the Salathé route run upward; we are glad we are not called upon to follow them. Twelve hundred feet directly beneath lies the base of the Arrow. Nerve tension mounts; we can not be entirely certain that our rope will stay on the top as we climb it. Jack smokes three cigarettes in succession. "Well, now or never," he smiles. He loops the second nylon rope from above about his waist for an upper belay to Bob. Another forms a lower belay to me, anchored on the ledge to pitons. We shout to Fritz that we are ready. Bob takes up his slack.

Jack begins the ascent, standing in slings wrapped around the fixed rope by Prusik knots which hold fast when weight is applied but can be slipped upward when weight is removed. My neck kinks as I watch Jack lead on and on straight up into the blue sky where little white clouds casually drift over the curious scene. If only Jack could find a crack for a piton it would improve by several times the usefulness of my belay by serving as a pulley point. After 50 feet he finds a good one. Twenty feet higher he finds another and a third. A fall would not hurt very much now. Nearing the summit pitch, Jack finds it indeed unclimbable, save by our method. He is 100 feet above me and his slight figure, wind blowing his hair and jacket, passes from sight.

Twenty feet to go. The angle tapers somewhat. Anticipation is unbearable. The most serious threat to success grows greater; although we could bring Jack down successfully, the chances are that he may pull the rope off to one side as he comes over the lip of the summit and before it gets him to the top. Ten feet to go. At 4:30 P.M. a man crawls safely onto the top of the Lost Arrow for the first time.

Cheers arise from friends who have come up to see the finish, and our own jubilant yodels resound from Columbia Cliffs, half a mile to the west. Jack's stature is dwarfed by the gigantic size of the great pinnacle. Although several men could stand erect on its sloping top, the exposure so near on every side justifies a prone position. He examines the top closely and reports that two slight protuberances have kept our ropes from sliding off. A slight crack is found also, and Jack anchors himself to it with a piton. Lest they fall and imperil retreat he anchors also his two belay ropes before untying them from his body. Then he unites them to form an upper belay running from the men on the rim over the summit and down to me and starts drilling a three-quarter-inch hole for an anchor bolt.

As the sun sinks low I place all our gear in my rucksack and tie to it one end of a 120-foot loose rope whose other end I tie about my waist, so we can pull the rucksack up later. Fritz relays my "up rope!" to Bob. In half an hour I join Jack on top. The sun is setting. Time, if ever it was, now is of the essence. I take over the drilling and Jack goes into conference with Bob and Fritz. A landing ledge on the home cliff about 60 feet horizontally from the summit is our goal for the return. A pine tree 90 feet above affords an anchorage at the proper angle. The ropes are shifted to this new point for the next phase of our adventure, the aerial traverse. I begin another hole to divide the strain of the double fixed ropes.

At one point the belay rope from the rim slips from Jack's grasp as he is handling it and, swinging across to the cliff, it wedges tightly in a fissure. This may complicate the whole venture. Will Jack and I have to lash ourselves to the pinnacle to spend the night shivering? "Pull," we yell despairingly to Fritz and Bob. The rope only wedges more tightly, then with a jerk it comes free. Our pulses beat more slowly as we haul it over on the fixed ropes. Our wonderfully good fortune has not deserted us.

We can now hardly see in the dusk. But the quarter moon peers through some clouds and casts an eerie light. Our return route lies over a black, forbidding abyss. We tighten the eyes of our anchor bolts. Both of us grasp the fixed ropes tightly as we remove them from the piton anchor, thread them through the two eyes, and join them again. Will the bolts, with two inches of granite holding them, be strong enough? Bob and Fritz strain them to the utmost. They seem reliable.

Jack, the lighter man, will again go first. The span on the ropes is nearly 150 feet between anchors. Even though we allow quite a bit of slack, the stress may exceed a ton. Belays are fastened before and behind, and then Jack ties the pack with our most important equipment in it to his back. Looping a sling of rope about his body, he snaps it to the fixed ropes with a carabiner to form a little trolley. Backing off the edge hand-over-hand, head first, he crosses his legs over the heavy line and slides away from me into the darkness.

"See you later, Ax."

Slack goes my rope. Fritz takes up slack on his. If a bolt should break, or the fixed rope, we belayers would have to try to bring our man up in mid-air before his fall gained momentum or he swung crashing into one of the walls. Every precaution has been taken and Jack has literally placed his life in our hands.

His figure is a dark blur out in space. The moon is clouded over. He comes to one of the large knots. Here he must hang by his knees and one elbow, unsnap his trolley arrangement, proceed hand-over-hand past the knot, and snap in again. Tenseness oozes from the darkness.

Suddenly an oath escapes Jack's lips as something drops from him. Is it the carabiner that will keep him from falling off? He reassures us that it is only a piton as we see a flash of sparks and hear it tinkle far below. Several seconds later we faintly hear it hit again. As though this development were not disconcerting enough, a blade of light suddenly stabs the night, blinding us. "Turn that thing off!" we shout spontaneously but futilely. Encouraged by more acid words it winks out after a bit. To comfortable tourists seated at the evening campfire program at Camp Curry the rangers announce that the Lost Arrow has finally been climbed, for they have sighted the white threads of our ropes in their telescopes. Perhaps it is as well that in the distance they did not note Jack hanging from them nor hear our harsh words!

Jack reaches the landing ledge and climbs to the rim above to be greeted warmly. The sporting thing to do now is for Fritz and Bob, the patient engineers of our four-man team, to come over on "The Lost Arrow Trolley and Scenic Railway." Fritz comes first, straining over the complication of the knot and up the arduous hand-over-hand pull from the low point of the traverse. He touches the mighty bulk of the Arrow tip and swings back, his strength beginning to ebb.

Descending to the ledge, Bob considers his turn. The ropes have become tangled. The night is advancing and the moonlight leaving the sky. The Lost Arrow has dealt kindly with its trespassers; we must not strain its generosity. He senses the responsibility of bringing back the last man. Disappointedly but wisely he calls, "Come on, Ax. I'm not crossing."

I stow some gear and loop the rest of our auxiliary ropes to a piton. I also fasten to the summit a little register to record the conquest of "The Last Error." In it are our names, the date of the first ascent, and the title, Sierra Club Rock Climbers. To retrieve our expensive nylon ropes we check them to see if they run freely through the eyes of the anchor bolts. They do, but the ropes are tangled out in mid-air. I must straighten them. Confident in the assistance of my three comrades, should it be needed, I back off, head down, into the blackness. After long, struggling minutes I swing onto the home cliff, feeling like a traveler returning from the moon. I untie one knot and throw off the rope end. Those above pull back our trolley cable and the Arrow is alone again. I am hauled up almost bodily. For the first time we all relax. The whole thing seems a climber's dream.

Friends who have waited patiently for hours have a warm fire to welcome us and hot broth waiting. Offering to help carry our heavy packs, they escort us down the trail. Our bodies are heavy with fatigue but our spirits exalted with the victory as our line of tiny lights, like so many fireflies, zigzags down through the night.

At Columbia Point we pause to rest. The three days of unforgettable adventure have forged a comradeship like that of a bomber crew coming through the perils of war. In the starlight we look back. There looms the Lost Arrow against its own black shadow, silent, implacable, a phantom in the night. Except for a point in time it is as lost as ever. Raising our arms toward it in a last salute, we comrades of the Arrow turn away and down into the night.

65

Five Days and Nights on the Lost Arrow

ANTON NELSON

1948

We have no record of Salathé's feelings on learning that others had topped the Arrow using a route he had pioneered, but he teamed up with Nelson for an assault on Half Dome a few weeks later. The goal was not the famed, nearly sheer "front" of the dome (that formidable wall, known as the "Northwest Face," awaited another generation of climbers) but the unclimbed shoulder toward Glacier Point, known as the Southwest Face. Salathé and Nelson started with a team of several climbers, but they found that the ascent could not be finished before dark. Only Salathé and Nelson were ready to spend the night on the dome, and they persisted after the others had dropped out, completing the ascent the second day.

The Half Dome climb was done by approved mountaineering methods, using only pitons; the Lost Arrow ascent had offended traditional climbers by its use of the ropes slung over from the rim and the "Tyrolean traverse" across that precarious suspension rope. Salathé and Nelson were determined to do the Lost Arrow all the way from the base, with no help from the rim. During the winter they mapped their strategy. And during the early summer of 1947 they watched one team after another make the attempt and fail. Their ultimate success was made possible not only by their technical mastery of climbing skills and Salathé's ingenious equipment but by a Spartan regime of self-denial. Their water ration, for example, was about one-half the minuscule amount climbers normally allow themselves. This classic account by Nelson has some important things to say, to non-climbers as well as climbers, about the meaning of self-mastery and the incredible achievements that may be possible, in any area of life, for those who can summon sufficient will and endurance.

The "class-6 climbing" to which Nelson refers is also called "Aid" or "artificial" climbing, where pitons, slings, and other devices are used to hold the climber's weight, rather than using the rock itself. Climbs in North America are ranked in difficulty from 1 (flat walking) through various gradations of class 5 (difficult climbing directly on the rock), with the sixth added to indicate the use of direct artificial aids. Europeans use a slightly different system —also including six grades —for classifying climbs. In fact, Europe's leading climber, Reinhold Messner, has recommended the addition of a seventh grade to indicate the style in which a climb is done.

WHAT IS REQUIRED to climb Yosemite's Lost Arrow? For years many determined men had tried to find out just that. In trying they succeeded only in showing how terribly close to unclimbable the Arrow really is. Then, on September 3, 1947, John Salathé and I completed a successful assault which we had begun 103 hours earlier at the base of the spire.

True, men had stood atop its summit one year before when a trip from the rim was ingeniously engineered by four Sierra Club climbers. Spectacular and effective though it was, this maneuver required very little real climbing; it was in effect an admission of the Arrow's unclimbability. The problem the Arrow poses for the climber is to ascend from the base up through the ramparts of the great chimney that cuts the spire away from the cliff, and past the three intermediate ledges, called Errors, until he reaches the summit, facetiously called the Fourth or Last Error.

A full story, although it ought to be exciting, would take too much space for present purposes. In its stead, a brief description of the preparations for the ascent is presented for prospective Arrow-climbers.

The equipment included a 120-foot nylon belaying rope, a 300-foot rappel rope; a 150-foot reserve rope for hauling up the thirty-pound pack and other purposes; three foot-slings per climber; eighteen pitons used and re-used in hundreds of places; about the same number of expansion bolts; twelve carabiners; and a "sky hook" invented by Salathé and used on the final summit pitch.

Weight and bulk of equipment was a limiting factor in personal needs, also. Water was the heaviest material, so the supply was limited to three quarts per person and was carried in a plastic bag. This will last up to five days if one does not sweat too much and can discipline the growing temptation to drink. It must be admitted that friends relieved our self-denial on the fourth day with liquid lowered from the rim to Third Error. A number 2 can of fruit juice was held in reserve for a victory toast at the top. Because of the exertions of the day we wet our mouths a little at dawn, took a sip or two at mid-day, and drank most of our liquid at night. Charles Wilts and Spencer Austin, who had reached the previous high point on this route, warned that too much liquid is a major drawback. The dozen or more cans of fruit juice they jettisoned made one wonder how they ever had the strength to haul it all up or how they ever got in through some of the narrow places.

What small amounts of food we ate were rationed in the same way as the water. We believe that the ideal food is raisins, dates, walnuts or peanuts, and fruit-flavored gelatin candies, and that heavier foods, such as starches or meat, would hardly be digestible under the strains of Arrow climbing. We needed no more than four or five pounds per man for five days. That we should lose a great deal of weight on the climb was assumed.

Our basic idea was that we would climb safely or not at all. We understood that rescue from an accident in the Great Chimney was not to be expected. Bombproof belays were in order and unprotected leads of more

258

Climbers
nearing the top
of the Lost Arrow.

than 10 or 15 feet were out of order. When the leader had to take a long chance he did so only when pitons (or bolts) that were sound enough for the anticipated fall were near by and the belayer was on special alert. Then the most that could happen (and not infrequently did happen) was that the leader would take a controlled fall and go right back to work.

For climbing on the Arrow, great strength is far less important than patience and endurance. On the first ascent each of us had been on the Arrow four times before and twice we had set out together for at least three days' work. On Memorial Day, 1947, the route became the bed of a waterfall and ended in a precarious rappel. On Fourth of July week end, much was learned during two days and a night on the rock, in which Second Error was attained for the first time. Better equipment was needed. We had thought ourselves in the pink of condition, but after only two days the state of nervous and physical exhaustion dictated retreat and far more rigorous preparation for the next attempt.

Several bivouacs on cliff walls, with or without warm clothes, taught us not to expect much rest on a climb. I took a hike the length of the John Muir Trail, practicing making long marches with little or no water. Doing that for four days in one's own home is good enough practice for mastering thirst — for learning, that is, how much thirst is to be safely endured. If one lacks time for long periods in the mountains, running steadily for an hour or so is a good way to build up the heart, lungs, nerves, and muscles for the long endurance at higher altitudes needed by any kind of mountaineering activity. To prevent the onset of cramps one needs brisk calisthenics to train climbing muscles far beyond their normal capacities. On the Arrow, failure to hold oneself to comparable preparations may be sufficient to scuttle a team's most carefully laid plans, and it has done so more than once.

For prospective Arrow climbers, it is important to have or acquire experience and competence with things mechanical; a manual acquaintance with forces, materials, and their relationships is a must.

This brings one to the matter of practical philosophy. One cannot climb at all unless he has sufficient urge to do so. Danger must be met — indeed, it must be *used* — to an extent beyond that incurred in normal life. That is one reason men climb; for only in response to challenge does a man become his best. Yet any do-or-die endeavors are to be condemned. Life is more precious than victory. In the safest possible climbing on the Arrow there is more than enough stimulus from probable and present danger. To know one's limitations and to keep within them is the essence of good sense. A comparatively weak party, sensitive to its weak points and keeping within their limits, will outlive and outclimb the strongest team which proceeds indiscreetly.

One thing is *not* an adequate motive for climbing; that is egotism or pride. Yes, most of us who climb usually play to the crowd, as such an article as this may demonstrate. However, mere self-assertion alone has a low breaking point. To keep going day after day under heart-sickening strenuousness requires a bigger, more powerful faith than in oneself or in any concept of superiority.

Conversely, I feel that a man who, through emotional temperament or habit, is used to the false stimulus of alcohol has two strikes against him before he undertakes a long climb. The psychological impact of continually new and increasing difficulties while one's physical resources seem to be running down is enough without being fettered by an undisciplined imagination or by emotional crutches. Human limitations are indeed more serious than the natural ones to be faced.

A brief description of the first ascent may illustrate some of the foregoing points. In 1937 the 350 feet to First Error took 6 hours; 35 pitons were used for protection. In the 1947 ascent of the Arrow, we passed that point, hauling our 30-pound pack between us, in just three hours, using no more than a dozen pitons. Time was a major limiting factor and all possible haste was made when there was a chance. Nearly half the distance, 650 feet, was beat out the first day in the 13 hours before darkness fell.

On the second day increasing problems really began slowing us down. We rope-traversed from the detour going out to Second Error back into the narrowest portion of the chimney where it slashes nearly 100 feet into

260

the heart of the cliff. At midday we arrived at the vertical headwall of the chimney where Wilts and Austin had turned back on their second attempt after two and a half days. From then on the class-6 climbing began in earnest; 350 feet were made the second day, 200 each on the next two, and the last 50 feet on the morning of the fifth day. The first pitch of this sort, 150 feet long, was mostly rotten granite. Salathé led for 8 hours without relief, save for the interruption of darkness. Two pitches above this point, massive, overhanging blocks had to be climbed by the exceedingly wide cracks between them. Often there seemed no evident route at all.

After the second day our muscles no longer cramped and we put thirst in its place. Bivouacking on the chockstones with our feet dangling, our backs aching where they were being nudged by granite knobs, and our shoulders tugging at their anchors, we got little sleep. Cold winds barely permitted us to keep warm enough for the rest essential to the digestion of food. The hours until dawn should permit the greater comfort of climbing were passed largely in talk. Food, sleep, and water can be dispensed with to a degree not appreciated until one is in a position where little can be had.

Frank Kittredge, then superintendent of Yosemite, asked if the 1947 Labor Day ascent of the Lost Arrow were not "the longest and most difficult high climb on record, presumably on sound rock. . . ." It is merely pointed out that Lost Arrow granite can often be far from sound. The Lost Arrow *can* be climbed again, perhaps in only four days. At any rate its superb challenge is there. To those who made the first vertical traverse of its Four Errors it stands as a symbol of high and unforgettable adventure.

Ordeal by Piton

66

ALLEN STECK

1951

Yosemite climbers next turned their attention from the Lost Arrow to an unclimbed wall across the valley — the north face of Sentinel Rock, 3000 feet above the valley floor. Salathé and Nelson looked it over, but decided to rest on their laurels. In the spring of 1950, a group of college climbers reached a point about halfway up before turning back. One of them was Allen Steck, who had climbed in the Alps, made a first ascent in the Dolomites, and was determined to force the Sentinel. Late in June he made an impulsive phone call to Salathé and asked the "elderly" Swiss iron monger, now fifty-one, to join him. Equally impulsively, Salathé accepted.

261

THIS STORY is not unique in the relatively short history of class-six climbing—there are many two- and three-day ascents listed today in the Swiss, Austrian, and Italian Alps; indeed, directly across from Sentinel Rock, in the Yosemite Valley, is the unmistakable spire of the Lost Arrow, climbed from its base for the first time in September of 1947. This five-day ascent by John Salathé and Ax Nelson was considered the greatest achievement of its kind in the history of tension climbing.

The Sentinel climb was of equal rank, perhaps even surpassed it—who can say? John used to tell me, as we waited out the sleepless bivouacs, that he couldn't decide which was "better." "You know, Al," he'd say, looking out across the valley at the Lost Arrow, "it's still a pretty good climb. You and Long ought to climb it next." My answer was a despairing grumble: my next climb was going to be Sentinel Dome in a wheelchair.

I lay awake many a night in Berkeley wondering what this north wall was like above the buttress; it was almost an obsession with me. This sort of feeling is indeed strange to the hiker or fisherman, yet it is typical of the climber.

Many have questioned the quality of this sort of achievement, deploring the use of pitons, tension traverses, and expansion bolts, but the record speaks for itself. This is a technical age and climbers will continue in the future to look for new routes. There is nothing more satisfying than being a pioneer.

The lure of the Sentinel Wall goes back to 1936, when Morgan Harris, William Horsfall and Olive Dyer made a reconnaissance on the north face. Rising a full 3,000 feet from the grassy floor of the Yosemite Valley, its sheer north exposure presented a fantastic problem in route finding; true, there was only one possible route (i.e., the Great Chimney), still there was the big question: how to use it? They reached the Tree Ledge, a prominent sandy terrace 1,500 feet above the floor, at the very foot of the north wall proper.

Several years later Morgan Harris and Dave Brower succeeded in reaching the Tree Ledge, and from the westernmost portion of this ledge they pioneered a route across the west face of Sentinel Rock and up its broken south side. The north wall remained untouched until the early 'forties, and, after several attempts by Robin Hansen, Jack Arnold and Fritz Lippmann, a high point was finally established some 150 feet above the Tree Ledge, to the right of the huge buttress that lies up against the lower portion of the wall. The difficulty was severe, but each attempt added to the knowledge of the route. It seemed of little concern that there was over 1,300 feet of tougher climbing yet to do. That problem would take care of itself eventually.

In the fall of 1948, Jim Wilson and Phil Bettler took the initiative and reached a ledge a hundred feet still higher, setting a new record. Then in October 1949 a four-man party—Phil Bettler, Jim Wilson, Bill Long, and I—arrived at the Tree Ledge prepared to make the first bivouac on the face, and were able to climb some 200 feet past the old high point. We passed the night on a loose, tilted chockstone directly beneath the 60-foot, 100-degree "Wilson Overhang." One person could stretch out comfortably, but unfortunately there were four of us. No one was able to sleep but Phil, who had taken one of Jim's backache pills to ease his headache — they were knockout pills, a decided must for any climber's bivouac equipment. Cursing Phil for his contented snoring, the rest of us waited out the night. Morning came and we continued up over the overhang, admirably led by Jim, to a new high point about 450 feet above the Tree Ledge. All eight leads were various degrees of class-six climbing, and over fifty pitons had been necessary.

Then came the remarkable ascent over the 1950 Memorial Day week end. Bill Long and Phil Bettler, in a two-day ascent, succeeded in reaching the top of the great 800-foot buttress, and thus the first major problem of the wall was conquered. Above the top of the buttress stretched the final 700-foot face, whose broad expanse was broken only by the Great Chimney, a large dark cleft easily seen from the valley. This still remained the only possible way to the summit.

"The first sixty feet (the Headwall Lead) above the buttress is smooth, vertical granite. The Great Chimney is over a hundred feet to the left; it seems impossible to reach even by a tension traverse. Three hundred feet above the Chimney narrows down to less than a foot and the walls are bare and overhanging. You may get into the Chimney, but 'The Narrows' looks doubtful." Thus had Long and Bettler reported the situation at the top of the buttress. The Narrows seemed — and ultimately proved — to be the most spectacular lead on the entire wall.

As on the Arrow, the route here was unmistakably clear; we joked about who was going to be the first to make the terrible 150-foot swinging traverse into the Chimney, but it seemed unlikely that this was the easiest way. There were a few small water cracks leading up the head wall that looked "feasible," to use the word loosely.

On June 30 John Salathé and I climbed up to the Tree Ledge, prepared for another long siege. At the foot of the buttress we sorted our supply of hardware: fifteen carabiners, ten or so horizontal pitons, about eight angle pitons, and 12 expansion bolts plus hangers. We also carried a 300-foot rappel and a 120-foot quarter-inch hauling line for the packs, along with a little dried fruit. Our water, more dried foodstuffs, and a small can of tuna were up on the ledge 200 feet above, where Jim and I had left them [earlier that year].

Two days brought us over now familiar ledges to the small cairn on the buttress — 800 feet and some eighty pitons later. From there on all was still unknown.

We were to be another two and a half days reaching the summit, only 700 feet above, but requiring seventy-six pitons plus nine bolts. The upper part of the chimney is broken, and many of the leads were composed of short class-four stretches between class-six overhangs. The last lead to the summit was a 110-foot class-four "scramble."

On the entire four-and-a-half-day climb, thirteen leads were made by John and twelve by me. The ascent of this wall was probably the toughest one that either of us had ever made, or ever hoped to make again. Though John has 51 years to my 24, the climb seemed to have little effect on his endurance; only toward the end of the third day, did he seem to show signs of wear, but then both of us were ready to acknowledge the pleasures of simple back-country hiking. It was just too damned hot. Each afternoon at two the sun came from behind the wall and turned the face into a veritable furnace; temperatures up to 105° were recorded down in the valley and there wasn't a breath of wind. We could watch the swimmers down in the valley, languishing in the cool waters of the Merced — one would dive in now and then and we could easily see the white foamy splash as he hit the water. The thought of suddenly finding myself in a cool fragrant spring was so maddening that it was hard to keep my balance. If only those swimmers would stop splashing! And this was only the third day! John never said much about it, but I knew he was thirsty. Standing there in slings, with his hammer poised over the star drill, John would turn his head and say, "Al, if I only could have just a little orange juice!" Up on that wall, oh what such a simple thing as a glass of orange juice would have been worth!

Inside the Great Chimney, I happened upon a little crack, glistening in the shadows. I remember watching, my lips tight and drawn, while a little bead of water seeped out and smoothly slid down the rock. It was barely enough to moisten my lips and wet my mouth, yet it was a wonderful sensation. We were so short on water that we could eat little during those five days. John left his dates in the chimney; he was tired of carrying them. I threw my food away upon reaching the summit. All in all I would guess that we ate half a pound of food apiece — as a liberal guess!

With ten expansion bolts already placed, the second ascent should do better, if there should ever be one. Six were needed on the Headwall lead. John stood in slings more than ten hours on that one. That day, the third, we made a total of only two hundred and forty feet. And after struggling over every foot of it, we were faced with the possibility of having to turn back. Not being able to go straight up, we climbed back into the chimney and eventually, through an inner chamber, reached a large ledge directly beneath The Narrows. Again the same old story — where to go? I can only say that there was little there with which to work. John finally made a bold attempt, using pitons upon which only he would ever rely (the double variety — back to back!); hanging almost horizontal, he was barely able to reach around to the outside of the chimney. The piton crack that he found made the lead. The Narrows were behind us!

The leads above here were agonizing in the hot sun. Still no wind. The packs got jammed in the chimneys, causing a great deal of wear on the nerves; there were bitter words, and we weren't afraid to let our tempers explode. When Ax Nelson heard of our plans, he remarked once to John, "If you expect to make the top, Al will have to be every bit as stubborn as you!" John agreed that I was.

The awful thirst. The overpowering heat cannot be described in simple words. Once on the top we could see the thin foamy line of the stream down in the gorge. We were on top, sure, but the ordeal wasn't over. We had yet to get down to the water that was staring us in the face. I slowed down for John as long as I could stand it, and then bolted down the couloir. I paid bitterly for my haste, for I descended into steep chimneys and had to claw my way

264

back up through the hot dusty deerbrush looking for another way. My judgment was numbed by the thought of water. I tripped over bushes, fell over unseen ledges, and finally collapsed fully clothed into a pool at the foot of a small waterfall. This was the climax of the climb, a supreme climax! And I can say, in retrospect, that it was well worth the effort. The reason, the incentive, the motive for all this? It is an intangible, provocative concept that I shall leave to the reader to explain. Some think they know why; others despair of ever knowing. I'm not too sure myself.

CLIMBING THE TWO BIGGEST WALLS

As if the Lost Arrow and Sentinel ascents had exhausted the possibilities for contemporary climbers, there were no further major first ascents in Yosemite for six years, although new routes were found up previously climbed summits. Then in 1957 and 1958 came two history-making climbs, one that was done quietly, with scarcely any notice, and one that was heralded by the greatest fanfare ever to accompany a climb in North America.

The first was the long-postponed assault on the "front" of Half Dome, the Northwest Face, by Southern Californians Royal Robbins, Jerry Gallwas, and Michael Sherrick, a five-day ordeal that had been preceded, like most Yosemite climbs, by several unsuccessful probes by various climbers. One of the precautions the team had taken was to arrange a system of flashlight signals to their support party at Mirror Lake. In order to avoid attracting attention, they signaled only at the time of the nightly Firefall, when most eyes on the valley floor were turned to Glacier Point. In Sherrick's Bulletin *account of this amazing first ascent of the steepest face of the world-famed monolith, he noted that the team was "fortunate to avoid publicity about an accomplishment which would only have been made into a sensation."*

It is understandable that climbers whose ethics made a point of avoiding publicity were dismayed at the hoopla that attended the razzle-dazzle assault on El Capitan by Warren Harding and party. Harding was a young civil engineer who, like the other Southern Californians, had trained on the mecca of rock climbers in the Los Angeles area—Tahquitz Rock near Mount San Jacinto, which towers above Palm Springs. In 1954 Harding had been a member of a team that made the second ascent of the Lost Arrow up the Chimney Route from the base, the route pioneered by Salathé and Nelson seven years earlier. His next goal was the Northwest Face of Half Dome, but when he and his team arrived there in June of 1957, he found Robbins, Gallwas, and Sherrick already well on their way up. He was severely disappointed but climbed the back of the dome by the regular cable route and greeted them when they scrambled triumphantly over the top on the sixth day.

Rebuffed at Half Dome, he determined to try something of similar magnitude—the 3000-foot face of El Capitan. He had no idea how long the climb would take, but felt it would require a new strategy that came to be known as "expeditionary" rock climbing, paralleling the intricate logistics of Himalayan expeditions. By going up and down the lower wall repeatedly over a six-day period, a large party of climbers and suppliers established a series of "camps" on the narrow ledges, the highest 1100 feet

265

up, all linked with fixed ropes. Each camp was stocked with food and water, ropes and hardware, laboriously hauled up on ropes from the bottom, hand over hand.

Since the base of the rocks was in easy view of Yosemite tourists, the climbers had a growing audience that threatened to stop all traffic. The mob scene was too much for Yosemite rangers, who after a week of turmoil ruled permanently against any further climbing on El Capitan during the tourist season from Memorial Day to Labor Day. Harding and company returned in September and inched farther up the wall before winter closed in. The "expedition" continued in spurts, over a period of seventeen months, as the difficulty steadily increased owing to an overhang near the top and the increasing weight of hauling food, water, and equipment a vertical half-mile up the wall. At dawn on November 12, 1958, after drilling bolt holes all night, Harding clambered over the top, followed by teammates Wayne Merry and George Whitmore. The climb had made page-one headlines across the nation and in Europe.

67

Realm of the Overhang

ALLAN MacDONALD

1962

After El Capitan, what next? Across the valley, immediately west of Bridalveil Fall, was the Leaning Tower, less spectacular than El Capitan but an even greater climbing challenge owing to the "lean" or overhang of the 1000-foot west face, far greater than any of the overhangs on El Capitan. There was little possibility here of "free" climbing, in which ropes and pitons are used only for safety, to check a fall. The alternative was to use them as direct aid, the only method feasible on an overhang.

The Bulletin account of the Leaning Tower climb was written by Allan Mac-Donald of Berkeley, a graduate of the Sierra Club rock climbing school and an advertising writer for Standard Oil. The article was put in context by some comments of Alfred W. Baxter, a former climber.

D AWN, on the last day of 1960, was cold, clear, and ominous. Although no snow had fallen, Yosemite Valley felt the hush of winter. The friendly burble of rushing water was gone. Bridalveil Fall hung above us in icy sheets, while the surrounding peaks retreated into silence, their smooth granite walls gray and cold. In these austere and solemn surroundings, we began one of the greatest adventures of our lives.

We were headed for the Leaning Tower, an impressive peak. Only 1860 feet above the Valley floor, its height is not great by Yosemite standards. But height is only one measure of a mountain. The severe and continuous overhang of the Tower's west face presents an extreme in difficult climbing. It might be compared to the Matterhorn in Whymper's day—a step beyond what any one had done. In the words of many climbers it was "for the next generation."

Considering the wall, we thought it seemed obvious that the ascent of the Tower would extend over many days, even weeks, causing supply and organizational problems encountered only in major mountaineering expeditions. A new method of climbing, introduced in the ascent of El Capitan's south buttress, would be required—expeditionary rock climbing.

Such a climb would also require a special type of leader. Without question, the perfect man for the job was Warren Harding, whose first ascents on El Capitan, the Washington Column, and many lesser known peaks are counted among the most difficult in the United States. Not only is he a superb climber possessing exceptional endurance, but he has experience, maturity, and organizational ability as well.

In the fall of 1960, Warren, ever in search of more daring struggles, turned his attention to the Tower's west face. The unattempted, seemingly unclimbable wall had offered a challenge he couldn't resist.

Warren led off into the gloomy forest beneath the west face, his wiry body dwarfed under a huge pack. Next, as porter, came Les Wilson, an old climbing friend of mine. I brought up the rear, following their intricate path through the giant talus boulders. The Tower loomed above us, massive and overpowering.

Across the valley, the top of mighty "El Cap" was catching the first rays of light as we reached a small ledge that traverses the face, separating it into upper and lower halves. The lower, sloping wall is almost vertical; above the ledge, it bulges sickeningly out into space, overhanging the entire distance to the summit in one grand sweep. Above a stunted tree, 150 feet across the ledge, several small bolts (placed earlier by Warren) projected from the wall in a line 60 feet high. Above these, a roof extending out from the cliff, which had stopped a previous try, posed our first real climbing problem. A thin but strong nylon rope, suspended from the topmost bolt, allowed us to ascend by prusik technique that portion of the wall already climbed.

Warren was soon ready for this airy trip up. With professional ease he stepped off the ledge into space to hang suspended 15 feet from the wall and 400 feet above the ground. He rose, rhythmically moving the prusik knots higher and higher, while a small breeze set the whole system, climber and rope, swaying like a giant pendulum.

In fifteen minutes he reached the high point where the serious climbing began up the right side of the roof. Placing direct-aid pitons behind a very loose flake of rock, Warren found that each piton he put in threatened to dislodge the one below it, or worse, the flake itself. Finally, to the great relief of Les and me, he changed to bolts. The angle at this point was more than 120 degrees. Warren worked tediously with rawl drill and hammer. After

267

twenty minutes of back-breaking work caused by the constant tension of the rope and back belt around his waist, he excavated a tiny hole one-inch deep and ¼-inch in diameter. This effort was so exhausting that many times Warren would collapse quietly in his slings, head and arms hanging down in complete rest.

After pounding in a small expansion bolt, he gained three more feet. Just above his head was another loose flake. In delicate balance, he carefully tested it. Deciding against pitons, he prepared to place another bolt, when without warning the flake broke off and crashed down on his head.

"Dammit! Dammit!" Warren's angry and painful words broke the silence.

"Warren! What happened? Are you hurt?"

A moan was the only reply.

I tied off the belay line and got out prusik slings. If he was unable to help himself we had only a short time to reach him before he would strangle in his own safety rope.

"Warren!" Les yelled again.

"My neck. I think it's broken."

"Do you want me to come up and lower you down?" I called.

"I don't know. Let me rest a second."

Small flecks of blood floated down. "You'd better go up, Al," Les said.

What a stinking mess, I thought. With adrenalin and butterflies both working on me at once, I tied the prusik loops to the climbing rope.

"I think I can make it down okay," said Warren.

"Be sure," I said. "How's your neck? Can you move your head at all?"

"Yeah. All the way around. I can see pretty good too—two of every-thing."

What a relief! That sounded like the old Warren. The situation which could very easily have had disastrous results was under control. After a careful and cautious retreat, we rushed Warren to the hospital where six or seven stitches were required to close the wound in his head. This incident put a rather ominous end to our first attempt.

SECOND ATTEMPT. JUNE 17–24, 1961

Heat, tourists, and smoke. That was Yosemite in June of 1961. And I mean heat. It was the warmest we had ever felt it in the Valley. The Tower was just as forbidding as it had been last December, but in a different way. Now it was the wall of an oven, reflecting heat and glare, painful to touch.

Saturday and Sunday, Warren and I, with the help of Chris Westphal, carried piles of climbing equipment and supplies (including nylon ropes, pitons, carabiners, five gallons of water, food, and personal gear) to our starting ledge. It wasn't until Sunday afternoon that we actually continued up the climb itself.

Warren again took the lead and bolted until after dark, ending the first pitch 135 feet up an immense granite wall. He prusiked down, a small dark object silhouetted against the night, a creature from another world. We

268

found the climb back across the ledge using the fixed ropes particularly exhilarating at night. The entire ledge is decomposing, and the frequency with which footholds dislodged and crashed hundreds of feet below made us particularly cautious. We worked our way down the talus using headlamps, and finally arrived at the ranger station at 11 P.M. We were a bit discouraged to find no word yet from George Whitmore, who was to be the third member of our party.

Nevertheless, on Monday Warren and I again climbed the talus, determined to force the route as high as we could. I was to belay in slings from the high point while Warren bolted above. I had only prusiked three or four times on a climb and nothing as severe as this. It was a mental block I had to overcome.

Taking a deep breath I pushed my chest prusik up and stepped off the ledge. Soon I was a full 25 feet from the wall! It was like being suspended from an airplane, a truly fantastic experience. When I reached the plumb line and began to rise, I started spinning like a twisted yo-yo. Warren, laughing like a madman, didn't help matters much. I discovered that if I concentrated solely on what I was doing and watched the rope right in front of me, the spinning wouldn't make me dizzy.

At the highest bolt I attached a wooden sling seat and was soon on belay to Warren. He came up and proceeded to pass over me in a tangle of ropes and slings. The overhanging wall pushed both of us out, impressing us with the prospect of a 500-foot free fall to the talus below. We started to laugh at what a ridiculous sight this must seem to the tourists watching from the Bridalveil Fall parking lot. It was rather strained laughter, though, as there was only one bolt holding the two of us.

Warren set to work at once. With tremendous endurance he pounded and pounded on the rawl drill. The extreme overhanging angle of the wall placed a great strain on Warren's feet and back, allowing him only ten or twelve strokes of the hammer before a rest. He also got cramps in his hands from constantly holding the drill above his head. Occasionally, during a rest period, Warren would haul up a plastic bottle filled with repulsively warm orange juice. All the while the sun seared into us, stifling desire and ambition. I found myself dozing on the belay, the last thing I thought I'd ever do. After what seemed an eternity, the sun reached the horizon and retreat for the night was in order. Our reward for the day — only 35 feet of burning granite.

That night, still no word from George. We met Glen Denny, a tall red-headed climber who had proved himself on the face climbs of Mount Conness and Keeler Needle. We didn't have to talk hard to persuade him to accompany us. Refreshed and encouraged by this piece of good luck, we slept at Camp 4 in hopes of an early start Tuesday.

In the morning, Glen and Warren started up the talus ahead of me as they would be climbing today. Our ascent was beginning to collect tourists like flies. One man, a tanned, bearded fellow, started up the talus behind me. It was George! At last the climbing party was complete.

Since George would be on the starting ledge, this gave me the day free to

269

photograph and watch the climb from below like a tourist. Borrowing binoculars and eavesdropping, I had a very interesting and enjoyable afternoon. One older fellow had a telescope set up that could focus on Warren's ear—absolutely unbelievable. Comments varied from "crazy fools" to the most elaborate but erroneous descriptions of "what was going on up there." I was amazed at how misinformed most people are about climbing. Some actually believed that we stood on the ledge and threw the rope up the cliff, and that after the rope mystically attached itself to the rock, we pulled ourselves up hand over hand.

By Wednesday Warren had reached the end of the second pitch beneath a large overhang. The three bolts to which he attached the second fixed line were bad, and I decided to belay from the first anchor bolt. High above, Warren continued the lead, while George, below, started up the first fixed line to straighten out some tangled ropes. While adjusting my belay seat I noticed white dust on my pant legs. My anchor bolt had bent down and appeared to be coming out. I shouted a warning and quickly stepped up into a sling attached to the bolt above. George, hanging in space below, set an Olympic prusik record for descending.

With a wildly beating heart I watched Warren lower the bolt kit down on the hauling line. I placed another ⅜-inch bolt and tied the two anchors together. Everything secure, a moment of anguish had passed.

Warren turned the overhang to the right and reached the beginning of a flaky crack where he ended the third pitch. I prusiked up the climbing rope and took out the bolts between us. We were short on bolt hangers and had to re-use them above. The bolts came out so easily I wondered if they would hold even a short fall.

It was 5:30 P.M. when, hot and tired, I reached the upper belay bolts. Sweat poured out of us and the warm orange juice couldn't quench our thirst. We decided against climbing on into the night and prusiked down.

Thursday, George and I awoke to sounds of tourists arriving in cars. News of the climb was really spreading. We met a television news photographer and carried his cameras to the beginning of the ledge where he spent the day photographing.

Above, Warren and Glen were hard at work on the flaky crack. Alternating pitons and bolts they climbed on through the day with the temperature hovering around 105 degrees. Since they were high up on the wall now, they decided to push on into the night and take advantage of the cooler hours. I waited at the traverse ledge by the hauling line, and George found a hole between two talus boulders 500 feet below. The acoustics were such that the climbing party could not talk directly to me, but we could relay messages with George as middleman. George promptly fell asleep, however, considerably confusing matters.

The night was beautiful—every star in sight. From above, the steady tap . . . tap . . . tap of bolts being driven kept me company. Garbled messages echoed off the buttress to the west. It wasn't until 3 A.M. that the noise stopped and I could lie down on the narrow ledge to catch a quick nap before morning.

Sometime that night, Warren and Glen had reached a sloping ledge they named "Guano" because of the birds' nests in the overhangs directly above. A 20-foot traverse to the left led to another ledge we called "Ahwahnee." Fortunately, Ahwahnee had dished-out sleeping places and was one of the best bivouac ledges we had ever seen. It was a monumental piece of luck and a real dent in the Tower's armor.

When I awoke Friday morning I climbed down to find George. After our short breakfast George yelled up to Warren, 1,000 feet higher, "What's it look like above?"

There was a long pause and a discouraging answer floated back, "It looks bad—real bad!" Our hearts dropped. Surely it couldn't be as hard as the portion we had just climbed. But above, the Tower's defenses multiplied—blank overhanging walls with small roofs jutting out here and there and near the summit a tremendous triangular overhang. If we could have tipped the Tower upside down it would have made an easy fifth-class climb.

George prusiked up with food and water and straightened out the hauling lines, which had become horribly tangled during the night. I followed, taking out more bolts on the fourth and fifth pitches, arriving on Guano in the afternoon.

The exhausted faces that met me showed defeat. The wall above looked unbelievably difficult. We couldn't go on. The suffocating heat plus the strenuous climbing and logistical problems had beaten us. Glen and I prusiked down by nightfall, and Warren and George came down the next day. Warren had been leading during the last six days in terribly hot weather and climbing all night Thursday, truly an incredible show of tenacity and endurance.

To escape the heat we piled all the climbing gear in George's car and sped to Tuolumne Meadows where we sorted the equipment on the cool grass. After lunch we headed home. It would be three months before we struggled on the great wall again.

THIRD ATTEMPT. OCTOBER 7–13, 1961

With renewed enthusiasm we spent the weekend of September 30, 1961, getting ready for our next assault. Saturday, Glen and I hauled supplies to Guano after first ascending the fixed ropes we had left last June. Warren tied on loads below while Dick Maroney, a photographer, documented the climb. George, much to our disappointment, was unable to come because of business commitments.

With blistering hands we managed to pull up five heavy loads. Warren joined us on the ledge in the evening, and we spent a glorious night on Ahwahnee with a candle weirdly illuminating the ledge and casting giant

271

shadows on the wall. We felt an immense sense of detachment and adventure—only a single nylon line connecting our world with the one below.

Warren had to leave for his home in Sacramento early Sunday morning, while Glen and I remained to rig a pulley system to ease the burden of hauling. When this chore was done we prusiked down (rappeling was impossible as the fixed ropes were pulled tight against the cliff to prevent our spinning on the way up) and reached Berkeley by dark, satisfied that we were ready for the big push, a week later.

The Tower's day of reckoning was approaching. We carried approximately 200 pounds of food and water as well as climbing equipment to the talus directly beneath Guano Ledge. Our food supply was composed of everything imaginable, including both canned and perishable foods from pomegranates to sardines. We took approximately 12 gallons of water, most of which we converted to Kool-Aid. Among the climbing equipment were drills, bolts, bolt hangers, all sizes of pitons, carabiners, 600 feet of $7/16$-inch nylon climbing ropes and 1200 feet of $3/8$-inch nylon hauling line. Ahwahnee Ledge fortunately was large enough to accommodate sleeping bags, so these were added to the list. All that remained was to get this huge mass up the wall to the upper ledges.

Warren and I prusiked up, towing the 1200-foot hauling line. The rope didn't even touch the cliff! It hung straight to the talus. When we were ready to haul, Glen tied on a load and we tried to pull it up. It was no use.

"Too heavy! You'll have to lighten the load," we yelled down.

"There's only two gallons of water in it now," came the reply.

Hauling directly from the talus, about 1,000 feet, obviously wouldn't work. The weight of the rope, the load, and friction where the hauling line rubbed over Guano Ledge were more than Warren and I could lift. This meant Glen had to spend most of the night carrying loads 400 feet higher to the traversing ledge. Meanwhile, Warren and I, spending a comfortable night on Ahwahnee in sleeping bags, thought highly of Glen for his noble efforts.

It was clear, cold, and windy Sunday morning. Despite heavy clothing we almost froze getting ready to haul. Now it was Glen's turn to rest while Warren and I pulled thirteen loads up, almost covering Ahwahnee with supplies. Hauling is arm-tiring, exhausting work. Hand over hand . . . 25 feet . . . 50 feet . . . 75 feet . . . rest. Rope piles up on the ledge, making it difficult to move around. And finally, when you think you just can't pull any longer, a scrape is heard and a duffel bag with its small treasure appears over the edge.

That afternoon, while Warren was stocking Ahwahnee Ledge with food, a sudden gust of wind inflated my sleeping bag and flung it at him. He yelled and all but fell off the ledge getting out of the way. The sleeping bag, defying gravity, floated upwards 50 feet out from the Tower like a flying carpet, then collapsed and dove madly toward the talus below. Glen thought a giant rock had broken loose and was headed his way. The bag eventually landed 40 feet up a tree about 100 feet out from the base of the cliff.

When Glen joined us, my sleeping bag in tow, he found me belaying Warren on the sixth pitch. Typical piton-placing went like this: a poor angle, a ¼-inch bolt, a tied-off knifeblade, an angle behind an expanding flake, a Simond channel that shifted and bent in half. It was a most formidable pitch. At almost every piton came the casual warning, "This one looks pretty bad. Be ready." Warren finally reached a point 100 feet diagonally up and to the right of Guano Ledge. He placed a small bolt there and prusiked down the climbing rope to the ledge well after dark. Glen, flashlight in hand, lit our way across to Ahwahnee.

As we had neglected to bring a primus stove with us, we had no warm meals. Sunday the main course was cold ravioli.

The next morning Warren resumed his lead with Glen belaying. Climbing a large deep crack using bong-bongs (over-sized angle pitons), he reached a belay stance on a small sloping foothold. It seemed like a ledge to us. We rated the pitch as very severe sixth class taking 34 pitons, three ¼-inch bolts, and eight hours to lead. Because this pitch was diagonal, the prusik was almost horizontal for some distance, placing a good strain on rather doubtful anchor bolts.

Glen had some trouble following Warren's lead, because a few of the pitons came out in his hand before he could step on them. Nonetheless, he soon reached Warren and continued the lead diagonally left on six pitons, most of them knifeblades (an extremely small hard piton for hairline cracks), and three tiny ³/₁₆-inch bolts. Darkness crept up the wall, bathing the Tower in splendid alpenglow, as Glen and Warren set up the ropes for retreat.

An early breakfast Tuesday morning meant that I was on belay before 8:30 A.M. Glen finished his lead, placing eleven more ³/₁₆-inch bolts. At the end of the pitch he placed a good ³/₈-inch bolt. For once the bolt drove in well, and the large flake of rock it was imbedded in seemed solid, too. A fixed rope was installed from this bolt to Guano Ledge 200 feet below.

Following this pitch I found that Glen, who is quite tall, had spread the pitons and bolts extremely far apart. Later, Warren and I talked about designing a "Denny-Arm," a device allowing you to make the absurd reaches prerequisite for anyone who follows Glen on a sixth-class lead. We left the bolts in on this pitch, but removed the hangers to re-use above. After reaching Glen, I was able to rappel down the rope 180 feet before prusiking into the ledge became necessary (a distance of about 25 feet). It was a wild free rappel, however, and we stuck to prusiking during the remainder of the climb.

Humor was building up to gigantic proportions, and rarely a moment went by when one of us wasn't laughing at something. It was a good way to relieve tension and bound our party even more closely together.

From our high point on Tuesday, an overhanging "open book" filled with mud and weeds led onward, blocked from time to time by small roofs. On

Wednesday I belayed in slings while Warren placed 29 pitons of moderate sixth class. The "Garden Pitch" was felt to be an appropriate name for this section. Warren would laugh and say, "Close eyes, please," as large masses of dirt and foliage rained down. A big, loose block of rock at the end of this pitch presented a problem. Somehow Warren managed to push it off. We could see the ground clearly and were sure no one was beneath the block. We also took the precaution of yelling "Rock!" several times before we let it go. The huge slab whooshed past me, 15 feet from the wall, and plummeted 1100 feet to the talus below. The loud crash echoed across the Valley. I removed the pitons from the pitch and we returned to Guano Ledge, dirty and worn out.

We were all getting tired of cold food. Stew was on the menu for tonight. It had almost no taste and left a cold, slimy feeling in my mouth. I ate very little, but Warren and Glen, having much sturdier stomachs than I, finished it off to the last drop. We passed another star-filled night telling climbing stories, a favorite pastime among climbers, and the party remained in high spirits.

Thursday was my rest day. Lying on my back on Ahwahnee Ledge, I soaked up sun and enjoyed the pleasurable experience of watching Warren and Glen climbing hundreds of feet above—a delicate ballet in air of two superb climbers.

Glen led a short, vertical pitch ending under the large triangular roof which is clearly visible from the Valley floor. This we were sure would be another crucial section. Warren took the lead. He was now climbing parallel to the ground in the most acrobatic fashion. The large bong-bong pitons he pounded in made strange music to accompany this impressive and awesome sight. The angle eased back to 140 degrees as he passed the outer edge of the roof. It was very strenuous sixth class. He climbed free the last 25 feet to two sloping ledges—the only portion of the climb made without direct aid.

Night was almost upon us. The Valley was already in shadow. From our separated points—Warren and Glen 500 feet above my spot on Ahwahnee Ledge—we held a council of war. We decided to bivouac on the tiny upper ledges, anticipating reaching the summit the next day.

The sun was just setting as I hastily threw some dried and canned apricots, fruit juice, flashlight, and clothing into a hauling bag and cleaned up Ahwahnee Ledge. After a last look at this fabulous place that had been our home for so long, I began the long prusik up. In a relatively short time I reached the bottom of the overhang and remained there in slings while Glen cleaned the pitons out of the roof. He finally reached Warren and they tied off the prusik rope. After another delay they were ready to haul up the sack. I dropped the line with the sack attached; it flew out incredibly far before disappearing in the darkness.

I then began one of the most frightening prusiks I have ever done. The rope dropped down from me, went straight out past the lip of the overhang and ascended into the blackness beyond. I was even confused as to how to start. I put an extra prusik loop in my mouth, more to bite on to ease tension than anything else. My mind was numb from trying to calculate the strain I would be placing on the system. If I could just be sure everything would hold! Finally, I realized there was nothing else I could do, and soon I was in my slings dangling 30 feet out from the wall.

The headlights of cars were an infinite distance below as they turned and twisted along the road. I couldn't help thinking about the tourists inside. What a contrast—tomorrow they might be swimming in the Merced River or taking pictures of El Capitan and Yosemite Falls, while we would be struggling upward, reaching for the top and the culmination of our climbing careers. And all within sight of one another. I finally reached the ledges and found the rope tied off to a small ¼-inch bolt and two doubtful pitons. I shuddered when I thought of the strain I had just placed on them.

We spent a long, cold, moonlit night under attack by small birds. The apricots and Lifesavers (a very appropriate name) helped stave off hunger pains. No comfortable ledge like Ahwahnee this time, and no sleeping bags either. Warren told us that the route above looked like easier climbing, maybe fifth class. The overhanging open book that greeted us Friday morning proved him wrong.

Warren led the last pitch, overhanging to the end, up fairly difficult sixth class, using 20 pitons and 5 bolts. Glen cleaned the pitch of pitons and I made the last prusik to the beautiful summit arête.

And then we were up. The struggle was over and the Tower was ours.

Our first feeling was one of intense happiness, bubbling up inside so we felt like shouting for pure joy. This soon gave way to deeper emotions: a contentment that we had savored life at its fullest for a short while—life stripped to barest essentials. No matter what the future held for each of us, the Tower had linked us in a bond of comradeship that most people never experience. We'll always feel respect and affection for that wall.

As we climbed down the sloping back side of the Tower, the soft play of afternoon sun and shadow gave a nostalgic beauty to the area. Between the Cathedral Rocks we paused for a last look at our huge granite friend, then plunged down into the dark depths of Gunsight Gully to a new world waiting below.

[*Alfred W. Baxter* comments: The ascent described in the MacDonald article typifies a kind of Yosemite rock climbing which is qualitatively and quantitatively different from Valley climbing prior to 1948:

1. Length of the climbs. The ascent of the Lost Arrow from its base (Salathé and Nelson) and the ascent of the north face of Sentinel Rock (Salathé and Steck) were done in five days of continuous climbing after some preparation of lower parts of the routes. In 1947 and 1950 these climbs were at the margin of length, strenuousness, and difficulty. Climbs in the new mode (the South Buttress of El Capitan—approximately 50 days, and the Leaning Tower here described—18 days) required continuous climbing after very substantial preparatory work. If these times are compressed, and not spread

275

as they were over months or years, they are of the magnitude of time involved in establishing camps, ferrying supplies, and ascending a major Himalayan peak. Indeed the logistic techniques on these climbs have a real resemblance to the relaying of supplies carried out on major peaks.

2. Demand for physical endurance. Most rock climbing is strenuous. In the current mode, however, leads of eight hours are not unusual. Piton pounding and bolt-hole drilling for such periods (even when leaders are occasionally alternated) is terribly demanding on strength, endurance, and body water. The levels and duration of fatigue and thirst accepted as routine are substantially above those of earlier periods.

3. Risks. Rock climbing, including that in the new mode, is seldom as hazardous as it seems. Notwithstanding this general qualification, the level of risks accepted in climbs such as the Leaning Tower is significantly higher than those of earlier years.

First of all there is an increased and more continuous dependence upon pitons and bolts of dubious quality and staying power, owing to the extreme limitation on alternative routes once a party is committed to a major face. Moreover, routes in the new mode are often selected *because* of their freedom from the more hospitable cracks, ledges, and rugosities which might provide frequent stances and occasional secure sections. There is inevitable compromise between speed and safety, since reliable bolts take longer to drill and set than marginal ones.

Second, in the case of accidents (and it should be noted that falls need not be considered accidents unless they are ill-prepared for or result in injuries), prompt and effective rescue efforts are unlikely. Last, is the difficulty in retreating back down a route or in reaching easier going by traversing. In the Leaning Tower climb, this difficulty was accepted knowingly and deliberately. With this acceptance of difficulty came the commitment to finish the climb over partially unknown ground or else face very serious difficulties should this ground prove impossible. Even on this point, which gives the account of the Leaning Tower climb much of its sweaty-palmed fascination, it is not clear what the bases of the party's judgment were when they relied on admittedly poor anchors to secure their lines of retreat. Warren Harding's decision may have been no less prudent than others he made during the course of the climb, given the party's skill, equipment, and what could be estimated of the difficulties of the final leads on this astonishing route.

These comments are meant to provide a context from which readers unfamiliar with Yosemite rock climbing may appreciate an account of a climb which typifies a new and distinct mode of mountaineering, and which places its extraordinarily skillful and enduring practitioners at a frontier of mountaineering aspiration and achievement.]

68

Everest: The West Ridge

RICHARD EMERSON

1963

With the ascent of the Leaning Tower, it might be said that the pioneering era in Yosemite climbing was over. During the 1960s, with the proliferation of new equipment and widespread publicity about the sport, climbers began to appear all over the Yosemite walls. The challenge now was to pioneer new routes up previously climbed summits; half-a-dozen routes were established up the walls of El Capitan, Half Dome, Sentinel Rock, and nearly every other valley monolith.

The new equipment included longer and stronger ropes; improved skyhooks (strips of metal with a hook at one end and a carabiner loop at the other); many types of pitons, mashies, and nuts (aluminum blocks that can be wedged into grooves or cracks in the rock and used in place of pitons); jumars (mechanical devices that replaced prusik knots as a means of "walking" up a rope by use of a stirrup); various aid slings (webbing that can be hitched to pitons to support the climber); and bivouac hammocks or "bat tents" for suspended sleeping.

Despite the mechanization, however, climbing still calls for skill, courage, tenacity, strength, and nerve. In these departments as well as technology, the Yosemite climbers of the 1960s and early 1970s were recognized as world leaders in the sport, as Chris Jones has noted in his excellent book, Climbing in North America.

Although Yosemite was the climber's Mecca, it was not the only locale for climbing achievements of interest to the Sierra Club. Americans made important climbs all over North America, and in Europe. Then, in 1963, an American expedition headed by Norman Dyhrenfurth, and including many Sierra Club members, among them director Will Siri, put three teams on top of Mount Everest and pioneered a new route traversing from the previously unclimbed West Ridge to the South Col.

Professor Richard W. Emerson was a longtime member of the club and a combat veteran of the 10th Mountain Division. From his account in the Bulletin *we excerpt an episode in which for complicated reasons, he found himself alone, carrying a load from one established camp to another. He faced a very different set of problems from those confronted by rock climbers in Yosemite. If in retrospect some of the experiences seem to resemble the more frantic moments of Charlie Chaplin in the snows of "The Gold Rush," the resemblance is deceiving. Daily the Everest climbers faced life-or-death decisions; one member was killed by a falling ice-block just above Base Camp.*

The numbers "3W" and "4W" refer to camps on the West Ridge; "3" and "4" are on the "normal" South Col route. This narrative was worked into Thomas Hornbein's Everest: The West Ridge, *published by the club in 1966 and long since a collector's item.*

LUTE [JERSTAD] counseled me against exposing myself to frostbite in a bivouac. However, there was one bottle of oxygen and a convenient crevasse at what had been the New-New Dump at a little over 23,000 feet. I had been down in the crevasse before, retrieving a fouled winch cable, and knew it to be suitable. If I slept on oxygen there would be no frostbite. Next day I started up, carrying an air mattress, which I concluded would be more useful than a sleeping bag. With the crevasse as my objective, I took a slow and steady pace, and arrived at dusk, feeling very well. I debated continuing the last 700 vertical feet to 3W, but it would be totally dark, and I was confident about the bivouac. In fact, I think I wanted the bivouac, but I don't know exactly why.

It must have taken me almost two hours to get myself prepared for the night. I found the bottle half buried, put it in my pack, anchored a piece of rope to a picket, and rappeled into the dark hole as light was failing. About thirty feet down, the crevasse closed to four feet wide, plugged with powder snow. I tamped it firm, then started to inflate the mattress. I stopped. (Stupid, you'd better get those crampons off or you'll puncture it for sure.) As I fiddled with things in the dark, I could hear the wind rising. (No worry—but it's dumping a lot of snow in here.) I removed my down gloves to work with the oxygen gear. (Careful! Put the right glove in the right pocket—now left in left. Don't misplace one. Don't let snow sift into them. Hold the hose in your teeth. Now, work fast with the metal attachments— hose to regulator; regulator to tank—keep the snow away and hope the threads seat well. Good, gloves. Now down pants, over the boots, wind shell, mask in place, regulator in reach. Flow? . . . one liter. And now for sleep. Wait! Let's review: Where's my ax? Upright, behind my head. Crampons? In the pack. Damn! I'll bet the flap's open. Goggles? Top left pocket.) This poor-man's countdown put my mind at ease, and I drifted into sleep in perfect comfort, never suspecting the storm I was creating at Base Camp.

Some time during the night I was awakened by cold around my eyes, where powder snow was sifting in. I was thoroughly warm otherwise, but slowly realized that I was totally buried. I rose to my feet, cradling the oxygen bottle like a baby in one arm. I pulled the mattress to the surface, remade my bed, and listening to the wind roaring past my cavern, immediately fell back to sleep.

At about that same time, the men at 4W were having difficulties. The wind had been tearing at their tent all night and finally it got under one edge. Lying in their bags, they felt it lift them from the ice, tear loose the moorings, and send them tumbling in a tangled mass of struts and fabric across level ground, over a crest, and down a slope. After some 150 feet, and in a partial lee from the wind, the two four-man tents and their occupants came to rest, none too soon.

All this time I enjoyed a cozy sleep, protected by snow and ice rather than man-made fabrics.

The second time I awakened, I brushed away snow and looked up. Soft light filled the crevasse, but I couldn't see the opening above me for the

Everest: The West Ridge

swirling snow. My watch said 7:00, yet the light suggested 4:00. (Radio contact is 8:15. Get on your way again by then so they can see you from Camp 2 and know all is well. But, no rush now.) So, I lay there marveling at the comfort of such a form-fitting bed, watching the snow sweep by above me with unbelievable velocity.

Eventually, I rose and started putting things in shape. (Will the weather block visibility from Camp 2?) I pulled the plug to let the mattress deflate and found that it had frozen up when only half deflated. I rolled it up under my pack flap and, using the front points of my crampons, started up the rappel rope to rejoin the elements.

It was 8:45, the sky was blue, and I could see the tents at 2, far below, yet I couldn't see my own feet in the blowing snow. I started up the home stretch for 3W, wondering if I could be seen in the ground blizzard. My route went straight up a 35° slope, scoured hard by the cross wind. Once, standing erect to see over the turmoil of moving particles, I was hit like a hammer by a wind change and did a self-arrest moving horizontally across the slope. I continued steadily, on front points and a pick. Soon, snow filtering through the air vents filled my goggles. Since there was no feasible way to clean them, nor any point in doing so, I put them away and continued, squinting out through the wolverine fur of my hood. All I had to do was go straight up. I didn't have to see. The wind tore the partly inflated mattress from my pack and I last saw it gaining altitude westward.

Meanwhile, the morning radio, May 17:

4W ([Barry] Corbet, from the remains of a tent): Let me fill you in. We've had a mishap during the night. Both Draw-Tite tents, the four Sherpas, and Al [Auten] and myself blew 150 feet down the slope and we're lying in the sack, held down with oxygen bottles . . . (garbled) . . . at midnight when it happened . . . roped us to the slope and I guess we're safe.

4W (Willi [Unsoeld], from the Gerry tent): Can you read 4 now, Bear? Over.

Base (Prather): I read you loud and clear, Willi. Did you get what Barry wanted? Over.

4W (Willi): I think I did. Yes. Right now it's going to be awhile yet, cause we're just barely holding on the Gerry tent. Over.

(There followed a long exchange between Jimmy Roberts, at 2, and Ang Dorje at 3W. Purpose: no carries to 4W; bring down sick Sherpa, and look for Emerson in the process. At about that moment, they spotted me approaching 3W.)

4W (Willi, 8:55 a.m.): Question, Bear. How's the wind down your way? Over.

Base (Prather): It's blowin' a bit. Not very hard though. . . . What? 20 MPH? 25 MPH. Over.

4W (Willi): I see. We may not be able to hold out much longer here. Tent's taking a beating. Blowing about 100 here pretty steadily. Over.

Base (Prather): We can see a hell of a lot of wind coming off Nuptse, and it really sounds bad. There's a big roar we can hear from down here even. Over.

279

4W (Willi): Yeah, I can believe it! Over.

2 ([David] Dingman): Willi, did you hear about Emerson? Over.

4W (Willi): No, I didn't, Dave. What's the latest word? Over.

2 (Dave): We looked out a few minutes ago, and lo and behold, we saw him between the new dump and the crest, still going up! Over.

4W (Willi): And that was *this morning?* Over.

Base (Prather): Roger. That's this morning. Just a few minutes ago. Over.

4W (Willi): Holy Cow, I can't believe it. Over.

Base (Prather): Roger. You're not the only one!

4W (Willi): That's great news, Dave. Great News. Now, if we can get out of this mess, we'll be fine. Over.

Then a few minutes later:

2 (Dingman): Do you have a weather forecast?

Base (Prather): High winds, low pressure over Punjab, . . .

4W (Willi): 4 to Base! 4 to Base! Over!

Base (Prather): Roger, Willi. Reading loud and clear. Go ahead.

4W (Willi): O.K. Here's the latest report, Bear. O-o-v-e-e-r-r-r!

Base (Prather): You want the weather report? Over.

4W (Willi): God damn! The tent's blowing away!

Base (Prather): Roger. The tent's blowing away. We'll stand by.

4W (Willi): Standby? We're headed over the brink! (*Base:* Roger) Barry! OUT! OUT!

Shortly, I arrived at 3W, and found three Sherpas preparing to descend. A little later the men from 4W came into Camp, and I learned for the first time that things had been rough all over. I was surprised to learn about the turmoil I had caused at Base Camp — after all, I had taken great care. But I was the only one who knew that, and I slowly started feeling foolish. (Now, in retrospect, an interesting question occurs to me: why did I not think to clear my plans through Base Camp?)

69

Dhaulagiri: A Mind Odyssey

JAMES JANNEY

1970

Both rock climbing and expeditionary mountaineering, properly pursued, are scarcely the suicidal activity pictured in the mind of the layman. We have never seen a survey on the subject, but it is at least a good guess that the careful climber is statistically safer on the Lost Arrow than he is in the car driving to Yosemite.

Nevertheless, climbers do die. The climber who experiences the loss of companions is likely to have some long thoughts about the matter, although they are seldom expressed as eloquently as in the following article in the Sierra Club mountaineering annual Ascent. Ascent *began publication in 1967 and replaced the* Bulletin *as the locale for articles on climbing. James Janney had climbed on the South Face of McKinley and in the Andes before joining the 1969 American expedition to Dhaulagiri in the Himalayas.*

THE WHITE MASS below rolls up the valley, mingling with other clouds above it, delivering its six-pointed message softly. Slowly each flake falls, lingering, before being flicked up by a slight breeze, not eager to reach the earth to be metamorphosed into water. The snow begins to fall fast, yet it is soft, feminine, gentle. The snow is cathartic; it is the calm after the violence, the silence after the avalanche's boom. Perhaps it was sent to us as a weak apology, as if Nature might be embarrassed at having taken so many at once, or perhaps, even more bizarre, for sparing Lou. The snow, at any rate, seems appropriate and beautiful.

As if in intentional countermotion to the snowfall, I ascend, though also lingering, thinking of those who have been free like the snow and now rest within the earth. This quiet emptying of the clouds seems to be both a white reminder of pale death and also a peaceful assurance of continuation — a confirmation of lives to come, lives which will attempt to carry on pieces of their spirits.

Seven of my friends have died. Ice hunks formed from similar soft snow fell on them and crushed them unmercifully. Only Lou survived to tell those of us below. The clouds sense the tragedy and send snow. They pay their respects, as does the full moon which now peeks sheepishly through the clouds, kindly assisting the forlorn search for any sign of life. We ascend. The procession, the wake, is good for us. Submerged in the pain of our upward paths, we forget some of the shock, some of the inexplicable ugliness of what has happened. For a time we forget the questions which may never be answered.

Yesterday, the day before their forever, my senses enveloped each's presence with sight. My senses incorporated each's sound in hearing. Now, totally unknown to my senses, they are dead. Dead. I cannot see, hear or touch them. Understanding the reality of their death is like seeing a vacuum, like listening for an echo which is never returned. Somethingness disappearing into nothingness; the final period of a sentence which was never completed. The full moon will wane. It speaks of the paradox that life also wanes. Life, even at its height, cannot escape the fact of death. In fact, lived at a mountaineer's rhythm, life tends toward death. Pushing hard against life, the seven have been pulled away by death.

We live in a world of cycles. *Samsara* it is called in Buddhist Nepal. The

Dhaulagiri.

cyclical make-up of existence. Water to vapor to snow, perhaps to ice, to water. The ever-changing moon, never constant yet always repeating itself. The wheel of life and death.

I ascend only to descend again. My footprints point upward and concur with others which have recently ascended. My footprints, after the ceremonial search, will return. Others' footprints will not. I make the ritual pilgrimage. For them the pilgrimage is over, cut off before completion, before maturation, some might say. Others will say they were cut off at the peak of involvement, of intensity, suggesting that the real joy of action is the process of achieving and not the achievement. Best, then, that they were cut off during the act and not the aftermath. Me—I do not know.

I do not know. My mind does not help, for it sends me on a wild shock trip, I cannot stand up even on an easy snow traverse. I become aware that now my sight has become round and the snow looks like an ever-changing concavity as I try to walk. Now my eyes are like telephoto lenses and focus only on small depth of field sections — first on my blue padded knee against a washed-out backdrop of snow, then on a precise snowflake which is falling five feet beyond. I do not know.

The night comes, cuddles with us, and passes; I do not sleep. I do not really exist, but the living must return. They do, although only with hesitant steps weighted with a curious guilt about being alive when others are dead.

Yet these steps are also filled with a strange joy, a thick, heavy joy about being alive and able to carry on what David, what they all stood for — a certain energy and vitality which caused them to die, yet which made all which went before bearable and more meaningful. Thoughts crystallize, perhaps too sharply.

It is not for us to ponder "Why he" or "Why not me." It is not for us to attach beautiful phrases apart from the fact as if to justify or attempt to give meaning. It is not for us to turn in desperation to some convenient concept of God which we neither accept nor understand. It is not for us to look above or beyond the incident, but to look directly, though seared by pain, into the undeniable fact of this accident.

There were five sahibs, and two Sherpas. Now seven no longer exist. Each was here for different reasons — some for pure adventure; some for companionship; some to prove something to themselves; some to gain a reputation; some to gain money; some only on a lark. All were trying to make up for a lack somewhere else in life; all were trying to complete themselves. All were human beings with many faults, yet all were there because they had the vitality to escape ordinary endeavor. They were attempting to find the answers to complex questions and to find out a little bit about themselves in this environment where they did not belong.

They could never have realized how much they took from us when they died, nor could they have realized how much they gave us. We take the energy and vitality of their souls and of their dreams. Taking a little bit of each individual which truly inspired us, we incorporate it into our lives, along with a knowledge of their faults, and descend. And continue living.

It is a time to look and a time to see. The pine forest with its fresh smells which permeate so deeply. The rhododendron. The clumps of grass. Nepal's spring breath. Down below it is spring, the youngest of the seasons. It bestows upon us its spirit. It is a time when the yaks are giving birth to their young. Though the evening comes, it is a time of newness, of recycling, of rebirth. As we descend we hear the sound of dogs barking. The candles within the homes cast a soft light, a quiet light on the families huddled around them. The children, young and inquisitive, greet us: "Namaste." Nice. For all the hurt we are more aware.

Downward we go: down. Down past familiar places where we had stopped along the way. Each prominent rock or bend in the trail initiates a force which prompts me to recall a conversation during the inward trek. Floating through my mind, the incidents fall into harmony with the river below. We had been marked as fellow travelers on a path we had dreamed of for many years.

Down we continue, past places where I had eaten with men now dead, had joked with those men, had sweated with those men. There are new footprints now but they do not matter any more than ours will; the footprints will disappear. The river will keep flowing, filled with a never-ending supply of glacial silt. The ecology of the valley will not change with their deaths.

283

But one day the river flow will be altered only so slightly by a tattered piece of cloth or a fragment of bone which has re-emerged from the white cave of its tomb.

Similarly, those of us who are walking back will not ostensibly change that much. Yes, we are preoccupied now and will be for months. But that preoccupation will pass. Except at those times when something, some incident or situation, will recall what has happened in this past week. The flow of our private river will then be altered and the man in us which has been added, the certain maturity somehow bred by tragedy, will emerge, making that small flow more sensitive, more able to respond with feeling, more able to be alive.

70

Waiting: Maroon Bells Campsite

MILLIE MARCHAND

1971

Unlike the days when Marjory Bridge Farquhar was a member of a party that ascended Higher Cathedral Spire in 1934, women climbers are no longer rare. Some have made historic ascents, such as the conquest of El Capitan by Beverly Johnson in 1978. Nevertheless, the women are still outnumbered on the cliffs by as much as one hundred to one. The principal role for women in climbing remains waiting behind and worrying while the men seek adventure and glory. Millie Marchand's lines appeared in Ascent *in 1971.*

I MOVE THROUGH dazzled mornings
In the shadow of your mountain
Conversing with my fear.
From it I draw my strength,
And from the river's motion.
I keep my waiting busy.

Since the cold, high darkness
Was scattered by the sun
I have been lost to sleep —
Since you struggled, born again,
Out of the quilted womb

284

Our bodies warmed
To stand full height
Upon the waking earth.

My spirit trembles now
Upon your mission. She rises
With the ropes upon your back
And quivers, like the aspen,
With the wind.

And here the timid flesh,
Bound to gentle valleys,
Tallies with unnatural precision
Morning chores completed.

Beyond this rush of water
High on the dying snow,
An apprehensive spectre
Marks the lost crevasse,
Or boulders on uncertain ground;
She fears a careless move, a weak belay.

Hold that anxious phantom
In your wary eyes
And make for her a refuge,
Though her flesh
Is long and far away.

71

The Ascent of Hummingbird Ridge

ALLEN STECK

1967

Fifteen years after his triumphant ascent on Sentinel Rock with the legendary John Salathé, Allen Steck was on Mount Logan in Canada's Yukon Territory with a six-man expedition headed for the unclimbed south ridge of the 19,850-foot peak, the second highest in North America, 500 feet lower than Mount McKinley. As noted in the first issue of Ascent *(1967), "the climb required thirty-seven days and the placing of eleven camps, or more accurately, the moving of one camp eleven times. . . . The name of the ridge commemorates a momentary, chance confrontation of man and hummingbird at 9000 feet—a good omen, perhaps."*

From Steck's account, we reproduce here the final passages, which culminate in the perennial question—why do we do it? Earlier in the story, Steck had described Mount Logan's "Osod Buttress" and explained that "Osod" was an "indigenous word connoting: hysteria, adrenal stimulation; hence, cumulative mental trauma producing an osodian chill in the back of the neck." Anyone adversely affected by accounts of osodosis is cautioned against reading this article.

It is not the role of *grand alpinisme* to face peril, but it is one of the tests one must undergo to deserve the joy of rising for an instant above the state of crawling grubs.

—*Lionel Terray*, 1965

I DREW THE LAST LEAD, took the shovel and bade farewell to John. The air was still. The cornices and ice towers were balanced on a slender spine of rock, the culmination of this giant ridge that formed a 7,000-foot barrier between two huge glacial cirques. A soft mist rose to the east of the crest, though it did not quite reach over the top. I turned for a moment and was completely lost in silent appraisal of the beautifully sensuous simplicity of wind-blown snow. Equating beauty with audacity has many connotations in our lives; the concept seems particularly meaningful to me as I think back on this particular moment. Such capricious interaction of wind, sun and snow!—the result made even more exquisitely delicate by gravitational forces. Snow is one of the most lovely manifestations of nature.

Each of us had our moments of rather personal involvement with this ridge and this seemed to be mine. This last 600 feet would in some way unlock the trail to the summit. Moving deliberately and without hesitation I began to excavate a path across the remaining cornices and ice towers. The thin quarter-inch dacron line tied to my waist led back to Evans who was now some 300 feet behind. I was entirely alone. I was deeply absorbed in this work when a small cornice on which I was standing broke with a strange squeaking sound. The sensation of falling is not new to me, though here it was more unpleasant than usual. I certainly cannot explain why my left arm happened to be extended, unless it was some sort of futile reflex action directed toward flight, for which I had the wrong equipment. In any case, it was indeed extended and I found that I had stopped with my arm fortuitously draped over the ridge crest formerly hidden by the cornice. The shovel hung below me on the cord we had tied for just this purpose. I lay still for a moment, watching the broken cornice disappear into the depths, and began to assemble the pieces of my shattered composure. Rather unnerved by this event, I finished the remaining 300 feet of the Traverse engaged in a unilateral conversation with the mountain, the first that I can ever recall. I explained forcefully, without restraint, that one of us was going to win and because of my shovel and uncontrollable desire, it would be me. Thus mentally fortified, I reached the end, called for John to come over, and together we surveyed the route up toward the summit before going back to Camp 5. The Traverse was completed!

Hunger was our companion now as we worked our way up through Camps 6, 7, and finally 8, just below the summit. We were on reduced rations to protect our margin of safety as much as possible, for we wished above all to be able to take a week of bad weather should it come higher up on the mountain as it did below. Emotional release was abundant on the day the lines were fixed to the summit plateau. The ridge was finished, the exposure gone. A four-foot picket, sunk to the hilt in the ice, still holds 2400 feet of fixed rope leading down to Camp 8.

As we neared the summit, the sun shone on us, beautifully diffused through thinning clouds in the upper sky. Words are such useless things at times, the mind preferring simply to be absorbent, drawing up impressions from all its senses. My eyes told me that Evans' tattered pants were in urgent need of repair; that Wilson's parka could use several trips to the dry-cleaners.

Hummingbird Ridge, Mount Logan.

I saw too that my friends shared my great inner joy of the simplicity of this moment:

> this is another earth, another sky
> no likeness to that human world below

to quote a Chinese poet whose lines will never lose their beauty throughout all human involvement on this earth.

Many persons have reached the summit of Logan with visibility down to less than 50 feet, while others, like ourselves, were blessed with unlimited views in all directions, the most lovely being a glimpse of the Malaspina Glacier and Pacific Ocean beyond the summit of Mt. Augusta to the west. We faced this magnificent panorama with emotions reminiscent of similar occasions on other mountains; the more dominant feeling bringing to mind the familiar phrase: "Descendamus de monte ineffabile, in nomine Osodi," which loosely translated reads: "in the name of Osod, let's get off this unspeakable mountain."

The trip was far from over, however. We spent another two days getting down to our cache in King Trench whence our flight out to the civilized, culinary smells of the 202 Club in Whitehorse was undertaken. Surely the most exciting moment of our travels occurred as the tiny aircraft groaned down the glacier at full throttle, while Jack Wilson desperately tried to get the thing into the air before reaching the icefall which lay directly before us in paralyzing proximity.

You will have discerned that the venture was not without substantial emotional and physical impact. We do not deceive ourselves that we are engaged in an activity that is anything but debilitating, dangerous, euphoric, kinesthetic, expensive, frivolously essential, economically useless and totally without redeeming social significance. One should not probe for deeper meanings.

I am reminded of an event that happened some years ago. I was with Pratt, Evans and Long on the ascent of the East Portal of Ribbon Fall in Yosemite Valley. It was after the second bivouac, while Evans and Long were leading the Guillotine Flake. Hungry and thirsty, I sought solace in hammering the date on the rock wall at my back, when Pratt, sensing perhaps my momentary loss of composure, suddenly proclaimed with excessive emphasis to no one in particular:

"I could climb for a million years and still not know why I do it . . . why? . . . why?" he cried, beating his fists against the wall, "am I here?"

I was overjoyed at this vocalization, generated as it was by neither alcohol nor other mind-loosening agents, of a nagging question that had been bothering me for some years. I know now how I should have replied:

"It's the grubs, Pratt, those crawling grubs we must rise above!"

Affectionately,
ALLEN [STECK]

72

The Climber as Visionary

DOUG ROBINSON

1969

One of the few systematic attempts to answer the question always asked about climbing—why do they do it?—is this essay from the 1969 Ascent. *Robinson was then a recent graduate of San Francisco State College, an aspiring English teacher, and an assistant in a Sierra mountaineering guide service.*

"Camp Four" referred to here is the Yosemite campground traditionally used as the climbers' base camp, southwest of the foot of Yosemite Falls. The National Park Service now calls it "Sunnyside Campground," owing to its warm location at the foot of the south-facing cliffs and its proximity to the ledge east of the falls named by John Muir "Sunnyside Bench."

IN 1914 GEORGE MALLORY, later to become famous for an offhand definition of why people climb, wrote an article entitled "The Mountaineer as Artist," which appeared in the British Climbers' Club Journal. In an attempt to justify his climber's feeling of superiority over other sportsmen, he asserts that the climber is an artist. He says that "a day well spent in the Alps is like some great symphony," and justifies the lack of any tangible production—for artists are generally expected to produce works of art which others may see—by saying that "artists, in this sense, are not distinguished by the power of expressing emotion, but the power of feeling that emotional experience out of which Art is made . . . mountaineers are all artistic, . . . because they cultivate emotional experience for its own sake." While fully justifying the elevated regard we have for climbing as an activity, Mallory's assertion leaves no room for distinguishing the creator of a route from an admirer of it. Mountaineering can produce tangible artistic results which are then on public view. A route is an artistic statement on the side of a mountain, accessible to the view and thus the admiration or criticism of other climbers. Just as the line of a route determines its aesthetics, the manner in which it was climbed constitutes its style. A climb has the qualities of a work of art and its creator is responsible for its direction and style just as an artist is. We recognize those climbers who are especially gifted at creating forceful and aesthetic lines, and respect them for their gift.

But just as Mallory did not go far enough in ascribing artistic functions to the act of creating outstanding new climbs, so I think he uses the word 'artist' too broadly when he means it to include an aesthetic response as well as an aesthetic creation. For this response, which is essentially passive and receptive rather than aggressive and creative, I would use the word visionary. Not visionary in the usual sense of idle and unrealizable dreaming, of building castles in the air, but rather in seeing the objects and actions of ordinary experience with greater intensity, penetrating them further, seeing their marvels and mysteries, their forms, moods, and motions. Being a visionary in this sense involves nothing supernatural or otherworldly; it amounts to bringing fresh vision to the familiar things of the world. I use the word visionary very simply, taking its origin from 'vision' to mean seeing, always to great degrees of intensity, but never beyond the boundaries of the real and physically present. To take a familiar example, it would be hard to look at Van Gogh's "The Starry Night" without seeing the visionary quality in the way the artist sees the world. He has not painted anything that is not in the original scene, yet others would have trouble recognizing what he has depicted, and the difference lies in the intensity of his perception, heart of the visionary experience. He is painting from a higher state of consciousness. Climbers too have their "Starry Nights." Consider the following, from an account by Allen Steck, of the Hummingbird Ridge climb on Mt. Logan: "I turned for a moment and was completely lost in silent appraisal of the beautifully sensuous simplicity of windblown snow." The beauty of that moment, the form and motion of the blowing snow was such a powerful impression, was so wonderfully sufficient, that the climber was lost in it. It is said to be only a moment, yet by virtue of total absorption he is lost in it and the winds of eternity blow through it. A second example comes from the account of the seventh day's climbing on the eight-day first ascent, under trying conditions, of El Capitan's Muir Wall. Yvon Chouinard relates in the 1966 *American Alpine Journal:*

With the more receptive senses we now appreciated everything around us. Each individual crystal in the granite stood out in bold relief. The varied shapes of the clouds never ceased to attract our attention. For the first time we noticed tiny bugs that were all over the walls, so tiny they were barely noticeable. While belaying, I stared at one for 15 minutes, watching him move and admiring his brilliant red color.

How could one ever be bored with so many good things to see and feel! This unity with our joyous surroundings, this ultra-penetrating perception gave us a feeling of contentment that we had not had for years.

In these passages the qualities that make up the climber's visionary experience are apparent: the overwhelming beauty of the most ordinary objects — clouds, granite, snow — of the climber's experience, a sense of the slowing down of time even to the point of disappearing, and a "feeling of contentment," an oceanic feeling of the supreme sufficiency of the present. And while delicate in substance, these feelings are strong enough to intrude forcefully into the middle of dangerous circumstances and remain there, temporarily superceding even apprehension and the drive for achievement.

Chouinard's words begin to give us an idea of the origin of these experiences as well as their character. He begins by referring to "the more receptive senses." What made their senses more receptive? It seems integrally connected with what they were doing, and that it was their seventh day of uninterrupted concentration. Climbing tends to induce visionary experiences. We should explore which characteristics of the climbing process prepare its practitioners for these experiences.

Climbing requires intense concentration. I know of no other activity in which I can so easily lose all the hours of an afternoon without a trace. Or a regret. I have had storms creep up on me as if I had been asleep, yet I know the whole time I was in the grip of an intense concentration, focused first on a few square feet of rock, and then on a few feet more. I have gone off across camp to boulder and returned to find the stew burned. Sometimes in the lowlands when it is hard to work I am jealous of how easily concentration comes in climbing. This concentration may be intense, but it is not the same as the intensity of the visionary periods; it is a prerequisite intensity.

But the concentration is not continuous. It is often intermittent and sporadic, sometimes cyclic and rhythmic. After facing the successive few square feet of rock for a while, the end of the rope is reached and it is time to belay. The belay time is a break in the concentration, a gap, a small chance to relax. The climber changes from an aggressive and productive stance to a passive and receptive one, from doer to observer, and in fact from artist to visionary. The climbing day goes on through the climb-belay-climb-belay cycle by a regular series of concentrations and relaxations. It is of one of these relaxations that Chouinard speaks. When limbs go to the rock and muscles contract, then the will contracts also. And at the belay stance, tied in to a scrub oak, the muscles relax and the will also, which has been concentrating on moves, expands and takes in the world again, and the world is new and bright. It is freshly created, for it really had ceased to exist. By contrast, the disadvantage of the usual low-level activity is that it cannot shut out the world, which then never ceases being familiar and is thus ignored. To climb with intense concentration is to shut out the world, which, when it reappears, will be as a fresh experience, strange and wonderful in its newness.

These belay relaxations are not total; the climb is not over, pitches lie ahead, even the crux; days more may be needed to be through. We notice that as the cycle of intense contractions takes over, and as this cycle becomes the daily routine, even consumes the daily routine, the relaxations on belay yield more frequent or intense visionary experiences. It is no accident that Chouinard's experiences occur near the end of the climb; he had been building up to them for six days. The summit, capping off the cycling and giving a final release from the tension of contractions, should offer the climber some of his most intense moments, and a look into the literature reveals this to be so. The summit is also a release from the sensory desert of the climb; from the starkness of concentrating on configurations of rock we go to the visual richness of the summit. But there is still the descent to worry about, another contraction of will to be followed by relaxation at the climb's foot. Sitting on a log changing from klettershoes into boots, and looking over the Valley, we are suffused with oceanic feelings of clarity, distance, union, oneness. There is carryover from one climb to the next, from one day on the hot white walls to the next, however punctuated by wine dark evenings in Camp Four. Once a pathway has been tried it becomes more familiar and is easier to follow the second time, more so on subsequent trips. The threshold has been lowered. Practice is as useful to the climber's visionary faculty as to his crack technique. It also applies outside of climbing. In John Harlin's words, although he was speaking about will and not vision, the experience can be "borrowed and projected." It will apply in the climber's life in general, in his flat, ground, and lowland hours. But it is the climbing that has taught him to be a visionary. Lest we get too self-important about consciously preparing ourselves for visionary activity, however, we remember that the incredible beauty of the mountains is always at hand, always ready to nudge us into awareness.

The period of these cycles varies widely. If you sometimes cycle through lucid periods from pitch to pitch or even take days to run a complete course, it may also be virtually instantaneous, as, pulling up on a hold after a moment's hesitation and doubt, you feel at once the warmth of sun through your shirt and without pausing reach on.

Nor does the alteration of consciousness have to be large. A small change can be profound. The gulf between looking without seeing and looking with real vision is at times of such a low order that we may be continually shifting back and forth in daily life. Further heightening of the visionary faculty consists of more deeply perceiving what is already there. Vision is intense seeing. Vision is seeing what is more deeply interfused, and following this process leads to a sense of ecology. It is an intuitive rather than a scientific ecology; it is John Muir's kind, starting not from generalizations for trees, rocks, air, but rather from *that* tree with the goiter part way up the trunk, from the rocks as Chouinard saw them, supremely sufficient and aloof, blazing away their perfect light, and from that air which blew clean and hot up off the eastern desert and carries lingering memories of snowfields on the Dana Plateau and miles of Tuolumne treetops as it pours over the rim of the Valley on its way to the Pacific.

I first began to consider these ideas in the summer of 1965 in Yosemite with Chris Fredericks. Sensing a similarity of experience, or else a similar approach to experience, we sat many nights talking together at the edge of the climbers' camp and spent some of our days testing our words in kinesthetic sunshine. Chris had become interested in Zen Buddhism, and as he told me of this Oriental religion I was amazed that I had never before heard of such a system that fit the facts of outward reality as I saw them without any pushing or straining. We never, that I remember, mentioned the visionary experience as such, yet its substance was rarely far from our reflections. We entered into one of those fine parallel states of mind such that it is impossible now for me to say what thoughts came from which of us. We began to consider some aspects of climbing as Western equivalents of Eastern practices: the even movements of the belayer taking in slack, the regular footfall of walking through the woods, even the rhythmic movements of climbing on easy or familiar ground; all approach the function of meditation and breath-control. Both the laborious and visionary parts of climbing seemed well suited to liberating the individual from his concept of self, the one by intimidating his aspirations, the other by showing the self to be only a small part of a subtly integrated universe. We watched the visionary surface in each other with its mixture of joy and serenity, and walking down the climbs we often felt like little children in the Garden of Eden, pointing, nodding, and laughing. We explored timeless moments and wondered at the suspension of ordinary consciousness while the visionary faculty was operating. It occurred to us that there was no remembering such times of being truly happy and at peace; all that could be said of them later was that they had been and that they had been truly fine; the usual details of memory were gone. This applies also to most of our conversations. I remember only that we talked and that we came to understand things. I believe it was in these conversations that the first seeds of the climber as visionary were planted.

William Blake has spoken of the visionary experience by saying, "If the doors of perception were cleansed every thing would appear to man as it is, infinite." Stumbling upon the cleansed doors, the climber wonders how he came into that privileged visionary position vis-à-vis the universe. He finds the answer in the activity of his climbing and the chemistry of his mind, and he begins to see that he is practicing a special application of some very ancient mind-opening techniques. Chouinard's vision was no accident. It was the result of days of climbing. He was tempered by technical difficulties, pain, apprehension, dehydration, striving, the sensory desert, weariness, the gradual loss of self. It is a system. You need only copy the ingredients and commit yourself to them. They lead to the door. It is not necessary to attain to Chouinard's technical level—few can or do—only to his degree of commitment. It is not essential that one climb El Capitan to be a visionary; I never have, yet I try in my climbing to push my personal limit, to do climbs that are questionable for me. Thus we all walk the feather edge—each man his own unique edge—and go on to the visionary. For all the precision with which the visionary state can be placed and described, it is still elusive. You do not one day become a visionary and ever after remain one. It is a state that one flows in and out of, gaining it through directed effort or spontaneously in a gratuitous moment. Oddly, it is not consciously worked for, but comes as the almost accidental product of effort in another direction and on a different plane. It is at its own whim momentary or lingering suspended in the air, suspending time in its turn, forever momentarily eternal, as, stepping out of the last rappel you turn and behold the rich green wonder of the forest.

293

PART VI

White Landscapes, Hickory Wings

THERE IS ONE TIME OF YEAR *in certain parts of the world when the known contours become elusive. This is winter, when each snowfall makes a new landscape and new footings must be found. In the Sierra, it was natural that the high country that beckoned club members in summer should intrigue them in winter, too. Around 1900, such titles as "A Glimpse of the Winter Sierra" began to appear in the* Bulletin. *The June, 1903, issue carried an article on how to make your own skis.*

For most people in California—and the United States—skiing was an unknown sport in 1903. In Western culture, men have traditionally shunned the cold of winter and in the Sierra there was an immediate memory to keep people out of the snowbound mountains. Most Californians grew up on the grim story of the Donner Party starving through the winter of 1846, caught by huge snow drifts near Donner Lake and finally turning to cannibalism to survive.

Skis themselves are not a new invention, as Scandinavian rock carvings thousands of years old show, but until a hundred years or so ago, they were used for utilitarian purposes only. Skiing for pleasure began in Norway around 1850, and after a few years spread rapidly across Europe. The new enthusiasm for the world of winter spread across the United States, too. It was in 1904 that the United States National Ski Association was formed.

The Sierra Club was quick to take up the new sport. With skis, members could enter the mountains in winter. New explorations, new achievements were possible.

In 1913, the club sponsored its first snow trip. Then and again in 1914, members went by train to Truckee, as Hazel King will mention. Twenty years later, Clair Tappaan Ski Lodge, constructed by club volunteers at Norden, near Donner Pass, was open for its first season. That it drew a capacity crowd was more than partly due to the efforts of Professor Joel ("Ski Heil") Hildebrand, a ski enthusiast of national reputation. Under Professor Hildebrand, the club organized ski classes in the late twenties and early thirties, and devised tests for determining levels of ability, and engaged in ski competitions.

The aspect of skiing, however, that lay closest to the hearts of many club members, was ski-mountaineering, a combination of two sports. In 1921, Harold Bradley crossed the range from a point near Placerville to Truckee, using skis fastened to his feet with little more than toe straps. Soon other mountaineers began to take to the "boards" to explore the mountains in winter: Bestor Robinson, Einar Nilsson, Oliver Kehrlein, Norman Clyde, Walter Mosauer—the list is long—explored the snow-covered slopes from north to south. They, too, started out with primitive ski bindings and heavy packs. Each winter, however, their packs grew lighter and their gear and ski-mountaineering techniques better. In World War II, the club's ski-mountaineers were able to give practical advice of the utmost value on the training and equipping of mountain ski troops.

In 1942 the club issued the first edition of the Manual of Ski Mountaineering. *Since then, three more editions of the manual have come out, the latest in 1969. All four editions have been edited by David R. Brower, one of the club's leading ski mountaineers. We will close with a statement by Brower, taken from the third edition, on what ski mountaineering has meant to him through the years.*

Most of these articles describe the early days of skiing, before concerns arose about what skiing —and ski lodges and ski tows —might do to the very wilderness the skiers

296

had come to enjoy. On the following pages we shall meet some members of the club who were preeminent on the Sierra slopes. We start, however, with one who was the pioneer skier of them all, long before the club was formed — "Snow-shoe" Thompson.

73

Snow-shoe Thompson

DAN DeQUILLE

1935

In the Overland Monthly, *October, 1886, appeared an account of the most remarkable skier in the history of the Sierra, a man whose deeds at times approach the exploits of such legendary heroes as John Henry and Paul Bunyan.*

This was "Snow-shoe" Thompson, who carried hundred-pound sacks of mail back and forth across the Sierra in winter for two decades, 1856–1876. What makes his story more incredible is the kind of skis ("snow-shoes," as they were then called) he wore. As Snow-shoe made them — based on childhood memories from Norway — the skis were eight to ten feet long. Their shape looked much like the skis of today, only Snow-shoe's skis were attached to the foot by the crudest of toe-strap bindings. This meant they would not respond to the turn of his foot. Some guiding could be done with a long pole he carried, but in general, his safety lay in choosing routes through moderately sloping areas, and in simply stepping off his skis when the going got too fast.

However, Snow-shoe and the others who tried skis in the 1850s and 1860s in the Sierra — chiefly young miners still working the gold mines — did not stick to mild slopes only. The ski meets they held — which may have been the earliest held in Europe or the United States — were daredevil events. They featured runs straight downhill at speeds sometimes surpassing eighty miles an hour. How many survived such runs is not recorded, but gradually the miners drifted away, and such feats, and skiing itself, became a matter of memory.

Snow-shoe Thompson's story is told by Dan DeQuille, who interviewed him only a few months before Thompson's death. DeQuille, at that time on the staff of the Territorial Enterprise *in Virginia City, did not publish the story until ten years later, and then in the* Overland Monthly. *That it appeared in the* Bulletin *in 1935 is due to the historical interests of its distinguished editor, Francis Farquhar. Snow-shoe's grave (his name is spelled "Thomson" on his monument) can still be seen in the cemetery of Genoa, Nevada, in the Carson Valley. Erected by his widow, the monument is decorated with a simple pair of crossed skis.*

J OHN A. THOMPSON, the man to whom the people of the Pacific Coast gave the name of "Snow-shoe Thompson," was born at Upper Tins, Prestijeld, Norway, April 30, 1827; and died at his ranch in Diamond Valley, at the head of Carson Valley, thirty miles south of Carson City, Nevada, May 15, 1876, after an illness of but a few days.

Mr. Thompson was a man of splendid physique, standing six feet in his stockings, and weighing 180 pounds. His features were large, but regular and handsome. He had the blonde hair and beard, and fair skin and blue eyes of his Scandinavian ancestors; and looked a true descendant of the sea-roving Northmen of old.

At the age of forty-nine years, he seemed in the very prime of life. His eye was bright as that of a hawk, his cheeks were ruddy, his frame muscular, and his *tout ensemble* that of a hardy mountaineer, ready to take the field, and face the dangers of the wilderness and the elements, at a moment's notice. His face wore that look of repose, and he had that calmness of manner, which are the result of perfect self-reliance, and a feeling of confidence in the possession of the powers to conquer.

In the year 1837, when ten years of age, Thompson left his native land, and with his father and family came to the United States. The family made Illinois their first halting place, but in 1838 they left that state, and went to Missouri. In 1841, the family left Missouri, and went to Iowa, where they remained until 1845, when they returned to Illinois.

In 1851, Mr. Thompson, then twenty-four years of age, was smitten with the "gold fever," and came across the plains to California. He landed at Hangtown, now known as Placerville, and for a time mined at Coon Hollow and Kelsey's Diggings. He presently became dissatisfied with the life and luck of a miner, and concluded to try the valleys. He went to Putah Creek, Sacramento Valley, and set up as a ranchman. He lived on his ranch during the years 1854–'55, but his eyes were constantly turned eastward toward the mountains — toward where the snowy peaks glittered against the deep blue sky.

Early in the winter of 1856, while still at work on his Putah Creek ranch, Mr. Thompson read in the papers of the trouble experienced in getting the mails across the snowy summit of the Sierra Nevada Mountains. At the time he was engaged in cutting wood on his ranch. What he heard and read of the difficulties encountered in the mountains, on account of the great depth of the snow, set him to thinking. When he was a boy, in Norway, snow-shoes were objects as familiar to him as ordinary shoes are to the children of other lands. He determined to make a pair of snow-shoes out of the oak timber he was engaged in splitting. Although he was but ten years of age at the time he left his native land, his recollections of the shoes he had seen there were in the main correct. Nevertheless, the shoes he then made were such as would at the present day be considered much too heavy, and somewhat clumsy. They were ten feet in length, were four inches in width behind the part on which the feet rest, and in front were four inches and a quarter wide.

Having completed his snow-shoes to the best of his knowledge, Thompson at once set out for Placerville, in order to make experiments with them. Being made out of green oak, Thompson's first shoes were very heavy. When he reached Placerville, he put them upon a pair of scales, and found that they weighed twenty-five pounds. They were ponderous affairs, but their owner was a man of giant strength, and he was too eager to be up and doing to lose time in making another pair out of lighter wood.

When he made his first public appearance, he was already able to perform such feats as astonished all who beheld them. His were the first Norwegian snow-shoes ever seen in California. At that time, the only snow-shoes known were those of the Canadian pattern. Mounted upon his shoes — which were not unlike thin sled runners in appearance — and with his long balance-pole in his hands, he dashed down the sides of the mountains at such a fearful rate of speed as to cause many to characterize the performance as foolhardy. Snow-shoe Thompson did not ride astride his guide-pole, nor trail it by his side in the snow, as is the practice of other snow-shoers when descending a steep mountain, but held it horizontally before him, after the manner of a tight-rope walker. His appearance was most graceful when seen darting down the face of a steep mountain, swaying his long balance-pole now to this side and now to that, as a soaring eagle moves its wings.

His first trip was made in January, 1856. He went from Placerville to Carson Valley, a distance of ninety miles. With the mail bags strapped upon his back, he glided over fields of snow that were in places from thirty to fifty feet in depth, his long Norwegian shoes bearing him safely and swiftly along upon the surface of the great drifts. Having successfully made the trip to Carson Valley and back to Placerville, Snow-shoe Thompson became a necessity, and was soon a fixed institution of the mountains. He went right ahead, and carried the mails between the two points all that winter. Through him was kept up the only land communication there was between the Atlantic States and California.

The load that Snow-shoe Thompson carried strapped upon his back would have broken down an ordinary man, though wearing common shoes and traveling on solid ground. The weight of the bags he carried was ordinarily from sixty to eighty pounds; but one winter, when he carried the mails for Chorpenning, his load often weighed over one hundred pounds.

In going from Placerville to Carson Valley, owing to the great amount of uphill traveling, three days were consumed; whereas, he was able to go from Carson Valley to Placerville in two days, making forty-five miles a day. Not a house was then found in all that distance. Between the two points all was a wilderness.

While traveling in the mountains, Show-shoe Thompson never carried blankets, nor did he even wear an overcoat. The weight and bulk of such articles would have encumbered and discommoded him. Exercise kept him warm while traveling, and when encamped he always built a fire. He carried as little as possible besides the bags containing the mail.

At the time Thompson began snow-shoeing in the Sierras, nothing was known of the mysteries of "dope"—a preparation of pitch, tallow, and other ingredients, which, being applied to the bottom of the shoes, enables the wearer to lightly glide over snow softened by the rays of the sun. Dope appears to have been a California discovery. It is made of different qualities, and different degrees of hardness and softness. Each California snow-shoe runner has his "dope secret," or his "pet" dope, and some are so nice in this respect as to carry with them dope for different hours of the day; using one quality in the morning, when the snow is frozen, and others later on, as the snow becomes soft. As Thompson used no dope, soft snow stuck to and so clogged his shoes that it was sometimes impossible for him to travel over it. Thus, it frequently happened that he was obliged to halt for several hours during the day, and resume his journey at night, when a crust was frozen on the snow.

Snow-shoe Thompson's night camps—whenever the night was such as prevented him from pursuing his journey, or when it was necessary for him to obtain sleep—were generally made wherever he happened to be at the moment. He did not push forward to reach particular points, as springs or brooks. He was always able to substitute snow for water, without feeling any bad effect. He always tried, however, to find the stump of a dead pine, at which to make his camp. After setting fire to the dry stump he collected a quantity of fir or spruce boughs, with which he constructed a sort of rude couch or platform on the snow. Stretched upon his bed of boughs, with his feet to his fire, and his head resting upon one of Uncle Sam's mail bags, he slept as soundly as if occupying the best bed ever made; though, perhaps, beneath his couch there was a depth of from ten to thirty feet of snow.

At times, when traveling at night, Thompson was overtaken by blizzards, when the air would be so filled with snow, and the darkness so great, that he could not see to proceed. On such occasions, he would get on top of some big rock, which the winds kept clear of snow, and there dance until daylight appeared; the lateness of the hour and the blinding storm preventing his making one of his usual camps.

Snow-shoe Thompson was one of those unfortunate persons whose lot in life it is to do a great deal of work and endure many hardships for very little pay. For twenty winters he carried the mails across the Sierra Nevada Mountains, at times when they could have been transported in no other way than on snow-shoes. After he began the business he made his home in the mountains, having secured a ranch in Diamond Valley, when for five winters in succession he was constantly engaged in carrying the mails across the snowy range. Two years he carried the United States mails when there was no contract for that service, and he got nothing. On both sides of the mountains he was told that an appropriation would be made and all would come out right with him; but he got nothing except promises.

If not the swiftest, it was universally conceded that, even up to the time of his death, Thompson was the most expert snow-shoe runner in the Sierra Nevada Mountains. At Silver Mountain, Alpine County, California, in 1870, when he was forty-three years of age, he ran a distance of sixteen hundred feet in twenty-one seconds. There were many snow-shoers at that place, but in daring Thompson surpassed them all. Near the town was a big mountain, where the people of the place were wont to assemble on bright days in winter, to the number of two or three hundred. The ordinary snow-shoers would go part way up the mountain to where there was a bench, and then glide down a beaten path. This was too tame for Thompson. He would make a circuit of over a mile, and come out on the top of the mountain. When he appeared on the peak he would give one of his wild High-Sierra whoops, poise his balance-pole, and dart down the face of the mountain at lightning speed, leaping all the terraces from top to bottom, and gliding far out on the level before halting.

Snow-shoe Thompson seldom performed any feat for the mere name and fame of doing a difficult and daring thing; yet W. P. Merrill, postmaster at Woodford's, Alpine County, writes me as follows, in speaking of some of Thompson's achievements: "He at one time went back of Genoa, on a mountain, on his show-shoes, and made a jump of one hundred and eight feet without a break." This seems almost incredible, but Mr. Merrill is a reliable man, and for many years Thompson was his near neighbor, and a regular customer at his store. Thompson doubtless made this fearful leap at a place where he would land in a great drift of soft snow.

Thompson was forty-nine years and fifteen days old, when he died. He was buried at Genoa, and now rests by the side of his son Arthur, his only child and a most promising lad, who died June 22, 1878, at the age of eleven years and four months.

Thompson left his widow a farm of one hundred and sixty acres, in Diamond Valley, just across the Nevada line, in California. She recently caused a tombstone to be erected over the grave of her former husband. At the top of the stone are seen a pair of artistically carved snow-shoes, crossed, and twelve inches in height.

John A. Thompson was the father of all the race of snow-shoers in the Sierra Nevada Mountains; and in those mountains he was the pioneer of the pack train, the stage coach, and the locomotive. On the Pacific Coast his equal in his peculiar line will probably never again be seen. The times and conditions are past and gone that called for men possessing the special qualifications that made him famous. It would be hard to find another man combining his courage, physique, and powers of endurance — a man with such thews and sinews, controlled by such a will.

74

A Glimpse of the Winter Sierra

BOLTON COIT BROWN

1901

Bolton Coit Brown was already a veteran mountaineer when he decided in 1900 to spend his Christmas vacation snow-camping. How novel this plan was is shown by the way he had to guess at the equipment he would need and improvise that which he could not get. His improvisations included a toboggan that was "in fact a single ten-pound sheet of rolled iron." Brown can tell the use to which he finally put this invention. What is important is that in spite of all the deficiencies in his equipment, he stayed on "for several days" and heartily recommended the experience.

Brown, professor of drawing at Stanford University, had explored extensively in the Sierra in the 1890s, particularly the country at the head of the Kings and the Kings-Kern Divide. He reported his findings in articles and maps published in the Bulletin. He was a charter member of the Club and made the first ascent of Mt. Clarence King in 1896. The same year, he joined J. N. LeConte in the first ascent of Mt. Gardner.

Brown entered the "arctic zone" at what was then General Grant National Park; today it is part of Kings Canyon National Park.

MY PLAN WAS to leave Millwood with a kind of mitigated arctic outfit, and to push back as far towards the great peaks as should prove practicable. My equipment consisted of two weeks' rations, two extra suits of underclothing, two pairs of blankets, a sleeping-bag of heavy canvas, an ax, a pistol, a pair of snow-shoes *(skies)* and a pole, a 5 × 7 camera with two dozen plates, a pocket camera with films, and a sled, this latter being simply a metal toboggan eight feet long by two feet wide—in fact, a single ten-pound sheet of rolled iron. My reason for adopting this remarkable article was that I wished to have matters so arranged that I could, at a pinch, travel over even the softest snow.

Arrived in due time at Millwood, there was only bare ground. Mr. Kanawyer, however, readily undertook to pack my stuff the three or four miles to the arctic zone. Soon after entering the gate of the General Grant Park we came to the snow, but it proved so hard that the horses readily walked upon its surface and passed the snowed-up eastern gate by walking over the fence on the crust. Of course, with snow at that depth "the trail" does not exist. The mountain-side along which in summer it runs now presents a steep snow-slope across which man or horse must go gingerly, clinging with an incisive edge of sole or hoof. Reaching presently an unusually steep descent, the animals pulled back amazed, snorting their disapproval. And as they positively refused to be dragged or bullied over the brow of the pitch, we were forced to change our route from east to south. For the next half-hour, as we wound and plunged along this crest, my attention was divided between avoiding hummocks and hollows and gazing far-off at the deepening sunset colors. For spread over the snow-fields of that tumult of Alps which filled the entire eastern horizon, glowed saffron and rose and wine-color and purple, beyond all imagination of tenderness, flushing over the vast snowy panorama and deepening down the mighty cavernous cañons to depths and intensities that thrilled like richest organ-music. And then it was night.

We tied up the horses to spruce-trees, fed them barley, and ourselves, in a rude camp there on the snow, lay in not unreasonable discomfort until daylight.

Morning came, and we again pressed on southeasterly, descending gradually into one of the gorges tributary to the Bearskin Meadow basin. At the bottom of this the horses broke through so often and floundered so badly that we gave up further packing, and lashing our load upon the toboggan, started to drag it by hand up the eastern side of the gorge. And drag it we did—although at vast expense of labor. In two hours we had hardly gone more than half a mile, nor ascended more than five hundred feet. At this point, owing to the necessity of his reaching Millwood before night, Kanawyer was obliged to leave me.

The sled with its load may have weighed 130 pounds. A very few minutes' experience with it showed me two things: first, that the sled itself would never stand any considerable journey, but would work itself full of holes, and ultimately to pieces, from the kinking of the iron; and, second, that over other than a comparatively even surface it would be folly for one man to attempt to haul it. So I tied it to a tree—it was so slippery that otherwise it would have scooted clear into King's River—and gave the afternoon to exploring among the ridges and snow-burdened rocks.

I found that I was just on the northern side of the crest of the divide between King's River and the Kaweah, about five miles south of Bearskin Meadow, three miles due east—as afterward determined by the North Star—of Finger Rock, and at an altitude of about 8,000 feet. The snow lay indefinitely deep, covering up into gentle mounds and long breastworks the bushes and logs, and giving to the forest something of a park-like character. The southern side of the ridge, however, was far less polar. Manzanita and all the familiar bushes enjoyed there the bright sun, and all about spread warm dry islands of odorous pine-needles whereon a man might lie and bask until he imagined it summertime. Woodpeckers rattled at the dead trees, and a few other birds swept from tree to tree. Nimble squirrels now and then dashed out of sight and the ever-present chipmunk scrabbled violently away in his usual panic. And across the snowy places trailed rows of holes made by the feet of bear, deer, and coyote.

Remaining for that night in the camp where I was, I next morning divided my luggage into four loads, which, at cost of half a day's hard work, I packed up to a cheerful spot on the crest of the ridge. Hardly, however, had I rolled the last burden from my shoulders when the sky began to cloud over and to threaten—so I thought—for the coming night a snow-fall. Now, in my wanderings I had, some half-mile away, come upon a ruined hut of shakes buried in the snow, and toward this, with feelings of keen sympathy for the laborious pack-mule, I now again began to pack my assortment of loads. The roof of the hut was crushed in and buried under several feet of snow, but there still remained along the wall an icicled cavity, into which I gratefully crept.

Next morning I went back and dragged up the abandoned sledge. Chopping it with the ax neatly into two unequal pieces, of the smaller I made an excellent stove and of the larger an excellent chimney. I melted up the glittering stalactites of my cave and made tea with them, which tasted, however, less like tea than like superior pine shakes. Cooking-water was better got by quarrying pure, crystalline chunks of hard snow from the heart of a snow-hummock.

On the whole, it seemed wisest to give over the idea of farther travel. My sled was a failure. My load was far too heavy. My rubbers had endured less than one day, while the shoes they had covered acquired great holes before the end of the next. I possessed, indeed, another and slightly heavier pair of shoes, but it seemed to me evident that the constant cutting of the harsh crust-edge would rapidly saw these also to pieces.

And so for several days, with this little camp as headquarters, I roamed about. I played, for the first time in my life, the rôle of photographer, lugging camera, plates, and tripod up hill and down dale with all the enthusiasm of the novice. I used my sleeping-bag as a dark-room for changing plates. And the amazing part is that, having now developed the plates, I find that, by mere luck and guesswork, the times of the exposures were right, and that I have a picture for every one of the twenty-four plates exposed.

One day I crossed the basin eastward, and climbed to the top of Finger Rock. The camera I hauled up from stage to stage by a rope. The summit of this crag commands a quite unobstructed view of the High Sierra, from the awful spikes away beyond the Middle Fork in the north round to Goat Mountain, King, Gardiner, Brewer, Milestone, Table Mountain, and the superb mass of the Kaweah, and all shone in the winter sunshine, dazzling, resplendent, and indescribably beautiful in their vast white blankets. I exposed four plates — three as a panorama—and all were surprisingly successful. As giving an idea of the practical rate of travel, I may say that this expedition, though its length, all told, could not have exceeded six miles, occupied one entire laborious day.

All the weather was perfect. During the middle of the day the thermometer, in the shade, probably remained somewhat below the freezing-point. At night it may have descended twenty or more degrees. The clouds proved false prophets, for not a snowflake fell. Still and sunny were the days—so still you could hear your ears ring—and still and starry were the nights. From the mysterious vastness of the fir forest the great owl hooted to the

304

sailing moon, and at dawn the shrill cry of the coyote came ringing over the frozen snow. A woodpecker at the corner of my cabin rapped me up for breakfast.

As looking towards some similar trip in future, by myself or by others, a few words of criticism may not be amiss. First, then, concerning the sled: The sled should be a pair of very low, light, and not too short "bobs." They should be so low and so smooth upon the under side that in very soft snow they slide on the under surface of the top board. The runners should be about three inches wide, and enable them to creep along hillsides without constantly slewing sideways down the slope.

I think that for warmth at night one should depend partly upon fire. A sheepskin sleeping-bag, wool inside, and one pair of blankets would be satisfactory. It is necessary to be able to resist a night temperature of about zero. A man equipped with, say twenty pounds of extra clothing, twenty pounds of condensed foods, and ten pounds of sundries—fifty pounds in all—could travel—well, almost anywhere.

Ski Running: An Impression

75

HAZEL KING

1915

In 1900 Bolton Coit Brown took "skies" on his snow-camping venture, but did not use them. Fourteen years later, however, Hazel King is skiing at Truckee, near Donner Lake, not expertly by any means, but with determination and spirit. The trip she tells of here was the second snow trip sponsored by the club. The participants slept and ate on a Pullman car parked on a siding.

Hazel King's experiences have been shared by all beginners, although not all have fallen and picked themselves up so cheerfully as she.

Eugene Sandow was a German strong man who, by royal appointment, was professor of physical culture to King George V.

COME AWAY FROM the rush and stress of life and follow on skis the flight of a mountain blue bird. To find those birds in the high mountains in winter is a rare privilege and to be able to observe them from skis is still another. So let the Pullman porter set you free at Truckee when he lifts his trap door, and glide away over the snowy slopes to the silent haunts of that wandering bird.

Already your soul has swung far out on the keen driving air to a snow-tipped pine tree; but your unmanageable and awkward body (it is all of that with strips of boards, half again as long as you are, attached to your feet), must struggle and push to make even a little headway up the hill.

It seems at the first careful lifting of one's feet that one needs the strength of a Sandow. There can be no doubt; the use of skis demands muscular effort. But this winter sport takes not alone physical ability, but mental agility as well—the art of looking ahead, determining one's course and swaying one's body accordingly. In the ascent you must place your weight forward. In the descent it is just the reverse. The extent of this forward and backward movement varies with the steepness of the slopes encountered. The steeper the declivity the more the body, in ascending, swings forward, whether you are traveling straight ahead, or are taking a zig-zag course. Again, the opposite movement takes place in the descent, while in any case the weight is always thrown from the knees.

You, of course, would suppose that the responsibility of keeping your equilibrium rests with your feet and ankles, they being in closer touch with the skis, but it is not so. They act merely in a steering capacity and as brakes, and must always move in connection with the rest of your quick and lithe body which swings like a pendulum.

In short, it is rhythm; it is the same intangible pulsing, the same beat that comes into the mind and dominates the body in skating and in dancing; it is the same undercurrent of mental movement with which all activity, physical or otherwise, is filled, and it is this harmonious blending of the body with the mind that enables you to travel easily and gracefully over the glistening snow.

But even with a sense of rhythm to your credit, you must not expect that it alone will instantaneously swing you up to that happy playground to which your soul rushed out, in the early morning. You must learn to be patient in your slips, and slides, and falls; to even anticipate the latter, so that you may tumble jauntily into the snow, thus causing you no bruises or pain.

It is a cosy place for half a minute (until you begin to thaw); that hole you have dug for yourself where the snow snuggles into every corner of your body. But such a snarl to disentangle, skis, stick and head all curled up in a knot, and when you are freed, erect and ready to start again, how humiliating to leave behind, for others to come upon, that hole for a signpost, "Here I fell!"

It takes quite a few pilgrimages to the skiing grounds to pass beyond that period of disfiguring the snow, and to glide with all ease and abandon down any sort of slope. To take bumps and dodge trees you must approach them without fear; with the realization that they are to be considered but with all the self-assurance and determination that you are master, and that they can have no terrors for you.

Here is where a knowledge of mountaineering is of advantage, for an understanding of heights and distances. A cautious alertness for precipices and crevasses, also, is most essential before attempting and hazarding too much. Again, another quality that is necessary to a ski-runner is endurance, especially in the case of journeying from place to place; for to travel steadily and easily, as the Indians do, is to win your goal with the least possible fatigue and trepidation.

Even after all is said, you will never learn to be quick and facile in strapping on your skis yourself, and skimming joyously over the freshly packed snow, unless you have a real love of adventure in your heart; unless you want to penetrate the winter's silences and mingle with and vanish away into them, with the hushed hope of stealthily tracking the mountain blue bird, or maybe coming upon a rocky fortress, where you can plant your skis endwise on the snowy threshold, climb upon its battlements and there stretch out in the warm sunshine, listening for the faintest stir of insect or wind.

Put on your skis and go up to the mountain top. There pause; gather yourself together in a crouching position, just as a bird does before it leaps into the air; then straighten out, with equal scorn of your moorings, with life and freedom tingling from your toes to the sparkle in your eyes, and you, too, will fly over that white world, alighting gradually and uprightly (we hope).

In any case, you have had the exhilaration of that wonderfully quick downward movement, and after you have gathered yourself together again to reascend the slope, you have the pleasure in the climb, of pausing to watch the changing clouds, of speculating as to "what is beyond that ridge," of noticing the whispering trees, until you find yourself once more at the top, ready and impatient to try again your ski wings.

76 Across the Sierra Nevada on Skis

H. C. BRADLEY

1922

"For many years I had hoped for the time when I should visit the Sierra in Midwinter," writes Harold C. Bradley.

The time came on New Year's Day, 1921, when he started from Berkeley with the plan of skiing from Placerville over Echo Summit to Truckee. As it turned out, he left from Kyburz.

It was a bold plan. There might have been a few who skied over the Sierra in winter — Bradley followed part of Snow-shoe Thompson's route — but there could not have been many, and, like Snow-shoe, Bradley skied alone. Moreover, the weather, which he had thought would be clear, was not; at Echo Summit it rained. Bradley's skis were not far advanced in design from Snow-shoe Thompson's; they still depended mainly on the toe strap for staying on the foot, and Bradley was still using the long staff that Snow-shoe had used for what guiding was possible. He did use "ski-dope"—ski wax, with which Snow-shoe was not acquainted. Bradley, however, was an excellent mountaineer, and well able to recognize both the possibilities and the limitations of his equipment.

Harold Bradley was the son of Cornelius Beach Bradley, one of the founders of the club, and was himself president from 1957 to 1959.

I HAD GONE OVER the equipment with the greatest care, taking only what seemed essential, and yet prepared for any emergency that might arise. As I had to make the trip alone, many little things had to be provided as accident insurance which might have been left out or at least divided in a larger party. For camping in the snow the lightest possible waterproof sheet (6 by 7) was taken as a shelter fly. A sweater, mackinaw coat, mittens, and extra woolen socks were included for cold weather. In addition, the pack included a miniature medicine-kit, camera and films, snow-glasses, automatic pistol, extra rawhide thongs for repairs, ski "dope," thirty feet of light, strong braided cord for tent lashings, and a two-handed axe of Hudson Bay model. The axe was taken in lieu of blankets or sleeping-bag, and thoroughly justified itself. Only the driest obtainable food was taken— sugar, chocolate, dry bean-and-vegetable soup cartridges, dried graham bread, cereal, bacon, butter, milk-powder, coffee and tea tablets. The cooking outfit consisted of an army mess-kit, an army tin cup rigged with a wire bail, and an aluminum bowl fitting the mouth of the cup. Axe included, the pack tipped the scales at forty pounds, and assured food enough for five days at least, with the possibility of making it last another day or so if necessary. For transportation a pair of hickory skis and a stout ski-staff were taken.

It was perfectly evident that the weather was all arranged to make the trip an entire success—at least so it seemed at the time.

From Sacramento to Placerville the journey was continued in the commodious Pierce-Arrow stage, the terminus being reached at one o'clock. Mr. Richardson, of the stage line, agreed to furnish auto transportation up the road at the rate of fifty cents a mile as far as a machine could go. This seemed somewhat excessive at the time, but, considering the condition of the road as we found it, its mud and snow, holes and bumps, I am inclined to think it was not. At two o'clock we pulled out of Placerville, passed the Pacific House at about four, and reached the bottom of the American River Cañon not far from Kyburz at about half-past four. It was impossible to drive farther on account of the snow, so the auto was abandoned for skis at this point. Twilight was already settling over the deep cañon as I shouldered my pack and started on, and by quarter-past five it was evidently time to make camp. In fact it was past time, for night shut in so rapidly that much of the preparation for camp had to be done hurriedly and in the dark. However, a

308

grove of pine, cedar, and fir on a level bench a few rods above the road made an attractive camp-site, and the fly was set up, a thick bed of fir boughs prepared under it, and at its mouth a crackling fire backlogged and platformed with the green butt-lengths of the small fir trees felled for bed-brush. By six o'clock supper was cooking, while the stars were blinking frostily above the black silhouettes of the forest trees. The wood supply was not of the best, for no really large dry timber could be located before dark, and the dead lower branches of the trees of my grove, while plentiful, were too small to make a lasting fire. However, they were easily obtained and in quantity, and together with a damp and punky standing dead pine, perhaps eight inches at the butt, they lasted till morning. The axe paid for itself that night, where a smaller belt-hatchet would have been worthless.

The night was clear and quiet. The firelight made a lovely picture of trees and snow against the curtain of blackness beyond. The river roared a wild lullaby from the gloom of the cañon below the camp. Inside the reflecting fly, with the fir boughs over the snow, all was dry and warm and fragrant. One could drop asleep luxuriously in the warmth of the crackling fire and an hour or so later wake up chilly when it had sunk to a bed of glowing embers. Another armful of wood purchased another hour of sleep. In this way the night was spent, interrupted more frequently than would have been necessary if the right sort of wood had been obtainable, but comfortable enough in spite of the interruptions.

Sunday morning was dawning as the start up the grade was made. The snow was dry after the frosty night, and in spite of the pack the going was all that could be expected. The road was smooth and billowy, with its surface marked by the broad pads of a mountain lion that had circled the camp at a respectful distance, and who was apparently also heading east across the range. His trail was so fresh that I half-expected to see his tawny form around each turn of the road, but after a mile his tracks turned down into a thicket above the river, and there was no further sign of him.

As the morning advanced the frosty temperature of the night gradually changed to the mild thawing climate of spring. Late in the morning two men on skis appeared coming down the road. They proved to be the caretakers at Phillips' Resort, near the top, bound out for a few days of civilization, and they hospitably offered me the use of their cabin for the night.

By noon I had reached Strawberry and camped on a rocky ledge blown free from snow, where a fire was soon blazing, and snow a–melt for tea and soup. The day had grown so warm, and the work had become so strenuous, that my clothing was wet with perspiration and I was parched with thirst. The best part of lunch was the brimming bowl of fragrant tea. What a delight it was to bask in the warm sunshine on my island of rock in this world of spotless snow, and all in the middle of winter! Now and then a young fir or pine, bent down and buried under the load of snow and looking like a mound or boulder, would free itself of its load and spring upright without a moment's warning. The first few times this occurred it startled me, like the sudden springing into view of game.

After a pleasant hour's nooning I buckled on my skis again and shouldered

309

the pack for the climb to the top. The snow had grown rapidly softer and more heavy. Every step was now sheer work for every foot gained. There was none of the extra slide at the end of the stride which under favorable conditions makes the ski such a splendid device in the snow. The skis sank deep, and the snow packed and clung heavily at every stroke. I found Strawberry [Resort] in winter much more beautiful than in summer—with no dust, no automobiles, no smell of gasoline. The soft hand of nature had wiped away all the ugly symbols of our civilization, and all was in perfect harmony again, as it might have been a thousand years ago.

But the long climb was ahead of me and I pushed on. The great cliff of Lover's Leap rose grandly to the right, but the higher ridges across the valley to the left were lost in cloud, so that I had no glimpse of Pyramid or his neighbors as I toiled up the steep grade to the top of the moraine. Under the conditions, two miles an hour was more than the best I could do. However, with the prospect of a cabin ahead for shelter, I was not at all disturbed either by my slow pace through the heavy snow or by the gathering gloom of the clouds, which were growing rapidly more ominous. From the top of the moraine on up to Phillips' the grade was delightfully easy and the landscapes increasingly beautiful. The yellow pines had given place largely to lodgepole pines and shapely firs, and no tree grows so charmingly in snow as does the fir. The decorations of the previous storm had all melted and dropped off and the branches stood out level and green, or massed in black against the pure white of the snow. The stream ran sometimes in the open, sometimes completely buried in the rounding drifts that had choked its valley and roofed it over. About four o'clock a sleety rain began, and an hour later I reached the cabin, glad of its stove and wood, its roof and bunks. There is no question about the work involved in skiing up-hill, through deep wet snow and under a pack. It was bedtime the instant supper was over, and the next instant the dawn was graying the east window.

It was still raining hard when I struck out Monday morning. I had seen it snow up here in summer; I hardly considered rain in winter a possibility; and I had to admit failure as a weather forecaster. But it was only a few miles to the summit of the pass, then a glorious down-hill stretch to Meyer's, and the Grove Hotel on the shores of Tahoe only eight miles beyond that for the night's stop, a total of but sixteen miles. Still the day before had given me more respect for sixteen miles than I had ever entertained before.

In spite of the rain and wet snow, the trip from Phillips' to the top was a lovely one. The snow was about six feet deep on the level, and the woods were silent except for the song of the storm-gusts that now and then crashed through the tree-tops. The sense of peace and calm repose was more tangible and definite here than anywhere else on the trip. I wished for the chance to spend a month or two with the snug cabin as a base from which to explore this new wilderness of white.

Finally the pass was reached, and the clouds blowing through the mountain rifts in long banners were tearing and whipping themselves to shreds in the great space to eastward. Every few moments the curtain would rise and disclose the valley below, with the Upper Truckee making a black meander pattern on the white valley-floor. Then the cloud streamer would shift and the big moraine south of Fallen Leaf Lake would dimly outline itself and fade into gray again. Once a lift of the clouds disclosed the bulk of Job and his fellows and the whole southern Tahoe Basin. I slipped off pack and skis and sat a few moments in the little snowed-up rest-house that stands in the pass. As I sat in its shelter out of the wind, the deep jarring crash and roar of a small avalanche off to the right and out of sight filled the Upper Truckee Valley with its thunder and its echoes. A few rods to the left across the road was the scar of another that had slid some days before. Evidently there were places where the heavy snow cornice blown through the pass was getting unsteady, and it seemed desirable to get by this first part of the descent as rapidly as possible before any more of it broke away from its moorings.

The descent was not up to expectations. Instead of a thrilling slide down the grade with moments of excitement in rounding the hairpin turns, as I had pictured it, it was just plain hard work. As a matter of fact I did not quite dare start straight down the scarp, ignoring the road and dodging trees and buried boulders. Particularly with the uncertain motions of the pack to disconcert every quick attempt at balance, I did not care to hazard the descent that way alone. It probably would not have worked had I tried it. The heavy snow canceled completely the advantage of the downward pitch, so that every step had to be made with effort. Slushy snow continued to fall, making clothing soggy and the pack heavier.

At Meyer's I found a room open, supplied with wood and a stove, left in true hospitable mountain style for the wayfarer to use. While tea was brewing and clothes drying I put a fresh coat of "dope" on the skis. In wet snow the "dope" becomes worth its weight in almost any commodity.

During the noon rest the rain abated and the storm blew by. The sun was shining fitfully as the start for the lake was made, and in an hour or two the sky was clear except for the cloud-banners streaming from the higher summits. The warmth of the sun, cheerful as it was after the rain, made the going still heavier, and two miles an hour was the best speed I could make, even along this level eight-mile stretch. The Grove Hotel was reached late in the afternoon. It was Monday evening, and on the next day the steamer was expected to make its circuit of the lake, stopping at Tallac. Under the conditions, two days would be required to skirt the lake on skis along the western shore to Tahoe City, and, as my time was limited, it was decided to shorten this portion of the trip by taking the boat.

The steamer arrived at eleven on Tuesday and the trip to Tahoe City was made by half-past two. Accommodation for the night was secured at the home of Mr. Schmidt. Leaving my pack and camera, I traveled down the Truckee Cañon a mile or two and climbed the ridge to the east of the river. The snow was deep and in fine condition for skis, and the views through the forest out over the lake in the late afternoon were superb. As the sun set, the eastern crest, Mount Rose, and the Job group were all tinted in brilliant tones of shell-pink, while the lake and lower forest were deep blue against the pale blue and lavender of the shaded snow. Lighted by a few flaming cloud-banners, I had an exhilarating slide down the ridge, through the forest to the lake shore. During supper the wind came up fresh from the southwest and blew a half-gale all night.

Wednesday morning broke with a sunrise as brilliant as the sunset of the night before. Long cloud-banners were blowing through the passes from the west, giving warning of an impending storm. The snow was excellent, however, and the way down the Truckee Cañon comfortably level. In the valley bottom there was little wind, but above on the ridges the trees were bending and thrashing in it. By nine o'clock fine snow was falling and soon the distant view was blotted out by the storm. The temperature rose and the soft fresh snow grew sticky and clinging. Nevertheless, the sixteen miles to Truckee were quite the easiest of the trip, and were covered in six hours of easy going. Before the town was reached about ten inches of fresh snow had fallen, and the whole world, trees and all, were covered with a spotless mantle.

If one can wait for his weather, under shelter while it is unfavorable, winter-camping with pack and skis offers many delightful contrasts to summer trips. Even on the old and beaten routes such as this one, there are no disturbing sights or sounds, no crowds of people, no dust or dirt or draggled evidence of former campers. The solitude is unbroken and refreshing, the prospect on every hand lovely and free from the disfiguring taint of careless occupancy. It is easy to fancy yourself the first white man to thread this wilderness, and as you see the untracked snow on every side you realize that in very truth you are.

It will not be long, I think, before the Sierra Club will route its winter trips, from cabin to cabin through the snows, as it now does its summer excursions, making possible, for a few enthusiasts at least, that return to the untouched primitive world which in summer grows each year more difficult to find.

77
Skiing in California

OTTO BARKAN

1931

Otto Barkan's article is interesting not only for his story of the ski trip from Donner Summit to Tahoe that he and his wife made in 1927, when such trips were still rare, but also for the account he gives of the development of skiing in the Sierra. This sequence must have paralleled that of other winter-sports areas in the country —with

one amusing exception. California had been promoted as the land of perpetual sum-
mer, and it took the State Chamber of Commerce some time to admit that California
ever had snow — anywhere.

Barkan, a doctor, was active in the winter sports sections in the club. His particular
interest lay in improved ski equipment. In 1921, when Harold Bradley was still
using the old single long ski pole, Barkan was using ski poles of modern design.

IT WAS IN THE WINTER of 1919– 20 that a small group of enthusiasts put about to find suitable skiing country in the Sierra Nevada of California. Up to that time skiing had been for the most part of the eight- or ten-foot pinewood variety, with primitive toe-straps — merely a means of locomotion for the lumbermen and railroaders of the Sierra. A few initiates may have penetrated the Tahoe region, a few boys may have performed some jumps at Truckee's snow carnival for the delectation of trainloads of metropolitan excursionists, or a very occasional knight-errant of the ski may have appeared for a snowy day; but skiing — the great and glorious sport of ski mountaineering — was practically non-existent in California.

So at least we were led to believe when two of us alighted in the snow-sheds from the train at the old Summit Station one chilly morning at 5 o'clock with our Norwegian ski and sticks. A huge fellow occupied the little station-room, spat on the remaining bit of floor, and remarked, "Going to ski?" — "Yes." — "Them sticks ain't no good — you want a big pole"; for the Sierrans were wont to ski forth with a single pole, acting as brake, hobby-horse, or balance, as the occasion demanded, much after the manner of the old Zdarsky one-stick method of the Austrians. Little did he guess that with these small ski and dainty bamboo canes it was possible to turn, swerve, or stop, at a speed of forty miles an hour and over, avoiding obstacles, shooting between and around trees, in a glorious flying descent of perfect control.

Out of deference to my companion, who was a novice, we spent the first two days in a secluded spot of the woods. On the third day, however, the writer, fresh from the Swiss Alps, climbed to the cliffs behind the rail-roader's settlement and "let her go," oblivious of everything but the sinuous flight down to a whirling stop. He was greeted by loud hurrahs and shouts from the various houses and shacks half-buried in the snow; for it was Sunday and the railroaders were at home. As they afterward confessed, they had watched the "fool city guys" climbing to the cliff with some amuse-ment, and had hoped they would break their —— necks. Sturdy skiers though they were over long distances and in any weather, they had never seen such turns or even imagined the possibility of their execution. That afternoon they shyly dropped in on our host, Bob Agnew, on various pre-texts, incidentally casting a glance at our skis and bindings. Later we heard a sound as of hammering from the neighboring cabins and before long saw them sally forth on quite modernized ski. Our Telemark and Christiania turns were imitated by our good mountain friends, some of whom in the course of the following years became expert skiers. With them we explored the surrounding country from Castle Peak to Mount Lincoln, and to our delight one day dropped into a skier's paradise, which we named the "Sugar Bowl"—the spot Charlie Chaplin at a later date chose for the first scene of his "Gold Rush."

In 1921 the writer's better-half, on her first arrival in California from Sweden, was greeted at Summit by fourteen feet of snow and a boxful of orange-blossoms. On that occasion, while skiing from Mount Lincoln to Mount Anderson and Tinker Knob, my wife and I saw in the light of the setting sun the opalescent glint of Lake Tahoe. To reach Tahoe across the mountains became our dream, the realization of which had to be postponed to a future occasion.

In 1926 the broad-gauge made it possible for the first time to go directly to Tahoe. Yet we regretted the passing of that fine sleigh drive up the Truckee River which we had enjoyed before the advent of the winter-train service. On this occasion we had a rarely beautiful tour, skiing west from the Tavern up Ward Creek to Ward Peak, from the top of which we dropped down north to Bear Valley and so to the Truckee River. The cliffs were aflame in the setting sun as we shot down in the shadow of the peak into the blue depths beneath us. The snow on this cold northern slope was so dry and powdery, and, except for a slight hiss, our descent so noiseless, that we became aware of the swiftness of the descent only through seeing the blazing crags to our right rapidly rise and thrust upward into the sky. After what seemed an endless series of downward shoots, punctuated with sharp turns and stops, panting, we reached the shadowed floor of the valley and its gentler slopes. The flaming cliffs were now high above us. With wings on our feet we coasted in gentle curves between the trees and into the starlit night.

As this tributary of the Truckee offered such a fine descent, my wife and I decided to carry out our cherished dream of crossing the mountains from Summit to Tahoe at the next opportunity. In 1927, one morning before daybreak, "the little woman," as the linemen called her, Scott Smith, and the writer started from Summit for Lincoln Saddle, which we reached as the sun was rising. We had decided upon the route to be followed from previous tours in the Summit and Tahoe regions and from the Geological Survey maps of the intervening portions. Due to the small scale of the maps, we were left largely to our own resources to find the route which would entail the least loss of altitude and of time—for it was imperative to reach the floor of Squaw Valley before nightfall. The trip took fifteen hours, including one half-hour of reconnoitering and one half-hour's rest. The distance covered was between thirty and thirty-five miles.

The first two hours from Lincoln Saddle took us underneath and past the wind-swept cornices of Mount Lincoln and Mount Anderson. At this early hour of the morning there appeared to be no danger from slides. Toward noon we lost altitude by being forced to descend into a cirque on the north side of Anderson. This was bad enough in itself; but when it began to thaw we wondered whether we should ever reach our goal. Hopeless though it seemed, we began the very hot and tedious climb up to Tinker Knob through abominably sticky snow that stuck a foot deep to our ski. The advisability of giving up the trip before it got too late was discussed. However, as we gained altitude and the shadows grew longer, the snow became less sticky, and at 4 o'clock we finally looked around Tinker Knob at our next objective, the watershed between the North Fork of the American River and Squaw Creek. We traversed the south slope, where the granular spring snow permitted us to swing along at a good speed, while the Granite Chief range, radiant in the afternoon sun, kept pace to the right. Just to our left, and seemingly within our grasp, cadmium-colored cliffs pierced a deep-blue sky. We had hoped that the descent from the watershed to Squaw Valley would prove to be a skier's reward for our previous labors. But, alas, after the first few excellent runs across wooded slopes we found the head of Squaw Valley to be broken up by a maze of boulders and cliffs. Time pressed; so good form was thrown to the winds. We slithered and skidded between the rocks any which way until our bones ached—albeit an interesting and fascinating descent—and reached the valley floor as night fell. Tired and hungry, we plowed our way for two hours along the Truckee River to Tahoe, where at last we thawed out our frozen clothes in the Pullman car.

In Europe the appreciation of winter in the mountains was not born until the latter part of the nineteenth century. It took some years for people to overcome their traditional attitude toward winter—let alone the mountains in winter—namely, that of a necessary evil, to be put up with as best one could in the shelter of towns and well-heated homes and relieved only occasionally by the pleasures of ice-skating. One need but cast a glance at any part of the Alps today to realize how totally the picture has changed and how the joys of winter have taken Europe by storm. One cannot but believe that the same will occur in California. It might be argued that the Californian has no need for this—indeed, Easterners come to the Pacific Coast to enjoy our balmy, snowless winter season. Yet, as variety is the spice of life, so also is it health-bringing, and there can be no question that for us lowland Californians a truly seasonal change such as is offered by the snows and altitudes of the Sierra is a priceless thing.

78

Ski-Experience

ANSEL ADAMS

1931

Here photographer Ansel Adams uses words as brilliantly as film to express the wonder of the natural world. This article was written four years after his first portfolio of photographs, The High Sierras, *was published. Since then he has published photographs in many distinguished books, including the landmark* This Is the American Earth, *done with the late Nancy Newhall. They have brought to Americans a new, vital awareness of their natural heritage.*

An active member of the club, Adams was chairman of the club's first winter sports committee. He also served as a director and as vice-president.

FRITSCH RESTS HIS SKIS upright on a brittle arm of albicaulis. "We should wax now; it is a long run down to the lake." While we wait for our skis to warm in the sun we search the gleaming skyline for old landmarks and the peaks and cañons of new adventure. . . .

Just two days before we had thrilled on the extensive snowy summit of Mount Watkins overlooking Yosemite Valley, where we made mile-long runs with the gigantic forms of Clouds Rest and Half Dome rising before us across the abyss of Tenaya Cañon. Beyond these somber masses of sculptured granite, profoundly accentuated by heavy robes of snow, shimmered in white majesty the Merced Range — Mount Clark (the Gothic mountain), and the colorful shoulders of Red Peak. We skimmed the very brink of the great valley; four thousand feet below lay the white threads of roads, and a tiny rectangle of gray, dotted with almost invisible moving specks, which we knew as the large ice-rink in the shadow of Glacier Point. Beyond, steel-toned foothill ranges notched the long vistas of the San Joaquin plain. And against the western sky leaned the coastal mountains, unbelievably blue and far away.

This very morning, at the hour of silence and frosty stars, we were edging along the base of Tenaya Peak, our skis rasping and crunching on the brittle snow. Climbing around the western shoulder of the mountain, we came into full sunlight and a thrilling view of the main-crest peaks, white and cold in the early light. Here the snow was powdery and swift under our skis, but we refrained from downhill running and soon emerged on the summit — the hub of a tremendous wheel of mountain grandeur. A hundred miles of glittering peaks encircled our pinnacle of granite, and far below stretched the shadeless, dazzling plain of frozen Tenaya Lake.

The familiar and intimate aspects of the Sierra that one has learned to love during the long summer days are not obscured by winter snows. Rather the grand contours and profiles of the range are clarified and embellished under the white splendor; the mountains are possessed of a new majesty and peace. There is no sound of streams in the valleys; in place of the far-off sigh of waters is heard the thunder-roar of avalanches, and the wind makes only faint and brittle whisper through the snowy forests. To us, four motes on an Earth-gesture of high stone, it appeared that great mountain spirits had assumed white robes of devotion and were standing in silence before the intense sun. . . .

Fritsch whips his skis on the snow and leaps down the long billowy slope; a cloud of powdery snow gleams in his wake. We follow; long spacious curves and direct plunges into the depths that take our breath with sheer speed and joy. Down and down through the crisp singing air, riding the white snow as birds ride on the wind, conscious of only free unhampered motion. Soon we are at the borders of icy Tenaya Lake — two thousand feet of altitude have vanished in a few moments of thrilling delight. . . .

Today we are moving on to Tuolumne Meadows. All the bright morning we were conscious of a deep stirring in the air, the world quickening to some obscure activity. Now, as we come upon the lower stretch of the meadows, we are aware of a remote, ominous sound, insistent as the murmur of a sea-shell pressed to the ear. Soon is this pulsing world-sound swelling to a deep and throbbing roar — the organ-tone of storm-wind sweeping the skies and mountains with immeasurable power. A huge dragon of cloud crawls out of the southwest, and with it comes a horde of gray demons, darkening the sun and veiling the summits. We arrive at our cabin under a leaden sky as the first snow is drifting down on the wind.

After several days, we emerge on a new and glorious environment, for the storm has piled a great splendor on the world, and peak and forest gleam with frosty beauty. The morning is clear and cold, the last stars burn with diamond light as we cross the meadows on our long run to Merced Cañon. The new day lifts over the silent range, Mount Conness takes sudden fire, blood-red and golden light flames on the long Sierra crest, and the crisp snow at our skis sparkles in the first sun. At Tuolumne Pass we find true alpine conditions — supremely fine snow, swift and dry; grand open areas above the last timber, undulating for miles under cobalt skies; peaks and crags flaunting long banners of wind-driven snow. A world of surpassing beauty, so perfect and intense that we cannot imagine the return of summer and the fading of the crystalline splendor encompassing our gaze.

The white magnificence yields to the clean motion of our skis, and we glide over the glistening dome of the world and launch our long descent to the Merced River. Down we rush, cutting the sharp air with meteor motion; always the cool rushing wind, and the shrill hiss of skis upon snow. Above us towers the noble Merced Range, wave upon wave of lofty stone glittering in the low winter sun. A huge ledge lifts suddenly on the curved face of the hill; we turn in a bright mist of ski-spun snow and slant anew along the cañon wall. The mountains soar higher into the flaming sky, and the blue depths rise to enfold us as we skim down through the dusk to the shadowed valley with the swiftness known only to the ski.

79

Ski Heil!

JOEL H. HILDEBRAND

1935

Joel H. Hildebrand served as manager of the first American Olympic Ski Team in 1932, and developed tests for skiing ability that were long used by the National Ski Association. A professor of chemistry at the University of California, Hildebrand's enthusiasms for both chemistry and skiing were contagious. Many students enrolled in his classes to find themselves not only studying the periodic table, but learning about skis, ski wax, and ski safety as well.

Within the club, he was an active promoter of the construction of Clair Tappaan Ski Lodge. Located at Norden, near Donner Pass, at 7000 feet, the site receives one of the heaviest snow packs in the United States. "Plenty to fall in!" was Hildebrand's smiling remark.

Hildebrand served as president of the club, 1937 – 40, and is at present an honorary vice-president. In 1976, at age ninety-four, he was acknowledged as Dean of American Chemists by the American Chemistry Association.

THE SIERRA CLUB is in the process of making a number of notable discoveries: that its beloved Sierra is the Sierra *Nevada,* or snowy range, and must be sought by devoted pilgrims not only in July, but also in January, to be known in the fullness of its glory; that winter at high altitudes is not bitter, but is warm and friendly, for the thin air easily transmits the radiance of the sun to bare brown backs; that twelve feet of snow affords a smoother path than even a national park trail, and runs anywhere you wish to go; that the purple shadows of the trees and the pure rose of the alpenglow are colors as rich as those of columbine and heather; that the smooth folds of sparkling virgin snow, the glitter of icicles, and the living green of firs showing beneath their heavy white mantles—all constitute an enchanted world which can be entered by the magic of the ski.

The delighted few who first made these discoveries have spread the gospel, for one simply cannot help telling it to others, till the converts are gathering like the children who followed the Pied Piper. They will disappear into the mountain, too, but not permanently, for each will quickly emerge, laugh and be laughed at, brush off the snow and try again.

Sufficient skiing proficiency to take full advantage of these facilities is rapidly being developed among our members. We have set standards by adopting the official tests of the British Ski Club. These comprise three classes: the first-class badge is given only to the very few who win first-class international races. We are not likely at present to go in for that sort of skiing. The second-class test is very severe, including, for example, a drop in altitude of 1000 feet over a standard course in not over four minutes, which is pretty swift going, and not all straight, either. The writer, who is a judge, has his eye on a few promising candidates, and one may expect to see several second-class badges strutting about by the end of the season. The third-class badge guarantees a rather good skier, well equipped for all ordinary touring. To earn it one must demonstrate climbing ability and stamina, telemarks, christianias, and continuous stem-turns on a gradient of 15 degrees, and run down a standard 1000-foot course within a fixed time limit, usually about seven minutes, but varying with snow conditions. Eight persons passed this test last winter. We have thought it well to encourage beginners by establishing a fourth-class test, designed to demonstrate ability to join in an easy tour without likelihood of having to be carried home. The fourth-class skier must ascend and descend 500 feet within specified time limits. He must demonstrate kick-turns, four successive stem-turns, a snow-plow to a stand-still and a short, straight run. Forty have passed this test.

It should be the ambition of everyone to pass at least the third-class test. The satisfactions of skiing confidently under control are very great. Do not emulate those who go wildly down a steep slope, out of control, waving arms and legs madly, holding poles so that a fall threatens impalement, only to crash to a mass of wreckage long before reaching the bottom.

Ski-touring in Wyoming below Gannet Peak, the state's highest summit.

319

No one who can use his legs should fear to try skiing. The first couple of days are very awkward, for one's natural reflexes are of little use and a new set must be acquired; but this need not take long, and it begins to be fun very soon. It is fun for those who watch you, right from the start. There are now a number of members who will be willing and able to help the novice.

I would urge our ardent mountain climbers to restrain their ambitions to climb peaks in winter till they have learned to ski. One should be ashamed to make a long descent by "sitzmarking" at every turn when it should be possible to run down under control in a beautiful series of christianias or telemarks. To one who has learned to ski, it is this, not the mountain-peak, that is the greater glory.

The winter greeting in the Alps is "Ski-heil!" *Heil* means health and happiness; it means long life and good luck; it means wholesomeness. The ski-runner knows that only on skis can these be realized in their fullness. Come to the mountains! To the Sierra Nevada, where the air is crisp and the sun is bright, where the only depressions are those that one takes with a flourish and whoop! Strap on your skis and shout with us, "Ski-heil!"

80

Beyond the Skiways

DAVID R. BROWER

1938

When you've had enough of the ski tows, the downhill slopes, and the crowds, it's time to try ski-mountaineering—if your skills are up to it.

This moment may have come for David R. Brower before April, 1938, when this article was published; but it is here that he vividly expresses the limitations of seeking the perfect "christy" rather than the perfect winter landscape.

Brower is among the best ski mountaineers in the club, and one of those who helped develop the equipment and techniques that served the mountain troops so well in the second World War. As we have said, he edited all four editions of the Manual of Ski Mountaineering.

Brower served as editor of the Bulletin *and as executive director of the club. He is now an honorary vice-president. In 1969 he founded Friends of the Earth, of which he is president.*

BEFORE SKIING had made its relentless surge toward universal popularity, there were still persons to whom the inherent beauty in snowclad hills was in itself sufficient cause for winter mountain trips. Skiing was the most practical means of reaching snow country, where men could pause amid the majestic winter scene to contemplate their sublime surroundings. This was the golden age of skiing. It passed when bindings were mechanized with rigid toe-irons and severe tensions. For with mechanization came a mania for speed. Steeper and steeper slopes were sought. Caution was cast aside. Mountains became mere proving grounds for exhibitions of tricks and technique. Men worshipped perfection in tempo, vorlage; were consecrated to mastery of controls and schusses, corridors and flushes; talked of waxes and edges, ski-meets and records. They admired their apparel, while the peaks went unnoticed. They slashed trails in the forests, built elaborate lodges, gashed mountains with highways, wired peaks with funiculars. They conquered the wilderness. Men now ski superbly. But what have they lost?

This is the attitude of the extremist. Although it may be a synopsis of a trend, few persons will maintain that it is entirely correct. Most of those concerned, however, are not so fearful of the complete ascendancy of ski-racing psychology. Its very nature requires the compensating values of ski-touring or ski-mountaineering. Ski-racing is a product of practice slopes; and everyone becomes aware, once in a while, of certain basic truths pertaining to practice slopes: (a) quest of the perfect christy is futile; (b) filling other persons' sitzmarks is monotonous; (c) it is less fun to fall on packed snow than on powder; (d) it is frightening when skis go too fast; (e) it is terrifying

Ski-touring. . . . why? Each would have his own answer, but the severe beauty and simplicity of a winter landscape would be part of the meaning.

321

to be mistaken for a slalom gate, with racers tearing by so close their poles don't clear. Conditions (a) to (e) may be endured most of the season. One may even enjoy them in a way. But now and then it's essential to have a change — to strike off on a ski-tour, or better still, to try ski-mountaineering.

"Ski-mountaineering" is a cumbersome term, but no other term so aptly describes the grand sport that results when skiing and mountaineering are combined. The ski-mountaineer's recipe, complex but not exacting, is this: find out how to handle skis reasonably well, gather winter equipment together, learn how to use it, find some trusted friends to carry most of it, then try to beard Old Man Winter in his den — out beyond the skiways. Out there one will find the timberline country, where temperatures are more invigorating, where snows are persistently drier and more powdery, where broad open slopes are tracked only by one's chosen friends, surroundings are rugged, yet marvelously adapted to ski-mountaineering. In such terrain even the most blasé of resort-skiers have been temporarily overcome with reverence. They have learned that the christy is more than a matter of accurately synchronizing the advance of the inside ski and the outside shoulder; it is a symbol of ski-control that broadens winter horizons.

Perhaps a tale of recent winter exploits will suggest how ski-mountaineering, with proper preparation, is really an inimitable way to enjoy the Sierra snows.

Mount Lyell, highest peak in Yosemite National Park, has been climbed without great difficulty during summer months by hundreds of persons; but until March, 1936, the peak had remained inviolate in winter. Three attempts had failed. In 1934 a party was driven to retreat by a blizzard, after having reached a 12,400-foot pass at the headwaters of the Maclure Fork of the Merced. A year later an attempt was stopped short of this point by a sub-zero, fair-weather blizzard of wind-whipped powder snow. A third attempt was made in January, 1936, but again the weather guarded the peak with nine successive days of storm.

February 29, 1936, at Happy Isles, in Yosemite Valley, Bestor Robinson, Lewis F. Clark, Boynton S. Kaiser, Einar Nilsson, and I started the fourth attempt. With fifty-pound packs, containing sleeping bags, tents, rope, ice-axes, emergency equipment, food and clothing, we followed the course of the Merced Canyon trail to Merced Lake Ranger Station. The next night, in a rising wind, a high camp was established at "Hell Hole" — nearly 2000 feet above Bernice Lake and timberline. Camping on snow, we again discovered, had pleasures all its own.

By the time sleeping bags, knapsacks, and men had been piled inside the two tiny tents the congestion was quite cozy. Sole evidence of the wind outside was the powder that sifted through every available aperture, to the syncopated accompaniment of flapping tent fabric. Having snow inside was an advantage, since it was no longer necessary to reach outside to get it for melting over our Primus stoves. Bestor, Lewis, and Bunco prepared the soup on their stove. Einar and I improvised an entrée of chocolate, cheese,

Ski-touring in the Northern Cascades. These skiers climbed within 300 feet of the top of the south side of Sahale Peak, where a snow-corniced ridge prevented them from going further.

and oatmeal—Bestor had left the macaroni at Merced Lake. With everything ready, dinner was served: a momentary lull in the gale was awaited, tent flaps were un-zipped, victuals passed frantically so that we could re-zipp before the next snow laden gust. The wind usually won.

By morning the wind had developed into a hurricane. Our next game, upon leaving camp, was to see who could stand up longest. On one occasion Lewis was upset by an errant gust, although he had braced against it with ski poles. Long snow-banners were torn from ridges and peaks to be flung far to leeward, and to avoid following suit while crossing the first spur of Mount Maclure, we dismounted and crawled, digging in hands and toes for anchorage. Bestor had forecast summit weather in which it would be possible to hold up a match and watch it burn!

Four hours later we were on the summit of Mount Lyell, with Bestor doing just that. We had left the wind far below the Lyell Glacier bergschrund, and in comparative comfort our rope of five had followed Bunco's lead up the final 65-degree pitch of snow and rock. As we settled down for a summit siesta the Sierra Nevada, from the Tuolumne to the Kaweahs, was revealed. We could now understand why Spanish explorers had called this "One Great Snowy Range of Mountains." The entire range had an Alpine aspect that we had never fully appreciated in forest-belt ski country. Even after the 7000-foot descent in afternoon and moonlight to

323

the ranger station, and the next day's 19-mile journey to Yosemite Valley we were still thinking of that view—of those incomparable north slopes, powder that lasts for months, square miles without a tree, the High Sierra above timberline—winter paradise, ear-marked for the ski-mountaineer.

81

A Trans-Sierra Ski Tour

WILLIAM W. DUNMIRE

1951

Here we meet a party of rock climbers ski-mountaineering in the Sierra. Some members we have encountered already in the previous section on climbers.
In the best tradition of the Bulletin, *Dunmire ends his account with some practical "how to do it" advice.*

THOSE THREE WEEKS were strenuous, but they did wonders for our wind. Rain or shine, day after day, a group of us ran the course we had laid out from the Berkeley campus of the University of California to Grizzly Peak, some fifteen hundred feet above. It was a workout, all right, but we needed the conditioning, even though most of us had spent an industrious seven weeks in the Coast Mountains of Canada just a few months before. For now we wanted abruptly to leave our books and make a ten-day ski crossing of the Sierra, at the apex of the range.

We began thinking of a long ski-camping trip last summer when Jim Wilson mentioned the possibility of a loop tour in the Humphreys region. When it turned out that eight people were interested, and that two of them had cars, we got a brilliant idea. We could make a trans-Sierra trip—one party traveling west and the other east—and exchange cars at the finish. The general plan we finally worked out was for George Bloom, Ray de Saussure, Bill Long and Bob Swift to start from Whitney Portal, east of Mount Whitney, while Norman Goldstein, Al Steck, Jim Wilson, and I would ski from Giant Forest. Our four would follow the High Sierra Trail to Kaweah Gap and then detour, via a knapsack pass north of the Kaweahs, to the pass across the Sierra crest between Mounts Russell and Whitney. We would carry food for fourteen days, the extra four day's rations to be used in case of storm. Being rock climbers first and skiers second, we could not forsake our rock-climbing gear—we knew that many peaks would beckon along the way.

It was fortunate that our plan also called for an overnight stay at Giant Forest before hitting our skis; for when we arrived at road's end we all had violent headaches due to monoxide fumes which had leaked from the motor of my ancient Chevy (since sold as junk by request). Next morning, after discussing our proposed route with the ranger, we hit the trail. Parkas and long johns were out of place that day, for on the south-facing slope the sun showed no mercy. This had been one of the driest of Kaweah-country winters and the trail was barely covered with snow, to the detriment of our base wax. It certainly didn't seem like the middle of January as we skied without shirts and camped that night on dry ground.

Above Hamilton Lakes the trail rises 2,000 feet in a very short distance and we knew from the concentration of contour lines on the map that this stretch would cause some difficulty if the snow were soft. Happily it was firm but a real problem arose. Although the trail looked as if it extended without interruption, we suddenly came upon a deep cleft in the slope. The rock overhung and the trail had been blasted into the granite wall of a couloir so deep that the winter sun hardly touched the snow, which was powdery and insecure. Al started without skis, cautiously probing with his ice ax, deliberately kicking footholds. We cheered when he reached the corner and firm snow and took our time as we followed—Hamilton Lake 1,500 feet below, seemed all too near.

By sundown we were on Kaweah Gap putting on those long johns; we knew we were in for a chilly night. Jim started the run down into the shadows of Nine Lake Basin and we all made the most of our first downhill skiing of the trip. In camp the thermometer dipped to 16°F.—no problem at all for ski mountaineers with a tent up and a small fire going (outside). Hot jello was welcome as always. The rest of our fare was not all taken from the manual, for we found that a dinner of instant potato and slow horse meat went well after a heavy day.

We had planned to spend a day or so climbing here in the Kaweahs, but next morning ominous clouds scudded overhead, and we knew we had better push on. We steered directly for the lowest notch in the Kaweah ridge, thinking this to be the correct pass. Halfway up the slope the wind-crusted snow became so steep that our sealskin climbers would not hold; packing skis on rucksacks, we kicked steps up into the mists which now swirled down around the high peaks. Haste seemed of great importance, and we looked forward hopefully to a speedy descent from the saddle. But instead of seeing a gentle snow expanse leading to Kaweah Basin from the saddle, we peered down the east face to see, as the only route, a steep couloir in which we could not hope to ski safely. The wrong pass! Taking off my pack I kicked a few trial steps but was glad to return quickly to the notch. We must have ropes on this one, for the snow was too powdery for comfort and there was a slight cornice. A few flakes drifted down to hurry us along. We picked out a belay spot 100 feet below and Jim headed for it with Al paying out rope. At the end of his rope, Jim sank his ski pole shaft for an improvised-ice-ax belay—we only had one ax, and it was left for me, the last man. When Al and Jim had progressed several hundred feet, Norm and I began the descent. It was cold and we wished—especially when belaying—that we could move faster, but discretion won. The couloir took eleven belayed pitches but we beat the storm. As one last gesture we shook our fists in defiance at the couloir, which was then vanishing in the mists. A short run took us down to the forest, where a huge dead log was soon merrily crackling in flames.

Not much snow fell that night and the next morning was clear. We were ahead of schedule so we could afford a layover day. During breakfast making the usual controversy ensued: "Should the oatmeal be thick or gruelly?" Jim is the proponent of "gruelly gruel," thinking for some reason that food at its best should be of about the consistency of blood. Norm and I, on the other hand, feel that in order to get a man started off right for the day, the mush should stick to his ribs even if it has to be cut with a knife. The gruel faction usually won out, however, since water was unlimited but oats were not.

No one was very energetic that day. After a few repairs were made, out came the Chinese puzzles which Jim had brought along. These little demons, bad enough to solve in a warm house, are quite a challenge when one is wearing mittens. No one was allowed to ski that day until he had worked all the puzzles. Nevertheless, three of us managed to get up to Milestone Basin that afternoon. The snow was too crusty for descent running, but we did get a first-rate view of the Kaweah Peaks.

By sundown clouds had closed in again and soon snow was falling heavily. Next morning it was still snowing. With the prospect of spending some time indoors, we settled down to the usual mountain-tent diversions. First it was Ghost, then a rhyming variation of Ghost, and then Twenty Questions. Was it alive? No. Was it singular? No. Were they real or imaginary? Yes . . . Al's object turned out to be the Russian salt mines; we got it on the seventeenth question. This went on until noon when someone had the flash of genius to open a tent flap. The clouds were dispersing, so we quickly packed up to take advantage of the break.

A foot of snow had fallen—fluffy powder snow, the kind we had so far looked for in vain. For several hundred yards at a time our ski tips would be hidden under the crystals as we schussed the gentle slope. Real skiing at last! Too soon our skis started to stick as the sun began its work, and before long we had to pole even on the steeper portions. I was getting fed up, and since we had a long downhill stretch ahead to Junction Meadow, I decided to try a little wax. I persuaded Al that wax would end our troubles, that a waxed ski was a controlled ski; Norm and Jim would have none of it. I'm not sure that Al has forgiven me yet; no sooner had we waxed than we got into steep terrain. Norm and Jim could slog straight down; Al and I picked up more speed than we could handle. To make matters worse, we were in a talus-brush combination, with just enough new snow to hide the obstacles. We'd snowplow and catch an edge, sideslip and catch an edge, and with each catch down we would go. The snow cover kept getting thinner, and Norm and

Jim's tracks, neat and parallel, went straight down it. We didn't dare follow. Rocks, brush, more rocks, more brush, and *crunch,* there went the rest of my base job. On one especially horrible section I sat down fully prepared to weep, but Al's distant curses raised my morale. I'll take any uphill grind any time over a day such as that one was! It was long after dark when we finally reached Junction and we were all pretty exhausted. Nevertheless, after supper we had a song festival, running through everything from our yodel repertoire to excerpts from Gilbert and Sullivan. Our jolly campfire seemed much cozier than sleeping bags on snow, so it was not until midnight that we hit them.

It was an easy uphill day to Wallace Creek. We arrived in early afternoon with plenty of time to pick out a good campsite. Just as we settled in one place Jim would rush ahead and find a better spot, and with loud grumbles we would move on. At the third site we decreed that no suggestions of new and better spots would be tolerated. We couldn't have found a better winter site. It had all the desirable features: water near by, dry-pine-needle bed sites, and most important, enough dead wood about for a whiteman's fire (i.e., any fire in which the flames rise at least eight feet and force its admirers back at least six feet). We would always camp far enough from trails not to leave our charcoal where summer travelers would find it. We wondered if winter travelers would find it either—namely, the westbound party, which should have passed us by now. We finally concluded that they must have had car trouble, and stopped worrying.

A climb was now in order—we were still ahead of schedule and we chose Mount Tyndall (14,025). That evening before retiring we recorded a temperature of 10°F. (our lowest), so we slept with boots on in order to get a headstart for the mountain. We were up by dawn and on our way after a breakfast of cold "gorp" (a dry cereal, powdered milk, sugar, raisins, cinnamon, nutmeg, etc., mixed together in a single pot). What a relief to be skiing without those packs! Although it was calm about us, all the major peaks bore snow banners—certainly the best I've ever seen. Many of the banners must have been at least 300 feet high; Mount Barnard had an especially fine one. Unlike Clarence King's, our climb of Mount Tyndall involved no shinnying on ice columns, nor did we have to lasso talus blocks and climb "sailor-fashion, hand over hand up the rope." In fact, when we realized that the west face was relatively free of snow, we left our skis and ropes in the bowl below. However, the climb was not entirely summer-like, for we were continually raked by windblown snow and ice particles—and the summit temperature was 19°F. Ours was presumably the first winter ascent of Tyndall, but we didn't pause long to celebrate. The threat of a new storm sped us back to camp.

We now decided that the other party must have turned back; we hoped that they would leave a car waiting for us at Whitney Portal but we planned on an extra day's travel to Lone Pine in case the car should not be at road's end.

The storm threat proved to be merely a bluff, so we were ready to push on toward Whitney country. That morning, to get us started right, we concocted a pot of stuff affectionately named "grease honey." We had hoarded until then a pound of solidified honey which, heated with a pound of margarine, comprised the morning meal. It was quite a change from the usual diet of oats and where would science be today without the experiment? For some reason we couldn't seem to average much faster than a mile an hour that day.

Fresh clouds the following day urged us over Whitney-Russell Pass, where there were extraordinary wind-crust formations, some of them in the making. The terrific wind blasts did not abate until we were well down the east side. Skiing here was better than we had expected, although our tracks did cause one minor avalanche.

At Whitney Portal next day we were relieved to find them from their note that the westbound party were all safe; before they reached the pass Bob Swift wrenched his knee, they were forced to spend a severe stormy night just beyond the pass, and then had decided that retreat was in order. Generously they had left their car for us and had hitchhiked home. That car was a mighty welcome sight, for Lone Pine was many miles away and we were in no mood for desert walking.

Ski touring today is certainly not the arduous undertaking it was twenty years ago, and the reason for this lies solely in improved equipment. I am not implying that persons who are in other than tip-top physical condition should attempt tours but rather wish to point out that the advent of the nylon tent, the nylon air mattress, and the lug-soled ski boot has meant lighter packs on the trail and greater comfort in camp. We have found the four-man army nylon tent, when pitched properly, to withstand very heavy winds; and wind, rather than cold, is the villain on any winter trip. Some sort of insulation is always essential for sleeping on snow, but until recently extra clothes had to be used above timberline. Now these clothes can be put to better purpose inside the sleeping bag since a nylon air mattress weighing only fifteen ounces has been developed. Of course the old rubberized mattresses weighing up to eight pounds are out of the question on tour. The lug-soled ski boot, also recently developed by the army, allows rock climbing to be combined with skiing, and a tour can often involve rock work, intended or not. A new safety binding has been developed that will give all the downhill tension one could need without requiring the monstrously heavy ski boots that have been the rage. These and other developments in mountaineering equipment have not only improved comforts, but have also increased the safety factor. With needless weight cut, greater amounts of emergency food and better repair kits may be taken along instead.

Judging from our recent experience it would seem that spring, rather than winter is perhaps the best time for ski touring in the southern Sierra, at least in a light snow year. Spring snow should have a better skiing surface and be generally more consistent. Most of our snow was breakable crust, unskiable at any speed so far as we were concerned. But maybe our trouble was the gorp!

82

Skis to the Winter Wilderness

DAVID R. BROWER

1969

We end the section with a paragraph by David Brower, in which he speaks of his experiences in ski-mountaineering, and what he hopes such experiences would mean to his sons. This is taken from the third edition of Manual of Ski Mountaineering *(1969).*

FINALLY I WOULD have tried to explain to them what ski-mountaineering has meant to me; about the peaks I had made first ascents of, for the most part on skis; of the high snow camps I had known and what it was like to be up on top in early winter morning and evening, when the world is painted with a very special light; of the kind of competence and even braveness, maybe, that one picks up from good friends and challenging peaks, up there when the storms hit and the snow pelts the fabric all through the night; of the kind of exhilaration we got when, after two winter struggles, the third put us on top of a fourteen-thousander and we were first to be there in winter and see how magnificently winter treats a high land we already knew well in summer but in a lesser beauty; of the long vibrant moments when we were back on our skis, skimming down the uncrevassed glacier on just the right depth of new powder, letting our skis go, finding that every turn worked, hearing the vigorous flapping of our ski pants even though the wind was singing in our ears and stinging our faces, sensing how rapidly the peaks climbed above us, those peaks that had dropped so reluctantly to our level in all the slow day's climb; of the care we had to take after night found us out and we sideslipped and sidestepped down into the tortuous little basins and then into the hummocky forest floor that lay in darkness between us and camp; I would have described that hot cup of soup I cuddled in my hand in exhaustion, sipping slowly to absorb its warmth and its energy at a retainable rate; and I would speak of the morning after and, not its hangover, but its glow as I looked back up to the rocky palisade above the glacier and was just pleased as hell to have got there at last—pleased with the weather, the companions, and the luck—and also forgivably pleased a little that I could do it.

But I didn't tell them all that. This is the sort of thing you find out for yourself, that comes when you escape into the reality of the wilderness and discover how amazingly well man has been designed to cope with just such reality. This is the sort of thing I would want them to find out for themselves. Maybe then, after that, we could compare notes. That would be the best reward of all!

Winter afternoon.

PART VII

The Club
Militant: Parks,
Wilderness,
and the
American Land

IN THE SUMMER OF 1966, millions of Americans who had never heard of the Sierra Club or knew little about it suddenly became aware of its existence as a crusading organization defending the scenic treasures of America with fighting vigor.

They read about it in the papers. On June 9 there was a full-page Sierra Club ad in The New York Times and The Washington Post. "IF THEY CAN TURN GRAND CANYON INTO A 'CASH REGISTER' IS ANY NATIONAL PARK SAFE?" And in larger letters: "NOW ONLY YOU CAN SAVE GRAND CANYON FROM BEING FLOODED . . . FOR PROFIT."

The ad described plans of the Bureau of Reclamation, an agency of the U.S. Interior Department, to build two dams on the Colorado river. It concluded: "Remember . . . There is only one simple incredible issue here: this time it's the Grand Canyon they want to flood. The Grand Canyon."

The following day, the Internal Revenue Service warned the club that its tax deductibility as a non-profit organization might be revoked because the club was making a substantial effort to influence legislation. Tax-exempt organizations are forbidden to do so.

The story that the IRS was putting the heat on the club for defending the Grand Canyon ran prominently in newspapers all over the country and generated thousands of letters of protest.

Two more full-page ads against the dams were published in July and August in national magazines and newspapers, in answer to the dam-builders' argument that more people could see the canyon walls from boats on the reservoirs. These asked, "SHOULD WE ALSO FLOOD THE SISTINE CHAPEL SO TOURISTS CAN GET NEARER THE CEILING?"

The result of the ads was what California's Senator Thomas H. Kuchel called "one of the largest letter-writing campaigns which I have seen in my tenure in the Senate." Another result was that Sierra Club membership rose from 39,000 to 67,000 in a little over a year, and doubled to 135,000 in the following three years.

The Grand Canyon holds a particular place in the hearts of Americans, whether they have seen it or not. It is perhaps the most spectacular piece of landscape on the continent, and the club's defense of the canyon from the dam builders captured the public imagination as no other single conservation battle had ever done.

The club had been a force on the national scene since early in the century. Hetch Hetchy was its first big fight, and the club had continued to battle for national parks and wilderness through the intervening years.

The successful struggles to create national parks in Kings Canyon and the North Cascades, for example, may have been less publicized than the Grand Canyon fight, but like all of the club's campaigns they were important to the nation's future and required immense outpourings of human energies. The stories of various battles in this section deal with the visible issues of each effort; they cannot show the hidden part of the iceberg—the uncounted hours of devoted work by thousands of members who planned strategy, wrote letters, conducted phone campaigns, mobilized opinion, got information to the news media, attended hearings, and lobbied legislators and government officials, at all levels from Washington to local planning commissions and town councils. The work of the paid staff is only a fraction of the effort devoted to the cause;

332

volunteers work nights, weekends, and vacations to preserve some beloved portion of the American landscape, from million-acre parks to fraction-of-an-acre nature preserves in metropolitan areas.

As the nation has grown in population and threats to the natural landscape have increased by quantum leaps, the emphasis on conservation has grown in relation to the club's other activities. The shift in the focus is reflected in the Bulletin, which for most of its life had been dominated by articles on natural science and enjoying the landscape. Conservation writings were relatively few. But in the late 1950s and particularly in the 1960s, interest in conservation steadily grew until it became by far the Bulletin's dominant concern.

Since this book is not a history of conservation or of the Sierra Club, we have made no attempt to cover every battle in which the club has been involved. The articles that follow deal with some of the club's major concerns in the years since conservation became the Bulletin's central focus. Inevitably the articles emphasize Sierra Club activities, but they are not meant to indicate that the club was acting alone. In some campaigns it has offered primary leadership; in some it has been involved as a partner in joint efforts; and in some it has supported campaigns initiated by others. On the national scene it has often worked shoulder to shoulder with such groups as Audubon, the Wilderness Society, the National Parks Association, the National Resources Defense Council, the Environmental Defense Fund, and Friends of the Earth. It has supported innumerable local organizations in their own conservation causes.

In all cases these battles have been far more than mere fights for particular stretches of territory. They have been expressions of a shared conviction that is felt with a well-nigh religious intensity. In the words of David Brower: "We seek a renewed stirring of love for the earth; we urge that what man is capable of doing to the earth is not always what he ought to do; and we plead that all people here, now, determine that a wide, spacious, untrammeled freedom shall remain as living testimony that this generation, our own, had love for the next."

83

Preserving
Dinosaur

DAVID R. BROWER

1954

The Sierra Club was well-seasoned for the Grand Canyon battle. The Colorado river had already received a share of the club's attention second only to that accorded the Sierra Nevada itself. The 1450-mile artery and its tributaries drain most of the vast Great Basin, the province between the Rockies and the Sierra. They have sculpted most of that region's spectacular land forms, and the river is also responsible for the civilization of the Great Basin. It is a lifeline, supplying water for irrigation and electricity to cities in the arid Southwest.

There are several major dams on the lower Colorado; Hoover is the largest. Although they destroyed scenic canyons, they were not opposed by the club; they provided water, power, and flood control for farmlands and cities.

But how many more dams on the Colorado are necessary? When do we reach the point of diminishing returns, the point at which the scenery destroyed is more valuable than any economic benefits?

This issue first surfaced in the 1940s, when the Bureau of Reclamation proposed two major dams in Utah. One would have been at Echo Park, the junction of two tributaries of the Colorado—the Yampa and the Green—and the other downstream at Split Mountain. Both locations were in Dinosaur National Monument, established to protect abundant dinosaur fossil beds. The club found itself back in the position it had occupied during the Hetch Hetchy struggle, defending National Park Service lands from invasion by economic development.

Some of the issues are explained here in congressional testimony Executive Director David Brower gave in January of 1954. As a preamble to his statement on Dinosaur, he told the House committee something about the Sierra Club, which was not yet well known in Washington. (It had 8000 members, compared to 175,000 in 1978.) We are not including here—partly owing to its technical nature—the portion of his testimony in which he demonstrated to the surprised congressmen that the Bureau of Reclamation had done some very bad arithmetic in calculating—and exaggerating—the benefits of the dam, errors later corrected by embarrassed officials.

LOOK AT THE SIERRA CLUB, which wants to persuade you to protect Dinosaur and the parks, just as other Congresses have done for so long. What kind of people are in it? Teen-age kids, out to climb, hike, and ski; office workers, teachers, professional men—we even have a mailman who comes on our Sierra outings to walk 90 or 100 miles during two weeks in the wilderness. Strange people, slightly odd? Some, perhaps. But also the past president of the American Society of Civil Engineers, the current president of the American Society of Radio Engineers, the next president of the American Chemical Society, the president of a major pharmaceutical house, of a major railroad, of a major mining firm, an Assistant U.S. Attorney General. We have these, too. All of them, whether kids getting away from too much homework or executives getting away from too many telephones ringing on one desk, all have this in common—a love for the beautiful, unspoiled places—places they work hard (at no pay) to preserve, and long after they themselves can no longer enjoy them.

It is a noble human endeavor that leads them to do this. It is this type of endeavor I am hoping I can communicate to you as something every bit as important as the type of enterprise so earnestly supported here—and entirely laudable in its place—the urge to produce, to grow, to develop, to profit, and to spend. This Sierra Club is a good organization, devoted to idealism, and I am proud of it. It is but one of many, all just as good. I wish you were all members. It would cost you only $3.50 per year.

Echo Park, Steamboat Rock on the right.

Yampa River coming into Echo Park from Harper's Corner.

Giant syncline, Echo Park.

Here are three questions which we feel have not been answered properly yet.

1. What are the important park values in Dinosaur?
2. Would they be destroyed by the Echo Park and Split Mountain dams?
3. Can Dinosaur's scenery be made accessible without dams?

As you may have guessed, our answer is that this area has superlative park values. They would indeed be destroyed by the proposed dams.

The Park Service has said in writing that the effects of these dams upon irreplaceable values of national significance would be deplorable. Deplorable is a mild word to describe what would happen to the scenery in Dinosaur were we to permit these dams to be built there. The Echo Park project alone calls for a dam 525 feet high, backing up 107 miles of reservoir, inundating the intimate, close-up scenes and living space with nearly 6½ million acre feet of water. There would be construction roads in the canyon and above it, tunnels, the whole power installation and transmission lines, the rapid build-up of silt at the upper end of the reservoirs, and the periodic draw-downs of the reservoir to enable it to fulfill its function—a fluctuation that would play hob with fish and wildlife. The piñon pines, the Douglas firs, the maples and cottonwoods, the grasses and other flora that line the banks, the green living things that shine in the sun against the rich colors of the cliffs— these would all go. The river, its surge and its sound, the living sculptor of this place, would be silent forever, and all the fascination of its movement and the fun of riding it, quietly gliding through these cathedral corridors of stone—all done in for good. The tops of the cliffs you could still see, of course. As reservoirs go, it would be a handsome one—but remember the 251 other reservoir sites in the upper basin and the hundreds of reservoir sites elsewhere in the country. We don't want Dinosaur to be just another reservoir. We want it to remain the *only* Dinosaur, which it is now.

If we should accept the amazing statement that Echo Park dam would not destroy Dinosaur, but would only alter Dinosaur, we should also accept such statements as these:

1. A dam from El Capitan to Bridalveil Fall would not destroy Yosemite, but just alter it.

2. Other dams would only alter Yellowstone, Glacier National Park, Mammoth Caves National Park, Kings Canyon National Park.

3. Removal of the rain forest would only alter Olympic National Park.

4. Cutting the 3,000-year-old Big Trees and making them into grapestakes would only alter Sequoia National Park. After all, the ground would still be there, and the sky, and the distant views. All you would have done is alter it, that is, take away its reason for being.

Maybe "alter" isn't the word. Maybe we should just come out with it and say "cut the heart out."

The axiom for protecting the Park System is to consider that it is dedicated country, hallowed ground to leave as beautiful as we have found it, and not country in which man should be so impressed with himself that he tries to improve God's handiwork.

84

Damming the Colorado River

RICHARD C. BRADLEY

1964

Dinosaur National Monument was not "altered" by the Bureau of Reclamation, partly owing to David Brower's testimony to Congress in the preceding article, partly owing to other forces described in the following account, which indicates what happened both before and after that Congressional hearing.

Newton B. Drury, who resigned as Director of the National Park Service in protest against the Dinosaur Dam proposal, had previously been Executive Director of the Save the Redwoods League, subsequently became California State Parks Director, and then returned to his longtime position with the league in San Francisco, where he climaxed his long and distinguished career in preserving natural America.

Ironically, until the mid-'60s, the club thought that nuclear power would soon supply a major part of the country's energy needs—both cheaply and safely. Coal-

fired generating plants in the southwestern desert were also endorsed as alternatives to dams on the Colorado. Times change.

Richard C. Bradley, the author of this article, was Associate Professor of Physics at Colorado College. The article was published on the eve of the Grand Canyon battle.

ONE DAY IN JULY 1943 Newton Drury, Director of the National Park Service, noted in the *Federal Register* that the Bureau of Reclamation had staked out a claim for two reservoir sites within Dinosaur National Monument — one at Echo Park and one at Split Mountain. The two reservoirs would flood Dinosaur National Monument's canyons from one end to the other. No one had bothered to consult him; this was the first news. In a letter of great restraint he suggested to the Interior Secretary that there may have been some misunderstanding; that perhaps the Reclamation Bureau had not realized that these sites were on lands already set aside for another purpose.

There had been no misunderstanding. Reclamation, conservationists were forced to infer, had not deemed it necessary to obtain consent from its impoverished sister bureau, the National Park Service. The Bureau was no longer an infant irrigation service, but a power elite that had built huge dams

Grand Canyon sunrise, Great Thumb Mesa.

and was now firmly in the business of producing hydroelectric power to help pay for irrigation. If some of the nine power dams it now proposed to build in the Upper Basin encroached on dedicated lands, this was regrettable but not terribly important. Echo Park in the heart of Dinosaur National Monument was one of the best power sites in the region and had to be included in any comprehensive development program. So said the Bureau of Reclamation.

Newton Drury, who had not discussed the Bureau's proposal outside the Department, protested vigorously, but was outflanked and outdistanced. Talk arose of putting in a defense plant to use Echo Park's power, and with the Korean war going on Secretary of the Interior Oscar Chapman reluctantly gave his approval to the Bureau's project—and accepted Mr. Drury's resignation. National defense, he said, had to take precedence over park preservation.

So ended the first round in the struggle for the big dam. The American public was about to surrender a scenic resource it scarcely knew it had—the magnificent canyons of the Green and Yampa rivers which Franklin Roosevelt had set aside for permanent preservation only a dozen years earlier.

The proposal for the Split Mountain dam was dropped by the Bureau, and the focus was entirely on Echo Park.

But now several important things happened to change the picture. Bernard de Voto, a long time champion of the national park system, sounded a call to arms in the *Saturday Evening Post.* As a result the nation, which traditionally has supported its national park system albeit frugally, began to show an interest in the controversy. At about the same time the plan to build a defense plant near Echo Park was abandoned; the plant was eventually built on the Ohio River. And finally, and perhaps most important of all, a retired general from the U.S. Corps of Engineers, Ulysses S. Grant III, a conservationist as well as a civil engineer of long experience, pointed out that the Bureau's own study showed there were other dam sites in the Upper Basin which the Bureau was not planning to use that would provide equivalent power and storage, would cost less to build, and would flood no parks.

Confronted with this new evidence, Chapman withdrew his approval, called for a restudy, and later flatly stated that Echo Park dam was "absolutely not necessary." Thus Round Two went to the conservationists, and particularly to de Voto and Grant.

But the proponents were not so easily dissuaded. An election year brought in a new Secretary, and Round Three opened with a bang. For about a year Secretary Douglas McKay had remained noncommittal while studying the proposal. The proponents must have been very busy behind the scenes, however, for when the action came it was a blitzkrieg—swift, smooth, and sure. McKay announced his approval of the dam in December 1953, several bills calling for its construction were introduced into Congress, and within three weeks the House of Representatives held hearings on them. The President and the Bureau of the Budget added their support.

The lineup at the hearings was an interesting study in contrasts. On the one side were the elite of Interior's engineering staff, including Under Secretary Ralph Tudor, who now presented in some detail the evaporation argument for Echo Park dam. They were accompanied by a battery of congressmen, senators, governors, mayors, heads of chambers of commerce, company presidents, and countless other luminaries. All had come to argue the merits of the storage project, and, nearly to a man, all pointed to the terrible loss of water the Rocky Mountain states would have to suffer if Echo Park were replaced.

Arrayed against this stellar assembly of competent professionals was a little group of amateur conservationists, variously referred to by the proponents as barefooted nature lovers, bird watchers, wildlifers, self-appointed do-gooders, so-called conservationists, fuzzy-headed thinkers, and well-meaning but misguided individuals. They came to defend the integrity of the national park system, and they came alone. Conspicuously missing from their ranks were their star witnesses—the Park Service officials who from a professional viewpoint could have discussed the effect of dams on park values, or the Geological Survey scientists who might have commented on the wasteful evaporation losses that take place from reservoirs built primarily for power, like Echo Park. These people, being in the Interior Department, were muzzled. The only experts were from the Bureau of Reclamation, and according to them dams would improve Dinosaur.

In spite of their handicaps the conservationists drew blood. They found the old error in subtraction being repeated and some unaccountable errors in simple arithmetic in Mr. Tudor's evaporation calculations. The errors, although favoring the Bureau, were undoubtedly accidental. But at the same time their existence showed that the whole argument was probably fictitious, its importance grossly exaggerated. If the Bureau was really worrying about evaporation losses it never would have been guilty of such carelessness. Indeed it never would have recommended a power dam for Echo Park in the first place, for even the evaporation from that reservoir would supply a major city and could be avoided simply by building a steam plant instead of a dam.

The well-oiled machinery lost enough momentum over this debacle so that the bills never quite reached the floor of either house that year, although they passed the Interior Committees of both houses. This delay may well have spelled the difference between success and failure, for by the following year the position of the conservationists was enormously strengthened. They had made a color movie of a boat trip through Dinosaur and were busy showing it all over the country. Alfred Knopf published *This Is Dinosaur,* edited by Wallace Stegner. This book, incidentally, was banned from sale in some of the national parks and monuments. That year thousands of people saw Dinosaur for the first time and many of them went down its rivers, tens of thousands saw the movie or read the book, and hundreds of thousands

Toroweap Overlook.

wrote their representatives in Washington, protesting the dam. The tide of opinion was heavily favoring the conservationists.

The gong had sounded on the final round. The proponents, meeting in Denver that autumn, reluctantly decided that Echo Park dam was a millstone which threatened to sink them all. So they offered to remove it from their plans if conservationists would withdraw opposition to the rest of the Colorado River project. Fearful that the dam might pop up again when no one was looking, the conservationists asked that the proponents write into the law: "It is the intention of Congress that no dam or reservoir constructed under this Act shall be within any national park or monument." They did.

At first glance it might seem like a clear-cut victory. Such a claim, however, would be extravagant. For one thing, conservationists can never really win any fight, they can only prevent someone else from doing so.

For another, the Bureau of Reclamation, rebuffed at Echo Park, turned to another scenic but little known gorge of the Colorado, Glen Canyon.

341

85

Glen Canyon

RICHARD C. BRADLEY

1964

How is it that an incomparably beautiful canyon in the West—one of the country's scenic jewels—now lies under hundreds of feet of water and silt held in place by a dam not needed?

True, Glen Canyon was called The Place No One Knew—but a few people had known it, Major John Wesley Powell, among others. On his explorations along the Colorado in 1869, Major Powell named Glen Canyon and described its beauty: "Past these towering monuments, past these mounded billows of orange sandstone, past these oak-set glens, past these fern-decked alcoves, past these mural curves, we glide, hour after hour, stopping now and then as our attention is arrested by some new wonder. . . ."

It was also true that Glen Canyon was not a part of a national park or sanctuary. Yet, the reservoir planned for Glen Canyon would flood the lower reaches of Rainbow Bridge National Monument—contrary to the act authorizing the Colorado River project.

Why was there so little protest until the dam was built; until the gates were ready to be closed; until it was too late?

One answer was given by Richard Bradley in his Bulletin *article,* Damming the Colorado River.

BY ALL ODDS the most crushing defeat which the cause of conservation suffered as a result of the passage of the Colorado River act was the tragic ruination of the incomparably beautiful Glen Canyon by the absolutely needless construction of a wasteful power dam. The trouble was that no one dreamed its construction would turn out to be needless, and so it was never seriously opposed. Besides, it did not have national park status. Wasteful, yes. Everyone knew it would annually evaporate enough water for several cities the size of Denver. But not needless. For hadn't the Bureau consistently argued that if the Upper Basin were to use its full share of the water and still meet downstream commitments, it would have to have large holdover storage dams on the main stem of the river to regulate its flow? During wet cycles these huge reservoirs would fill; during dry ones they would empty, and the water released to the lower Basin could be maintained at exactly the right amount to satisfy the Colorado River Compact of 1922, which parcels the river's water out to the various Basin states. Indeed river regulation was allegedly the primary purpose of the nine-dam storage complex proposed by the Bureau. Power generation was to be strictly a by-product, albeit an important one; its sale was supposed to help pay back the cost of the dams and eventually help finance irrigation dams elsewhere. It all seemed so reasonable then and sounds so hollow now!

No sooner was the storage project well started than the Geological Survey, now no longer muzzled, published a report which vitiated the River Regulation argument.

According to this report, which was written by the Chief Hydrologist, the Colorado River can be regulated by 30 million acre-feet of storage capacity. In 1950 there already existed 38 million acre-feet on the main stem, most of it being in Lake Mead. Adding Glen Canyon has increased this to 66 million, more than twice the needed amount. Unfortunately, extra regulation does not mean extra water for anybody; once the flow of the river has been made uniform, further storage cannot make it more uniform. On the contrary, further storage can only reduce the water resource for every one because of reservoir evaporation. In fact it would be perfectly possible to dry up the entire river simply by building enough storage dams, and the Reclamation Bureau, which once was so anxious to conserve water by building a dam at Echo Park, seems to be well on its way toward this dubious goal.

And it will be more ridiculous if it should come to pass, as now seems likely, that even the power benefits claimed for Glen Canyon cannot be realized. Hydropower appears to be obsolete in the Upper Basin even before Glen Canyon's generators go on the line. And if it is obsolete in 1965, what will it be in the year 2040 at the end of the 75-year payout period? To provide a benefit that could more economically have come from other sources, a superb canyon was destroyed, its tombstone a concrete slab that should never have been poured.

86

The Place No One Knew

ELIOT PORTER

1963

Before going on to the Grand Canyon battles, we cannot leave Glen Canyon without an epitaph. The following words by Eliot Porter, in his Sierra Club book, The Place No One Knew, *were written about one of the last trips ever made down the canyon.*

THE ARCHITECT, the life-giver, and the moderator of Glen Canyon is the Colorado River. It slips along serenely, riffled only in the few places where boulder-filled narrows confine it, for nearly two hundred miles. For all the serenity, the first canyon experience is too overwhelming to let you take in more than the broadest features and boldest strokes. The eye is numbed by vastness and magnificence, and passes over the fine details, ignoring them in a defense against surfeit. The big features, the massive walls and towers, the shimmering vistas, the enveloping light, are all hypnotizing, shutting out awareness of the particular.

Later you begin to focus on the smaller, more familiar, more comprehensible objects which, when finally seen in the context of the whole, are endowed with a wonder no less than the total. It is from them that the greatest rewards come. Then you see for the first time the velvety lawns of young tamarisks sprouting on the wet sandbars just vacated by the retreating flood, or notice how the swirling surface of the green, opaque river converts light reflected from rocks and trees and sky into a moire of interlacing lines and coils of color, or observe the festooned, evocative designs etched into the walls by water and lichens.

It is an intimate canyon. The feeling of intimacy comes partly from your being able to travel through it by boat — from a close association unknown in a canyon seen only from above or dipped into at only a few places. The intimacy also comes from the calmness and congeniality of the river and the closeness of the walls. Life along the banks and bars is unhurried. Every bend offers a good campsite. Clear springs are not far apart, providing in a shaded setting of mossy, dripping rocks and wildflowers welcome respite from the heat of noon. At evening, in the glow of burnished cliffs, a quiet peace settles on the boatmen gathered close to their campfire, their subdued voices accentuating the faint gurgling of the big river slipping past its banks. With night spreading fast and stars appearing in the diminished sky, the canyon's dimly silhouetted walls give comfort and security.

In the canyon itself the days flow through your consciousness as the river flows along its course, without a break and with hardly a ripple to disturb their smoothness. Problems fade from the forefront of your mind. Duration becomes a serene timeless flow without landmarks, without interruptions, without the insistant beckoning of obligations. The river supplies and in a sense supplants the need for a measure of time. The current becomes the time on which you move. Things happen and days pass. They exist simply in a heap of impressions and memories, all different and yet all of one kind. There is no more liberating or healing experience. It penetrates to the very core of being, scattering anxieties, untangling knots, re-creating the spirit.

To put the world, and yourself at the same time, in a valid perspective you must remove yourself from the demands of both. The world's demands fade the faster, but nonetheless surely your own will shrink to acceptable proportions and cannot sally forth to attack you. In the wilderness of Glen Canyon you do not assail yourself. You glide on into the day unpursued, living, as all good river travelers should, in the present.

Rainbow Bridge from the east. When Lake Powell (formed by the Glen Canyon dam) is full, water from the reservoir regularly floods the base of the Bridge, whose status as a national monument does not seem to afford it much protection.

345

87

Dams in the Grand Canyon—A Necessary Evil?

SIERRA CLUB STAFF

1965

Oddly enough, the battle over the two dams that the Bureau of Reclamation proposed for the Grand Canyon included controversy over what stretch of the river's gorge could legitimately be called the Grand Canyon. For historical reasons, the area under the jurisdiction of the National Park Service was divided into Grand Canyon National Park upstream and Grand Canyon National Monument downstream. Still farther downstream is Lake Mead National Recreation Area, behind Hoover Dam. Most river trips through the canyon begin at Lee's Ferry, Arizona, below Glen Canyon dam, and end at or near Lake Mead, a distance of nearly 300 miles.

The Bureau of Reclamation pointed out that neither proposed dam—at Bridge Canyon and Marble Canyon—would be within the national park or the national monument. However, the U.S. Board of Geographic Names defined the Grand Canyon as including Marble Canyon—as well as the portions of the canyon within the park.

The following excerpts from the Sierra Club broadside on the controversy describe, among other things, precisely what each dam would do to the entire canyon, inside the parks and out.

UNDERSTANDABLY ON THE DEFENSIVE concerning the impact of dams on Grand Canyon National Park and National Monument, the Bureau of Reclamation stresses the fact that Bridge Canyon dam would be downstream from the monument and Marble Gorge dam would be upstream from the park. Bridge Canyon dam, however, would back water all the way through the monument and 13 miles into the park. This would convert the living river, chief architect and artery of the Canyon, into a dead reservoir. It would halt the processes that created the Canyon, and turn a living laboratory of stream erosion into a static museum piece. It would flood the habitat of wildlife that through the ages has depended on the living river for its own life. It would make invaluable archaeological and geological records inaccessible. It would inundate campsites on beaches and sandbars,

346

and the sheer walls of the new shoreline would offer no substitute. Fluctuations in reservoir level would stain the walls between high and low water. Dambuilders' access roads would disfigure the scene, as would transmission lines. And dams in Grand Canyon would extinguish for all time one of the great experiences available to modern man: the boat trip on the living river through the whole length of the Canyon from Lee's Ferry to Grand Wash Cliffs at the head of Lake Mead.

What about Marble Gorge dam? The Bureau of Reclamation asserts that "Construction of the Marble Canyon Dam and Reservoir would have no effect on the National Park since the dam and reservoir would be upstream from the park boundary."

There is a superficial plausibility to the Bureau's contention. But the flow of water through the park and monument would be metered through valves. Debris floated down tributary canyons and stranded is now flushed out by periodic high-water stages, and regulation of flow could destroy this natural flushing action. "It is anticipated," says the Bureau, "that a minimum flow of at least 1,000 cubic feet per second will be maintained below Marble Canyon Dam through the Grand Canyon." It was "anticipated," too, that the Bureau would protect Rainbow Bridge National Monument from the waters of Lake Powell, rising behind Glen Canyon Dam, as provided by law. But the legally prescribed protection was never provided. In any case, 1,000 cfs is a

During the Grand Canyon battle, the Internal Revenue Service removed the tax-exempt status of the club.

Cartoon by Conrad: "Back just a little further . . . back . . ." Reprinted with permission of Register and Tribune Syndicate. Copyright 1966.

pitiful trickle incapable of floating boats down what the Bureau calls "this 104 mile undisturbed stretch of river" between the foot of Marble Gorge dam and the head of Bridge Canyon reservoir.

Although it may appear comparatively innocuous, Marble Gorge dam is as great a potential threat as Bridge Canyon dam. It would be a long step toward realization of a cherished dream of the Bureau: the Kanab diversion. This is a plan to divert 90 percent of the Colorado's flow from Marble Gorge through a 45-mile tunnel to a hydroelectric plant at Kanab Creek—which, uncoincidentally, is at the head of Bridge Canyon reservoir. This would reduce to the vanishing point the Colorado's flow through the national park.

In a rather pathetic attempt to offset damage that the dams would inflict, the Bureau claims tremendous recreation values for the proposed reservoirs. The most extreme statement of its case was made by Regional Director A. B. West: "We think the recreational, fish and wildlife values accruing from these developments—aside from their other multipurpose water benefits—are ample justification for their construction."

This extraordinary contention can be most conveniently disposed of by quoting a report of the Bureau of Outdoor Recreation, which, like Reclamation, is an agency of the Interior Department:

"No additional recreation benefits can be claimed for the proposed Bridge Canyon dam because of the unusual existing recreation values of the proposed reservoir area and the adverse effects the dam and reservoir would have on these values.

"Water-oriented recreation cannot be considered one of the primary purposes for constructing the Bridge Canyon and Marble Canyon dams because less costly alternatives for expanding recreation facilities in this area are available.

"The types of water-oriented recreation which could be supplied by the reservoirs are available at Lake Mead and Glen Canyon National Recreation Areas. These recreation areas serve the same population centers, and facilities could be added as recreation demand expands."

Flaming Gorge, Navajo, Glen Canyon, Hoover, Davis, Parker and Imperial Dams already furnish 600 miles of reservoir recreation in the Colorado basin. This is far more than the mileage of recreational swift-running water.

Sensitivity to encroachments upon Grand Canyon National Park and National Monument, by defenders and detractors of the dam proposals alike, has tended to obscure the fact that the park and monument contain less than half of Grand Canyon proper. Neither damsite is within the boundaries of the park or monument, *but both dams and both reservoirs would be wholly contained within Grand Canyon.* Parts of the canyon not within the park and monument are in no way inferior to other parts that are included. The Sierra Club has long advocated national park or equivalent protected status for the entire Grand Canyon from Lee's Ferry to Grand Wash Cliffs.

Whether or not the dams and reservoirs would impair Grand Canyon National Park and Monument is the key legal question. But in broader perspective, the key question is whether the dams would impair the integrity of Grand Canyon as a physical entity and as a priceless national resource. Marble Gorge dam is at least as offensive as Bridge Canyon dam in this respect, if not more so, and the Sierra Club is as unalterably opposed to one as it is to the other.

The Grand Canyon brochure, presented as part of the club's testimony to Congress, went on to point out that the two dams would not save water but waste it (by evaporation and seepage), would generate electricity that could be more economically provided by fossil-fuel and (or) nuclear plants, and would imperil other national parks by creating a precedent for invasion of the parks by the dam builders. They were, in short, "cash register" dams.

The battle continued in and out of Congress for two more years. The Bureau of Reclamation admitted that the chief purpose of the dams was not to save water but to sell power to pay for the giant irrigation works of the Central Arizona Project. The backers of the project offered various compromises, including deletion of one or the other of the dams and expansion of the national parks to include Marble Gorge if the Bridge Canyon dam were built. The club's position on these compromises was succinctly expressed in the following exchange at a 1967 hearing of a House subcommittee chaired by Morris K. Udall of Arizona, an advocate of the dams as part of the Central Arizona Project.

MR. UDALL. . . .
One of the things that has troubled many of my colleagues here is what they deem the impossibly adamant noncompromising position of the Sierra Club. We have 104 miles of living river, the longest stretch of national park in the country. We enlarge that to 158 miles. We are willing to enlarge the Grand Canyon to take in Marble Gorge and Vermillion Cliffs and all of that. We are willing to talk about going downstream another 13 miles. What would the Sierra Club accept? If we have a low, low, low Bridge Canyon dam, maybe 100 feet high, is that too much? Is there any point at which you compromise here?

MR. BROWER. Mr. Udall, you are not giving us anything that God didn't put there in the first place, and I think that is the thing we are not entitled to compromise. That is the primary scenic resource of this country. If there are no other ways to go about getting your water, I would still say that the compromise should not be made—that Arizona should be subsidized with something other than the world's Grand Canyon, or any part of it. . . .

We have no choice. There have to be groups who will hold for these things that are not replaceable. If we stop doing that, we might as well stop being an organization and conservation organizations might as well throw in the towel.

MR. UDALL. I know the strength and sincerity of your feelings and I respect them.*

The club's campaign of nationally published, full-page ads ("If They Can Turn Grand Canyon into a 'Cash Register' Is Any National Park Safe?") and the subsequent threat of the IRS to revoke the club's tax deductibility prompted editorials

*From Congressional Quarterly, Nov. 1, 1968

in newspapers across the country and a deluge of letters to Congress. A Sierra Club book of Grand Canyon photographs with text by Francois Leydet, Of Time and the River Flowing, *helped convey a sense of what would be lost.*

The storm of public indignation could not be ignored. In July of 1968, Senate and House conferees agreed on a Central Arizona Project bill that prohibited dams anywhere in the Grand Canyon—between Glen Canyon Dam and Hoover Dam.

In the words of the Congressional Quarterly: *"The Sierra Club took on—and defeated—a powerful coalition of interests which included the Interior Department's Bureau of Reclamation, the Colorado River Association and like-minded lobbies in the Southwest, the American Public Power Association as well as several large private power companies. The club was also opposing the united position of the seven Basin states, with their 51 seats in the House and 14 seats in the Senate. . . ."*

Against such odds are historic victories won. The beneficiaries would be all future generations of Americans.

Some years after the battle, the entire canyon, from near Lee's Ferry to the head of Lake Mead, was included in Grand Canyon National Park.

The club had achieved a long-sought goal, but it is an axiom that in conservation there are no final victories. Some future Congress, pressured by who-knows-what interest, could still dam the Grand Canyon. The sites were surveyed and debris from the preliminary construction work of the 1960s still mars the canyon walls. Fifteen thousand people each year enjoy the incomparable boat-ride down the canyon, and they can see the scars.

88   Dams Unlimited

JOHN V. YOUNG

1967

Anger at the Bureau's follies, and technical discourses on its poor arithmetic, weren't the only tools conservationists used in protecting the Colorado. Lyricism had a vital role—and so did sarcasm and satire.

A S A LIFELONG CONSERVATIONIST and nature lover, and a Sierra Club member of 1931 vintage, I protest your continued antediluvian opposition to such forward-looking proposals as Marble Gorge and Bridge Canyon dams and other progressive measures of their ilk.

You should get with it. Everyone knows that all such projects automatically make more recreation available to more people than the scenery they happen to replace could ever be worth. Besides, the power they produce perhaps in a few hundred years or so might pay the interest on the investment. Then there is the water they will divert (if there is any water to divert) to irrigate land to produce more crops to increase food surpluses so more farmers can be paid not to raise crops with the water the dams divert. This is obviously a matter of simple economics, easily grasped by simple-minded people.

Instead of opposing big dams, the Sierra Club should escalate them. The club should start the Big Think. For example, why not pile Marble Gorge dam on top of Bridge Canyon dam, add some superstructure, and thus fill the Canyon from rim to rim? This would immediately become the world's largest dam, of inestimable international prestige value, possibly as much as putting a monkey on the moon and probably no more expensive.

With the addition of a couple of hundred miles of dikes along the South Rim and a few dozen smaller dams on some of the side canyons, it should be possible to create a lake extending the entire length and width of the Grand Canyon. Then, instead of the present primitive and uncomfortable travel across the Canyon by mule, one could easily paddle his own canoe from El Tovar to Point Sublime.

Imagine the thrill of water skiing up the Little Colorado, and speedboat races past Toroweap! Think of the beneficial effect on the economy of the vastly increased sales of boats, outboard motors, water skiis, life jackets and sunburn lotion! The three or four million people who get to see the Grand Canyon annually would be doubled or tripled, and away we go!

Of course, there are a few trivial problems. One minor matter is that of preserving the status of Grand Canyon National Park. Here again, you have not been noodling big enough. There is nothing in the act that says Grand Canyon (or any other national park) shouldn't be an *aquatic* park, is there?

89

The Battle of the Redwoods

EDGAR and PEGGY

WAYBURN

1967

While the Grand Canyon fight was going on, the Sierra Club was engaged on other battlefronts—one to create a North Cascades National Park among the glacial peaks of the state of Washington, one to preserve the near-wild Point Reyes peninsula near San Francisco, and still another to save the last and tallest of the redwoods by establishing a national park on California's north coast. The latter struggle had gone on sporadically for an incredible ninety years. As noted here, a Secretary of the Interior had proposed just such a park thirteen years before the Sierra Club was founded.

Edgar Wayburn is a long-time director and past president of the club; Peggy Wayburn has written frequently for the Bulletin *and edited* The Last Redwoods *and* The Parklands of Redwood Creek.

THEY WERE THERE long before mankind had known there was a Pacific, those immense, incredible forests. From the Big Sur country they extended northward four hundred miles along the wild, rocky, beautiful coast — crowding the broad river flats, clothing the steep slopes, and crowning the ridges. They were forests such as man had never seen, anywhere, with trees so huge it sometimes took a dozen men to circle one — trees so tall no one could know their height until they fell.

The trees were somber Greek columns in muted colors, branches held high, needles delicate against the distant sky. Sunlight slanting through sought out the big-leaf maples, the alders, the dogwood, and the oaks. And in spring, even without sunlight, myriad small flowers brightened the forest floor.

Redwoods at Prairie Creek, Humboldt County.

The coast redwoods, *Sequoia sempervirens*, are among the survivors of a great genus. Crowded westward by geological and climatic changes, the tallest living things make their last stand along the rim of the Pacific. From the time of the dinosaurs to the time the white man came.

Spaniards found them, the Russians and Englishmen followed, and the tough pioneers came. The early records are scant, and some are difficult to believe: A tree 32 feet in diameter stood on the Oakland hills above San Francisco Bay, one naturalist noted. Others there were so tall that English sailors in 1816 used them to sight a course from beyond the Golden Gate. Around Bolinas, great groves of redwoods stood "as fine as any," and the Bolinas harbor rivaled San Francisco as a timber port until it silted in.

Eureka was forest. Crescent City was forest. On the Elk River in Humboldt County, a tree yielded 420 feet of logs, and the salmon ran so thick in Bull Creek a wagon couldn't cross it in the spring. It took 15 years of steady logging to cut the great trees of Jolly Giant Creek near Arcata. And everyone thought the redwood forests were without end.

Disappointed goldseekers swelled the ranks of loggers in the 1850's. They turned from the Mother Lode to mine the coastal forests instead. They sailed north from San Francisco, and at almost every creek they discovered a new strike—a grove of trees to stagger a man's imagination. By 1860, they were all the way to Crescent City, and the blue smoke of a sawmill drifted from the mouth of every sizable stream.

In 1879, when the first major proposal was made for a redwood national park (by Secretary of the Interior Carl Schurz), the young industry was becoming Big Business. During the next two decades—while small sporadic attempts were made locally to save trees—busy entrepreneurs succeeded in gathering into private hands virtually all the redwood forests. By 1900 the chance had been lost for the nation to save a redwood park out of the public domain. Parklands would have to be bought back from private owners, and on the owner's terms.

The park idea persisted, and logging went inexorably on. In 1911 a California Congressman introduced a House joint resolution to investigate the "advisability and necessity" of establishing a coast redwood park. His resolution failed. The donkey engine and band saw sped up operations, and by the time passable roads penetrated the redwood region, thousands of devastated acres were suddenly on display. The Save-the-Redwoods League was formed in 1918 to rescue the redwoods, and high on its agenda was the establishment of a national park.

A redwood national park bill passed the House in 1923, but died in the Senate. Logging continued vigorously behind some of the roadside strips the League had begun to acquire. By 1942 half the primeval forests had been cut.

The depression brought a chance to buy redwood parklands. Largely through the efforts of the Save-the-Redwood League, the state acquired some of its finest redwood groves—at Bull Creek, Prairie Creek and Mill Creek. The redwood industry was glad to get the money. In 1946 Congresswoman Helen Gahagan Douglas proposed the Roosevelt Memorial

Forest, 2.4 million acres to be administered by the Forest Service, and 340,000 acres, including state parklands, to be set aside in four memorial park units. But the economy had improved, and her ideas lost out.

Timber operations continued to accelerate. Chain saws and bulldozers moved into the woods. The great trees fell faster and faster; it now takes less than an hour to fell a giant. The Save-the-Redwoods League fought to make the state parks bigger, and the roadside strips longer. The dream of a redwood national park faded.

But the dream still has one place to be realized—at Redwood Creek. It is some measure of the redwood forests that, after 115 years of steady logging, such a place remains at all. For one last chance.

Redwood Creek: Tall Trees Grove, Redwood National Park.

90

Bridge Creek—1973

EDGAR WAYBURN

1973

The battle to create a Redwood National Park was far more fiercely fought than most previous efforts to create national parks. Earlier parks had been created out of the public domain—lands already owned by the federal government—but this one involved private lands and a booming industry devoted to converting the tall trees into lumber.

A chain of state parks along the Redwood Highway already included some of the finest groves, but nowhere was there a complete watershed or even a major portion of a watershed within a park. The result was to leave the groves open to erosion from nearby logged-over hills.

Since California's redwoods were as well known as the Grand Canyon, the struggle to save them aroused almost as much national attention as the fight against dams on the Colorado. Again there were full-page Sierra Club ads in national newspapers and magazines, and again Congress was bombarded with letters. In 1968 Congress created a Redwood National Park, including three state parks, lands along the Smith River, and a narrow strip along Redwood Creek, designed to save the grove containing the world's tallest trees. As a result of legislative compromises, however, the slopes above the strip were left in the hands of the loggers, who proceeded to go about their business with the results noted here. So the long campaign to save the trees had to be resumed.

I T WAS ONE OF THE EARTH'S loveliest places. Through a shadowy canyon a wild clear stream leapt and tumbled, making its own free way, wandering with the land. Where a log lay across its course it broke into a white dazzle of waterfall. Like the forest floor beyond, its banks were clothed in a richly colored tapestry of leaf and needle and moss, which had a deep and easy spring beneath a walker's feet. In summer the maples along the stream illumined the mid-story of the forest with a soft green glow. In fall, the maples turned a brilliant gold as though celebrating the turn of the seasons. Above them and around them, the great old redwoods soared, their deep brown and gray fluted trunks solid and straight and somehow reassuring: those trees had stood at least a half a millennium in their places, and their ancestors had stood nearby for untold millennia before.

To one who stopped on the bank of this stream and listened, there were elemental earth-sounds to hear. There was the voice of the stream, quick and dancing and full of freedom. Behind it, there was the steadier, more insistent call of the nearby river that soon would claim its waters. And overhead, there was the tranquil wind — music in the high trees — a music as old almost as the land itself, and as elemental as the sound of waves against the shore.

The stream was known as Bridge Creek. Visitors to its confluence with Redwood Creek a few years ago experienced so profound a feeling that they returned to their seats in Congress and voted to incorporate this place in the new Redwood National Park.

But today, that place is no more. The wild free stream, the elemental earth-sounds, and the beauty are gone. I stood on the banks of Bridge Creek a few weeks ago and wondered if I had traveled to the right place on Redwood Creek — gone far enough upstream or found the canyon I had come to see. Where the bright clear waters of Bridge Creek had wandered freely, a hard straight race of silt-dulled waters poured between high levees of gravel, heaped up straight and even. The banks were rough and jagged underneath my shoes. The maples still stood, but uphill they blazed against an empty sky: for just beyond the national park boundary, a quarter-mile from the confluence of Bridge and Redwood creeks, the redwood trees were gone. I stopped to listen and sorrow. Above the hard new flow of Bridge Creek are the sounds of cats and chain saws and at intervals the thunder of a falling tree.

Five years after the above was written, conservationists pressured Congress to halt the logging. In 1978 the park was finally expanded to include the slopes above Redwood Creek — after large portions of them had been logged over. But some of the giant trees on the hillsides were saved, and the cut-over land could be at least partially repaired and reforested, so that the tall trees in the bottom would receive some seasonal protection, and in a few centuries visitors might again stand at Bridge Creek and view a scene like that described by Dr. Wayburn.

Clearcutting of redwood forest, Gold Bluffs Beach Road, Prairie Creek, Humboldt County.

91

Are the Everglades Forever?

JOHN G. MITCHELL

1970

We are accustomed to think that America's remaining wilderness areas are all in the West, but the East still has wildlands, too, and a unique portion of them are "preserved" in Everglades National Park. The "preserved" is in quotes because it ignores what is too often forgotten. Parks are vulnerable to what goes on outside their boundaries. In the redwoods it was possible for the government to buy—at great expense—most of the lands that directly affect the park. In the Everglades this solution is not feasible, as the following article, an excerpt from a Sierra Club book, The Everglades, *makes clear.*

The author, a former Sierra Club editor, is gloomy about the prospects for the Everglades. However, one heartening event has occurred since the article was written. The Cross-Florida Barge Canal—under construction at the time of writing by the Army Corps of Engineers—would have seriously impaired the ecosystems of much of the Florida peninsula of which the Everglades is a part. A long campaign against the canal was successful in the early '70s, when President Nixon ordered the work abandoned. But the Everglades is still in deep trouble.

EVERGLADES IS A deceptive word. It has to be split. The second part comes from the old Anglo-Saxon *glyde* or *glaed,* meaning a bright, shining open space in the forest. And that fits. But the first part is tricky, for it promises an eternity of grass and shining water, together, without limit in time or space, as if they always were and always will be, world without end, never changing and forevermore. The promise of permanence is everywhere. In the visitor's center at Everglades National Park, where tourists stop first to find out what it is they have come so far to see, a modest sign informs them that they are guests in "a land of subtle charm and complexity, preserved forever for the inspiration and enjoyment of mankind." The message echoes what Harry Truman said in 1947 when he dedicated this park at the tip of the Florida peninsula. "We have," said the President, "permanently safeguarded an irreplaceable primitive area." Who, then, is qualified to challenge the language of optimists, or question the meaning of permanence, as he starts down the park road toward Flamingo, pausing along the way to stand at the edge of the grass, to look at the grass shimmering like a green sea, even and unbroken until it reaches that point in the curvature of the earth where grass becomes sky? How far does it go on? *Forever?*

A man can be fooled by the Everglades, but not for long if he moves about. For the grass does end. Now there is the darker, rougher green of bunched mangroves, and beyond them the turquoise shallows of Florida Bay peppered with flotillas of waterfowl. The islands of the bay are also mangrove. The tops of the trees are salted white with roosting birds. The birds rise from their rookeries, wedges and clouds of them, not all white now but mottled pink or brown by spoonbills and pelicans. The sky fills with birds until they, too, seem to go on without limit in time or space, world without end of wings flashing across an earthscape that is neither charming nor subtle, but strong and captivating, and wondrously wild. Yet even the wilderness ends. Now there is a highway. It is raised above the wet grass on the berm of a canal. Then more canals appear, and highways and gas stations and cultivated fields and groves of trees arranged symmetrically and houses; and still more houses until finally, on the outskirts of the cities, the land begins to disappear entirely under cubes of tile and plaster. Now you are in an altogether different world, a world that is pressing hard against the outer limits of the natural one next-door. The sign in the visitors' center at the national park does not acknowledge the presence of this larger world of people. Thus it can claim enduring preservation of an area that in fact is too fragile to endure the circumstances—and excesses—of encroaching development. Everglades become neverglades without water, and without water there can be neither grass nor wildlife, only fossils. So the myth of permanence is shattered. Yet the challenge to save what is left of the Everglades still remains.

There is no other wilderness like it in the country, nothing like it on this planet. That is why it must be saved, the part that is left. Down the long tunnel of time it will all be gone someday, eons hence. But not because of man; because of nature, which has been shaping and reshaping the landforms and life-forms of the planet, ever so slowly, since land and life began. Only man can hasten the process. What might take ten thousand years, in nature, man can now accomplish in less than a century. In less than a century, he has already reduced the living Everglades to half their original size. The half remaining could disappear in a generation.

The record of man's manipulation of nature in the Everglades is replete with examples of remedies which were never fully analyzed before they were applied—remedies that inevitably turned out to be more disastrous than the troubles they were intended to cure. It was man's judgment, for example, that the rich muck of South Florida was going to waste under water; so man drained off the water only to discover that muck, exposed to the heat of the sun, oxidizes into thin air. In some agricultural districts now, as much as 40 per cent of the organic soils are gone. Some farmers will be ploughing limestone by the year 2000. But they won't be raising any crops. Similarly, drainage undertaken to increase food production in one area has inhibited productivity in another: in periods of drought, the long canals became arms of the sea and saltwater intruded on the land. In 1945, salinity in the soil killed off 18,000 acres of vegetables in southeast Dade County. Now increasing salinity in Florida Bay, caused by the decreasing outflow of fresh water from the Everglades, threatens the natural nursery ground of the Tortugas shrimp and a $20 million-a-year commercial fishery.

It would be wholly unfair and inaccurate to single out agriculture—and the public works instituted on agriculture's behalf—for all the havoc that has been wrought in the Everglades. There is yet another pressure on the ecosystem, and in many ways it is the stronger of the two. It bears repeating, for it is the pressure of people—people in houses and office buildings, people sunning themselves on the fabulous beaches, people shopping for land to invest in, people turning faucets, eating melons, buying steaks.

Florida's population growth represents a booster's dream-come-true: a net increase of 119 per cent since 1950. The chambers of commerce are delighted. The Florida Development Commission is ecstatic. Now it can boast that Florida has twice as many people per square mile—111 to be exact—as the national average. And that, the commission explains, doesn't even account for the half-million tourists from out-of-state who are in-state on any given day. Now the coasts are getting crowded, and inland is the only way the people can spread.

The spread is most noticeable in Collier County, where, according to the billboards, developers have been busy "building new worlds for a better tomorrow." Here, in the mid-Sixties, the Gulf-American Land Corporation raised its model country club community of Golden Gate City, then proceeded to drain some 200 square miles of adjacent cypress swamp. They called the swamp Golden Gate Estates, in anticipation of the spacious homes that would never be built here because the "developer" declined to provide either landfill or the necessary utilities, such as electricity. Nevertheless, more than 20,000 people have bought lots in the Estates, though only a fraction of that number have ever set foot on their individual properties, which is understandable; few investors in real estate are known to be handy with machetes. In any event, there it is—a pathetic gridiron of unpaved roads spaced a quarter mile apart, and a system of canals that is sucking the lifeblood from the western edge of the Big Cypress. To accomplish this, Gulf-American retained the services of a remarkable machine called the Tree Crusher. Fifty-five tons and two stories high, Crusher made short work of the cypress. "The wilderness has been pushed aside," claimed one promotional brochure, quite accurately. "We are literally changing the face of Florida."

In Miami, there is a cattle rancher whose name I will not mention but whose philosophy, I think, demands to be put down in the record, for the man and his beliefs seem to me to epitomize all that is wrong today in the Everglades. No, not only in the Everglades. In America. He is a good man, I am sure. On the basis of one brief conversation, I know this man would stop his car to help a wounded dog on the side of the road, that he gives to

359

charitable causes, abides by the law and loves his country, in his own way, as much as any honored patriot. But he does not understand. He has lived in South Florida for more than half a century. He has witnessed its fires and floods. He has been alone and on foot deep in the saw grass glades. But he does not understand. He is still back there somewhere with all the ancient ones who are long dead on the vanished frontier. Yet he is alive and does not understand.

We talked about water and people. And ecology. He didn't like that word, ecology. He called it "a phony issue." He said he didn't want people to be denied water for a phony issue. So I suggested that we forget for a moment about ecology and just talk about water and people. If there get to be too many people, I said, there won't be enough water for cows. And pretty soon, there won't even be enough water for people.

The rancher's teeth made a sound like marbles when you have a handful and start to squeeze. And he said: "Horseshit. The good lord takes care of things like that."

92

The Tall Grass Prairie: Vanishing Landscape or National Park?

LINDA M. BILLINGS

1977

The best introduction to this article is supplied by Walt Whitman: "While I know the standard claim is that Yosemite, Niagara Falls, the upper Yellowstone and the like, afford the greatest natural shows, I am not so sure but the Prairies and Plains last longer, fill the esthetic sense fuller, precede all the rest and make North America's characteristic landscape."

The author of this article served as a Sierra Club representative in Washington. Bills to establish a Tall Grass Prairie National Park in Kansas are regularly introduced into Congress and supported by the club, but the intransigence of the cattle industry has stymied them.

FEW LANDSCAPES are more evocative of the unique aspects of American history and culture than the prairies. Indians, early explorers, sod busters, homesteaders, wagon trains, cowboys, cavalry, buffalo, antelope, elk, wolves, coyotes and eagles—all these and more lived in close association with the famous North American Prairie. For those few left who remember it as it was, the grand sweep of grass and sky must have been awesome. At one time, the heart of America's inland sea of grass, the tall-grass prairie, stretched in a broad swath of 250 million acres from Canada to Texas and Indiana to Kansas. Now, only remnants are left, and these are fast disappearing.

Perhaps because we have thought of the prairie as such an integral part of the American landscape, it comes as a shock to us to realize that only very small parts of it remain in public ownership—as parts of wildlife refuges, in parks or as small research plots. We have no parks containing a large expanse of native tall-grass prairie. Development pressures, changes in land ownership and agricultural methods, and other threats to the last remaining stretches of tall-grass prairie make it imperative that we act quickly to establish a Tall Grass Prairie National Park.

Between 1937 and 1975, the National Park Service and other federal agencies conducted studies and issued reports on possible grassland sites in Montana, the Dakotas, Colorado, Nebraska, Kansas and Oklahoma. These studies eventually focused upon the Flint Hills, in Kansas and Oklahoma, the last remaining intact stretch of tall-grass prairie.

The Flint Hills, running north and south, offer wide, rolling vistas and are characterized by flat-topped hills, deeply dissected scarps and woody alluvial valleys. While they lack the flat topography and deep rich soils characteristic of "true prairies," their distinctive physiographic character does offer richer and more diverse natural and scenic qualities.

The tall-grass prairie is a remarkably stable ecosystem, but once it is disturbed or destroyed, it is very hard, if not impossible, to reestablish. Gone, too, would be the way of life, the buildings, the artifacts and the potential archaeological sites, that could give future generations an understanding of their cultural heritage. The National Park Service sees a twofold purpose for a Tall Grass Prairie National Park: "to preserve and protect a relatively undisturbed portion of the national prairie environment, and to interpret its role in shaping the American culture."

At first glance, most people would wonder what could be so important about a lot of wild grass ("weeds," some would say). What makes the tall-grass prairie so special? What are its unique and compelling qualities? In some ways, it is not entirely unlike a forest, with its all-enveloping silence punctuated by occasional bird songs, a rustle of underbrush from a small animal or reptile, the whooshing sound of the wind. Yet, it also has the broad, expansive vistas characteristic of the ocean—gentle undulations of green as far as the eye can see, with a huge, vivid sky above.

Within this seemingly uniform environment exists a diverse and complex ecosystem. The dominant and distinctive feature is the native grasses:

primarily big blue stem, Indian, little blue stem, and switchgrass, variously reaching heights of three to eight feet. Failure to set aside a significant portion of the remaining tall-grass prairie could well mean the loss to the gene pool of these and other species, grasses that one day might prove invaluable to botanists and agronomists interested in developing new strains for forage or even human consumption. This reason alone is enough to warrant the establishment of a Tall Grass Prairie National Park. The tall-grass prairie of the Central Lowlands should not be confused with the short- and mixed-grass prairies of the Great Plains region, to the west, though combinations of tall, mixed and short grasses do exist. The tall grasses generally require more rainfall and richer, deeper soils. Throughout the spring, summer and fall, wildflowers are everywhere, including gay-feathers, sunflowers, black-eyed susans, asters and lupines. The prairies support hundreds of different kinds of plants.

They also support eighty species of mammals, which at one time included bison, pronghorn antelope, gray wolf, mountain lion and elk. Today, there are the deer, bobcat, coyote, fox, jack rabbit, opossum, muskrat, raccoon, badger, and many more. Over 300 species of birds are found there, including the prairie chicken, hawks, falcons, various waterfowl and an occasional eagle. Over 1,000 kinds of insects and other animals are also inhabitants of the tall-grass prairie.

The first human inhabitants of the prairie region were native hunters, who came there some 10,000 years ago. Later, farming cultures were established in the fertile river bottoms and valleys. At one time, the great Indian tribes of the Comanche, Kiowa, Gros Ventre and many others dominated the region. Later came the early European explorers such as Coronado, and still later, Lewis and Clark and Zebulon Pike. They were followed in turn by countless processions of trappers, miners and settlers going west over the Santa Fe and Oregon trails. The Homestead Act of 1862 brought still more settlers to the prairies, though they found the chert-laced soils of the Flint Hills too rocky for plowing and cultivation. Consequently, the area has been used mostly for grazing to this day. The great cattle drives of the late 1800s went through the Flint Hills. Millions of head of cattle were brought over the Chisholm and other trails from Texas and Oklahoma to the Kansas railheads. Where the early settlers once cursed those rocky, unyielding soils, we can now give thanks. For without them, there would not be any large expanses of tall-grass prairie left.

However, recent changes in the Flint Hills make us concerned about what the future might bring. Power plants, power lines and reservoirs encroach increasingly upon the landscape. Small towns are losing out to big cities, and today, many rural dwellers earn some or all of their living in surrounding urban areas. Economic pressures are forcing some pastures to be consolidated and turned over to corporations. In search of more winter-grass resources, some landowners are plowing up prairie pasturelands and planting fescues.

These pressures and more add up to the final assault on the great American prairie. Unless the public is moved to express its concern for the tall-grass prairie, and unless Congress takes action quickly, future generations of Americans will never know an integral part of their natural and cultural heritage.

93

The Mountains
and the
Megalopolis

JOSEPH E. BROWN

1973

Until the 1960s, the National Park Service had been preoccupied with preservation of the nation's natural and historic wonders, regardless of their location. But with the creation of Cape Cod and Point Reyes National Seashores in 1962 (the Sierra Club supported both and led the fight for the latter), the Park Service turned a corner in its history. For the first time, recognizing urban pressures, it began to provide recreation space in metropolitan areas. Scenic values were still important, but equally important was access—proximity to large centers of population.

Inevitably the Park Service also became involved in big money. Buying private land near urban areas was considerably more expensive than the process by which earlier national parks were created—transferring federal lands from one jurisdiction to another. But in the precedent-breaking cases of Cape Cod and Point Reyes, Americans proved willing to spend whatever might be required to acquire breathing space for the multitudes. The two national seashores were followed a decade later by two major national recreation areas—Gateway in New York and New Jersey and Golden Gate in northern California.

Badly needed was a comparable park for the teeming Los Angeles area. Amazingly there remained a largely undeveloped region in the midst of the metropolis. The author of this article is a former editor of Oceans magazine and a freelance writer in southern California.

O N A BALMY SPRING MORNING a lizard, in retreat from the sun's increasing heat, slithers beneath a sumac bush. Not far away, a young gray fox pauses to slake his thirst at a small stream, flanked by graceful laurels and willows standing motionless on this breathless, windless day. Then he scurries up a ridge toward a sandstone peak. To the southwest, beyond the shoreline at the mountains' feet, beyond sight or hearing of either lizard or fox but surveyed by a flock of terns, three California gray whales lumber northward. Their destination: the Arctic, their annual migration to the Baja California calving grounds fulfilled once again.

There is much more in these Santa Monica mountains, along this seashore—hidden valleys, steep cliffs, submarine canyons, placid ponds, and shady groves. Companions of the fox: bobcat, coyote, ground squirrel, deer. Waterbirds and shorebirds. And an archaeological treasure: more than 600 Indian sites dating back nearly 7,000 years identified so far, possibly only a tenth of the number still awaiting discovery.

The Santa Monica Mountains, running roughly east-west parallel to the meandering Pacific shoreline, rise abruptly out of the agricultural Oxnard plain in the west; and in the east the range buries its feet beneath the asphalt of freeways and the concrete and glass of highrises almost at the heart of downtown Los Angeles. To the north lies the sprawl of the heavily populated San Fernando Valley, but to the south the range adjoins one of the most outstanding marine areas left between Santa Barbara and San Clemente, containing an extremely rich marine biota, kelp beds, and a spectacular stretch of sand beaches and rocky headlands. Together, mountains and shore contribute to Los Angeles' physical identity, provide a clean airshed for smog-contaminated inland cities, offer recreational alternatives to overused Southern California beaches, and support a surprising variety of plant and animal species.

They are not Alps, these mountains. One would hesitate to equate them with some of California's other natural wonders—Lake Tahoe, for example, or Yosemite, or the giant redwoods. Yet to the ten million residents of the Los Angeles megalopolis, the 46-mile-long, 10-mile-wide, 220,000-acre Santa Monica mountain range and its neighboring shoreline are far more important. For Los Angeles has fewer public lands and parks than any other American city, including New York. Worse, open space continues to shrink as the population expands. The Santa Monicas constitute the last surviving unpreserved open space close by the nation's second most populous urban area. So to Los Angeles' millions, this geologically, biologically, and geographically diverse mountain range is a backyard Big Sur, an Everyman's Sierra Nevada—so close that from downtown Los Angeles, the most distant point of the range is only 90 minutes away by automobile.

Ironically, the very attribute that makes this range especially valuable as open space—its proximity to a giant urban area—also makes it attractive to developers.

The bulldozer is at work on the Santa Monicas at the eastern end, near the heart of megalopolis; on the north, close to the heavily trafficked Ventura Freeway; and increasingly along the scenic Pacific Coast Highway to the south. Already, homes and apartments occupy about 32,000 acres. Another 1,000 acres now support a welter of commercial and industrial enterprises,

364

ranging from shopping centers to gas stations and from movie studios to warehouses. Still another 5,800 acres remain as farmland. Out of a total 220,000 acres, only 150,000 — most of it in private ownership — remain in the Santa Monicas for badly needed open space.

For years, the Sierra Club and other conservation organizations have advocated preserving the Santa Monicas as open space. They represent precisely that sort of terrain on which development should not occur. Seventy-eight percent of the slopes west of the San Diego Freeway are in gradients over 25 percent; nearly half of them, 50 percent or more. Building on slopes this steep requires extensive cuts and fills which destroy the ecology of an area and contribute to further weakening of already precarious strata. The highly erodible soil and rock formations of the Santa Monicas' steeper slopes present a formidable slide hazard even without human meddling. Furthermore, fires, floods, and earthquakes scorch, soak, and shake the range at distressingly frequent intervals.

But in the Santa Monicas, nature can also be benevolent. Because of clean, prevailing winds blowing off the Pacific Ocean, the mountain range serves as a valuable airshed, diluting the already critically polluted air over the Los Angeles basin. Development of these mountains would not only add new smog as more and more two- and three-car families commute to work, school, and store from their split-level hillside perches, but would also remove the giant natural air cleaner that keeps pollutants in the metropolitan basin from becoming worse than they are.

Los Angeles conservationists began years ago to protect the diminishing, precious natural resource of the Santa Monicas and the adjoining seashore. Considering the enormous opposition from developers, who are abetted by a tangle of tax dollar-hungry local governmental jurisdictions, even the conservationists' smallest victories today loom as milestone achievements. In 1968, for example, they managed to block plans to "upgrade" Mulholland Drive to what is deceptively called a "scenic drive" — as if it weren't already. Their argument was devastatingly simple: how "scenic" can any road be when it is converted to a mini-freeway. They also convinced the state to remove the proposed Malibu and Pacific Coast freeways from future maps.

The $300-million pricetag for the proposed 100,000-acre urban park is staggering to be sure, but the cost of preserving the Santa Monica Mountains to the ten million residents of the Los Angeles area and eight million annual visitors is only about $17 per person. Few could deny they would be getting one of the world's great bargains.

The "omnibus parks bill" of 1978, shepherded through Congress by Representative Phillip Burton, was good news for conservationists in many parts of the country. Near Los Angeles, the bill created a Santa Monica Mountains National Recreational Area.

94

From Sea to Shining Sea or Through the Rockies at 31 Knots

JONATHAN ELA

1972

One of the Sierra Club's most consistent opponents over the years has been the Army Corps of Engineers, the agency charged by Congress with flood control, navigable waterways, and a host of allied activities. Along with the Bureau of Reclamation, which is responsible for irrigation projects, the Corps' military and civilian engineers are the nation's chief dam-builders. It was inevitable, perhaps, that there would be irreconcilable conflicts between building dams and canals and preserving scenery. Some of these conflicts are vividly illustrated in the following article on the Corps by the club's Midwest representative and author of the Sierra Club book, Faces of the Great Lakes.

CONSERVATIONISTS ARE expressing concern over a proposal just announced to construct a Cross-Continent Barge Canal linking Boston with San Diego. The joint project of the U.S. Army Corps of Engineers and the Atomic Energy Commission would be the largest public work ever constructed in the United States, and would utilize the technology recently perfected by the AEC in its Cannikin explosion on Amchitka Island in Alaska.

The Cro-Con Canal is officially described as "a multiple use project in the highest sense of the term," but it is generally understood in Washington that the major justification for the project is to aid movement of aircraft carriers. Pentagon sources point out that the Panama Canal is too narrow to handle the newer carriers, necessitating enormously expensive and time-consuming voyages around Cape Horn. Plans to construct a new, sea-level canal across Panama have been blocked by Panamanian nationalists and by aroused environmentalists in the United States who have pointed out the possibly disastrous effects on the mating and migrating patterns of certain endangered species.

Supposed benefits of the Cro-Con proposal are spelled out in the Corps of Engineers' "Preliminary Framework Analysis," a 640-page document released on May 18th of this year. These include: enhanced capacity to transport coal from the fields of Kentucky and southern Ohio; creation of deepwater ports for such cities as Cincinnati, Louisville, Tulsa, and Aspen; flood control and water supply; and water-oriented recreational activity of a linear nature. The corps indicated that the Cro-Con Canal has a projected benefit-cost ratio of 1.001:1, "thus more than justifying the substantial public funds that will go into the project."

The public "Framework Analysis" fails to give a detailed route for the canal beyond the Charles River at Watertown, Mass., but a member of the Sierra Club's Washington staff has procured a Xerox of a sketch map through the good offices of a disgruntled associate of Jack Anderson. Corps of Engineers' sources warn that the leaked route map is a "rough guesstimate" and that details will be worked out after construction starts.

Early critics of Cro-Con contend that the corps has not sufficiently taken into account the scarcity of water in the arid western states. Corps Public Relations Director Lt. Gen. B. R. "Brute" Thwackem disputes this point, saying that the Corps can generate more than enough water to float even the largest aircraft carriers that the nation is likely to construct. Revival of the dormant NAWAPA water plan will bring enormous quantities of Canadian water into the arid areas, where it can be stored in specially constructed reservoirs. To avoid problems of evaporation, these reservoirs will be located in underground cavities created by detonation of five-megaton nuclear devices in the style of Cannikin.

It is now conceded in Washington that Cro-Con was the real reason for the Cannikin test, and for the earlier Project Rulison explosion in Colorado. Environmentalists in the Midwest also speculate that Project Old Oaken Bucket in Kentucky is a related feasibility study. This project, now one-third completed, consists of filling Mammoth Cave with water diverted from the Red River in eastern Kentucky. The explained justification of Old Oaken Bucket has always been to meet the water supply needs of Cub Run, Kentucky, but local conservationists have never been completely satisfied by this explanation.

Environmental groups have been alarmed that evidently no Environmental Impact Statement, as required under Section 101(2) (c) of the National Environmental Policy Act, is to be issued for the Cro-Con Project. General Thwackem has given three reasons for this. First, it is argued that there is no conceivable way in which significant environmental damage could occur. Second, corps personnel take the position that NEPA is nonretroactive and that Cro-Con is simply a routine departmental updating of Albert Gallatin's April, 1808, report on proposed domestic improvements, including canals. The corps' argument is that since Gallatin did not have to write an impact statement, neither should they. Finally, the corps argues that the only slight risk of environmental damage would be from the AEC's still novel means of excavation through the use of nuclear devices. The corps feels that for this reason the impact statement is out of its jurisdiction, and should be prepared, if at all, by the AEC. Attempts to reach an AEC official associated with Cro-Con were unsuccessful (although more than 2,000 are said to be employed on the project), but one contact within the AEC's sprawling Germantown, Maryland, headquarters indicated that there are "compelling reasons" for not issuing an impact statement, although he could not divulge them "because of national security considerations."

Conservationists appear to have an ally within the Nixon Administration in the President's Council on Environmental Quality. The CEQ takes the position that it should have been consulted, and is agitating within the Administration to have alternatives considered. The Council finds that some impact from the Cro-Con is likely, and has quickly brought forward a different route. CEQ suggests improving the Intracoastal Waterway along the East Coast, constructing the Ochlawaha (Cross-Florida) Canal, developing the Intracoastal along the Gulf Coast, dredging up the Rio Grande as far as Alamosa, Colorado, cutting due west to Lake Powell, and following the corps proposal from that point. The Council points out that its proposal involves far less construction in areas that do not currently have rivers, and that the portion of the Rocky Mountains that would have to be leveled by nuclear explosions is "much less valuable, estheticwise."

The corps rejects the council's alternative for three reasons. First, it would expose the aircraft carriers to enemy submarines. Second, the CEQ route would have less value for movement of coal, development of inland ports, flood control, mid-continental water sports, and other benefits. Third, the corps proposal is so designed that a branch canal could be extended to Seattle, using basically the Missouri and Columbia Rivers, thus aiding the movement of supertankers from Puget Sound refineries to northeastern markets.

It is clearly too early for environmentalists to voice a unified opinion on the Cro-Con Canal, as the facts are not yet all in. Yet the corps has already accused the Sierra Club of "irresponsibility" in "raising baseless questions." "These environmentalists want us to return to the Stone Age," says General Thwackem. "National Security and economic prosperity demand a canal. They've blocked us in Panama and now they want to block us here. But here in the Corps we believe in Cro-Con, just as we believe in America, and no posy-plucker is going to tell us how to run our shop."

95

The Tocks Island Dam Fight

PETE du PONT

1972

Sharp-eyed readers will doubtless have discerned that the preceding article was a bit of satirical fantasy. For a more factual account of the fate of one Corps project we offer the illuminating adventures of a freshman member of Congress who innocently ran into the pork-barrel interests in the House of Representatives. The author was later elected governor of Delaware.

HAD I BEEN approached on the day of my swearing-in in January, 1971, and told that six months later I would be on my feet on the floor of the House of Representatives, opposing the powerful House Appropriations Committee, not to mention many of my colleagues in neighboring states, over an environmental dispute involving Tocks Island Dam and the National Environmental Policy Act, I would have returned an incredulous stare. After all, I had come to Congress intent on sinking my teeth into such knotty issues as drug abuse, foreign policy, the economy, and congressional reform. Such acronyms as NEPA were as new to my lexicon as I was to Capitol Hill. And though I cherished the beauty and heritage of the Delaware River Valley, I knew nothing about a certain tiny sliver of land lying north of the famed Delaware Water Gap known as Tocks Island.

This was all to change within a few months in a process which I can best describe as the "greening" of Pete du Pont. I would soon find myself girding for a solo attack, Don Quixote style, against some of the institutions which the elders in Congress revere the most—the Appropriations Committee, public works projects, and silent freshmen congressmen.

But my motive was more than a penchant for masochism. I sought to sharpen the teeth of NEPA and focus the concentration of the Congress on the need to stand firm in our national environmental policy. And, too, there was something truly worth saving—the Delaware Water Gap and the Delaware River itself.

From above Milford, Pennsylvania, to the famed Water Gap, the Delaware flows through one of the most beautiful river valleys in the country. To the east, in New Jersey, looms the forested ridge of Kittatinny Mountain, along which runs the Appalachian Trail. On the west, in Pennsylvania, swift streams and waterfalls splash over the rim of the Pocono upland and cut steep gorges filled with dark hemlock trees and rhododendron. Farm fields and woodlands quilt the valley itself along broad river bottoms and across rolling lands veined by brooks spangled here and there with ponds. Central to all is the majestic silver ribbon of the Delaware. Whether riffling or serenely pooled, this central reach of the river's overall Z-shaped course flows straight to Wallpack Bend, writhes back upon itself in a great double curve and then heads onward, smoothing its tones, to a dramatic thrust through the great gap near Stroudsburg, Pennsylvania.

This is historic country, with memories of Indian times. Dutchmen settled here before William Penn founded his colony. Wars came, and the valley linked George Washington's revolutionary forces in upper New York with those near Philadelphia. Today, the valley still retains that same peaceful, rural charm. And it is just "over the mountain" from the sprawling megalopolis, 62 miles from the heart of New York City, and 75 miles from the center of Philadelphia.

But late in 1962 much of this bucolic landscape was threatened by congressional authorization for construction of the Tocks Island Dam. The area would be flooded by construction of a 3,200-foot-long dam upstream from the Delaware Water Gap, 100 feet downstream from Tocks Island. The result would be a 37-mile-long lake extending as far north as Port Jervis, New York.

The dam was authorized by the Flood Control Act of 1962 primarily to prevent flooding, but also to provide supplies of water, hydroelectric power, and recreation opportunities.

The wheels of the Corps grind slowly, and construction on the dam was delayed for almost ten years for lack of available funds.

The passage of the National Environmental Policy Act of 1970 declared a whole new ball game in water resource development; for beyond the elaborate review procedures set out in the statute (which mean very little by themselves) lay the first major step towards development of comprehensive national resource planning.

The Corps' first gambit was to ignore the intent of NEPA. There were enough available studies on Tocks Island to "line the bottom of the reservoir" claimed one Corps official. The Tocks Island library was indeed voluminous, but the major environmental issues still remained undisclosed and unstudied. Prior to the Appropriations Committee deliberations in May of 1971, the Corps made a *pro forma* attempt to comply with NEPA by submitting an eight-page stagement on the projected environmental impact of the project. An eight-page report on the environmental impact of a $300 million dam! The supporters of the project were ready to begin construction.

In conjunction with my general objections to the Corps' build-now-study-later attitude, which seemed to violate the spirit of the National Environmental Policy Act, there were numerous questions concerning the impact of the dam on upper Delaware Bay. Meetings with local scientists convinced me that a serious ecological imbalance might occur with the impoundment. Biologists predicted that by shutting off annual spring flows, the lower part of the river would be robbed of nutrients, and certain areas of the upper bay would not be flushed out with fresh water. Many forms of fishlife — oysters in particular — could be adversely affected.

On the basis of this local environmental concern and in the belief that the National Environmental Policy Act would be meaningless if we simply used the impact statements as postscripts to construction, I decided to seek deletion of construction funds from the annual public works appropriation bill.

This decision marked the beginning of what was to be an initiation into the intricacies of the power structure on the Hill and of the frustration of trying to convince half of my 434 colleagues that a dam that had been under study for ten years needed further study. My first attempt at persuasion was with the House Public Works Appropriations Subcommittee. Delighted in having secured one half hour to present my views, I went to the hearings armed with voluminous memoranda and two experts from the University of Delaware. After receiving a gracious southern welcome from Chairman Joe Evins of Tennessee, I was quickly informed that I had only five minutes to present my testimony. Even that was divided three ways. My expert witnesses had just enough time to identify themselves before we were politely informed that the pressing business of the committee unfortunately prevented further testimony. In the eyes of the committee, it seemed to me, I was as unwelcome as the many concerned and articulate citizens who also came to plead with it.

Upon leaving the hearing room, I thought the prospects of convincing the rest of the House to be remote indeed. This feeling proved to be an underestimate of the difficulties that lay ahead.

As expected, the House Appropriations Committee reported out the annual Public Works Appropriation bill with some $3.7 million dollars designated for the construction of Tocks Island Dam. Only two days lay between the day the bill was reported out and its consideration on the floor. Engaging the enthusiasm — or even the attention — of harried Members of Congress for the amendment I was going to offer was a monumental task. We churned out "Dear Colleague" letters, called the offices of members who had good environmental records, and began the unfamiliar task of cornering members on the floor to request their assistance. Most were skeptical, some sympathetic, and none could understand why I insisted on this form of self-immolation. Most incredulous of all was our local newspaper reporter, seasoned by years of log rolling and pork barreling. "The Appropriations Committee? Joe Evins? Do they let Christians in too, or just the lions?" I did, however, receive able support from three colleagues: Hamilton Fish of New York, Guy Vander-Jagt of Michigan, and Pete McCloskey of California. Each promised to give floor speeches supporting my amendment.

"Let there be no mistake about the real issue in this case," I doggedly continued to a disinterested audience of tired colleagues. "It is not the Tocks Island Dam, it is not the Delaware River. The real issue here is whether we are going to have any teeth in our environmental laws." It was a hot July night, the kind Washington is famous for, and Congress wanted a vacation.

371

For hours I waited for the reading of the bill to progress as one issue after another sapped the patience of the world's greatest deliberative body. Then came the perennial dogfight over the Dickey-Lincoln hydroelectric project in Maine. As usual, a debate on the merits of public power vs. private power ensued. But even politicians become bored listening to politicians. Determined that this phoenix-like project was not going to be resurrected, the leadership terminated debate amid shouts of "Vote! Vote!" Dickey-Lincoln was reduced to dust.

Tired from the rigors of defending or abusing public power projects, members drained out of the hot chamber as my remarks concluded. Interrupted by groans of boredom, pleas to vote the amendment down, and the clap of the Speaker's gavel attempting to keep the House in order, I argued against build-now-study-later, and my time had expired.

Now the proponents of the project were recognized. A series of memorable oratories followed—the most acerbic of which exist only in my mind, since their authors later used their right to "revise or extend" their remarks to expunge them from the record. Representative Frank Thompson of New Jersey suggested that "everytime we want to erect a seesaw, someone objects that it will hurt the bunny rabbits."

The House grew impatient. And the end came swiftly. The record shows only that the motion offered by the gentleman from Delaware was rejected. In fact, a few young voices said "Aye," and the "Noes" rolled across that chamber like thunder. The lions had won, of course. And some miles upriver, the yellow bulldozers of the Corps of Engineers were fueled and ready to begin corrective surgery on the earth.

Despite the fact that the battle had been lost in one house of Congress the war continued elsewhere. In the course of the controversy over the Corps' draft of the environmental impact statement, Senator Clifford Case of New Jersey led a forceful and effective one-man crusade to have the project thoroughly reviewed by an impartial and independent body of experts. He called upon the Council on Environmental Quality, which oversees the NEPA process, to appoint the National Academy of Science or some such group to the task. Eventually CEQ arranged a compromise involving an interagency federal review of the Corps' final impact statement. The key finding of the review was contained in a 100-page report prepared by the Corps of Engineers' own consultants. The report, which confirmed the fears of conservationists, concluded that because of the high level of agricultural run-off and wastes from poultry farms along the Delaware, any impoundment would result in rapid eutrophication, jeopardizing the quality of the water supply and recreational aspects of the project.

CEQ immediately requested a moratorium on the project until the pollution sources could be identified and controlled.

The House and Senate Appropriations Committees responded in unprecedented fashion by deleting construction funds until these environmental problems are resolved. In the meantime, they have earmarked more than $15 million for land acquisition. This action suggests what may be the only rational alternative to the Tocks Island Dam, one long advocated by conservationists and most recently by the Park Service itself—a national recreational area utilizing all of the land intended for the original project plus 10,000 "extra" acres of scenic riverside lands that would otherwise be inundated. In other words, a park without a dam.

This revised plan would in effect represent the first and major step necessary toward protecting the river and riverscape from the urbanization of New York, New Jersey, and Pennsylvania. Complementing the park would be the proposed Delaware National Scenic River along the upper reaches of what is probably the East's most widely enjoyed canoeing stream.

The future of Tocks is still uncertain, but it appears that one major step has been taken. After years of subsidizing inefficient water management projects, the Congress is beginning to scrutinize the value of these investments, not only from a fiscal, but from an environmental standpoint. To strike a balance between efficient water resource management and minimal environmental damage, the government must embrace new, flexible alternatives to the big dam: the use of minor structures, flood plain zoning, water recycling, flood plain insurance, or high flow-skimming. This year Congress took its first step toward accepting the new science of water resource management. I hope it continues to go forward.

By 1977, even the Corps was persuaded that the Tocks Island Dam was a bad idea. Along with the Delaware River Basin Commission and the Department of the Interior, the Corps asked Congress to deauthorize the project. But hard-line dam lovers in Congress were hanging tough and putting up a battle against bills to add the Middle Delaware to the National Wild and Scenic Rivers System. However, this status was awarded to the Middle Delaware under the "omnibus parks bill" of 1978—a Congressional action which should spell the end of the Tocks Island Dam.

Before we leave the Corps of Engineers, we should note that the agency has been officially commended by the Sierra Club for several actions, including the protection of San Francisco Bay marshlands from filling, and restoration of a large tidal marsh in the Bay which had been diked as a salt pond. Nationally, the club has also backed the retention of Corps jurisdiction over wetlands under a law that gives the engineers a strong environmental mandate to protect wildlife ponds and marshes. The Corps has also been active in developing water-recycling projects of the kind strongly approved by environmentalists. The Corps now has many environmentally minded people on its staff. However, the club still actively opposes Corps projects that conflict with environmental goals.

96

America's Beleaguered Coasts

ELLEN WINCHESTER

1977

If we want a coast bristling with oil rigs, polluted with human and industrial wastes, lined with hotels, power plants, and second homes, we can have it—easily. What will be difficult is to make the decisions for a coast that will meet many different human needs, including those of contemplation and spiritual renewal. As the author points out, the legislative tools to assure this kind of coast are available if conservationists will use them.

Ellen Winchester has served as chairman of the Sierra Club's National Energy Committee and as secretary of the Board of Directors.

In the mid-'70s, with the support of the club and other conservation groups, California voters enacted a plan that preserves scenic areas of the coast, and confines development to areas where industry, tourism, or housing are already located.

THE COASTS OF AMERICA are under siege. New job opportunities and the almost mystical attraction of these vulnerable margins of land and sea are swelling population growth in coastal areas three times as fast as elsewhere. Half of all Americans now live within a fifty-mile coastal strip. This pressure is destroying the land they occupy. Where stretches of the coast are not already overcrowded, polluted, bristling with oil rigs or converted to commercial corridors or industrial wastelands, they are almost everywhere candidates for similar destruction. Soon, unless many people quickly organize to influence implementation of new coastal legislation, the only seascapes left to lift the hearts of poets, lovers, and weary pilgrims seeking spiritual renewal will be limited to national and state parks and wildlife refuges.

The loss is not merely one of aesthetics; it is also one of food in a world hungry for protein. Coastal estuaries are the nurseries of marine life, and coastal waters are the richest fisheries. Already, a quarter of all estuaries in the United States have been destroyed or severely damaged; all the rest have been degraded to some degree. Fish catches are decreasing, and large oil slicks shift with the wind on the waters of our bays and fishing grounds.

Florida's 150-mile-long Big Bend, where the peninsula curves northwest and west at the base of the continent, is the strip of coast I know best. Because most of its shore is marshland, and its fishing and forest-products economies have always been depressed, the land is little developed and sparsely populated. Real estate billboards advertise "Selling Florida's Last Frontier." Yet even a thinly settled remnant of coast like the Big Bend suffers from hazards common along the coastline of North America.

Erosion: As elsewhere in the Southeast where land is sinking, wave action alone causes beach erosion, without help from man or wind. In late summer, when nature moves our sand beach out to a sand bar, high tides lap the exposed roots of our pines, and the grisly cemetery of stumps and snags at low tide reminds us of the destiny of our whole property. When people carve up naturally dynamic oceanfront property into plots, erosion can cause knotty legal problems. For example, should a beach owner be entitled to build a bulkhead and fill behind it to capture new erosion-caused land? When groins and bulkheads are built to protect one person's beach by interrupting natural sand transport to the beach, who has what rights in court? A concept of shifting and rolling easement to permit ownership to follow changing shorelines is gaining favor among environmental lawyers.

With the Army Corps of Engineers' beach-restoration projects costing more than a million dollars a mile, Florida is slowly, county by county, establishing beach set-back lines determined partly by flood tides, partly by vegetative criteria. Their purpose is to allow enough room for natural processes to operate. New housing, put on pilings to comply with the National Flood Insurance Act, does less harm to wetlands and primary dunes than filling or bulldozing to build on poured concrete slabs, once the common practice.

Development: Directly across St. George Sound from us lie the sloping, sleepy-looking prominences of a twenty-eight-mile-long, dune-covered barrier island of the same name. A combination of a state park at one end, land speculators and the Franklin County commissioners have together saved it from high-density vacation homes following the construction of a bridge. The bay produces eighty-seven percent of Florida's oysters. The sewage, sediment runoff, and pleasure-boat traffic that would result from 20,000 to 50,000 new residents on the island would ruin the world of the oyster. So far, fortunately, the county commissioners have not been persuaded they could do better fleecing summer residents than maintaining a fishing economy.

Dredging: Other threats bear down on the bay shellfish. The wooded, 107-mile-long Apalachicola River already serves as a shallow barge canal for industry in Alabama and Georgia. It is annually threatened with dredging and damming by the Corps of Engineers to accommodate bigger barges. The deeper the barge channel, the greater the threat that toxic sediments from upriver industrial development, induced by the cheap transportation, will pollute the estuarine system. As things stand, the forested floodplain both absorbs pollutants before they reach the bay and produces organic detritus upon which marine life depends.

Another barge channel, the Intracoastal Waterway, threads behind barrier islands from the Mississippi River to Carrabelle, a Big Bend port for shrimpers. There, shipping moves into the Gulf around Alligator Point and St. Marks Wildlife Refuge, site of the waterway's so-called missing link. St. Marks contains a 17,500-acre wilderness area, is wintering ground for birds of the North, and year-round home for egrets, gallinules, limpkins, white pelicans, ibis, bald eagles, osprey, turkey, alligator, deer and mosquitoes. Perhaps wilderness designation can save the refuge from the waterway, but the Army Corps' canal projects have more lives than a cat.

Oil Pollution: From St. Marks, the marshes of the Big Bend, formed by the deltas of a thousand little streams, extend a hundred miles to Cedar Key. In coastal marshes and estuaries nature is at her most productive, often exceeding on a per-acre basis agricultural yields by a factor of two or more. Here, decomposing grasses provide a rich broth to nourish phytoplankton, food for tiny crustaceans and zooplankton. These in turn are the nursery diet of shellfish and fishes consumed by larger aquatic creatures, some of which, particularly red snapper, grouper, mullet and flounder, are the basis of the sport and commercial fishing in the northeastern Gulf of Mexico. In 1973, part of the outer continental shelf (OCS) due west of these marshes was leased, along with other tracts, for oil and gas drilling at a cost of $1.5 billion to the oil companies. As yet no oil has been found.

Unfortunately, another source of oil trouble looms ahead: supertankers. Two deepwater ports, LOOP off Louisiana and SEADOCK off Freeport, Texas, have permits for construction. One supertanker catastrophe could irreversibly destroy the marshlands of the Big Bend, where no barrier islands like those to the west stand offshore to stem the tide of oil. Fifty-one thousand tons of crude spilled by the tanker *Metula* two years ago coated seventy-five miles in the Straits of Magellan with an oil emulsion fifty to 200 feet wide and one to four inches deep. Since the recent epidemic of Liberian tanker spills, even the Coast Guard has admitted that no adequate means exist of containing or cleaning up spills at sea.

Even without a catastrophic spill, the chronic small ones associated with tanker traffic—Exxon has already chartered ships to bring Alaskan oil to Gulf and East Coast ports—are a threat to Gulf sea grasses, another marine food source, and other life forms inhabiting the marsh. Hydrocarbons stored in the fatty tissue of fish and shellfish adversely affect their life cycles and productivity in ways not yet fully understood.

The threats to Florida's Big Bend from various human enterprises, in both their variety and the complacency with which they are pursued, typify the situation along all our coasts. Far to the north, a real coastal frontier 6,640 miles long awaits swift, irreversible change from oil and gas development.

Oil and gas development anywhere on the Alaskan OCS, from the Beaufort Sea—summer home of myriad birds; refuge of beluga whales, polar bears, seals and sea lions — all around the peninsula, will be done under the most adverse conditions the industry has ever encountered, including earthquakes, undersea landslides, tidal waves, pack ice and high seas and winds.

As an example of risk, spills on tracts near Kodiak Island in the Gulf of Alaska, to be leased in November unless delayed by Secretary Andrus' review of leasing schedules, will endanger the breeding grounds for scallops, salmon, crab and shrimp that have made Kodiak home of the second largest fishing port in the nation. On tidal flats in this gulf, densities of more than 250,000 shorebirds per square mile have been observed.

Once OSC or Prudhoe Bay oil safely leaves Alaskan waters, its potential for coastal damage continues — all the way around the continent.

Other Pollutants: Oil from marine sources has taken the headlines this year, yet it is a relatively new stress on coastal habitats. More familiar and still dangerous are the effluents from chemical industries; sulfite from pulp mills; fertilizer, pesticide and sediment run-off from agriculture and lumbering; and used lubricating oil dumped in sewers, which is perhaps greater in volume even now than oil from tankers. Whether the ocean can safely serve as a dump for the sewage of the continent's coastal cities is another question raised with growing concern by marine biologists. Red tides of mysterious origin seem to be increasing. The closing of shellfish beds and bathing beaches because of high coliform-bacteria counts is common. Sewage-caused disease among fish has been documented, but the extent and gravity of the problem has not been studied sufficiently.

The rapid proliferation of coastal electric-power plants has created a new stress on water quality. Cooling towers recirculate water and build up mineral concentrations that periodically must be flushed. Thermal discharge has been known to disrupt an ecosystem for a distance of thirty-five miles, kill corals and harm marine grasses. With an open cooling system, thirty percent or more of the annual brood of estuarine spawning fish can be killed by the operation of a single 1,000-megawatt plant located in a semi-enclosed system, such as the Indian Point nuclear-power plant on the Hudson River.

Dredge and Fill: But damaging as pollutants are now, and promise to become, the worst harm to the coastal zone historically has been its steady obliteration by earth-moving machinery, the harbor dredging and wetlands-fill construction that has built much of present-day Seattle, Boston, New York, and other major and minor coastal cities.

Port Development: The development of supertankers too large for existing ports, and the nation's escalating energy appetite have increased demands for new oil and coal ports. As of this writing, site selection for West Coast ports to receive Alaskan oil and gas is the focus of much controversy from Long Beach to Puget Sound. Deepwater ports are being studied for Maine, North Carolina, and New Jersey. A coal port on Lake Superior to supply power plants in Chicago, Detroit, Cleveland and Buffalo is predicted to double lake shipping, with attendant dock-side dredging and chronic oil spillage.

Behind the barrier islands of South Carolina and Georgia is one of the least industrialized coastlines in the continental United States. It consists almost entirely of wetlands—easy picking for ports, submarine bases, oil refineries, power plants and paper mills. An unanswered question of particular concern to the southeastern states is the effect that the Gulf Stream, with its unchartable swirls and eddies, would have on the transport of pollutants.

Unrelenting Nature: All of this human misuse and overuse of the coastal zone would be less costly if the forces of nature were more kind. Seismic catastrophes make headlines, but the steady loss of cliff shorelines on the West Coast, under the attack of Pacific storms or the pace of erosion on low-lying Gulf Coast deltas, is less publicized. Between the Brazos and Colorado rivers in Texas, erosion has pushed back the shoreline 300 feet in sixteen years. The fact that people have, by dams and divisions, steadily reduced the supply of river sediments to the ocean may well have contributed to these problems.

The Open Space Institute and the National Resources Defense Council have found that forty-three of eighty-one barrier islands from Georgia to Virginia are in danger of destruction through real estate development that eliminates the natural defense of dunes and vegetation to the violence of wind-driven water. All of the Maryland and Delaware ocean shorelines and all but seventeen miles of the New Jersey shore are considered critical erosion areas.

So it goes.

Our grandchildren will not let us off with a Vonnegut shrug, however, especially since we have the legislation to protect their heritage. Our major tool, the Coastal Zone Management (CZM) Act of 1972, as amended in 1976, is designed to strengthen state control of coastal land and water. All states and territories to which the act applies are working on state plans for coastal management to be submitted to the Secretary of Commerce for approval. Merely to comply with this first step required that each governor designate a state agency to inventory that state's coastal resources, pinpoint areas of special concern and see that a plan to protect them gets down on paper. In many states this was the first effort ever made to focus state attention on coastal problems.

The Clean Air, Ocean Dumping, and Federal Water Pollution Control Acts (FWPCA) can also be forceful tools for protecting coastal values if damaging amendments are not passed by this Congress.

Saving a continental margin under siege is not a task for people who discourage easily. Unless enough determined people, the kind who join the Sierra Club, lead the effort to stop the destruction of beaches and estuaries, the degradation of air and water quality, and unplanned urban coastal land use, even the farthest mountains and the most remote forests cannot compensate us for the consequences.

97

Long Island Sound—The Urban Sea

DONALD F. SQUIRES

1972

Sketched here is an all-too-real scenario that may mean the end of Long Island Sound as we know it. Dr. Squires' assessment of the present and future of Long Island Sound could apply to most of the country's other "urban seas": Puget Sound, Chesapeake Bay, Narragansett Bay, the Great Lakes.

Yet, even as we reprint this article, the future for Long Island Sound has brightened. A bill has been introduced into Congress that would create a federally owned and supported system of parks, beaches, and wildlife areas on both the New York and Connecticut shorelines. The Long Island Sound Heritage Program, proposed in the bill, is supported by the Nassau County Group and the Atlantic Chapter of the Sierra Club, as well as other conservation organizations.

At the time this was written, the author was Director of the Marine Sciences Research Center at the State University of New York, Stony Brook.

SOME 10,000 YEARS AGO the great wall of ice which covered most of northern North America stalled in its advance, retreated and advanced again. Two great ridges of sand and gravel, over 100 miles in length and up to 30 miles in width, were piled up on the Continental Shelf ten to fifteen miles off the Connecticut shore forming, when the ice withdrew, Long Island. As the ice continued its retreat a fresh water lake was formed in the embayment between the glacial ice on the Connecticut shore and Long Island. This soon was replaced by sea water, forming what is now Long Island Sound.

Because of this geological history, Long Island Sound is not a typical estuary with a great river at one end, the sea at the other. The Sound is an enclosed arm of the Atlantic Ocean, with several important rivers such as the East Housatonic, Connecticut and Thames Rivers, draining into it. But this is not what makes Long Island Sound of interest today, but rather the fact that this body of water has become an urban sea.

Today the Sound is a playground for some 12 million people. On its shores the citizens of New York and Connecticut bathe (where possible), boat, race, fish, bird watch, dig for clams (where possible), and earn a living through shell fishing and fin fishing. Today the Sound is also used as a dumping ground for 1.8 million tons of dredge tailings, materials from metropolitan excavations, and for waste products of certain industries. Additionally, sixty municipal sewage treatment plants discharge over 170 million gallons of waste water per day into the Sound, and it receives the waste heat of power plants generating more than 3,000 megawatts.

What makes this urban sea interesting is that from the Metropolitan complex of Queens and Westchester Counties on the western boundaries of the Sound, the scene changes slowly and steadily to the east as urbanization gives way to suburbia and finally to the agricultural areas of eastern Long Island and eastern Connecticut. (Suffolk County, Long Island, is the leading agricultural county in New York State.) Here, at the eastern end of the Sound, the cluttered, industrialized shoreline and the hustle and bustle of harbor, airports and bridges has given way to the open coasts which still have vestiges of their earlier maritime history. Mystic Seaport, Connecticut, with its whaling museum and square riggers, is matched by the quaint village of Sag Harbor, Long Island and its whaling museum and traditions. Old oyster industries, once a multi-million dollar venture in Long Island Sound, still hang on, but only a few companies are still fighting the increased costs of labor, starfish, and pollution. The famous Stonington fishing fleet still operates and the Stonington dragger, though no longer built, is still a familiar sight in this area.

Long Island Sound presents the full spectrum of man's impact on the sea from the urban sea at the western end to the open, relatively unpolluted waters at the eastern end. The eastern end of the Sound is relatively open and has good exchange of water between the Atlantic Ocean and Block Island Sound. At the western end, access to the sea is greatly constricted through the East River.

What has happened to Long Island Sound over the years? Nothing dramatic. Just a slow, general, wasting through misuse coupled with a general indifference because the problems were not observable by the public.

The most pressing problem of Long Island Sound, to isolate the one single factor to which to attribute its present decay, is the concentration of sewage outfalls in the western end. The impact of sewage and the resulting biological stimulation from the nutrient materials placed in the waters has caused responsible reporters to project the imminent death of Long Island Sound — the difficulty is to define "death." In the westernmost portion of the Sound, the concentrations of nitrogen and phosphorus are among the highest in marine waters anywhere in the world.

Each year the tiny plants of the sea, the phytoplankton, the base of the entire food chain of the sea, respond to the lengthening day and the slight warming of the water temperatures by increasing in numbers. This rapid growth of the phytoplankton is termed a bloom, and the growth intensity of the bloom is governed to a large extent by the nutrient materials in the waters. As man has increased the nutrient levels of the Sound through introduction of sewage, the intensity of the blooms has increased with time until they have reached the critical point at which the wildly developing populations of phytoplankton have gone beyond the point of being beneficial to the environment and have become, at their peaks, detrimental.

The problem of extreme phytoplankton blooms, the result of a process called eutrophication, has many dimensions. Upon death of the phytoplankton individuals, many species of which have very short life spans, the organic material of the cells sinks and is oxidized by the dissolved oxygen contained in the waters. Organic material added to the Sound through sewage also utilizes oxygen in the waters, further reducing amount of oxygen available to organisms living at or near the bottom. Depletion of oxygen in the western portion of the Sound has reached levels which are now critical for many months of the year—and new sewage plants being developed by communities on both the Connecticut and Long Island Shores call for additional outfalls. Despite the fact that the sewage will be "highly" treated, the treatment is not sufficient to remove the nutrients from the waters and the situation can be expected to worsen.

Long Island Sound once boasted a commercial fishery of consequence, but today there are very few commercial fishing activities left. Shell fisheries, once an important industry for Long Island Sound, are hard pressed on many fronts. Oyster spat produced in Connecticut were formerly taken out to beds in Long Island Sound to grow to market size. High quality marketable oysters were produced in large quantities until the mid-1950's when the industry was decimated by an influx of predatory starfish. The cause of the invasion is still unknown and the starfish remain. Their presence alone, but with the situation worsened by pollution, has resulted in the almost complete collapse of the Long Island Sound oyster industry.

Long Island Sound is the unhappy recipient of 1.8 million tons of debris dumped yearly in its nineteen designated dumping grounds. The materials dumped here consist primarily of dredge spoils from harbor management programs. These spoils present a very real hazard, creating yet another drain upon the oxygen of its waters through release of contained nutrients. It may also release various toxic or deleterious chemicals derived from industrial wastes into the waters of the Sound.

Dredging operations are manifold in the waters of Long Island Sound. They range in scope from the maintenance of major channels for commercial shipping to the opening of shallow embayments for recreational boating and the construction of marinas. To meet these demands, local authorities dredged wetlands at increasing rates. Recently the trend has slowed as pressure from conservation groups and the environmental community has led, in certain areas, to the placing of very high priority upon public acquisition of wetlands and their preservation as open space and vital segments of the marine ecosystem. However, the action came sufficiently late so that between 1954 and 1964 over 29 percent of the wetlands of Long Island were lost.

Oil is a perpetual problem. Both sides of the Sound are dotted by tank farms and oil transhipment facilities. In 1970 and 1971 major spills of over

300,000 and 600,000 gallons occurred. However, potentially more serious, and more difficult to assess, is the cumulative effect of the small spills occurring at transhipment points over long periods of time.

The catalogue of woes of Long Island's waters has been scarcely touched. Unwritten here are the effects of pesticides, PCB's, agricultural run-off, changes in freshwater run-off through increasing utilization of ground-waters on Long Island, the effects of highway expansion upon recreational areas, and the process of urbanization. To end on such an unhappy note is to do Long Island Sound's clamoring public a great disservice. There is a great deal of positive action and, to a large extent, it has been generated by pressures from the public who now clearly see the deteriorating water quality.

Citizens' groups have emerged as an active and potent force in guiding public opinion and governmental action. Groups such as the Nature Conservancy, the Audubon Society, and more recently the Sierra Club, are continuing long standing efforts to conserve the natural resources of the Sound.

Will the recuperative forces of Long Island Sound be pushed to the point beyond which environmental quality precipitously declines? The prospects for the urban sea are linked to the future of the cities. If we save the cities, restoring the quality of their environment and life experiences, we can do the same for the urban sea which provides so much life enhancement for the populace living on its shores.

98

Picking Up the Pieces of the Tuolumne

RODERICK NASH and

ROBERT HACKAMACK

1976

The National Wild and Scenic Rivers System would not amount to much if it only applied to rivers that are wild and scenic from headwaters to mouth. Few such rivers remain. But there are significant stretches of many rivers that retain many of the pristine qualities of their natural condition. One of these is the Tuolumne, the focus of the Sierra Club's biggest early-day battle, and the scene now of an effort to preserve what is left.

Roderick Nash of the University of California at Santa Barbara is author of Wilderness and the American Mind, *and Robert Hackamack is a member of the Sierra Club's Northern California Regional Conservation Committee.*

PROTECTING WILDERNESS VALUES and natural beauty does not always involve saving large expanses of virgin land. Increasingly it means picking up the remains after the developers have had their innings. The landscape that results is a patchwork: some development, some wildness—satisfaction of man's material needs and recognition that he cannot live by bread alone.

The 158-mile long Tuolumne River drains the western Sierra north of the Merced River and its Yosemite Valley. In 1913 Congress authorized a dam on the Tuolumne at the lower end of the spectacular Hetch Hetchy Valley within Yosemite National Park. With his last energy, an aged John Muir fought savagely to keep the developers out of his "temple." But Muir lost, and the Tuolumne began supplying drinking water and electricity, largely to San Francisco. Today five major dams and powerhouses squeeze still more from the river. Yet, unbelievably, the Tuolumne remains alive, if not altogether well, as a wild river. In fact, a twenty-six-mile section downstream from Hetch Hetchy is, mile for mile, the most formidable whitewater river run in the American West.

The developed portions of the Tuolumne now serve civilization. The undeveloped sections serve man's need to escape, periodically, from that civilization. Today's Tuolumne is a realistic compromise; tomorrow's is the subject of an intensifying local, state, and national controversy. The same vertical drop of fifty-four feet per mile (seven times that of the Colorado in the Grand Canyon) that makes the twenty-six-mile reach of the middle Tuolumne a mecca for trout fishermen, whitewater boaters and connoisseurs of river scenery also attracts dam builders. Both contingents have specific agendas for the Tuolumne. Developers propose three more dams and two more powerhouses on the middle river. Preservationists argue that this same stretch of the Tuolumne should be protected in the National Wild and Scenic Rivers System. There is no more room for compromise. The Tuolumne's future hangs squarely in the balance of America's values.

San Francisco's aqueduct draws some water from Hetch Hetchy. But the city is required by the Department of the Interior to maintain the trout habitat with a minimum flow. However, seven miles downstream from the national park boundary, the discharge of the Dion Holm Powerhouse on Cherry Creek augments the river. There are also natural increments from tributaries such as the south, middle and north forks of the Tuolumne, Jawbone Creek, Clavey River, Indian Creek and Big Creek. The upshot is that thirteen miles below Hetch Hetchy the Tuolumne gets its act as a river together again. It is big enough for kayaks, whitewater canoes and modified rafts at this point, and the fishing is excellent. Eight miles farther downstream, at Lumsden Campground, river runners confront eighteen incredible miles.

The dirt road that snakes down the steep southern wall of the Tuolumne Canyon to Lumsden is the last one seen until Ward's Ferry Bridge at the head of the Don Pedro Reservoir. It is easy to spend three days making the whitewater run between the roads and, because of the special challenge of the Tuolumne, feel as if you had been away for a week. In theory, the river can be run in a matter of hours. But the Tuolumne often spoils the best laid plans. Particularly during the high water of the spring runoff, it is relentless. One rapid blends into another. Only occasionally can a boatman find an eddy in which to catch his breath. Then, looking back upstream, the river seems like a white staircase descending the Sierra. At Clavey Falls it pounds through one of the West's undisputedly great rapids.

Even the most hardened whitewater veterans are stunned when they see Clavey Falls for the first time. Caused by the confluence of the Clavey River on the right side and a two-hundred-foot cliff on the left, the rapid begins with a fifteen-foot drop—a maelstrom of green and white water crashing over ominous black rocks. In a successful run boats drop over the falls inches away from dagger rocks on the left and right. And this is only the beginning of Clavey Falls. There is a cliff to slam, rocks to smash boats upon or wrap them around, "holes" ready to flip boats, ledges waiting to tear out their bottoms and, finally, a hundred yards of run-of-the-mill ten- to twelve-foot waves. Clavey is, as they say on the rivers, a "hummer."

Within a half-day's drive of fifteen million people, it is astonishing that the middle Tuolumne was not run until the 1960s. Kayaks pioneered, in 1965 and 1968, and in 1969 the first inflatable rafts challenged the Tuolumne. The following year saw the hesitant beginning of commercial river-running. In time came confidence and better equipment. The United States Forest Service, which regulates the runnable section of the Tuolumne, estimates that 6,500 persons, about equally divided between commercially guided parties and private groups, travel on the Tuolumne annually. With the Stanislaus River, just to the north, slated for submergence behind the bitterly contested New Melones Dam, the popularity of the Tuolumne as one of California's last runnable whitewater rivers will certainly increase.

Whitewater boating on the Tuolumne no sooner began than it appeared destined to end. On December 4, 1968, the San Francisco Public Utilities Commission released a report proposing more intensive use of the Tuolumne's "remaining power drop" for hydroelectric generating capacity. Indeed, the proposal was for near-total use. A new dam and reservoir were proposed for the river below O'Shaughnessy Dam near the Cherry creek confluence. From there, water would be conducted by tunnel through Jaw-bone Ridge into the Clavey River six miles upstream from the Tuolumne and Clavey Falls. The water would then be channeled to a power plant located at the foot of Clavey Falls. A twelve-mile-long reservoir created by a dam at Ward's Ferry would complete the destruction of the last runnable section of the Tuolumne.

Initially the San Francisco proposal did not elicit much opposition. Most Americans did not know what was at stake. They assumed that the value of the Tuolumne as a recreational resource ended with the closing of the gates of O'Shaughnessy Dam. Few could correct this impression. River running was in its infancy as a sport.

The Sierra Club, however, was instinctively suspicious of San Francisco's plans for the Tuolumne. Like the Alamo, Hetch Hetchy's loss was remembered. Indeed, recollection of that lost valley helped fuel the successful campaign against dams in Dinosaur National Monument in the 1950s and in the Grand Canyon of the Colorado a decade later. So when the first river-runners reported that there was a remarkable river worth protecting below Hetch Hetchy, the Sierra Club swung into action. The result was a publication by Robert W. Hackamack and Thorne B. Gray entitled *The Tuolumne River: A Report on Conflicting Goals with Emphasis on the Middle River* (1970) and a recommendation: instead of placing more dams in the Tuolumne watershed, the Club proposed to delete some. Eleanor Dam, built in 1918 on a tributary of the Tuolumne to generate power for the larger Hetch Hetchy project, could, it was argued, be removed without great loss to anyone. Some went further. Michael McCloskey, Sierra Club executive director, made San Francisco headlines with the suggestion that O'Shaughnessy Dam be removed and the Tuolumne allowed to return to its ancestral course through Hetch Hetchy. "We've already had the experience of reclaiming logged-over land for parks," McCloskey reasoned. "We think it's time the same concept be applied to dams." McCloskey's position drew force from the fact that the new Don Pedro Dam, completed in 1971 on the lower Tuolumne, could provide all the flood-control and irrigation services expected by residents of the San Joaquin Valley. And San Francisco could explore alternate sources of municipal water supply including waste-water recycling and drawing from the Sacramento-San Joaquin Delta. It was also possible to think the unthinkable: use less.

On January 3, 1975, the controversial middle stretch of the Tuolumne was designated a "study" river under an amendment to the federal Wild and Scenic Rivers Act. Ensuing public hearings, conducted during the death throes of the Stanislaus, revealed overwhelming support for protection. Congress will have the final word, probably not before 1980. Meanwhile the hydropower interests stepped up their campaign. In June 1976 the Modesto and Turlock irrigation districts filed an application with the Federal Power Commission for a three-dam, $473-million complex on the Tuolumne. San Francisco joined the application in September, with Commissioner Larsen dissenting. The proposals rested on suspicious and self-serving benefit-cost ratios that drew heavily on air conditioning and other peak-power uses, which many felt constituted insufficient reasons for completing the destruction of the Tuolumne as a living river. Representative of the developers' point of view was the statement of Oral L. Moore, general manager of the

Hetch Hetchy system. "As I see it," opined Moore, "it's just another hot canyon—a kind of Disneyland."

Looming over the determination of the future of the last runnable white-water on the Tuolumne is the memory of the drowned Hetch Hetchy Valley. The 1913 decision to build a dam there closed options. Four other major dam-powerhouse complexes similarly curtailed choices in other parts of the watershed. Protection of the free-flowing Tuolumne below the Hetch Hetchy keeps options open. If the agribusinesses and utility conglomerates ever become so starved for water, energy and revenue that it seems in the nation's interest to complete the conquest of the entire Tuolumne, that possibility still exists. But if, on the other hand, wild rivers continue to win friends and favorably influence the quality of people's lives, the middle Tuolumne will still be dancing in the sun.

A final truth must not be forgotten in deciding the future of the Tuolumne. There is nothing inherently wrong with dams and hydropower installations. We all are the beneficiaries of these things. But of every new proposal involving the loss of living rivers society must ask if the increased benefits of extending the control of technological civilization really compensate for the loss to our culture of an increasingly rare wildness. This should be the ultimate cost-benefit analysis. Performing one is never simple given the diverse priorities in American society, but surely the intensity of civilization in a given region is an important determinant. Dammed rivers and flatwater reservoirs are common in California. The whitewater Stanislaus is apparently doomed. Much of the Tuolumne is already dammed. The preservation of the magnificent pieces that are left should be an imperative that the state and the nation cannot ignore.

99
The West Against Itself

BERNARD DeVOTO

1947

The late Bernard DeVoto, pen dipped in acid, habitually took out after the plunderers of our natural resources with a vehemence and biting eloquence that at its best recalled the more pungent prose of Mark Twain. Here his attack is upon economic interests who were trying in the late 1940s to "liquidate all public ownership of grazing land and forest land in the United States" in order to plunder that land

386

without government restraint. Their efforts were unsuccessful, partly owing to De-Voto's exposure of their tactics in Harper's *magazine, whose editors gave kind permission for the material to be reprinted in the* Bulletin *and now in this book.*

The Taylor Grazing Act of 1934, to which DeVoto refers, was the first Congressional effort to protect the public lands from overgrazing. In 1977 Congress passed the Forest Land Policy and Management Act (the "BLM Organic Act") that set more stringent regulations and, just as important, gave the Department of Interior's Bureau of Land Management effective enforcement authority.

Time and tactics have changed since DeVoto wrote these words, but, as we shall see in succeeding articles, the danger of private exploitation of public resources continues in new forms—and demands new DeVotos to sound the alarms.

Historian, novelist, essayist, literary critic, and theorist of the martini, DeVoto wrote "The Easy Chair" column in Harper's, *and, as we have seen earlier, helped win the early Colorado River battles.*

IN HARPER'S FOR AUGUST 1934, I called the West "the plundered province." The phrase has proved so useful to Western writers and orators that it has superseded various phrases which through generations of Western resentment designated the same thing. We must realize that it does designate a thing; that, whatever the phrases, there is a reality behind them. Economically the West has always been a province of the East and it has always been plundered.

The first wealth produced in the West was furs, mainly beaver furs. It made a good many Easterners rich. Partnerships and corporations sent technical specialists—trappers and Indian traders—into the West to bring out the furs. . . . They cleaned up and by 1840 they had cleaned the West out. A century later, beaver has not yet come back.

The development of the mineral West began in 1849. Mining is the type-example of Western exploitation. . . . Mining is liquidation. You clean out the deposit, exhaust the lode, and move on. Hundreds of ghost towns in the West, and hundreds of more pathetic towns where a little human life lingers on after economic death, signalize this inexorable fact. You clean up and get out—and you don't give a damn, especially if you are a stockholder in the East.

So we come to the business which created the West's most powerful illusion about itself and, though this is not immediately apparent, has done more damage to the West than any other. The cattle business.

The cattlemen came from elsewhere into the empty West. . . . They thought of themselves as Westerners and they did live in the West, but they were the enemies of everyone else who lived there. They kept sheepmen, their natural and eventual allies, out of the West wherever and as long as they could, slaughtering herds and frequently herdsmen. They did their utmost to keep the nester—the farmer, the actual settler, the man who could create local and permanent wealth—out of the West and to terrorize or bankrupt him where he could not be kept out. And the big cattlemen squeezed out the

387

little ones wherever possible, grabbing the water rights, foreclosing small holdings, frequently hiring gunmen to murder them. . . .

Two facts about the cattle business have priority over all the rest. First, the Cattle Kingdom never did own more than a minute fraction of one per cent of the range it grazed: it was national domain, it belonged to the people of the United States. They do not own the range now: mostly it belongs to you and me, and since the fees they pay for using public land are much smaller than those they pay for using private land, those fees are in effect one of a number of subsidies we pay them. But they always acted as if they owned the public range and act so now; they convinced themselves that it belonged to them and now believe it does; and they are trying to take title to it. Second, the cattle business does not have to be conducted as liquidation but throughout history its management has always tended to conduct it on that basis.

The Cattle Kingdom overgrazed the range so drastically—fed so many more cattle than the range could support without damage—that the processes of nature were disrupted. Since those high and far-off days the range has never been capable of supporting anything like the number of cattle it could have supported if the cattle barons had not maimed it. It never will be capable of supporting a proper number again during the geological epoch in which civilization exists.

There remains lumbering. It perpetrated greater frauds against the people of the United States than any other Western business—and that is a superlative of cosmic size. It was a business of total liquidation: when a tree is cut, a century or two centuries may be required to grow another one and perhaps another one cannot be grown at all. . . . The effects of denuding a forest extend as far as fire may go and beyond that as far as any of the streams on the watershed it belongs to may be used for human purposes or are capable of affecting life, property, or society.

Lumbering, however, shows several deviations from the Western pattern. First, though a greater part of the timber came into Eastern ownership, . . . an important fraction of it came into the hands of Westerners. Second, the national government got on the job in time to protect vast areas of forest from liquidation—and to protect the heart of the West from geological extinction. Third, a good many of the big operators got the idea in time and it is mainly they who are now trying to maintain privately owned Western forests as a permanent source of wealth, whereas the drive to liquidate all forests comes most vociferously from small operators, who have neither the capital nor the timber reserves for long-term operation.

These then, with power and irrigation which we may skip for the moment, are the businesses founded on the West's natural resources.

New Deal measures slowed the liquidation of resources and substituted measures of permanent yield. They operated to rehabilitate depleted resources, halt and repair erosion, rebuild soil, and restore areas of social decay. . . . The West greeted these measures characteristically: demanding more and more of them, demanding further government help in taking advantage of them, furiously denouncing the government for paternalism, and trying to avoid all regulation.

The West with its hat held out beseeching the expenditure on its behalf of federal money. . . . You can hardly find an editorial page in the West that is not demanding as Western right, as compensation for the West, and as assistance toward Western liberation, the expenditure of more federal funds. More government money . . . the improvement of Western agriculture, the replenishment of soils, the instruction of farmers; . . . the improvement of stock and range, quarantine, research; for fire protection in the logging business; for drainage; for reseeding and reforestation of private lands; for roads; for weather service; and always for dams, canals, and the whole program of reclamation. But at the same time: hands off.

The second column of the editorial page is sure to be a ringing demand for the government to get out of business, to stop impeding initiative, to break the shackles of regulation with which it has fettered enterprise, to abjure its philosophy of suppressing liberty, and to stop giving money to people who will only fill the bathtub with coal.

It shakes down to a platform: get out and give us more money. . . . It reveals the West's attitude toward the federal intervention which alone was powerful enough to save Western natural resources from total control and quick liquidation by the absentee Eastern ownership. For that preservation the West is grateful to the government. But there was and still is a fundamental defect: federal intervention has also preserved those resources from locally owned liquidation by the West itself. So, at the very moment *when the West is blueprinting an economy which must be based on the sustained, permanent use of its natural resources,* it is also conducting an assault on those resources with the simple objective of liquidating them. . . . The West as its own worst enemy. The West committing suicide.

The main objectives of the Western assault on the natural resources are the remnants of the national domain, the Taylor Act grazing lands, and the national forests. I have heard this assault called a conspiracy but it is in no way secret or even surreptitious; it is open and enthusiastically supported by many Westerners, by many Western newspapers, and by almost all the Western specialty press. Openly engaged in it are parts of the lumber industry (though other important parts of that industry are opposing it), some water users (though water users would be its first victims), the national associations of cattle and sheep growers and an overwhelming majority of the state and local associations as such and of their members individually, large parts of the mining industry, the U.S. Chamber of Commerce (some of whose local chambers are in opposition).

Right now the stockmen and woodgrowers are carrying the ball. . . . Their limited objectives are:

1. Conversion of the privilege which cattlemen and sheepmen now have of grazing their stock on Taylor Act and Forest Service lands—a privilege which is now subject to regulation and adjustment and for which they pay

389

less than it is worth — into a vested right guaranteed them and subject to only such regulation as they may impose upon themselves.

2. Distribution of all the Taylor Act grazing lands, which is to say practically all the public domain that still exists, to the individual states, as a preliminary to disposing of them by private sale. (At an insignificant price. . . . The price most commonly suggested was ten cents an acre.)

3. Reclassification of lands in the national forests and removal from the jurisdiction of the Forest Service of all lands that can be classified as primarily valuable for grazing, so that these lands may be transferred to the states and eventually sold. Immediately in contemplation is the removal of all government regulation of grazing in about 27,000,000 acres of forest lands and their distribution to the states — and to stockmen and wool-growers as soon thereafter as possible.

But that is just a start: a further objective is to wrest from Forest Service control all lands in all forests that can be grazed. And beyond that is the intention ultimately to confine the Forest Service to the rehabilitation of land which lumbermen and stockmen have made unproductive, under compulsion to return it to private ownership as soon as it has been made productive again. The ultimate objective, that is, is to liquidate all public ownership of grazing land and forest land in the United States. . . .

The immediate objectives make this attempt one of the biggest land grabs in American history. The ultimate objectives make it incomparably the biggest.

This is your land we are talking about.

The public lands are first to be transferred to the states on the fully justified assumption that if there should be a state government not wholly compliant to the desires of stock growers, it could be pressured into compliance. The intention is to free them of all regulation except such as stock growers might impose upon themselves. Nothing in history suggests . . . that cattlemen and sheepmen are capable of regulating themselves even for their own benefit, still less the public's. And the regulations immediately to be got rid of are those by which the government has been trying to prevent overgrazing of the public range.

Everyone knows that the timber of the United States is being cut faster than replacements are being grown, that the best efforts of the government and of those private operators who realize that other generations will follow ours have not so far sufficed to balance the growth of saw timber with logging. Everyone knows that regulation of grazing is the only hope of preserving the range. Open the public reserves of timber, the national forests, to private operation without government restriction and not only the Western but the national resources would rapidly disintegrate. . . . Turn the public range over to private ownership, or even private management, and within a generation the range would be exhausted beyond hope of repair.

But that is, by a good deal, the least of it. Most of the fundamental watersheds of the West lie within the boundaries of the Taylor Act lands, the national forests, and the national parks. And overgrazing the range and liquidating the forests destroys the watersheds. In many places in the West today property in land, irrigating systems, and crops is steadily deteriorating because the best efforts of the government to repair damage to watersheds — damage caused by overgrazing the ranges and overcutting the forests — has not been enough.

If the watersheds go, and they will go if cattlemen and sheepmen are allowed to get rid of government regulation of grazing, the West will go too — farms, ranches, towns, cities, irrigating systems, power plants, business in general. Much of the interior West will become uninhabitable, far more will be permanently depressed. The United States cannot afford to let that happen — you cannot afford to.

100

Canyonlands and Compromises

EDWARD ABBEY

1971

Maybe partly as amends for having drowned Glen Canyon a few years earlier, Congress in 1964 created Canyonlands National Park, a region of incredibly sculptured rock formations at the junction of the Colorado with the Green. Although the intention of the National Park Service was to preserve it as a wilderness park, pressure immediately built up to open it to large-scale tourism, and the smokestacks of proposed power plants in the Southwest threatened the air not only of Canyonlands but a half-dozen other national parks and monuments in that region.

Edward Abbey is the author of Desert Solitaire, *and the Sierra Club book,* Slickrock, *from which the* Bulletin *took the following passages.*

WHEN I FIRST SAW THE LAND this book is about, I thought that a more utterly worthless region could hardly be imagined. In other words, I thought such a beautiful land so full of marvels was fairly safe from the cash-register mentality. Wrong, of course. As the genius of American commerce has discovered, *almost anything can be sold.* But for a while it seemed as if the canyonlands might somehow be overlooked. Wrong.

Even as late as 1948 most of southeast Utah appeared as a blank space on the maps. Terra incognita. All that unbreathed air. A reserve of clean air and unfenced space sufficient for the needs of all 150 million Americans. Wrong. A sweaty scramble began in Utah's canyon country for the rare metal uranium. It was found, too, culminating in the big strikes of 1955, and within a few years the canyon country was overlaid with a network of jeep and truck roads and sprinkled here and there with hastily bulldozed landing strips. The assault was under way.

When a portion of the canyon country adjoining the conjunction of the Green and Colorado rivers was set aside by Congress as a national park, presumably to protect it from commercial exploitation, the pressures began at once to open it up to the road builders. For roads, paved roads, are the primary essential in creating an industrial tourist market. Without paved roads you get only the people who want to visit an area for obscure private reasons, probably of an immoral nature. With paved roads, however, you attract as if by magic every American who owns an automobile and knows how to back it out of the garage and how to point it down the highway. The profit lies in heavy volume, as any business-administration major knows.

Efforts were made to save Canyonlands National Park from becoming another "scenic drive" type park, complete with "auto nature trails," but as usual compromises had to be made because of political pressure from Utah business interests. A paved road has already been built as far as Squaw Spring; this road will be extended to a point overlooking the confluence of the two rivers, and from there a loop drive will be constructed close to the entrance to Chesler Park, center of The Needles area. This loop drive, in turn, will probably be joined to a road leading south to Natural Bridges National Monument. Another paved road will be built to Grandview Point and Upheaval Dome. Present jeep trails except the one inside Chesler Park will remain in use.

A few words on the word "compromise." Compromise used to mean an agreement whereby two parties to an issue each gave up something in return for something. Nowadays, in conservation controversies, it seems to mean an agreement whereby one party (the conservationists) yield up part of what they wish to save in order not to have to lose it all. That's called a compromise. If the term were strictly applied, it should mean that every time a road is built into a previously unspoiled area, then an equivalent length of road would be closed off, rolled up or otherwise removed from some other area. The same goes for dams, power plants and uranium mills.

The American Southwest was once famous for its pure air, vivid light and dazzling visibility. There was a time, since forgotten, when Eastern physicians would send their serious respiratory cases to Arizona or New Mexico. Thanks to the efforts of regional economic boosters, much of the air of the Southwest has been "brought up to standard" — to use the terminology of the Four-Corners Regional Commission. Our air is just as dirty as your air. Central Arizona, for example, is now a good place to catch a disease known locally as "valley fever," a debilitating lung fungus borne far and wide by the winds in our almost-always dusty air. Visibility also suffers. According to Dr. Otto Franz, an astronomer at the Lowell Observatory near Flagstaff, the air of northern Arizona, once renowned for its clarity, has undergone a light loss of 25 percent since 1962.

The canyon country escaped most of this pollution until recently, except for the haze added to the air by a few potash and uranium mills. Then, with the opening up of a huge coal-burning power plant near Shiprock, New Mexico, the pollution assumed a more serious aspect.

After only six years of operation this plant [Four Corners] has become the most notorious single polluter of public air in the entire Southwest. The refuse from its stack can be seen for a radius of 100 miles and has been the object of complaints from citizens as far away as Durango, Colorado, and Albuquerque, New Mexico. American astronauts orbiting the earth were able to identify the Four Corners Plant, thanks to its gaseous garbage, as one of the few man-made objects visible from space.

Soon to begin operation is the Mohave Plant near Davis Dam on the Arizona-California border, owned like other plants by an interstate consortium of utilities and public agencies. Now in the initial phase of construction is the Navajo Plant at Page, Arizona, close to Glen Canyon Dam; this plant, if completed, will have a total installed capacity of 2,310 megawatts, making it one of the biggest in the United States. Others in the project or proposal stage are the San Juan Plant, to be located sixteen miles northwest of Farmington, New Mexico, the Huntington Canyon Plant twenty-nine miles southwest of Price, Utah, and the Kaiparowits Plant twelve miles north of Page. The last-named will be the monster of them all, with a projected ultimate capacity of 5,000 to 6,000 megawatts.

These power plants would half-encircle the canyonlands. The effect of their smokestacks, cooling towers, strip mines, truck roads, waste disposal dumps, pipelines, railways, and transmission lines on the surrounding landscape can easily be imagined. The pollution of the atmosphere would be far worse, an insidious smog of fly ash and sulfur dioxide which would spread as sure as the winds will blow over the entire air space of the canyon country.

Fly ash, as all urban readers know, is an exceedingly fine grade of dirt — "particulate matter" in the jargon of the engineers. It diffuses through air like a dye through a glass of clear water. The effect on the atmosphere of the canyonlands will be the same. Visibility will be reduced from the customary 60 to 100 miles to more like 15 miles, or little more than the width of the Grand Canyon at Bright Angel Point. Swimmers and boaters on the Glen Canyon Dam reservoir will plow through a film of soot; hikers will find a coating of the black dust on the ancient monoliths of Rainbow Bridge, the Arches, the Needles — everywhere, *hic et ubique*.

Like the network of new highways proposed for the canyon country, these power plants are meant not for current needs but for "anticipated" needs. "Planning for growth," it's called. The fact that planning for growth encourages growth, even forces growth, would not be seen as a serious objection by the majority of Utah-Arizona businessmen and government planners. It would merely excite them to greater enthusiasm. They believe in growth. Why? Ask any cancer cell why it believes in growth.

393

In spite of Mr. Abbey's pessimism—or more probably because of it and the cries of outraged conservationists—the paved roads planned for Canyonlands were subsequently cancelled, or at least deferred, by Congress in 1977. In 1976 the Kaiparowits power plant was cancelled thanks to determined opposition by environmentalists. All the other plants mentioned by the author are now in operation.

101

The Scourge of Clearcutting

NANCY WOOD

1971

The beginnings of conservation in America can be traced back to the classic Man and Nature, *by George Perkins Marsh, published in 1864. Marsh warned of the disastrous chain of consequences resulting from the destruction of the American forests by rapacious loggers who levelled the woods and moved on. One eventual result of Marsh's book was the creation of the first national forests by President Grover Cleveland in 1891. The purpose of the forests, as developed by Chief Forester Gifford Pinchot, was to manage selective logging on public lands in such a way as to produce a "sustained yield"—so that a crop of lumber could be harvested virtually forever.*

Later came the concept of "multiple use" of the national forests. They were to be managed not merely for timber production but also for such other purposes as recreation, wildlife habitat, and watershed protection.

In our generation, however, under the pressure of the increasing demand for lumber, the levelling of the woods over large areas has been introduced into the national forests on a controlled basis known as "clearcutting." Many conservationists feel that clearcutting violates both the principles of sustained yield and multiple use.

This Bulletin *article is excerpted from the Sierra Club book,* Clearcut: The Deforestation of America.

THE AMERICAN FOREST is a battleground. What is left of it. On one side is the timber industry. Having overcut its own lands, it now seeks to raid the national forests where half the remaining softwood supply stands. On the other side are individuals from all walks of life who believe that the national forests belong to the people and who decry the fact that each year one million acres of wilderness fall to industry's chain saws. In the middle is the Forest Service, painfully aware that timber has been given priority over all other uses, yet apparently powerless to regulate that industry or even to justify the strangle hold that timbermen have on the national forests.

Within this framework, the struggle over the national forests and who controls them and for what purpose is largely a political one. As always, the bureaucratic structure yields to pressure from powerful lobbyists and powerful congressmen. It becomes bogged down with red tape and master plans which, while theoretically sound, do not work on a practical basis because there is neither adequate management personnel nor money. It loses sight of the goals it had in the beginning. In the case of the Forest Service, now sixty-six years old, those goals were not only to furnish a continuous supply of timber to the nation but to protect the forests, soil and watersheds as well.

The Forest Service has failed to render this protection. Although it speaks reverently and convincingly of multiple use, the service ignores all other values when timber is in question. Recreation, wildlife, watershed protection are given sparse attention.

The Forest Service is adopting and implementing on a wide scale various forms of even-age management, or clearcutting. Under this form of so-called "sound forest management," entire mountainsides are stripped of trees, thousands of acres at one whack, running as much as three miles in length and a mile or more in width. Such a practice has an enormously devastating environmental effect which includes soil destruction, stream siltation, and a stinging blow to the aesthetic sense. It is also in violation of the Multiple Use Act of 1960.

Aside from political and legal considerations, money is at the heart of the matter, for industry must pay a fee to the U.S. government for the privilege of removing timber from the national forests. With $312 million in timber receipts anticipated for 1971, and an increase of $40 million expected in 1972, the Forest Service is one of the government's major money-making operations. It is no small wonder, then, that the Forest Service acquiesces to the demands of the industry for more areas to be opened up to the sale of billions of board feet.

The manner of cutting in the national forests disturbs many observers even more than any projected increase in the yield of logs. Clearcutting is total cutting, whether a given piece of land measures 5 acres or 2,000. It is this practice which has caused fiery debates, congressional hearings, endless attacks on the Forest Service and industry — and a challenge to both to prove that clearcutting does not harm soil, water and the ability of the forest to regenerate in perpetuity.

As far as industry is concerned, clearcutting is the most scientifically sound way to keep the forest producing trees forever. Industry foresters say that they can get second crops of trees to grow faster and better once the land is stripped of its "century-old, dark, dank Douglas fir forests." They insist that the only way they can stay in business is to grow second, third and fourth crops of trees as rapidly as possible with the assistance of such deadly poisons as DDT, endrin and dieldrin.

Lumbermen use the clearcutting method because it is easier. Roads are put down and across creek beds because it is easier. When the second growth of trees is all lined up in even stands ready to cut, it is easier. When these fairly uniform logs reach the sawmill, it is easier. And after all, the lumbermen point out, clearcutting *does* produce more timber. In 1969, 50.2 percent of the timber taken from eastern forests was clearcut from only 39.6 percent of the area logged. In the western forests, 30.1 percent of the logged area was clearcut, producing 60.8 percent of the volume of timber. With statistics such as these, what does a little erosion matter? Or some siltation in the water? Or the side of a mountain that begins to take on the appearance of Viet Nam after bombing? Yet the timber industry and the Forest Service, while admitting that some mistakes have occurred in the process of clearcutting, argue that no real damage is done to the land.

The truth is that clearcutting is the most destructive tool ever applied to the American forest. The most severe effect of clearcutting is the disruption of age-old soil conditions in the forest, which could leave the land barren in less than 200 years.

The next worst effect of clearcutting is sedimentation caused by erosion when logging occurs on steep slopes or upon unstable soils. Sedimentation from poor logging practices chokes stream beds many miles downstream. This causes loss of natural stream vegetation and destroys fish habitat. Clearcutting also leads to greater spring runoff, increasing the danger of floods.

What does a clearcut area look like?

Imagine the mountains, ridge after ridge of them, rolling slopes of dark green conifers punctuated with aspen — an emerald empire of stately trees against the severity of granite.

But now there are no trees. They have been cut down.

The slope in the foreground is denuded — not a single tree remains nor a shrub nor a flower.

It is ugly on the next ridge where another thousand acres have been cut over. And on the next where the clearcut jumps a watershed and spans two slopes. It is an odd sight, this clearcut, done in clean lines right up to the next stand of virgin forest, intact until a timber sale brings it down. What is left — a checkerboard of trees throughout a million-acre forest — does not please the eye. And what is left looks as if it ought to come down too. To sort of put it out of its misery.

To cut the trees down over 20 million acres or 30 million in patches of 10 acres up to 3,000, is bad enough in itself. And so are the gouges — running into the hundreds of thousands of miles — which the Forest Service calls logging roads. They crisscross the clearcuts as if laid out by a drunken engineer. They do not go anywhere — except to a sea of stumps. One main road leads out of the forest to the nearest sawmill. And when the timber is all gone, the Forest Service will say this road is for recreation.

102

Responsible Forestry

GORDON ROBINSON

1971

If clearcutting is destructive, what kind of forest management would produce timber continually while accommodating recreation and watershed control? An answer is provided by the Sierra Club's forestry consultant.

THE BEST KEPT SECRET in this period of great concern about the declining quality of our environment is the condition of our forest lands. Concern for forests prompted the beginning of American conservation. Forests are the source of the bulk of our water, the home of our wild life, the scene of much of our recreation, and the resource base of one of our largest and oldest industries. Yet the forests of America have been relentlessly plundered ever since Europeans began their conquest of the North American continent five hundred years ago. The destruction continues almost unabated today.

During the past twenty years forest industries have been vigorously campaigning both through administrative and legislative channels to require the United States Forest Service and the Bureau of Land Management to vastly increase the sale of timber from our public forests. Their rationale is that this country is in the midst of a critical housing shortage, requiring low cost housing which in turn ostensibly requires increasing quantities of wood. What these industries hesitate to admit is that private forests are being increasingly depleted, because of their own consistently poor logging practices, and that is why they look to national forests as a new resource base.

Until about 1950 the timber industry cut and sold all the timber they could profitably handle. The volume of timber sold annually remained nearly constant from 1900 to 1970 in spite of increasing population. During the same period the per capita use of wood gradually declined and lumber prices gradually but steadily increased. Yet in the early 1950's, a new situation had evolved which threw the industry into a panic: many operators had liquidated their resources and for the first time were having difficulty purchasing new supplies of virgin timber. Fearing self-defeating price increases and the resulting widespread introduction of wood substitutes, industry representatives pressured Congress and administrations of both political parties into helping them find new ways of increasing their purchase of timber from public lands.

In 1900 all of the lumber used in the United States was cut from private lands. By 1950 about 15 percent was coming from public lands. Since then the ratio has steadily increased until now about 40 percent is from the public lands. Meanwhile, prices have been artificially maintained at relatively low levels since around 1960 by using excessive quantities of public timber.

Who decides how much virgin timber on public lands will be put up for sale? The public agencies, principally the Forest Service. Operating under laws requiring that *sustained yield* and *multiple use* values be maintained on national forest lands, the agencies periodically measure the total inventory of timber in each of their working circles, their administrative units for timber management. They determine the amount, growth rates, and condition of timber; from their findings they then determine the "allowable cut" for each working circle. "Allowable cut" is the amount of timber that can be sold annually under a timber management plan. It may be more or less than the sustained yield.

Having done this, each national forest then offers timber for competitive bidding to lumber companies, supposedly in such volumes and locations as to best conform to the needs of local industry and other users of the forest. Multiple use laws stipulate that timber harvesting on public lands shall not impair other land values relating to water quality, recreation, range and forage, watershed, wildlife and plant life, and the preservation of wilderness.

Yet in the past two decades, the Forest Service has employed some interesting statistical maneuvering in order to continue to arrive at higher and higher figures for their "allowable cut." One method is the continuous shifting of criteria for classification of forest lands. In 1928, the passage of the McSweeney-McNary Act along with subsequent amendments gave the Forest Service responsibility for measuring the forest resources of the United States. The first survey under the Act was published in 1945 and showed a total of 73 million acres of commercial forest land in the national forests of the contiguous forty-eight states. However, when the second inventory was published in 1953, the total had risen to 81 million acres and in the third, published in 1963, the total had reached *91.5 million acres.* The reported increase does not reflect any change in the area of our national forests; that has comprised a total of 186 million acres throughout the entire period of the surveys, except for minor variations due to acquisitions, exchanges and withdrawals for parks and wilderness areas. *The 18 million acre increase in eighteen years was the result of reclassification of forest from non-commercial to commercial.* For example, the definition of commercial forest land was recently changed from land capable of producing 25 cubic feet of wood per acre annually to land capable of producing 20 cubic feet. Consequently, some of the increase in the volume of national forest annual timber sales consists of marginal species of timber growing on steep unstable soils, in scattered stands, and of timber that has taken a long time to mature because of poor growing conditions.

Another way in which the cut has been increased on the national forests has been by combining working circles. A working circle is a compact unit within which the forester balances cut and growth. In recent years, these units have been merged so that now many national forests as a whole are regarded as a single working unit. This has had several destructive results. Forest statistics are gathered by sampling techniques and the people who collect the data do not see the results of their work. Data is forwarded to a computer center where it is processed and delivered to others than those who did the sampling. Some of the most important decisions concerning how much and which timber to sell are consequently made by people not directly familiar with the forest. The practicing forester has generally lost ultimate control and the forests are run by people high in the bureaucratic echelons who are closer to industry than they are to the living forest they administer. Thus scattered timber and timber on unstable soils is not recognized for what it is by those making the management decisions and allowable cuts are thereby increased in the readily accessible high quality timber — all brought about by the gerrymandering of working circles.

A forest which has been well managed for multiple use is fully stocked with trees of all sizes and ages and is generally composed of a variety of species. Trees will often occur in clumps of more than one age. The land is growing about all the timber it can and most of the growth consists of high quality, highly valuable material in the lower portions of the large older trees. No erosion is taking place. Roads will be stable and attractive, having the appearance of being lain on the land rather than cut into it. The soil will

Forest detail,
Kings Canyon National Park

399

be intact, the forest floor will be covered with leaf litter and other vegetative matter in various stages of growth or decomposition. This absorbent layer holds rain and melting snow while it soaks down into the ground through animal burrows, pores such as worm holes, channels dug by ants, and tracks left by the decaying roots of past generations of vegetation. In this way the forest becomes a vast reservoir for water which gradually seeps down through the land and comes out in springs as fresh, clear cool water. This is how the forest stabilizes stream flow and this is what is referred to when one reads of the forest serving to protect our watersheds. In the well-managed forest there are frequent small openings stocked with herbs and browse, which provide food and shelter for wildlife. Finally, such a forest maintains its beauty and will continue to serve the recreational needs of people as long as it is so managed.

It will require many years to restore the nation's millions of acres of depleted forest and to return the even-age stands to a reasonable semblance of multiple use, but this must be our objective.

In 1976 Congress passed the National Forest Management Act, which directed the Forest Service to develop guidelines for clearcutting in National Forests that would reflect the "multiple-use" concept of land management. In spite of this legislation— and the protests of conservationists—ninety-five percent of all land in the National Forests is managed under various forms of "even-age" management—a euphemism for clearcutting.

103

Whose Home on the Range?

LESLIE HOOD and

JAMES K. MORGAN

1972

As Bernard DeVoto had noted a quarter-century earlier, western forests and range-lands have historically been the victims of raids on our natural resources. Overlogging and overgrazing have been the scourge of the land, destroying irreplaceable soils that had been slowly created over thousands of years. The destruction continues in new forms. The fate of the bighorn sheep is one of its symbols—a warning to the humans who depend on the soil of the continent for sustenance.

Leslie Hood is executive director of the California Natural Areas Coordinating

Council. *James Morgan is an authority on wildlife, who made a five-year study of the Rocky Mountain bighorn sheep for the Idaho Fish and Game Department.*

As we have noted, Congress passed the Forest Land Policy and Management Act in 1977, which called for more stringent range management in accordance with the concept of multiple use.

THE SAGEBRUSH desert blankets the Western rangeland, a dreary landscape relieved by an occasional deer and the ever-present cattle and sheep. Yet less than a hundred years ago this same land supported the greatest assemblage of game animals found on the continent. Bison, elk, deer, pronghorn, and the prize of all, the bighorn, grazed the lush mountain valleys, the vast grasslands of the foothills, and the broad uplands that separate range after snow-capped range of jagged peaks.

The fate of the bighorn, banished now to the more inaccessible recesses of the mountains, is an indicator of the degradation of the environment that has taken place in less than a century. Some animals were hunted to the verge of extinction for the supposed threat they posed to man and his livestock, others for transitory economic gain. Now the bighorn, harmless and free of obvious utilitarian value, balances precariously close to oblivion in much of its range, the passive victim of the damage wrought by cattle and sheep to an environment which must, ultimately, preserve all of us from oblivion.

The decline of the bighorn is only one of many consequences of the exploitation and ravaging of this once-rich land, a waste subsidized by the American public. Before it is too late for both bighorn sheep and us, we must examine our public grazing land policies and chart a new course more in accord with the needs of our times and more attuned to our increasing knowledge of environmental necessities.

Today we realize that energy use is the measure of the quality of an environment. In the highest quality environments, plants and animals have achieved a dynamic equilibrium where all of the available energy is fully utilized. Such a system perpetuates itself, adapting to fluctuations, continually evolving to make the most efficient use of the energy. Evolving over thousands of years, the bighorn sheep made the most efficient use of a relatively stable habitat, the semi-arid grasslands of the western mountains.

For hundreds of generations, each spring as the grass turned green the bighorn began their annual trek up the ridges of the backbone of the continent, from the Sangre de Cristos of New Mexico to the Canadian Rockies, following the receding snow to the rich grassy pastures in the high mountains. The gravid ewes stayed behind to lamb in May and June, but as soon as the young were born they, too, climbed to the high pastures. Then, each fall, when the snows began to cover the increasingly sere pasture, the herds in small bands, always led by a ewe, wended their way back down the ridges to the winter feeding grounds on the foothills and in the valleys. Here on the snow-free slopes they could forage the grasses and forbs and, when the snow covered the ground too deeply, browse the shrubs. The abundance of the bighorn was a sensitive indicator of the quality of the environment: any disruption in the energy flow would immediately be reflected in the size of the herds.

To illustrate: the area around Challis, Idaho, is a microcosm of much of the present bighorn world. Located here on the headwaters of the Salmon River, Challis is in the heart of what was ideal bighorn country. In the 1870's the Middle Fork of the Salmon alone supported a herd of 2,500 animals. Today remnant bands of these thousands straggle through their traditional territories — perhaps a total of 300, half of what there were even a decade ago.

The cause is readily apparent. Overgrazing has stripped the hillsides and valleys of grasses and shrubs that once flourished, leaving sagebrush. On the south slopes, where the snow cover is lighter and the animals, wild and domestic, can find food during the winter, the sagebrush takeover is almost complete. On the north slopes, where the snow is deeper, some grass still remains, maybe a quarter of the total cover. This is not a localized condition. Over two-thirds of the western ranges have suffered similar damage as a result of overgrazing by livestock.

The decline of the bighorn, and the range, set in with the rise of the cattle industry after the Civil War. Cattle swept through the West almost as fast as the animals could be driven. In their wake came the sheep. Within a few short decades the West was won; cattle and sheep could be found virtually anywhere the grass grew.

In the rush to settle, the mountain valleys with their rich meadows and year-round streams were the first to be homesteaded. Control of a stream — or a waterhole — gave the owner effective control of large stretches of land.

Lands away from the valley bottoms and the forests remained in the public domain. They were there for the taking, free to anyone wishing to exploit them. And exploited they were.

The forests were hurt first. Great tracts were logged off for mine timbers, fencing and railroad ties. Stockmen seeking richer grazing burned off thousands of acres, for thick grass carpets would spring up in their stead. Itinerant charcoal burners, supplying smelters, were permitted to work only burned-over lands, so they, too, fired the forests. By the 1890's, realizing that soon there would be no forests left unless some protection was given, the federal government put millions of acres into forest reserves.

In 1905, the newly established Forest Service instituted a permit system for the grazing lands it administered. Such an infringement of "individual rights" was bitterly fought by the stockmen, as was the modest grazing fee when it was imposed a few years later. These controls have continued to the present, and though not overwhelmingly successful, they have afforded a measure of protection to the forest rangeland.

With the prime timber protected and the choice lands taken, there still remained several hundred million acres in the public domain. The old adage that "everybody's land is nobody's land" might well have been coined to apply to these lands which have taken the brunt of abuse. Considered "free" by the stockmen, these lands were ruthlessly exploited. All too soon, ranchers could tell the progress of the nomadic herds by the great clouds of dust they raised as they moved across the range. The clouds portended more than approaching animals; the end of the grass was in sight, for grass-covered land does not stir into dust with the passage of animals.

The ecological impact of this rush to "get it before somebody else gets it" was dramatic and drastic. Today it is impossible to tell accurately in many areas just *what* the original plant cover was because so many of the more valuable species have disappeared completely. Others, more resistant to grazing or less used by livestock or other animals that like good grass, have increased, creating unpalatable plant communities. The relatively inedible big sagebrush, which commonly grows in association with wheatgrass and was present in moderate amounts, literally exploded on the rangeland as a result of overgrazing the grasses. Today over a third of the public range — 96 million acres — is primarily sagebrush.

As the conversion to sagebrush desert was so swift, early ecologists were led to believe that sagebrush was the climax stage on the Western rangelands. Only a few tiny areas of the range escaped the violent change brought about by overgrazing to provide a clue to the original plant cover.

The alteration of the true climax plant cover radically reduced the numbers and changed the distribution of the bighorn as well as many of the other native animals. Both the summer and winter ranges of the bighorn have suffered the effects of overgrazing. The most acute problems are in the lower altitudes on the winter ranges. Here the animals are in competition not only with the domestic livestock but with the displaced deer, elk and pronghorn.

The livestock industry itself became a victim of its own greed in the absence of any effective control of the public grazing lands. Before 1900, overgrazing had become apparent in parts of the range, yet despite the rising concern of conservationists over the next few decades, little was done to correct the abuses.

By the 1930's, the situation was becoming desperate, as Professor Paul Gates describes in *The History of Public Land Law Development:* "The failure of Congress to adopt legislation to halt the destructive use of the public rangelands and to prevent the continued breakup of natural grazing areas by homesteading, which was taking the land with access to water and leaving useful grasslands without any water, brought about an increasingly critical situation by 1933. Overgrazing, destruction of the better grasses and survival of poisonous plants, erosion of steep hillsides, and silting up of reservoirs, all emphasized the need for control."

Realizing the gravity of the situation, the ranchers sought protection, which came in the form of the Taylor Grazing Act of 1934. This act set the pattern for public grazing land policies as we know them today.

There is no denying that the Taylor Grazing Act was long overdue. Yet in operation it stressed one stated purpose of the act — to stabilize the livestock interest — at the expense of another which called for "preventing overgrazing

403

and soil deterioration." No one even bothered to make an assessment of the long-term impact that the policies of continued heavy grazing would have on the land. Only recently have such assessments been made—and the results are appalling.

Of the 410,000 square miles of public rangeland, 30.5 percent (125,000 square miles—an area almost the size of Montana) is considered to be in poor condition, and 50 percent (250,000 square miles—an area greater than Wyoming and Colorado combined) is in only fair condition. These figures were developed by the Public Land Law Review Commission. After more than 60 years of "management," overuse and unsatisfactory conditions prevail on over two-thirds of our public range.

But the loss of plant cover and wildlife is only the beginning of the destruction. In an account of the erosion of the range, the Bureau of Land Management states, "According to the best estimates now available, about 50 percent of the federal range lands are in a state of severe to critical erosion, 32 percent are eroding moderately, and only 18 percent are in a condition of slight or no erosion."

To stem and correct the damage brought about by overgrazing, millions of dollars are spent annually on soil conservation projects, stream channelization, dam building, fish restocking, and stream rehabilitation programs. Ironically, not only is the public taxed to repair the damage but, in this curious wonderland of politics and bureaucracy, it continues to underwrite, at a cost of more millions yearly, the very cause of the destruction of its own lands and wildlife.

These tax-supported subsidies—though they aren't called that—come in a variety of guises. Fire protection, improved access to public lands, or other pretexts justify slashing roads across the land—roads for which the main use is to haul stock and equipment. Wildlife range improvement is a guise for gouging out waterholes—wildlife may benefit but the new waterholes open previously unusable range to the livestock. Other tax-supported programs are frankly designed to protect the livestock.

The most grotesque subsidies have been in the "predator control programs." Ever since cattle and sheep first grazed the West, any creature that walked or flew that could be considered even remotely harmful has been relentlessly persecuted. Though dubiously necessary in certain areas on a limited basis, the indiscriminate killing of cougars, bears, wolves, coyotes, bobcats, even hawks and eagles, has all but eliminated them from much of their former ranges. The unnatural absence of predators throughout much of the West has been responsible in no small part for the explosion of deer, rabbits, ground squirrels, mice and other animals and even insects that the ranchers find to be *truly* economically dangerous pests.

Sagebrush deserts, denuded hills, vanished wildlife, depleted fisheries, eroded gullies, silted rivers, flooded lowlands and, above all, the loss of productivity on the rangelands are the price we are paying for allowing overgrazing. It will take a long time to rejuvenate and restore the range to a point even approaching its original productivity.

The first step in such a program is the reduction of all grazing allotments for a five-year period. Reductions up to 50 percent and more, depending upon the condition of the range and its safe carrying capacity, should be made by curtailing spring grazing when the grass is most susceptible to damage. Fall grazing, which is less detrimental and may even help restore the grass, should be continued. During this time detailed objective studies of the public lands, district by district, range by range, would be made to determine their best potential use. (Ostensibly this has been done, but too many studies have been economically rather than ecologically oriented.) As the studies are completed, the land would be classified according to its best use: watershed, recreation, wildlife, timber, minerals and grazing. Grazing then would be restricted to those lands best suited for grazing.

During the five-year study period the money used to subsidize the livestock industry on the public land could be channeled directly to range restoration and rehabilitation projects, reseeding with native grasses and forbs, repairing damage, cleaning up the range, and so on. Individuals seriously affected by the partial closure of the range could be employed in these projects or given aid in relocating. To further soften the impact, grazing fees could be maintained at the present low levels.

Grazing would be closely controlled through the use of range analysis to maintain grazing pressures that would not interfere with the reestablishment of natural, healthy ecosystems. It is quite conceivable that large numbers of animals might be grazed on suitable parts of the range when it is restored to its original productivity. When the land was first subjected to rancher exploitation it often supported herds larger than those of today—it is overgrazing that has injured productivity of the land, and only careful husbandry can bring it back.

Management of our land must be firmly based on biological principles, for ultimately these are the principles that determine our fate. To do less, to avoid these realities, is to quicken our own footsteps along the bighorn's path. Eons in the making, our land is sluicing down our rivers in a few short decades.

The clock cannot be turned back one second, let alone a hundred years. No one will ever again see the great spectacle of the wild herds that once ranged the grasslands of the Rockies, the bison, deer, elk, pronghorn and the bighorn feeding on the seemingly endless grass. The rangelands will never be entirely the same—but they can be restored, brought back to a natural, self-perpetuating ecosystem. They can once again approach the same smooth energy flow, the same ecological efficiency that created those vast herds. When they do, then the bighorn will move back from that precarious stance on the edge of oblivion, back to the abundance of the range, their future secured. And ours, too.

104

Alaska: The Last Opportunity

PEGGY WAYBURN

1976

In his book, The Quiet Crisis, *Stewart L. Udall, former Secretary of the Interior, wrote: "There are, today, a few wilderness reaches on the North American continent— in Alaska . . . where the early-morning mantle of primeval America can be seen in its pristine glory, where one can gaze with wonder on the land as it was when the Indians first came."*

It is one of the more amazing facts of New World history that after nearly five centuries of colonization, westward expansion, and urbanization, such a spectacle as Udall described remains on such a colossal scale.

One of the major priorities of the Sierra Club during the 1970s has been to ensure that in the face of intensifying pressures to develop Alaska's economic resources, the state's priceless wilderness will itself be regarded as an irreplaceable resource. Peggy Wayburn is co-author of the Sierra Club book Alaska: The Great Land.

MANY BELIEVE Alaska's wilderness to be unmatched on the planet. Also unmatched is the challenge it now presents. For this wilderness, still intact in many places, is at this moment largely in uncommitted public land. Congress is deciding its fate: the terms of the Alaska Native Claims Settlement Act (ANCSA), passed in December, 1971, provide for classifying large areas as "national interest lands." Thus, while there are enormous pressures to exploit all of Alaska's energy resources, there is also a real chance to protect what is unquestionably this country's greatest remaining wilderness resource. There is a chance to profit from our old mistakes and, at long last, to exercise wisely our stewardship of the land.

Consider the opportunity. Some 235 million acres of Alaska lands have now been earmarked for future use, and the great majority of this land will be available for development. As much as possible of the approximately 140 million acres remaining can, and many advocates feel must, be protected for their wilderness values. Considering the magnitude of these values, and the total land-use pattern emerging in Alaska, this amount hardly seems unreasonable.

To describe the beauty of Alaska's wilderness has always been a challenge. The Aleuts, among the first settlers, met the challenge by simply naming the place "Alaska," which means "The Great Land." Bob Marshall, one of

Alaska's early and eloquent advocates, spoke of its "most staggering grandeur," and he provided a classic description of the Arctic when he wrote of it: "All was peace and strength and immensity and coordination and freedom."

Quite aside from aesthetic considerations, however, Alaska's wilderness has many incalculable values. It is an unequaled natural laboratory for the biologist, the botanist, the anthropologist, the archaeologist, the geologist, the meteorologist and the ecologist. It is one of the few places on earth left for the adventurer and explorer. Most important, it is the only home remaining for our last large populations of free-roaming animals: the caribou, the Dall sheep, the bear, the wolf, the wolverine, the moose, the mountain goat. These animals cannot survive close to people nor live in altered, restricted habitats. Having evolved in terms of space and freedom, they require wilderness on what John Milton calls poignantly "the old vast scale."

Add to the land mammals the mammals of the sea — the seal, the sea lion, the sea otter, the walrus, and the many kinds of whales, all of which Alaska's wilderness nurtures — and the millions upon millions of migratory birds that wing their way from nearly every part of the planet to nest and rear their young in Alaska's coastal areas, along its wild river banks and lakes, and in the rich wetlands of the interior and the great river deltas. There are also the

Snow banners, Alaska.

407

fish, like the salmon that in John Muir's time so thickly crowded the rivers of southeast Alaska during spawning runs that he wrote there were more fish than water in the streams. Even terribly depleted as they are today, Alaska's salmon feed the people of at least three countries, and they are essential to Alaska's natives for their subsistence. Like the animals of the land, the animals of the sea, the birds and the fish have evolved in a wilderness habitat. Their future is threatened as more and more of this wilderness is lost.

Following the congressional guidelines of ANCSA, and observing the realities of established use, conservationists have outlined six areas in Alaska where superb wilderness remains and can be protected. These regions — along with thirty-nine identified wild rivers, thirteen of which lie outside these regions — have peerless scenic and recreational values, but more important, contain unique ecosystems whose integrity can be maintained only by wilderness protection. Four of the six regions contain established national wildlife refuges and/or national parks.

Here, broadly sketched, are the six Alaskan areas proposed for wilderness protection:

The *Arctic-Subarctic Region* sweeps from the Arctic Ocean and Beaufort Sea over the crest of the Brooks Range and south of the Yukon. Being irrevocably divided by the Trans-Alaska Pipeline, it has been fractured into two regions, one to the east, one to the west. In the *Eastern Arctic-Subarctic Region,* the nine-million-acre Arctic Wildlife Range provides a major encounter between the Arctic land and sea.

This is the land of the caribou. Tens of thousands (once hundreds of thousands) of these creatures, which link us to prehistoric times, subsist on the feathery lichen that curls from the tundra. They move with the seasons, traveling hundreds of miles in pursuit of their food. The lichen they eat may require as long as forty years to replace itself once it is grazed.

The caribou crowd south through the mountain passes of the Brooks Range in age-old migratory patterns. Through the southern foothills runs the Porcupine River to swell the muddy waters of the Yukon. Even as people do, the salmon use the Yukon as a lifeline, and at least twenty species of wildfowl depend upon the Yukon wetlands in this interior region for their nesting and breeding places.

Within roughly thirty million acres of undisturbed wilderness, the fragile ecosystems of the eastern portion of Alaska's *Arctic-Subarctic Region* still persist.

West of the trans-Alaska pipeline, the Arctic land mass contains some of the most magnificent scenery on earth. The beautifully colored and folded metamorphic rocks of the Brooks Range culminate in rough young granite spires, the Arrigetch Peaks. Nearby broods Mt. Doonerak, the Devil Mountain; and Mt. Boreal and Frigid Peak form the Gates of the Arctic, which open the way to the Arctic slope. This land lies rigid in the grip of cold for more than three-quarters of the year. For nearly two months, the winter sun does not show above the horizon, and the dark lies deep and icy in the shadows of the high mountains. But the slope thaws into myriad lakes and

Yukon Flats, Alaska.

ponds when summer's endless days and starless nights release it. Thousands of birds nest here.

To the west, the Noatak, one of the last extensive unmolested river-drainage ecosystems anywhere, extends from Mt. Igikpak to the Bering Sea. In the Noatak country, the tundra and the forests form unique encounters. Southwest of the Noatak, there are huge, mysterious inland sand dunes, and the ancient wild lands of the Seward peninsula, which contain vast frozen lava flows. Here, a few thousand years ago, the land of the North American continent was linked to Siberia. Across this land bridge wandered the animal forebears of today's Alaskan wildlife, as well as many species now extinct. Pursuing these animals came the early hunters and fishermen who became the forebears of Alaska's native peoples. This area is a unique resource for archaeologists and anthropologists, many of whom are now working with the natives in excavating digs.

This *Western Arctic-Subarctic Region* supports caribou, polar bear, grizzlies, wolves, Arctic foxes and whales, as well as gyrfalcons, peregrines, emperor geese and countless other wildfowl.

Where the western sea meets the tundra-clothed land, cool winds sweep in from the water. Days are often fog-shrouded. Stretching along these western

409

shores are some of the world's greatest remaining wildlife sanctuaries. Nearly three dozen different mammals thrive along these coasts. This is a crossroad for birds that winter widely throughout the Pacific. Thirty million acres here in *Western Alaska* now support an invaluable living resource.

The mountains of the *Alaska Range and Aleutian Range* form a unique landform. In the northern portion, lying in Alaska's interior, the continent swells to its greatest height in Mt. McKinley. The Alaska Range and its vast tundra-covered foothill country is watered by immense glacial streams, which rise in the high peaks. Lake Clark and Lake Iliamna (the country's seventh largest freshwater lake and home to both the Beluga whale and the only freshwater seal colony in the United States) offer exceptional recreation — and subsistence — for fishermen, hunters and ordinary beauty-lovers. The rivers in this region provide unmatched opportunities for kayakers and rafters.

In the Aleutian Range, the land changes character dramatically. This volcanic area, part of the Pacific's Ring of Fire, has many active peaks, including the Mt. Katmai complex, where eruptions in 1912 formed the Valley of 10,000 Smokes. This is prime brown-bear territory. (One brown bear, it should be noted, requires about 64,000 acres of range to support itself.)

Some twenty million acres of the *Alaska-Aleutian Range* contain wilderness habitat that is immensely important to moose, caribou, wolves, sea lions, sea otters, seals, sea birds, wildfowl, and red salmon, as well as people.

The scenery of south-central Alaska and southeast Alaska is overpowering in its beauty. In south-central, the Wrangell Mountains, massive volcanic peaks, lift their snow-covered heads more than three miles into the sky. Some of their deep-cleft sculptured canyons could hold a half-dozen Yosemites.

To the southwest curve the Kenai-Chugach mountains, capped with one of North America's great ice-fields, laced with superb canoeing streams and dotted with clear deep-green lakes, where trumpeter swans nest and rear their young. These mountains dip westward until only their snow-streaked peaks rise above the water to cradle the idyllic Kenai Fjords. Within more than twenty million acres of Alaska's *South-Central Region* there are exceptional wilderness qualities.

To the south and east, the mountains of the St. Elias and Fairweather Ranges soar directly from the sea. Their lower flanks and coastal lands are carpeted thickly with Sitka spruce and hemlock forests. This is the domain of the United States Forest Service, which has committed almost all of these forests to logging. In the more than sixty years of its administration, the service has failed to establish any wilderness for protection. West Chichagof Island and Admiralty Island still contain meaningful samples of the home of the bald eagle, brown bear, "blue" bear, Sitka deer, moose, beaver and countless birds. With Glacier Bay National Monument, these additional Forest Service lands constitute *Southeast Alaska's* finest remaining typical wilderness.

Such then is the incomparable wilderness potential of Alaska.

If we are to meet the great challenge Alaska's wilderness offers, if we are to be true stewards of this last great land resource, we need to revise some of our land-use priorities. Instead of having to justify the protection of each acre of Alaskan land we are trying to retain as wilderness, we should begin instead to require justification for the development of each acre turned over to economic exploitation. And the justification for development must be in terms of long-range needs, not just immediate economic or energy demands. Our own survival, as well as the survival of many of our fellow creatures who share our planet home, may be at stake.

105

Wilderness Myths and Misconceptions

BROCK EVANS

1976

"On a cold, wet night in the timber country of southwest Oregon," Brock Evans relates, "I found myself facing a crowd that had gathered to hear me debate officials of the timber industry on their home ground. . . . One angry woman approached me and said, 'Here you are, you and your people, trying to turn the Northwest into one vast wilderness area, locking up all the forests for an elite few who hike every now and then while we starve.'"

In answer to such attacks, Evans, who now heads the Sierra Club's office in the nation's capital, wrote this myth-shattering article. It should be clear that national parks and national forests are not wilderness, although there may be wilderness zones within them. Under the Wilderness Act of 1964, wilderness areas designated by Congress are roadless areas where no logging or construction is permitted.

MYTH #1: Only a tiny minority of people use wilderness areas.

ANYONE WHO BELIEVES this statement probably has not been in a wilderness area for some time or has not talked to the Forest Service or the Park Service, which administer the Wilderness Areas we now have. Use of most Wilderness Areas in the United States is not only very heavy, but has been increasing rapidly in recent years. For example, figures available for Wilderness Areas in Idaho, Washington and Oregon show that since 1941, wilderness use in this region has increased from ten to fourteen percent per year.

In some areas, the increase in use has been astronomical. In California, between 1969 and 1970, use of all Wilderness Areas went from about 100,000 persons to almost 300,000 a year—a 300-percent increase. About two million people (nationwide) used the Wilderness Areas in National Parks and Forests in 1960. Today at least twelve to fifteen million persons a year visit the back-country areas of the National Parks and Forests.

Those who believe "Wilderness Myth #1" do not give up easily: they contend that even if twelve to fifteen million people do use wilderness each year, this is still a minority of our population; that the wilderness system reserves far too much land for such a small group.

Although those who actually walk into Wilderness Areas do constitute a minority, it is a very substantial one. In addition are the millions who "use" wilderness in many other ways: those who live far from Wilderness Areas, but buy books about it; those who think or dream about it, who write letters to support it, who go to movies about it, or who drive into park and forest roads and look into it. These people are also "users" of wilderness, and they must be counted among those who benefit from knowing it is there. Another important point is that we live in a country that believes in protecting minority rights.

Wilderness is part of our culture, our American heritage. The theme of contact with wilderness has been a source and inspiration for much of our art, music, philosophy and folklore.

As a nation, we have consistently and strongly supported government endeavors to protect and support cultural institutions, even if only a minority of Americans ever makes use of them. The wilderness idea and Wilderness Areas themselves are also a part of our national culture, as much so as parks or the National Gallery of Art, and they should be supported and preserved for the same reasons.

MYTH #2: Wilderness is an "elitist" concept: wilderness areas are playgrounds for the affluent, the leisure class, the physically fit.

A wilderness vacation is one of the least expensive recreational activities. The total cost of a good pair of boots, a backpack, a sleeping bag, and other equipment is between $150 and $300 amortized over a useful life of at least five years. This amount is far below the cost of ski togs and a weekend on the slopes, a snowmobile, a motorcycle or a motorboat. It is untrue that "only the rich" can afford to visit the wilderness. Furthermore, the decision to vacation in the wilderness is a matter of preference, as is going to Yankee Stadium, the symphony, the drag races or a football game. It is not necessary to deny wilderness to those who prefer it in order to support other forms of recreation or the pursuit of other interests.

Some studies have tended to show that generally, the higher the educational level, the more likely a person is to seek a wilderness experience, which may account for the belief that wilderness is only for the rich. But the fact remains: wilderness itself is free, and the expense necessary to enjoy it is minimal. Wilderness use is a matter of preference, not of income.

Nor does wilderness require more leisure time than other forms of outdoor recreation. A study done in the Three Sisters Wilderness Area in Oregon showed that most use there consists of day hikes, or weekend trips at most. A recent Forest Service study of the Mission Mountain Wilderness in Montana showed that at least fifty percent of the use of that area consisted of one-day trips by people with low incomes. Wilderness use depends not on having unusual amounts of leisure time, but on personal preference.

Finally, wilderness is not only for the physically fit, or the "hardy." The amount of physical conditioning required depends on the kind of wilderness experience one wants. Some Wilderness Areas have trails through flat, low, gentle valleys, trails most people can walk on. Other Wilderness Areas can be visited by boat or by walking on the beach. In addition, there are many vantage points from which one can look into the wilderness, especially along roads such as those through Great Smoky, Yellowstone or Yosemite national parks.

MYTH #3: Wilderness represents a single use of National Forests that "locks out" other uses.

The only people locked out of wilderness areas are those who want to build roads, ride motorized vehicles or log the trees: these are the *only* uses that are forbidden. Wilderness Areas are open to hunters, fishermen and walkers; to scientists for study, even to miners (under an unfortunate compromise in the Wilderness Act of 1964). Grazing is also permitted. In addition, Wilderness Areas are often valuable sources of water supply for many cities. Thus, of the so-called "Multiple Uses," the only ones precluded by Wilderness designation are logging and motorized recreation.

There is ample opportunity to enjoy motorized recreation within our National Forest System. In fact, about 100,000 miles of roads now exist within the National Forests. Surely it is not too much to ask that some areas be reserved as islands in this vast network of roads.

MYTH #4: Locking up vast areas of wilderness will pose a severe drain on our nation's economy and reduce opportunities for local employment.

The argument that setting aside Wilderness Areas will adversely affect the timber industry has been raised in almost every wilderness and park dispute in the West over the past century. But in every case, studies have shown that the actual amount of timber involved would have supplied local mills only for a few days each year and that mills looking for new sources of timber would do far better to concentrate on better reforestation and utilization of what they already have.

413

National Parks, which are essentially wilderness reserves, and Wilderness Areas are big business. The National Park System, for example, brings about $5.7 billion a year into the nation's economy. Olympic National Park, consisting almost entirely of wilderness, has been estimated to contribute about $70 million per year to the state of Washington's economy. Everywhere across the country, the sale of pictures, books and articles about parks and wilderness areas, and the sale of backpacks and other wilderness equipment, is big business indeed, running into many millions of dollars.

In many areas with wilderness nearby, guiding and packing users in and out is also a significant part of local economies. For example, testimony on hearings dealing with the proposed Scapegoat Wilderness in Montana revealed that the existence of that wilderness was essential to the local guiding business, which contributed about $850,000 a year to the local economy. Unlike the timber resource or the mining resource, the wilderness resource is there forever, to be used year after year in just the same way.

PART VIII

The Club Militant: The Environment

LONG BEFORE THE ECOLOGY MOVEMENT burst upon the nation, the Sierra Club had begun to expand its concerns beyond the traditional ones of preserving scenic landscape. Land use, pollutants, energy resources, social issues, all were to be dealt with as parts of the interconnected, whole environment.

Although the theme was clearly a minor one until the mid-'60s, there was discussion of the impact of population, for example, at the club's biennial Wilderness Conferences beginning in 1957. By the end of the 1960s, the message was getting through. Conservationists were becoming environmentalists.

Saving the land is still a top club priority, but now it shares the stage with other environmental matters. We can only be concerned here with a few of the subjects that demand the club's attention every day under such headings as energy, pollution, environmental law, and population.

During most of the club's existence, the most popular quotation from John Muir was, "Climb the mountains and get their good tidings." In recent years another insight has been more often quoted: "Whenever I try to separate out anything by itself, I find it hitched to everything else in the Universe."

Being concerned with the universe makes the club's life complicated, but its leaders and members can take satisfaction in helping begin a major turnaround in American thought. The emphasis is shifting from the way things work separately to the way they work together. The specialists still play a vital role, but the future would seem to belong to the generalists, who can see not merely the trees but the whole forest—and the whole earth.

106

The Rape of
Black Mesa

WILLIAM BROWN

1970

The Sierra Club has been involved with energy ever since its unsuccessful fight against the dam at Hetch Hetchy, which was a hydroelectric facility, and its fights against similar projects proposed for Dinosaur National Monument and the Grand Canyon.

In recent years the energy picture has become much more complicated, but the club's basic position remains the same: all proposals to generate energy must be evaluated for their impact on the physical environment. At Black Mesa, located in the Navajo-Hopi country in northern Arizona, William Brown considers another kind of environment: the web of ancient ways that sustain a people.

Such eloquent protests as this did not stop the stripmining of Black Mesa. It now supplies fuel to several coal-fired power plants, including the giant Four Corners plant near Farmington, New Mexico. The San Juan plant near Farmington, the Navajo plant at Page, Arizona, and the Mohave plant on the Arizona-California border, all mentioned in the article, are also currently in operation.

The author is a former "environmental awareness specialist" for the National Park Service.

DOT KLISH CANYON is a long way from Los Angeles. In fact, it's a long way from any place, unless you think of Navajo trading posts like Pinon and Shonto as places.

But Los Angeles and Las Vegas, Tucson and Phoenix, and even Washington, D.C., have come to Dot Klish Canyon in a big way. They have ripped across it to get to Black Mesa's coal fields. They will strip mine the coal, then ship it to power plants being built at Page, Arizona, and Mohave, Nevada.

A few days ago I stood in Dot Klish Canyon and looked at the mess. The road to the coal plant smashes across the canyon twice. The bulldozers hit a steep ridge the first time, so they just turned around and rammed through another one. The double roadbed dams the wash in the bottom of the canyon, destroying the natural drainage. A Navajo garden downstream lies dry and abandoned in the sun. A nearby hogan stands vacant. It is a scene of brutal devastation, compounded by the most careless scalping kind of non-engineering. It made me mad.

Why were Dot Klish Canyon and the rest of Black Mesa and the people who live there chosen for sacrifice? Hanging from this question is a tale of environmental tragedy. It is a tale of the industrial octopus, created by the insatiable demands of its customers, reaching into remote places and tearing them apart. This is the hidden story of environmental destruction. It's what happens to people who speak quietly in strange tongues, to places away from highways and headlines. . . .

The far Southwest and Southern California keep booming. Nobody asks if the growth is wise, if the earth can provide. These things are assumed. So utility companies and government agencies scramble to get power and water to fuel the growth.

All parties to this process reinforce each other. The Federal Power Commission warns of brownouts in Los Angeles. Business, industry, and local government take heed and join the chorus that demands more power. Tucson and Phoenix must have more water from the Colorado River, because they have already mined groundwater far in excess of natural recharge. The U.S. Bureau of Reclamation needs more power to pump water from the river into the Central Arizona Project. So it becomes the lead federal agency pushing coal-fired power plants, which are trade-offs for the dams it couldn't build in Grand Canyon.

And, as cities become more crowded and unlivable, their victimized people have to blow off steam somehow, so Las Vegas has to have more casinos, advertised by more obscene neon signs. Finally, to cap this complex of functional and frivolous forces, all parties can join the moral cause of helping the poor Indians by industrializing their reservation. So the deals were made, the contracts signed.

Conservationists and ecologists are concerned about the coal-fired power plants operating, being built, and proposed in the Southwest. One that is operating near Farmington, New Mexico, daily spews fly ash and invisible poisonous gasses. Aerial tracking of the visible air pollution shows that this single plant (not yet in full operation) soils air, water, land and people over an area 100,000 square miles in the Four Corners region of New Mexico, Arizona, Colorado, and Utah.

What's going to happen when the Farmington plant is joined by its sister San Juan plant, by two more proposed in Utah, by two now under construction at Page and Mohave? Projecting the answer from the observed effects of the Farmington plant, Dr. Joseph J. Devaney of Los Alamos Scientific Laboratory paints a noxious smear from Southern California to the Rocky Mountains. Long-term weather inversions typical of this region will concentrate the smog. It simply means goodby to the distances and spaces and mountain ranges floating over the plateaus and canyons of this great country.

But the effects of this huge power complex go far beyond esthetics. Thousands of tons of oxides of sulfur and nitrogen will poison the visible pall. These poisons have cumulative, and largely unknown, impacts on living things, including man.

Water from the Colorado River and its tributaries will be heated and consumed in vast quantities. This will concentrate the river's already high

418

Coal stripmined at Black Mesa is fed into the notorious Four Corners Power Plant that emits wastes in such volumes that they show up clearly in photographs taken from space satellites.

salinity, with serious effects on domestic, agricultural and industrial water uses in California, Arizona and Nevada, not to mention our good neighbor Mexico.

On and on the questions go — what about coal dust, pipelines, ash dumps, transmission lines, leaching of soil, road and railroad construction, runoff from chemical and industrial processes? What will be the direct and indirect environmental results of all these insults? No wonder ecologists are worried.

Black Mesa is a great highland in the Navajo and Hopi Reservations of northeast Arizona. It is hundreds of square miles of high valleys, dry washes, and aspen-laced piney canyons descending from a surrounding rim to a basin-like center. Navajo Indians live in the northern part — gardening and grazing sheep and cows. The southern end breaks away in a series of deep canyons interspersed by high peninsulas of the mesa. Here the Hopi Indians have their villages. These remarkable people have lived here nearly a thousand years — just about the way they live now.

An island of forest and grass in the desert, last outpost of ancient cultures — that's part of what Black Mesa is about.

But then there is the coal. It is spread thin over the 64,000-acre mining lease in the Navajo Indian Reservation and the Navajo-Hopi joint use area. That means extensive stripping and wide-spread devastation. It means networks of roads, big roads to carry 100-ton capacity loaders.

Today, the main road from U.S. 164 to the coal processing plant steals the scene. From the point where it leaves the highway and climbs the north rim of Black Mesa, then cuts across drainages and ridges for 15 miles to the coal plant, this road is a monument to all that is ecologically and esthetically wrong. It straight-lines and crosscuts the land in a massive swath of destruction. It is a line-of-sight road that violates every engineering principle. This means flooding and washouts and all manner of drainage destruction and clogging. Cuts through the ridges make no attempt to run with the contours. Huge expanses of bare, wounded earth will slump and slide, and the bulldozers will come back to shove the debris into the washes. The road is a crime, a gash, and a folly.

This road is 15 miles long. Debris alleys along the sides (where all trees and vegetation have been grubbed out) make it 150 feet wide in places. Add to this the parallel, equally devastated power line swath. Add to this the full network of mine roads. Add to this the thousands of acres of strip-mine devastation. Upshot: goodby Black Mesa.

What about the people? They are traditional Navajos. Few of them speak English. They and their ancestors have lived here for a long time. They will be displaced; "relocated" is the term. But to where? For traditional Navajos (not the urbanized, Anglicized progressives of Window Rock who signed the lease contracts), there simply aren't any places to go. All favorable areas of the largely barren Navajo Reservation are already occupied. Functionally illiterate and unemployable for industrial and urban life, deprived of their gardens and pastures, these people will be refugees. But what the hell? This is progress.

You might be tempted to say, "Too bad about the Navajos, but at least the Hopis will be okay. They're a long way from the coal fields."

That would be hasty. Because now we come to water. The coal mining lease lies athwart the drainages that head on Black Mesa's high rim, then flow southerly and southwesterly to the Hopi farmlands and beyond to the extensive Navajo farms in Moenkopi Wash. Spring snow melt and summer rains turn these usually dry washes into streams that water the Indian farms.

Once the strip mining starts it will interdict this flow of surface water. Artificial channels through the mine fields will be only partially effective. Much water, held in check by the torn up landscape, will leach into the ground. Water that does get through will carry in solution undetermined amounts of sulfuric acid. What does this portend for the Indian farms?

Another problem: the coal that goes to the Mohave plant will be pumped through a slurry line 275 miles long. It takes lots of water to make slurry and push it through a pipe 275 miles long. That water will be mined out of Black Mesa by deep wells. According to the pump operator it will take 2,000 gallons of water a minute.

Now for some geology. Black Mesa, though topographically a highland, is geologically a structural basin. In terms of groundwater, that makes it a low point. Skeleton Mesa to the north is higher. So are the Hopi villages, and the springs that give them life. The main aquifer of the region (that's where the groundwater is) is the Navajo Sandstone. This sandstone formation is 3,000 feet deep under the Black Mesa. It is higher in the surrounding areas. And, water flows downhill.

Pumping 2,000 gallons per minute out of Black Mesa will produce unknown effects on the surrounding parts of the Navajo and Hopi Reservations. Life on these reservations is pretty hard already. Take away the water and it will be impossible.

That about sums it up. The land, the water, and the people of Black Mesa are expendable.

It might ease the pain a bit to hear about the environmental protection plans put out by the public relations people of the Salt River Project. This is the managing utility for the Navajo Power Plant.

The best short statement of the Navajo Power Project's environmental policies is the one entitled "Environmental Policy." Part of it states: "The policy of the Salt River Project is to take whatever steps are technologically and economically feasible to protect the environment, while fulfilling our primary responsibility of providing adequate low-cost water and power. We will inspect and survey all new facility sites so that any historic or archaeological materials can be saved for posterity."

I wonder where the ecologists were (much less plain journeymen engineers) when they built the road? I wonder if the Salt River Project and its coal mining and processing agent, the Peabody Coal Company, have gone beyond dollars and gallons per minute in their hydrologic studies of Black Mesa. I wonder, when they piously talk of historical and archeological salvage, if they include living cultures a thousand years old? I wonder if they could care less?

107

The Stripmining of America

WAYNE DAVIS

1971

The proposal that the U.S. depend on coal as a basic fuel to replace dwindling stocks of petroleum seems likely to result in stripmining ever-larger areas of the American earth. The devastating impact of this technique in the past, particularly as it has affected the coal-rich state of Kentucky, is explored here by a professor of zoology at the University of Kentucky, Lexington. A compromise federal strip-mine bill was enacted in 1977 to modify some of these practices—but many of the basic problems remain.

KENTUCKY IS BEING destroyed by stripmining. Not slowly and surely, but rapidly and at an ever accelerating rate. And the disease that affects Kentucky soon may spread to more than half our other states.

Compare the irretrievable desolation of this eastern stripmined area with the pleasant farmland in the background.

Most Sierrans are aware of the problem of acid mine drainage. Sulfur impurities in coal, when excavated and exposed to the air, invite invasion by bacteria which manufacture sulfuric acid. The result is streams with a pH so low that nothing survives but bacteria. The damage is permanent; some sickly red streams run dead a hundred years after mining operations have ceased, with little prospect of improvement in sight.

The extent of the problem is enormous. Keith O. Schwab, of the Federal Water Quality Administration in Cincinnati, has data showing 12,000 miles of degraded streams from mine acid drainage in the Appalachian states. "We can ill afford to lose more streams to mining pollution," he said, "but this is exactly what is happening."

Acid mine drainage has been with us as long as we have been mining coal. It comes from deep mines and surface mines. It has long been accepted by most local people as a price they must pay for an economy which removes the coal and burns it up as quickly as possible. Progress means removing the wealth, destroying it, and leaving the land and streams permanently impoverished.

Acid mine drainage, considered one of the most vicious of industry by-products, is trivial however compared to the massive onrush of destruction caused by the incredibly rapid move to surface mining.

In surface mining heavy machinery removes the soil, including trees, grass and everything else on the surface, to expose the coal seam beneath. In the steep hill country of Eastern Kentucky, this means pushing massive amounts of spoil down the mountainside. Even the largest trees are broken and pushed over. The magnitude of the devastation is difficult to imagine for anyone who has not seen it. Man's ever accelerating technology, now rushing forward faster than the speed of thought, has designed machinery which will move 100 cubic yards of dirt with a single bite. Such shovels, standing as high as a 12 story building, are used around the clock, as is the smaller equipment at many of the mountain stripping sites. With profits running as high as 50 percent annual return on the dollar invested and the minimum price of Eastern Kentucky coal having doubled over a 6 month period last year, the rush is on while the getting is good. Western Sierrans who watched the timber barons' frenzied efforts to cut as many big trees as they could before Congress established a national park will understand the rape of Kentucky. As stripping grows and as people become more informed, the opposition forces encompass an ever larger segment of the public.

When rain falls upon a strip mine site massive quantities of mud wash into the streams.

Silt kills streams by destroying the nature of the bed. Many aquatic invertebrates upon which fish feed live beneath stones in the gravel-covered bottom of a stream. A fine load of silt from the clay-banks above glues down the stones, making them inaccessible and preventing the free movement of oxygen-carrying water among the gravel and beneath the stones.

The effect upon spawning of fish is similar. Most species of game fish lay eggs in the gravel of the stream bottom. If a fine layer of silt washes off the strip mine spoils and covers the eggs, they are deprived of sufficient oxygen for development and fail to hatch.

Although land destruction occurs, and acid mine drainage and silt are the best known effects of stripmining, a less known but equally dangerous factor may be the raising of the mineral ion concentration of the water affecting its usability by man and his industries. The U.S. Public Health Service sets standards for drinking water quality and the various industries have their own tolerance levels depending upon the purpose of the water they use.

The U.S. Forest Service has done studies on the effects of stripmining on water quality in Eastern Kentucky. In a report they point out that although the U.S. Public Health Service's Maximum Permissible Level for sulfates in water is 250 ppm, on severely disturbed watersheds in Eastern Kentucky they found concentrations ranging up to 2100 ppm. Whereas the tolerance level for manganese is 0.05 ppm, concentrations of up to 74 ppm were found, and for iron, whose recommended maximum level is 0.3 ppm, concentrations ranged up to 88 ppm.

In the steep Appalachian hills of 9 states strip mine benches now extend for 20,000 miles. Since only 4.6 billion of the estimated 108 billion tons of strippable coal have been harvested, one can see what the future holds.

The states with the largest reserves of strippable coal are North Dakota, Montana and Wyoming. If we draw a line from Pennsylvania to the coal-laden northwestern tip of Georgia, every state west of the line except Wisconsin, Minnesota and Hawaii has some coal deposits. With the industry's trend toward building power plants where the coal is, the destruction of parts of your state may be even now on the shallow horizon.

An example of what we are up against is illustrated by the opinion of James D. Riley, a vice president of Consolidation Coal Company, who spoke to the American Mining Congress in Pittsburgh in 1969. To the thunderous applause of the assembled strip miners, Mr. Riley declared that the conservationists who demand a better job of land reclamation are "stupid idiots, socialists and commies who don't know what they are talking about. I think it is our bounden duty to knock them down and subject them to the ridicule they deserve."

What can be done? First we must insist that Americans take their heads out of the sand and recognize the fact that power demand cannot continue to rise as it has been. Nothing—whether the power demand, the production of coal, the number of people, the number of cars, or the gross national product—can continue indefinitely to rise at an exponential rate in a finite world. The sooner we face reality on this the sooner we can begin to attack the problems.

So the next time the power tycoons tell you they must double power capacity by 1980 you should reply, "Nonsense—long before 1980 we must plan and put into practice a program to level off power consumption at something like present levels or less."

Stripmining coal from the Rosebud mine in eastern Montana.

424

Second we must have federal regulations of mining practices. Any local efforts to regulate this or any other industry encounter the standard and somewhat justified reply that regulation would put them at a disadvantage with their competitors in other states.

The culmination of oil production in this country is now at hand and the culmination of natural gas will arrive at the end of this decade. We are now dependent upon foreign sources for 20 percent of our oil supplies, and by the end of this decade this is expected to rise to 40–45 percent. Although coal reserves are much greater, we should not continue to treat them as the common enemy to be destroyed with all speed by the system found to be so effective in getting rid of our oil and gas.

108

Oil and Trouble in the Louisiana Wetlands

WILLIAM FUTRELL

1974

In our desperate rush for oil, we may be needlessly inflicting great damage on other resources, as this case history from Louisiana indicates. The author is a professor of law at the University of Georgia and served as president of the Sierra Club in 1977–1978.

IN FEBRUARY, 1970, when a blowout at Chevron's platform Charlie off the Louisiana coast resulted in a major oilspill, many conservationists along the Gulf Coast shifted their attention for the first time from the classic conservation issues of parks and wildlife to the problems of environmental pollution. At first, they focused on the more dramatic problems associated with offshore drilling—oilspills, for example. But in time, following the lead of career conservation officials in state and federal agencies, they came to understand that the most severe environmental impacts of offshore oil development were not the results of oilspills, but of the construction of onshore support facilities. Conservationists discovered they were dealing mainly with a land-use problem, a problem in coastal-zone management, for in the previous 30 years about 200 square miles of Louisiana's coastal wetlands had been destroyed as a result of onshore petroleum facilities. And in all this time, Louisiana had had no coastal zone management.

The economic development of Louisiana during this same 30 years has been intimately connected with the petroleum industry—offshore oil in particular. The bumper sticker often seen in southern Louisiana—"Oil feeds my family"—is true. More than 25,000 wells are in production along its coast, and more than 90 percent of all the offshore wells ever drilled in this country have been off the Louisiana coast. Offshore production in California and Texas is minute by comparison.

The history of Louisiana's coastal zone over the last generation is one of exploitation of *non*renewable resources and the deterioration of the natural environment on which renewable resources depend. The oil industry moved into the estuarine areas of the state in the mid-1930's, when drilling barges plied the inner waterways to drill for oil at the bottom of the many shallow lakes. In the late '30's, canals were dredged to provide access to previously inaccessible marshes and bayous so that submersible drilling barges could be moved into position. The first well out of sight of land was drilled in the Gulf of Mexico in 1937. Since then, the coastal zone has produced 90 percent of Louisiana's oil, with the majority of the producing wells located in swamp and marsh areas.

The petroleum industry's impact on the economy of Louisiana has been significant, largely because the oil boom led to the secondary development of an associated petrochemical industry. The population of the state, which had remained static, shifted from the northern region to the coastal zone, where the population increased 51 percent between 1950 and 1970. The area of highest growth, of course, was the oil coast. From 1936 to 1971, approximately 80 percent of all new investments in manufacturing facilities in the state was in the coastal-zone parishes. More than five billion dollars was invested in the petrochemical industry in the Louisiana coastal zone during those years, when approximately 100 major petroleum and petrochemical plants were built.

Naturally, such rapid development caused great changes in the coastal marshes. A recent study entitled, *A Louisiana Wetlands Prospectus,* published by the Louisiana Advisory Commission on Coastal and Marine Resources, states that increasing acreages are being closed to oyster harvesting because of pollution, that oyster yields per acre have decreased tenfold in the last 30 years, that the shrimp catch per boat has decreased ninefold in the same period, and that saltwater continues to intrude farther inland.

In the wetlands and coastal waters of Louisiana, a single structure or activity—whether it be an oil well, a refinery, or a highway—will not by itself decisively affect the health of the environment, but the cumulative effect of such projects results in an irreversible environmental decline. No matter how rich a state's coastal area may be, there is a limit to the amount of environmental stress that it can withstand. A number of respected observers believe that Louisiana's coastal zone has reached that limit, that there is no longer an excuse for allowing the oil companies, agricultural drainage projects, urban developers, and the mining industries to work unimpeded in the coastal marshes.

Dr. Sherwood Gagliano of Louisiana State University's Center for Wetland Resources has warned that another 30 years of abuse at the present level will probably destroy the viability of the Mississippi Delta system. The coast of Louisiana is no longer gaining new lands, as a delta coast should and as the Mississippi Delta has done for the past 4,000 years. Rather, it is now losing land at the rate of 16.5 square miles per year. In the past 30 years the Louisiana coast has lost almost 500 square miles.

Dr. Gagliano has further concluded that a major portion of the marsh destruction has resulted from the actions of the petroleum industry. Other contributing factors are canals, roads, flood control projects, and service facilities to service the secondary development of the oil-associated industries. The cumulative effect of onshore facilities for offshore drilling — the dredging and filling for sites, the use of the marshes as a dumping ground for waste — has led to the destruction of a large percentage of Louisiana's coastal wetlands. The introduction of a heavy industry such as offshore oil into the marshes presents a major crisis for the coastal zone.

In Louisiana, city and local governments, which once welcomed every increase in oil-company activity, now have reversed their position to the extent of bringing suit to enjoin the oil companies from further destroying the marshes. At public hearings, local officials are beginning to speak out for the protection of the renewable resources of the wetlands and to question the uncurbed dredging and pollution of the coastal zone during the past years.

The President's call for a tenfold increase in offshore-oil production, together with the opening of the Atlantic outer continental shelf, is a policy with profound and disturbing implications for our coastal lands. The lessons learned in Louisiana should be a warning against any such hasty development.

427

109

700,000,000,000 Barrels of Soot

DAVID SUMNER and

CAROLYN JOHNSON

1974

When all the oil is pumped out of the ground, the argument goes, there's plenty more to be had, embedded in certain kinds of shale. But oil-shale mining can be as devastating as the stripmining of coal. Some authorities doubt that it can produce more energy; the energy squeezed out of the rock may be less than the energy required to do the squeezing. Other questions about shale mining are raised here by David Sumner, a member of the Sierra Club's National Wildlife Committee, and Carolyn Johnson, a geologist who was affiliated with the Colorado Open Space Council.

THE OIL COMPANIES of America have a dream. The dream is oil shale, a dull gray rock that holds hundreds of billions of dollars worth of crude oil. The landscape of the dream is a 17,000-square-mile semi-wilderness area that encompasses major portions of southwestern Wyoming, east-central Utah, and west-central Colorado. The mechanics of the dream include the creation of a machine civilization in the West on public-domain land, land set aside for this purpose by an accommodating Department of the Interior. The occasion for the dream is what our government has chosen to call the energy crisis.

For the land, the dream is a nightmare.

Today, there are many who have said goodbye to the oil shale country, accepting as inevitable its transformation into a post-industrial wasteland, perhaps assuming that the land is of such indifferent quality that it doesn't really matter—particularly when weighed against the nation's orgiastic consumption of fossil fuels. If so, they are dead wrong. The country is generally high (elevations range from 4,800 to 9,000 feet) and semi-arid (rainfall is from eight to 24 inches annually), but this rolling, broken expanse of hills, valleys, ridges, holes, draws, breaks, washes, canyons, gulches, and meadows contains pockets of strikingly lovely country—such as the deep, ragged, sculpted, fluted canyons meandering into the southern margin of Colorado's Piceance Basin, or the sheer, stark Cathedral Bluffs westward in the same region, the ghostly eroded buttes and badlands along the White River in Utah, or a tough, severe landmark in Wyoming known as Kinney Rim. The land's cover is principally sage, assorted grasses, brush, and middling forests of squat, gnarled juniper, and pinon pines. Roads, even of the dirt variety, are few and far between; human population density is a scant 3.5 people per square mile.

This tri-state region is one of the truly superior wildlife habitats remaining in the lower 48 states.

In Colorado alone, more than 300 different species of mammals, birds, and reptiles have been inventoried, and in the three-state area, 20 rare or endangered species are thought to exist. The oil shale country is one of the only places left in the United States outside of Alaska where one can still see not only rare animals, but *lots* of animals—in numbers approaching those that must have existed before the white man came West.

Most of the oil shale land is public domain; all of it is irreplaceable. Once destroyed, it will be as extinct as the virgin hardwood forests of Manhattan.

The immediate impact of oil shale development will vary from site to site in all but its pernicious effect on the land. A "Preliminary Development Plan" for one Colorado tract (Gulf-Amoco) anticipates a 300,000-barrels-a-day production capacity from an open-pit mine two miles long, one mile wide, and 1,000 feet deep, in addition to an underground mine. Another site, where the area's saucer-shaped shale beds dip beneath the earth, will require "room and piling" mining methods similar to those now common in the coal industry. This method will extract only about 20 percent of the available shales, and only 65 percent of the horizon actually mined. The rest will be left in place, in hopes of preventing cave-ins and land subsidence. However, this site could present acute ground-water problems. Estimated at 25 million acre-feet (enough to supply a city like Boston for more than 15 years), a deep aquifer of subsurface brine underlies much of the Piceance Basin. In places, it is three times saltier than the ocean; obviously, it will have to be pumped from the mines before and during operations. Since the oil shale country occupies the upper Colorado River Basin, and since that river's salinity problems are already legion, the entire water quality problem is now a subject of intense political concern.

Along with the prospect of increased salinity levels, the need for removing water from the mines raises another problem: as the deep brines are pumped elsewhere, the surface water table is bound to drop. Springs and seeps will dry up, depriving the wildlife of what little water it already has; vegetation patterns will change after the present growth withers and dies.

The disposal of the processed shale presents enormous problems—especially since the material occupies 25 percent more volume *after* processing than it did before. The prospect of filling up the canyons of the Rocky Mountain West with billions of cubic yards of oil shale residue (the color of lampblack and the consistency of silt) poses some interesting questions. Since canyons have a way of running downhill, what will happen during periods of seasonal rain? Will the stuff be carried into the creeks, streams, and rivers of the Colorado watershed? Will it seep into the springs that help support the animals of the region? Will the Green and Colorado rivers (already thoroughly harassed by the works of man) run black with the contamination? And to what degree would this suspended soot add to the load of silt that is already beginning to fill up Lake Powell behind Glen Canyon Dam? Aside from potential contamination of the natural world, man himself could be victimized, according to a preliminary study by the University of Denver Research Institute: "Approximately 6,000 tons of carcinogenic material" could exist in the piles of waste, with undetermined effects on local inhabited areas.

The mining operations will require prodigious amounts of water. Fortunately for the oil companies, the Mineral Leasing Law of 1920 earmarks 52.5 percent of all oil shale receipts for the Bureau of Reclamation. Not only will this cash be used to build more and bigger dams, but in a classic case of public funds serving the private good, the money will build dams especially to benefit the oil shale industry.

Finally, there are the thousands of people, the executives, workers, merchants, wives, and children—as well as all the support facilities that go with them: the housing tracts, sewers, electrical lines, towns, service stations, boutiques, hamburger stands, bars, restaurants, and drive-in theatres. No one knows exactly how much land all this will affect, but a rough idea can be obtained from the prediction of the Colorado State BLM office that a "mature" million-barrel-a-day industry in the state will require 41 new schools handling 63,000 new children, who will live in 47,000 new housing units. One estimate predicts the population of the three affected Colorado counties will leap from its present level of 72,000 to 310,000 by 1987.

The impact of such a population on a previously semi-wild environment is predictable and hardly unprecedented. We can wonder, however, what the quality of life is likely to be for those thousands who find themselves trapped in a land that does not welcome them, their lives defined by the hard edges of a transplanted industrial civilization, with all the sterility, pollution, ugliness, and tawdry clutter common to such a world. And 30 or 40 or 50 years from now, when the land has been gutted of its shale and the people are gone, what will this transient civilization leave as its legacy?

The environmental provisions in the oil shale leases are so feeble, so shot through with debilitating qualifications, that any possibility of even mitigating possible environmental damage, much less of avoiding it, is extremely remote. The perfunctory bows to "restoration," an elusive notion that has evaded the coal strip miners for years, seem more like sedatives for conservationists than a remedy for the injured land. No one can agree on exactly what restoration entails, nor how it would be carried out even if it were possible.

Disturbed areas must be replanted with a cover sufficient to support pre-existing wildlife. A nice idea, to be sure, even encouraging—but virtually impossible. Regrowing any self-sustaining flora on the thin soils of the semi-arid West is an uncertain proposition at best. With oil shale, the difficulty is compounded because revegetation must proceed on the sterile, salty wastes that will issue from the processing plants by the cubic mile.

The dream machine moves on, but can it be stopped—or at least slowed down long enough for us to take a hard, long look at what we are doing?

The present techniques for mining oil shale are crude; the probable effects of charging ahead, disastrous. We cannot afford to learn from our mistakes. The land cannot afford our ignorance.

110

The Crisis We Won't Face Squarely

ROBERT ENTWISTLE

1973

Despite previous blackouts in certain areas, most Americans first discovered the energy crisis in 1973 when suddenly there was not enough gasoline to run the family car. The flow was subsequently restored at higher prices, but as this article points out, the great gasoline shortage was only a minor symptom of a much more serious disease in our society.

The reader should note that in 1977, the U.S. was importing 46% of all the oil it used, at a yearly cost of some $42 billion. The cost makes an obvious contribution to the U.S.'s foreign trade deficit of $35 billion, and one of its results was inflation, ever-higher prices for the American consumer to pay. The author's predictions would appear to be on target.

ARNOLD TOYNBEE has suggested that civilizations rise because of some fortunate set of characteristics and usually fail from an excess of those same characteristics. These days, the average American uses more energy in a week than a man living 150 years ago used in a lifetime. Our production and distribution of cheap energy is far beyond anything known before in history. Cheap energy in huge quantities is at the root of our affluence—and may be at the heart of our imminent demise.

Since 1945 our domestic consumption of oil has been rising at the rate of 5.4 percent a year, and this pattern of exponential increase shows every sign of continuing. Yet in 1971 our domestic extraction of oil, which had been following the upward trend of demand and use, suddenly stopped increasing.

The oil supply crisis is bracketed between our geometrically increasing

431

consumption and the plain fact that we are in the first stages of running out of domestic oil supplies. We mistake the real problem when we talk about a shortage of oil, for what we are actually facing is a consumption rate far in excess of a rational oil budget.

There is strong evidence that much of our oil consumption is more a habit of consumption than something essential to our affluence or standard of living. An all-out "crash" program of oil conservation is our best hope, perhaps our only hope.

The United States has six percent of the world's population, nine percent of the world's oil reserves—and uses 49 percent of the world's energy. The difference between domestic extraction and consumption is our "oil deficit." It is, simply, the difference between what we have and what we use.

That deficit is increasing at the rate of about 300 million barrels a year. By 1981, the oil deficit will approximately equal every barrel of oil we can suck out of our own ground and tidelands. There *is* no solution so long as the problem continues to be viewed in terms of meeting our growing levels of consumption.

We may be able to alleviate the deficit for the next several years by increasing our importation of foreign oil. To think this is a solution, however, is a snare and a delusion, for importation is economically dangerous and ultimately self-defeating. The cost of importing our oil needs could be as high as 15 billion dollars a year within five years.

This is ruinously expensive, obviously, but it has another effect which is more insidious—and damaging. We have had a negative balance of trade for some years now, and increasing prices for imported oil are not likely to help the situation.

There is no way that this writer can detect to increase our oil supply to actually meet our ever-growing demand. As noted, there are a number of things we can do to maintain our present supply level for the next 15 or 20 years, perhaps even increase it slightly. But the real problem simply will not go away. That problem is the consumption rate, compounded of our increasing population and an increasing per-capita use of energy. It is clearly telling us, as it has been telling us for years, that we have been extracting oil at rates which were not in our long-range best interests. We apparently have chosen to ignore that lesson in the past; we cannot afford to ignore it any longer.

The information that we would begin to run out of oil in the early 1970's has been known for at least 25 years. But consider only the past 10 years, how have we reacted?

We permitted automobile efficiency to decline almost 9 percent.
We permitted our mass transportation systems to almost disappear.
We doubled our use of oil to produce electricity.
We spent almost $50 billion on an interstate highway system.

Suppose we had taken just one of those highway billions and put it into the research for a truly economical 100 mpg personal transportation system;

432

not only would this have saved us billions of barrels of oil, and improved our international economic situation by perhaps billions more, it could have cut our automobile emissions by more than half. Suppose we had put a couple more of those billions into modernizing the 19th-century technology of the railroads. Suppose we had put one of those billions into research that would have shown us how to use high-sulphur coal without pollution in generating plants, instead of oil.

The fact is that the choices we made with respect to energy were more often the wrong choices. We were approaching oil bankruptcy and we ignored the fact. We tended not toward an oil conservation policy, but toward increased use of energy-inefficient systems. This is well illustrated in the transportation sector.

We use 61.8 percent of our oil consumption, or 9.8 million barrels per day, for transportation. Have we made the most efficient use of our transportation technology in terms of conserving oil? In *Energy Trends and Their Future Effect on Transportation*, W. E. Mooz used the term "energy intensiveness" to describe the relative energy efficiency of the various transportation systems. Driving an automobile requires more than three times the energy of a bus, and 17.4 times more energy than riding a bicycle. In the typically congested urban situation a bicycle is about as fast as a car. The use of the airplane is growing faster than any other mode and illustrates that we are actually trending toward the *lowest* energy-efficient system.

The automobile accounts for 4.6 million barrels of oil a day, or more than 29 percent of our total consumption. Suppose we could double the energy-efficiency of cars. That would cut oil consumption by almost 15 percent and would reduce emissions very greatly. After years and billions of dollars worth of advertising, about the only way we have to change the big car habit is to recognize what big cars are *really* costing us and to add part of that cost to their price.

An annual tax, which would be zero for 30 mpg cars and gradually rise to $1,000 for cars getting less than 10 mpg, could be an effective approach.

The transportation of freight uses 3.3 million barrels of oil per day, or 21 percent of our total consumption. The patterns away from energy-efficient systems are almost identical to the passenger sector.

Mode	Energy Intensiveness BTU/Ton Mile
Airplane	63,000
Truck	2,400
Rail	750
Ship	500

Of the oil used for freight transportation, 60 percent is used by trucks, but they only carry 19 percent of our freight. The $40 billion spent on the interstate highway program stands in stark contrast to the $900 million doled out to the near bankrupt railroads in the same period. Clearly, the Highway

Trust Fund amounts to a significant subsidy of the relatively inefficient trucking industry.

The long-range fact of the matter is that automotive and trucking fuel is almost a minor part of the problem. Indirectly, the automotive industry alone employs one in every seven people. The energy used to produce and support the automobile and truck is almost as large a part of our budget as the fuel. Automobiles and petroleum are the single most dominant influence on both the American and the international economy and upon our usage of raw materials, and the great majority of our seemingly unregulated conservation problems can be directly traced to their influence.

The short-range question asks if we can make the transition from our assumption of an unlimited supply of oil to the realistic position of living within a declining oil budget. Can we make that transition in an orderly fashion, seeing it as an opportunity, or will we resist reality and produce economic chaos? We taught ourselves and the world the affluence produced by a production/consumption society. Now can we lead the world toward the acceptance of quality rather than quantity, toward population control and an economy that serves the people while living within a rational natural resource budget? And the answer is: If we want to.

111   # Net Energy

THOMAS A. ROBERTSON

1975

"Our conventional wisdom is no longer working. It was made for a simpler time."

—WALTER LIPPMANN

The new concept of net energy analysis could revolutionize our understanding of what energy is all about—a revolution we need, as we enter the era of scarce resources. It is particularly essential to an appreciation of the limits to energy growth. And it throws new light on the causes of inflation. The ramifications of the idea are too complicated to be explored here, but the following excerpts provide a brief explanation of the basic idea. The author is coordinator of the Energy Center at the University of Florida and an associate of Howard Odum, who developed the concept; Odum is a specialist in energetics.

NET ENERGY BEGINS as a simple concept. *It takes energy to get energy.* What counts for use by society is the net energy "profit" from the work we (society) do to extract the given supply of energy. The accounting must be done in terms of both energy and money. Money alone as an accounting medium is not working. In other words, net energy is the amount of energy available from a given resource for use by society after subtracting the energy required to search for, extract, process, and transport the energy derived from that resource.

The energy/dollar problem is one involving two different but not separate functions in our economy, and the best way to understand this subtle distinction is first to consider energy alone. Our effort as a society to find, process, and use fossil fuels can be likened to that of a family fueling its members with food. In our case, the family at first lives next door to a grocery store that is fully stocked but charges nothing for the food. The family's only cost is the energy they burn in walking to and from the store. As long as the store is nearby and the trip is short, the family is unaware of any significant "price" and happily assumes either (a) that the store will never be exhausted, or (b) that another full store will spring up alongside the first by the time the first runs out of food.

Unhappily, the store runs out, and no new store takes its place. The family must now go to a store several blocks away—a trip that begins to exact a noticeable amount of food-energy cost to the family. Eventually, the only stores that can be found still stocked with food the family must have are a half-day's trip away. One day, the family realizes that it is spending the same amount of energy in traveling to and from the distant store as is contained in the food they pick up during the trip. There is, in other words, no net energy.

Now add dollars to the above story. We start with each unit of energy having an equivalent unit of money attached to it. The family gets money for all work it does outside of going to the store. After the family gets food/energy from its nearby store, it is able to use its surplus energy to do non-store-going work for which the family receives money. With this money the family can buy still other kinds of work. (Work, in this sense, means the goods and services available from society.) The non-store-going energy is net energy. It is easy to see that as the family spends more and more of its energy going to those more distant stores, it has less and less energy to do its money-making work.

The fundamental cause for inflation can be seen as changes in net energy. As our concentration of resources diminish (the stores are more distant and harder to get to), we do more work to bring in less and less net energy. Consequently, the amount of work done per unit of money diminishes.

The net energy available to an economic system can be seen as an energy return on the energy invested. This "energy-investment ratio" changes over time as concentrated resources become more dilute.

The energy-investment ratio and other elements of energy systems analysis form a new economics. Using energy as an accounting medium along with money can re-establish the information quality of our economic system so necessary to the best understanding and use of scarce resources by our society.

112   # Energy: Tomorrow Starts Today

JAMES SPAULDING

1972

The usual answer for the energy crisis, emphasized by the energy industry and most government agencies, is "Produce more." But environmentalists for many years have had another answer: "Waste less." The author of the article from which these paragraphs were excerpted was on the faculty of the Graduate School of Journalism at the University of California, Berkeley, and was past president of the National Association of Science Writers. His recommendations are based on a 1972 federal study, "The Potential for Energy Conservation."

THE MOST EFFECTIVE WAY to save energy in the home appears to be through more insulation, but significant savings are possible immediately without structural changes. If all home thermostats were set two degrees higher in summer and two degrees lower in winter, the 1980 projected energy savings would amount to 600,000 barrels of oil daily.

Other simple steps to reduce needless expenditure of energy in the home and office include: shutting off lights when leaving a room; drawing blinds and draperies in unoccupied rooms; operating washing machines and dish washers only when fully loaded; repairing faucet leaks promptly; having furnaces cleaned and adjusted at least annually; keeping the damper closed in an unused fireplace; cleaning condenser coils periodically in air conditioners, refrigerators and freezers; selecting light colors for roofing and house paint; and changing filters often in air-distribution systems. Many of these steps would save electricity, and for every BTU of electricity saved in the home or office, three BTU of energy will be saved ultimately because the conversion of fuel to electricity wastes about two-thirds of the fuel. A federal report says that the price of energy must be raised, or other strong incentives offered, to induce widespread adherence to these energy-saving steps. As it is now, a homeowner who conserves electricity might save energy but pay a higher bill, owing to a rate system that charges more per kilowatt the less fuel consumed.

More efficient home air conditioners represent another possibility for saving energy. The federal report says that many of the units being sold today are so grossly inefficient that they use about twice as much electricity to accomplish the same cooling as efficient units. The federal government specifies a minimum efficiency for the window air conditioners it buys. If these specifications became standard nationwide, the energy required for air conditioning would be cut 20 percent by 1980 at a savings of 500 trillion BTU per year.

Another 350 trillion BTU could be saved, according to the federal report, by changes in lighting. Fluorescent lamps, for instance, are more than three times as efficient as ordinary incandescent lamps. The report said that interior lighting in some new buildings is thought by some architects and lighting engineers to be excessively high, and the *Wall Street Journal* recently reported that a small group of these experts contend there is 10 to 20 times too much light in most modern schools, factories, and office buildings. They blame the makers of lighting equipment and the power companies for encouraging what the experts consider excessive lighting. In many new buildings lighting is so intense, the *Wall Street Journal* article says, that lighting experts estimate that except for the very hottest days, the main function of office air conditioning is to remove the heat caused by the indoor lighting.

Many scientists and engineers are coming around to the position taken by the Sierra Club and other conservation groups that an energy crisis exists only to the extent that we continue to ignore the sound management of existing resources. What remains to be done is to convert this growing awareness of the potential for conserving energy into a comprehensive national policy and program. In this effort, both scientists and environmentalists have much to contribute.

113

The Radioactive Risks of Nuclear Pollution

JEROLD LOWENSTEIN

1971

In the beginning, even the Sierra Club held the hope that "clean" nuclear energy would eliminate the need to build any more giant, scenery-destroying dams to generate electricity. But doubts arose when some of the hazards of nuclear fission plants became known. Some of these doubts were raised in this article by a member of the Radioactivity Research Center at the University of California's San Francisco medical center. His article begins with the effect of nuclear radiation on the oceans and goes on to discuss the effects of radiation on all life.

Surprisingly, the 1955 figure for the total body dose of radiation permitted yearly to radiation workers has still not been lowered.

DUE TO FALLOUT that will continue for another generation from nuclear weapons already tested, the world's oceans have already been contaminated with approximately twenty million curies of strontium-90 and cesium-137, isotopes with half-lives of thirty years, which enter the metabolic cycles of all living organisms. There are, at present, measurable amounts of these two radioactive isotopes in all living creatures, including man. There is considerable scientific controversy as to the "safe" concentration of these materials, or whether there is a safe concentration. But it is important to realize that if at some point we should decide that the "safe" concentration has been exceeded, we must then wait at least 30 years for that amount to be reduced by fifty percent.

Present levels, whether safe or not, are low indeed compared with those that may be projected to the end of the century. Radioactive wastes are either stored in tanks as corrosive liquids that will boil for more than a hundred years, or incorporated into glassy materials and stored in abandoned salt mines. By 1980, it is estimated that ten trillion curies of accumulated wastes will be stored, of which one trillion will be strontium-90. Although precautions are taken to prevent these lethal and long-lived radioactive poisons from entering the environment, a number of storage tanks have already developed leaks, and the heat from wastes stored in salt mines could deform the walls of the mines and raise the ground temperature at the surface by several degrees. Inevitably some of these radioisotopes will find their way into the world's waters and into the hydrobiosphere.

What I have outlined so far takes the most optimistic view of future radioactive pollution, for it assumes that present U.S. standards will be adhered to, and that there will be no major accidents. But some other nations already have less rigorous controls of nuclear wastes, and it cannot be expected that developing nations, which are viewed as possible customers for nuclear power plants exported by the advanced nations, will adhere to waste disposal techniques which are expensive and require a high level of technology.

Nuclear shipping presents an even more direct threat to the aquatic environment. Not only does it discharge fission products into the water, especially during warmup, but a nuclear vessel carries all its radioactive power source and radioactive wastes with it, and in case of accident, the entire amount eventually may go into the ocean. One Soviet and two U.S. nuclear submarines have already been lost, with millions of curies of fission products on board. Although the reactors of these vessels are strongly contained so as to prevent accidental release, it seems likely that over many years these corrosive radioactive wastes, with half-lives of thirty, a hundred, or a thousand years, will escape into the sea. Collisions in closed harbors, where most such accidents occur, could endanger large population centers and result in closure of a harbor to commercial activities for months or years.

From these sources—continued fallout, effluents and wastes from nuclear power and nuclear shipping—we see the prospect of steadily rising radioactive pollution of the ocean for several decades. During the next ten years, there will be a ten-fold increase in the production of radioactive wastes and, as yet, there are no international agreements limiting the disposal of these wastes into the oceans.

So violent are the disagreements among scientists regarding the biological hazards of radioactivity, that the general public has become quite confused. Citizens' groups in the U.S. have succeeded in blocking the construction of several nuclear power plants and are fighting legal battles against several others. The power companies have counter-attacked by a massive advertising campaign to persuade the public that nuclear power is safer and cleaner than conventional power.

What are the facts?

As usual, they are complex enough to provide arguments for both sides.

Many aquatic organisms concentrate radioactive elements. Some investigators point out that though the concentration factors may be high, the absolute amounts of the radionuclides in sea animals and plants are still small, and that one would have to eat very large amounts of any species in order to exceed the "allowable limit" for a particular isotope.

Other scientists insist that many of the present limits are set too high, that they are based on ignorance of the detailed or long-term effects of the radionuclides.

In humans, the allowable limits of radiation have been reduced progressively, as effects have been observed at lower and lower levels. For example, the permitted total body dose to radiation workers was set at 2500 rem/yr in 1902 (this is about three times the mean lethal dose, if given all at once); it was reduced to 100 in 1925, to 25 in 1936, to 5 in 1955; and Gofman and Tamplin believe it should be reduced now to 0.5, which is just the value that the previous downhill slope would predict for 1970!

Gofman and Tamplin, vocal critics of the present radiation standards, have compiled voluminous evidence that there are increased rates of cancer and leukemia at currently permitted radiation levels. Other experts have denied this and supported the concept of a "threshold" radiation dose below which no ill effects occur. Against the "threshold" concept and supporting the Gofman and Tamplin view, is a recent study by Stewart and Kneale, in England, showing that children whose mothers had x-rays taken while pregnant are more likely than other children to develop cancer, and that the probability increases with the number of x-ray pictures taken. The radiation dose in these cases is extremely small and, until the time of this study, was considered completely safe for humans at any age. It appears now that unborn babies and infants may be a hundred times more sensitive than adults to the carcinogenic effects of radiation.

As with DDT, the direct effects on man may prove to be less important than the indirect ecological impact due to eradication of vulnerable species.

Radiation literally breaks a link in the helical chain that transmits genetic information, causing abnormalities and death in descendants. These effects, while they occur at the lowest levels of radiation, may not become apparent for several generations. Therefore some of the most serious delayed consequences of radioactive pollution may not appear for ten to fifty years in affected species, which includes all species on earth. It can be argued that some mutations are useful, that improved strains of food plants have been produced by deliberate irradiation of seeds, that the process of evolution may ultimately depend on radiation-induced mutations. But the ratio of harmful to useful mutations is at least a million to one, so radioactive pollution constitutes genetic experimentation on a global scale, with unpredictable consequences to all life on earth.

I am very much disturbed by the massive advertising campaign which has been launched by power companies in the United States, aimed at convincing the public that nuclear power is clean, virtually free of radiation, good for the environment, and necessary to meet the power demands which their advertising has helped to create. The parallel with the cigarette companies, which for years made unsupported health claims for their products, and have persisted in their promotional efforts despite the proved carcinogenic and other disease-inducing results of smoking, are only too striking. It seems to me grossly irresponsible to substitute the techniques of mass persuasion for the scientific investigation and careful search for answers which only many years of experience and observation will assure. In the meantime, restraint and careful planning in nuclear exploitation of the oceans, and worldwide agreements limiting radioactive pollution, are urgently needed.

114

Radioactive Wastes: An Aspirin Tablet per Person?

JOHN P. HOLDREN

1977

John Holdren is a physicist at the University of California's Lawrence Berkeley Laboratory and a member of the U.C. Energy and Resources Group. This selection was taken by the Bulletin *from* Ecoscience: Population, Resources, Environment, *published by W. H. Freeman. Holdren was co-author with Paul and Anne Ehrlich.*

IT IS NOT UNCOMMON to hear from the public-relations arm of the nuclear industry that the radioactive wastes from nuclear power are equivalent in size to no more than an aspirin tablet per year for every person whose electricity is provided by nuclear plants. Probably the most misleading aspect of this analogy is that toxicity, not volume, is the important characteristic of the wastes. If a "tablet" were an apt comparison, it would have to be a cyanide tablet, and even this does not do justice to the magnitude of toxicity of the fission products.

It turns out, moreover, that a tablet per person is far from correct, even in respect to volume. If the high-level radioactive wastes from the reprocessing plant are solidified in their most concentrated form—the process to which the aspirin-tablet view presumably refers—the resulting volume per 1000-megawatt light-water plant per year is 2.5 to 3.0 cubic meters. Since such a plant, running at a generous average of seventy-five percent of full capacity, could meet the full electricity demand of 750,000 Americans in 1975 (this includes not only their residences but the associated commerce and industry), the volume of high-level solid waste per person served is 3.3 to 4 cubic centimeters. The volume of an aspirin tablet is about 0.4 cm³, so the solidified high-level wastes are about the size of ten aspirin tablets per person.

This figure, however, is only the tip of the iceberg. Most of the high-level wastes have not been solidified yet and federal law requires only that solidification take place within ten years of the creation of the wastes. The volume of the liquid form before solidification is ten times greater than that of the solid (100 aspirin tablets per person). Additionally, there are the highly radio-active remains of the fuel cladding (2 cubic meters per reactor year, or five aspirin tablets/person).

Unfortunately, even this is only the beginning. The reprocessing plant also produces annually for every 1,000-megawatt reactor about twenty-five cubic meters of "intermediate-level" liquid wastes and 1200 cubic meters of "low-level" liquid wastes. These amount to sixty and 3,000 additional aspirin tablets per person, respectively. "Low-level" solid wastes from the reprocessing plant and from the reactor itself add up to between eighty and 160 cubic meters per year (200 to 400 more aspirin tablets per person). These wastes contain alpha-emitting radioisotopes of very long half-life.

All this adds up to a volume equal to that of 3,300 to 3,600 aspirin tablets per year per person served. If the Nuclear Regulatory Commission (NRC) approves the routine recycling of plutonium, an additional 340 cubic meters of plutonium-contaminated wastes per reactor per year will appear at the fuel-fabrication plants—another 850 aspirin tablets per person served. The total is still not an overwhelming volume—around 1,500 cm of waste per person per year—but remember, the toxicity of this material is what is really important. It is disquieting, in any case, to find the nuclear industry—so quick to complain about "irresponsible" statements from environmentalists—glibly dispensing information that is both qualitatively misleading and quantitatively in error by a factor of thousands.

115

Nuclear Exports: The Perilous Enterprise

GREG THOMAS

1977

Nuclear dangers in the U.S. are impressive enough, but what happens when wastes from nuclear power plants, including deadly plutonium, which can easily be used to make nuclear bombs, are spread around the world? The author is a lawyer with the Sierra Club Legal Defense Fund.

WHEN THE ATOMIC BOMB made its grim debut in August, 1945, at Hiroshima and Nagasaki, the United States alone possessed the secret. Soon after, there were two nuclear powers.

Today, there are six. The prestige and tactical advantage of nuclear weapons continue to provide an incentive to other nations to join the nuclear club. The worldwide proliferation of nuclear power technology provides the means. Unchecked, the current drift toward increased access to nuclear explosives threatens to put at the disposal of governments and, ultimately, individuals, the ability to inflict at will enormous damage on one another and on the natural world. It is improbable that the power, once possessed, will not ultimately be used.

The difficulty in insuring that nations do not misuse atomic power is that in the process of generating heat for electricity, nuclear reactors transform much of their uranium fuel into other radioactive substances, including plutonium, which accumulate in the fuel rods. Natural systems have evolved no tolerance for plutonium. But in addition to its extraordinary toxicity, plutonium is also the material of choice for fabricating nuclear explosives. With as little as ten pounds of plutonium, equipment and materials that can be readily purchased, and technical information freely available, an atomic bomb can be fashioned in a matter of days even by a person who is not a scientist.

Recent events indicate that little exists to deter the diversion of the peaceful atom to weapons production if the will to do so exists. In 1974, India shook a complacent world by such an exercise of will and thereby joined the ranks of the United States, the Soviet Union, Great Britain, France and China as a nuclear weapons state. But unlike the other members, India's credentials were forged of materials produced in a reactor designed to furnish electricity. India simply diverted plutonium from a power reactor, which it had imported from Canada under an agreement that contemplated only "peaceful" uses. A new era in the course of nuclear proliferation had dawned.

Mad rulers, internal revolutions and desperate military responses within national governments are all too common in history. The current era has been plagued by terrorists, who have grown increasingly sophisticated in their tactics and manipulation of available resources. The allure of nuclear capability may be irresistible to them; it surely opens terrifying new horizons for everyone else. The existence of separated plutonium, however well guarded, may put such groups a giant step closer to such capability than does the existence of plutonium within spent fuel rods.

As the number of fingers on the nuclear trigger increases, so do both the incentive and the means to join the club. Contemplating this spiral, David Lilienthal, the first chairman of the U.S. Atomic Energy Commission, reflected during the course of recent Senate hearings: "If a great number of countries have arsenals of nuclear weapons, I am glad I am not a young man, and I am sorry for my grandchildren. That would produce a terrifying prospect for the young men and women who are looking forward to a future."

In searching for a solution, the most compelling fact is that the options are becoming fewer.

It is imperative that the United States act now at least to establish a selective and discriminating export policy that rewards those countries that agree to stringent limitations on their nuclear activities. Fuel services and all other nuclear assistance should be immediately confined to countries that:

Forswear additional nuclear explosives for all purposes;

Place all nuclear facilities under effective safeguards and physical security;

Forego the development, acquisition or export of fuel reprocessing or enrichment facilities;

Require the same set of conditions of those countries to whom they might in turn sell nuclear materials and technology.

The reprocessing moratorium is certain to be the most controversial. It is also the most important. Nothing short of leaving plutonium in the spent-fuel rods will be sufficient, over the long run, to keep it away from those who aspire to the bomb. Even then, the spent fuel must be assiduously protected.

It seems most likely that in the face of the considerable moral persuasion of the United States, a framework and incentive would be established for meaningful negotiations. If success cannot be guaranteed, at least a break will have been made with current trends that, in sum, amount to a prescription for disaster.

116

How We Can Live Without Nuclear Power

MICHAEL McCLOSKEY

1976

In 1976, concern with nuclear hazards was so high that an anti-nuclear initiative appeared on the ballot in California. The following article by the Sierra Club's executive director was published in connection with that campaign (the measure did not pass); much of it is applicable to the rest of the country as well. It is designed to answer the argument that whatever the risks of nuclear power may be, we must have it to keep going.

FORTUNATELY, we have not yet really become "hooked" on nuclear power—it now only provides ½ of 1% of the total energy this state uses.

The people of California have at least five possible options to choose from to replace projected nuclear output.

1 They can employ energy conservation to cut our future use by the year 2000 to one-half of what it might otherwise be;

2 they can accelerate development of geothermal power, solar energy, and conversion of organic materials;

3 they can use a surplus which is likely to exist on the west coast over the next twenty years of domestically produced oil as a result of development in Alaska, at Elk Hills, and in Pacific outer-continental-shelf waters;

4 they can import sufficient quantities of oil, or

5 they can rely on abundant U.S. coal reserves which may be deep-mined from places like Utah to produce synthetic gas or oil for use in properly located steam plants equipped with scrubbers.

These options are not mutually exclusive; they can be combined in varying mixes according to changing circumstances.

Let's look at what is involved with each of these alternatives.

1 *Energy Conservation.* Much of the debate over future energy needs centers on the question of how fast demand will grow. Slowing population growth and rising prices have already cut the rates of high-growth familiar in the 1960's. A vigorous program of energy conservation can cut the projections even more. Instead of growing at a rate of 3.4% annually, California's energy use is now growing at about 2.3% annually, with the higher prices now prevailing and energy conservation measures which have already been initiated. With additional energy conservation measures, the rate may be cut to something ranging from 1.6% to 0.6%. By the year 2000, these differences in growth rates would produce widely contrasting projections of needed supplies. Instead of needing 14 quads (quadrillion BTUs) of energy by 2000, we may need only 7 quads or less (we now produce 6 quads for use in California).

Further improvements in auto fuel economy, greater appliance efficiency and thermal efficiency in industry, and better thermal standards for buildings as a result of state and federal programs can rein in growth rates to produce these savings. With such savings, three-quarters or more of the projected nuclear plants would not be needed, and very little added power capacity may be needed at all. Present installed capacity, plus already planned hydro and geothermal facilities, might handle really low growth in demand for as much as twenty years. Thus, prudent money-saving techniques to save energy might save all the capital that would have been used to produce more nuclear power and spare us exposure to nuclear risks. We could put the same capital to work to produce jobs in other more socially useful pursuits.

445

2 *New Energy Sources.* Of all the states, California has the best opportunity to make the most of geothermal power (though it is not without its own environmental problems). Presently, California has the largest installed capacity; federal leasing is most advanced here; and research is most advanced in solving corrosion and scale problems with wet steam in places like the Imperial Valley, which has a huge potential. By the year 2000, geothermal power might supply as much as 40% of our electricity in California. Also, by converting organic wastes into power, taking them from municipal sewage and garbage as well as from farms and feedlots, we could procure another 8% of our power in that fashion (bio-conversion). And by replacing demand for electricity and gas with rooftop solar collectors for heating on more and more houses and businesses, we can efficiently reduce the need for so many power plants of any sort. Through a combination of these strategies, plus moderate efforts of conservation, Commissioner Ronald D. Doctor of the California Energy Resources Conservation and Development Commission believes we can have the power we need in the future without more nuclear power.

3 *Surplus Oil on the West Coast.* At the present time, more electricity in California is generated from oil than any other fuel. Some studies suggest that with moderate growth in energy use, there may be a substantial surplus of oil on the west coast through the year 2000. With the resumption of federal oil leasing in waters offshore of Southern California and completion of the Alaskan pipeline, the share of the national production of oil supplied by the west coast may double by the year 2000. As a result, two or three times more oil than we can consume may be available for shipment east via a pipeline or tankers (cf. 1162 million barrels, under low growth, with 885 million barrels under medium growth). If nuclear power is not available, about one-third of this oil could be used to fire power plants here instead. There is some question, in any event, about whether enough pipeline capacity will be available to get all the oil out of California. If the federal government proceeds to release oil from the Elk Hills reserve, there may be an even bigger oil surplus. To solve problems of air pollution from oil-fired plants, the troublesome sulfur should be removed at the refineries (producing ultra-low sulfur oil with less than 0.1% of sulfur instead of 0.5% sulfur; the cost of this is estimated to be only 30¢/barrel).

4 *Imported Oil.* California now imports only about 29% of its oil supply from foreign sources (principally Indonesia, Iran, and Saudi Arabia), in contrast to 40% for the country as a whole. With burgeoning Alaskan and OCS production, California might not need to import any oil after 1980. However, if the entire surplus of oil were instead to be moved to eastern markets, California could easily replace nuclear power by continuing to import oil, but at a rate that would still be under the current relative levels of importation. The nuclear component could be replaced by importing only slightly more oil than we now do. (To replace 300 billion KWHs of nuclear electric-

ity by 2000, we would need about 190 million barrels of oil, in contrast to our current importation of 176 million barrels/year.)

5 *Coal.* Of all conventional energy sources, none is more plentiful in the United States than coal (we have a supply that may last more than 400 years even with high growth rates). An ample supply of it exists in Utah and New Mexico, and much of this can be reached via deep mining (with proper ventilation and safety precautions, deep mining can be safer than most industries). One study, which projects current growth rates to the year 2000, estimates that coal usage in California will grow at the rate of 8.4% even with nuclear power. If nuclear power is replaced entirely by coal, the growth rate for coal would then increase to 11% per year. If power plants which burn coal are equipped with the best available emission control technology (e.g., scrubbers), air pollution problems can be minimized. Plants with such equipment should be located away from air basins which suffer severe air pollution problems and away from national parks, monuments, and other such reservations. By 1990 fluidized bed facilities may have been perfected to eliminate NOx problems from coal-fired plants. An even better solution may be to convert coal into low BTU gas, which can be burned by a power plant without causing air pollution. Continuing research may solve enough problems with such conversion to bring such gas into the market in the late 1980's. While coal may be the least environmentally attractive replacement alternative, nonetheless it is abundant, and it is bound to become a growing factor in the supply picture. We cannot avoid grappling with the process of finding solutions to its environmental problems.

It will take further study to determine what constitutes the best combination of alternatives to nuclear power as time progresses. The important point to stress, however, is that we have *plenty of choices.*

We are not yet sure what would be the best combination from an environmental point of view. However, we have prepared a supply scenario for the year 2000 in California for electricity which we think is plausible. It is the kind of scenario that needs to be seriously studied. It assumes that population will continue to grow slowly, and that the state will have the good sense to institute an effective and economical energy conservation program (including managing peak loads). Under these assumptions, electrical usage would grow at a rate of only about 2.5% per year (about 0.5% for energy as a whole), and we would need not quite twice as much electricity by the year 2000 as we now use. The electricity would be obtained from the following sources: oil—24%; geothermal—21% solar/wind power—16%; hydro—13%; bioconversion—10%; coal—9%; gas—7%; nuclear—0%.

We have lots of alternative sources of supply—most of which are available at acceptable environmental and economic costs.

447

117

Defusing Old Smoky by Plugging into Nature

JOHN P. HOLDREN

1971

Solar energy as an alternative to nuclear energy is discussed here in an excerpt from Energy: A Crisis in Power. *This was a Sierra Club book, published in 1971.*

IN THE YEAR 1970, mankind consumed an amount of energy equal only to the amount of solar energy that strikes earth's outer atmosphere in fifteen minutes. Because solar energy is clean, free and abundant, why did we not use it to solve our energy problems long ago? There are two main reasons. First, the solar energy reaching the surface of the earth is dilute: to acquire enough for large projects it must be collected over a large area, which makes solar energy, although free, expensive. Second, solar energy is variable: on cloudy days not much gets through, none at night, and in winter less is available than in summer. Storing large amounts of heat or electricity is difficult and expensive. But these problems are not overwhelming. Much progress has been made during the past few decades, despite woefully inadequate financial support for the research.

Two misconceptions about solar energy should be dismissed at the outset. One that can unfortunately be found in many recent books and articles is that harnessed solar energy would cost "one thousand times as much" as electricity does today. The basis for this statement is the high cost of the sophisticated photovoltaic cells which convert sunlight directly to electricity in running space satellites. These cells cost $175,000 per kilowatt electrical (kwe) of capacity, or about one thousand times as much as a coal-burning power plant. But there are dozens of other ways to harness solar energy. The extremely expensive solar cells for space flights are so unrepresentative that one might think this misconception was planted by the coal industry or the nuclear interests.

The second misconception is that harnessing solar energy necessitates covering sixteen square miles of flat land with solar collectors in order to build a single 1 million kwe power plant. Again, the measurement has some technical basis. But it is misleading because heavy reliance on centralized power plants is not the only way to exploit solar energy. After all, one of the great built-in advantages of energy from the sun is that transmission and distribution are free. Many household, commercial and even industrial consumers of energy could be served by roof-top solar collectors, with the higher construction cost of the numerous small facilities (as opposed to a few centralized ones) being partly offset by savings in transmission and distribution.

Solar energy is already used for domestic water heating in many parts of the world, especially where electricity or fuel is expensive. The usual method exploits the fact that a black surface absorbs almost all the solar energy falling on it. Water pipes are laid over black panels of metal or wood; glass is placed over the pipes to reduce heat loss by radiation and convection. The water is heated while circulating through the pipes and is then stored in an insulated tank. An adequate system for a typical family requires ten to fifty square feet of panels, costs between $100 and $500, and can heat water to 200 degrees Fahrenheit. For decades, a few experimental houses have been successfully heated with solar energy in climates as cold as Boston's. Usually, water or a bed of rocks has served as a storage medium for the heat until needed, but we can probably anticipate important advances in chemical storage.

Larger amounts of energy can be obtained by building collectors that follow the sun in its path across the sky; higher temperatures can be achieved by using lenses and mirrors to concentrate the sun's energy on a small area. Using such techniques, small solar-driven steam engines have been built for $1,000 per kwe — not one thousand but only five times as expensive as a large nuclear or fossil fuel power plant.

A solar unit providing heat in winter and air conditioning in summer is an attractive possibility. A particular virtue of solar air conditioning is that the period of peak demand coincides rather closely with the period of peak solar energy flow. Within ten years, such dual-purpose units could compete with electrical heating and air conditioning in many parts of the United States. They could employ relatively simple collectors like those described above.

New coatings superior to glass in increasing the "greenhouse effect" (solar energy gets in but heat doesn't get out) may put an end to conventional assumptions about the efficiency of solar collectors.

Even the solar cell may eventually become an economic proposition for large-scale terrestrial use. Some experts believe that solar cells manufactured in quantity, with lenses or mirrors to reduce the necessary surface area, could be one hundred times cheaper than they are today. It has also been suggested, for the longer term, that large collectors in earth orbit could tap solar energy before any is lost in reflection and absorption by atmosphere and clouds. While in orbit the energy would be converted to electricity, then beamed to earth on microwaves. The difficulties of such an enterprise should not be underestimated, but it would be foolish to state flatly that it cannot or will not be done within the next thirty or fifty years.

118

The Windmill Renaissance

VOLTA TORREY

1977

Every mountain climber knows that in order to go forward, it is sometimes necessary to go backward to some point you have passed and chart a new route from there. Windmills, which supplied energy for thousands of years, were largely abandoned in industrial countries when cheap electric power came in over the wires. Now that electricity is becoming increasingly expensive, energy experts are taking another look at that ancient power source and devising ingenious variations on it. The writer of this article is author of a book on the subject: The Wind Catchers *(Stephen Greene Press, 1976).*

THE MOST NEARLY inexhaustible source of energy yet available to us is the sun. It bathes the earth with radiation, and the wind derives its strength directly from this energy. Windmills have often enhanced both the earth's productivity and its beauty, without ever polluting the air, water, or soil, But when nuclear power was first demonstrated at Alamogordo, New Mexico, thirty-two years ago this summer, further development of wind-energy conversion systems in the United States virtually ceased, and was not resumed until recently.

Our biggest wind-energy conversion system today is a 100-kilowatt machine designed by space engineers and erected on the Ohio Shore of Lake Erie near Sandusky. On this machine, ERDA expects to test new concepts and components for more powerful wind turbines, and several aerospace companies are competing for contracts to produce them.

Although the Ohio plant is the largest one now running, many other new types are generating smaller amounts of electricity elsewhere. Almost any home handyman can build a windmill that will pump water, but building an economical, efficient aerogenerator is still a complex technical challenge.

At Albuquerque, New Mexico, in the Sandia laboratories that ERDA inherited from the Atomic Energy Commission, a small team of aerodynamics specialists has built a modern rotor that revolves parallel to the ground, the way the world's first windmills did. Instead of catching the wind with simple sails, this one does it with scientifically designed bow-shaped airfoils. Engineers call this a "vertical axis wind turbine" because the axis of rotation is perpendicular both to the earth's surface and to the windstream that drives it. Several similar turbines are being tested in other states and Canada. The Sandia team believes this kind of machine will prove to be best for generating electricity, and ERDA has applied for a patent on its experimenters' innovations.

At Mukwonago, Wisconsin, a technological commune called "Windworks," sponsored by Buckminster Fuller, has been especially interested in small aerogenerators that anyone handy with tools might assemble. This group has devised new kinds of vertical rotors, towers and power converters. With one of the latter, the owner of a Windworks system might make his utility company's meter run backward whenever the wind produced more power for him than he was using.

At Stillwater, Oklahoma, a newly organized firm called American Wind Turbine, Inc., began manufacturing another new type of windmill last year. The rotor on it is built like a bicycle wheel, with a rim around it so that power can be drawn from it at either the hub or the rim. The wheel weighs less than the old type of fan and is easier to support at an appropriate height. This turbine can either run a pump mechanically or generate electricity.

Both on our big ranches and in many other places still remote from transmission lines, some machine of this sort may be the most economical type of power plant yet feasible. The wind that drives these and other new experimental machines costs nothing, and this accounts largely for the windmills' ability to survive competition from alternative energy sources.

Few authorities expect a windmill ever to generate as many megawatts of energy economically as a big thermal or nuclear plant, but most experts agree that wind-driven engines can provide supplemental power during peak loads. The most desirable sizes and types of wind-energy conversion systems can soon be determined, and economic as well as environmental and sentimental motives all suggest that more attention should be given to solar energy, including the wind, in formulating policies to provide our country with adequate energy.

119   # Of Poison, Man, and Indifference to Life

NANCY BUDER

1974

It is dismaying to count the poisonous products in our cabinets and closets—and probably impossible to count the number of poisonous substances used in industrial processes. While laws affecting the use and disposal of such poisons have been passed, in many cases they have proved difficult to enforce.

The author served as consultant to the Sierra Club on solid waste management while working under a grant from the Environmental Protection Agency.

NOT LONG AFTER moving to Maryland's Little Elk Valley in 1967, Dr. Petro U. Capurro and his family began to fall ill with increasing frequency, exhibiting strange symptoms that Dr. Capurro, a pathologist and toxicologist, suspected were connected with the activities of a local chemical plant. So he set out to discover just how widespread these symptoms were among the people in the valley. He learned that 12 of the 43 residents were hospitalized from 1967 to 1970, showing signs of damage to the pancreas, liver, or kidneys. Seven of the eight residents he examined personally also showed malfunctions of the liver and pancreas.

The Galaxy Chemical Company, the only industry in the valley, has been the center of controversy among local residents since 1961, when it began to reprocess solvents in its local plant. The company uses a distillation process to purify more than 20 different solvents, most of which are deadly in high concentrations. One of these—benzene—is known to inhibit the production of red blood cells and to cause leukemia. Others can damage the liver, kidneys, pancreas, and central nervous system. In the course of his investigation, Dr. Capurro identified more than 25 of these solvents in the air and water of the valley. He reported in *Medical World News* that he had found nine of these solvents in blood samples from various valley residents. The nine solvents were benzene, carbon tetrachloride, methyl chloride, methylene chloride, methyl ethyl ketone, methyl isobutyl ketone, tetrachloroethane, and toluene.

Most of the solvents processed by Galaxy contain an unknown number of impurities that are discarded as wastes. No one—not even company

452

officials—knows what all the impurities are. These wastes are illegally dumped in a nearby sand-and-gravel quarry because Galaxy does not have the dumping license required by the state. Residents of the community have continually complained to the county health authorities about odors emanating from the quarry. In April, 1973, it caught fire, and fumes from the burning chemicals were dispersed throughout the valley. After the fire, the residents' complaints and health problems greatly increased.

The state of Maryland forced Galaxy to eliminate its open evaporating ponds, but residents of Little Elk Valley must still rely on wells for water that the EPA has determined is contaminated. The valley's air is so polluted that some parents will not allow their children to play outside because the fumes make them act "dopey." As one mother recently explained to a reporter from the *Baltimore Sun,* "We'd have to house ourselves up like bears and hibernate." Looking outside, she went on to say that she could "see a blue fog settling through here laying right close to the ground—or yellow, it would get real yellow looking."

Little Elk Valley provides an extreme case of the threat to human health and environmental quality posed by the careless or mindless disposal of hazardous substances. But we must not mislead ourselves into thinking such instances are unique. We are all, in some degree, in the position of the valley residents, for the entire country—if not to say the world itself—has been repeatedly exposed in the past century to a staggering variety of toxic substances. Industrial society has routinely trafficked in poison, and we are beginning to pay the price. The common wastes of home and industry have become a greater threat to human safety and environmental quality than anyone could have foreseen. Even our best attempts to contain many of these toxic substances have proven futile, not to mention the appalling number of occasions when few if any precautions were taken. Not only is the production of hazardous wastes continuing, now increasing by some five to ten percent annually, but the wastes of past generations—wastes assumed to be long buried—are returning to plague us.

The practice of burying toxic substances in the ground on the assumption they would eventually decompose into natural elements and remain permanently as benign constituents of the soil has proven disastrously wrong in many communities. For example, a large municipal landfill in the state of Delaware, where both domestic and industrial wastes had been buried for many years, was closed in 1968, and its contents forgotten. Four years later, it was discovered that chemical and biological pollutants had percolated into the local groundwater. The Environmental Protection Agency estimates that some $26 million will be required to correct this dangerous situation and to stop further deterioration of an underground aquifer that provides drinking water to over 40,000 people.

The kindred practice of confining certain wastes to holding ponds has proven just as unreliable. In too many cases, the pond has held little beyond our hopes. For example, since the 1940's, a New York electroplating firm has been discharging its waste-water into what it considered to be safe settling ponds. Even though the ponds were well constructed, they lacked protective linings. As a result, seepage of toxic cadmium and chromium has contaminated the local groundwater.

Our air may also become the unfortunate destination of migrating wastes, as is demonstrated by the hexachlorobenzene mystery of Geismar, Louisiana. Hexachlorobenzene, along with other benzene derivatives, is noted for its carcinogenic properties. So when the U.S. Department of Agriculture discovered that unusually high levels of the substance had accumulated in the fatty tissues of local cattle, it placed the entire herd, numbering some 20,000, under quarantine. It turned out that one of the many chemical plants in the area, following a practice common to all, had dumped its hexachlorobenzene wastes on adjacent land, assuming they would remain intact until they could be properly treated. But weather conditions caused the hexachlorobenzene to evaporate into the atmosphere, from whence it proceeded to settle with the morning dew on nearby pastures, where it was ingested by the grazing cattle.

Substances such as hexachlorobenzene and the host of solvents emanating from the Galaxy Chemical Company are relatively new arrivals in the world. They were created in the retorts of modern science in an age when "progress through chemistry" seemed not only promising, but inevitable. We may regret our foolishness in so cavalierly handling these exotic substances, in blithely assuming that the miracle of modern chemistry was entirely benign, but at the same time we can understand, perhaps, how it

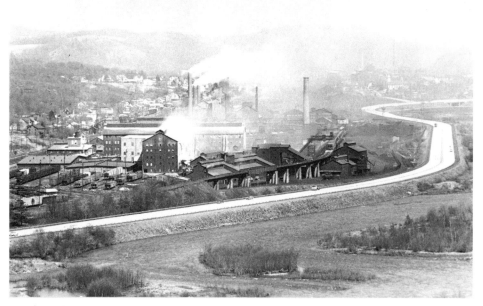

Smokestacks in Pennsylvania.

was that we failed to recognize the deadly aspect of these new substances. It is far more difficult to understand our similar casualness with such naturally occurring poisons as arsenic, surely one of the most notorious poisons in history.

Because it is a naturally occurring element in our soil and water, we long believed that if buried in the ground, even arsenic would eventually be rendered harmless. Today, we know differently, we know that this element will remain indefinitely and reappear to infest later generations. For example, in the late 1930's, a pesticide containing arsenic was buried in western Minnesota. Thirty years later, a building contractor expanded his facilities by building a warehouse and office outside the city of Perham. A well was drilled for his water supply. Almost immediately, workers developed symptoms of arsenic poisoning.

We would be fortunate indeed if all we had to do in order to solve the problem of hazardous wastes was to, say, shut down a chemical company, or restrict the uses of certain substances, or regulate how such substances are handled and disposed. Such steps are necessary, and we should do whatever possible to assure that they are taken at once, but unfortunately, the problem is far too complex to be so easily solved.

We have become hooked on a whole array of poisons, and a major shift in our life-styles will ultimately be necessary if we are to escape further intoxication. Hundreds of household items — nylon stockings, paints, synthetic fabrics, pesticides, floor polishes, solvents, cleaners, detergents — are either poisonous themselves to some degree, or rely on poisons for some aspect of their production. We have all become so accustomed to these and similar materials that we have grown careless, or even apathetic about the consequences of using them. We need not die at once in order to be counted among their victims. Like the residents of Little Elk Valley, we may simply begin to suffer inexplicably from an assortment of ailments whose origins we may never suspect. The passage and enforcement of legislation to regulate strictly the production, availability, and disposal of hazardous wastes is vital to the good health of both people and their environment, but ultimately the people themselves may have to break the poison habit altogether.

455

120

The Alternative
to Pesticides

ROGER OLMSTED

1972

Nature places its own controls on plant-eating insects. Those controls can be used by man to avoid poisoning the biosphere with pesticides. The author is an environmental writer who has served as Associate Editor of the Sierra Club Bulletin.

I T IS TEN YEARS since Rachel Carson took on the American pesticide industry single-handed and showed us that careless assaults on the environment in the name of pest control must certainly lead to ecological disaster. The impact of *Silent Spring* is a classic example of the influence that one thoughtful and dedicated person can have on public sensitivity to complex and little understood problems that are really very close to us.

The battle begun by Miss Carson against indiscriminate use of persistent chemical toxins has been taken up by others with growing success. Yet while most of us have heard that DDT is on the way out, few have much knowledge of the obvious alternative to chemical pesticides — biological control. Biological control of native pests is not an entirely new concept, but work in a field that does not lend itself well to packaging, marketing, and advertising has not been well publicized and has often been as lonely as Miss Carson's efforts.

Development of effective biological control of native pests has been painfully slow — although in the last two or three years many applications of what would have seemed novel techniques a decade ago have proved successful. The big-time poison industry was born, grew to grotesque proportions, and now may be on the verge of dying of its own excesses. One exciting biological control experiment can give us special insight into the state of the art: an imaginative one-man campaign against a tent caterpillar infestation in the aspen forests of New Mexico during the 1930's.

"The entire region was made unfit for recreation, fishing, riding, or hiking. Streams were clogged with the dead bodies, polluting drinking water supplies. The ugly, furry things dropped from the trees as one walked beneath. Trout streams were dammed up every ten or 20 feet with caterpillar bodies. A pervasive stench filled the air for miles."

This was the scene in the aspen forests around Santa Fe that confronted Norman Appleton at the height of a devastating tent caterpillar invasion in

456

the 1930's. Appleton, trained as a biologist, but known to the Santa Fe community for his activity in art and music and for his Aspen Ranch School, decided to try to do something about the infestation which had defoliated some 1,200 square miles of the most scenic mountain areas of New Mexico, including his own beloved Aspen Ranch. The outcome of seven years of almost single-handed study and experimentation was then and still is today a novel and promising approach to the use of beneficial insects in the control of native pests.

In the last 25 years the quick answer to the problem would have been aerial spraying of pesticides, and this was also the initial idea of Norman Appleton. But he found the fish and game department opposed to potential poisoning of wildlife, and airplane pilots averse to navigating the mountain gorges where the aspen clustered thickest.

In desperation, Appleton went back to first principles — he started collecting and opening tent caterpillar cocoons. To his surprise, he found in a large number of cases tiny parasites feeding on the pupae. From his graduate studies at the University of Pennsylvania, Appleton was aware that almost no work had been done in the area of using native parasites to control native pests. Until then, the spectacular successes of biological control had been restricted to identifying and introducing *foreign* insect parasites or predators to control accidentally introduced foreign pests who had arrived on a scene where they had no native enemies. The first really dramatic use of biological control in America was in such a case, when the Australian cottony-cushion scale, which was destroying the orange groves of Southern California, was suppressed in the years following 1888 by the introduction of the Australian vedalia beetle.

But if foreign pests could be controlled by insects from their native environment, why couldn't native predator or parasite populations also be manipulated to control native pests? Of course, nature would eventually provide the control insects, but often only after a substantial time lag (up to six years in the case of the Rocky Mountain tent caterpillar, Appleton concluded), during which time astonishing damage might be wrought. Appleton reasoned that outbreaks of tent caterpillars resulted from their being reintroduced to areas that had been free of them for some time, areas in which

As we know, pesticides do more than kill crop-eating insects. This photograph taken at the San Diego Society of Natural History shows the effect of DDT on pelican eggs.

457

the population of their natural enemies would therefore also be low. If predators and parasites could be reared in the laboratory and introduced at the first sign of infestations in new areas, perhaps man could significantly cut down the time it would take natural forces to limit the pest.

In order to put his theory to any kind of test, Appleton first had to learn all he could about the tent caterpillar and the predator and parasite insects that attacked it. At the outset, he found scant entomological information about tent caterpillar species other than those of the Eastern states. The species that was eating up the aspen groves of New Mexico and Southern Colorado he found lived always above 6,500 feet, and for this reason he settled on the name "Rocky Mountain tent caterpillar." When he started his work, Appleton found only five species of parasites recorded for what appeared to be this caterpillar. During his study, however, he identified 28 kinds of insects that affected the life cycle of the Rocky Mountain tent caterpillar and was able to work out the life histories of many of them and use them in control operations.

Disease also plays a large role in controlling many pest infestations, and Appleton observed a viral disease of the tent caterpillar that was destroying up to 25 percent of the population in some cases. He concluded that *Sarcophaga* flies might materially assist in spreading this disease, as both male and female flies were found crawling all over the pests and flitting from one caterpillar to another as they lapped up the exudations from the mouth and cuticle.

From the outset of the study Appleton had assumed that deliberate introduction of some of the most important parasites at the time an outbreak was first observed might avert a serious infestation. The opportunity to test this theory came soon after the identification of beneficial insects was in hand, and methods of collecting them had been established. On July 14, 1937, the Supervisor of Carson National Forest called from Taos to report a small but heavy infestation of tent caterpillars in some 50 acres of aspen just north of a division of the Santa Fe National Forest that had been heavily infested for some years. The challenge was to see whether or not timely introduction of parasites might not save the Taos forests from the scourge that had devastated the Santa Fe forest.

In the spring of 1938, Appleton's team caught 3,000 big female digger wasps and introduced them to the infested site. In Appleton's words, "It was thrilling to watch these allies of man pounce upon their prey as soon as they were liberated from their cages." In addition to the ichneumon flies (also parasites) and the diggers, 45,000 *Sarcophaga* flies were brought in. These had been hatched out in the laboratory by stacking mesh-bottomed trays of caterpillar cocoons known to have a high incidence of *Sarcophaga* over a base filled with moist sawdust. When the *Sarcophaga* maggot emerged from the caterpillar cocoon, it dropped to the ground and burrowed; thus, Appleton wound up with sawdust trays of *Sarcophaga* puparia that could be kept dormant in the refrigerator until needed. When they were allowed to complete their metamorphosis and mate, they were introduced to trays of diseased caterpillars. Released at the infested site, they presumably not only added their numbers to the present parasite population, but helped to spread infection to the caterpillars.

Egg-gathering in the winter of 1937–38 produced 1.5 million more *Tetrastichids*, and a like number the following season. In the summer of 1939, some 60,000 more *Sarcophaga* were also introduced. Close examination of the infested area in 1940 could not turn up a single tent caterpillar. This single field trial does not prove beyond doubt the efficacy of the method; more extensive trials with adequate control populations for purposes of comparison would have been necessary for systematic development of the idea.

Unfortunately, the possibilities inherent in this imaginative control attempt were not followed up. Norman Appleton's low budget program disappeared beneath the gathering clouds of war. The obvious next step of setting up a well equipped state program that could engage in precisely controlled experiments was never taken. Incredibly, his idea of manipulating native parasite populations to mitigate the cycles of native pest explosions is still considered novel—and this first published report of his work is as timely now as it could have been thirty years ago.

121 Precedent on the Hudson

MAXWELL C.

WHEAT, JR.

1966

The venerable American sentiment that "There ought to be a law!" is shared by conservationists, particularly when they behold some outrage against the natural environment perpetrated by the pursuers of power or profit. Sentiment has led to political action; and action, particularly in the late '60s and the '70s, has resulted in not just one law, but a whole battery of laws to defend the environment, including most notably the Wilderness Act of 1964, the National Environmental Policy Act of 1969, and national and state legislation providing for clean air and water.

But conservationists have found that getting a law passed was only the beginning of a long, hard struggle. Laws do not enforce themselves, and very often governments do

*not enforce new laws with any zeal until prodded to do so by vigilant citizens'
organizations.*

*As a result, the conservation troops now include almost as many lawyers as
political activists or naturalists, and the battleground on which the natural environment is protected has been extended from the legislatures and Congress to the courts.
The next three articles deal with this newer battleground.*

*Of the court cases that have been signal victories for conservation, two bear the
names of kings. Storm King is a mountain in New York; Mineral King is a valley in
the Sierra. Neither is out of jeopardy, but the legal battles to preserve them have
resulted in monumental precedents of environmental law that would have been cheered
by John Muir. Storm King is explained by a resident of Freeport, Long Island, a
teacher and New York conservation activist.*

WHEN I FIRST SAW Storm King Mountain ascending 1,340 feet above
the Hudson—the *Grande Riviere* to its discoverer, Giovanni da
Verrazzano—the stars above the steep Highlands backdrop were
sparkling sharply in the clear black sky on a night that was frigidly windy.
From where I stood shivering on the deserted east bank at Cold Spring, the
riled waters of the river appeared strangely narrower than their three quarters of a mile width because of the almost disproportionately huge, dark
hump of a mountain looming up towards the heavens like some ancient
Leviathan heaved out of its watery depths. This was Storm King—"solemn
and wild," as a Revolutionary War chaplain reported—overshadowing the
village, the river, and the very night itself.

Cupping an ear I strained to hear, between chill blasts, a faint echo of the
thunderous peals rolling off the Highlands that for generations of Hudson
folklore have heralded the ghostly charge of some redcoat or continental
regiment. Or to hear Henry Hudson's crew—his Half Moon was harbored
300 years ago near Storm King's flanks—again playing ninepins among the
mountain tops as Rip Van Winkle heard them.

"Inside us," said New York State's folklorist-historian Carl Carmer about
the Hudson recently, "there is a conviction that everything that happens in a
place lingers in some form or other."

I wonder if I could have been so haunted that night by the Hudson's
beauty and past—by high-pooped Dutch sailing ships plying the waters, by
pirates lurking in wait for unlucky sailors, by Ichabod Crane and his headless
pursuer—if parts of that mountain had been efficiently illuminated by a
$162,000,000 pumped storage hydroelectric plant. The Consolidated Edison
Company plans to build the biggest pumped storage plant in the world here,
blasting a site for it out of the side of Storm King. The plant would be
capable of sucking more than one million cubic feet of water per minute
from the river and pumping it more than 1,000 feet up the mountain through
a tunnel 40 feet in diameter to a 240-acre reservoir—all this to create, in
effect, a massive storage battery. At peak demand periods, when New York
City's millions are switching on their air conditioners or lighting their

Storm King Mountain seen from the east bank of the Hudson River.

Christmas trees, Con Ed would unleash the pent-up water to cascade un-naturally back down the mountain and send 2,000,000 kilowatts surging through transmission lines strung from 100- to 150-foot towers through 25 miles of town and country.

No wonder Carl Carmer demanded "that the time for opposing those selfish interests that would defile the Hudson is now." For this river is deep in myth and tradition, resources necessary to the feeling for one's native land. Who can imagine the picturesque frigates of old navigating up and down the river past a "scenic" view dominated by a powerhouse 800 feet long?

The scenic and historic values of Storm King Mountain and the Hudson River were recognized by the U.S. Court of Appeals in an epoch-making decision handed down December 29, 1965. Setting aside Federal Power Commission orders granting Con Ed a license to construct a powerplant at Storm King, the Court ruled that the FPC had fallen short in failing to concern itself with the fact that the plant was "to be located in an area of unique beauty and major historical significance."

This wasn't all. The Court declared that the FPC had failed to adequately consider the disruption of local planning (transmission lines would march through the site of a proposed junior high school in Yorktown), the inunda-

461

tion of trails maintained by the New York-New Jersey Trail Conference in the proposed reservoir area, and the consequences of locating the hydroelectric plant amidst the spawning grounds of perhaps 88 percent of the river's striped bass.

"What's good for Con Ed is good for the country" seems to have been the attitude of the FPC. Unfortunately, there is a pronounced tendency for regulatory agencies to feel more of an identity of interest with the industries they are supposed to regulate than with the public they are supposed to serve. This stems from an obsession with so-called growth and development, which has often transformed the useful concept of "progress" into the horns of a moral dilemma. Armed with the argument that "you can't stop progress," a powerful utility is able to assert intimidatingly: "You are not going to stand in the way of New York's getting more power, *are* you?" With that the person who likes to watch the sun set behind the Hudson Highlands, who likes to wade into the water casting for stripers, or who likes to explore woods that appear much as General Washington might have seen them, is supposed to mutter "I'm sorry" and slink to a seat in the back.

The Court of Appeals ruled that people who like to hike, watch sunsets, fish, birdwatch, absorb history, or live in scenic surroundings, belong in the front row at hearings alongside the professional experts and public relations personnel of big corporate entities. This court decision affirming the right of all such interests to equal and full consideration is a precedent that will be noted by other courts ruling on conservation controversies involving highway departments or federal agencies such as the Corps of Engineers and the Bureau of Reclamation.

The favorable court decision at Storm King was in part the result of a potent case marshalled by Sierra Club lawyer David Sive of New York. The club and the Scenic Hudson Preservation Conference, a coalition of local organizations defending Storm King, were given the right to bring before the bar the cause of natural beauty.

The Sierra Club Legal Defense Fund was set up in 1972 to organize strategy before the courts. But the club's standing to sue on behalf of the environment was still challenged in case after case. The challenges reached a climax in the case of Mineral King. There the club was opposing a Forest Service permit to allow Disney Enterprises to build a $35-million ski resort in a Sierra valley almost entirely surrounded by Sequoia National Park. The valley had been left out of the park (but remained in Sierra National Forest) because of claims that valuable minerals could be mined there. (Mining is prohibited in national parks but permitted in national forests.) The mining claims did not pan out, but the valley remained outside the park. Opponents argued that the Sierra Club had no legal right to claim any interest in the case, but the U.S. Supreme Court affirmed that right in 1972 and said that the club could bring suit whenever it could demonstrate that injury has been done or will be done to the recreational, environmental, and esthetic interests of its membership and programs.

As a result of that landmark case the club continued its efforts on behalf of Mineral King. The result was a notable victory: in 1978 Congress made Mineral King part of Sequoia National Park.

122

The Power of NEPA

ROBERT GILLETTE

1972

Perhaps the most powerful legal weapon ever given to conservationists was the National Environmental Policy Act of 1969, which has been called the Magna Carta of the environment. Its passage was not only a victory for conservation but for the democratic process as well. It enabled private citizens and their organizations to haul powerful government bureaucracies into court for failing to give sufficient attention to the environment in their plans and projects.

For a brief explanation of NEPA, we excerpt here a Bulletin *article by Robert Gillette, a reporter for* Science *magazine. James Moorman was later appointed President Carter's Assistant Attorney General for Land and Natural Resources.*

NEPA IS THE LAW that environmental lawyers, led by James Moorman, now the executive director of the Sierra Club Legal Defense Fund, invoked to delay construction of the trans-Alaska pipeline; it was used to stop the Tennessee-Tombigbee waterway. NEPA played a pivotal role in killing the Cross-Florida Barge Canal and it was the tool that the Sierra Club and the Natural Resources Defense Council used to force the Interior Department to postpone its plans to sell oil and gas leases on vast tracts of coastal waters in the Gulf of Mexico.

This is also the law that has delayed the operation of half a dozen nuclear power plants and — to the consternation of the White House — let two young Cleveland lawyers throw a monkey wrench in the Nixon administration's elaborate water discharge permit program, the government's main scheme for curbing industrial water pollution.

All of these nettlesome setbacks dealt by NEPA have stemmed from federal district and appeals court rulings in which one or more judges ruled that a federal agency — whether by reason of innocent misunderstanding or bold intransigence — had failed to comply fully with NEPA procedures in analyzing the impact of various projects.

NEPA was largely the handiwork of two Democrats — Senator Henry M. Jackson of Washington and Representative John D. Dingell of Michigan. Although as a bill NEPA had wide bipartisan support (and still does), the White House took little interest in it until after its passage through Congress in late 1969. President Nixon then gave it symbolic prominence when he signed the bill as his first official action of the new decade. The President has made extensive use of the three-man Council on Environmental Quality (CEQ), established by NEPA, taking its advice in such issues as predator control and the fate of the Cross-Florida Barge Canal.

As federal legislation goes, NEPA is brief and not very complicated. As its name implies it is mostly a statement of policy, and one couched in rather sweeping terms at that. The first part of the law, section 101, declares, among other things, that it is the government's responsibility to "assure for all Americans safe, healthful, productive, and esthetically and culturally pleasing surroundings." Later on, this section holds that "each person should enjoy a healthful environment and that each person has a responsibility to contribute to the preservation and enhancement of the environment."

NEPA's rather limited complement of teeth is found in the next part, section 102. Here is the language that has triggered the reappraisals, the arduous analyses of public works, and the current fuss.

Very simply, section 102 stipulates that whenever an agency contemplates a "major action" that is likely to have a "significant" impact on the environment, the agency must first prepare a formal description of its action, the probable impact, and the alternatives to the proposed action. (For example, the Interior Department's proposal to grant a right-of-way through federal lands for the trans-Alaska pipeline.) Implementing guidelines drawn up by the CEQ call for making drafts public in advance of the proposed action, soliciting comments from the public and from other agencies, and then issuing a final impact statement to take account of comments on the first.

In short, NEPA demands that before any federal agency takes any major action—be it building a highway or issuing a permit for a pipeline—that agency is supposed to *think* about the consequences and the alternatives. But applied on the scale of the federal government, the straightforward directive to think before acting has engendered a major new occupation in Washington—that of preparing environmental impact statements.

Dozens of agencies, including a few like the Securities and Exchange Commission and the Department of State that have never before thought of themselves as impinging on the environment, have had to make adjustments in their organization and compose guidelines of their own to comply with NEPA.

As much of a paper-shuffling exercise as it is, compliance with NEPA has had some far-reaching and beneficial spinoff. It has opened administrative procedures to public view that formerly were closed. And it has given the government a handle on the difficult and pervasive problem of "technology assessment"—the anticipation of technology's adverse effects. It has also prompted the legislatures of Washington, California, Montana, Delaware and Puerto Rico to adopt similar environmental disclosure laws.

But perhaps most important, some astute observers think that NEPA is having a tangible effect on the way decisions are made in key federal agencies; that, for some at least, the advent of NEPA continues to be a consciousness-expanding experience.

464

For example, Roger Cramton, a former professor of law at the University of Michigan and now chairman of the Administrative Conference of the United States, notes that under NEPA, "an agency that attempts to grapple meaningfully with environmental issues is forced to recruit a phalanx of professionals with different values and perspectives than its old-line operatives." Initial reaction to NEPA by older, middle-level bureaucrats tends to be one of anger and stubborn resistance, Cramton continues, but once the new employees begin mingling with the old, "new sets of shared attitudes and goals may replace those that have been hardened into the bureaucratic structure."

Similarly, Secretary of Interior Rogers Morton, who has some strong complaints about court decisions under NEPA, nevertheless thinks that it has resulted in "more informed decision making." In particular, he believes that if the trans-Alaska pipeline is built it will be safer and less detrimental than it would have been in the absence of the studies and public hearings required by NEPA.

For all the law's attributes, however, it's equally important to realize what it is not: it is not an environmental police law; it grants no one veto power over any federal action, regardless of how destructive a project is revealed to be by its impact statement.

"This is an informational statute," says Frank Potter, a staff aide to Representative John Dingell of the House Merchant Marine and Fisheries Committee. "It is built on the supposition that once the facts about a given action are made known, the political process will come to an appropriate decision."

Even without explicit provisions for enforcement, NEPA is no paper tiger, as the tooth marks in half a dozen arms of the executive branch will attest. On the contrary, the federal courts have given the law a substantial bite, one the government cannot conveniently ignore.

123

The Club, the Cause, and the Courts

JOHN D. HOFFMAN

1977

Here are specific illustrations of how conservation lawyers are defending the American earth under existing environmental law. This excerpt was written in

465

America's bicentennial year by the executive director of the Sierra Club Legal Defense Fund.

A colossal coal-fired power plant was proposed for the Kaiparowits Plateau in Utah, to supply electricity to Arizona and California. Conservationists maintained that smoke from the plant would foul the air for hundreds of square miles and send smog into the "golden circle" of national parks and monuments in the Southwest. Tongass National Forest, the largest of the national forests, is in southeast Alaska.

I N 1976, THE SIERRA CLUB LEGAL DEFENSE FUND (SCLDF) completed its fifth year of operation as the Club's arm for environmental law. A review of some of last year's key battles can tell us something about the nature of environmental law and the Club's role as a major force in its development during the first half of the seventies.

The proposed 3,000-megawatt Kaiparowits plant was an outlaw — a Jesse James among power plants. Environmentalists accustomed to challenging such projects in proceedings for a federal license and/or a state certificate of public convenience and necessity were startled to learn that Kaiparowits might not need either of these and that its sponsors had no plans to obtain them. Although power was to be generated in Utah, transmitted across Nevada, and used in Arizona and California, the Federal Power Commission did not have licensing jurisdiction over Kaiparowits. The Utah Public Service Commission was the next logical candidate since the plant would be constructed within that state, but only Utah's environment — neither its power companies nor its consumers — was involved. (Even if jurisdiction technically existed in Utah, that state's enthusiasm as an environmental guardian could reasonably be doubted.) This left California, where the great bulk of the power was to be consumed, but except for transmission lines, there was to be no construction within that state's borders. It is arguable that California's environment would even benefit from Kaiparowits, at least insofar as other coal-burning or nuclear projects within the state would be postponed or perhaps cancelled if Kaiparowits went forward.

Ultimately, a petition was filed on the Sierra Club's behalf with the California Public Utilities Commission (PUC) asking it to exercise full licensing jurisdiction over Kaiparowits, which would entail public hearings, official findings as to the need for the plant, environmental review under California's equivalent of NEPA, and no construction until completion of the proceedings and the PUC certification.

When the PUC hearings on the petition opened last April, a full-scale battle over jurisdiction was expected. Rumors were rife that Interior Secretary Kleppe would announce any day his approval of Kaiparowits' construction on federal lands, but as the hearings began in Los Angeles, the sponsors of Kaiparowits rose and announced they were dropping the plant from their construction schedules.

The utilities gave several reasons for this decision, including increased costs, reduced rate of growth in power demand, and the strong opposition to

Kaiparowits' construction on environmental grounds. Also mentioned prominently by the utilities, however, was the rising interest of the PUC and the California State Energy Commission in supervising out-of-state power-plant construction. Inasmuch as the PUC staff had recommended to the full commission that it take jurisdiction over Kaiparowits, the utilities may have anticipated an adverse decision from the commission. In any event, a dramatic victory was won. Kaiparowits had waived extradition and surrendered.

SCLDF's Tongass National Forest litigation resembles Kaiparowits in that it ended by a private decision rather than a court ruling, but here the resemblance ceases. The Tongass case began in early 1970, before SCLDF was even founded, and did not end until 1976. The suit was designed to force at least a major reconsideration of the fifty-year, 8.75-billion-board-foot Admiralty Island/Juneau Unit timber sale, largest in the history of the U.S. Forest Service. It achieved even more—an agreed cancellation of the contract by the Forest Service and Champion International, the contract holder. How this all came about is a fascinating story. The legal record, however, shows two major trials—one lost and one that remained undecided for well over a year after final evidence was submitted—plus an intervening appeal that was never decided because of newly discovered evidence that resulted in the second trial. In retrospect, it was this new evidence—a devastating critique of the sale's effect on wildlife habitat issued after the first court decision by consultants for Champion itself—that turned the case around and led to its eventual conclusion.

But though the "Tongass case" has ended, the controversy continues, and SCLDF is already involved in fresh litigation over Admiralty Island that in some ways is more complex than the original. Various native groups have asserted conflicting claims to key areas of the island, including many formerly covered by the Juneau Unit sale. These competing groups have strongly differing views concerning the nature and intensity of the uses to which they would put these lands; the aims of some are highly compatible with the Club's environmental goals, but others envision major timber-harvesting operations not unlike those once planned by Champion. Although not quite so immediately threatened as they once were by the Juneau sale, vital conservation interests are again at stake, and SCLDF is in the middle of the battle.

A full review of SCLDF's scoresheet for the past year would require a good bit more space. Rather than survey the field at length, it would be more useful to identify a few key attributes of environmental law as it stands today and as SCLDF expects to practice it over the next several years.

• The Supreme Court is beginning to exercise a major influence on the development of environmental law and will no doubt continue to do so. For almost three years after its mid-1972 decision in the Mineral King case, the court issued no decision of comparable interest to environmentalists. In the past two years, however, it has been issuing such decisions regularly on matters as diverse as attorneys' fees, NEPA and the Clean Air Act. What is more, almost all the decisions have been adverse, except for a few in which environmental groups were not directly involved and in which the court upheld the government's regulatory position *vis-à-vis* private industry. Some of the latter, though, may prove very helpful to the Club in its future environmental battles.

So far as the Supreme Court is concerned, then, the appropriate axiom for environmental lawyers in the next few years may be "he who litigates least litigates best." Unfortunately, one does not always have a choice in these matters.

• Pollution-control laws and other statutes that place definite limits on the conduct of government and private parties are likely to dominate environmental litigation in the late seventies, as opposed to laws, such as NEPA, that primarily regulate the manner in which environmental decisions are made.

The ascendancy of pollution-control laws can be traced to several causes. It has taken time, as well as considerable litigation effort, to get a basic regulatory framework established under the Clean Air Act and the federal Water Pollution Control Act, but this process is now well advanced, even if not completed. These laws now mean something, and increasingly they present major roadblocks in the path of projects that conservationists find objectionable on these as well as broader environmental grounds.

NEPA, on the other hand, has undergone a transformation, at least from the lawyer's standpoint. Its role is not unlike that of the erstwhile star player who can still perform brilliantly in a back-up role, but no longer can carry the team. A few years ago, a sort of consensus began to form in the appellate courts regarding the outer limits of NEPA. In general, the courts concluded they would not second-guess government agencies' substantive decisions on proceeding with their projects and would not require them to refute conflicting expert opinion in their environmental impact statements, only to report it. Once this judicial consensus became apparent, it was only a matter of time before NEPA yielded its stellar position. Now NEPA's main value to environmental lawyers lies in the information impact statements disclose, however murkily, and in the safeguards the EIS process erects against environmental ambush.

• The growing importance of "pollution-control" cases will have several significant corollaries. For one, the three-ring circus in which industry, government and conservationist each urges a sharply divergent interpretation of a statute upon the same court will have numerous performances. Common sense and case law to date both suggest government will win more of these frays than either of the other participants, which means the real battle may not be in court, but long before, when EPA or whatever agency is involved arrives at its administrative position. Thus environmental lawyers may increasingly find themselves arguing their cases in conference rooms rather than courtrooms.

• The shift in emphasis to interpretation and enforcement of regulatory statutes in environmental law means that larger national groups such as

SCLDF and the Sierra Club have an increased responsibility to the rest of the environmental movement. Such groups are in the best position to identify key administrative rulings that may be decisive in later applications of a statute to specific controversies, and to marshal the scientific and technical resources that may be needed to challenge effectively an erroneous official position.

124

Minorities and Conservation

THOMAS BRADLEY

1972

The fact is undeniable: Conservation has long been a cause supported primarily by the relatively affluent. The poor and the minorities were too worried about jobs and discrimination to be concerned, and conservationists seldom gave much thought to the relation of their work to low-income families. But the situation is beginning to change. Sierra Club chapters, for example, conduct special outings for inner-city youngsters and work for parks and open space in inner-city areas. In 1979, the club sponsored a major national urban environment conference in Detroit. There is still much to be done to bridge the gap, however, as the following article indicates. Thomas Bradley, a UCLA graduate, was a Los Angeles City Councilman when he delivered this speech to a Sierra Club Education Conference and the Bulletin *published it. He subsequently was elected the first black mayor of Los Angeles.*

TWO OF THE NATION'S most fundamental problems demanding solution today are environmental disruption—pollution and destruction of natural resources—and the continuing inequities which degrade the daily lives and expectations of millions of minority citizens. Both problems are urgent, and they are related. Yet in practice, we find supporters of one cause frequently at odds with supporters of the other. Although minorities and conservationists share many goals in common and ought to be working together, too often—as one observer put it—they "squabble over pieces of a shrinking pie." Should this divisiveness continue unchecked, the dangers for all are manifest.

It is surely clear to most of us that ecological problems are inseparable from the other ills of society. The social pollution which minorities suffer spreads its toxins to every element of our society, and no one can escape environmental pollution. Today, 70 percent of our population lives in the midst of traffic tangles, suffocating smog, poisoned water, deafening noise and terrorizing crime. These problems are real, not illusory. Nevertheless, to many of our nation's 20 million blacks, the conservation movement has about as much appeal as a segregated bus.

Why?

The reasons are not hard to find. Blacks generally regard ecology as irrelevant to their most pressing needs — jobs, housing, health care, education. Worse, they fear that concern with environmental problems diverts attention from the problems of poverty and racism. As Richard G. Hatcher, mayor of Gary, Indiana, expressed it, "The nation's concern with environment has done what George Wallace was unable to do: distract the nation from the problems of black and brown Americans."

Basically, of course, the problem is not a conflict between ethnic minorities and white Americans. It is an economic problem. It results from the schism between poverty and affluence.

Poor whites, as well as blacks and Latin Americans, have always lived in polluted environments. Air pollution is thicker and more persistent in the slums than in the suburbs. The steel-workers of Pennsylvania and Indiana haven't breathed fresh air in all their lives — nor did their fathers before them.

Contemporary planners design freeways to go through low-income areas, just as their forerunners sent elevated trains racketing past the tenement windows of the poor. And migrant workers continue to accumulate dangerous concentrations of pesticides in their blood.

Perhaps what the poor minorities resent most of all is that our nation has always been able to mobilize massive resources to meet almost any challenge it really wants to. We funded the rehabilitation of the entire Western world after World War II. We put men on the moon. We spend billions subsidizing agricultural enterprises and hundreds of billions for military adventures. If all this is possible, they ask, why then is the nation unable to mount a similar attack on the related problems of poverty and racism? Their answer: because the United States has not committed itself to solve these problems.

The minorities are aware that widespread concern over social pollutants is generated when they affect the lives of middle- and upper-income citizens. High unemployment rates were acceptable until aircraft workers and aerospace scientists and engineers lost their jobs. Affluent white Americans turned their backs on the problem of drug abuse as long as the drug user was a shadowy figure in the ghetto: It is a central issue now that the victim is often the suburbanite's own child.

And now, the poor minorities see that everyone is in an uproar because pollution is no longer confined to the slums. Everyone is up in arms because affluent neighborhoods are also full of traffic, dirt, smog and airplane noise. So it is no wonder that many among the minorities view ecological woes as symptoms of the deeper ills infecting society. Indeed, they feel they are double victims. They suffer from pollution as much as anyone, but they are not the beneficiaries of the affluence which produced the pollution.

The people of the minority communities want ecological pollution eradicated as much as those of the white communities do. But they want social pollution eliminated at the same time. They will not be satisfied by cleaner ghettos if they are still denied access to suburbia. They will not be content with a ban on DDT if exploitation of migrant laborers continues. They will not be appeased by a company that cleans up its shop if it still excludes blacks from its executive suite.

But it is not enough to understand why the ethnic minorities and the poor are wary about the conservation movement. It is important that we realize that the battle against environmental pollution and the battle against poverty and racial discrimination are not mutually exclusive. Far from it: both involve a concern for preserving and bettering the opportunities for every human being to fulfill himself. America ought to be able to lick social pollution *and* environmental pollution. Perhaps only by doing both can we achieve either. And that suggests the need for a broad-based coalition of both conservationists and minorities to fight simultaneously for mutual objectives.

If we are to be effective participants in the struggle to make this a better world, we must have a sincere concern for every issue that involves human beings. We must realize that the problems of man and his environment are inextricably interrelated. As environmentalists we must recognize that a movement dedicated to the survival of man and his habitat is itself ecologically unsound if it remains irrelevant to the needs of so many people living in squalor.

125

Labor and the Politics of Environment

LEONARD

WOODCOCK

1971

The issue of jobs versus the environment has been a major headache for both workers and environmentalists almost from the start and has too often driven a wedge between the two movements. But there are strong grounds for cooperation between the two, as the following article indicates.

Leonard Woodcock retired as president of the United Automobile, Aerospace and Agricultural Implement Workers of America (UAW) in 1977. This article is taken from a statement he delivered before the Subcommittee on Air and Water Pollution of the Senate Committee on Public Works.

We should emphasize at this point that this article does not represent the official position of the Sierra Club. The club would perhaps be more likely than Mr. Woodcock to see American industry not as a monolith but as a mixture; it would give credit to some industries for a conscientious regard for the environment, while still condemning those that have no such scruples.

A NEW ENVIRONMENTAL "game plan" is emerging in American industry. Employers under notice to comply with governmental anti-pollution standards are seeking to enlist workers, their unions, and their communities in campaigns of resistance to the enforcement of these standards through overt or implied threats that such enforcement would result in loss of jobs and income through shutdowns and layoffs.

Our passage from a pollution-prone to a relatively pollution-free society, even under the best of circumstances, is bound to be long and difficult. But we can be sure that the best of circumstances will not prevail, if through inaction we tolerate an industrial strategy of playing on the economic fears of workers and communities to create widespread political opposition to cleaning up the environment. Giving workers the right to sue would put an end to that strategy and, at the same time, would create a new and powerful financial incentive to induce polluting employers to step up to their environmental responsibilities.

Throughout our history, we have measured growth, profitability and progress by a much too narrow and shortsighted calculus. For a century or more, industry, especially large corporate industry wielding a high degree of market power and political clout, has made its way on the basis of an irresponsible indifference to the adverse impact of its operations on the physical and social environment. Many of the social costs of "doing business" were never assumed by business. They were sloughed off as "negative externalities" (in the jargon of economists) to be borne by the most vulnerable segments of society—mostly workers and their families—in various kinds and degrees of economic insecurity and the disabilities flowing from such insecurity. These insecurities and disabilities, according to the laissez-faire gospel, were the price that had to be paid for progress. Workers, their families and their communities were still paying most of that bill.

As for the other major social cost of doing business—environmental pollution—to the extent that it was paid at all, it was also borne primarily by workers in the form of unsafe and unhealthful working conditions. In addition to polluting the work environment, the wastes of American industry were simply thrown off onto the land, air or water. Our reckless exploitation of natural resources was not perceived as a threat to the quality of life except by a few conservationists. Exploitation was defined optimistically as development and development was the national business.

Now tomorrow is here. The bills for generations of recklessness and greed are coming due. The social and environmental costs of doing business at the same old stand and in the same old way can no longer be tolerated. Growth, given the way it has been and is being achieved, can no longer be defined optimistically as a higher standard of living; it must also be defined as a deterioration of the quality of life, urban congestion, suburban sprawl, the poisoning of the air we breathe, the water we drink and the soil that nurtures us, the accumulation of garbage, and the steady pressure of a rising population on a finite resource base.

A member of President Nixon's Council of Economic Advisers, Mr. H. S. Houthakker, speaking on "The Economy and the Environment," said: ". . . any ambient air standard implies a value judgment on the social importance of clean air relative to the social cost of achieving it. There is no obvious reason why this value judgment should lead to the same conclusion everywhere. It is conceivable that a depressed area may want to attract industry at the expense of a less stringent ambient air standard; the citizens of that area should be able to have some influence on the choice involved. . . ."

If this proposition is translated into plain language, it emerges as the old and ever-new government-industry partnership against the unorganized, the unemployed, the poor and their communities. Just as poor states and communities have long been invited to compete for industry and jobs by maintaining the open-shop and keeping unemployment compensation and other social charges on employers low, they would now be invited to maintain or create a suitably polluted environment—toward the same end of getting jobs, paychecks and a brisker trade at the local stores.

This doctrine also constitutes a warning to employed workers already breathing polluted air in and out of the plan as the price of having jobs. That warning is clear: "cough and visit your doctor regularly, but don't get environment-happy or we may have to shut the operation down and move away."

What we really need is a new *social* ethic, which would affirm and implement the basic proposition that we have the right to, and the means to assure, both a wholesome environment and economic security.

Unions, such as the UAW, take very seriously the degradation of the environment in the United States and throughout the world. But we also feel obliged to remind Americans who share our environmental concern that the natural and social environments are one. If we are to succeed in making the difficult transition to a society living in harmony with the natural world, we must make a parallel, simultaneous commitment not just to the rhetoric of social justice but to specific legislation and institutional reforms which will insure an equitable sharing of the costs and benefits of environmental improvement, based upon a realistic appraisal of responsibility.

The environmental movement has been too slow to grasp the social and economic aspects of the environmental issue which the movement has so effectively brought to national attention. Non-labor members of that movement have done yeoman's service in creating an awareness of environmental policies. But in failing to come to grips with the politics of environment, they have exposed themselves, as well as the working men and women who should be their strongest allies, to the trap being set for them by corporate polluters.

The challenge of environmental degradation is also too important to be left to the environmentalists, because without support from the American people as a whole, especially from workers and the urban poor or near-poor who are pollution's worst casualties, the environmentalists will be fighting a lost cause. They are the bearers of bad news, and industry is already moving to discredit them as extremists. The new scapegoats, in fact, may well be not those who are most actively polluting the nation and the planet, but those who are sounding the alarm.

American workers, perhaps more than the rest of the nation, have good reason to be foes of pollution. They have confronted it, resisted it, and to a dangerous degree have had to endure it over decades on the job. These in-plant hazards have increased with the proliferation of new toxic substances in recent years. Moreover, workers and their families are most apt to be exposed to the pollution released by industry into the surrounding community, for they are less likely than executives and professional workers to live in residential suburbs. The problem is not that they are advocates of pollution, but that their economic circumstances require them to think first of jobs, paychecks and bread on the table. The Congress has no more serious challenge than that of taking specific actions which will assure American workers and their families of a valid alternative to paychecks earned through working and living in a polluted environment. That alternative is the alternative of jobs, paychecks, bread on the table—*and* a *clean* environment.

126

Numbers
Against
Wilderness

DANIEL B. LUTEN

1964

We have already seen some of the problems in continuous growth in the use of energy resources—partly, at least, a product of population growth. The Sierra Club's concern with population goes back at least to 1957, when Executive Director David Brower told the club's biennial Wilderness Conference: "A serious problem, upon which no conservation organization I know of has adopted a policy, is the population problem—an especially touchy cat to bell."

No one was ready to bell the cat at that time, but the subject received increasing discussion at the Wilderness Conferences. At the 1963 conference Secretary of the Interior Stewart Udall became the first high government official to raise the problem: "It is not time to give serious consideration to the ecology of man—the relation of human population to its environment? Is it not time to ask whether man, as part of nature, is subject to the laws that govern other species, particularly the law that for every species in a particular environment there is an optimum population?"

The following article puts the population problem in historical perspective and relates it to club's traditional concern with wilderness. Professor Luten has been a research chemist for Shell Development Company and geographer on the faculty of the University of California at Berkeley.

MEN HAVE LIVED on this earth for a long time: 600,000 years is an adequate guess. Growth of the world's population at the time of Christ was perhaps 0.04 percent per year; today it is almost 50 times as great. What happened in a century back then happens in two years now.

Can this growth continue indefinitely? No. Today's population growing at today's rate would require only 800 years to reach SRO Day, the standing-room-only population, five square feet per person, land and sea. Perhaps 2,000 years later the periphery of the earth's mass of humanity would be expanding outward at the speed of light.

My only purpose in playing with these numbers is to convince you utterly and irrevocably, finally and remorselessly, mathematically and logically, that the growth so familiar to us today was unknown to all but the most recent of our ancestors and that it must be unknown to all but the most immediate of our descendants.

Of all these 600,000 years, man has had to contend with appreciable growth for less than 6,000, and most of that growth can be limited to the 600 years beginning with 1500 A.D. Its peak will probably lie in a 60-year period centered in this century. We live in a unique age. It will not continue; it probably will never recur.

The world's population reached a half billion in about the year 1650 A.D. In the next two centuries it doubled, reaching a billion in about 1850. In the next 80 years it doubled again. The doubling time is now 40 years.

As I have said, such growth must end. How it will end cannot be predicted with assurance but the alternatives are limited.

The alternatives for the equalization of birth and death rates are limited to two. An increase in the death rate would mean a world where few people live to a great age; where many, perhaps a major fraction of infants die in their first year of life. It is a world not entirely unfamiliar to us, but to most of us it is familiar only by report. It is the grinding world of the Bolivian Altiplano, the deprived world of India in the famine of 1943, the hazardous world of an Eskimo hunter. We would not be eager for it.

A reduced birth rate would mean a world of smaller families. Given a choice between long life and a large family, which will man choose?

No solution is to be found in long-range efforts to increase the world's food supply. For the short run, we must, in practical humanity, do what we can to extend it; but the long-range efforts we must, in good conscience, oppose.

Some people extol the algae farm as the answer, pointing to the vast yields obtainable per acre. Rarely do they mention the vast costs of creating such farms. Scarcely ever do they mention that such extensions of food supplies, almost inevitably at the cost to all other human values, suggest an entire Malthusian world. Such a course provides no solution; it only postpones the day of reckoning, and each forty years' delay doubles the piper's bill.

Let me say what I believe to be basic: A society which can discern the limits of its environment will guide its conduct and will control its population so as to remain within those limits.

The deliberate limitation of populations is not new. Throughout human history, societies that found the incentive to limit their populations managed to find techniques. A. M. Carr-Saunders (1932) has catalogued them by the score. The techniques are as varied as human imagination; each year the anthropologists and sociologists get wind of new ones. Some of the techniques we all deplore, others are deplored by some of us, and a few simply remain unexplained mysteries.

Incentive to limit populations, I am coming to believe, existed in and was recognized by any human group able to measure the relation between its needs and the capacity of its environment to meet those needs. Within an environment whose limits are simple and obvious, even simple-minded groups could get the message. Such societies also tried to tread evenly on their environment, so that no part of it was destroyed through poor management. It seems plausible that the concept of property, as a piece of land a given man owns, developed as a mechanism to assure protection of the environment, even as territoriality develops in birds and other mammals.

Game laws among the Choctaws were as strict as those of today (Swanton, 1931). The amount of game killed was reported to the chiefs; the amount that could be killed each season was regulated on the basis of the expected supply.

But with the coming of the white man, these practices deteriorated, and the record is full of destruction of game by the Indians. Can we read into this that it had now become impossible for them to see the limits of their environment? Perhaps we should write it in our books that the coming of broader horizons brings with it not merely greater opportunity, but also greater responsibility.

What is the limit of our environment? How clearly must we see this limit before we find the character to keep within it?

Our limit must be defined carefully. We are not a Malthusian society, deprived, existing at the very margin of life itself. We have a society of great richness, of opportunity. We cherish ideas which, if not new, had at least been submerged in the press of the early industrial societies: the idea of progress is recent and the idea of human dignity, of individuality, is still almost brand new. Perhaps these ideas have no survival value and will be scoffed at by our descendants. If we intend them to persist, we will have to do a great deal more than to boast about them. We will have to take great care that what made them possible also persists. We cannot talk of the limits of our environment in food, clothing, and shelter alone.

Those of us who have time to think about it feel that an essential component of our lives is the opportunity to know the natural world—the world which has shaped man.

Aldous Huxley wrote in *Brave New World* (1932): "The purpose of life was not the maintenance of well-being, but some intensification and refining of consciousness. . . ." The major opportunity for the intensification of consciousness lies in nature. Any infringement in the opportunity for free contact with the natural scene diminishes the quality of our lives. Once we lose touch with nature, our society loses its values, its purpose. And this should concern us more than bricks and mortar. It is one of our great failings that few of us have the spirit to hold spirit above material welfare.

I can already hear the voices: "Let's be realistic about nature; you can't eat the natural scene. It makes no jobs and is worthless on the tax rolls." I would ask you who speak in this voice to dedicate one day to a conscious effort to erase all the influences of nature from your life. Should you see a flight of geese overhead, as I just did, avert your eyes, close your ears to their clangor, and remember: *last year we reduced our waterfowl to its lowest level yet.* When you walk out to your car, turn your eyes from your lovely garden: *it will look better done up in high-rise apartments or under pavement.* As you step across the parking strip into your car, cross out the trees in that parking strip: *we will widen the pavement; hail the marvelous ducts beneath the asphalt that bring our energy, water, communication, and take away our effluents!*

I can go on. In your offices and homes, turn your eyes away from all the decorations with symbols of nature. Turn to the walls all paintings except the abstractions devoid of nature. Hear no birdsong; smell neither seashore nor violets. Taste only the synthesized foods. Touch plastic and never a river-worn stone. Try all day to put yourself in such a world and then decide how much of the natural scene you and your children should settle for.

There is today a crisis in wilderness; from now on, there will be a crisis in wilderness. The ever-growing population is absolutely and uncontrovertibly incompatible with the preservation of our wildlands, which is the mission we have above all others. It must follow, if reason was granted to man for any purpose at all, that these wildlands cannot survive reckless parenthood, uncontrolled birth, whether in poor lands or rich. Each of us is responsible, not just our experts or our statesmen. It also follows that a conservation organization concerned as it must be with the wholeness of man, needs to have a population policy. What should it comprise?

As a suggestion: Wildlands conservation organizations should willingly acknowledge that population is the common denominator of all resources problems. They should acknowledge that if wildlands in the United States are to endure together with a high level of living, then here, no less than in the poor lands, a cessation of population growth is imperative. The world's population growth derives from a humane diminution in death rates. Termination of growth can be humanely sought only in reduced birth rates.

If we are afraid to come to a decision, then the wilderness movement will end as other romantic movements have ended — in obscure history books.

It may be worse than that. Man has not demonstrated in any convincing way his ability to survive without wildlands. In prudence, he ought to take the most important step toward saving them or there may be no writers at all to record his failures.

A few months after this article appeared in the Bulletin, *the Sierra Club Board of Directors adopted this policy: "The 'population explosion' has severely disturbed the ecological relationship between mankind and its environment. . . . The Sierra Club supports a greatly increased program of education on the need for population control."*

127

Progress Against Growth

DANIEL B. LUTEN

1972

Here Professor Luten, who had some years earlier raised the population problem as it related to wilderness, attacks the American gospel of growth in cities and suburbs. He points out that while progress, properly defined, is possible and desirable, unending growth can only bring misery.

IN A YOUNG LAND that has experienced development at an unprecedented pace, it is not surprising that we struggle with the confusion between growth and progress. Historically, growth and progress have been to us almost interchangeable, so much so that even though we may not buy the shopworn idea that bigger is better, we still do not act as though we understand a distinction that seriously affects our lives and will determine the quality of life that our children will live.

Growth can be something other than progress. Our dictionary gives "augmentation" as a synonym for growth—but it also lists "excrescence." There is the rub: growth can go quite beyond healthy increase into the realm of pathology, and here we find that growth is "an abnormal proliferation of tissue, as in a tumor."

[Healthy] growth is appropriate to the juvenile condition, not to maturity. Nearly all living organisms adapted to survival go through periods of rapid early growth. But upon attainment of maturity, control mechanisms come into play to insure that the organism remains of the right size to fulfill its purpose. Lacking such controls, continued growth would lead only to disaster.

While living organisms commonly have developed regulatory (usually hormonal) systems which come into play when they reach the right size, human societies have been less successful. Small groups of people living close to the land seem ordinarily to have come to terms with their environment and to have developed institutions for stabilizing their numbers and their impact on the environment. In contrast imperialistic, dynamic, innovative societies have left their mark on the earth but have not long endured. Such societies may not have had the time or introspection to see and accept their own maturity. Could it be that our 20th century conservation movement might become a controlling "social hormone"?

The reality of urban subsidy to suburban growth is clearly shown in a $250 million bond issue passed in 1958 to provide water for the growth of metropolitan San Francisco's East Bay area. Berkeley's burden was some $20 million. What did Berkeley get in return? Essentially nothing, because the growth was not in Berkeley, but in Walnut Creek, Upper Pinole and Lower Slurbovia. But since it was promised that taxes would not increase, Berkeley citizens voted for the bonds four-to-one, without realizing that water rates could be half as high were it not for the need to support new suburban growth. How many cities have paid for their own schools, then chipped in to pay for the schools in successive suburban rings?

It is not surprising that California, the focus of the growth mystique, should generate the strongest opposition to growth. Force begets counter-force. Where the fever of growth is hottest, the antibodies form fastest. The conservation movement grows best on the site of worst abuse. Today, many in California question burgeoning development and when they are told that growth is good, are prepared to look the developer in the eye and ask him how much of that good will end up in his pocket.

In California, as in other places, an aversion to needless growth waxes:

• Palo Alto, persuaded by a Livingston and Blayney report, has concluded that it is wiser, and more economical to boot, to buy its hills for parkland than to permit subdivision.

• Marin County has rejected a new water supply on the grounds that it will only stimulate growth. (The voters are unlikely to have considered the issue of subsidy for newcomers.)

• Bolinas and Stinson Beach have rejected an oversized sewer project because they believe it will lead to undesirable growth.

• Petaluma has proposed to limit its growth to 500 new homes per year.

Those who extol growth keep saying, "growth means jobs." Yes, jobs for today and for immigrants, but none guaranteed to local unemployed. Growth looks good to small business—up to a point. For winners can become losers with frightening suddenness: the local grocery store in a growing neighborhood until the supermarket moves in; the frontage on an increasingly busy street until the freeway bypasses it; the easy drive to work, and then the traffic jam. The longer you ride the tiger of growth, the more dangerous it becomes. The walls of growth press in on the city, shrink room to maneuver, bleed bargains dry, bankrupt the central stores, drain support from schools and libraries. Then the loss of pride, the strife that succeeds sense of community, the rubbish in the streets all suggest a condition where "the mass of men lead lives of quiet desperation."

How do we turn from pathological growth to humanistic progress?

1 We need more sophistication. When your mayor tells you that growth broadens the tax base, laugh in his face and ask him to count for you the growing cities with growing tax bases—and with declining tax rates. When your antagonists tells you that your love of beauty is emotional, reply that love of money is an emotion, and hunger, too.

2 We need to be more skeptical. When the power industry warns us that energy needs for environmental protection and mass transit will require great expansion, common sense should tell us that the incremental needs in these area will be trifling in comparison with the other "growth needs" that the utilities have in mind to promote.

3 We can vote down bond issues, try to limit facilities, but I think this will do more to publicize our feelings than to end growth. Dasmann suggested denying water to Southern California; water control authorities have come close to denying sewers to San Francisco; the Sierra Club suggests denying electric power. Facetiously, it has been said that this won't work but will, instead, trade the present population for one which drinks only alcohol, doesn't wash, and uses outhouses and kerosene lamps. Yet such measures might help if we were to increase water rates to the point where per capita consumption would level off, and if we were to require new developments to pay for all of the services provided rather than only for their incremental costs.

4 Can migration to growing areas be restricted? Probably not. Proposals to exact a California immigration fee of $1,000 would be judged unconstitutional. But what of a carefully measured fee reflective of the facilities available to new residents but paid for by prior residents? If it is a denial of the privileges and immunities clause of the Fourteenth Amendment to restrict interstate migration, is it not a denial of the due process clause to force prior residents to contribute their property to the support of immigrants?

5 We must modify our institutions. They were developed for a juvenile, growing society, a poor society in an empty land. We now have a rich society in a full land, a mature society past its era of growth. Above all, it is time that we abandon our treasure-hunt philosophy of economics and reward productivity, not opportunism.

6 If growth is to end, we must abandon the growth mystique. Can our generation close its eyes to growth when we know that the next generation must face up to it? Shall we live our lives as addicts to growth and then, having addicted our children, tell them in our wills to kick the habit? Let us say instead, and say it in our plans, that we expect growth to end soon; let our plans cover the period until growth has ended. Let our planning schools begin to produce planners who do not themselves believe in growth.

128

Parson Malthus
Tolls the Bell

CHARLES WARREN

1975

The most alarmingly immediate impact of an exponentially growing world population is not on wilderness or cities but on the food supply. The 1975 United Nations World Food Conference, held in Rome, was haunted by the gloomy ghost of Thomas R. Malthus, who maintained nearly 200 years ago that the number of people on earth always increases faster than the amount of food, unless the population is diminished by starvation, disease, or war.

How well the assembled delegates met the challenge of Malthus is assayed here by a delegate who was at the time a member of the California State Assembly. In 1977 he was named by President Carter as Chairman of the Council on Environmental Quality, the environmental branch of the White House.

W E ARE AT THE BEGINNING of an epoch marked by events unanticipated by most and characterized by all as "crises": food, energy, inflation, unemployment, environment, government credibility, among others. Almost without exception, each is viewed as a separate event with scant relationships to the others. Each crisis is parceled out to its particular bureaucracy, which responds with its conventional wisdom and solutions.

Thus the United Nations will continue to have world conferences to resolve this or that crisis, while individual nations attempt to adjust their own policies and programs to the particular crisis-impacts to which they are especially subject.

The confluence of these events is more than coincidental. It is a harbinger of a radical change in man's relationship with his earth. Simply put, such events are manifestations that exponential growth in the consumption of finite resources has reached a critical stage, and that conventional wisdom does not relieve, but aggravates the problem.

Reality requires a perspective of man and his earth lengthier than those that presently rule his institutions. For example, if we were to carry single-purpose planning to its ultimate conclusion, malnutrition might be eliminated within ten years: strip the forest, develop all maximum fertilizers from feed stocks, and build massive water projects. But at the end of ten years what would be the consequence?

If we single-mindedly determine to meet all needs and requirements, there is no shortage of oil, nor will there be for the next 10 or 20 years. But to squander petroleum reserves leads to impoverishment far beyond the depletion of fossil fuels, and on a scale that touches not just those who plundered the till to perpetuate growth.

The conference planners were voluble and myopic. They talked endlessly of shortages and little of solutions. They saw a food shortage based primarily upon: intervention in the world market by certain nations that had not previously participated; shortages in fertilizer and fuel created by petroleum-price inflation; and *unusual* weather—particularly floods and drought cycles in the Indian subcontinent and in Africa. The planners demonstrated nothing of that broader perspective which recognizes that the food crisis is not an isolated phenomenon, but part of a larger complex of problems that together constitute the crisis of industrial society.

The fallacy of modern industrial states is their commitment to growth at exponentially increasing rates in a world where resources are finite. The inevitable result is system collapse. The symptoms of pending collapse may go unrecognized until it is too late to prevent it. For example, within the next ten years, it is probable that over 250 million persons will die of starvation. They will die in Asia, Africa, and Latin America. In the United States, to the extent our production is available to the world market, prices of food products will rise disproportionately to other products and a larger percentage of our countrymen will be malnourished and hungry. The *demand* for food and increased inability of the earth's resources to accommodate demand is at the heart of the problem.

In 1850, world population was one billion; in 1920, two billion; in 1975, four billion; and today, our population is primed to double to eight billion in the next 32 years. The time it takes for the population to double is getting shorter and the amount being doubled is expanding.

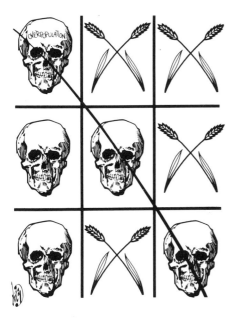

Cartoon by Tom Darcy, Newsday, *Los Angeles Times Syndicate, that won first prize in the Third Annual Population Cartoon Contest sponsored by the Population Institute.*

483

To minimize and eventually eliminate famine, we must bring into equilibrium the world's need for food as determined by population, nutritional levels, and the earth's food-producing capacity, represented by land, water, fertilizers, and energy. Since the food-producing resources are limited, our efforts, incontestably, must directly address the cause of burgeoning demand — population. Instead, Micawberites in government perversely take comfort in optimistic estimates of man's ability to tinker with and adjust our resources.

A common claim is that there are vast acreages of land still uncultivated in the world. In truth, all of our best lands are already in production. The remaining land is marginal and will require immense and perhaps impossible capital investment. Overall, probably 500 million additional acres have crop potential. This represents only a little more than ten percent of the land currently cultivated. As it happens, this additional land is situated in the United States, Canada, Argentina and Australia. The amounts available will be insufficient to provide the 40-percent increase in global food production necessary in the next ten years.

Another assumption is that we can make the desert bloom. In fact, it is becoming increasingly clear that water, not land, may be the crucial limiting factor of food production.

The role and significance of fertilizer in the development of agriculture is a recent phenomenon. Fertilizer use has increased 400 percent in 20 years while crop yields have increased only 50 percent. This lopsided relationship is due to the diminishing returns stemming from each additional increment of fertilizer applied to a portion of land, and to the larger fraction of the available fertilizer being used in the richer nations, where rates of fertilizer application are already high. The rising price will serve to put fertilizer out of reach of those who need it most.

Energy is another material central to the development of world food supplies. Much of the world's agriculture is labor-intensive, but even in these countries energy can have a crucial role in increasing output — diesel irrigation pumps, tractors, and farm-to-market trucks, for example. Energy price hikes quickly foreclose increases in production, since fuel energy purchases usually absorb a large fraction of a farmer's income in these countries. Thus, rising fuel costs will doubtless reduce production.

Many of the potential techniques for increasing agricultural yields will require increased reliance on chemicals such as herbicides and insecticides. Worldwide use of such chemicals has tripled in the last 20 years, but increasing use is again complicated by the energy crisis as both are petrochemical products and thus are tied intimately to fossil-fuel shortages.

Finally, there are the vagaries of the weather to contend with. Meteorologist Paul Berghorrson has carefully pieced together a record of the earth's weather over the last thousand years. It shows that the past 50 years have been a period of unprecedented warmth and climatic stability. Though some meteorologists do not agree, Berghorrson and others conclude from this that we are about to enter a more typical period, when the temperatures will be cooler and the climatic pattern more variable. Evidence is also accumulating that suggests a cooling trend resulting from atmospheric pollution. When food is in short supply, even small weather changes can have devastating consequences.

With all these improbables, is it possible to expand production at the rate necessary to accommodate anticipated demand?

Until 1970, numerous countries produced more food than they could consume, so food was available for export. The United States had prime agricultural land in storage; food surpluses were sufficient to feed the world for four months; the fish catch was bountiful. The "Green Revolution," with the application of petrochemical fertilizer and pesticides, was increasing yields of wheat and rice.

Since 1970, all has changed. There are only four countries which produce food for export: the United States, Canada, Australia, and Argentina. Now, there is no agricultural land in storage. The fish catch is declining. The "Green Revolution" was quelled by the force of a four-fold increase in the price of fertilizer and pesticides essential to its success. Our world grain reserves have dwindled perilously.

The choice before the world is clear: either decrease population growth rates to permit subsistence consumption levels of available resources, or condemn increasing numbers of people to malnutrition and starvation.

The only attempt by any organization to require a more comprehensive view of the implications of food demand given exponential growth in global population and other resource limitations was made by the Sierra Club's representatives to the World Food Conference. The club's proposal included a *30-year* demand forecast on food, together with an assessment of the world's agricultural lands now in, or suitable for, agricultural production. The assessment would be made by analyzing the productive capacity of the land, requirements for energy, capital, and irrigation. In addition, the proposal included a method of preserving world options by controlling the urbanization of farmlands now in or potentially able to be used for production, except in extraordinary cases of health, safety, and welfare. A monitoring system as well as a passive early warning system was recommended for the earth's oceans to determine the extent to which toxic wastes and other pollutants were reducing the ability of the sea to provide food.

The solution that must be adopted not merely for the sake of posterity, but for millions of people alive today, is to establish a balance between available resources and rates of consumption. In the short term, mankind must recognize its plight and begin to plan for the increasing shortages of foodstuffs and other raw materials that seems to be its unavoidable lot. But most importantly, it must recognize that the food shortage and other contemporary resource problems are but separate symptoms of a common malady—namely, exponential growth in a finite world. Population growth coupled with increasing per-capita consumption of resources conspire to inflict on people everywhere and on governments at all levels one crisis after another.

485

129

Nobody Ever Dies of Overpopulation

GARRETT HARDIN

1971

Professor Hardin, whose "Tragedy of the Commons" may be the most an-thologized environmental article of recent times, and whose "lifeboat ethic" has caused furious debate around the world, here points out in an ironic way that millions of deaths attributed to natural disasters are actually the result of overpopulation, although various taboos prevent us from recognizing the fact. This Bulletin *editorial was reprinted from* Science *and is used here with the permission of that magazine.*

THOSE OF US WHO ARE deeply concerned about population and the environment—"econuts," we're called—are accused of seeing herbicides in trees, pollution in running brooks, radiation in rocks, and overpopulation everywhere. There is merit in the accusation.

I was in Calcutta when the cyclone struck East Bengal in November, 1970. Early dispatches spoke of 15,000 dead, but the estimates rapidly escalated to 2,000,000 and then dropped back to 500,000. A nice round number; it will do as well as any, for we will never know. The nameless ones who died, "unimportant" people far beyond the fringes of the social power structure, left no trace of their existence. Pakistani parents repaired the population loss in just 40 days, and the world turned its attention to other matters.

What killed those unfortunate people? The cyclone, newspapers said. But one can just as logically say that overpopulation killed them. The Gangetic delta is barely above sea level. Every year several thousand people are killed in quite ordinary storms. If Pakistan were not overcrowded, no sane man would bring his family to such a place. Ecologically speaking, a delta belongs to the river and the sea; man obtrudes there at his peril.

In the web of life every event has many antecedents. Only by an arbitrary decision can we designate a single antecedent as "cause." Our choice is biased—biased to protect our egos against the onslaught of unwelcome truths. As T. S. Eliot put it in *Burnt Norton:*

> Go, go, go, said the bird: human kind
> Cannot bear very much reality.

Were we to identify overpopulation as the cause of a half-million deaths, we would threaten ourselves with a question to which we do not know the answer: *How can we control population without recourse to repugnant measures?* Fearfully we close our minds to an inventory of possibilities. Instead, we say that a cyclone caused the deaths, thus relieving ourselves of responsibility for this and future catastrophes. "Fate" is *so* comforting.

Every year we list tuberculosis, leprosy, enteric diseases, or animal parasites as the "cause of death" of millions of people. It is well known that malnutrition is an important antecedent of death in all these categories; and that malnutrition is connected with overpopulation. But overpopulation is not called the cause of death. We cannot bear the thought.

People are dying now of respiratory diseases in Tokyo, Birmingham, and Gary, because of the "need" for more industry. The "need" for more food justifies overfertilization of the land, leading to eutrophication of the waters, and lessened fish production—which leads to more "need" for food.

What will we say when the power shuts down some fine summer on our eastern seaboard and several thousand people die of heat prostration? Will we blame the weather? Or the power companies for not building enough generators? Or the econuts for insisting on pollution controls?

One thing is certain: we won't blame the deaths on overpopulation. No one ever dies of overpopulation. It is unthinkable.

130   # False Starts in Detroit

ART HOPPE and

STEVEN JOHNSON

1976

Art Hoppe is a columnist for the San Francisco Chronicle *and 100 other newspapers, and Steven Johnson's cartoons have appeared in the* Bulletin *and elsewhere.*

WITH WHIRLING SEARCHLIGHTS, beaming smiles and carnations in their buttonholes, the nation's auto makers have unveiled their all-new, 1977 models, each heralded as The Great American Car designed to be released during this, our Bicentennial Year. The reaction of the motoring public was perhaps best summed up by Hector Woolsey of Falls Church, Virginia, who, after visiting nine dealers' showrooms, said glumly, "I didn't even bother to kick the tires."

The Great American Car the motoring public has demanded for years, of course, is a small, roomy, gas-saving, high-powered automobile with a low price tag and a plethora of chromium-plated accoutrements to enhance its owner's sense of status, and incidentally, security on the highway.

With the quality of the environment at stake, patriotic motorists were more than willing to accept a compact car that offered thirty-five miles to the gallon and a smog-free exhaust system—just as long as they didn't have to sacrifice roominess, comfort, a massive grille and an engine that would take them from zero to sixty in ten seconds flat. That was the clear-cut challenge Detroit faced once again in this Bicentennial Year. Once again, Detroit failed to meet it.

The problem was not lack of intent. ("God knows we tried," said one General Motors executive with a touch of bitterness.) During the past year, thousands of imaginative designs flowed from the drawing boards in a feverish effort to produce what the public demanded. Yet each, for one arcane reason or another, proved impractical. In fairness to the auto makers, here is a smattering of these aborted attempts.

With the dismal failure of their attempts to create The Great American Car in our Bicentennial Year, it was back to the old drawing board for the nation's auto designers, who even now are creating mock-ups of the 1978 models. What they have in store for us cannot definitely be known. Most industry analysts agree, however, that the closest Detroit has yet come to meeting the demands of the environment-conscious American motorist was the innovative Chevette. Here was a small, economical, gas-saving, no-frills car. Unfortunately, it lacked a large bumper, four headlights, room for eight passengers and an engine that went, "Va-room! Va-room!" Sales were disappointing.

Nevertheless, General Motors plans to continue production of the Chevette as its contribution to a more beautiful America. The new model will, of course, incorporate "minor design changes."

The Chevette 2

Cadillac Coupe de Grille

The aforementioned, somewhat-bitter G.M. executive declined to confirm the authenticity of the pirated photograph above, which purports to show the 1978 Chevette 2. All he would say was, *"If we can't give the public what they like, we'll give 'em, by God, what we like!"*

It was Cadillac ("The Standard of the World") that first applied both longitudinal and latitudinal maximinimization. Shortening the length of its 1976 models proved no problem. Narrowing the width by 27.4 inches, however, required narrowing the sparkling, heavily chrome-plated front end by a like amount. At first, this seemed an overwhelming obstacle to consumer acceptance. *"After all,"* said General Motors' consulting psychologist, Dr. Herman Fishbein, *"why else does anyone buy a Cadillac?"* But a design task force, working around the clock for three months, eventually scored the breakthrough shown here—the 1977 Cadillac Coupe de Grille. A pilot model was tested for eight days in the Los Angeles area. In that time, it was ticketed twice for parking illegally in parallel zones and caused several nasty accidents on the Ventura Freeway when other motorists, upon glancing out their right-hand windows, swerved with undue haste to avoid side-on collisions. At this point, the U.S. Bureau of Automotive Safety obtained a cease-and-desist order from Federal Judge Albert Swinnerton and the project was regretfully terminated.

Chrysler New Yorker Crescent

489

At Chrysler, meanwhile, the father-and-son team of Herbert and Robert Stitwiler had come up with an ingenious application of longitudinal maximinimization in this mock-up of a 1977 New Yorker Crescent. *"We realized that the longest distance between two points is a curved line,"* explained the elder Stitwiler. *"Thus, by arching the frame, we were able to reduce the wheel base 19.4 inches without sacrificing roominess, comfort, or stability. Moreover, this design provided easy access for under-body maintenance."* It was not so much the inconvenience of the portable boarding steps (an optional accessory) that caused the project to be abandoned as it was the tendency of the curved drive shaft, when rotating more than 30,000 revolutions per minute, to emit what one automotive analyst described as "strange noises."

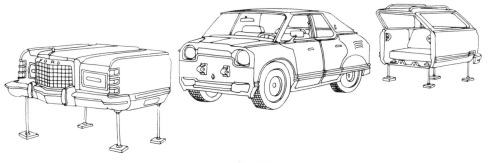

Ford Gallia

The concept that came closest to being placed in production was this 1977 Ford Gallia, all of which was divided into three parts. *"It is optional accessories that have made our industry what it is today,"* proudly explained Justin Forestone, a senior Ford accountant, when the model was first unveiled to applauding company executives. "The Gallia is the ultimate in its field." The basic unit with its four-cylinder engine achieved the compactness, fuel economy and low price tag the public had long demanded of Detroit. Employing an advanced link-up device that was a technological spin-off from the Apollo-Soyez space mission, the driver, by careful maneuvering, was able to lock on to the ornate hood accessory which contained its own four-cylinder engine, thus doubling the car's horsepower and prestige for trips to country clubs and restaurants with valet parking. This left only the challenge of roominess, one easily solved by the purchase of the rear-end station wagon accessory shown here. This, then, appeared to be The Great American Car at last — small, roomy, gas-saving, high-powered, low-priced and prestigious. After market-testing fourteen models, however, Ford executives reluctantly decided to stick with their traditional, one-piece, eight-cylinder $7,500 Country Squire station wagon. It was not so much the difficult maneuvering involved (this required driving forward into the garage to pick up the front accessory, backing out, turning around, and backing in again to pick up the rear accessory), as the fact, proved conclusively by the

Pontiac Grand Prix Hardtop Garage

studies, that once American motorists had locked on their accessories, they would be psychologically incapable of releasing them.

Probably the most innovative approach was taken by Pontiac officials. "The basic technological hurdle was to combine a small economy car with a large luxury car," said the company's chief engineering analyst, Godfrey Jonah. "While other designers have long attempted to build the features of a large luxury car within the confines of a small economy car, we saw at once that the challenge was insuperable. So we simply reversed the process." The result was this 1977 Pontiac Grand Prix four-door hardtop garage. Parked permanently in front of the owner's home in full view of the neighbors, the Grand Prix offered what Jonah termed "the zenith in low fuel consumption" due to its lack of an engine. For trips, the hatchback raised and a ramp descended automatically, thus enabling the small economy car it contained to back out and be on its way in a jiffy. While the concept looked good on the drawing board, tests in several urban areas showed that the Grand Prix not only required a parking place for itself, but an empty parking place behind it to permit the egress of the small economy car it contained. This resulted in numerous altercations and the filing in Chicago of an assault-and-battery complaint. *"I still feel strongly that this problem can be licked,"* said Jonah, but he declined to speculate on precisely how.

131

Save the Seas:
Save the Earth

JACQUES COUSTEAU

1976

Our ancestors came from the ocean, and the life of the seas is still vital to the support system of life on the lands. In poisoning the seas we are poisoning the source of life, at no little risk to our own survival. No one is more qualified to speak on the seas' role in our survival than Jacques Cousteau, who has sailed the surfaces and probed the depths, finding everywhere evidence of man's heedless disregard for the waters that gave us birth.

Following are excerpts from a speech he delivered at the Sierra Club's annual banquet in San Francisco where he received the club's highest honor: the John Muir Award.

JANUARY 1973—Having crossed the Antarctic circle, *Calypso* heads south along Adelaide Island, en route to Marguerite Bay. I am on the bridge, to make a decision about sending my son Philippe in our helicopter, as our vanguard, to the British Station at the southern tip of Adelaide. A wind, force five, blows; the sea is agitated. On our path, scattered blocks of ice oblige us to alter our course occasionally. It is three o'clock in the morning. A low sun showers the scenery with a pristine, unreal pink dye. A cavalcade of huge tabular icebergs files across the horizon. Along the coast, a thick mist rises from the sea, and above, low clouds of cold steam. The majestic glaciers and ice-capped mountains of Adelaide emerge and stretch up toward a half moon of silver engraved in a purple sky. At a cable's length, a few orcas loudly cough their blows of vapor. Everything, here, is water: water solid, water liquid, water in fog and cloud, water alive, water immense, overwhelming, but, also, water little, humble, fragile. Surrounded by a majestic beauty that still haunts me today, I know that here, the sea is only a couple of degrees from freezing solid, that life teems at the edge of death. In the Antarctic, the vulnerability of our magnificent world is exposed, a message that we refuse to read.

Cruising three months in the Antarctic waters, flying 120 hours by helicopter in search of cetaceans, we have observed only two humpback whales, two groups of sei whales, half a dozen packs of orcas. Not one single blue, not a single finback! But everywhere, heaps of bleached bones, tragic monuments to human folly. The seals were scarce, but seal hunting was about to resume. Penguins proliferated, fattening from the krill left over since the slaughter of whales. But dead penguins were found, poisoned by distant pesticides, brought here by oceanic currents.

Every two weeks, a liner poured two thousand tourists on the Antarctic peninsula. The scientific stations, whatever their nationality, however conscious of the damage done by their guests they may be, are surrounded by heaps of litter that may accumulate there and will remain for near eternity. I knew that 2,000 miles from us in another part of Antarctica, the sinister silhouette of the first off-shore drilling ship announced the approaching new fate of the last near-virgin continent: today, investigations have discovered coal, gas, oil, iron and about as many ore deposits as in any other land mass.

Oh! I know that the Antarctic deep-sea coring operation was only for science! The tragic irony of the social systems we live in is that such a monumental hypocrisy is forged by very sincere people. The drillers, the sailors, the geophysicists are all working for scientific institutes; the results will be published in learned magazines. It is none of the scientists' business, by definition, to deal with what may be done with their findings. The geologist and the nuclear physicist work for the advancement of knowledge and wash their hands of any responsibility. This "Pilatic syndrome" has been institutionalized, so that inventors and finders simply surrender all their substance to the elected adventurers who rule our so-called democratic world. And, if at the end of a career, a respectable scientist revolts and protests, he will be given half a column of the 23rd page of a local newspaper.

Our fears about the Antarctic have a special origin: a nostalgic feeling or premonition that the continent of ice may be our last wilderness. But everywhere else, abuses of technology and forgeries of information are even worse than in the Antarctic. Never before has the marine environment been misrepresented, and then raped, cut-up, poisoned, as it is today:

• All urban and industrial effluents from 500 million Europeans and Africans flows freely, practically without treatment, into the Mediterranean, the near-closed sea that was the cradle of civilization.

• Most large cities systematically dump their refuse offshore.

• Millions of tons of toxic chemicals find their way into the ocean through direct dumping, or indirectly in rivers or rain.

When the *Cavtat* sank off Otranto with drums containing hundreds of tons of highly poisonous lead tetraethyl, nations and companies quarreled, but nothing was done to defuse such a time-bomb. When in France the Supertanker, *Olympic Bravery,* the unsinkable pride of the Onassis fleet, recently ran aground in Ouessant, nothing was done for one full month until a storm broke the ship in two and generated a near-catastrophic oil spill.

Dumping nuclear wastes in the sea, after the irresponsible operations of France, the European Organization Euratom and the United States, was suspended because deep sea photographs had demonstrated that some of the drums were crushed open. Nevertheless, major grants are given today to resume this horrible practice, hopefully with a higher degree of ephemeral

Jacques Cousteau

security. And licenses are granted to extradite the dangerous nuclear power plants offshore, on floating barges. Madness could not go farther.

Meanwhile, swamps are filled, coastline development neutralizes the natural and only breeding grounds of thousands of species of marine creatures, huge industrial complexes are built on the seashores or along rivers, with no significant protection. Multinational corporations now build their plants in those developing countries that have no environmental-protection regulations. Overfishing is such that the whale population has decreased at least 92 percent. The catch of most commercial fish like herring, sardines, anchovies, tuna and swordfish has dropped by an average of 40 percent in the past ten years in spite of an increase in tonnage of the fishing fleet and in spite of the availability to industrial fishermen of scientific and technologic data. An estimate of two miles of coral reef is destroyed every day with crowbars to furnish souvenir shops, often those of scientific institutions, with shells and pieces of coral. Highly evolved creatures like dolphin and orca are exhibited as clowns in anti-educational marine zoos. Spearfishermen kill or scare away the last groupers and lobsters of the reefs.

This overview, far from being pessimistic or exaggerated, is, on the contrary, incomplete and carefully toned down.

The earth is the only planet where liquid water is to be found in an appreciable quantity. And even that quantity is small. The United Nations' poster for Environment Day, June 5, illustrates a comparison that I had made in 1959: if the earth were reduced to the size of an egg, all the water in the oceans, the lakes, the rivers, the ice caps, would amount to one single drop, hardly capable of moisturizing the egg. When we contemplate the vastness of the ocean, it is only a measure of how minuscule our persons are. In fact, there is on our planet only a very small, very finite, very precious and very vulnerable water reserve.

In this large expanding and cooling universe, in at least one tiny corner, life was born. It may have been born in other places as well, but, needing water quantity and quality, life must be exceedingly rare. Life, as we know it, made its appearance in water about three billion years ago and still depends on water. The "life expectancy of life" on earth extends probably until the sun becomes a red giant, in another four billion years. The miracle of life, the adventure of life is not yet halfway through its possible existence, and as our species is about two million years old, the human race could continue to thrive 2000 times as long as it already has. In order to fully realize our responsibilities in the face of such a future, we must abandon our individual consciousness and develop a global consciousness. We must switch from the motivation of individual profit to that of profit for humankind.

Today, in the fury of misguided progress, destructions have become exponential, hysterical, catastrophic! But, paradoxically, the same science and technology used for reckless pilfering of resources, have also developed, available on a shelf, all the means, all the solutions to reverse the trend. Yesterday, our ancestors did not know, and they could do nothing anyway. Today, we know, and we can, but we don't. We are living a nightmare, when our hands desperately reach for an easy, accessible cure, while incomprehensible forces paralyze us. Let us awaken from this nightmare, a world where any reasonable solution is declared utopian.

Meanwhile, the little pulse of life, thriving on water, still turns shining drops of water into living jewels. At least locally and apparently, life defies the universal law of degradation, creating highly complex organic molecules, organizing chaotic matter into unbelievably well-programmed structures of trillions of cells, like my grandchildren, for example. It is the contemplation of life that inspired Father Teilhard de Chardin to envision three infinites: in addition to the infinitely big and the infinitely small, Teilhard told us there also was the infinitely complex—life. This is what we should all be fighting for.

PART IX

Wilderness, the Whole Earth, and the Spirit of Man

LIKE THE SIERRA CLUB ITSELF, *the philosophy that motivates its members has evolved over the generations. It began as a concern with the relation of the individual to nature—particularly the Sierra Nevada—and with the preservation of wilderness—particularly in national parks. Over the decades it has broadened to encompass the need for the human race to adapt to the limits of the planet. Yet such considerations as overpopulation, resource depletion, forestry, park policy, and energy conservation are necessarily abstractions; they lack the power to move people deeply unless they are grounded in the individual's feeling for the visible signs of nature around him.*

The philosophy shared by the club's members recognizes this vital fact: It is essential that in today's high-level environmental contests over those abstractions, we maintain contact with our sources of personal strength and renewal in the plants and trees, the birds and animals, the forms of the land and the flowing currents of water and air.

132

Trustees of the Future

JAMES BRYCE

1913

Next to John Muir, the most famed member of the Sierra Club in its early years was his fellow Scot, James Bryce, mountaineer, British politician, diplomat, and historian. His masterpiece, The American Commonwealth, *published in 1888, is one of the two most acclaimed nineteenth-century European views of the United States. The other is de Tocqueville's* Democracy in America. *At the time he wrote this address to the American Civic Association in Baltimore he was British Ambassador to the United States. It appeared in the* Bulletin *in 1913.*

EUROPE IS A POPULOUS overcrowded continent; you will some day be a populous and ultimately perhaps even a crowded continent, and it is well to take thought at once, before the overcrowding comes on, as to how you will deal with the difficulties which we have had to deal with in Europe, so that you may learn as much as possible from our experience, and not find too late that the beauty and solitude of nature have been snatched from you by private individuals.

The love of nature is happily increasing among us, and it therefore becomes all the more important to find means for safeguarding nature. The population is increasing, too, and the number of people who desire to enjoy nature, therefore, is growing larger, both absolutely and in proportion. But, unfortunately, the opportunities for enjoying it, except as regards easier locomotion, are not increasing. The world is circumscribed. The surface of this little earth of ours is limited, and we cannot add to it. When a man finds his house is too small, he builds more rooms on to it, but we cannot add to our world; we did not make it, it was made for us, and we cannot increase its dimensions. All we can do is to turn it to the best possible account. Now, let us remember that the quantity of natural beauty in the world, the number of spots calculated to give enjoyment in the highest form, are limited, and are being constantly encroached upon.

I beg you to consider that, although your country is vast and has scope of natural beauty far greater than we can boast in little countries like England or Scotland, even your scenery is not inexhaustible, and with your great population and the growing desire to enjoy the beauties of nature, you have not got any more than you need. Fortunately, you have made a good beginning in the work of conservation. You have led the world in the creation of national parks. I have seen three or four of these. I have been in the Yosemite twice, in the Yellowstone twice. The creation of such national parks is good, and it has had the admirable effect of setting other countries to emulate your example.

Let me try to give some logical quality to my statements by submitting some few propositions in order.

The world seems likely to last a long, long time, and we ought to make provisions for the future.

The population of the world goes on constantly increasing, and nowhere increasing so fast as in North America.

A taste for natural beauty is increasing, and, as we hope, will go on increasing.

The places of scenic beauty do not increase, but, on the contrary, are in danger of being reduced in number and diminished in quantity, and the danger is always increasing with the accumulation of wealth, owing to the desire of private persons to appropriate these places. There is no better service we can render to the masses of the people than to set about and preserve for them wide spaces of fine scenery for their delight.

From these propositions I draw the conclusion that it is necessary to save what we have got, and to extend the policy which you have wisely adopted, by acquiring and preserving still further areas for the perpetual enjoyment of the people.

Let us think of the future. We are trustees of the future. We are not here for ourselves alone. All these gifts were not given to us to be used by one generation, or with the thought of one generation only before our minds. We are the heirs of those who have gone before, and charged with the duty we owe to those who come after, and there is no duty which seems clearer or higher than that of handing on to them undiminished facilities for the enjoyment of some of the best gifts that the Creator has seen fit to bestow upon his children.

133

The Mountain and the Sea

CHESTER ROWELL

1921

Chester Rowell was the kind of person who has played a leading part in the life of the Sierra Club from its beginning—the busy, successful executive who maintained a deep sensitivity toward the wilderness. Rowell was editor of the Fresno Bee *and later of the San Francisco* Chronicle, *a mainstay of the liberal (Hiram Johnson) wing of the Republican party, and a Regent of the University of California. (A university regency has been called California's equivalent of knighthood.)*

This article was an address delivered at the Annual Reunion Dinner at the Palace Hotel in December of 1921. These affairs brought together the participants in the previous summer's annual outings, which in those days included most of the club's members. The tradition is continued nowadays in dozens of reunions held by participants in the various trips. One problem Rowell mentions is still with us—how to recognize, in their town finery, those you last saw in their wilderness fatigues, covered with mountain dust.

M R. CHAIRMAN AND FELLOW MOUNTAIN LOVERS: — Let me first congratulate you on your good looks, and hope that friends have recognized each other in spite of those good looks. I have seen you when you looked otherwise, and I have, on those occasions, observed some other things than looks—for instance, a new aspect of femininism. Even our great-grandparents recognized that women were our moral superiors. It took our generation to discover, by humiliating experiences, in schools and lately in politics, that women are our intellectual superiors; but it took the Sierra Club to reveal that they are our physical superiors. I used to think I was a pretty good mountain "hiker" myself; but no matter how long or how hard a walk I took, there was always some Sierra Club girl ahead who had beaten my record.

You are to be congratulated not merely on your membership, but on your mission, for you are dedicated to the doctrine that no matter how thick this earth may be piled with the works of man, there shall still be preserved on it some of the works of God. We may scratch the earth for our crops and pile up baked earth for our dwellings and factories to supply the needs of our bodies, but also we still need the earthly symbols of the Infinite to minister to the infinite soul within.

The earth has two symbols of the Infinite—the great mountains and the great sea. But there is one creed of the mountains and another of the sea. The mountain is a theist; the sea a pantheist. The mountain points upward to heaven; the sea dissolves into Nirvana.

On the mountain the finger of God has written the story of creation. There is beginning and middle and end, and a multitude of episodes and digressions. The mountain itself is a growth, a visible handiwork. Upheaved in the morning of time from the metal bowels of Earth; corroded into earthy salts by rains of boiling acid; laid down in the bed of a steaming sea and upheaved again; buried and metamorphosed into granite; outcropped and ground by the first glaciers, spread out as soil and silt, the home and the grave of living creatures; washed by softer rains and compacted into sedimentary rock, with the fossils of its children hidden in its matrix; crumpled and tilted into a new mountain range, with its crown of living verdure, its veil of shifting cloud, its diamond cascades; its face scarred with the

501

glaciers and the storms of ages and buried in its structure the record of all the ages before—that is a tale, not of death, but of life. Vast time and vast forces have gone to the making of the mountain, but they are comprehensible and finite; the projection, not the immediate symbol, of the Infinite. The mountain inspires to thought and to work. There are things to understand and things to do, all on a scale grand enough to uplift, but not overwhelming enough to cast down. Humanly the mountain speaks the language and preaches the creed of the occidental man. One can be a Christian in the mountains, and believe in a personal God and an individual immortality. Also, one can work and think and study, and remember and plan.

A mountain's life is a man's life multiplied by billions, but not a changeless infinity. The mountains call us, not to rest, but to work. A great peak is a frowning challenge, until we have scaled it; a strong and trusted friend thereafter. We can share the life of the mountain; we can search its history until we are as old in knowledge as it is in experience; we can stand on its summit and be lifted up in spirit as if we had grown to its height and expanded in soul to the whole reach of a broadened horizon. The glaciers have carved a castle for us whose ceiling the sun emblazons with cubic miles of filmy gold; the winds fling banners from the bleak peaks; the winters of ages have piled our partitions; the summers of centuries have grown the pines for our bedposts, and God has scattered the firmament with stars, to give us courage by contemplating their infinity, to measure our pygmy finitude against the giant but also finite mountains. The torrents and the pines sing to us, the birds and the busy squirrels speak to us, the rocks preach to us, and the mind is at stress with the muscles as the soul breathes deep with the lungs. So the mountains enter into our lives as we enter into theirs. We are lifted up in the high places, not beyond ourselves, but to our best selves.

But the sea preserves no marks of the finger of God, and its God has no fingers, nor any parts or members. The sea itself is neither new nor old, and has no past nor future—only an eternal Now. It has not even Here nor There, for all places are one to it; the very navigator has to locate himself, not by any fact, but by a mathematical abstraction, computed by tangents and cosines. The sea has no measure, for there is no unit to measure it by—no part to be applied to another part, and then to another, and the number of applications counted. Individuality, separateness, are illusions in the sea; the only reality is The One. There is one wave, and another wave, but presently they are the same wave, and then no wave. The drop of spray flashes a moment a separate unit, and then sinks back again into the undivided One. Since the world was, the sea is; but the spirit of God still broods on the face of the waters, changeless forever. Not the grasp of thought, but only the rapt vision of the Plotinist can apprehend the vastness of the sea. Its lessons are not written in a book, but whispered in mystic oracles. Its language, to humans, is the occult speech of the Orient. Its creed is not Christianity, but Theosophy or esoteric Brahminism. Its God is the Inscrutable; its destiny Nirvana.

502

And so we have the seashore to rest and forget; the sea to muse and dream; the mountains to work, to think, to feel, to grow, to be inspired and uplifted. And then the office and the shop, to grind once more our little cog in the great mill of life.

134

Prolegomena to a Philosophy of Mountaineering

ELMO A. ROBINSON

1938

The contemporary American who finds delight in the mountains is the heir of a tradition that has been evolving for more than 2000 years. Historian Elmo A. Robinson here chronicles the growth in that tradition, from a mild interest in the pastoral and the picturesque to a passion for the most remote wilderness.

OCCASIONALLY ON A Sunday afternoon members of the Sierra Club, arriving at an intersection of trail and highway, speculate concerning the thoughts of the autoists dashing by. "What do they think of us?" we ask ourselves. "Are they also speculating about us and wondering how we have become the queer-looking folk we seem to be?" If they really do have such thoughts, they are at the beginning of a fascinating inquiry. How *did* we get this way? Why is it that we camp and hike and ski and climb cliffs and scale peaks? Until the last two hundred years such things simply were not done. What brought about the change? What is its significance? "The most important aspect of all culture," says Powys, "is the gathering together of the integral self into some habitual way of response to Nature. . . . No refining of one's taste in matters of art or literature, no sharpening of one's powers of insight in matters of science or psychology, can ever take the place of one's sensitiveness to the life of the earth."

Among the peoples we are accustomed to call "the Ancients" there were apparently no activities resembling those of the modern hiking or mountaineering club. Appreciation of nature was not entirely lacking, but it seems to have been directed towards the more familiar and livable aspects. Remote, strange, forbidding regions—if one may judge from the records—were avoided. The Hebrew poetic and prophetic literature contains many allusions to objects of natural beauty. Isaiah has been called a nature-lover, and Jesus has immortalized the lilies of the field. But there is no indication in the gospels that "Nazareth is set on a hill overlooking one of the fairest mountain prospects in all Judea." And as for mountains, they are spoken of either merely as backgrounds or as scenes of unusual events—the transfiguration, the temptation, the strange adventures of an Elijah, the revelation to Moses, the grounding of the Ark. Hebrew appreciation of nature was, rather, a love of the pastoral. Eyes might be lifted to the hills, praises be sung to the cedars of Lebanon, but bodies and voices remained in more comfortable and conventional locations.

Among the Romans country life was prized and travel was common—for purposes of sightseeing, change of climate, edification, and relaxation. Interest in the past led men to visit temples, for these often served as historical museums. Interest in art was also a motive for travel, but an even stronger one was interest in nature. The Roman appreciation of nature, however, was more limited than ours. Objects in nature which were famous (like our Niagara Falls), or rare (like Point Lobos), or regarded as sacred (like Plymouth Rock), were the usual destinations. Valleys, low hills, and coastlands were charming; grottos and sources of streams were particularly enjoyed; but there was no admiration for the wild or savage or for the majestic or sombre.

In fact, there were those who emphatically denied any beauty to mountains. "Horrible rock" is a characteristic phrase. By the beginning of the Christian era several passes through the Alps were well known, but a pass was merely an occasion for making, in return for safety, a votive offering of thanks to some god.

Ascents of actual mountains by Romans were apparently rare. Mount Etna, an exception, was visited chiefly for "scientific purposes," or perhaps to see the sun rise; the records usually omit any reference to the view or the beauty. Occasionally one finds claims that genuine enthusiasm for mountain scenery is to be discovered among Roman writers, but the usual report of scholars is to the contrary.

After the breakdown of the Roman administrative system and on into medieval times, the poor condition of the unrepaired trails, the uncertainty about inns, the likelihood of meeting brigands, combined to reduce transalpine travel to a minimum. Pilgrims on their way to Rome for Easter had to brave the passes at the worst season of the year when the danger from avalanches was at its maximum. Records speak of the horrors of the journey, the glare of the sun, the chill of the air. We are accustomed to associate indifference to *all* the beauties of nature with medieval religiosity and other worldliness, but this is doubtless an error. Among the early Christians there had been some appreciation of nature. Rather early in the development of the church, St. Basil struck a modern note when, in his description of the retreat which he had selected for the period of his readjustment from the life of a "college professor" to that of an ecclesiastical administrator, he wrote:

There is a high mountain, covered with a thick forest, watered on its northerly side by cool and transparent streams. At its base is outstretched an evenly sloping plain, ever enriched by the moisture from the mountain. A forest of many-coloured and multifarious trees, a spontaneous growth surrounding the plain, acts almost as a hedge to inclose it. . . . For it is, in fact, by no means far from being an island, since it is shut in on all sides by barriers. Two ravines break off abruptly on two sides, and on a third side, at the bottom of the cliff, the river which glides gently by forms a wall, being itself a continuous and impassable barrier. . . . The mountain stretches along the fourth side. . . . Adjoining my land is another neck of land, as it were, which supports at its summit a lofty ridge, so that from the former the plain below lies outspread before the eyes, and from the elevation we may gaze upon the encircling river. . . . roughened by the rock which borders upon it. As the river recoils from this rock, it coils itself into a deep whirlpool, furnishing me, and every spectator, with a most pleasing sight. . . . The highest praise, however, which I can give for this place is that. . . . it attracts not even a wayfarer, except the guests who join me in hunting.

In the Middle Ages monasteries were established in inaccessible regions of the Alps and other mountain systems, largely as retreats from the turmoil of the world, but perhaps with some degree of appreciation for nature. Gautier de Coinci, a monk of the thirteenth century, shows his sensitiveness to beauty when he says:

Therefore will I do even as he does who seeks flowers in a meadow the which is all springlike and bedecked with flowers and who sees all round him so many divers ones, crimson and violet and yellow and dark blue, that he knows not the which to pluck first.

Theoretical discussions were not lacking, for at least two of the great philosophers of the Church, John Scotis Erigena and Thomas Aquinas, had something to say about the significance of beauty. There were differences of opinion, but one widely accepted view held that those objects are beautiful which symbolize God's glory and power and goodness.

But in all this there was nothing of mountain climbing. What was advocated is comparable to advice to walk in Golden Gate Park or perhaps through the orchards of Santa Clara Valley. Except for a record of six priests who were punished for an attempted ascent in 1307, Petrarch (1335) stands out as the only known individual of this period who climbed a mountain from motives comparable to ours, and he was apparently the first to record his "deep and grave reflections."

With the Renaissance there came a new love for nature, or at least a new freedom to express in literary form that love which had perhaps never been absent from medieval life. Especially is it noteworthy that writers upon education now began to assert that growing boys should be taken upon nature trips. Vegio recommended that schoolboys should walk by streams, woods, and seashore, engaging in fishing, bird-catching, and teaching birds to talk. But even the humanist was likely to be blind to mountain scenery. Erasmus crossed the Alps in 1506 when he was about forty years old. It has been remarked that: "Although the journey was made through some of the grandest and most stupendous of Nature's wonders, there is not one word in any of the great man's letters to show that he was even conscious of their presence, and, though he was engaged in writing during the whole period, he could find nothing better to write about than his approaching old age, of which he had been reminded by discovering some gray hairs on his temples," according to J. J. Mangan.

Humanistic interest in man, and his affairs in this world, found almost simultaneous expressions in many fields. Artists began to discover new subjects and techniques of painting, writers became conscious of the beauties of native tongues, classicists turned back to forgotten periods of man's achievements, scientists looked out at nature with new eyes, astronomers found new worlds, and navigators began to explore this one. The year 1492, famous in American history, is also the date of the first full and precise account of a mountain expedition. Under orders from the King of France, several persons led by Domp Julien de Beaupré made a climb of Mount Aiguille, involving a stay of one week in the high elevations. Some of the party were terrified by their "horrible and frightful passage," since, in addition to the unknown physical dangers, there was the additional fact that by climbing they were tempting God to become very angry with them. De Beaupré himself was of a different mind, for to him the horrors were more than compensated for by the beautiful meadows and the herds of chamois.

During the next fifty years portions of the Alps became familiar to Swiss town-dwellers, particularly scholars, although true mountain ascents were rare. Indeed, if a man climbed one mountain, that was sufficient for a lifetime. Conrad Gesner was the first to profess boldly a love of climbing for its own sake. In 1543, at the age of twenty-seven, he wrote:

I have determined for the future, so long as the life divinely granted to me shall continue, each year to ascend a few mountains, or at least one, when the vegetation is flourishing, partly for the sake of becoming acquainted with the latter, partly for the sake of suitable bodily exercise and the delight of the spirit. For how great the pleasure, how great think you, are the joys of the spirit, touched as is fit it should be, in wondering at the mighty mass of mountains while gazing upon their immensity and, as it were, in lifting one's head among the clouds. In some way or other the mind is overturned by their dizzying height and is caught up in contemplation of the Supreme Architect.

The first English party came to the Alps in 1563, and by the end of the century there were numerous resorts for the traveler, and numerous treatises available for the reader. But for a period of a hundred and fifty years little advance was made either in mountaineering itself or in attitudes toward the mountains. At the opening of the eighteenth century the mountain world was practically unknown to the cultured European. Natural scenery was still generally regarded as hideous and gloomy; it could become attractive to the eye only by artificial landscaping. Pope and Addison were among those who attacked this view. At times the attack was rather weak, as when Addison wrote that the mountains "fill the mind with an agreeable horror." But presumably an agreeable horror is a step in advance of a disagreeable one.

The older views were undermined, also, by scientific expeditions, as well as by painters and poets. By the last quarter of the century, around 1780 and 1790, one hundred accounts of Alpine journeys had been published; the Alps had become a European playground, it was now fashionable to climb, and John Moore had observed that mountaineers, as do American vacationists of today, like to boast of what they have done and seen.

Perhaps the most significant name in the story of the modern attitude toward nature is Jean Jacques Rousseau. "Back to nature" is the slogan usually associated with him. But he was confused in his concept of nature. Sometimes he pled for a return to a less artificial design for human education and human nature, sometimes for the superiority of country life over town life, sometimes for the beauties of natural scenery, sometimes for a romantic idealizing of the savage over the civilized. All of these were "nature" to Rousseau. Love of nature in our sense meant to him either love of wild scenery or the love of domesticity in the country. In many respects the secret of his influence is difficult to understand. He made one walking trip into the mountains. He never made a second, nor visited a glacier, nor crossed a pass except from necessity. Of "torrents, rocks, dark woods, mountains, rough paths, and frightful precipices," he wrote eloquently. But what he actually valued most highly was not the high country but the lower wooded regions. What he has to say about "local walks" will touch a responsive chord in hikers of today:

I can only think of one way of travelling pleasanter than travelling on horseback, and that is to travel on foot. You start at your own time, you stop when you will, you do as much or as little as you choose. You see the country, you turn off to right or left; you examine anything which interests you, you stop to admire every view. Do I see a stream, I wander by its banks; a leafy wood, I seek its shade; a cave, I enter it; a quarry, I study its geology. If I like a place I stop there. As soon as I am weary of it I go on. I am independent of horses and postillions; I need not stick to regular routes or good roads; I go anywhere a man can go; I see all that a man can see; and as I am quite independent of everybody, I enjoy all the freedom a man can enjoy. . . .

What varied pleasures we enjoy in this delightful way of travelling, not to speak of increasing health and a cheerful spirit. I notice that those who ride in nice, well-padded carriages are always wrapped in thought, gloomy, fault-finding, or sick; while those who go on foot are always merry, lighthearted, and delighted with everything. How cheerful we are when we get near our lodging for the night! How savory is the course food! How we linger at table enjoying our rest! How soundly we sleep on a hard bed! If you only want to get to a place you may ride in a post-chaise; if you want to travel you must go on foot.

It is difficult to compress into a few words a statement of all the satisfactions and values of mountaineering. Perhaps this sentence by Shuster does it about as well as it can be done:

The glorious heat of noonday, the majesty of the night, the marching stars, the wide vision, the suggestion of peril, the rhythmic movement of the body, the fellowship of toil, the attainment — all these together make some new and precious thing which lives in us and which will till thought and feeling die.

507

To review the development of human attitudes and behaviors with respect to mountains is to assemble evidence that human nature can be changed, or at least that it has changed. This proposition must of necessity form a part of any philosophy based upon mountaineering. To say that human nature changes is not to claim that the fundamental wishes or needs which motivate behavior are altered; presumably they are not. Rather is it an assertion that the change is in the behavior itself, by which men seek to meet their needs. In seventeenth-century Europe to climb mountains for pleasure was not even thought of; it was contrary to human nature as then constituted. In twentieth-century Europe and America it is human nature to love mountains and mountaineering. The change which has come about suggests the possibility of modifying a great many other aspects of behavior which are now commonly regarded as fixed and unalterable characteristics of human nature.

Among the many possible directions in which human nature may change in the future is one in which is specifically implied by mountaineering. This is a diminishing evaluation of the profit motive. Critics of mountaineering often exclaim, "Well, I just can't see what anybody gets out of risking life and limb in that fashion!" Beneath such impulsive outbursts lie the common assumptions of our age, or at least of the age which is passing: that a man should do only what will bring him profit; that there abideth three kinds of profit—political power, social prestige, and economic wealth; and that the greatest of these is wealth. There is no activity of man which is more directly opposed to such a philosophy than mountaineering. Our commercial civilization assumes that in the absence of the struggle for economic existence there can be no adequate urge to action, no sustained striving, no admirable achievement. Every man or woman who climbs for the love of it is proclaiming a denial of this point of view. Is there not significance in the fact that mountaineering never became a popular activity until after the industrial revolution and the rise of capitalism? Superficially this relationship might be thought to rest upon the improvements in transportation which have rendered the mountains accessible. But such an assumption hardly explains all of the changes of attitudes, especially the almost religious consecration to the task, which characterizes many climbers. Certainly the genuine mountaineer constitutes vital testimony for the existence of powerful motivations upon which it is conceivable that the society of the future may place greater reliance.

One other aspect of mountain philosophy is the recognition that the irregularities of the earth's surface offer unexpected testimony of beauty and friendliness. "The two most obvious characteristics of Nature. . . . are loveliness and power. The beauty dawned later upon human intelligences than did its power," wrote Alfred North Whitehead. To sleep on a high mountainside a few centuries ago was to suffer the maximum torments of fear. Even Emerson of our own time, with all his love for nature, was too timid to spend a night in the open among the big trees, although his fears were "scientific" rather than "theological," fears of disease rather than of divinity. Parts of the earth's crust that were once regarded as at least uninteresting, or more probably as ugly, repelling, and inimical, are now looked upon as bits of marvellous beauty, inviting, and friendly. From horror to "agreeable horror," to agreeableness without horror, to fascinated delight—such has been our heritage of attitudes.

Something of this same development is occasionally recapitulated by the initiate Sierran, to whom the first days among the crests may seem terrifyingly overpowering, but in whom this depression is soon replaced by an unexpected yet welcome elation. What was once lonely and forbidding becomes a spot in which to curl up comfortably and confidently in one's blankets and lay onesself down to rest. The mountaineer has been one who, "passing through the Valley of Baca, maketh it a well." He has given the lie to those who deny the evidence that the universe is in some respects friendly to man and man's aspirations. Any complete philosophy must incorporate these racial and individual experiences into its final description of the nature and meaning of the cosmos.

135 Mountain Photography

CEDRIC WRIGHT

1941

Like Ansel Adams, Cedric Wright was a skillful musician as well as a photographer. In the article excerpted here, he combines the two elements that made him successful, a meticulous attention to the details of the craft and an intuitive grasp of the message he was trying to convey.

A S IN MUSIC, or anything else, rules condense in the wake of fine original and vital expression. There is an emotional and psychological grace about work done when rules and creativeness are kept in proper relationship.

Now, after this warning, I might mention some of the generalities which are worth thinking about:

1 Try to simplify subject material. Often a shift of camera position of but a few inches will eliminate insignificant detail.

2 Do not divide the picture space into equal parts, horizontally or vertically.

3 If the chief interest is in a fine cloudy sky, put the horizon below the center. If a fine landscape is burdened with an uninteresting sky, put the horizon near the top.

4 Keep the main object of interest off center. Try to find a camera position which brings some smaller mass to the opposite side of the picture and nearer the edge.

5 Try to find subjects with long, graceful lines, which lead into the picture and into the distance, within the picture.

6 In framing subject matter, one main center of interest is usually best and enough.

7 Study the picture margins, avoiding anything which attracts much attention near the picture edge. Avoid lines parallel to margins. (Trees don't count!) Avoid light foreground or light areas near the edges. Segments of area along the margins usually don't look too well if one to one, or one to two, in size.

The most important consideration of all remains—to try to cover the relationship of photography to our serious reactions to nature. And in this it will be hard to avoid making a noise like an oracle. In photography one is translating, somewhat, from one language to another. Rock, cloud, water, and fire, in all their aura of light and sound and depth, must be translated into the language—the materials—of a photographic print. For this, both languages must be thoroughly felt and understood. This begins to be possible only when one's range of dynamics and tones is that of a full-scale keyboard, and at the fingertips. Then photography is an ample voice, a resonant language. Our materials then become rich in resource.

The mountain photographer is interpreting the face of nature—that mysterious infinity, eternally a refuge, a reservoir, an amplifier of the spirit; a mother of dreams; a positive though elusive voice in whose depth lies its subtlety. They will interpret best who are never so content as when under the influence of situations where silence is rich in the mute assurance and beauty of mountain surroundings. The quality of emotional knowing has a finer integration with our spirit than anything that comes from barren intellectual processes. This point of view only accumulates slowly, out of long experience and contact with wordless influences. Under the spell of solitude and of natural beauty the root system of this kind of awareness establishes itself.

Great art is usually created under some such saturation of awareness. The work is then permeated with an inner perception of beauty and an inner personal philosophy. The hope for our photography is that it shall retain these high lights of more than beauty, that through it symbols shall be preserved of response to our mountains, keeping them to flow, a golden thread, in our experience.

136

Problems of Interpretation of the Natural Scene

ANSEL ADAMS

1945

Here Ansel Adams tilts his lance at some distorted views of nature and enlists photography not merely in the task of seeing and interpreting wilderness, but also in preserving it from human predators.

I BELIEVE A PHILOSOPHY of appreciation has taken root in the consciousness of the American people. Even though distorted by the false emphasis and exaggerations of commercial exploitation and advertising, the *facts* of our magnificent land are nevertheless slowly rising above the tides of confusion. Now as vulnerable as the first seedlings after rain, they may in time become firm elements of our national life — but only if we nourish them and expand the positive directions of their growth. The sum of our *response* is the sum of our experience of a myriad minute actualities and forces; the sum of our *appreciation* lies in the mood and understanding which we bring to these intimate experiences.

One weakness in our appreciation of nature is the emphasis placed upon *scenery,* which in its exploited aspect is merely a gargantuan curio. Things are appreciated for size, unusuality, and scarcity more than for their subtleties and emotional relationship to everyday life. Even some of the most sincere proponents of the National Parks speak of "the oldest living thing," or "the highest waterfall," or "the greatest collection of geysers in the world," unmindful that such extremes are merely coincidental and have little to do with true spiritual and emotional values. The moon rising beyond a great mountain establishes an emotional actuality which has nothing whatever to do with size, distance, or coincidence. Likewise, common grass growing against stone may be of more poignant beauty than an entire grove of sequoias in their most conventional "tourist" aspect.

Having been intimately associated for many years with the Sierra and with the problems of conservation and the interpretation of the Natural Scene, I have experienced — as a photographer — the persistent enigma, the finding of some basic key of statement and communication. This key depends upon more than the esthetic factors; the problem as a whole must be explored, for the implications — social and otherwise — are far-reaching and intricate. Interpretation is more than a factual enterprise; it relates not only to the communication of literal aspects, but to the revelation of the deeper impulse of the world. It must stimulate response and activate understanding. In addition it should *prepare* — create an anticipatory mood. Unfortunately, the present inundation of superficial images usually associated with commercial advertising propaganda serves to weaken and distort what should be a clear and accurate mood of expectation. Herein lies the great value of images, photographic and otherwise, which convey impressions of the Natural Scene to the people.

Every person would rise in indignation were he to observe careless destruction of marketable timber, flooding of mines, or poisoning of lakes and rivers. Any tragic waste of our natural resources would arouse alarm and protest. But now let us pause and think — are not the intangibles of the natural world an integral part of our national resource? And are they not of incalculable importance to the development of our civilization and to the generations to follow us? Can we let them be wasted?

We must fight for *integrity of experience* as well as for the more obvious benefits of existence. We are confronted with a terrifying danger to the Parks and to the Wilderness, and to all that they represent in our culture and way of living. Predatory interests desiring to enlarge their rightful share of the natural resources clamor for additional exploitation and invasion of these preserved areas.

Facing this problem with considerable first-hand observation of selfish exploitation and the stupid misuse of priceless resources, I have developed a concept of interpretation through the camera of the qualities of the natural world, hoping to reveal them with sufficient impact and clarity to aid definitely in the coming struggle for true conservation. The miracle of photography makes possible the interpretation of both great and small aspects of the world, destroying the false emphasis on *size* and the equally false anthropocentric concepts.

Now that the camera has become a universal instrument of expression and communication it is conceivable that a great number of sympathetic photographers will make a constructive interpretation of the natural world. Photography, more than any other visual medium, effectively reveals not only the aspects of the natural world, but also the tragic results of its violation.

137

A Day with Aldo Leopold

ALFRED G. ETTER

1963

Aldo Leopold's two books, Round River *and* A Sand County Almanac *called for an American land ethic. They have taken a place alongside the writings of Muir and Thoreau as preeminent examples of American nature literature. In 1947, the year before Leopold died of a heart attack while fighting a fire on his Sand County, Wisconsin, farm, he was visited by Alfred Etter. Etter was then working for the Department of Fisheries and Wildlife at Michigan State University; he later became a lecturer for the Audubon Society. This account of the visit was written in 1947, published in* The Land *in 1948, and reprinted in the* Bulletin *fifteen years later.*

"Our children are our signature to the roster of history. I hope to leave them good health, an education, and possibly even a competence. But what are they going to do with these things if there are no more deer in the hills, and no more quail in the coverts? No more snipe whistling in the meadow, no more piping of widgeons and chattering of teal as darkness covers the marshes; no more whistling of swift wings when the morning star pales in the east? And when the dawn wind stirs through the ancient cottonwoods, and the gray light steals down from the hills over the old river sliding softly past its wide brown sandbars — what if there be no more goose music?"

— ALDO LEOPOLD in *Round River*

WE DROVE FROM CEMENT to gravel to dirt to a narrow pair of ruts that wound their way past successively poorer farms. The first barn after the junction was red and round-roofed and large enough to store small crops of hay and to accommodate a fair herd of dairy cows. The second barn had once been red, but now there was only a faint glow to the old wood under the angled roof. As the road grew grassier between the sandy yellow ruts the barns gradually became nothing but bleached walls and sagging roofs, muddy yards, and tangles of old machines.

The river ran alongside the road, pinching in and out between low islands of willow, cottonwood, and elm, and steep banks of oak. Clumps of prickly ash invaded the grass of old fields. A hog pasture, pocked with upturned sod, blanketed a hillside. On its broken ground were corn ears recently spread for the hungry animals. On another hill were the remains of a meager crop of dwarfed corn, the shocks a hundred feet apart. Drifting sand piled in small crescents about each broken stalk.

Farther down the road, a boxlike house, a yard of litter, and a flock of chickens huddled together in a field of scrubby oak. Still the road declined, and in the low places silt and water made shallow puddles. After passing through several of these dips, Professor Leopold let his dog, Flick, out of the car to run the rest of the way to the "Shack." We had come to land that both of them knew intimately. Here the distractions of the bigger-and-better way of city life were shut out by expanses of sterile land, marsh, and meandering rivers.

Whether the Professor or Flick knew the farm more intimately was hard to say, for they knew it differently. Flick knew the ground, the smell of the soil. He knew the sedge in the marsh from the rustle of its keeled blades against his nose and the dry bluegrass for its tickle and maze of essential pleasure. He was familiar with the softness of moss, and patterns of tracks in the sand blow, and with the sensation of his own feet sinking into the sand. Flick liked to investigate the dark mystery of burrows and the black windows of brush piles. Each new patch of scrub held the possibility of pheasant, woodcock, or grouse. The wind was his pleasure, and his companion, and his competitor. Flick was the first to investigate the morning dew, and from it learned a mass of facts important to his day's adventures.

To the Professor the farm was earth and soil too, and full of pleasant sensations. It gave him the satisfaction of planting a pine, of building a brush pile, of finding a deer track in the cool silt along the river. His eyes fed on the brilliant green expanse of spike rush that bordered the islands in early summer, and on the brilliant leaves of blackberry in the fall.

The farm was a place to satisfy a craving for beauty and simplicity, and yet it was much more than that. It was where the Professor worked out the subtle pattern that became his life. It was a place where he could gain information from the tallest tree or the most insignificant spring flower, from a casual squirrel or a cached fawn. Here he tried to piece together answers to the questions that nature so often tempted him to solve. From pads of moss or patches of quack grass he learned a bit of history. From a tangle of ash logs a suggestion of some principle dawned upon him. From a broken pine a brief diagram of the balance of the forces in the environment was devised. Above all, this farm was a place where his children could learn the meaning of life and gain confidence in their ability to investigate small problems and discover things that no one knew.

I had heard Professor Leopold refer frequently to the "Shack" on his farm. When we made the last turn up the road I was surprised to find this familiar name a very descriptive one. At the time this property first felt the Professor's step there were two feet of stale cow manure in this building. It had been a barn and stable for many years. The energy and ingenuity of his family had converted it into a roughly yet comfortably furnished week-end home with a substantial fireplace, heavy iron pots, hewn wooden tables and benches, and a string of decoys for decoration. Bunk-beds spoke of the healthy robustness of this life, and suggested the repose of sleep in the silence of the misty Wisconsin River valley.

I had come to the farm on a field trip in company with the Professor's Wildlife Ecology class. This field trip was essential in his experience of spring. To assist a group of people in understanding nature was for him a yearly goal and a pleasant undertaking. He was proudest of his pine plantations. Perhaps that is why our trip began there. Much effort of the Leopolds had been spent in planting pines, and already several thousand trees garnished the old fields. We dug up some young stock which had been "heeled-in" behind the Shack for future use. He showed how they were planted. Soon the class had enlarged the grove by twenty pines. We took the trail through the woods, and he made new discoveries as he walked. Crouching in the grass at the edge of the sand blow, he searched for the first pasque flower. He found it, and in his face was the confidence of spring. On the open sand he smiled again as he described the experiences this sterile place knew when rains drenched the surrounding vegetation. Then it was that new grouse broods wrote long sentences in the sand.

By the river was the place where beaver had been two years before. A chiseled cottonwood testified to this. In the darkness among the river-bottom elms, black ponds lingered from the high water. Fox sparrows sang above them. A trip toward the lake brought a flock of wary geese into the air, barking, making the valley ring. Hundreds of them circled, then poured back like maple leaves into the marsh. Careless mallards passed overhead in courtship flight, craving to touch wings in mid-air.

In a lighter vein, we were shown the spacious no-hunting signs that the Professor had posted. In the center of each sign ample room was left for frustrated hunters to unload their shots without damaging the printed warning.

The day would not have been complete without the revelation of a favorite secret, a nesting woodcock. Here was a bird that made the ground itself look camouflaged. Certainly there were some students who, through sheer embarrassment at their blindness, at first claimed to see the female on the nest when actually they had discovered only a shadow on an oak leaf. But before they left, there were none who had not seen this small favorite of the Professor's.

I had no idea of not returning home that evening. But when the Professor offered to share his dinner with me, I lost all idea of leaving. I sent word home with those returning, and then relaxed in the silence that two men enjoy when the twilight finds them alone.

When the nearby bushes slowly merged and became difficult to distinguish, that was the time to take the path toward the gathering dimness of the marsh; for that was when the woodcock did his sky-dance. It was not long before we heard the peenting of the male bird from his stand on the bare moss. But not for long; for soon the calling stopped, and for a moment the whole marsh was silent. Then from some unknown height, a thin cascade of song turned down through the dusk. A long silence—then the peenting started again. The whole marsh came alive with the sounds of night, drawing one's spirit into the sleeping marsh grass.

We made our way back to the lamp-lit cabin and stirred up the fire. Flick drew himself close to it. The Professor entered the day's gleanings in his log and began to prepare our meal. The conversation took many directions. We talked of mouse cycles or deer habits, of nutrition, and especially of phenology. For Professor Leopold, every day in spring marked some new happening—first skunk, first horned owl ears above a nest, first pasque flower—these were the events of life. I wondered if there were not some persistent owl about the farm which kept phenology on the Professor, recording when he cut his firewood, when he didn't go back to the city because of the floods, when he first shed his winter coat, or when he first lay down on the sand blow and watched the clouds bring geese into his farm.

The river mist was seeping into the room when the fire died down. The dog was asleep. We sought the comfort of our beds. I settled into a bunk and the Professor climbed into the old sleeping bag that had once belonged to his father. We slept, waking only briefly in the night to hear the geese call.

Morning for Professor Leopold did not begin with daylight: it began with the silence just preceding it. He was dressed when I awoke and was blowing on the coals. A fire crackled as I clambered into the room and coffee was ready for the flame. The Professor hung the pot in place, took his light meter and chart for recording bird songs, and went out the back door and listened. I watched him silently as I finished dressing. He looked closely at his watch and his light meter and made an entry in his book. "Cock pheasant was first again," he said, opening the door. The coffee was ready. He poured each of us a cup and returned to the wooden bench outside. Each waking bird voice became an entry in his book, and yet was more than just that in the Professor's morning. The orderly, predictable succession of birds' songs was implicit in his concept of a day.

When the voices of late-rising species began to confuse the early pattern, he came in, returned the coffee to the fire, and put eggs and bacon in the skillet. Soon we were having breakfast in the quiet, misty dawn, our conversation mingled with the honking of geese. We hastened through our meal, stacked the dishes, and left the cabin. The path through the river bottom led toward the old pines of the neighboring farm, passing the fenced-off garden plot along the way. It bore a crop of green winter rye, wet with dew.

We came out of the low growth of scented willow and ash and elm, and crossed a weak, wire fence. Ahead of us, hundred-foot pines, scattered and clustered, seemed to converse in an interminable monotone. These were what the Professor wanted, if not for himself, then for those who would follow in his spirit. He was heartsick with fragments and remnants of the beauties he had once known. Somewhere he wanted them restored to inspire his successors with the knowledge of what could be, what once was.

We continued through the pine woods for a little way, catching its wet resin scent, brushing our faces deliberately against the needles. The low motor of a drumming grouse halted us in our tracks. It was the first I had ever heard. The Professor was pleased. We then turned away from the woods into an opening, and came eventually to the same grassy ruts that had

516

brought us into the farm the day before. There was something good about walking down a poor road like this, two ruts with a grassy strip between them. It was not a lonesome trail, nor a cosmopolitan thoroughfare. It was a pathway for two people who could share its peace.

The Professor took out his small black address book in which he kept his daily observations and pointed to the sky above the marsh. "Geese." He took the stubby pencil, a constant companion to the little notebook, and began recording flock counts. Flock after flock passed on its way from feeding. They were magnificent and loud as they swept down into the lake beyond the farm. The Professor was moved by their demonstration. "It is rare now," the Professor said, "to see any kind of wildlife like this in excess. There is something satisfying in it. There is some symbol of freedom here that we're losing rapidly elsewhere. I'm glad we have something in excess on this farm; we don't have to skimp on geese. They find something here that suits them." So did those who watched.

138 Wilderness and Culture

A. STARKER LEOPOLD

1957

Aldo Leopold's son, a University of California zoologist, leading authority on wildlife, and former member of the club's Board of Directors, here takes up an aspect of the historic relation between man and nature examined above by Elmo Robinson. Robinson was concerned with the relation of the individual to nature; Leopold considers the next step, the effort to preserve natural areas by governmental action, a breakthrough of immense historic significance.

IN SEARCH OF SECURITY, comfort, and ease, man has labored in the past few thousand years to conquer and civilize the wilderness. Having done so, and while enjoying the fruits of physical well-being, he developed a taste for activities that satisfy his soul as well as his body. To these activities we apply the collective term "culture." The relationship between culture and the original wilderness is perhaps worth exploring.

Historically speaking, the relationship has been an inverse one—culture and the humanities have flourished as the wilderness was conquered. This is easily understandable in the early stages of social advance. The cave dweller,

517

faced with the daily task of gathering fresh food, had scant time for letters and arts, although all primitive people have left expressions of these. But as man institutionalized the exploitation of the earth around him, his daily bread became assured, and leisure time, at least among the upper social classes, permitted more indulgence in the pleasures of cultivating the mind.

Periodically through the pages of history we meet indications of surges of liberal thinking about man's activities and social relationships. The term "humanities" means the study of human values throughout history. Beginning with the Renaissance and the revolt against religious pedagogy, men of learning looked back to the philosophers of earlier eras for leads to what is important and what is worth knowing. But not often were man's relationships to nature seriously explored. When at last the study of natural phenomena was accepted as worthy of the dignity of the sages, the objectives were principally practical, not philosophical. Modern medicine, engineering, and agriculture are a few of the applied fields of natural science that have flourished and have accounted for much of the recent advance of civilization, without, however, any commensurate advance in the philosophy of man's relationship to the world around him.

It is only in very recent years—less than a century in fact—that an attentive attitude toward undisturbed and unutilized nature has begun to emerge. It is surprising that in the long history of man's conquest of the earth there is no evidence of sustained effort on the part of any people to preserve native landscape for its own sake, until our own national park system began to take form late in the nineteenth century.

There were of course elaborate programs of preserving and culturing certain elements of flora and fauna for purposes of man's use. For example, one of the most complete plans of wildlife management ever devised was observed by Marco Polo in the realm of Kublai Khan. The Great Khan maintained fields of grain and adjoining shelters for the use of partridges and other wild animals, so that he might find good sport when he went afield to fly his falcons. Most of the so-called parks and forests of mediaeval Europe were similarly managed for specific purposes—usually game and forest products combined.

Throughout history there are records of zoos and botanical gardens maintained by rulers and men of means, proving that people had an avocational interest in natural history even if they lacked appreciation of the undisturbed wilderness *per se*. Curiously, two of the most elaborate zoological parks were on this continent in the capitals of the Aztec and Tarascan empires in Mexico, although these peoples were not far advanced by European or Asiatic cultural standards.

But there is a world of difference between the creation of a zoo or a botanical garden and the maintenance of an undisturbed natural area. In a zoo man is rearranging and managing nature for his own interest and amusement. In the wilderness he is showing respect for nature as it existed in the first place. It is the emergence of this element of *respect* that deserves special attention, for it marks a turning point in man's view of the earth.

That the peoples of the world were receptive to a philosophy of nature preservation was manifested by the way the national park idea swept from continent to continent once it was announced in the United States. In a few decades natural preserves of one sort or another were created in many parts of the earth. European countries that had no wilderness left at home applied the idea to their colonies and dependencies. The British Empire was outstanding in this regard, but Germany, Belgium, Holland, and some others followed suit. Many Latin American countries and even some independent nations of Asia and Africa joined in the new movement. The dedicated areas went by many names — parks, game refuges, crown forests, or simply nature preserves. But the basic idea was the same — the preservation of unexploited and more or less unmanaged natural areas.

The implications of this new look toward the outdoors can scarcely be overemphasized. From a tradition of conquest and subjugation of nature and the wilderness, extending back to the earliest pages of history, man suddenly finds within himself a desire and an obligation to preserve untrammeled some remnants of the natural scene he has labored so long to bend to his material needs. That all nations have not succeeded equally well in bringing about this reform is beside the point. The issue is one of intent and acknowledgment of something that is right, even if it is not completely attainable.

Coming back to the origin of this idea in the United States, I have difficulty in seeing any logical reason for the sudden and inexplicable emergence of so sweeping a reversal in traditional philosophy at the time and place where it occurred. One would have supposed that appreciation of wild country would have emerged first in some overpopulated region where wildness was at a premium. Instead, Yellowstone National Park was created in 1872 when the United States was still considerably underpopulated and major effort was being directed to the conquest and settlement of the West. Yet the Congress and the people readily accepted the idea of setting aside this large block of country for recreational needs which at that time scarcely existed. Thinking as a biologist I see this emergence of a new idea as comparable to a macromutation in organic evolution — one of those sweeping shifts of evolutionary direction that come suddenly, and without forewarning, like the emergence of the flatfishes from the normal teleost line. There is no gradual approach.

Once born, the concept of nature preserves spread rapidly, and at the same time evolved. Let us consider the evolution of thought regarding the national parks of this country — prototypes of all to follow. The initial idea in the first half dozen parks was to preserve for public access such natural geologic features as geysers, hot springs, spectacular mountains, and canyons. Fauna and flora were less seriously considered. The first botanical features to be emphasized were the big trees on the west slope of the Sierra Nevada. Consideration of native animal life came later, and then on a classified basis. The "good" species like deer were protected, but the "bad" actors, including wolves, coyotes, and mountain lions, were controlled in accordance with the common-sense policy of the day. Bears were fed garbage and elk were fed hay. There was a carry-over of the outdoor-zoo idea which took some years to die out, during which period wolves and lions unfortunately were exterminated in many Rocky Mountain parks. This event has led directly to the difficult problems of overpopulation by deer and elk that plague the National Park Service today.

Likewise, the idea of leaving substantial blocks of park land undeveloped and in true wilderness status came long after the parks were created. The initial hope was to build roads, railroads, and hotels anywhere within the parks that people wanted to go. But this utilitarian concept of park development and management gave way gradually to the informal zoning idea that guides park programs today.

In short, the national parks as preserves of unmanaged nature did not spring forth in full bloom. They tended always toward naturalness, except in the heavily developed centers of activity where, unfortunately, the trend up to now has been strongly in the other direction.

Even as the National Park Service was being created, other types of natural areas were coming into being in this country. Some of the national wildlife refuges were created. The great system of Forest Service wilderness areas came soon after, along with state and municipal parks, and various types of national preserves controlled and operated by a host of agencies, organizations, and even individuals. We take for granted that preserving native associations of fauna and flora is in the public interest and is to be encouraged. The basic concept is scarcely open to challenge any more in this country — we disagree and wrangle only over what areas are to be preserved, by whom, and how it should be done.

And so it is in much of the rest of the world. It is agreed that most renewable natural resources are to be used, wisely and with due provision for sustained yield. But some areas are to be excluded from this plan and kept for the wonder and edification of the citizens. These two concepts are not always realized, but they are recognized, on an international level. The natural scene now commands respect. Its preservation is accepted as moral and proper. From the Serengeti Plain to the Great Smokies, from the Brooks Range to Tierra del Fuego, conscientious people are struggling to preserve samples of native landscape. Often the pressures of economic need and human populations make the cause seem almost hopeless. Yet my over-all impression is that the effort is gaining in strength, not losing.

Wherein lies the appeal of this movement? What forces motivate its spread?

The need is not solely for recreation in the sense of new playgrounds for people to get some fresh air. In many countries the preserved areas are used scarcely at all for recreation by the citizens. Nor are the educational and scientific values of wilderness, of which we often speak, weighed heavily into the equation.

The only possible force that could be motivating the effort to preserve natural areas is the moral conviction that it is right — that we owe it to ourselves and to the good earth that supports us to curb our avarice to the extent of leaving a few spots untouched and unexploited.

When one considers the spread of this idea over the earth in sixty-odd years it is cause indeed for wonder. Here is an addition to the accepted mores of people in all continents, imposed suddenly on codes of ethics that have been evolving for many centuries.

And so when we find cause for alarm and discontent with the progress of the wilderness movement it may help perhaps to take the long view—to see how astonishingly far the idea has progressed in the few decades of its existence.

I think that when future philosophers scan back through the records of human history and human thought they may put their finger on this century as a time of outstanding advance in man's feeling of responsibility to the earth. Whether man can succeed in preserving an attractive and livable world is the problem that lies ahead.

139   Little Deaths

T. H. WATKINS

1974

John Muir and most of his followers have had little to say about the problem of cruelty in man and nature. Some of the moral ambiguities involved in that perplexing question are confronted in this narrative. The writer is an editor of American Heritage, *author of several books, and co-author of the Sierra Club's* The Land No One Knows: America and the Public Domain.

I T HAS BEEN MORE than ten years since the day my cousin let me walk his traplines with him. We never see each other now. Our worlds, never very close, have grown even farther apart. He left California several years ago to become a trapping supervisor somewhere in Nevada, while I have joined the ranks of those who would cheerfully eliminate his way of life. He would, rightly enough, consider me one of his natural enemies, and it is not likely that we would have much to say if we did meet. Still, I am grateful to him for giving me a glimpse into the reality of a world normally hidden from us, a dark little world where death is the only commonplace.

At the time, my cousin was a lowly field trapper at the beck and call of any rancher or farmer who made an official complaint to the trapping service about varmint troubles—coyotes or wildcats getting after newborn lambs, foxes sneaking into chicken coops, that sort of thing. His current assignment was to trap out the varmint population of some ranchland high in the Diablo Hills southeast of Oakland, a country of rolling grassland, scrub oak, and chaparral dominated by the 3,000-foot upthrust of Mount Diablo. His base was a house trailer planted on the edge of one of the ranches he was servicing near Livermore, although he got into Oakland quite a lot for weekend visits to a lady of his acquaintance. I lived in Oakland at the time, and he usually made a point of stopping by to see my children, of whom he was particularly fond.

I was then a practicing student of western history and thoroughly intrigued by the glittering adventure that pervaded my reading—especially in the stories of the mountain men, those grizzled, anarchic beings with a lust for far places and far things, stubborn individualists who had lived freer than any Indian and had followed their quest for beaver pelts into nearly all the mysterious blanks of the American West, from Taos, New Mexico, to Puget Sound, from the Marys River of the northern Rockies to the Colorado River of the Southwest; hopelessly romantic creatures with a predilection for Indian women, a talent for profanity, and a thirst for liquor profound enough to melt rivets. And here was my cousin, the literary—if not lineal—descendant of the mountain man. True, he was neither grizzled nor given much to profanity, nor had he, so far as I knew, ever offered his blanket to an Indian woman. Still, he was a *trapper,* beGod, and when on one of his visits he invited me to accompany him on his rounds, I was entranced with the notion.

Late one spring afternoon I bundled wife and children into the car and drove down to Livermore and out to the ranch where he was staying. After a dinner cooked in the trailer's tiny kitchen, my wife and the children bedded down in the trailer's two little bunks. "When we get back tomorrow afternoon," my cousin told the children, "I'll take you out and show you some spring lambs. You'd like that, right?" he added, giving them a pinch and tickle that set them to giggling in delight. He and I bundled up in sleeping bags on the ground outside.

It was pitch black when he woke me the next morning at five o'clock. After shocking ourselves out of sleep by bathing our faces in water from the outside faucet, we got into his pickup and drove off for breakfast at an all-night diner on the road. Dawn was insinuating itself over the dark hills by the time we finished breakfast, and had laid a neon streak across the sky when we finally turned off the highway and began climbing a rutted dirt road that led to the first trapline (we would be walking two traplines, my cousin explained, one on the western side of the hills, one on the eastern; these were two of the six he had scattered over the whole range, each of them containing between 15 and 20 traps and each checked out and reset or moved to a new location every ten days or so). As we bumped and rattled up the road, daylight slowly illuminated the hills. For two or three months in the spring, before the summer sun turns them warm and brown, these hills look as if they had been transplanted whole from Ireland or Wales. They are a celebration of green, all shades of green, from the black-green of manzanita leaves to the bright, pool-table green of the grasses. Isolated bunches of cows and sheep stood almost motionless, like ornaments added for the effect of contrast, and morning mist crept around the base of trees and shrouded dark hollows with the ghost of its presence. Through all this, the exposed earth of the road cut like a red scar, and the sounds of the pickup's engine and the country-western music yammering out of its radio intruded themselves on the earth's silence gracelessly.

We talked of my cousin's father, whom he worshipped and emulated. My cousin was, in fact, almost literally following in his father's footsteps, for "the old man" had been a state trapper himself and was now a trapping supervisor. Before that, back in the deep of the Depression, he had been a lion hunter for the state, when a mountain lion's ears were as good as money, and before that he had "cowboyed some," as he put it; at one time, according to family tradition, his grandfather's ranch had encompassed much of what became the town of San Bernardino in Southern California. At one point in his life, he had led jaguar-hunting trips to the jungles of northwestern Mexico, and he was still a noteworthy hunter, though now he confined himself principally to an occasional deer, antelope, or bear. My cousin had grown up in a house where skins of various types served as rugs and couch-throws, where stuffed heads glared unblinkingly from the walls, where sleek hounds were always in-and-out, where hunting magazines dominated the tables, hunting talk dominated the conversations, and everywhere was the peculiarly masculine smell of newly oiled guns, all kinds of guns—pistols (including an old Colt once used by my cousin's great-grandfather, legend had it, to kill a man), rifles, shotguns. It was a family that had been killing things for a long time, sometimes for meat, sometimes for a living, sometimes for what was called the sport of it, and one of my cousin's consuming ambitions was to bag a bighorn sheep, something his father had never managed to do.

I had never killed anything in my life except fish, and since fish neither scream, grunt, squeal, nor moan when done in, it had never seemed like killing at all. In any case, I was by no means prepared for the first sight of what it was my cousin did to earn his bread. I don't know what I had expected with my romantic notions of the trapper's life, but surely it was something other than what I learned when we crawled up the road through increasingly heavy underbrush and stopped to check out the first of my cousin's traps.

We got out of the truck and beat our way through the brush to a spot perhaps 30 feet from the road. I did not see the animal until we were nearly on top of it. It was a raccoon, the first raccoon I had ever seen in person, and at that moment I wished that I never had seen one. It was dead, had been dead for several days, my cousin informed me. "Hunger, thirst, and shock is what kills them, mostly," he said in response to my question. "That, and exhaustion, I reckon." The animal seemed ridiculously tiny in death. It lay on its side, its small mouth, crawling with ants, open in a bared-tooth grin, and its right rear leg in the clutch of the steel trap. It was easy to see how the animal had exhausted itself; it had been at its leg. A strip of flesh perhaps three inches in width had been gnawed away, leaving the white of bone and a length of tendon exposed. Tiny flies sang about the ragged wound and over the pool of dried blood beneath the leg. There was a stink in the air, and it suddenly seemed very, very warm to me there in the morning shadows of the brush.

"Once in a while," my cousin said, prying open the curved jaws of the trap, "one of them will chew his way loose, and if he doesn't lose too much blood he can live. I caught a three-legged coyote once. Too stupid to learn, I guess."

"Do you ever find one of them still alive?" I asked.

"Sometimes."

"What do you do with them?"

He looked up at me. "Do with them? I shoot them," he said, patting the holstered pistol at his waist. He lifted the freed raccoon by the hind legs and swung it off into the brush. "Buzzard meat," he said. He then grabbed the steel stake to which the trap was attached by a chain and worked it out of the ground. "I've had this line going for over a month, now. The area's just about trapped out." He carried the trap back to the road, threw it in the back of the pickup, and we drove up the increasingly rough road to the next trap. It was empty, as was the one after it. I was beginning to hope they would all be empty, but the fourth one contained a small skunk, a black-and-white pussycat of a creature that had managed to get three of its feet in the trap at once and lay huddled in death like a child's stuffed toy. It, too, was disengaged and tossed into the brush. A little further up the ridge, and we found a fox, to my cousin's visible relief. "Great," he said. "That has to be the mate to the one I got a couple of weeks ago. Pregnant, too. There won't be any little foxes running around this year." Into the brush the animal went.

By the time we reached the top of the long ridge on which my cousin had set his traps, the morning had slipped toward noon and our count had risen to seven animals: three raccoons, three skunks, and the pregnant fox. There was only one trap left now, but it was occupied by the prize of the morning, a bobcat. "I'll be damned," my cousin said, "I've been after that bugger all month. Just about give up hope." The bobcat had not died well, but in anger. The marks of its rage and anguish were laid out in a torn circle of earth described by the length of the chain that had linked the animal to its death. Even the brush had been ripped and clawed at, leaves and twigs stripped from branches, leaving sweeping scars. Yellow tufts of the animal's fur lay scattered on the ground, as if the bobcat had torn at its own body for betraying it, and its death-mask was a silent howl of outrage. My cousin took it out of the trap and heaved it down the side of the hill. Buzzard meat.

We had to go back down the hills and around the range in order to come up the eastern slopes and check out the second trapline, and on the way we stopped at a small roadhouse in Clayton for a hamburger and a beer. I found I could eat, which surprised me a little, and I certainly had a thirst for the beer. We sat side-by-side at the bar, not saying much. Something Wallace Stegner had once written kept flashing through my mind. "Like most of my contemporaries," he had said, "I grew up careless. I grew up killing things." I wondered if my cousin would know what Stegner had been talking about, and decided it would be best not to bring it up. I could have cancelled out right there, I suppose, asking him to take me back to his camp, explaining that I had seen enough, too much, of the trapper's life. I could always plead exhaustion. After all, the day's hiking had been more real exercise than I had had in months, and I was, in fact, tired. A stubborn kernel of pride would not let me do it. I would see the day through to the end.

So the ritual continued. We climbed back up into the hills on the east side of the range in the oven-heat of a strong spring sun. The day's count rose even more as the pickup bounced its way up the ragged weedgrown road: two more skunks, another fox, two more raccoons. The work went more slowly than the morning's run, for this was a new line, and each trap had to be reset. My cousin performed this task with an efficient swiftness and the kind of quiet pride any craftsman takes in his skill, snapping and locking the jaws of the traps, covering them with a thin scattering of earth and twigs, sprinkling the ground about with dog urine from a plastic squeeze bottle to cover up the man-smell. By the time we were ready to approach the last three traps of the line, it was well after three o'clock. We were very high by then, well up on the slopes of Mount Diablo itself, and we had to abandon the pickup to hike the rest of the way on foot. We broke out of the brush and walked along a spur of the hills. About 1,500 feet below us and some miles to the east, we could see the towns of Pittsburg and Martinez sending an urban haze into the air. Ahead of me, my cousin suddenly stopped.

"Wait a minute. Listen," he said.

A distant thrashing and rattling sound came from the slope below us. "That's where the trap is," he said. "Might be a bobcat, but I didn't expect to get him so soon. Come on."

The slope was very steep, and we slid much of the way down to the trap on our bottoms, slapped at and tangled by brush. The animal was not a bobcat. It was a dog, a large, dirty-white mongrel whose foreleg was gripped in the trap. The dog snarled at us as we approached it. Saliva had gathered at its lips and there was wildness in its eyes.

"*Dammit,*" my cousin said. He had owned dogs all his life. "A wild dog. Probably abandoned by somebody. They do it all the time. Dogs turn wild and start running in packs. Some people ought to be shot."

I didn't know what he wanted to do. He hadn't pulled out his gun. "Can we turn him loose? Maybe he isn't wild. Maybe he just wandered up here on his own."

My cousin looked at me. "Maybe. There's a noose-pole in the back of the truck—a kind of long stick with a loop of rope at the end. Why don't you get it?"

I scrambled back up the slope and made my way back to the pickup, where I found the noose-pole. As thick as a broomhandle and about five feet in length, it looked like a primitive fishing-pole. When I got back down to the trap, the dog was still snarling viciously. My cousin took the pole from me, opened the loop at the end, and extended it toward the dog. "If I can hook him," he said, "I'll hold his head down while you open the trap. You've seen how I do it."

It was useless. The dog fought at the loop frantically in a madness of pain and fear. After perhaps 15 minutes, my cousin laid the pole down. "He just isn't going to take it."

"What'll we do?" I asked, though I'm sure I knew.

He shrugged. "Can't just leave him here to die." He unsnapped his holster and pulled out the gun. He duck-walked to within a couple of feet of the animal, which watched him suspiciously. "I'll try to do it with one shot," he said. The gun's discharge slammed into the silence of the mountain. The dog howled once, a long, penetrating song of despair that rang in echoes down the hill. My cousin nudged the animal with his boot. It was dead. He opened the trap, freed the leg, and heaved the body down the slope. The crashing of its fall seemed to go on for a long time. My cousin reset the trap. "Come on," he said. "It's getting late."

The last trap of the day held a dead raccoon.

My cousin was pleased with the day's work. "If it keeps up like this," he said as we rattled down the highway toward his trailer, "I could be out of here in a month."

"What's the hurry?"

He indicated a small housing development by the side of the road. "Too much civilization around here for me. Too many people. I need to get back up into the mountains."

There was plenty of light left when we got back, and true to his promise, my cousin took the children out into the fields to see a newborn lamb. While its mother bleated in protest, he ran one down and brought it to my children so they could pet it. I watched his face as he held the little creature. There was no hint in it of all the death we had harvested that day, no hint of the half-eaten legs we had seen, no hint of the fearful thrashing agony the animals had endured before dying. No hint, even, of the death-howl of the dirty white dog that may or may not have been wild. There was neither irony nor cynicism in him. He held the lamb with open, honest delight at the wonder my children found in touching this small, warm, live thing.

My cousin is not an evil man. We are none of us evil men.

140

On Coming to Terms with Our Environment

PAUL B. SEARS

1959

Along with Aldo Leopold, one of the first to call for a new relation between man and nature was Paul B. Sears, eminent biologist, chairman of the Yale University Conservation Program, and past president of the American Association for the Advancement of Science. Sears' emphasis was different from Leopold's; his was one of the first voices calling attention to the consequences of unrestricted worldwide population growth and resource consumption. In the 1950s such voices were lonely and seldom heard.

The following article (adapted from a 1958 Phi Beta Kappa address) was a precursor of the wave of concern for the future of the planet that swept the nation in the early 1970s.

Reading Sears' essay two decades after it was written, we can find bases for both pessimism and optimism. He notes that in the 400 years since Dr. Rabelais made the statement he quotes, the population of the earth had multiplied by four times. In the two decades since Sears wrote, the world population has increased by more than the total number alive in Rabelais' time. We also note that since Sears wrote, the taboos that he described—taboos against confronting the population threat—have been lifted. Informed people have become aware of the problem; revolutionary techniques have been developed for population control; and population growth has slackened in the industrialized countries, although globally it is still increasing at an alarming rate.

Coming to terms with the environment, Dr. Sears points out, includes applying to human affairs certain laws of the physical sciences, including the concept of the "steady state."

THE DREAM OF UNIVERSAL HARMONY is an ancient one. Often it has taken the nostalgic form of a Golden Age, long past. Again it appears as future promise. The dreamer who looks ahead often sees it all very simply. Let him and all who think alike with him have their way. Never has this been better set forth than by Dr. Rabelais:

"Then, ah then . . . then plenty of all earthly goods here below. Then uninterrupted and eternal peace through the universe, an end of all wars, plunderings, drudgeries, robbings, assassinates unless it be to destroy these cursed rebels, the heretics."

There are today four times as many human beings in the world as when those words were written. Old and stable social orders have broken up. New powers, through new knowledge, are at man's disposal. He has, in truth, become a geological force. The dream of ultimate harmony still persists, but the old cleavage remains. There are those who think the blessed state must come by eliminating all who do not think as they do. There are others who hope for a condition of mutual tolerance and restraint, founded upon some measure of common understanding.

These are moral problems, using that term in its broad and classic sense. But morality today involves a responsible relationship toward the laws of the natural world of which we are inescapably a part. Violence toward nature, as the Tao has it, is no less an evil than violence toward fellow man. There can be no ultimate harmony among our own species in defiance of this principle. But more than that, we can find in certain concepts of natural science an invaluable guide as we struggle to attain a better order in our own affairs.

A disturbing paradox of this scientific age is the fact that its most profound implications have not sunk into our minds and become manifest in our behavior. Commonly—too commonly—we hear such glib phrases as "man's control of nature," "the necessity of an expanding economy," and "the conquest of space." As Ortega y Gasset has said, the effect of the industrial revolution has been to create an illusion of limitless abundance and ease, obscuring the ancient doctrine that effort and struggle are the price of human survival.

Thus in one sweep are brushed away the lessons of history, the wisdom so painfully gained through disciplined thought and intuition in the fields of ethics and aesthetics, as well as those aspects of natural science that could afford us perspective, rather than immediate convenience.

We can isolate certain qualities in a system and study them profitably on their own merits. A notable instance is afforded with respect to mere increase in human numbers within a finite space. Obviously we cannot apply the laws that govern the dynamics of gas molecules strictly unless we are all playing blind man's buff with motion at random. This we are not doing, for eyesight and judgment enable human beings to pick open pathways, which molecules cannot do. Yet the general principle that freedom tends to diminish (or stress to increase) as numbers multiply not only applies in theory, but in historical fact.

The application may be pressed still further. When energy is introduced into a system, the stress increases. This obviously applies to the molecules in a kettle of heated water. I am unable to see why it does not apply with equal rigor to modern man who, through the internal combustion engine, is drawing upon the fossil energy of oil deposits, now being consumed at an estimated rate one million times faster than they have accumulated. By virtue of this process the average American moves, I should judge, some ten times faster than he did in 1900, and if so, covers one hundred times more territory. The evidence of stress as a function of numbers and energy is manifold. Yet we have reassuring voices telling us not to be disturbed, because the earth can support an indefinitely increased population.

Perhaps, with so much at stake, it is time to make certain we understand what science is, and what is its role in human affairs.

Science is the discovery and formulation of the laws of nature. In our enthusiasm we may forget that a law not only tells you what you can do, but what you cannot do. When we use our knowledge of natural law for specific problems we are practicing technology, not science. And because scientific technology has placed an estimated minimum equivalent of three dozen servants at the disposal of the average American, we are, quite naturally, more inclined to listen to promises than to warnings.

Yet the necessary warning can be stated quite simply. *The applications of science must be guided, managed, controlled, according to ethical and aesthetic principles and in the light of our most profound understanding.* Unfortunately we cannot set up an equation to show that because a thing is possible, it is necessarily wise and proper. If we could, it might simplify matters.

Certainly the application of science has been selective. An astute student of cultural processes, examining the western world, would note that science has been applied in spectacular fashion to the elaboration of consumers' goods, the reduction of mortality rates, and the tapping of fossil energy. He would also note certain consequences of this situation. Among them would be an explosion of human population without known precedent in the biological world, a lessening of the need for muscular effort, increased leisure, a startling multiplication of the rate of individual movement, dissipation of nonrenewable resources, and disruption of natural cycles in the landscape. Nor would he be likely to overlook the signs of increasing tension upon the individual and the disintegration of value systems, which, whatever their limitations, have always exerted a stabilizing effect on human societies.

Our observer would find the question of man's relation to environment relegated to the fringes of serious scientific inquiry. He would uncover a widespread belief in the possibility of and necessity for a perpetually expanding economy. He would find economists well pleased if they could look ahead twenty-five years while a few scientists try honestly to peer much farther into the future. He would see that a great deal of effort is being given by the latter group to estimating the maximum number of human beings that could possibly be kept alive on earth, such estimates ranging from three to ten or more times the present population. Concerning the quality of existence possible under such conditions he would discover a strange silence broken only by such bold prophets as Orwell, Huxley, and Sir Charles Darwin, the physicist.

Persisting, he would recognize other interesting conditions. Although the devising of means of human destruction continues uninhibited, frontal attack on the control of population pressure—difficult enough for technical reasons—is largely taboo. So are suggestions that human happiness might well be possible under a far less wasteful and consumptive economy. And while analysts are beginning to demonstrate that, beyond a certain limit, the expansion of any urban center means economic loss, not gain, their warnings carry little weight.

Personally I am far less interested in guessing how thickly mankind can be amassed on this planet and still survive than I am in the optimum quality of existence for those who do.

[We need a] realistic understanding of the natural world of which we are a part. We must know its possibilities and respect its limitations. We must scan it for hints and models, remembering that the organized system of life and environment has been operating more than a thousand times as long as the experience of our own species. Our knowledge of the vicissitudes of geological and climatic change, of organic competition, conflict, even extinction, should not blind us to the essential order behind it all. In our consumptive age we hear much talk of the danger of depleting our environment. A far more profound threat lies in our power to disrupt its orderly transformations of material and energy.

The confidence with which the physical scientist faces his task rests essentially upon a few basic assumptions with respect to the orderly behavior of energy and matter. One of the important concepts corollary to these principles is that of the steady state. Systems tend toward conditions of minimum stress and least unbalance—that is, toward equilibrium. Energy flowing into a system operates to upset this trend, unless the system is so organized as to transform that energy in orderly fashion, using it meanwhile to keep the system in good working condition. Such a system, that is, an open steady state, is approximated in living communities. Green plants utilize solar energy to build carbon compounds that sustain themselves and animals as well, while complementary processes return materials for fresh re-use.

The heat from a stove—energy—will keep the pot boiling so long as there is water in it. But it will not replace the water when it is gone, nor mend the pot when it melts. By contrast, an organized pattern of living communities is self-maintaining if energy is available.

These circumstances have long since caught the imagination of men. Harrison Brown and other analysts point out that if man continues to increase in numbers and per capita requirements his fate will depend on his success in tapping additional energy sources rather than on lack of materials. For example, the mineral content of a ton of granite or a cubic mile of sea water is most reassuring. The hitch comes in the energy cost of reclamation, yet the literature abounds in optimistic assurances that man is clever enough to turn the trick. Now and then, but not always, we see the added proviso that he must first learn how to behave himself better than he does. On a less responsible plane we continue to hear talk of an expanding economy, the conquest of nature, and man's unlimited future.

Why not divert more of our scientific enterprise to studying the model

530

that is before us, that has operated for more than a billion years, and has made our own existence possible?

Again, why continue, not only to tolerate, but to sponsor reckless and irresponsible multiplication of human numbers? Why accede to the notion that in a world where millions are hungry and malnourished through failure to apply the knowledge we now have, industrial enterprise must concentrate so largely on the mass production of what a philosopher would consider toys for adults?

Why worry so much about the other side of the moon when our cities, bursting at the seams, are erupting into an unplanned chaos? Why dream of escape to other planets when our own would respond generously to kinder treatment? Right and proper it is to push knowledge to the uttermost limits, but why not use what we have to clean the open sewers we call rivers, purify the air we must breathe, slow down the tragic waste of human ability, and get things about us shipshape? We are sweeping too much stuff under the bed, locking up too many closets.

Probably men will always differ as to what constitutes the good life. They need not differ as to what is necessary for the long survival of man on earth. Assuming that this is our wish, the conditions are clear enough. As living beings we must come to terms with the environment about us, learning to get along with the liberal budget at our disposal, promoting rather than disrupting those great cycles of nature—of water movement, energy flow, and material transformation that have made life itself possible. As a physical goal we must seek to attain what I have called a steady state. The achievement of an efficient dynamic equilibrium between man and his environment must always, in itself, have the challenge and the charm of an elusive goal. The infinite variety and beauty of the world about us, the incalculable facets of human experience, the challenge of the unknown that must grow rather than diminish as man advances in stature and becomes at home here—these are sufficient guarantee that a stable world society need never be a stagnant one.

141

Mountain Talk: Thoreau at Katahdin

FRED GUNSKY

1960

In the late 1950s and early '60s, the Bulletin *featured a regular page by Fred Gunsky, newspaperman and California fair-employment official, entitled "Mountain Talk," informal reflections on life and wilderness. This column is vintage Gunsky—and vintage Thoreau.*

O NE TOUCH OF WILDERNESS makes the whole world kin, as we have been saying here in one way or another. Looking back to our Sierran elders—Muir, the LeContes and their contemporaries—we have not yet taken note of one of the founders of the fellowship, whose kin they were whether they mentioned it or not. Henry David Thoreau was touched by Nature, early and late, and wrote a classic book under her inspiration.

Readers of *Walden* know that the author was a great stay-at-home, camping in that little cabin less than two miles from his mother's kitchen in Concord. He was born and lived and died in the village, now a Boston suburb; his famous sojourn at Walden Pond lasted only two years and two months. In the 1840s and 50s, while adventurous men were crossing the plains and searching out the secrets of the Western mountains, Thoreau was insisting in word and act that adventures of the mind and spirit were best enjoyed without leaving one's native township. "Be the Lewis and Clark of your own streams," he demanded, "explore your own higher latitudes."

Thoreau nevertheless did travel occasionally. He had an insatiable curiosity about things of nature, and even of man, beyond the bounds of Massachusetts. He would not have protested his hearthside faith so strongly if he had not been tempted by the Western prospect. Even during his stay at relatively tame Walden he had a vacation trip (not mentioned in the book) which gave him a first taste of genuine wilderness.

For two weeks in 1846, with a few companions, Thoreau hiked, camped and fished in the Maine woods, sometimes in areas affected by primitive logging operations but often in terrain hardly known except to the Penobscots. Maine was a frontier, bypassed in the sweep toward the West. It was canoe country, Indian country, wild country, as Thoreau found on this and two later visits. The trout were fabulous, while the river men made him think of ancient mythical heroes.

As it often is on our own summer outings, the climax of this trip was a mountain climb. The party had traveled for days through an uninhabited, swampy land of "countless" lakes and "immeasurable" forests to reach Mount Katahdin in the heart of the wilderness. Not high by our standards — elevation 5,273 — the tallest peak in Maine was sufficiently impressive to the young man from Concord.

In the magazine piece he wrote about his adventure ("Ktaadn," the long first chapter of his posthumous book, *The Maine Woods*) Thoreau presents an interesting straightforward narrative. Any mountain camper who reads it will enjoy it and recognize the marks of an authentic fellow wanderer. All the way up Katahdin, as he and his companions taste the juicy berries, discuss bears, and laboriously bushwhack to the correct, highest summit, he has the twentieth-century peak fancier right there with him, breathing hard.

Then something astonishing happens. It is a passage no less authentic, no less recognizably true to those of us who have had similar moments of awareness in the earth's high, wild places. But it is, for a page or so, no simple account of a travel experience; it is a powerful report of a spiritual adventure in Thoreau's inmost higher latitudes.

Descending from the summit by the way of a particularly desolate slope, he was suddenly conscious of a world not made for man:

. . . Nature was here something savage and awful, though beautiful. I looked with awe at the ground I trod on, to see what the Powers had made there. . . . This was that Earth of which we have heard, made out of Chaos and Old Night. Here was no man's garden, but the unhandselled globe. It was not lawn, nor pasture, nor mead, nor woodland, nor lea, nor arable, nor waste land. It was the fresh and natural surface of the planet Earth, as it was made forever and ever — to be the dwelling of man, we say — so Nature made it, and man may use it if he can. Man was not to be associated with it, and was Matter, vast, terrific — not his Mother Earth that we have heard of, not for him to tread on, or be buried in — No, it were being too familiar even to let his bones lie there — the home, this, of Necessity and Fate. There was clearly felt the presence of a force not bound to be kind to man. It was a place for heathenism and superstitious rites — to be inhabited by men nearer of kin to the rocks and to wild animals than we. . . . What is it to be admitted to a museum, to see a myriad of particular things, compared with being shown some star's surface, some hard matter in its home! I stand in awe of my body, this matter to which I am bound has become so strange to me. I fear not spirits, ghosts, of which I am one — *that* my body might — but I fear bodies, I tremble to mee them. What is this Titan that has possession of me? Talk of mysteries! Think of our life in nature — daily to be shown matter, to come in contact with it — rocks, trees, wind on our cheeks! the *solid* earth! the *actual* world! the *common sense! Contact! Contact! Who* are we? *where* are we?

If he had never written *Walden* or the half-dozen shorter essays on which his fame rests, or the *Journal,* Thoreau would have left the wilderness fellowship in his debt for this fragment of scripture, this token of a revelation, this question.

142

Serenity in Yosemite

LEWIS P. MANSFIELD

1960

No matter how furious the struggles, or how beleaguered by controversy the club may be, there has always been room for the quiet reflections, the perceptions of nature that nourish the spirit and provide the strength to go back into battle. Lewis P. Mansfield is a San Francisco financier and mountaineer.

TRY YOSEMITE VALLEY in November. The armies of summer have retreated and the regiments of winter have not yet invaded. You can enjoy in peace the fine weather and the clear air laden with that sad, pungent smell of autumn.

Where you hike up the trail to the base of Vernal Fall, broadleaf maples and oaks paint the landscape with russet, copper and gold. The dogwoods flash their salmon-pink when the sun touches their delicate leaves, and the pines, firs and incense-cedars hold their steady green in the symphony of color. Backdrop to this glory, the gray, scarred walls of the High Sierra stand implacably silent.

The Merced River hurls its silver over the black rocks of Vernal, but it is a small refined stream now compared with the torrent of early July. Most of the dozen falls in the Valley are stilled at this season or reduced to mere trickles. Even Bridal Veil shows only a token of water.

But rivers, creeks, waterfalls and lakes are only one form of treasure which nature has hidden in this enchanted region. Indeed, the grandeur of its geological evolution through the ages is most apparent as the year comes full-circle. Now the impressive bastion, towering two thousand feet above the Valley speaks its tale of primal action and glacial movement. El Capitan, North Dome, Half Dome, Glacier Point, Sentinel Rock and the rest fill the eye with wonder.

You need attempt no great feats of climbing or exploration, but can wander as inclined. One day, you may follow the low, shadowy trail from Mirror Lake into Tenaya Canyon, thence up the steep north trail to Snow Creek, having Basket Dome to the northwest, until you see the sun peeping over Half Dome. One day, you may take the long trail toward Upper Yosemite Fall; and again a short trail to the Lower Fall and along the north side of the Valley. Or, you are content to stroll in the level valley itself for a circular view of the surrounding peaks.

Wherever you walk, on trails, through woods, across meadows, you are sure to encounter something of special interest. For this is the joy of walking. There is always a surprise in store. It may be a pretty bird, a squirrel, an old Indian cave or a family of deer. All are important. Even a fallen tree with a boulder held in its roots tell its tale. To be free from highways, cities and the maddening crowd is a grateful, healing experience.

November in Yosemite! The still world awaits the long, cold winter in a mood of solemn calm. In communing with it you may recall the words of Thomas Starr King, who loved Yosemite—"The truth of nature is a part of the truth of God; to him who does not search it out, darkness; to him who does, infinity."

143

The Magic of Gypsy Woods

ALFRED G. ETTER

1963

In the following article, Alfred G. Etter explores a concern that conservationists have had for decades—that all parents have, for that matter. How do you pass your values along to your children? Today's youngsters grow up in a paved-over, urbanized world, in the glare of the television tube. Nature, elemental things, could sharpen their senses—but how do you bequeath that understanding, that enjoyment?

IN SPARE MOMENTS I am occasionally entertained by the vision of a clear creek and a spring feeding it through a green tongue of crisp watercress. Along the bank are camped in comfortable disarrangement wagons of gypsies. Their shaggy horses stand silent and black beneath the deep shade along the stream. This vision is now undoubtedly embellished with the romance of time past, but the realness of the scene is unmistakable. It is a memory of the Saturdays when some of us, as children, used to come with a lunch of sandwiches to Gravois Creek. There at the spring we would wash away the heat of tramping along country roads, and we would drink, from the pale blue mirrored pool, water which was magic and good.

We seldom allowed our backs to turn upon the gypsies, for they were dark people of somewhat unknown nature, imbued with the mystery of much childhood fantasy. And so, while we walked the woods, picking violets or

535

sweet-william or buttercups that grew in the spongy black mold, or waded in the stream and sought snails, mussels, and silver bream, or as we stood surrounded by a copse of wild crab, or leaned on the trunk of an old redbud as the early spring sunshine filtered down through the canopy of trees, we enjoyed the vague danger of gypsies. Along the streams were sycamores so large that they encircled whole meanders in the palms of their roots. Wild grapevines, tangled in the branches, hung to the ground and gave us a brief new power of touching the high, otherwise remote, limbs of trees. And there were banks of moss, deep green and soft; and fallen, fractured rocks supported ferns and made innumerable cavities where animals could live.

The childish reverence for a place of gathering flowers was our possession, and we seldom took the trip home through the dusty roads that lived so intimately with the bordering fields without a handful of clean green violet stems clutched firmly, the coolness of the petals brushing our hand. And yet the secret enjoyment of such bouquets was that they had been gathered in the gypsies' woods. Our pride in this was great and full of grave significance.

It was never clear to me as a child exactly why we gradually forewent this pleasure. It is strange to realize the full story now, after nearly twenty years have passed. The road by the creek that squeezed between the trunks of trees and almost lost itself with turning slowly disappeared as the years went by in rank lanes of nettles and became a source of painful lessons learned. The gypsies were not seen any more, and the silent old horses that had lent so pungent an odor to the camp no longer rubbed themselves against the worn trunk of the sycamores. The search for mussels and minnows was a dangerous and unprofitable one in the now slippery and cloudy stream. Moss (I would have to call it algae now) was growing heavily on the gravel, and the smell that rose from the water on the quiet sunny day was unpleasant. The violets were there, and the buttercups, but the blue crystal of the spring had broken and we were forbidden to drink from it. The sewage of suburbs now made the name of Gravois Creek more famous for its odor than it had ever been for its gypsies or its flowers or clear water.

I suspect that the construction of a broad concrete highway through this area had as much to do with the disappearance of the gypsies as anything else. Though we are inclined to look upon good roads as the means for making areas accessible, for the horse-wagons of the gypsies they became impassable barriers to long uninterrupted days of journey along quiet rural roads.

The highway soon enticed a lumber mill which set up its saws in one of the flats of the creek. With it came the shacks of workers, crowded along the stream banks. Junk accumulated in the creek: old bedsprings, Ford chassis, tin cans, mattresses, rags, bottles, chicken feathers. Stacks of lumber and barrel staves grew, feeding on the trunks of white and black oaks from the hills, the sycamores of the valleys. Sawdust towers were built to the memory of Gravois woods. Skinny children played in the creek bottom, catching the few remaining crawfish, throwing mud at the emerald dragon flies. Then a nurseryman bought the spring and bricked it in for irrigating his platoons of evergreens. Billboards and tourist cabins have since completed the annihilation of this peaceful scene.

Science so far has devoted itself to many fields, but up to the present has never concerned itself with the preservation of simple beauty and landscapes for the creation of childhood memories. At the same time, artists and illustrators continue drawing colorful pastoral scenes rich in flowers and animal life as decorations for children's stories. Psychologists have from time to time condemned fairy stories for the illusions and complexes that they build up in the minds of children. What complications then will arise, or are arising now for that matter, from the use of peaceful country-sides and profuse floras and faunas in the child's book? Certainly there is no greater illusion for the city child than the idea that such scenes are enduring, well-taken-care-of parts of the world in which he is growing up. Personally, I am not inclined to believe that the neglect which these matters have so far received is indicative of their importance in a society destined to become more complicated and unnatural.

City children have no concept of wildness, of the rhythm of natural events, of the significance of non-human forms of life, of the inter-relationships of living things and the land. At the same time present and future generations are faced with the very difficult problems of dealing sensibly with matters such as river and stream control, erosion control, human nutrition, and prevention of diseases, both physical and mental, resulting from abnormal developments in society. Even a brief consideration of these problems demonstrates the need for a public familiar with the land and conscious of the existence of natural laws. If, as children, adults have had contact with the beauty, peace, organization, or thrill of wild plants and animals in their natural habitat, it will be that much simpler for them to understand the problems involving man and his environment.

Highways radiating from the city gradually force wild places into the distance, and the quiet of country lanes is forgotten in the thrill of speed. Rare indeed is the opportunity for people to become a part of a natural scene and to look with wonder and astonishment at something which is not man-built, something which represents a power greater, by far, than their own.

Gravois Creek, with its woods and wildflowers, was not only *my* retreat but provided pleasure to many families. Now, as a sewer, it breeds repulsiveness and disease. The secret beauty of the valley, however, still exists in my mind. But the gypsies with their mysterious wagons and their smoking fires, the crystal spring, and the cool violets are gone. If I tell my son I knew these things, he will scarcely believe me. I often wonder where my child can go to learn what this earth was like before he was born.

144

Nature and the Value of Diversity

WILLIAM O. DOUGLAS

1964

During his four decades in the federal government, Supreme Court Justice William O. Douglas has been the highest-placed advocate of wilderness in the United States. From 1960 to 1962, he was a member of the club's board of directors. In the speech excerpted here he raised the need to give children a new education in nature, stressing the imponderables that are beyond the reach of science. Justice Douglas retired from the bench in 1975.

THE LICHEN HAS A built-in device that gives it capacity to reproduce without outside help or intervention. Year after year the avalanche lily grows on the edge of snowbanks, producing delicate petals that have a consistency, a symmetry, and abandon that technology does not know.

The saguaro cactus during a rainstorm multiplies its tiny hair-like roots so fast that the process is visible; its central intelligence center seemingly is aware that when the drought is broken, the time has arrived for storage of water within the plant against the exigencies of the next dry cycle.

The ironwood tree of Australia lays on an outer layer of criss-crossed lattice that is so tough that an ax bounces off it, and so strong and wiry that a gale will seldom level the tree even though termites have eaten out its inner core. How did its central intelligence learn without benefit of a slide rule that a given weight of cellulose fabricated in the form of a hollow, criss-crossed lattice cylinder is stronger than the same weight of material made into a round, solid shaft?

The examples from nature multiply endlessly from the purple-eyed grass to the pasque flower to the pitcher plant. Science can displace or destroy, it can interpret, it can imitate; but science cannot take the place of the wonders of creation nor explain them. An eminent doctor recently said that after decades of work on the human ear, he had come to believe in God. I asked why; and he replied "God is the only explanation of ear wax."

Francis Thompson, the English poet, said last century:

> Thou canst not stir a flower
> Without troubling of a star.

Rachel Carson added, "but the poet's insight has not become part of general knowledge."

Where does one start with this new education? Certainly the first grade is not too soon. How does one go about it? By teaching the virtues and values of diversity and some of the "social costs" of so-called "progress."

Exposure of the young to nature under the guidance of sensitive and knowledgeable adults is one necessary starting point. This is virtually impossible in modern cities of asphalt and concrete where even playgrounds are paved. It means planning years ahead so that blighted areas are reclaimed and returned to nature, so that our suburbia retain woodlands and swamps immune from throughways and other developments. Our urban plight is due to the fact that we have left our future in the hands of engineers and landscape architects. We need to bring in the botanists, zoologists, biologists, ornithlogists and geologists if wonder, reverence, and awe are to become values in our society.

Every school needs a nature trail; and every person—adult or young— needs a bit of wilderness, if wonder, reverence and awe are to be cultivated. The wild areas are fast disappearing. Science and technology have transformed our concepts of recreation. Recreation today is not generally related to exertion but to transportation by auto to picnic grounds, to a scenic lookout, to a place where other people are engaged in exercise or games. The car, people urge, now needs to go wherever engineers can build a road. Once a road enters, the wilderness is at an end. Loggers usually go where roads go. All the debris of civilization follows roads. Roads are a death sentence to the quiet and repose of wilderness sanctuaries. Roads mean the end of certain species of game, such as elk that need larger zones to survive.

A return to the mysteries of nature is necessary for members of a society that honors diversity and teaches it. That return requires many paths. It entails among other things, the inculcation of a new land ethic.

Those who streamed through Cumberland Gap, headed west, saw mostly unbroken forests; and those barriers had to be levelled so that farms could be established, towns built, and a network of roads constructed. First the ax and later the bulldozer became the symbol of power and achievement, our mark of distinction. They are also the Russians', who we resemble in many particulars . . . [but]. . . . The leveler has had no one political ideology. The leveler of forests is, indeed, the extrovert, whether he be capitalist, socialist, or dictator. But the energies of the extroverts must be re-directed lest every valley be paved and every mountain peak have a chair lift. If we are to have a new land ethic, a child of five needs a new symbol of American power; he needs to be directed not to the bulldozer but to the wildlife and wild flowers of the woodlands and to the endless wonders of nature.

145

Facets of Wilderness

MARGARET OWINGS

1965

From "Wild Bird," the Big Sur eyrie she shares with architect Nathaniel Owings, Margaret Wentworth Owings has crusaded valiantly and successfully to save endangered wildlife—the California mountain lion, the sea otter, the porpoise. Her writings have more than a touch of poetry and often a perceptive feeling of the wild shoreline. Here, in a closing statement to the Ninth Wilderness Conference, she evokes the first-hand experience with the sights and symbols of the natural world. Sigurd Olson, a previous speaker, is the author of numerous books of nature writing.

THESE TWO DAYS we have been turning over in our hands a great rough rock with many facets. It is a treasured rock. We call it "wilderness." Each facet is one variety of this wilderness, and the reflection from each facet is a human response to that experience.

There are those of us who look at wilderness primarily as a dimension—an immensity, a grand proportion. These may be people who work by expansion and think by expansion, fanning out their interests. It's the broad, deep picture they find rewarding.

Then, there are those who turn primarily to the intimate savor of landscape: the detail, the scent of nettle and mint, the lazy buzz of a mountain fly, the careless grace of a flower opening. These people are selective and concentrate their attention, finding their reward in infinite detail.

But neither approach seeks confinement. Both pursue the sense of the unexplored landscape. For each man is his own eager explorer.

It was Rachel Carson who unrolled the long vistas before our eyes and described man's place as a mere moment of time. "This particular moment of time that is mine," she repeated again and again to help us see our place and our role and the perils of our future in the long view.

It is the perceptive explorer who can glimpse this view, who can uncover the links and bridges of history and find his own particular place in the moment of time.

Having a landscape to oneself is an exclusive pleasure. Many of us stumble upon this by surprise. Suddenly it is there—unshared, solitary. One may well experience a reckless moment of freedom, a penetrating moment of understanding. A meaning that was elusive is suddenly clear! And in the words of Freya Stark, one can carry long afterwards "a secret sense of exile."

Promise is a word I associate with wilderness. Promise and independence are rare qualities found deep in solitude. Promise renews faith. Independence is found only when the sense of belonging is understood.

Sigurd Olson spoke of "the animal oneness with the earth," the sense of close relationship, of belonging.

How can we recapture this relationship?

How can we return to this "oneness"?

What kind of a ceremony can lead us back: The Mountain Chant of the Navajos in their dark circle of branches? The Hopi Snake dancers at Walpi, stamping on the Sapupai—the door to the inner earth?

Sigurd Olson quoted Pierre Teilhard de Chardin (that rare soul who could make an experience flare with a presence) as saying that only if man is receptive, contemplative, and aware can he open these doors to what the universe and life really mean—can he open these doors to belonging. But for most of us, under the pressures and conflicts of human society, it is only in the setting of wilderness that this revelation can unfold.

I, myself, experienced a form of revelation one autumn morning. In an unexpected moment, I witnessed a thin slice of wilderness, fleeting and brief, but filled with a meaning somehow intensified by the counterpart of its setting.

I was on the sidewalk of 55th Street in the heart of New York City. Around me was the noise and confusion, the frantic strain of traffic, horns and whistles. Tall buildings cast their shadows over the deep chasm of the street. It was the essence of the man-made world.

At that moment, as if by signal, every city sound about me was suddenly hushed. All mechanical uproar was arrested abruptly, as if the power had been shut off. And in the silence of that instant, I heard but one thing—the delicate honking of geese high overhead. I looked up through the slot of buildings to another dimension, as a V of geese moved south, calling to one another as they passed out of view.

One world gave way to another.

It was one of those "burning instances of truth," referred to by Sigurd Olson, "when everything stands clear."

Now Loren Eiseley admonishes emissaries returning from wilderness to record their marvel, not to define its meaning. But I am tempted to call your attention to several potent words used by Sigurd Olson: timelessness, majestic rhythms.

Each of you alone can read your own symbols into the incident I have tried to describe. But it seems appropriate, with the dedication of the Dag Hammarskjold Memorial Grove of redwoods, to close with these lines from his diary:

A wind from my unknown goal
Stirs the strings
In expectation.
Shall I ever get there?
There, where life resounds
A clear pure note—
In the silence.

541

146

An American Land Ethic

N. SCOTT MOMADAY

1970

A descendant of the Kiowa tribe here evokes the spirit of his ancestors and the land ethic that had evolved on this continent before the coming of Europeans. N. Scott Momaday has taught English at the University of California and is the author of The Way to Rainy Mountain *and* House Made of Dawn.

I

ONE NIGHT a strange thing happened. I had written the greater part of *The Way To Rainy Mountain* —all of it, in fact, except the epilogue. I had set down the last of the old Kiowa tales, and I had composed both the historical and the autobiographical commentaries for it. I had the sense of being out of breath, of having said what it was in me to say on that subject. The manuscript lay before me in the bright light, small, to be sure, but complete; or nearly so. I had written the second of the two poems in which that book is framed. I had uttered the last word, as it were. And yet a whole, penultimate piece was missing. I began once again to write.

During the first hours after midnight on the morning of November 13, 1833, it seemed that the world was coming to an end. Suddenly the stillness of the night was broken; there were brilliant flashes of light in the sky, light of such intensity that people were awakened by it. With the speed and density of a driving rain, stars were falling in the universe. Some were brighter than Venus; one was said to be as large as the moon.

I went on to say that that event, the falling of the stars on North America, that explosion of Leonid meteors which occurred 137 years ago, is among the earliest entries in the Kiowa calendars. So deeply impressed upon the imagination of the Kiowas is that old phenomenon that it is remembered still; it has become a part of the racial memory.

"The living memory," I wrote, "and the verbal tradition which transcends it, were brought together for me once and for all in the person of Ko-sahn." It seemed eminently right for me to deal, after all, with that old woman. Ko-sahn is among the most venerable people I have ever known. She spoke and sang to me one summer afternoon in Oklahoma. It was like a dream. When I was born she was already old; she was a grown woman when my grandparents came into the world. She sat perfectly still, folded over on herself. It did not seem possible that so many years—a century of years—could be so compacted and distilled. Her voice shuddered, but it did not fail. Her songs were sad. An old whimsy, a delight in language and in remembrance, shone in her one good eye. She conjured up the past, imagining perfectly the long continuity of her being. She imagined the lovely young girl, wild and vital, she had been. She imagined the Sun Dance:

There was an old, old woman. She had something on her back. The boys went out to see. The old woman had a bag full of earth on her back. It was a certain kind of sandy earth. That is what they must have in the lodge. The dancers must dance upon the sandy earth. The old woman held a digging tool in her hand. She turned towards the south and pointed with her lips. It was like a kiss, and she began to sing:

> We have brought the earth,
> Now it is time to play;
> As old as I am, I still have the feeling of play.

That was the beginning of the Sun Dance.

By this time I was back into the book, caught up completely in the act of writing. I had projected myself—imagined myself—out of the room and out of time. I was there with Ko-sahn in the Oklahoma July. We laughed easily together; I felt that I had known her all of my life—all of hers. I did not want to let her go. But I had come to the end. I set down, almost grudgingly, the last sentences:

It was—all of this and more—a quest, a going forth upon the way to Rainy Mountain. Probably Ko-sahn too is dead now. At times, in the quiet of evening, I think she must have wondered, dreaming, who she was. Was she become in her sleep that old purveyor of the sacred earth, perhaps, that ancient one who, old as she was, still had the feeling of play? And in her mind, at times, did she see the falling stars?

For some time I sat looking down at these words on the page, trying to deal with the emptiness that had come about inside of me. The words did not seem real. The longer I looked at them, the more unfamiliar they became. At last I could scarcely believe that they made sense, that they had anything whatsoever to do with meaning. In desperation almost, I went back over the final paragraphs, backwards and forwards, hurriedly. My eyes fell upon the name Ko-sahn. And all at once everything seemed suddenly to refer to that name. The name seemed to humanize the whole complexity of language. All at once, absolutely, I had the sense of the magic of words and of names. Ko-sahn, I said. And I said again KO-SAHN.

Then it was that that ancient, one-eyed woman Ko-sahn stepped out of the language and stood before me on the page. I was amazed, of course, and yet it seemed to me entirely appropriate that this should happen.

"Yes, grandson," she said. "What is it? What do you want?"

"I was just now writing about you," I replied, stammering. "I thought—forgive me—I thought that perhaps you were . . . that you had. . . ."

543

"No," she said. And she cackled, I thought. And she went on. "You have imagined me well, and so I am. You have imagined that I dream, and so I do. I have seen the falling stars."

"But all of this, this *imagining*," I protested, "this has taken place—is taking place in my mind. You are not actually here, not here in this room." It occurred to me that I was being extremely rude, but I could not help myself. She seemed to understand.

"Be careful of your pronouncements, grandson," she answered. "You imagine that I am here in this room, do you not? That is worth something. You see, I have existence, whole being, in your imagination. It is but one kind of being, to be sure, but it is perhaps the best of all kinds. If I am not here in this room, grandson, then surely neither are you."

"I think I see what you mean," I said meekly. I felt justly rebuked. "Tell me, grandmother, how old are you?"

"I do not know," she replied. "There are times when I think that I am the oldest woman on earth. You know, the Kiowas came into the world through a hollow log. In my mind's eye I have seen them emerge, one by one, from the mouth of the log. I have seen them so clearly, how they were dressed, how delighted they were to see the world around them. I *must* have been there. And I must have taken part in that old migration of the Kiowas from the Yellowstone to the Southern Plains, for I have seen antelope bounding in the tall grass near the Big Horn River, and I have seen the ghost forests in the Black Hills. Once I saw the red cliffs of Palo Duro Canyon. I was with those who were camped in the Wichita Mountains when the stars fell."

"You are indeed very old," I said, "and you have seen many things."

"Yes, I imagine that I have," she replied. Then she turned slowly around, nodding once, and receded into the language I had made. And then I imagined I was alone in the room.

II

Once in his life a man ought to concentrate his mind upon the remembered earth, I believe. He ought to give himself up to a particular landscape in his experience, to look at it from as many angles as he can, to wonder about it, to dwell upon it. He ought to imagine that he touches it with his hands at every season and listens to the sounds that are made upon it. He ought to imagine the creatures there and all the faintest motions of the wind. He ought to recollect the glare of noon and all the colors of the dawn and dusk.

The Wichita Mountains rise out of the Southern Plains in a long crooked line that runs from east to west. The mountains are made of red earth, and of rock that is neither red nor blue but some very rare admixture of the two like the feathers of certain birds. The yellow, grassy knoll that is called Rainy Mountain lies a short distance to the north and west. There, on the west side, is the ruin of an old school where my grandmother went as a wild young girl in blanket and braids to learn of numbers and of names in English. And there she is buried.

III

I am interested in the way that a man looks at a given landscape and takes possession of it in his blood and brain. For this happens, I am certain, in the ordinary motion of life. None of us lives apart from the land entirely; such an isolation is unimaginable. We have sooner or later to come to terms with the world around us — and I mean especially the physical world, not only as it is revealed to us immediately through our senses, but also as it is perceived more truly in the long turn of seasons and of years. And we must come to moral terms. There is no alternative, I believe, if we are to realize and maintain our humanity, for our humanity must consist in part in the ethical as well as the practical ideal of preservation. And particularly here and now is that true. We Americans need now more than ever before — and indeed more than we know — to imagine who and what we are with respect to the earth and sky. I am talking about an act of the imagination essentially, and the concept of an American land ethic.

It is no doubt more difficult to imagine in 1970 the landscape of America than it was in, say, 1900. Our whole experience as a nation in this century has been a repudiation of the pastoral ideal which informs so much of the art and literature of the nineteenth century. One effect of the Technological Revolution has been to uproot us from the soil. We have become disoriented, I believe; we have suffered a kind of psychic dislocation of ourselves in time and space. We may be perfectly sure of where we are in relation to the supermarket and the next coffee break, but I doubt that any of us knows where he is in relation to the stars and to the solstices. Our sense of the natural order has become dull and unreliable. Like the wilderness itself, our sphere of instinct has diminished in proportion as we have failed to imagine truly what it is. And yet I believe that it is possible to formulate an ethical idea of the land — a notion of what it is and must be in our daily lives — and I believe moreover that it is absolutely necessary to do so.

It would seem on the surface of things that a land ethic is something that is alien to, or at least dormant in, most Americans. Most of us in general have developed an attitude of indifference toward the land. In terms of my own experience, it is difficult to see how such an attitude could ever have come about.

IV

Ko-sahn could remember where my grandmother was born. "It was just there," she said, pointing to a tree, and the tree was like a hundred others that grew up in the broad depression of the Washita River. I could see nothing to indicate that anyone had ever been there, spoken so much as a word, or touched the tips of his fingers to the tree. But in her memory Ko-sahn could see the child. I think she must have remembered my grandmother's voice, for she seemed for a long moment to listen and to hear. There was a still, heavy heat upon that place; I had the sense that ghosts were gathering there.

And in the racial memory, Ko-sahn had seen the falling stars. For her there was no distinction between the individual and the racial experience, even as there was none between the mythical and the historical. Both were realized for her in the one memory, and that was of the land. This landscape, in which she had lived for a hundred years, was the common denominator of everything that she knew and would ever know — and her knowledge was profound. Her roots ran deep into the earth, and from those depths she drew strength enough to hold still against all the forces of chance and disorder. And she drew therefrom the sustenance of meaning and of mystery as well. The falling stars were not for Ko-sahn an isolated or accidental phenomenon. She had a great personal investment in that awful commotion of light in the night sky. For it remained to be imagined. She must at last deal with it in words; she must appropriate it to her understanding of the whole universe. And, again, when she spoke of the Sun Dance, it was an essential expression of her relationship to the life of the earth and to the sun and moon.

In Ko-sahn and in her people we have always had the example of a deep, ethical regard for the land. We had better learn from it. Surely that ethic is merely latent in ourselves. It must now be activated, I believe. We Americans must come again to a moral comprehension of the earth and air. We must live according to the principle of a land ethic. The alternative is that we shall not live at all.

147

Wilderness and the Geography of Hope

WALLACE STEGNER

1961

The uses of wilderness for such purposes as recreation and scientific research have received increasing attention in recent years, but Wallace Stegner is here concerned with something quite different. The wilderness idea, he writes, is a resource in itself: "Being an intangible and spiritual resource, it will seem mystical to the practical-minded — but then anything that cannot be moved by a bulldozer is likely to seem mystical to them."

This article was originally written as a letter to a federal recreation agency and was presented by Secretary of the Interior Stewart Udall at the club's seventh biennial wilderness conference in 1961. It was published in Wilderness — America's Living Heritage, *the proceedings of that conference.*

Stegner is a Pulitzer Prize novelist (Angle of Repose) *and a former member of the club's board of directors.*

SOMETHING WILL HAVE GONE OUT of us as a people if we ever let the remaining wilderness be destroyed; if we permit the last virgin forests to be turned into comic books and plastic cigarette cases; if we drive the few remaining members of the wild species into zoos or to extinction; if we pollute the last clear air and dirty the last clean streams and push our paved roads through the last of the silence, so that never again will Americans be free in their own country from the noise, the exhausts, the stinks of human and automotive waste. And so that never again can we have the chance to see ourselves single, separate, vertical and individual in the world, part of the environment of trees and rocks and soil, brother to the other animals, part of the natural world and competent to belong in it. Without any remaining wilderness we are committed wholly, without chance for even momentary reflection and rest, to a headlong drive into our technological termite-life, the Brave New World of a completely man-controlled environment. We need wilderness preserved — as much of it as is still left, and as many kinds — because it was the challenge against which our character as a people was formed. The remainder and the reassurance that it is still there is good for our spiritual health even if we never once in ten years set foot in it. It is good for us when we are young, because of the incomparable sanity it can bring briefly, as vacation and rest, into our insane lives. It is important to us when we are old simply because it is there — important, that is, simply as idea.

We are a wild species, as Darwin pointed out. Nobody ever tamed or domesticated or scientifically bred us. But for at least three millennia we have been engaged in a cumulative and ambitious race to modify and gain control of our environment, and in the process we have come close to domesticating ourselves. Not many people are likely, any more, to look upon what we call "progress" as an unmixed blessing. Just as surely as it has brought us increased comfort and more material goods, it has brought us spiritual losses, and it threatens now to become the Frankenstein that will destroy us. One means of sanity is to retain a hold on the natural world, to remain, insofar as we can, good animals. Americans still have that chance, more than many peoples; for while we were demonstrating ourselves the most efficient and ruthless environment-busters in history, and slashing and burning and cutting our way through a wilderness continent, the wilderness was working on us. It remains in us as surely as Indian names remain on the land. If the abstract dream of human liberty and human dignity became, in America, something more than an abstract dream, mark it down at least partially to the fact that we were in subtle ways subdued by what we conquered.

547

The Connecticut Yankee, sending likely candidates from King Arthur's unjust kingdom to his Man Factory for rehabilitation, was over-optimistic, as he later admitted. These things cannot be forced, they have to grow. To make such a man, such a democrat, such a believer in human individual dignity, as Mark Twain himself, the frontier was necessary, Hannibal and the Mississippi and Virginia City, and reaching out from those the wilderness, the wilderness as opportunity and as idea, the thing that has helped to make an American different from and, until we forget it in the roar of our industrial cities, more fortunate than other men. For an American, insofar as he is new and different at all, is a civilized man who has renewed himself in the wild. The American experience has been the confrontation by old peoples and cultures of a world as new as if it had just risen from the sea. That gave us our hope and our excitement, and the hope and excitement can be passed on to newer Americans, Americans who never saw any phase of the frontier. But only so long as we keep the remainder of our wild as a reserve and a promise—a sort of wilderness bank.

As a novelist, I may perhaps be forgiven for taking literature as a reflection, indirect but profoundly true, of our national consciousness. And our literature, as perhaps you are aware, is sick, embittered, losing its mind, losing its faith. Our novelists are the declared enemies of their society. There has hardly been a serious or important novel in this century that did not repudiate in part or in whole American technological culture for its commercialism, its vulgarity, and the way in which it has dirtied a clean continent and a clean dream. I do not expect that the preservation of our remaining wilderness is going to cure this condition. But the mere example that we can as a nation apply some other criteria than commercial and exploitative considerations would be heartening to many Americans, novelists or otherwise. We need to demonstrate our acceptance of the natural world, including ourselves; we need the spiritual refreshment that being natural can produce. And one of the best places for us to get that is in the wilderness where the fun houses, the bulldozers, and the pavements of our civilization are shut out.

Sherwood Anderson, in a letter to Waldo Frank in the 1920's, said it better than I can. "Is it not likely that when the country was new and men were often alone in the fields and the forest they got a sense of bigness outside themselves that has now in some way been lost. . . . Mystery whispered in the grass, played in the branches of trees overhead, was caught up and blown across the American line in clouds of dust at evening on the prairies. . . . I am old enough to remember tales that strengthen my belief in a deep semi-religious influence that was formerly at work among our people. The flavor of it hangs over the best work of Mark Twain . . . I can remember old fellows in my home town speaking feelingly of an evening spent on the big empty plains. It had taken the shrillness out of them. They had learned the trick of quiet. . . ."

We could learn it too, even yet; even our children and grandchildren could learn it. But only if we save, for just such absolutely non-recreational, impractical, and mystical uses as this, all the wild that still remains to us.

548

It seems to me significant that the distinct downturn in our literature from hope to bitterness took place almost at the precise time when the frontier officially came to an end, in 1890, and when the American way of life had begun to turn strongly urban and industrial. The more urban it has become, and the more frantic with technological change, the sicker and more embittered our literature, and I believe our people, have become. For myself, I grew up on the empty plains of Saskatchewan and Montana and in the mountains of Utah, and I put a very high valuation on what those places gave me. And if I had not been able periodically to renew myself in the mountains and deserts of western America I would be very nearly bughouse. Even when I can't get to the back country, the thought of the colored deserts of southern Utah, or the reassurance that there are still stretches of prairie where the world can be instantaneously perceived as disk and bowl, and where the little but intensely important human being is exposed to the five directions and the thirty-six winds, is a positive consolation. The idea alone can sustain me. But as the wilderness areas are progressively exploited or "improved," as the jeeps and bulldozers of uranium prospectors scar up the deserts and the roads are cut into the alpine timberlands, and as the remnants of the unspoiled and natural world are progressively eroded, every such loss is a little death in me. In us.

I am not moved by the argument that those wilderness areas which have already been exposed to grazing or mining are already deflowered, and so might as well be "harvested." For mining I cannot say much good except that its operations are generally short-lived. The extractable wealth is taken and the shafts, the tailings, and the ruins left, and in a dry country such as the American West the wounds men make in the earth do not quickly heal. Still, they are only wounds; they aren't absolutely mortal. Better a wounded wilderness than none at all. And as for grazing, if it is strictly controlled so that it does not destroy the ground cover, damage the ecology, or compete with the wildlife it is in itself nothing that need conflict with the wilderness feeling or the validity of the wilderness experience. I have known enough range cattle to recognize them as wild animals; and the people who herd them have, in the wilderness context, the dignity of rareness; they belong on the frontier, moreover, and have a look of rightness. The invasion they make on the virgin country is a sort of invasion that is as old as Neolithic man, and they can, in moderation, even emphasize a man's feeling of belonging to the natural world. Under surveillance, they can belong; under control, they need not deface or mar. I do not believe that in wilderness areas where grazing has never been permitted, it should be permitted; but I do not believe either that an otherwise untouched wilderness should be eliminated from the preservation plan because of limited existing uses such as grazing which are in consonance with the frontier condition and image.

Let me say something on the subject of the kinds of wilderness worth preserving. Most of those areas contemplated are in the national forests and in high mountain country. For all the usual recreational purposes, the alpine and forest wildernesses are obviously the most important, both as genetic banks and as beauty spots. But for the spiritual renewal, the recognition of identity, the birth of awe, other kinds will serve every bit as well. Perhaps, because they are less friendly to life, more abstractly non-human, they will serve even better. On our Saskatchewan prairie, the nearest neighbor was four miles away, and at night we saw only two lights on all the dark rounding earth. The earth was full of animals—field mice, ground squirrels, weasels, ferrets, badgers, coyotes, burrowing owls, snakes. I knew them as my little brothers, as fellow creatures, and I have never been able to look upon animals in any other way since. The sky in that country came clear down to the ground on every side, and it was full of great weathers, and clouds, and winds, and hawks. I hope I learned something from knowing intimately the creatures of the earth; I hope I learned something from looking a long way, from looking up, from being much alone. A prairie like that, one big enough to carry the eye clear to the sinking, rounding horizon, can be as lonely and grand and simple in its forms as the sea. It is as good a place as any for the wilderness experience to happen; the vanishing prairie is as worth preserving for the wilderness idea as the alpine forests.

So are great reaches of our western deserts, scarred somewhat by prospectors but otherwise open, beautiful, waiting, close to whatever God you want to see in them. Just as a sample, let me suggest the Robbers' Roost country in Wayne County, Utah, near the Capitol Reef National Monument. In that desert climate the dozer and jeep tracks will not soon melt back into the earth, but the country has a way of making the scars insignificant. It is a lovely and terrible wilderness, such a wilderness as Christ and the prophets went out into; harshly and beautifully colored, broken and worn until its bones are exposed, its great sky without a smudge or taint from Technocracy, and in hidden corners and pockets under its cliffs the sudden poetry of springs. Save a piece of country like that intact, and it does not matter in the slightest that only a few people every year will go into it. That is precisely its value. Roads would be a desecration, crowds would ruin it. But those who haven't the strength or youth to go into it and live can simply sit and look. They can look two hundred miles, clear into Colorado; and looking down over the cliffs and canyons of the San Rafael Swell and the Robbers' Roost they can also look as deeply into themselves as anywhere I know. And if they can't even get to the places on the Aquarius Plateau where the present roads will carry them, they can simply contemplate the *idea,* take pleasure in the fact that such a timeless and uncontrolled part of earth is still there.

These are some of the things wilderness can do for us. That is the reason we need to put into effect, for its preservation, some other principle than the principles of exploitation or "usefulness" or even recreation. We simply need that wild country available to us, even if we never do more than drive to its edge and look in. For it can be a means of reassuring ourselves of our sanity as creatures, a part of the geography of hope.

Very sincerely yours,
WALLACE STEGNER

550

148

Homecoming

CHARLOTTE MAUK

1947

Charlotte Mauk was a member of the club's board of directors for many years; the editor of Yosemite and the Sierra Nevada, *combining writings of John Muir with photographs by Ansel Adams; and head of commissary on unnumbered High Trips. In these paragraphs from her report on the 1946 High Trip, she invokes the spirit that has animated the Sierra Club from its beginnings—the deep sense of awe and delight in the wilderness experience.*

The article's title derives from the fact that this was the first High Trip following the hiatus during World War II. It may be taken in a more symbolic sense as well. Each return to the wilderness is a homecoming.

THE HAPPINESS of a mountain day is not a thing, and cannot be analyzed into so many distinct parts. It is a nonmaterial entity to be experienced and cherished by all the senses, but not to be questioned. Perhaps a part of the charm of mountains is that there the very joy of existence is in itself sufficient answer to almost any question. It is enough to recognize, without trying to catalog, the brilliance of the sunshine; the clear blue vault and the answering blueness caught in shadowed clefts; the fragrance that the sun draws from a pine tree; the silver glint on willows dancing in the wind; the crystal smoothness of a streamlet curving through a meadow; those rugged, thrusting crags against the sky; the tender, graceful pattern of tiny plants against a boulder; the sound of wind in branches overhead, from gentle whisper to a surflike roar; the rough and satisfying feel of sun-warmed granite.

Out of solitude may grow a sharper perception of the quiet life about us, a deeper appreciation of its features, a fuller understanding of the world's wild beauty. Alone, or with a sympathetic companion, the wanderer in the mountains is receptive to what amounts to religious experience. It may be the culmination of a lengthy crescendo, as the final dazzling brightness of a blazing sunset; the ultimate step onto a summit and the scanning of a horizon which has become ever wider as ridge after intervening ridge dropped below it; the long-awaited breaking of a magnificent thunderstorm which has grown through hours of swelling clouds and brooding purple-gray shadows. Or it may be but a fleeting moment of revelation, as a glimpse of exquisite grace and rhythm in a wind-stirred columbine, the mysterious poignant sweetness of the song of a hermit thrush, the irised flash of flying spray above a pool.

These things, perhaps unanalyzed but surely recorded, make up man's deepest memory of mountain experience. He may never mention to another his own inmost feelings, nor even admit to himself that there is something poetic about his personal response to surpassing beauty. He may scarcely recognize its absorption into his spirit. But the unrecognized recall of myriad strangely moving moments of awareness blends into the nostalgia which is evoked by a photograph or a painting, a word picture, or the vivid memory of some mountain scene.

"Awful in stern, immovable majesty, how softly these rocks are adorned . . . the snow and waterfalls, the winds and avalanches and clouds shine and sing and wreathe about them . . . I am hopelessly and forever a mountaineer."

John Muir

Bibliography

Abbey, Edward. "Canyonlands and Compromises." *Sierra Club Bulletin,* 56 (1971), no. 1, p. 12.

Adams, Ansel. "Problems of Interpretation of the Natural Scene." *SCB,* 30 (1945), p. 47. "Ski Experience." *SCB,* 16 (1931), p. 44.

Anonymous. "Instant Vacation." *SCB,* 45 (1960), no. 2, p. 3.

Badè, William Frederic. "The Water Ouzel at Home." *SCB,* 5 (1904), p. 102.

Barkan, Otto. "Skiing in California." *SCB,* 16 (1931), p. 39.

Billings, Linda M. "The Tall Grass Prairie: Vanishing Landscape or National Park?" *SCB,* 62 (1977), no. 4, p. 19.

Bohn, Dave. "Francis Farquhar at 84 Speaks of the Sierra Club Then and Now." *SCB,* 57 (1972), no. 6, p. 8.

Bradley, H. C. "Across the Sierra Nevada on Skis." *SCB,* 11 (1922), p. 292.

Bradley, Richard. "Damming the Colorado River." *SCB,* 49 (1964), no. 9, p. 73. "Glen Canyon" (excerpted from "Damming the Colorado River"). *SCB,* 49 (1964), no. 9, p. 77.

Bradley, Thomas. "Minorities and Conservation." *SCB,* 57 (1972), no. 4, p. 21.

Breckenfeld, Robert R. "Knapsaga." *SCB,* 32 (1947), p. 99.

Brower, David R. "Beyond the Skiways." *SCB,* 23 (1938), p. 40.
"Cedric Wright." *SCB,* 44 (1959), no. 8, p. 2.
"Francis P. Farquhar." *Not Man Apart,* 4 (1974), no. 18, p. 6.
"Preserving Dinosaur." *SCB,* 39 (1954), p. 1.
"Skis to the Winter Wilderness." Reprinted from *Manual of Ski Mountaineering. San Francisco: Sierra Club Books, 1969.*

Brown, Bolton Coit. "A Glimpse of the Winter Sierra." *SCB,* 3 (1901), p. 242.

Brown, Joseph E. "The Mountains and Megalopolis." *SCB,* 58 (1973), no. 2, p. 4.

Brown, William. "The Rape of Black Mesa." *SCB,* 55 (1970), no. 8, p. 14.

Bryce, James. "Trustees of the Future." *SCB,* 9 (1913), p. 28.

Buder, Nancy. "Of Poison, Man, and Indifference to Life." *SCB,* 59 (1974), no. 10, p. 12.

Butler, Vincent. "Walter Augustus Starr, Jr." Introduction to *Guide to the John Muir Trail and the High Sierra Region,* by Walter A. Starr, Jr. 4th ed. San Francisco: Sierra Club Books, 1951.

Cahill, J. Lloyd. "Puma." *SCB,* 56 (1971), no. 3, p. 18.

Cephalopod, D. "Say What You Want About Me, But Spell My Name Right." *Yodeler,* 38 (1976), no. 4, p. 9.

Clark, Lewis F. "Down the Narrows of the Virgin River." *SCB,* 36 (1951), p. 6.

Colby, William E. "How It All Began—or Almost Didn't" (excerpted from "Twenty-Nine Years with the Sierra Club"). *SCB,* 16 (1931), p. 1.
"Knapsacking Across the Kings-Kern Divide." *SCB,* 8 (1912), p. 163.

Bibliography

Condit, Daniel H. "Burro Tripping" (excerpted from "Sierra Interlude"). *SCB*, 30 (1945), p. 56.

Cook, William Bridge. "Wilderness Fungi—The Silent Scavengers." *SCB*, 42 (1957), p. 38.

Cousteau, Jacques. "Save the Seas; Save the Earth" (excerpted from "Reasonable Utopias"). *SCB*, 61 (1976), no. 6, p. 25.

Davis, Wayne. "The Stripmining of America." *SCB*, 56 (1971), no. 2, p. 4.

DeQuille, Dan. "Snow-shoe Thompson." *SCB*, 20 (1935), p. 8. Reprinted from *The Overland Monthly*, 1886.

DeVoto, Bernard. "The West Against Itself." *SCB*, 32 (1947), p. 36.

Douglas, William O. "Nature and the Value of Diversity." *SCB*, 49 (1964), no. 5, p. 18.

Dunmire, William W. "A Trans-Sierra Ski Tour." *SCB*, 36 (1951), p. 82.

Du Pont, Pete. "The Tocks Island Dam Fight." *SCB*, 57 (1972), no. 7, p. 13.

Easton, Ethel Olney. "The Founding of the Sierra Club." *SCB*, 54 (1969), no. 11, p. 13. "Hetch Hetchy" (excerpted from "The Founding of the Sierra Club"). *SCB*, 54 (1969), no. 11, p. 15.

Ela, Jonathan. "From Sea To Shining Sea Or Through the Rockies at 31 Knots." *SCB*, 57 (1972), no. 6, p. 26.

Emerson, Richard. "Everest: The West Ridge" (excerpted from "The Traverse of Mount Everest"). *SCB*, 48 (1963), p. 5.

Entwistle, Robert. "The Crisis We Won't Face Squarely." *SCB*, 58 (1973), no. 10, p. 9.

Ernst, Emil F. "The Disappearance of Yosemite's Meadows." *SCB*, 46 (1961), p. 21.

Etter, Alfred G. "A Day with Aldo Leopold." *SCB*, 48 (1963), p. 46. "The Magic of Gypsy Woods." *SCB*, 48 (1963), no. 6, p. 3.

Evans, Brock. "Wilderness Myths and Misconceptions." *SCB*, 61 (1976), no. 9, p. 53.

Farquhar, Francis P. "The First Ascent of the Middle Palisade." *SCB*, 11 (1922), p. 264.

Farquhar, Samuel T. "John Muir and Ralph Waldo Emerson in Yosemite." *SCB*, 19 (1934), p. 48.

Frugé, August. "River Journal: Yampa and Green Rivers." *SCB*, 39 (1954), p. 15.

Futrell, William. "Oil and Trouble in the Louisiana Wetlands." *SCB*, 59 (1974), no. 7, p. 14.

Gibbs, George. "The Descent of Tenaya Cañon." *SCB*, 3 (1901), p. 230.

Gillette, Robert. "The Power of NEPA" (excerpted from "Will Success Wreck NEPA?"). *SCB*, 57 (1972), no. 4, p. 12.

Gilliam, Harold. "Norman Clyde: Old Man of the Mountains." *SCB*, 46 (1961), no. 7, p. 13. Reprinted from "This World," *San Francisco Chronicle*. August 13, 1961.

Gompertz, Helen M. "A Tramp to Mt. Lyell." *SCB*, 1 (1894), p. 136.

Gunsky, Fred. "Mountain Talk: Thoreau at Katahdin." *SCB*, 45 (1960), no. 2, p. 19.

Hackamack, Robert. "Picking Up the Pieces of the Tuolumne." *SCB*, 61 (1976), no. 10, p. 6.

Hardin, Garrett. "Nobody Ever Dies of Overpopulation." *SCB*, 56 (1971), no. 3, p. 2. Reprinted from *Science*, 12 February 1971.

Heald, Weldon. "A Wartime High Trip" (excerpted from "High and Dry"). *SCB*, 26 (1941), p. 16.

Hildebrand, Joel. "Ski Heil!" *SCB*, 20 (1935), p. 1.

Hoffmann, John D. "The Club, the Cause, and the Courts." *SCB*, 62 (1977), no. 2, p. 41.

Holdren, John P. "Defusing Old Smoky by Plugging into Nature." *SCB*, 56 (1971), no. 8, p. 24. Reprinted from *Energy: A Crisis in Power* by John Holdren and Philip Herrera. San Francisco: Sierra Club Books, 1971.
"Radioactive Wastes: An Aspirin Tablet Per Person?" *SCB*, 62 (1977), no. 3, p. 20. Reprinted from *Ecoscience: Population, Resources, Environment*, by Paul R. Ehrlich, Anne H. Ehrlich, and John P. Holdren. San Francisco: W. H. Freeman and Company, 1977.

Hood, Leslie. "Whose Home on the Range?" *SCB*, 57 (1972), no. 5, p. 5.

Hoppe, Art. "False Starts in Detroit." *SCB*, 61 (1976), no. 10, p. 13.

Howell, John Thomas. "Carbonated Landscape." *SCB*, 31 (1946), p. 18.
"Mono Mesa, Sierra Sky-Island." *SCB*, 32 (1947), p. 15.

Hutchinson, J. S. "Joseph N. LeConte: Some Recollections." *SCB*, 35 (1950), p. 1.

Janney, James. "Dhaulagiri: A Mind Odyssey." *Ascent*, 1 (1970), no. 4, p. 12.

Johnson, Carolyn. "700,000,000,000 Barrels of Soot." *SCB*, 59 (1974), no. 4, p. 25.

Kehrlein, Oliver. "An Ascent of North Palisade from the Glacier." *SCB*, 14 (1929), p. 58.

Kellogg, Vernon. "Butterflies of the Mountain Summits." *SCB*, 9 (1913), p. 85.
"The Great Spruce Forest and the Hermit Thrush." *SCB*, 4 (1902), p. 35.

King, Hazel. "Ski Running: An Impression." *SCB*, 9 (1915), p. 271.

LeConte, J. N. "The Sierra Club." *SCB*, 10 (1917), p. 135.

LeConte, Joseph. "A Journal of Ramblings through the High Sierra of California." *SCB*, 3 (1900), p. 1.

Lehmann, B. H. "Marion Randall Parsons." *SCB*, 38 (1953), p. 35.

Leopold, A. Starker. "Too Many Deer." *SCB*, 38 (1953), p. 51.
"Wilderness and Culture." *SCB*, 42 (1957), p. 33.

Lowenstein, Jerold. "The Radioactive Risks of Nuclear Pollution." *SCB*, 56 (1971), no. 7, p. 22.

Luten, Daniel B. "Numbers Against Wilderness." *SCB*, 49 (1964), no. 9, p. 43.
"Progress Against Growth." *SCB*, 57 (1972), no. 6, p. 22.

MacDonald, Allan. "Realm of the Overhang." *SCB*, 47 (1962), p. 5.

Mansfield, Lewis P. "Serenity in Yosemite." *SCB*, 45 (1960), no. 8, p. 3.

Marchand, Millie. "Waiting: Maroon Bells Campsite." *Ascent*, 1 (1971), no. 5.

Mason, Herbert. "Do We Want Sugar Pine?" *SCB*, 40 (1955), p. 40.

Matthes, Francois E. "The Little 'Lost Valley' on Shepherd's Crest." *SCB*, 18 (1933), p. 68.

Mattison, James A. Jr. "Sea Otters." *SCB*, 55 (1970), no. 10, p. 12.

Mauk, Charlotte. "Homecoming, 1946." *SCB*, 32 (1947), p. 19.

McCloskey, Michael. "How We Can Live without Nuclear Power." Speech delivered at press conference, Los Angeles Press Club, March 9, 1976.

McLean, J. K. "The Upper Sacramento in October." *SCB*, 1 (1893), p. 54.

Merrill, Samuel. "Personal Recollections of John Muir." *SCB*, 13 (1928), p. 24.

Mitchell, John G. "Are the Everglades Forever?" *SCB*, 55 (1970), no. 6, p. 4. Essay in *Everglades*, by Patricia Caulfield. San Francisco: Sierra Club Books, 1970.

555

Bibliography

Momaday, N. Scott. "An American Land Ethic." *SCB,* 55 (1970), no. 2, p. 8.

Morgan, James K. "Whose Home on the Range?" *SCB,* 57 (1972), no. 5, p. 5.

Muir, John. "Explorations in the Great Tuolumne Cañon." *SCB,* 12 (1926), p. 65. Reprinted from *The Overland Monthly,* 1873.

Nash, Roderick. "Picking Up the Pieces of the Tuolumne." *SCB,* 61 (1976), no. 10, p. 6.

Nelson, Anton. "Climbing the Lost Arrow." *SCB,* 32 (1947), p. 1.
    "Five Days and Nights on the Lost Arrow." *SCB,* 33 (1948), p. 103.

Newberry, Todd. "The Seashore: Wilderness Between the Tides." *SCB,* 52 (1967), no. 3, p. 7.

Olmsted, Roger. "The Alternative to Pesticides." *SCB,* 57 (1972), no. 7, p. 4.

Owings, Margaret. "Facets of Wilderness." *SCB,* 50 (1965), no. 10, p. 96.

Parsons, Marion Randall. "John Muir and the Alaska Book." *SCB,* 10 (1916), p. 33.
    "Will Colby's Last High Trip" (excerpted from "The Twenty-Eighth Outing"). *SCB,* 15 (1930), p. 9.

Perry, Harold E. "Native Daughter." *SCB,* 37 (1952), p. 17.

Pollock, Robert. "What Colors the Mountain Snow?" *SCB,* 55 (1970), no. 4, p. 18.

Pope, Bertha Clark. "The High Trip of 1925." *SCB,* 12 (1926), p. 213.

Porter, Eliot. "Voices of Spring." *SCB,* 52 (1967), no. 9, p. 18. Reprinted from *Summer Island,* by Eliot Porter. San Francisco: Sierra Club Books, 1966.
    "The Place No One Knew." Reprinted from *The Place No One Knew,* by Eliot Porter. San Francisco: Sierra Club Books, 1963.

Price, Jennie Ellsworth. "A Woman's Trip through the Tuolumne Cañon." *SCB,* 2 (1898), p. 174.

Proctor, A. Phimister. "An Ascent of Half Dome in 1884." *SCB,* 31 (1946), p. 1.

Randall, Marion. "Why Camp with a Crowd? (excerpted from "Some Aspects of a Sierra Club Outing"). *SCB,* 5 (1905), p. 22.

Robertson, Thomas A. "Net Energy." *SCB,* 60 (1975), no. 3, p. 20.

Robinson, Bestor. "The First Ascent of Shiprock." *SCB,* 25 (1940), p. 1.

Robinson, Doug. "The Climber As Visionary." *Ascent,* 1 (1969), no. 3, p. 6.

Robinson, Elmo. "Prolegomena to a Philosophy of Mountaineering." *SCB,* 23 (1938), p. 50.

Robinson, Gordon. "Responsible Forestry." *SCB,* 56 (1971), no. 10, p. 4.

Rogers, Elizabeth. "The Work Trip" (excerpted from "Trip No. 103"). *SCB,* 54 (1969), no. 9, p. 10.

Roth, Berry. "Native Mollusks: Little Known and Little Loved." *SCB,* 57 (1972), no. 6, p. 4.

Rowell, Chester. "The Mountain and the Sea." *SCB,* 11 (1921), p. 261.

Rowell, Galen. "The Rings of Life." *SCB,* 59 (1974), no. 8, p. 4.

Sears, Paul B. "On Coming to Terms with Our Environment." *SCB,* 47 (1959), p. 37.

Sierra Club Staff. "Dams in the Colorado—A Necessary Evil?" Special publication issued by the Sierra Club in 1965 and presented as part of the club's testimony before the Subcommittee on Irrigation and Reclamation of the House Committee on Interior and Insular Affairs. Washington, D.C., 1965.

Siri, W. E. "A Fractured History of the Sierra Club." Excerpted from a speech delivered at the Sierra Club Annual Banquet, 1966.

Smith, Grant H. "Late Autumn in the Sierras." *SCB,* 12 (1924), p. 1.

Solomons, Theodore S. "A Search for a High Mountain Route from the Yosemite to the Kings River Cañon." *SCB,* 1 (1895), p. 221.

Spaulding, James. "Energy: Tomorrow Starts Today." *SCB,* 57 (1972), no. 10, p. 11.

Squires, Donald F. "Long Island Sound—The Urban Sea." *SCB,* 57 (1972), no. 2, p. 12.

Stallings, Blanche. "The Lore of the Cup." *SCB,* 25 (1940), p. 64.

Steck, Allen. "Ordeal by Piton." *SCB,* 36 (1951), p. 1.
"The Ascent of Hummingbird Ridge." *Ascent,* 1 (1967), no. 1, p. 3.

Stegner, Wallace. "Wilderness and the Geography of Hope." Reprinted from *Wilderness, America's Living Heritage,* edited by David Brower. San Francisco: Sierra Club Books, 1961.

Sumner, David. "700,000,000,000 Barrels of Soot." *SCB,* 59 (1974), no. 4, p. 25.

Sumner, Phoebe Anne. "Last Citadel." *SCB,* 35 (1950), p. 77.

Thomas, Greg. "Nuclear Exports: The Perilous Enterprise." *SCB,* 62 (1977), no. 3, p. 17.

Torrey, Volta. "The Windmill Renaissance." *SCB,* 62 (1977), no. 3, p. 41. Reprinted from *The Windcatchers,* by Volta Torrey. Brattleboro, Vermont: Stephen Greene Press, 1976.

Vandevere, Judson E. "Sea Otters." *SCB,* 55 (1970), no. 10, p. 12.

Warren, Charles. "Parson Malthus Tolls the Bell." *SCB,* 60 (1975), no. 3, p. 7.

Watkins, T. H. "Little Deaths." *SCB,* 59 (1974), no. 9, p. 34.

Wayburn, Edgar. "Bridge Creek—1973" (excerpted from "Last Days of the Emerald Mile"). *SCB,* 58 (1973), no. 10, p. 26.

Wayburn, Edgar and Peggy. "The Battle of the Redwoods" (excerpted from "Prologue"). *SCB,* 52 (1967), no. 9, p. 48.

Wayburn, Peggy. "A Carol in Praise of the Hat Monticolous." *SCB,* 46 (1961), p. 39.
"Alaska: The Last Opportunity" (excerpted from "Alaska Wilderness—The 140-Million Acre Challenge"). *SCB,* 61 (1976), no. 9, p. 43.
"O Tempora! O Mores!" *SCB,* 60 (1975), no. 3, p. 28.

Wheat, Maxwell C. "Precedent on the Hudson." *SCB,* 51 (1966), no. 3, p. 5.

Winchester, Ellen. "America's Beleaguered Coasts." *SCB,* 62 (1977), no. 4, p. 4.

Wood, Nancy. "The Scourge of Clearcutting."*SCB,* 56 (1971), no. 8, p. 14. Reprinted from *Clearcut; The Deforestation of America,* by Nancy Wood. San Francisco: Sierra Club Books, 1971.

Woodcock, Leonard. "Labor and the Politics of the Environment." *SCB,* 56 (1971), no. 10, p. 11. Reprinted from testimony given before the Subcommittee on Air and Water Pollution of the Senate Committee on Public Works. Washington, D.C., 1971.

Wright, Cedric. "Mountain Photography." *SCB,* 26 (1941), p. 83.
"Trail Song." *SCB,* 30 (1928), p. 20.

Young, John V. "Dams Unlimited." *SCB,* 52 (1967), no. 4, p. 10.

Picture Credits

Index

561